SINOPHONE STUDIES ACROSS DISCIPLINES

Global Chinese Culture

GLOBAL CHINESE CULTURE

David Der-wei Wang, Editor

Mingwei Song, *Fear of Seeing: A Poetics of Chinese Science Fiction*

Robin Visser, *Questioning Borders: Eco-Literatures of China and Taiwan*

Cheow Thia Chan, *Malaysian Crossings: Place and Language in the Worlding of Modern Chinese Literature*

Michael Berry, ed., *The Musha Incident: A Reader on the Indigenous Uprising in Colonial Taiwan*

A-Chin Hsiau, *Politics and Cultural Nativism in 1970s Taiwan: Youth, Narrative, Nationalism*

Calvin Hui, *The Art of Useless: Fashion, Media, and Consumer Culture in Contemporary China*

Shengqing Wu, *Photo Poetics: Chinese Lyricism and Modern Media*

Sebastian Veg, *Minjian: The Rise of China's Grassroots Intellectuals*

Lily Wong, *Transpacific Attachments: Sex Work, Media Networks, and Affective Histories of Chineseness*

Michel Hockx, *Internet Literature in China*

Jie Li, *Shanghai Homes: Palimpsests of Private Life*

Andrea Bachner, *Beyond Sinology: Chinese Writing and the Scripts of Culture*

Shu-mei Shih, Chien-hsin Tsai, and Brian Bernards, eds., *Sinophone Studies: A Critical Reader*

Alexa Huang, *Chinese Shakespeares: A Century of Cultural Exchange*

Michael Berry, *A History of Pain: Literary and Cinematic Mappings of Violence in Modern China*

Sylvia Li-chun Lin, *Representing Atrocity in Taiwan: The 2/28 Incident and White Terror in Fiction and Film*

Michael Berry, *Speaking in Images: Interviews with Contemporary Chinese Filmmakers*

A Reader EDITED BY

HOWARD CHIANG

AND SHU-MEI SHIH

Columbia University Press

New York

Columbia University Press wishes to express its appreciation for assistance given by the Chiang Ching-kuo Foundation for International Scholarly Exchange and the Council for Cultural Affairs in the publication of this series. The conference organized in preparation for this volume was funded by the UCLA-NTNU (National Taiwan Normal University) Taiwan Studies Initiative, which also provided half of the funding for publication subvention and indexing. The Lai Ho and Wu Cho-liu Endowment in Taiwan Studies at UCSB provided the second half of funding for publication subvention. Indexing has also been made possible by a Diversity, Equity, and Inclusion Fund from the Department of East Asian Languages and Cultural Studies at UCSB.

Columbia University Press
Publishers Since 1893
New York   Chichester, West Sussex
cup.columbia.edu
Copyright © 2024 Columbia University Press
All rights reserved

Library of Congress Cataloging-in-Publication Data
Names: Chiang, Howard, 1983– editor. | Shih, Shu-mei, 1961– editor.
Title: Sinophone studies across disciplines : a reader / edited by Howard Chiang and Shu-mei Shih.
Description: New York : Columbia University Press, 2024. | Series: Global chinese culture | Includes index.
Identifiers: LCCN 2023056213 (print) | LCCN 2023056214 (ebook) | ISBN 9780231208628 (hardback) | ISBN 9780231208635 (trade paperback) | ISBN 9780231557528 (ebook)
Subjects: LCSH: Chinese diaspora. | Chinese—Foreign countries—Ethnic identity. | Chinese—Foreign countries—Intellectual life. | Interdisciplinary approach in education. | National characteristics, Chinese.
Classification: LCC DS732 .S573 2024 (print) | LCC DS732 (ebook) | DDC 305.800951—dc23/eng/20240116
LC record available at https://lccn.loc.gov/2023056213
LC ebook record available at https://lccn.loc.gov/2023056214

Cover design: Julia Kushnirsky
Cover image: Hung Chang (circa 1959, Paris), oil on canvas. By permission of the estate of Hung Chang

Contents

Introduction: Sinophone Studies Across Disciplines
　　Howard Chiang and Shu-mei Shih　1

PART I　Interdisciplinary Conjunctions

1　The Question of Chinese Empire　*Shu-mei Shih*　23

2　Stonewall Aside: When Queer Theory Meets Sinophone Studies
　　Howard Chiang　55

3　Written Out: Dance and the Sinophone　*Emily Wilcox*　73

4　Cantonese Opera and Sino-Soundscape in North America
　　Nancy Yunhwa Rao　89

5　Ann Hui, Hainan, and the Sino-Vietnamese War: A Sinophone
　　Inter-Asian Recasting of *Boat People*'s Transpacific Refugee Critique
　　Brian Bernards　108

6　Sinophonic Affects: Kyle Dargan's *Anagnorisis* and the Poetics
　　of Infrastructure in Chan Tze Woon's *Yellowing*　*Lily Wong*　125

PART II　Theories, Methodologies, Controversies

7　Geocritical Sinophone and Transgressive Community
　　Yinde Zhang　147

8　Sinophone Postloyalism　*David Der-wei Wang*　161

9   Parasite: Conceptualizing a Sinophone Approach and Ethics
    E. K. Tan   176

10 Queer Hong Kong as a Sinophone Method   *Alvin K. Wong*   193

11 Enjoy Your Sinophone!   *Chien-heng Wu*   209

12 The Lure of Diaspora and Sinophone Malaysian Literature in Taiwan
    Wai-Siam Hee   226

13 Conditions of Theory in Taiwan: Americanism and Settler Colonialism
    Shu-mei Shih   243

PART III   Places of Differentiation

14 Chinese Settler Colonialism: Empire and Life in the
    Tibetan Borderlands   *Carole McGranahan*   265

15 Beyond Musical, Political, and Linguistic Boundaries: The Influence of
    the Hong Kong Rock Band Beyond in the PRC in the 1990s and Its
    Legacy   *Nathanel Amar*   281

16 Translanguaging as a Transcultural Marker in the Italian Sinophone
    Play *Tong Men-g*   *Valentina Pedone*   299

17 From Multilingualism to Mandarin: Chinese Singaporeans as a
    Sinophone Community, 1945–1990   *Jason Lim*   315

18 Adaptation and Identity Building Among the Ethnic Chinese
    Communities in Vietnam: A View from Ritual Transformation
    in Popular Religion   *Tho Ngoc Nguyen*   332

19 The Misconstrued Reader: Contemporary Sinophone Literature in
    Thailand   *Rebecca Ehrenwirth*   361

List of Contributors   377

Index   381

SINOPHONE STUDIES ACROSS DISCIPLINES

Introduction

Sinophone Studies Across Disciplines

HOWARD CHIANG AND SHU-MEI SHIH

Since the initial conceptualization of Sinophone studies over a decade ago as the study of Sinitic-language cultures and communities marked by difference and heterogeneity around the world, scholarly work in the field has become progressively interdisciplinary, involving not only literary and film studies but also history, anthropology, musicology, linguistics, art history, dance, political science, and others.[1] Nowadays, *Sinophone* routinely appears as a specific signifier with multiple implications that are no longer merely denotative, enabling, on the one hand, marginalized voices, sites, and practices to come into view and, on the other hand, an expanded conversation with such fields as postcolonial studies, settler colonial studies, migration studies, ethnic studies, queer studies, and area studies.[2] There have been vibrant debates at the definitional and conceptual level about critical issues and standpoints, such as the mis/uses of the diasporic framework (diaspora as history versus diaspora as value),[3] the difficulty of overcoming compulsory Chineseness, the strength and pitfalls of language-determined identities, imperial and anti-imperial politics, ethnoracialized assimilationism and the self-determination of minority peoples, place-based cultural practices, the dialectics between roots and routes, and the question of (de)politicization, among others. Given that scholars in disciplines other than literary and film studies have begun to join these conversations, the present juncture affords an opportunity to take stock of where this inherently interdisciplinary field has been, where it is going, and where it might go in the future.

Even though Sinophone studies grew out of debates in literature, this book argues that its conceptualization of power is what distinguishes its cross-disciplinary contribution and intervention in topics concerned with overturning the status quo, which is maintained by the supposedly unmarked and depoliticized center(s) across the Sinophone world. As the field broadens beyond literary studies—including matters of categorization and inclusionary parameters—not only does Sinophone studies have the capacity to attract a wide range of interlocutors, but it can also bring to light the variegated mechanisms by which power operates at different levels of society and across national and transnational terrains. One aim of this book, then, is to highlight the convergence of disciplinary traditions in the way they approach the questions of colonialism, hierarchy, oppression, resistance, and plurality, marked by the (dis)aggregated categories of race, ethnicity, class, language, nationality, gender, sexuality, and culture against their enforced isomorphic coherence and equivalence. By expanding history and historiography as a potent conceptual building block in Sinophone studies, the following essays seek to reveal how time, space, and place function as catalysts for cross-disciplinary contestations, such as in the form of temporal dissonances, historic flashpoints, epistemic formations, spatial practices, and place-based articulations. Moreover, scholars who are typically alienated within their own disciplines have come to voice urgent and critical insights that cohere around the relatively young field of Sinophone studies. To that end, in addition to the self-reflexive treatment of text, time, and place as webs of interrelation, a significant part of this volume will situate another dimension of materiality—corporeal politics—as a new theoretical cornerstone in Sinophone studies.

This book is organized into three sections. The first section, "Interdisciplinary Conjunctions," introduces some of the most representative cross-disciplinary synergies that have blossomed in the last decade. In their engagement with empire studies, queer theory, dance studies, musicology, cinema studies, and affect theory, these essays open the book with definitive touchstones for documenting modalities of cultural heterogeneity and resistance in a relational world.[4] The second section, "Theories, Methodologies, Controversies," proposes paradigm-shifting rubrics that best frame the critical intervention of Sinophone studies by proposing a vibrant toolkit of Sinophone methodologies along the insights of geocriticism, Indigenous studies, parasitism, trialectics, diaspora politics, and homophonic/homonymic transliteration. The third section, "Places of Differentiation," hones in on the place-based fulcrum of Sinophone studies, executing an in-depth investigation of a series of regional sites where the geopolitical differentiation from the centers of power and hegemony has acquired a distinct shape. The various deconstructions of queer, postcolonial, religious, ethnic, migration-based, and non-Mandarin-based identities locate their potency in some of the most urgent "hotspots" in Sinophone studies, such as Tibet, Hong Kong, Italy, Singapore, Vietnam, Taiwan, Thailand, and the United States. An undercurrent of this book charts a fresh horizon of Sinophone studies in which the signification of the body and performance politics assume center stage. Through case studies in dance history, Cantonese opera, docudrama, rock and roll music, and theater, a subset of essays develops an innovative program for approaching how bodies mediate the relation between word and world, why performance and performativity are at once illusory and real, and the way historical discrepancy constitutes the record(ing) of Sinophone diversity.

Across all three sections, contributors grasp their own subject position through their object and method of analysis. The kind of transdisciplinary framework underscored in this book captures the lingering unevenness, vulnerability, and triviality that some of them experience with respect to established disciplines and scholarly conventions. In spite of, or precisely due to, this unsettling effect, the framework of interdisciplinarity also helps to augment a practice to overcome such peripheral ontology in the wider academic profession. Taken together, this book considers power as both an object and a condition of knowledge-making in Sinophone studies, notwithstanding its detractors' move to political innocence and fictive neutrality, which ultimately recenters that which the Sinophone seeks to launch a "multidirectional critique" against.[5] This introductory chapter gives an overview of how each essay engages with the analytic of power and when brought together, furnishes a distinctively Sinophone episteme—a necessary regime of knowledge-formation for interrogating the temporal collisions that mediate the hegemony of the present and out of which new coalitions of marginal relations are sutured and made possible.

Interdisciplinary Conjunctions

Building on her earlier critique of Eurocentrism in empire studies, Shu-mei Shih opens this volume with a critical look at the ways in which multiple discursive positions have coproduced the moralistic injunction against any conception of the People's Republic of China (PRC) as an empire that deserves a careful examination and critique. From the misconception that empires and imperialism are prerogatives of the white race and the lingering Third-Worldist romanticism toward China to the Chinese state's and statist intellectuals' vociferous defense of China strictly and as ever an object and victim of empire, these discursive positions in the West and China, within and without academia, have contributed to a strident ideological purism and a driving ressentiment that coalesced into an injunction that China cannot be criticized—in fact, in any form or any way. The Western Left's moralism and ideological purism that China must be defended has functioned, in effect, as a kind of racialized essentialism and even Orientalism, not unlike the Western Right's racialized vilification of China, while Chinese nationalism of all hues is seemingly winning discursive wars through self-victimology. What this discursive conjunction, which also constitutes an affective community of power, defensiveness, and ideological righteousness, disavows, then, is the power dynamics within the geopolitical boundary of China and its global consequences. In this context, Shih emphasizes the ethical imperative to reengage with empire studies from Sinophone perspectives, both historically and historiographically, so as to allow us to see the discursively displaced objects of empire within the geopolitical boundary of China (whether in the form of settler colonialism in the Uyghur homeland or not) and without (expansionism abroad covered over with a discourse of victimology and outdated Third-World solidarity).

Building on Shih's theorization of the Chinese empire, Howard Chiang, in chapter 2, probes the cross-fertilization between Sinophone studies and queer theory. Both fields acquired salience in a particular moment in the academy as a response to the changing nature of the wider political environment. Queer theory evolved from the earlier identitarian concerns of gay and lesbian scholarly activism; Sinophone studies emerged to address the many blind spots where area studies and ethnic studies have persistently failed to speak to their very intersections. Since the late 1980s, a reigning tenet of queer theory has been the fluidity, instability, and subversiveness of gender and sexuality. In other words, queer critique has been most powerfully imagined from the peripheries of social norms, not unlike the way Sinophone communities are situated on the margins of China-centric statism, colonialism, and Chineseness. The conjunctive peripheralisms of the queer and the Sinophone coactivate their interdisciplinary synergy. In a double move to decenter Chinese history and the history of sexuality, Chiang's chapter reroutes mainstream concerns in queer historiography from the 1969 Stonewall riots to other turning points in Sinophone history: the 1987 lifting of martial law in Taiwan, the 1989 Tiananmen Square incident, and the 1997 handover of Hong Kong. An important example of queer Sinophone production is the emergence of *tongzhi* ("comrade" or "common will") as an LGBTQ category across the Sinophone Pacific, especially since the term's circulation in socialist mainland China precluded such a queer register. Chiang's discussion of Wong Kar-wai's *Happy Together* (1997) shows the centrality of geopolitics to the contestation of heteronormativity. Emphasizing cross-cultural encounter and displacing outdated paradigms of area studies,

Chiang's queer Sinophone approach maps an alternative genealogy of temporal coordinates—a new engine of historiography—both from below and beyond the nation-state.

Defined chiefly around matters of language and linguistic communities since its inception, Sinophone studies has found some of its leading interlocutors in the field of literature. A growing body of scholarship, however, has attempted to explore the technological, bodily, and sonic implications of Sinophone interventions, ranging from cinema studies to the medical humanities and trans historiography.[6] Such a fruitful cross-disciplinary encounter that places corporeal politics at the center is thematized in a number of essays in this volume. By probing the Sinophone analytic through examples in dance, music, and theatre, it becomes possible to raise new questions about place-based expressions of identity, power, border, social relation, cultural negotiation, and way of being. In this spirit, Emily Wilcox's chapter provides a long overdue analysis of Sinophone dance. The question of what constitutes Sinophone dance denotes an animating fulcrum for Wilcox's exploration. On the one hand, the answer can be formulated from a place-based vantage point, and as such, one can look at dance performances in regions typically associated with the Sinophone world at large, including Taiwan, Hong Kong, and Asian America. However, in chapter 3, Wilcox pushes for a deeper engagement with other dimensions of dance studies, including disciplinary norms and the very content and form that dance takes. Not only is Sinophone dance appropriate for challenging the hegemony of Euro-American centrism in dance studies, but it also draws attention to the legacy of dance forms created by minoritized/marginalized groups in the broader Sinophone world. Because dance is not a text-based medium, it offers a rare opportunity to question all sorts of essentialist assumptions about Chineseness, frequently articulated in linguistic terms, in the realm of the performing arts. In fact, Wilcox delivers a surprising discovery overlooked by scholars in both dance studies and Sinophone studies: What is now often recognized as "Chinese dance" has historically been invented through the bodily discourse of non-Han or minoritized Chinese dancers.

Musical performance offers another underappreciated lens through which it is possible to expand the corporeal politics of Sinophone studies. Later in the volume, Nathanel Amar's chapter (chapter 15) considers the porousness of rock music by which the politics of democracy and dissent comes to assume relevance across the Hong Kong-mainland China border. Nancy Rao's chapter (chapter 4) shifts the focus to the other side of the Pacific: the history of Cantonese opera as a Sinophone expression in Asian America. Developing the notion of "Sino-soundscape," Rao argues that the popularization of this form of theatrical arts, especially within the Chinese American communities, revises both the transatlantic focus of American music and the China-centrism (e.g., the prominence of Peking opera) in the global circulation of Chinese drama. With roots in the gold rush era, the popularity of Chinese opera waned in the early twentieth century due to anti-Chinese sentiment in the United States. Yet, the genre witnessed a comeback in the 1920s that accompanied several new trends: the growth of second-generation Chinese Americans, the maturation of Chinatown cultures, new recording technologies, and the increasing affordability of phonograph records. A key example of Sinophone subjectivity was embodied by youngsters who eagerly learned to sing Cantonese opera songs. This was not purely catalyzed by their experience in accompanying their family to attend Cantonese operas, which was a multisensory and collective experience and established a sentiment of familial and community belonging. Their admiration of Cantonese opera also featured the sonic dimensions of Sinophone expression. Performing Cantonese opera involved the renarration of well-known cultural "repertoires" (historical legends, romance stories, and so forth), as well as the vocalization of a particular style of singing. Linguistic nativity did not play a necessarily determinant role in their Sinophone embodiment, but, rather, what mattered most was their vocal production of melodies and memorization of lyrics by phonetic pronunciation.

In addition to highlighting new dimensions of Sinophone cultural production, an interdisciplinary perspective brings urgency to the contingent nature of a historical *event*, which could serve as a flashpoint of futurity and even a fracturing of possibility. Howard Chiang's chapter already underlines a number of such events in queer Sinophone historiography. The critical treatment of turning points in history enables new forms of cultural alliance, ways of historical periodization, and styles of cross-temporal reasoning. One such rupturing event long neglected by Sinophone scholars is the 1979 Sino-Vietnamese War, the focus of Brian Bernard's chapter (chapter 5) on Ann Hui's *Boat People* (1982). Ann Hui's film restages communist Vietnam through the eyes of a Japanese photojournalist, while its production—from casting, language, and source material to where the film was shot, Hainan—was made possible by its close ties to the PRC and Hong Kong. When the film was released, its initial reception often led to an allegorical interpretation of Hong Kong's impending postcolonial transition. However, Bernards reorients our lens by foregrounding the Sino-Vietnamese War, showing why the war serves as a flashpoint for both the allegorical and realist depictions in Sinophone inter-Asian production. According to Bernards, *Boat People* not only acknowledges multiple forms of Asian imperialism (including contemporary Chinese imperialism), but it also gives Vietnamese refugees, whose stories crucially sourced Ann Hui's production, a localized identity in Hong

Kong. The film accomplishes what has been called a "de-Cold War" mode of thinking since the backdrop of the war breaks down a homogenous rendition of communist Asia.[7] The authorization of Ann Hui's shooting in Hainan required the PRC government to recognize the difference between itself and the Vietnamese communist government and, like the ideology of U.S. involvement, announced to the world Chinese losses and sacrifices. By drawing *Boat People* into a transpacific network of filmic production, Bernards loosens the affective tropes of statelessness and agentlessness often affiliated with the Vietnamese refugee figure.

Turning points can be both strange and familiar. Whereas Bernards reroutes the oeuvre of a famed Sinophone director through an often-neglected flashpoint, in chapter 6, Lily Wong centers on a legendary incident of Sinophone resistance—the 2014 Umbrella Movement in Hong Kong—to generate unforeseen synergies between the disciplines, areas, and modes of analysis. Wong has pioneered the merging of Sinophone studies and affect studies to "unsettle more centripetal theorizations of identity (e.g., territory, locality, or nationality) with an emphasis on relationality, dynamism, and temporality." The fact that the Umbrella Movement occurred in Hong Kong does not constrain the significance of its cultural articulation in relation to Chineseness or the Chinese nation-state alone. In the context of the African American writer Kyle Dargan's poetry collection *Anagnorisis* (2018), Hong Kong's democracy protest is situated in relation to American minority politics and the growing visibility of Xinjiang oppression. The Sinitic script offers a material and conceptual infrastructure in which the emotions for thinking across Afro-Asian relationality are explicable and the double critique of China- and U.S.-centrism becomes meaningful. While Chan Tze Woon's *Yellowing* (2016), a documentary of the Umbrella Movement, might seem to be an unequivocal record of Sinophone resistance in light of its subject, Wong instead draws attention to the film's affective register and what she calls the poetics of infrastructure—both material (city streets, skyscrapers, etc.) and metaphorical (aesthetic configurations, such as the inscription of Sinitic scripts on the hands of protestors). These embodied arrangements of resistance exceed neoliberal ideologies of power by activating synergies among "unevenly stratified bodies, discourses, and spaces that are put into contact on the margins."[8]

Theories, Methodologies, Controversies

As Sinophone studies enters a vibrant phase of interdisciplinarity, it must persist in advocating a heterogeneous way of thinking about history's relation to the present. Whereas the first part of this reader highlights the collision of temporalities as a motor of Sinophone production and the Sinophone recasting of historic flashpoints through interdisciplinary conjunctions, the second cluster of essays seeks to put a spotlight on theoretical and methodological conversations—on diaspora politics, queer resistance, critical theory, and Sinophone Malaysian literature, for instance—in new directions. In so doing, these chapters take cues from what Foucault, following Nietzsche, has termed genealogy: a deep probing into the conditions of possibility for certain styles of existence and the ways in which new epistemic formations displace older ones.[9] Indeed, we already live in the world of a Sinophone episteme. The resulting reorganization of social relations and knowledge apparatus cast new light on debates and controversies over the definition, boundary, and object of critique in Sinophone studies. In addition to the excavation of new regions, areas, and basis of identification, the Sinophone episteme, above all, introduces new concepts as organizing rubrics of investigation across disciplines.

In chapter 7, Yinde Zhang announces the arrival of what he calls the "geocritical Sinophone." A range of literary and artistic creations have synchronized geocriticism—a method of enabling transgressivity with respect to spatial and territorial organization—with the standpoint of Sinophone epistemology. Zhang identifies three thematic threads in this growing body of work: the deconstruction of centrality, the criticism of territorial expansion, and the disintegration of hegemony. When Sinophone writers such as Han Song, Liu Cixin, Yan Lianke, Qiu Zhijie, Dung Kai-chung, Chan Koonchung, and Lee-chin Lin deploy cartographical rhetoric and concepts, a geocritical paradigm coalesces from their work, redrawing the map of possible alliances and reorienting the conditions for speaking to power. Although cultural geography has implicitly shaped the programmatic contouring of Sinophone studies, Zhang's chapter makes the critical tools of geography explicit and central to the future of the field.

Another rubric for analyzing the convergence, divergence, and rupturing of competing temporalities has been offered by David Der-wei Wang and is delineated in his chapter on Sinophone postloyalism (chapter 8). In Wang's understanding, the work of Shu-mei Shih and Jing Tsu each provides a different conceptualization of Sinophone literary production, with the former framing it in terms of colonialism, difference, and resistance and the latter diasporic governance.[10] While the production of Sinophone culture on the margins or outside of China has received some attention, Wang prefers to conceptualize postloyalism as a framing rubric to test the field's value *within* the nation-state of China. The word *postloyalism* comprises two parts, and Wang acknowledges the tensions that arise out of this coupling. The standard

Sinitic word for loyalism, *yi*, captures at least three etymological meanings: losing something, leaving something, and bequeathing something. With the postmodern hermeneutic of *post-* attached to this tripartite concept, postloyalism makes visible a Sinophone subject's ambivalent positionality vis-à-vis China. If, as Wang seeks to demonstrate, the Sinophone marks an interface between China and the world, Sinophone subjects continue to remake the meaning of their relationship to the past, something often understood under the umbrella of the Chinese past. These engagements with the signifier "Chinese" are evident in the work of four writers, and by analyzing their work, Wang proposes to shift the understanding of modern Chinese literature from what Chih-Tsing Hsia calls the "obsession with China" to the Sinophone "intervention with China."[11]

When Sinophone studies has aimed to critique power as manifested and operative in all places where Sinophone communities reside, the postloyalist framework tends to tie the Sinophone subject to China. This is in direct opposition to Shih's emphasis on place-based critique wherever Sinophone communities reside. Postloyalism thus maps the uneven temporality of Sinophone production in perpetual relation to China, even as spectral remains or a hauntology, and ends up risking a different kind of obsession with China, in this case, a kind of Chinese civilizationism from which no Sinophone subject is supposed to escape. Perhaps one of the boldest moves advanced by Wang's postloyalist framework comes from its continual rethinking of the parameters of Chineseness from within the PRC.

Another rubric that exposes a different temporal and spatial collision is the idea of the parasite. Chapter 9, by E. K. Tan, develops the parasite as both a descriptor and a functionary model to "imagine the Sinophone . . . that exists in the form of a continuous nuisance and irritation to the main(stream) body."[12] In developing the concept of Sinophone parasite, Tan's purpose is two-fold. First, he aims to rethink the power relation between Sinophone communities and China. Notable social movements in Taiwan and Hong Kong, such as the Indigenous rights movement, the independence movements, the Umbrella Movement, and the anti-Extradition Amendment Bill protest, continually pressure the legitimacy and political governance of the PRC. When residents of Taiwan and Hong Kong envision forms of temporality in which they seek to situate their future that differ from the temporality mandated by Beijing, the resulting rupturing promises a critical edge of Sinophone studies that fastens such disjunctive ways of being rather than, as the Chinese government would have it, diminishing them. Second, Tan reminds us that the singularity of China-centrism is not an exclusive concern in Sinophone studies, a field that considers multiple forms of political and cultural hegemony, including, but not limited to, the Chinese imperial order. Sinophone temporalities can become parasitic to the temporality of the American nation-state in the context of Sinophone America, for instance, or the temporality of ethnic and racial ordering in Sinophone Malaysia. By grounding this theoretical provocation in grassroots politics, Tan puts to rest any insistence on a binary relation with China and only China as a kernel referent in Sinophone studies.

Recent events, such as the Umbrella Movement examined in Lily Wong's chapter and the anti-Extradition Amendment Bill movement in 2019–2020, have identified the precarity of Hong Kong, a topic taken up by Alvin K. Wong in chapter 10. Formally a special administrative region since 1997, Hong Kong has become increasingly culturally and politically contested in at least three ways. Due to its growing dependence on the PRC, what critics have variously labeled "Mainlandization," the city is witnessing a decline in political and legal autonomy, a loss in its cultural uniqueness, and a marginalization of its regional intellectual orientation by the growth of China studies. In light of these trends, and echoing Howard Chiang's chapter, Wong asserts that Hong Kong studies, postcolonial theory, and queer studies can learn meaningfully from one another. In the 1990s, not only did postcolonial critics such as Rey Chow discuss the in-betweeness of Hong Kong, but this very liminality of the region also bears striking similarity to the concurrent discussion of gender/sexual antiessentialism. Because the political condition of Hong Kong can only but claim instability, its queer formations provide a heuristically useful window into the promise and perils of cultural ontology. Through a thick reading of three texts—Wong Bik-wan's *Portraits of Martyred Women* (1999), Jacob Cheung's *Intimates* (1997), and Ma Ka Fai's *Once Upon a Time in Hong Kong* (2016)—Wong sets various temporal ruptures as the backdrop of queer Sinophone formation: the 1967 riots, the tradition of sworn spinster sisterhood in the Canton Delta, and the interimperiality of British colonialism, Japanese aggression, and multiple Chinese political forces in the twentieth century. If the city's history and culture remain on the periphery of postcolonial critique, a queer Sinophone approach also calls into question any heteronormative rendition of Hong Kong's status quo.

As a multidirectional critique, Sinophone studies observes the role of all power actors, not just perpetrators of Chinese hegemony, in shaping politics and culture. Hence, while it is important to deconstruct the meaning of the native and the local in Han settler colonies of Taiwan, Singapore, Tibet, and the Uyghur homeland, where the local has attempted to usurp the Indigenous to different degrees, it is equally important to acknowledge the increasing precarity of a complexly articulated Hong Kong localism threatened first by British colonialism and then by the ever-oppressive political and cultural (post)loyalism to China. Building on this set of power triangulations, Chien-heng

Wu's chapter (chapter 11) offers a meticulous response to a short, incendiary, online review of Shih's 2017 book *Against Diaspora: Discourse on Sinophone Studies* by the Sinophone Malaysian, Taiwan-based writer Ng Kim Chew. In this review, Ng willfully misconstrues Shih's arguments on settler colonialism and refuses any engagement with Indigeneity with his "will to non-knowledge." Wu argues that by denying the presence of multiply-determined modalities of power, Ng risks overlooking "a trialectics that complicates the process of mediation by factoring in the often-neglected perspective of indigeneity." What Wu calls "the structure of reversibility" compels us to consider how the position of the victim can easily turn into that of the oppressor if we are not sensitive to our own positionality in multiply-variegated structures of power. By expanding the horizon of Sinophone studies beyond (1) the obsession with Chineseness as the sole organizing principle and (2) the decisive lack of engagement with other disciplines, it becomes possible for Sinophone epistemology to merge the politics of time and the politics of place, as place is also simultaneously predetermined and indeterminable due to its openness to change in the future, wedding phenomenology with ontology. This form of temporal collision is one that disrupts any straightforward determination of the future; that is, a disturbance that keeps the future indeterminate. In Wu's words, this constitutes "a future that includes both the thriving and the vanishing of the Sinophone culture and, of course, everything in between." To bring back the example of the Umbrella Movement, then, its historicity and urgency were never fully predicted or predicated by the establishment of the one country, two systems mandate, nor was its meaning and significance at different historical moments past the moment of the movement. We can thus interpret the surfacing and transformation of Sinophone dissent as being specific in its criticality in a given historical time and yet contingent upon the mutating historical landscape and open to different futurities.

Historicity and context: Their mutual production has anchored a central tenet of the Sinophone episteme, namely, the troubling of diaspora. The antilocalization sentiment of the Chinese diaspora in Malaysia, as notoriously embodied by Ng Kim Chew, is the subject of Wai Siam Hee's chapter 12. To understand the complex history of the Chinese Malaysian experience, Hee calls attention to the different waves of Chinese Malaysian migration out of Malaysia in the late twentieth century. The state-backed Bumiputera privileges and the suppression of the Chinese Malaysians led individuals like Ng to seek residence abroad in the late 1980s. However, Hee argues that the "master-slave" template through which Ng continues to articulate his diasporic subjectivity (the master being the Malay and the slave being the Chinese Malaysians) has an expiration date. After the Asian financial crisis, domestic political turmoil, and the rise of China in the 1990s, Ng's insistence that localization represents a backward, undesirable expression for Chinese Malaysians becomes similarly outdated. Based on a bird's-eye reading of Ng's oeuvre, Hee demonstrates the feasibility of Sinophone Malaysian subjects to recreate the fluid locality of Chinese Malaysian culture in Malaysia. In Hee's words, "Chinese Malaysian diaspora discourse is not wholly an anti-localization discourse [as Ng would have it] and . . . that a clear border does not have to be drawn between the diasporic and the local."[13]

At issue here is Ng's mistaken equation of localization with assimilation to the dominant group, the Malays, when, in fact, Shu-mei Shih's conception of the local, while not conflating it with the Indigenous, is a site of inscription by all those who partake of it. Hence, the Chinese Malaysians do not at all need to compromise their cultural sovereignty but instead contribute to the local to make it truly multicultural. To put it differently, localization does not mean succumbing to assimilation; rather, it is a way of resisting assimilation by making discreet claims on the local by minority subjects, such as those by Asian Americans in the United States. Localization means making claims on the local, challenging the Malay-dominant conception of belonging, thereby *remaking* the local in the case of Malaysia. The Sinophone episteme recognizes the Sinophone subjects' claims on the local—"Everyone should be given a chance to become a local," as Shu-mei Shih noted[14]—but this local is not a fixed essence. Hence, the Sinophone episteme entails a nonessentialist understanding of the local across national and transnational terrains to understand why people produce different localisms even as they may move fluidly between their ancestral lands and places of residence.

In this sense, in chapter 13, Shu-mei Shih explores the conditions of possibility for local theory in Taiwan, or Taiwan as the site and producer of theory, not merely the object to which theory imported from the West is applied. Understanding that all theory arises out of particular historical contexts to later acquire universal appeal, often thanks to the epistemological reach of empires' power, in this case, French and American, Shih's question is naturally whether something like universalizable theory can be derived from the particularity of Taiwan as a small peripherized nation. But the project of epistemological justice also needs to be based on scrupulous self-understanding and self-critique, hence the identification of Americanism and settler colonialism as two of the major conditions of theory in Taiwan: Taiwan as a protectorate of the United States and Taiwan as a settler colony of Han people over Indigenous peoples and land. In order to expand the scope of understanding and constructing theory out of Taiwan's unique experience in the broadened context of the world, Shih does not directly engage with Chinese civilizationism that has served as the foundation of settler legitimacy in Taiwan and instead emphasizes understanding empire and settler colonialism as global processes with which Taiwan was deeply entangled, including the prehistory of Dutch colonialism in Taiwan, which was directly related to the emergence of international law that had governed settlements. From the ways in which writers in and outside Taiwan responded to these two local and global conditions emerge creative theoretical concepts, including a uniquely Sinophone practice of homophonic and homonymic transliteration, which Shih identifies as having potential for general application in thinking of other parts of the world and other non-Sinitic languages. Thus, we may fruitfully ask: How may the transmutations between source and target languages in mutual translation and transliteration suggest something structural to theoretical thinking in different languages? The local, always informed and inscribed by the global and always in flux, may yet produce particular theories with potentialities of significance beyond the local.

Places of Differentiation

The third section of this volume follows the above discussion of the site of the local—place—and builds on the final section of *Sinophone Studies: A Critical Reader* (2013), "Sites and Articulations," in which literary expressions from different geohistorical contexts denote "the quintessential endeavor . . . [and] the most concentrated exploration of what it means to be Sinophone, in all its multifarious, contentious, and paradoxical ways."[15] Yet the cross-disciplinary synergies that have enriched Sinophone studies in the last decade, as shown in the first two sections of this book, point to the production of Sinophone communities beyond the literary sphere. Therefore, this section of the book draws on perspectives from anthropology, political science, theater, religious studies, and literature to capture the ways in which power and resistance in global Sinitic-language cultures have been differentiated across geopolitical sites.

With respect to place-based differentiation, the rupturing effect of Sinophone production on normative time can be easily seen in the history of Tibet. When the People's Liberation Army invaded Tibet and defeated local resistance in 1950, it solidified the apparatus of settler colonialism. As documented in Carole McGranahan's chapter (chapter 14), Chinese settler colonialism in Tibet features political administration, settlement incentives, resource and economic extraction, land renaming and redistribution, and cultural assimilation, including the (unsuccessful) elimination of religion. This colonialist temporality clashed with the Tibetan independence temporality, which reached a crescendo in the first half of the twentieth century. Such rupturing of the time and timing of Tibetan modernity conditioned Sinophone dissent in the region. Some of the classic features of imperial violence are evident in what McGranahan calls "settler colonialism with Chinese communist characteristics." For instance, the ongoing Education Aid for Tibet project exemplifies the complex Han Chinese civilizing mission toward Tibetans. Justification for such a project rests on a moralistic reinscription of the Han superiority vs. Tibetan inferiority dichotomy. New forms of tension, struggle, and inequality among Tibetans also emerge from the PRC's evolving policy toward nomads, farmers, and urban residents. Whereas the government may hide the Han oppression of Tibetans behind the official discourse of ethnic (*minzu*) minority, a Sinophone perspective draws attention to a different rhetoric of time and place to foreground Tibetans' right to self-determination.

One of the mottos of the Umbrella Movement, "Today's Tibet, Tomorrow's Hong Kong," underscores not only temporal and spatial politics of Chinese empire but also the affective linkages between Tibet and Hong Kong. A political inquiry into popular culture could thus trace the geopolitical genealogy of Chinese rock and roll back to the student protests of 1989 while foregrounding Hong Kong-China linkages. In chapter 15, Nathanel Amar shows why the Tiananmen democracy movement has cast a long shadow over the exchange between Sinophone communities, on the one hand, and the uneven power relations behind music creation and reception, on the other. In particular, the bourgeoning popularity of the Hong Kong band Beyond in the PRC exemplifies the political saturation of popular music. While the history of Chinese rock dates further back, with singers such as Cui Jian carrying symbolic weight, Amar discovers that for many PRC youths who grew up in the 1990s, their main frame of reference in rock and roll is Beyond. This extends the insight of scholars who have already documented the propagation of Hong Kong Cantopop and Taiwan Mandopop on the mainland.[16] But Amar brings to light another intriguing phenomenon: Beyond's songs have fueled a new wave of karaoke culture, thriving especially outside of Beijing, where Mandarin is not commonly used, such as Wuhan, Yunnan, Guangxi, and Xinjiang. Even to this day, mainstream Chinese musicians and artists continue to mobilize vintage Hong Kong fashion and sounds, including images of Beyond, in their latest cultural creations. Meanwhile, Hong Kong youths have recuperated the band's iconography for other political purposes in the twenty-first century. As such, the case study of Beyond illustrates why the Tiananmen crackdown of 1989 (both on the democracy movement and the Beijing rock and roll scene) pivots a nodal turning point for cultural reappropriation: Consumed for leisure or not, Cantonese rock songs undermine the imposition and hegemony of the Mandarin language in popular music.

While Sinophone subjects and cultures have a long history in Europe, they have not been the topic of systematic investigation in the field of

Sinophone studies. Already, in chapters 3 and 4 by Emily Wilcox and Nancy Rao, we learned the ways in which Sinophone dance and operatic performance challenge both China-centrism and Western-centrism in the history of these performing arts. The interest of minoritized Sinophone subjects to contest dual forms of domination can also be seen in the example of dramatic arts.[17] In chapter 16, Valentina Pedone uses a Sino-Italian play, *Tong Men-g*, to illustrate how its writer and actor, Shi Yang Shi (a China-born Italian actor), practices a politics of transcultural linguistics. Cultural brokers like Shi carve out a place for themselves in a world where their marginalization continues to be voided under dual cultural hegemony. *Tong Men-g*, for instance, is a play in part about Chinese culture (sometimes reductively understood through the Orientalist gaze of Europe), in part about Italy (especially as it is experienced by Chinese migrants) but, above all, about the liminal "third" space in between (a subject position difficult to pin under the ambit of Italian or Chinese nationalism). The various transcultural markers in the play exceed a nominal bilingual caricature: The interlacing of Chinese and Italian linguistic and cultural cues embedded in the dialogue speak to more than just two monolingual audiences. It is precisely the site of cultural contestation, conflict, and negotiation that the play draws attention to rather than seeking to tame.

Whether our spotlight is put on Tibet, Hong Kong, or Italy, the frictions and fissures between regimes of temporality are often drawn over linguistic lines. This basis for demarcating Sinophone production can also be seen in the history of another British postcolony, Singapore. Jason Lim, in chapter 17, shows that on the path to Singaporean independence, achieved in 1965, two temporalities collided among the Chinese population in Singapore. On the one hand, Lee Kuan Yew's government increasingly promoted Mandarin as the only legitimate Chinese language. On the other, most Sinitic-language subjects in Singapore spoke languages other than Mandarin (in order of decreasing usage): Hokkien, Teochew, Cantonese, Hainanese, and Hakka. In fact, the kind of language spoken among the Chinese population in Singapore is often a mixture of Mandarin, other Sinitic languages, English, and Malay. This collision reached a climax in the Speak Mandarin campaign promoted by the Lee government starting in the late 1970s. In the post-1945 era, the Chinese in Singapore formed their own clans, associations, and groupings, sometimes based on occupations. An important example was the founding of the Singapore Federation of Chinese Clan Associations in December 1985. The Sinophone diversity of these clans and associations is first and foremost rooted in the history of colonial and postcolonial Singapore. By delineating this history closely, Lim redirects our attention from the flattening effect of such concepts as the "overseas Chinese" or "Chinese diaspora."

The origins of a new episteme in popular religions constitute the focus of chapter 18 by Tho N. Nguyen. While the standardization of gods in the history of the Sinosphere has been studied extensively, Nguyen uses the liturgical transformation of Guandi and Tianhou as a window into the development of Sinophone religious communities in Vietnam. Early modern Vietnamese dynasties executed a system of official registration for their Sino-Vietnamese residents. The five main congregations included the Cantonese, Hokkien, Teochew, Hakka, and Hainanese (as we saw, these are also the major Sinophone language groups found elsewhere in Southeast Asia). Unlike other European colonies in Southeast Asia, French power in colonial Vietnam tried to control and diminish the importance of Chinese communities (other powers tended to make use of Chinese immigrants for business and diplomacy with the Qing empire). Against this historical backdrop, Guandi became localized in Vietnamese culture, providing a powerful source of cross-ethnic solidarity, while Tianhou came to be preserved as an icon of "Chineseness" over time. Nguyen documents the selective ways by which Sinophone communities appropriated the religious symbols and rituals associated with these two gods, establishing hybrid expressions of popular religion. Not only does such a genealogy suggest the local roots of this new episteme in Vietnamese society (rather than, say, China or France), but it also reiterates the idea that a study of Sinophone cultures and communities must never lose sight of their contextual contingency and specificity in time and place.

Since literature played a leading role in the first reader of Sinophone studies, this volume concludes by centering literary history. In particular, the reorganization of social relations and knowledge apparatus in Thailand, the focus of Rebecca Ehrenwirth's chapter (chapter 19), has often been overlooked in existing accounts of global Sinophone production. While the establishment of the Society of Sinophone Writers in Thailand in 1986 is undoubtedly a landmark event, Ehrenwirth chronicles a deeper historical formation of the Sinophone cultural episteme in this region. Three major periods of "highs"—the 1920s–1930s, the 1950s–1960s, and the late 1980s–1990s—are interlaced with two periods of "lows"—the Second World War and the era of high socialism in China, when the political climate curtailed the literary production of Sinophone Thai writers. This is a genealogy that many contemporary writers themselves reference time and again in order to reflect on how they came together and what their future prospects might be. Throughout the twentieth century, Sinophone writers in Thailand reworked the meaning of Chineseness, fused it with their localized Thai identity, and sustained the desire for rooting their legacy in either Thailand or a more global literary community. The majority of Sinophone writers in Thailand came from

Chaoshan, a region in eastern Canton, Southern China, and spoke Teochew. Similar to a transcultural process that transpired in other Southeast Asian regions (e.g., Singapore and Malaysia), Sinophone writers in Thailand, such as Sima Gong, invented new strategies and techniques of literary narrativity. They often hybridized Teochew and Thai, mixing symbols of "Chineseness" and cultural signifiers of "Thainess" in their work. Today, the Society of Sinophone Writers in Thailand has its own publishing house, and this adds to a growing number of supplements to Sinophone newspapers as avenues of literary production. The contemporary exchange between Sinophone Thai authors and Sinophone writers and communities outside Thailand is best understood in the long historical formation of this culturally creolized Sinophone sphere.

The Historical and Historiographical Time of the Sinophone

When we begin to appreciate the evolution of historical versus historiographical time, cross-disciplinary synergies in Sinophone studies deepen scholarly dialogues around overlapping matters of concern.[18] In the frame of world historical time, the Sinophone frameworks dissected in the following nineteen chapters occupy a space of both alterity and mimesis in relation to the tooling and fabrics of the Hispanophone and Lusophone empires, followed by the Anglophone, Francophone, and Germanophone empires, since at least the fifteenth century. On the historiographical time scale, the diversity of Sinophone cultures analyzed here both extends and upends ongoing efforts to rekindle the contested meanings of being "Chinese," among other forms of cultural rootedness. This latter point is imperative. At the heart of yielding a critical lens on Sinitic-language communities and cultures marked by difference and heterogeneity worldwide lies the saturated experience of everyday life. The tempo of immobility, subjugation, and normativization—at once vulgar, invisible, and suffocating, among other characteristics of violence—occurs at all registers of society in dispersed locales around the world. To think through these variegated experiences together meaningfully, and minor transnationally, a critical step entails acknowledging that the ruse of ethnic and national identities often collapses with those modalities of power structure that can never be untethered from the embeddedness of resistance.[19] As Foucault reminds us, where there is power, there is resistance.[20] Against depoliticization, this book invites scholars from discrepant disciplines to forge new connections, imagine unforeseen possibilities, and continue to make trouble in our shared history.

Notes

1. Howard Chiang attributes the coinage of the term *Sinophone* and its conceptualization into a field of study, Sinophone studies, to the pioneering work of Shu-mei Shih, the coeditor of this volume. The concept first appeared as an analytical category in her essay, "Global Literature and the Technologies of Recognition," *PMLA* 119, no. 1 (2004): 16–30. For a more substantial development of this framework, see Shu-mei Shih, *Visuality and Identity: Sinophone Articulations Across the Pacific* (Berkeley: University of California Press, 2007; Mandarin translation, 2013, 2015, 2018; Korean translation, 2021), and later, *Fan lisan: huayuyuxi yanjiu lun* (*Against Diaspora: Discourse on Sinophone Studies*) (Taipei: Linking Press, 2017, 2018; Korean translation, forthcoming). Scholars have subsequently engaged with the Sinophone paradigm from a variety of perspectives. See, for example, Jing Tsu and David Der-wei Wang, eds., *Global Chinese Literature: Critical Essays* (Leiden: Brill, 2010). The definitive reader is Shu-mei Shih, Chien-hsin Tsai, and Brian Bernards, eds., *Sinophone Studies: A Critical Reader* (New York: Columbia University Press, 2013). There has been a range of publications in Mandarin Chinese, too, including Yu-lin Lee, ed., *Ten Lectures on Sinophone Studies* (Taipei: Linking Publisher, 2020). In 2019, Shu-mei Shih organized a major retrospective and prospective conference entitled Sinophone Studies: Interdisciplinary Perspectives and Critical Reflections at UCLA. Many of the chapters in this book were originally presented at that conference. At the conclusion of the conference, furthermore, the Society of Sinophone Studies was established, whose inaugural chair was Howard Chiang.

2. One important example of field formation that moves in both directions is the synergy between queer theory and Sinophone studies. See, for example, Howard Chiang and Ari Larissa Heinrich, eds., *Queer Sinophone Cultures* (New York: Routledge, 2013); Zoran Lee Pecic, *New Queer Sinophone Cinema: Local Histories, Transnational Connections* (New York: Palgrave Macmillan, 2016); and Howard Chiang and Alvin K. Wong, eds., *Keywords in Queer Sinophone Studies* (New York: Routledge, 2020). The *Keywords* volume contains research in the social sciences.

3. For distinctions between "diaspora as history" and "diaspora as value," see Shu-mei Shih, "The Concept of the Sinophone," *PMLA* 126, no. 3 (May 2011) 709–718.

4. On the notion of relational world, see Shu-mei Shih, "World Studies and Relational Comparison," *PMLA* 130, no. 2 (2015): 430–438.

5. For "multidirectional critique," see Shih, "The Concept of the Sinophone," 709–718.

6. See, for example, Audrey Yue and Olivia Khoo, eds., *Sinophone Cinemas* (New York: Palgrave Macmillan, 2014); Howard Chiang, *After Eunuchs: Science, Medicine, and the Transformation of Sex in Modern China* (New York: Columbia University Press, 2018); Howard Chiang, *Transtopia in the Sinophone Pacific* (New York: Columbia University Press, 2021).

7. Kuan-Hsing Chen, *Asia as Method: Toward Deimperialization* (Durham, NC: Duke University Press, 2010).

8. The two quotes in this paragraph are taken from Lily Wong's chapter (chapter 5) in this volume.

9. Michel Foucault, *The Order of Things: An Archaeology of the Human Sciences* (New York: Vintage, 1973).

10. Shih, *Visuality and Identity*; Jing Tsu, *Sound and Script in Chinese Diaspora* (Cambridge, MA: Harvard University Press, 2010).

11. C. T. Hsia, *A History of Modern Chinese Fiction*, 2nd ed. (New Haven, CT: Yale University Press, 1971 [1961]).

12. This quote is taken from E. K. Tan's chapter (chapter 9) in this volume.

13. This quote is taken from Wai Siam Hee's chapter (chapter 12) in this volume.

14. See Shih, *Visuality and Identity*, 185.

15. Shu-mei Shih, "Introduction: What Is Sinophone Studies?" in *Sinophone Studies: A Critical Reader*, ed. Shu-mei Shih, Chien-hsin Tsai, and Brian Bernards (New York: Columbia University Press, 2013), 1–16, on 14.

16. Marc L. Moskowitz, *Cries of Joy, Songs of Sorrow: Chinese Pop Music and Its Cultural Connotations* (Honolulu: University of Hawai'i Pres, 2010).

17. For an insightful analysis of the problem of dual structural hegemony, with particular relevance to Sinophone studies, see L. Ling-chi Wang, "The Structure of Dual Domination: Toward a Paradigm for the Study of the Chinese Diaspora in the United States," *Amerasia Journal* 21, nos. 1–2 (1995): 149–170. This influential article was also included in *Sinophone Studies: A Critical Reader*.

18. Bruno Latour, "Why Has Critique Run Out of Steam? From Matters of Fact to Matters of Concern," *Critical Inquiry* 30, no. 2 (2004): 225–248. In contrast to historical time, historiographical time is marked by purposive reflexivity. On the distinction between historical and historiographical time, see Prasenjit Duara, "Oceans as the Paradigm of History," *Theory, Culture & Society* 38, nos. 7–8 (2021): 143–166.

19. François Lionnet and Shu-mei Shih, eds., *Minor Transnationalism* (Durham, NC: Duke University Press, 2005).

20. Michel Foucault, *The History of Sexuality*, vol. 1: *An Introduction*, trans. Robert Hurley (New York: Vintage, 1990).

INTERDISCIPLINARY CONJUNCTIONS

The Question of Chinese Empire

SHU-MEI SHIH

> Every single empire in its official discourse has said that it is not like all the others that its circumstances are special, that it has a mission to enlighten, civilize, bring order and democracy, and that it uses force only as a last resort. And, sadder still there always is a chorus of willing intellectuals to say calming words about benign or altruistic empires, as if one shouldn't trust the evidence of one's eyes watching the destruction and the misery and death brought by the latest *mission civilizatrice*.
> —Edward Said

There is a consensus that Britain and France were modern empires that behaved imperialistically, but the question of Chinese empire and imperialism has been beset by ambiguity, controversy, and very strong emotions. China having suffered from Western imperialism for over a century, many maintain that it could only ever be the object of empire, never the subject of empire. Furthermore, if we take as literally true what J. M. Blaut succinctly states in the opening sentence of his classic essay on imperialism, imperialism is "white exploitation of the non-white world."[1] According to this racial logic, China, being of the nonwhite world, cannot possibly be an empire and exercise imperialism on others in the modern world. The double condition of China having been the object of empire and being a nonwhite nation has provided China a strong degree of immunity to any serious considerations of Chinese empire and imperialism in the modern and contemporary era.

Reading Blaut's essay beyond the first sentence, we find an analysis of the enabling conditions of Western imperialism, which bears a curious similarity to the contemporary conditions in which China finds itself. The white exploitation of the nonwhite world, Blaut argues, was legitimized by what he calls an entire ethnoscience of the white Western world, containing "a set of beliefs and social-science generalizations about the Non-White World as well as the White."[2] In this racialized scheme, the white world boasts of a coherent "civilization" whose advance is generated by its own internal processes. This civilization clearly demarcates the inner (white) and outer (nonwhite) spaces, where the nonwhite world is deemed not only primitive, unprogressive, barbarous, and heathen but also less strong, less intelligent, and less virtuous than the white world.[3] There is, of course, nothing surprising in Blaut's argument, which has by now become a mainstream argument about the West, having been extensively elaborated on and critiqued by scholars of postcolonial studies, critical race studies, and empire studies. What is surprising is how this argument was never considered in relation to China, not as an opposite or an object of white empires but possibly as a parallel or similar case. The focus on China has been consistently about difference, not similarity, resulting, in my view, in a fetishism of differences when it comes to the question of China and Chinese empire.[4]

Anyone familiar with China's own civilizational discourse should find that Blaut's description of the white ethnoscience bears an uncanny resemblance to what can be called China's own ethnoscience, at least in terms of their broad contours and general substance, found in the age-old imperial discourse of the "all under heaven" (*tianxia*). Recently revived in China, this discourse similarly demarcates inner and outer spaces marked by racial and civilizational differences. In fact, the discourse of racial and civilizational superiority of the majority race in China, the Han, has persisted throughout Chinese history except for very brief interruptions.[5] Even during what the Chinese call the "hundred years of shame"—from the Opium Wars of the 1840s to the founding of the People's Republic of China (PRC) in 1949—when China was clearly an object of empire, racial and civilizational discourses that consolidated the Han self against the non-Han others flourished. In the Chinese racial discourse of the late nineteenth and early twentieth centuries, for instance, the yellow race of the Han was placed on the most advanced evolutionary spectrum alongside or even surpassing the whites, as opposed to the condemned black, brown, and red races of the world. While I will analyze some of the representative Chinese discourses on civilizational and racial organization of the world below, if only to provide documentary evidence to show that such discourses have both a long and contemporary genealogy, I want to proceed first with the question of why Chinese empire has been so beset with the ambiguity, controversy, and very strong emotions mentioned above. For one thing, in the seven decades from the 1950s to the 2020s, an affective community constituted by various agents promulgated and guarded the injunction that China *could not* be the subject of empire, nor could it practice imperialism. While the global community in the early 2020s seems to have awakened overnight to the reality of Chinese power and wealth—leading to simple-minded and right-tilted condemnations of problematic Chinese colonial and imperial practices at home and abroad— the ideological Manicheanism governing Western intellectual discourses on the left has not yet loosened its hold. Some on the left continue to displace Uyghur genocide as right-wing conspiracy and new cold-war propaganda, taking an anti-imperialist attitude toward the West and lauding China's rise as creating a multipolar world that checks Western imperialism. In so doing, they disallow the possibility of Chinese imperialism, as if we cannot be critical of Western and Chinese imperialisms at the same time.[6]

In fact, the discursive injunction against Chinese empire and imperialism has been coproduced by multiple actors, which explains why it has been so durable. While it is easy to understand why, for purposes of displacement and disavowal, PRC state-controlled discourse indignantly insists that China can never be the subject of empire, it is not as readily apparent why it should be the case in Western academic and intellectual discourses. I suggest that this is the result of a convergence of multiple intellectual positions, born of ideological struggles and contestations in the West, with the aid of China's statist discourse and that of its statist intellectuals. Broadly speaking, I see three parties at work to form a discursive trinity that has made the injunction so powerful as to be virtually inviolable until the early 2020s: Western leftist intellectuals who were sympathetic toward socialist China and held onto outdated romantic visions of China as the alternative to the capitalist West; U.S. left-leaning China studies scholars who were similarly aligned with socialist China, albeit under a specific logic of area studies; and Chinese nationalist intellectuals of all hues, whether state-sponsored, state-compliant, or state-resistant, and whether considered leftist or liberal. How the voices of the Western left collapsed with the voices of the Chinese statist left in their shared defense of China is the story that must be analyzed if we are to demystify the sanctity of this injunction. How those daring to violate the injunction must, therefore, suffer the charge of being Western imperialist apologists, right-wing hawks, or Cold War hysteria-mongers is also part of this story of simplistic ideological Manicheanism. Of course, there are apologists, hawks, and hysteria-mongers, but not all those who criticize China or see China as imperialistic can be summarily reduced to these stereotypes. Such summary condemnations have, unfortunately, had the effect of silencing critical conversations on the left, encouraging ideological myopia, and unwittingly serving China's statist discourse of victimology, displacement, and denial. There has been, to say the least, more than sufficient ideological inflexibility on both the left and the right.

A discourse of Chinese exceptionalism is both the underlying principle and the logical conclusion for all three parties, ultimately not unlike the European exceptionalism that gave Eurocentrism and Western imperialism their most formidable substance, justification, and durability. For many left intellectuals in the West, the need for the Chinese alternative to Western capitalism had been necessary, especially after their disillusionment with the Soviet Union. China was made to be the exception to capitalist hegemony. As for the left-leaning China studies scholars who often supplied data supporting the left's need for the Chinese alternative, they were able to do so thanks to the area studies logic of expertise. The logic of expertise dictates that only those with the requisite training and language skills can know China, which encouraged a sense of monopoly and ownership over such knowledge and the belief that everything about China is particular and different, thereby precluding any attempt at generalist understanding. Otherwise, the knowledge would not need to be learned with such great effort and so much time. Hence, all knowledge obtained about China was made to carry the ethnonational marker "Chinese." Such a logic in area studies that mandates Chinese particularity was to become the basis of a powerful exceptionalism. Chinese nationalism, fueled by the erstwhile wounding by Western imperialism, has given further ammunition to this exceptionalism, its self-defensiveness and powerful censorship of contrary views having already reached global dimensions.

The power of this discursive trinity is further derived from it being an affective community. What has made both the mutually enforcing injunction and the exceptionalism so inviolable is the coalescing of strong affect expressed by these three discursive positions. Western leftists generally bore guilt toward the so-called Third World, feeling responsible for its colonization and underdevelopment, while maintaining a romantic attachment to those Third World countries that have engaged in socialist experimentation, however failed those experiments turned out to be. Until recently, for instance, there has been a persistent denial that China is no longer of the Third World or socialist. The deniers failed to see Chinese Third Worldism, carefully crafted since at least the Bandung Conference, as a strategic and self-serving discourse that has not only facilitated China's entry into the capitalist world but also engendered sympathy from left-leaning intellectuals globally.[7] For the leftist China studies scholars in the United States, who tended to take positions coalescing with that of the Chinese state, there has been not only sympathy toward China but also indignation felt on behalf of China, which has translated into a surprising degree of coyness when it comes to behavior for which China may be criticized. As scholars who have spent their lives studying China, it is not surprising that they may internalize to some extent the indignant emotions of the dominant Han Chinese toward the West. The degree of this indignation can be measured by the harshness of their antagonism toward critics of China. If one had criticized China for a specific failing, the rejoinder was that the United States had already done the same or worse. Finally, for the Chinese nationalists, the memorialization of wounding and injury by Western imperialism helped make their ressentiment unassailably justified, even sacred, so that China was beyond criticism. After all, according to all parties in this affective community, China was and, to some, is still *the* victim.

For the affective community to have been effective for so long, it turned affect into fetishism, which also strengthened its inflexibility. It made a fetish, first, of Chinese victimhood at the hands of Western imperialism to such an extent that China could only be the object of empire, thus creating a semantic and logical impossibility for China to be the subject of empire. Secondly, it fetishized China's ideological sanctity, which seemingly acquired metaphysical or even divine qualities, leading to the euphemization of Chinese power as just achievement attained by itself, i.e., self-generated, which further supports its exceptionalism. Fetishization, as Latin American intellectual Enrique Dussel has shown, is the process of making divine.[8] The necessity for the important work of critique was thus relinquished to the right while the left, from a self-satisfied moral high ground, dismissed, in a knee-jerk fashion, anyone criticizing China's failings as stoking Cold War hysteria and speaking in support of U.S. empire and imperialism. This position has proven to have a lasting power that stymied genuine critical work so long as China appeared to deserve empathy, admiration, and indignation on its behalf.

Giovanni Arrighi is probably typical of the Western left. In his highly acclaimed *Adam Smith in Beijing* (2007), he argues that, contrary to the conventional position that there is no market road to socialism, China's economic development has proven to be an example of Smithian noncapitalist market economy, able to counter U.S. empire and bring about a "socially more equitable and ecologically more sustainable" future for the world.[9] He writes that, in contrast to European colonialist practices and prior to the European arrival, the "China-centered system" in East Asia had enjoyed "five hundred years of peace" by way of the tribute trade system, the "near absence of intra-systemic military competition and extra-systemic geographical expansion," and the absence of "any tendency" to build overseas empires or engage in an arms race. The Manchu Empire, which Arrighi considers Chinese, had been a much more benign empire than European empires, and in the eighteenth century, it was the "exemplar of Smith's 'natural' path to opulence."[10] Given such a track record, he continues, it is not surprising that contemporary China's ascent in the world is on an alternate path from that of neoliberal capitalism via the development of a noncapitalist market economy, a gradualist reform process, the subordination of capitalist interests to national interests, the practice of "accumulation without dispossession," and the practice of a "distinct Chinese brand of Marxism-Leninism" in the social arena oriented toward egalitarianism.[11] He concludes that if this China continues its path, we shall see the emergence of a new Bandung era, where China, in its leadership role of the Global South, shall be in a position to "contribute decisively to the emergence of a commonwealth of civilizations truly respectful of cultural differences." But if China veers from this course of noncapitalist market development with socialist egalitarianism, China will turn into the epicenter of social and political chaos, which will leave the Global North, the West, to lead the world again via its usual violent practices.[12]

Erudite and persuasive as Arrighi's book is in his analysis of Smithian economics in relation to China, his is a hopelessly romantic vision, very much in the tradition of Western Marxists habitually and insistently seeing China as the *ontological* alternative to the capitalist world order since the heady days of the global sixties.[13] If China should be unable to serve its ontological purpose, Arrighi expects that China will fall into chaos, leaving absolutely no room for the other potential outcome: China itself emerging as an imperialist power. In 2007, when the book was published, it was not at all the case that China still belonged to the Global South. As indicated above, China's Third Worldism had been deliberately engineered in a way that allowed China to succeed in the capitalist world order, which meant an economic departure from the Global South while maintaining solidarity with the Global South rhetorically—a practice that continues to the present day. Since time immemorial, China has always been the North, in both political and economic terms, to most of its neighboring countries in Asia, especially in Southeast Asia, not to mention Taiwan. This has also become abundantly true across Africa, where China is increasingly involved in the twenty-first century. By the 2020s, it has become clear that neither Arrighi's hope nor his fear would be materialized, as China has neither become an egalitarian world leader nor plunged into chaos. While he built much of his argument on the work of China studies scholars such as Arif Dirlik and others, Western leftist romanticism toward China has gradually lost its emotional object, as China has refused to adhere to the image held dear by them. In a remarkable reversal, furthermore, Dirlik himself penned a scathing indictment of China's complicity with global capitalism in a tellingly titled book, *Complicities: The People's Republic of China in Global Capitalism* (2017), which came out ten years after Arrighi's book. In this book, Dirlik argues that, instead of a socialism aimed to achieve a just society, China has relentlessly pursued wealth and power; instead of socialism as a means to national liberation, China has not only exercised colonial occupation of Tibet, Xinjiang, and Inner Mongolia but also created its own overseas colonies in enclaves of Chinese laborers sent abroad; instead of being a revolutionary leader against global capitalism, China has aimed for global "imperial hegemony" in the world, creating a new tribute system that is driven by political interests while exercising censorship globally through economic as well as academic blackmail. In view of these facts, Dirlik admits that U.S. academics writing about China have been nothing less than "servile" to China.[14]

This dramatic reversal by a Western Marxist who is also a China studies scholar—and a self-styled anarchist in Dirlik's case—seems to finally reckon with a reality that has been in the making since the 1950s. However, Dirlik's clarion call has not been widely followed within the China studies scholarly community, with the exception of those scholars who study minority and Indigenous populations within the PRC, such as the Uyghurs and the Tibetans, whose existential duress has increased exponentially in the twenty-first century under pervasive and intensifying Chinese settler colonization. Mainstream U.S. China studies scholars, who frame Han Chinese as *the* Chinese and Han culture as *the* Chinese civilization, continue to be either silent or coy about criticizing China in any sustained way, lest their leftist ideological position be seen as compromised and mistakenly collapsed with that of the U.S. right-wing hawks.

Ironically, it is mostly the work of non-China studies scholars, whose research and livelihood do not depend on China and the Chinese state and who are not wedded to China as the ontological alternative, that, at the beginning of the twenty-first century, began to consider China's rise as the contemporary manifestation of a long, durable, and continuous imperium. For example, Jane Burbank and Frederick Cooper, U.S. scholars of world history, argue that the years between 1911 and the establishment of the PRC in 1949 were, in fact, merely "another interlude in a very long imperial history" of China. Contemporary China clearly has an "imperial map" in mind and has been "innovating and reinvigorating its imperial tradition once again," its policies another transformation of "the long-lived Chinese imperial tradition."[15] A British scholar who lived for a long time in South Africa, Adrian Hadland, even compares the European "scramble for Africa" during 1880–1914 with twenty-first century China-African relations and shows many similarities between the two scrambles, from "the multiple agendas of the actors and the role of compradors through to patterns of investment and financing" and characterizes Chinese practices in Africa as "neo-imperialism."[16] Alfred McCoy, a U.S. historian of the Philippines and the United States, makes a geopolitical argument as to why China is emerging as a global empire. He draws from Halford J. MacKinder's 1904 address at the Royal Geographical Society entitled "The Geographical Pivot of History," which challenged the maritime argument for world power and instead proposed that it is the control of Europe, Asia, and Africa—not as three continents but as one unitary landmass—that makes world empires. Accordingly, it is present-day China that has carefully unified and increased control of the Eurasian landmass by building a massive transcontinental infrastructure through the One Belt, One Road Initiative, fulfilling MacKinder's vision and successfully competing with and even supplanting the United States to emerge as a global empire.[17]

I believe it is not a coincidence that Hadland is a scholar of Africa and McCoy a scholar of the Philippines; both areas are squarely in the Global South and under different degrees of Chinese imperial aegis. As in the proposal that the oppressed or the marginalized have a degree of epistemic privilege in understanding the workings of power,[18] I surmise that Hadland and McCoy perhaps see China more clearly because they view China from the perspectives of Africa and the Philippines and thus are more critical of China, as opposed to those Western leftists who prefer to see China as the ontological alternative to the West. Similarly, China studies scholars who study the minority and Indigenous populations in China tend to be much more critical of the PRC state, as opposed to those who study the mainstream, majority China, who tend not to question Han-centric and statist perspectives. Such is also the case for those who take the epistemic position of Taiwan under direct threat of Chinese invasion, Hong Kong under punishing Chinese authoritarianism, and the millions of Tibetans, Uyghurs, Kazakhs, and Mongolians residing within the geopolitical boundary of China.

In the following, I find it imperative to provide a short genealogy of Chinese empire, even if an unorthodox Foucauldian one,[19] as discursive support to the argument that the rise of Chinese empire is not a historical accident. The genealogy will begin with a question of the empire that immediately preceded modern China, the Manchu Empire, followed by a review of Chinese discourses of race, nation, and empire since the late nineteenth century to arrive at the question of Chinese empire at our historical moment.

Is the Manchu Empire Chinese?

Like all signifiers, the two words, China and empire, that form the compound term "Chinese empire" (Zhonghua diguo) are both empty signifiers in and of themselves. *China* (Zhonghua/Zhongguo) is a construction with a contested historical and textual genealogy, each instance of construction implicating the questions of who defines it, who claims it, and doing so on what grounds and for what reasons. Even in the most general terms, there are striking spatial and temporal variations to its construction. Spatially, what we call "China" has been a changing geographical entity with dramatically different territorial boundaries over time: At its smallest, it was about one-tenth of today's China. What territorial China has been over time is, therefore, not a given but a process, bounded contingently in specific historical periods only to shift and change again. Furthermore, what we call "China" was not even the correct nomenclature for most periods of its history, especially when it comes to those historical periods prior to the Sui dynasty (581–618) when the territory about the size of one-fourth of today's China was unified under Han rule;[20] during times of intense fragmentation such as the Six Dynasties (222–589); and during those long periods of non-Han rule such as the Mongol Empire (aka Yuan dynasty, 1205–1368) and the Manchu Empire (aka Qing dynasty, 1644–1912). To determine whether contemporary China is an empire or not, therefore, requires a retrospective view, especially of the Manchu Empire that immediately preceded modern China, if only for the fact that the PRC has largely inherited the territory of the Manchu Empire with an intact imperial infrastructure. The more crucial question here, then, is whether the Manchu Empire could even be considered "Chinese," as this pertains not only to the (il)legitimacy of inheritance but also to the periodization of Chinese empire.

So, was the Manchu Empire Chinese?

This was the topic of an intense debate in the field of Chinese history in the United States between the proponents of the Sinicization thesis and the scholars of the so-called New Qing History. Briefly, the Sinicization thesis is largely a unidirectional assimilationist thesis. As explained by Crossley, Siu, and Sutton, it assumes that "the inherent charisma of Chinese culture" as the single civilizing force emanating from the "Chinese imperial center" has assimilated all alien cultures and peoples throughout history, including, and especially, during the periods of alien rule. For this narrative of assimilation to work, which is also a narrative of inherent Chinese superiority over all those they had come into contact with, the history of violent military conquests is minimized on the one hand, and the participation of local societies and Indigenous populations in the state-making process is dismissed on the other.[21] According to this thesis, everyone, ineluctably, *becomes Chinese*, thanks to the superior civilization that is Chinese. Mongols became Chinese, so the Mongol Empire was the Chinese Yuan dynasty. Similarly, Manchus became Chinese, so the Manchu Empire was the Chinese Qing dynasty.

The Sinicization thesis thus effectively sanctions a narrative of Chinese history as an unbroken succession of Chinese dynasties since time immemorial.

New Qing historians disagree. First and foremost, they argue for the "Manchu-ness" of the Manchus as an ethnoracial group in their public and private practices within the Qing Empire. They document how the Manchus deliberately maintained their unique ethnicity, language, and culture by way of, for instance, the ethnicity-specific, hereditary Eight Banner system, which began as military divisions that included some separate Mongolian and Han banners but ended up being mainly identity markers for the Manchus, who, through this system, were granted land and income for no other reason than for the purpose of preserving their "ethnic sovereignty."[22] The banner people, until the overthrow of the Manchu Empire in 1911, lived apart from the Han in their separate Manchu cities, did not intermarry with the Han, and practiced their own distinctive culture.[23] As a multiethnic empire, the Manchu court ensured Manchu separation from the Han also by way of deliberate denigration of Han Chinese values, especially since the Manchus were not the demographic majority.[24] As it consolidated Manchu-ness as an ethnicity—by way of distinctions in language and customs (such as hairstyle, clothing, food, and wedding and funeral rituals)—it simultaneously reinforced the Han as a distinct ethnicity called the Nikan in the Manchu language.[25] In its official multilingual policy, it also designated the Manchu language as the preferred language of the empire.

One may argue that the Manchu Empire became more Han-ized as Han people increasingly took up official positions by the mid-nineteenth century, but having more Han people at the court is fundamentally different from asserting that the Manchu Empire became Chinese, or Sinicized.[26] James Millward shows that the notion of Sinicization of the Manchu Empire was a retrospective construction by Han nationalists in the middle of the twentieth century, decades after the end of the Manchu rule.[27] In fact, Han antagonism against the Manchus had long been in existence during the Manchu Empire, initially articulated as the conquered against the conquerors by Ming loyalists living in the empire or in exile after the Manchu conquest in 1644. By the late nineteenth century, after the continuous humiliation suffered by the Manchu Empire at the hands of Western imperialism, Han intellectuals developed a sophisticated anti-Manchu discourse, as in the work of the renowned thinker Zhang Taiyan (1869–1936), who advocated Han racial unity and the overthrow of the Manchus.[28] The leader of the Republican Revolution, Sun Yat-sen, also deliberately reinforced the idea of the Han as a distinct race in order to cultivate and promote an anti-Manchu discourse in support of the revolution.[29] The revolutionary party members' oath began with the phrase, "expelling the northern barbarians and restoring China" (qüzhu dalu, huifu Zhonghua), where the "northern barbarians" refer to the Manchus and "China" unequivocally refers to the Han ethnoracial nation. In this slogan, which served as the raison d'être of the Republic of China established upon the overthrow of the Manchu Empire, the Manchus and the Chinese (read, the Han ethnorace[30]) do not belong to the same community; in fact, they are enemies to each other. Han ethnoracialism had, in fact, been on broad display during and after the Republican Revolution of 1911, in the widespread race-based violence against the Manchus that reached the level of a "threat of racial annihilation," where the Manchus were separated out for their dress, accent, physiology (women with unbound feet), and any other sign of ethnoracial difference to target them for vengeance.[31]

New Qing historians argue that the Manchu Empire was a decidedly Manchu polity, dissimilar from the Han-dominant polities that had come before. Military conquests by the Manchus added to the existing seventeen provinces of the Ming dynasty the vast lands of Xinjiang (literally, "the new dominion"), Tibet, Taiwan, and Mongolia, which, together with Manchuria, constituted about five-eighths of the entire empire. Territorially then, the so-called China proper before the Manchu conquest was less than half of the Manchu Empire. The Manchu Empire was, scholars also note, not only a military empire that committed acts of conquest and massacre, quite contrary to what Arrighi asserted, but also a colonial empire that used population transfer to establish settlements in the geographically contiguous colony of sparsely populated East Turkestan (aka Xinjiang). The Court of Colonial Affairs (*tulergi golo i hafan* in Manchu; *lifanyuan* in Sinitic) was a distinctly Manchu bureaucratic innovation that practiced a complex and effective colonial administration of Mongolia, Tibet, and East Turkestan.[32] The School to Colonize the Borders (*zhibian xuetang* in Sinitic) was also a Manchu invention established to train colonial officials specifically to rule Mongolia and Tibet.[33] Colonial administration was extensive and thorough, including making Xinjiang a province, upgrading the Court of Colonial Affairs into a ministry, setting up the Department of Colonization (*jichuan si* in Sinitic) in charge of emigration to Mongolia, and several other colonial administrative organizations.[34] The Manchu Empire was thus, in many ways, similar to early modern European colonial empires that combined military conquest with well-articulated and instituted colonial policies of ethnic, religious, and gender management, which demonstrates the "completeness" of Manchu colonization efforts.[35] It was an empire that was unlike any dynastic empires that had come before, and, in effect, Manchu rule of Inner Asian dependencies more closely resembled the acquisition of overseas colonies than the conquest of adjacent territory, which disputes the notion that colonialism can only be applied to overseas rather than geographically contiguous territories.[36]

Furthermore, this new greater empire in Inner Asia implemented a specifically Manchu view of universal empire and is, in short, a Manchu creation.[37]

It follows then that, according to New Qing historians, the answer to the question, "Was the Manchu Empire Chinese?" is a "no." If we agree with their argument that the Manchu Empire was not Chinese, it follows then that the lands conquered by the Manchus and added to the empire are not "Chinese" either. For these lands to be included in Chinese sovereignty claims made since the Republican revolution, the answer to the question of "Was the Manchu Empire Chinese?" has to be a "yes." Hence, the Republic of China, even though its revolutionary rhetoric was clearly anti-Manchu, had to change its founding ideology of Han-centrism into a new national policy of "federation of five ethnicities" (wuzugonghe) of Han, Manchu, Mongol, Hui, and Tibetan peoples, so as not to relinquish lands conquered by the Manchus. Similarly, for the Chinese Communist Party that established the PRC in 1949, its early policy of granting political autonomy to all oppressed minority nationalities and areas, including Taiwan, was dramatically altered after coming to power. The rhetoric of restoring and maintaining "territorial integrity" by the PRC now encompasses all the territory conquered by the Manchu Empire at its height, with the exception of (outer) Mongolia, which later became independent. This is the "China" that is framed today as the natural consequence of five millennia of presumed continuous history and political unity, and the "China" as attributed and sanctioned by the international community. The logic goes that everything that belonged to the Manchu Empire belongs to China because the Manchu Empire was Chinese. If this logic is correct, then we must posit that the Mongol Empire was also Chinese. Then we may wonder whether Chinese sovereignty should extend to such countries as today's Iran, Iraq, Romania, and Turkey, which were all under Mongol rule.

In any event, it is an indisputable fact that, with the exception of now independent (outer) Mongolia, the PRC claims the vast lands conquered by the Manchus, whether these claims have legitimacy or not. This much we all agree on. However, not all scholars agree that the Manchu Empire was imperialist, nor do they agree that contemporary China is an empire that engages in imperialistic behavior. Some say that the Manchu Empire was an empire, a *diguo*, as acknowledged by Han intellectuals during the Manchu Empire who used this term interchangeably with the older term "all under heaven" (tianxia), but not imperialist.[38] Contemporary Han Chinese historian Ge Zhaoguang disagrees with the tortuous semantic disentanglement between the two words, *empire* and *imperialism*, by simply stating that the Manchu Empire had "imperialist tendencies," even if these tendencies might be different from those of Western empires.[39] Even for Ge, however, while his three books on the question of "China" emphasize the contingent territorial boundaries of "China" as caused by colonialist practices, military conquests, and assimilation of its peripheries,[40] he carefully avoids extending his discussion to contemporary China by limiting his discussion to "historical" China, meaning China before the PRC. Suffice it to say that to discuss contemporary China using the terms that he offers can be very risky in China, as they challenge the primordialism of Chinese sovereignty claimed by the PRC over the conquered lands.

Race and Colonialism in Pax Sinica

In this context, it is helpful to review some of the representative discourses of Chinese imperium within China both during the hundred years of shame, when China was clearly the object of empire, and in the twenty-first century after China achieved the status of world power. Four figures within my unorthodox genealogy include the influential Han intellectuals Zhang Taiyan and Liang Qichao (1873–1929), who, writing in the late nineteenth and early twentieth centuries, formulated the vision of a future Chinese empire with a distinct theory of race, nation, and culture simultaneous with the production of a new genre of futuristic fiction projecting the coming Chinese empire; historian Li Changfu (1899–1966), who was part of the Jinan University group tasked by the ROC government to study Nanyang, i.e., Southeast Asian, cultural affairs and wrote a major book on the history of Chinese colonialism; and philosopher Zhao Tingyang, whose work lent scholarly support to the revival of the Chinese imperial discourse of all-under-heaven in the twenty-first century and showcased the conjunction of the temporalities of the past and the future in the present time of empire.

As the person who coined the name "Republic of China" (Zhonghua minguo) in 1907, which was later adopted by the government of the new republic in 1911, Zhang Taiyan penned some of the most influential essays on the relationship between race and nation. Even though these essays were written over a century ago, his views, along with the views of Liang Qichao, have had a foundational significance and indelible legacy, presaging with surprising consistency the ideas that underlie the racialized policies of the contemporary PRC state. Being a staunch racialist, Zhang, as the title of his influential 1901 essay "Zheng chouman lun" (On the correct hatred of the Manchus) suggests, advocated racial discrimination against the Manchus, whom he saw as an alien race diametrically different from the Han.[41] A few years later, in an effort to reconceptualize the new republic to encompass all the peoples within the Manchu Empire, he moved to a more assimilationist position, similar to the views of his peers, but without giving up on his Han-centric racialism. In "Explaining 'The Republic of China'" (1907), the article bearing the future name of the republic, he continued to denigrate the Manchus as "indolent," "greedy," "lazy," "corrupt," and "parasitic" people, who "commit disgraceful acts" and can achieve nothing beyond "looting and extortion." Short of letting the Manchus as well as the peoples of the "three wild domains"—Mongolians, Tibetans, and Muslims—form their own separate and independent countries since these peoples and their territories ("dependencies") were "taken over" rather late in Chinese history, he reasoned, these alien races may be incorporated into the future republic through assimilation with the Han. How would this assimilation work? According to Zhang, the future republic will be a racial state par excellence constituted by the Han people as the only sovereign subjects. The name Republic of China (Zhong-Hua-min-guo) means the "Republic of the Central Hua," where the "Hua" refers to the Hua people, as Hua is a synonym for Han, the "national race" (guozu). He, therefore, intended that the name of the republic retain its racial sense as a Han Republic. The word Hua was later retained by the People's Republic of China (Zhong-Hua-ren-min-gong-he-guo), again showing the consistency. According to Zhang, the Hua/Han constitutes "one race," the "one uniform majority blood lineage constituting [the] main body" of the republic. Once this main body achieves its sovereignty after overthrowing the Manchus, the Han may then consider allowing "alien races to assimilate with us." In other words, the first precondition for inclusion of the alien races is the sovereignty of the Han, and, to rescue them from their inferiority, the second precondition is that they become assimilated. The assimilation process would require "taming" these people first through an "enlightened despotism" as well as twenty years of education before they would be allowed to assimilate and participate fully in the new republic. Furthermore, to this Han-centric assimilation of the Manchus, Muslims, Mongolians, Tibetans, and others, and the incorporation of their territories, Zhang believed the republic should also add Vietnam, Cambodia, Myanmar, and Korea to its territory in the future.[42] As this summary shows, Zhang's vision for the republic clearly exceeded that of a nation-state and approached that of a supranational empire, constituted by a clearly laid-out, hierarchical ordering of races and nationalities with the Han race at its center and apex.

Zhang's emphasis on Han racial unity, superiority, and sovereignty as the foundation of the new republic and as the precondition for the assimilation of other races is, in fact, quite mild when compared to the views of many of his contemporaries, such as the unabashedly racist Zou Rong (1885–1905), who called for the rape and massacre of the Manchus.[43] Consider also the work of his other contemporary, Liu Shipei (1884–1919), whose polemical

Rangshu (Book of expulsion; 1903) argued for the expulsion of the non-Han peoples from the Han Chinese polity altogether since they would "pollute" the purity of the Han and therefore the latter's ability to build a new nation. In Liu's *Zhongguo minzu zhi* (Record of China's ethnicities; 1905), he revived the stereotypical taxonomies of the non-Han peoples as beasts, raptors, insects, dogs, and worms, who must be expelled by the might of Han civilization ("yi wenming rangyi").[44] It is, therefore, unsurprising that the founding father of the Republic of China, Sun Yat-sen, would hold similar views: "When we speak of China, no matter what peoples may be included in the future, they must be assimilated into our Han race"; "assimilating the Tibetans, Mongols, Huis and Manchus into our Han race" is necessary to construct "the largest possible race-state" in the world, all of which is premised on the "self-determination of the Han people."[45]

The other major Han thinker from the period, Liang Qichao, shared with Zhang a persistent racial imagination that emphasized Han racial power and superiority as the basis for a hopeful vision of a future Chinese nation. Liang's racial imagination, however, while equally directed toward the non-Han peoples within the Manchu Empire, was infused with an acute awareness of the place of the Han as the representative yellow race in the context of the global white supremacy of his time. In many of Liang's essays on the question of race, he showed a clear inclination toward what I would describe as Hegelian racism with a Chinese twist, where geographical and environmental determinism are combined with racialized historicism. In his thinking, the yellow Han race occupies the same exalted place as the white race, destined to be superior in development due to geographical and climatic advantages, and is, therefore, a people with history, in contradistinction to those without. Liang follows Hegel closely here, except substituting Hegel's white race with the yellow Han race.[46] Indeed, in all these discourses of race, civilization, and nation, there is a persistent race envy toward the whites, to the extent of direct transposition of yellows in place of whites, as well as a desire to surpass the whites.

In "The Future of the Chinese Race" (1899), Liang makes the case for the superiority of the Han Chinese race, in a specifically species sense of race (renzhong), in the global context. He argues that the future belongs to the Han race due to their four natural endowments: the Han are most capable of "governing themselves"; they are endowed with the "nature of adventure and independence"; they are "strong in scholarship and hence thought develops easily"; and, finally, since China has a large population and rich natural resources, the Han are most adept at business, and since Han labor is inexpensive, China will become *the* major power in the world economy. With these four endowments, the yellow Han race is superior to white people who are "proud and cannot tolerate hardship" and black and brown people who are "lazy and lack wisdom," and so it is to be expected that only China can control the entire world in the future and the "Chinese race will be the most powerful race in the world." Just as Australia and North America were colonies of white people at that moment, South America and Africa would surely become Chinese colonies in the future, given the Han's ability for self-government (zizhi 自治), which is the basis for their self-motivated colonization (zizhi 自殖).[47] The futurity of global Chinese power is, furthermore, predetermined by China's position in Asia and the world: "Asia is sovereign of the world, China is sovereign of Asia, and China Proper is sovereign of China."[48] From "China Proper," the Han area at the center of China, China extends and assimilates all alien races. China is thus the sovereign of Asia and, by extension, sovereign of the world, as Chinese civilization is peerless in its superiority and reaches outward through the entire world.

Liang's theory of Han civilization's assimilative power would become the direct starting point for the "Sinicization thesis" of China studies scholars in the United States discussed earlier.[49] Again, here we see China studies scholars replicating a Chinese discourse, however problematic it might be. Again as well, Liang's is by no means an imagination restricted to the nation-state but a global vision wherein China is projected to colonize South America and Africa to take an equal share of the world with the Western powers and, furthermore, to dominate the world. In hindsight, it is as if Liang had predicted the intense Chinese engagement with South America and Africa in the twenty-first century, offering a blueprint for the future Chinese empire with global ambitions.

To project such a powerful global future, however, requires some evidence of success in the past, especially in terms of the Han race's innate capacity as colonizers. On par with Hegel's white Europeans whose desire for "life to step beyond itself" helped them "found" colonies,[50] Liang uses the same rhetoric to describe the Han as endowed with the spirit of "adventure and independence" to qualify as the best colonizers. He discusses Chinese colonialism on several occasions in his works, but the article titled "Zhongguo zhimin bada weiren zhuan" (Biographies of eight great heroes of Chinese colonialism, 1905) offers the most focused discussion. Essentially a hagiography of Han colonists, this article is, in fact, the earliest work of its kind to use the modern sense of the terms *colonialism* (zhimin) and *colony* (zhimindi) in China. In this article, which would become the major reference for numerous similar discussions up to the present day, Liang argues that Chinese settlements in Southeast Asia should be considered "natural Chinese colonies" even though the Manchu state did not directly control them. In fact, unlike Western colonialism, Chinese colonialism does not need the sponsorship of the state, as the Han are natural rulers, settlers, and colonizers due to their independent spirit that propels them to not only govern themselves but also colonize others without needing state support. As in the historical case of the global voyages of Zheng He in the fifteenth century, which Liang deems comparable to those of Christopher Columbus, Ferdinand Magellan, and Vasco da Gama, the Han are endowed with the capacity for maritime expansion. This is evidenced by the many kingdoms established or ruled by the Han/Hua race (Huazu) in Thailand, Sumatra, Vietnam, Java, Borneo, Myanmar, Vietnam, Philippines, and the Malay Peninsula between the fourteenth and nineteenth centuries. He emphasizes that these heroic colonists were all of the Han race—Cantonese, Hakka, and Hokkiense—and, as a matter of fact, were superior to Columbus, Magellan, and da Gama, as they did not even need the state sponsorship of the Ming or Manchu courts. He hopes that writing this genealogy would "carry our nation's glory forward and inspire fellow countrymen to open up new lands." The description of self-motivated colonization in this article and this call to "open up new lands" are as close as it gets to classic definitions of settler colonialism.[51]

Liang's call was to be echoed later in popular eugenics discourses, ethnology, and, most interestingly, works of fiction, given that Liang advocated for the importance of fiction in the edification and governance of the people. In many examples of the new genre of science fiction or speculative fiction in China in the early twentieth century, the black, brown, and red races are depicted as having met a steep decline so that the world is left to be contested over by only the white and yellow races, with the yellow race ultimately emerging victorious. *Xin Jiyuan* (The new century, 1908) portrays Han settlements in Africa, Australia, and the Americas becoming Chinese "extra-territories," while *Dian Shijie* (Electric world, 1909) sees China emerging as the master of the entire world after vanquishing the Europeans.[52] Many other novels about colonization were published during this period, with such titles as *Auzhou lixianji* (Adventures in Australia), *Shizi hou* (Lion's roar), and *Huangjin shijie* (Golden world), while translations of Western colonialist texts, such as the works of Henry Morton Stanley (1841–1904) on Africa, were also popular. Most notable among these works of fiction is the 1905 novel by He Jiong titled *Shizi xie* (Lion's blood), whose telling subtitle is *Zhina gelunbo* (Chinese Columbus). This novel offers an expansive imagination of Han colonization and settlement in Mexico, Java, Africa, and even farther afield to the Arctic Ocean. It is especially noteworthy for the part set in Africa where the Chinese Columbus, unlike the real Columbus, is presented as a benevolent colonizer who frees slaves, opens up lands for agriculture, develops industries, and offers education and enlightenment to enable the moral and civilizational transformation of the "odorous and dirty" natives.[53] The Han colonizers are, in short, better at the colonization of Africa than the Europeans.

Retrospective and prospective discourses on Chinese colonialism by Han intellectuals during the waning years of the Manchu Empire did not cease with the founding of the republic and would, in fact, become an institutional project. The Chinese colonial discourse would receive a much fuller treatment in the work of Li Changfu and others during this period. Li was a member of a group of more than thirty researchers at the Department of Nanyang Cultural Affairs (Nanyang wenhua shiyebu) established in 1927 at Shanghai's Jinan University—the department that published two periodicals, more than thirty books, and numerous other documents such as maps, references, and textbooks about Southeast Asia.[54] Li Changfu's *Zhongguo zhimin shi* (A history of Chinese colonialism, 1937), which is a classic of its kind, offers perhaps the most comprehensive overview of Chinese colonialism of its time. Li uses a distinctly modern definition of colonialism to refer to economic as well as political relationships involving military conquest, economic dependence, and settlement/immigration, with copious references to and comparisons with scholarship in French, English, Japanese, Dutch, and German. By this time, the republic had claimed all the territories of the Manchu Empire, however unstable its grip might have been, and fostered a national discourse of a multiethnic republic to legitimize that claim, the discourse no longer limited to the Han but invoking the inclusive "Chinese" (Zhongguoren, literally, people of the Chinese nation). Now the "Chinese" included non-Han groups, especially those alien people, like the Manchus, who had colonized lands that Republican China was happy to lay claim to.

Li Changfu divides the history of Chinese colonialism into four periods: the period of early Chinese colonialism, the height of Chinese colonial power, the period of intercolonial rivalry between China and Europe, and, finally, the period of the ascendance of European colonial power. The first period covers China's contacts with Western Asia, South Asia, Japan, Korea, and Southeast Asia from around 400 BC to the end of the thirteenth century, which led to the establishment of a vast tributary system where "foreign kings sent their emissaries to express submission by offering tributes to China," even as these tributes had underlying economic purposes.[55] During this period, Chinese emigrated and settled as far away as Persia and Iraq to the west, Japan to the east, and throughout Southeast Asia to the south. The second period begins with the expansion of the Mongol Empire and its "colonial invasion" of vast areas of the world, constituting the largest landed, transcontinental empire in human history. After the fall of the Mongol Empire—claimed as Chinese here—Ming China, though reduced in size geographically, still functioned as a colonial power, evidenced by the seven sea expeditions of the Muslim eunuch Zheng He in the fifteenth century. Against the view that Zheng He's journeys were mainly peaceful displays of Chinese wealth and technological superiority, he argues that, like the Mongol invasion of Java, Champa, and Burma, they were, in fact, for purposes of "political and military expansion."[56] He notes that these expeditions toppled regimes in Ceylon, Sumatra, and Palembang and brought dozens of other states into the Chinese tributary system, constituting a particularly "glorious" chapter in the history of Chinese colonialism. This was also the time when Chinese settlers in Southeast Asia either set up their own regimes, as in Palembang, Datani, and Sumatra, or seriously contested European and local regimes, such as in Luzon. Li argues that, before the eighteenth century, much of Southeast Asia had largely been "subject to Chinese colonial power," evidenced by the Manchu invasion of Burma and the Chinese settler regimes in Siam, Hatien, and Songkla.[57] Zheng He's large-scale "overseas invasions" (haiwai qinlue) and the Mongol and Manchu invasions of Southeast Asia are evidence that Chinese colonialism had a maritime character, just like that of European colonialism, again refuting Hegel's European exceptionalism and making China equal to the task of maritime colonialism, as Liang Qichao did thirty years earlier.[58]

Li's historiography on early Chinese colonialism was partially corroborated by Western scholarship on Chinese colonialism and settlement in Southeast Asia that came much later. This scholarship was done by scholars in Southeast Asian studies, not China studies, who, due to their standpoint, were more likely to present a bottom-up view from Southeast Asian perspectives. According to them, prior to the arrival of the Europeans during the early and relatively open stage of interactions, the Chinese did actually create ruling dynasties in Southeast Asia, notably in Ayutthaya, Brunei, Melaka, and Demak. They also established autonomous Chinese polities at Hatien in the Vietnam-Cambodia borderland and in the gold fields of western Borneo, and the powerful Thonburi and Bangkok dynasties in Siam were themselves half-Chinese.[59] Among them was the independent republic in western Borneo, the Lanfang Republic, which lasted over one hundred years (1777–1884) and was one of the earliest republics in the world. Li himself describes these colonies as the "colonialism of the overseas Chinese" (huaqiao zhimin), for which he coined the term "immigrant colonizers" (yizhimin 移殖民), thereby connecting immigration with colonization, similar to the concept of settler colonialism. Indeed, the Lanfang Republic is probably the clearest case of a Chinese settler colony in Southeast Asia for the period, as are today's Taiwan (whose Indigenous people are Austronesian) and Hainan (whose Indigenous people are Thai).

Li continues that even during the fourth period, when European ascendency seemed to have supplanted Chinese colonialism in Southeast Asia (approximately 1821 to 1901), the Manchu Empire did not give up its power in Southeast Asia that easily. As the suzerain (zongzhuguo) of Burma and

Vietnam, the Manchu court fought a war with the French in Vietnam in 1884 and signed a treaty with the British in 1886 in which Great Britain acceded to the Manchu Empire's demand that Burma continue to pay tribute to China for ten years. This is the era when the Chinese in Southeast Asia became *tusschenhandelaar* (Dutch for "middlemen merchants") between the natives and the European colonizers. During this period, the Chinese also started emigrating to the Americas, the Pacific islands, Europe, and Africa, and this was not simply immigration (yi) but also colonization (zhi), as they formed diasporic secret societies and independent polities, such as the Lanfang Republic, which Li calls an "independent nation-state" (duli guojia), and the Selangor state under the control of one Chinese *kapitan* (captain) called Ye Lai. The history of Chinese coolies is also recounted in a matter-of-fact manner, including the history of anti-Chinese exclusion and racism around the world and the little-known history of 150,000 Chinese coolies and laborers brought to Europe and Russia during World War I. The book ends with a description of the contributions made by the overseas Chinese to the Republic of China up to Li's present time in 1933. It also explains the necessity for the republic to provide protection for its overseas populations so that they do not experience any oppression.[60] Throughout, the history of Chinese colonialism is seen as a glorious one of economic, political, and cultural conquest of other territories until the European contestations of Chinese power, which needs to be confronted and overcome.

In the work of his colleagues in the same department, such as those of Wen Xiongfei and others, the history of Chinese colonialism was more heavily influenced by both social Darwinism as well as European and Japanese ideas and practices of imperialism. They argue that "oceanic spaces are free and open, climate determines human attributes and activities, and settlers of the new frontier should civilize the natives for control."[61] In short, they assert that Chinese colonialism is a civilizing mission aimed at the inferior natives everywhere, while overseas Chinese in Southeast Asia are superior beings equal to and sometimes even surpassing the Europeans. Southeast Asia, the so-called Chinese South Seas, is therefore seen as an empty arena free for the taking by China and the West. Mandated by the Republican government to imitate Japanese research activities about Southeast Asia in preparation for future colonial projects there, while all the while trying to best European colonialism and lamenting China's present weakness as something to be overcome, the Jinan scholars offered historical accounts and justifications for Chinese colonialism both retrospectively and prospectively.[62] Considering the research activities of the department as a whole, furthermore, it is fair to characterize it as the colonial research office aimed at studying and promoting Chinese colonialism, settler or otherwise.

If the Chinese discourse of racial and civilizational superiority as the condition for Chinese colonialism continued unabated during the hundred years of shame, the rise of China has given unprecedented impetus to the revitalization and enhancement of the discourse in the contemporary context. But since the contemporary Chinese state has skillfully eschewed the language of imperialism and colonialism as exclusively belonging to the West, different terms needed to be either recuperated from the past or newly invented. This follows, initially, U.S. China studies scholarship on the form of the Chinese state as an incomplete transition from a (Manchu) empire to a nation-state. As the vast multiethnic territory exceeded the modern framework of the nation-state, China was termed a "civilization-state" or an "empire-state," again showing how China studies scholarship in the United States easily coalesced with Chinese nationalist discourses.[63] Han Chinese intellectuals then only picked up the notion of a "civilization-state" (wenming guojia) after U.S. scholarship.[64] They also claimed that China, being a supranational country that nonetheless must be granted the Westphalian notion of sovereignty, is thus a "multi-systemic state," where the logic of incorporating a vast frontier—especially the Greater Tibet and Xinjiang—is deemed unique to China.[65] The Chinese state form is exceptional, after all.

A popular version of this trend to focus on the form of the Chinese state, as China gathers power and influence across the world in the twenty-first century, is the revival of the ancient imperial discourse of tianxia referred to earlier. Generally speaking, the discourse of tianxia was cosmological-cum-political, involving the emperor in the center as the son of heaven (tianzi) who, with the mandate of heaven (tianming), rules over the realm under heaven. Tianxia as a political theory evinces a concentric structure of power with the son of heaven at the center or apex, emanating his dominion over inner subjects, outer subjects, tributary states, and barbarians in the four directions of north, south, east, and west who inhabit the "outside lands," or the "realm beyond civilization" (huawai zhi di). The renowned U.S. sinologist John K. Fairbank, who analyzed this concept in 1966, translated tianxia as "the Chinese world" and explained that this Chinese world may reach beyond the borders of China but only in "gradually decreasing efficacy, as parts of a concentric hierarchy." Fairbank noted that unlike the theoretical equality presumed by the European ideology of nation-states, the Chinese world order "was not organized by a division of territories of sovereigns of equal status but rather by the subordination of all local authorities to the central and awe-inspiring power of the emperor." Its organizing principle is "superordination-subordination."[66]

Within this political structure, all those outside the center—the so-called China Proper—constitute various barbarian peoples with corresponding synonymous nomenclatures—barbarians (man) in the south, barbarians (di) in the north, barbarians (yi) in the east, and barbarians (rong) in the west—who are wild and beastly peoples in need of both subjugation and appeasement by the son of heaven and awaiting civilizational assimilation (hua or jiaohua).[67] In other words, the theory of tianxia has been historically imbued with the barbarization and primitivization of non-Han others, revealing a deep-seated Han racism, which is geospatially and literally informed by Han centrism, the Han at the center from where the four directions of the world are organized. In the twentieth century, these frontier peoples in China began to shed their stereotypical beastliness, if only in name only: for instance, the northern barbarians have become Mongolians, while today's Uyghurs and Tibetans are the erstwhile western barbarians.[68] Whether packaged as cosmopolitanism (shijie zhuyi) or the Great Unity (datong), as in the work of Han thinkers from the late Manchu Empire, it is a discourse of empire that presumes "the radiance of the civilizational center" that concentrically organizes a hierarchy of races according to their relative distance from the center.[69]

Almost picking up where Fairbank and others left off, Zhao Tingyang, a philosopher at the august institute of academic research in China, the Academy of Social Sciences, along with several other prominent intellectuals, revived tianxia as a Chinese theory of world order in the early twenty-first century—as a matter of fact, as a *world system*—deemed to be much more preferable than the current world system organized around Western ideas.[70] Using Wallerstein's notion of the world system, Zhao characterizes the current one as a system of nation-states, where the nation-states are represented by the United Nations, which he criticizes as nothing but a "political market for nations" where the powerful nations impose their will on the weaker ones. He also criticizes democracy for its mass orientation, noting that the masses "always make the wrong choices for themselves." Instead of the current world system thus described, Zhao proposes tianxia as the superior theory of governance and world order, which is a "universal knowledge system" that China, as a "knowledge-producing great nation," is offering to the world.[71] According to Zhao, tianxia is an ideal form of empire, a "perfect empire," where the world, rather than the nation-state, is primary; it sees the entire world as one family—"family-ship"—and it has the mandate of "the hearts of all peoples," leading to a world society governed by a world institution superior to the United Nations. Such a world society—tianxia—existed in ancient China before the centralized government of the Chinese empire was established in 221 BC and has never existed ever since. This ancient Chinese society was the ideal empire, consisting of many substates, which were economically, militarily, and culturally independent but "politically and ethically" dependent on the empire's institutional core, the suzerain center.[72] Zhao's theory of the Chinese world order has become influential beyond China as well, prompting a two-year dialogue and correspondence between French Marxist philosopher Régis Debray and Zhao, which was published in book form as *Du ciel à la terre: la chine et l'occident* (From Heaven to Earth: China and the West) in Paris in 2014 as well as several academic conferences and publications in the United States.

Essential to the Chineseness of the theory of tianxia, as explained by another prominent theorist of tianxia, Han Yuhai, is the capacity of China to "incorporate four kinds of barbarians," echoing the age-old imperial thinking. His book, *Tianxia: baona siyi de Zhongguo* (All under Heaven: China incorporates four kinds of barbarians), further connects this theory to the early twentieth-century discourse of China's assimilative power I discussed above, showing the lasting power of the work of Han intellectuals such as Liang Qichao in the late Manchu Empire. Han Yuhai uses the character *yi* as a synecdoche for the four kinds of barbarians (siyi) who reside in the four directions from the imperial center. He emphasizes how Chinese empire has always incorporated barbarians into its realm through strategies of "governing the barbarians" (zhiyi), especially by learning the best techniques from the barbarians to, in turn, govern them (yiyi zhiyi). In short, it has always been and continues to be China's "historical mission" to transform barbarism into civilization.[73]

In all the theories of Han Chinese civilizational and racial superiority discussed thus far, the logical implication is that assimilationism is premised on the separateness of the civilizations, races, and realms/territories. In such a formulation, "China" (Zhongguo) is viewed as a geographical, cultural, and racial entity distinct from where and what the four barbarians are. Otherwise, China has no need to incorporate them. This embedded contradiction clearly undermines the imperial discourse of China's historical claim to the lands of the so-called barbarians. As in all the discourses of China's assimilative power, their unintended implication is precisely this: Those people under Chinese assimilative subjection were not originally Chinese nor were part of China, hence requiring assimilation or incorporation. We may observe this as a typical double talk of colonialism: claiming the conquered lands as historical inheritance on the one hand while instituting a hierarchical membership within the colonial empire by a carefully articulated politics of exclusion and inclusion on the other. The Chinese empire, like Western empires, has no lack of such theories to support the double talk.

As we move further to the contemporary moment, Zhao and others can be seen to skillfully connect the language of tianxia with empire, now strongly tinged with nationalist, if not imperial, pride. Echoing Michael Hardt and Antonio Negri's argument in their book *Empire* that empire is the new universal order of the world, contemporary Chinese theorists see tianxia as the universal world order that is essentially Chinese, governed by the Chinese empire. In fact, the first chapter of Zhao's book, *Tianxia tixi* (The Tianxia system), begins with an epigraph from Hardt and Negri's *Empire* and proclaims that we are witnessing, with our own eyes, how empire has become a reality.[74] Between the opening epigraph on empire and the rest of the book on tianxia, the implications are clear and overt.

This is the contemporary vision of Pax Sinica, the Han-centric Chinese world order where Chinese imperial hegemony, emanating from the Han-centric China Proper, first expands to the four contiguous barbarian realms and then, in concentric circles, to all realms under heaven, a vision that has been nurtured for almost two centuries. There has been an unbroken continuity and a remarkable internal coherence to this discourse. This is what I call Han Chinese ethnoscience, à la Blaut. In this ethnoscience, the Han, however fictive as an ethnorace it may be, has been persistently theorized as coterminous with Chinese civilization, as a bioracial category in contradistinction from other races but with the ability to assimilate all, and as a political-geographic unit constituting China's "geobody" with boundless expansionist ambitions.[75] Ultimately, Han-ness has become thoroughly conflated with Chineseness, the language of the Han people has become *the* Chinese language, Han culture has become *the* Chinese civilization, while the cultures of the non-Han peoples are subjected to oftentimes violent assimilation or Han-ization. In its presumed inclusive universality and its exclusivist particularity, Han-ness functions in ways very similar to whiteness in the West. Whether white or yellow, the presumed simultaneous universality and particularity are not a contradiction in terms, as the discourse and practice of hegemony depends precisely on both the solidity of the dominant race's superiority and its simultaneous flexible ability to absorb and contain the nondominant, whether using the rhetoric of assimilation or multiculturalism, whether in China or the United States. As in the ways in which colonial assimilationism reaches its limit when the colonized's similarity to the colonizer becomes threatening, the colonizer will always demand assimilation only to the point where the colonized can still be kept in their place. In empire, assimilationism is nothing but a tactic of colonial racism.

As in the case of racial hegemony of the Han, furthermore, the conception of the Chinese world order combines both the particularistic claims (the Chinese case is unique) and universalistic claims (the Chinese world order is more universal than that of the West). Universalism premised on exceptionalism, though logically contradictory, is the exact same mode of discourse for Western empire and imperialism, just as Blaut so persuasively argued. *All empires claim universalism, and China is no exception; all empires claim exceptionalism, and China is no exception.*[76]

To return to the discursive trinity that I started this chapter with, I repeat that Chinese exceptionalism is coproduced by mutually interacting discourses in China and the West. The kinship of Chinese discourse in China and the China studies scholarship in the United States has continued in a dynamic of cross-fertilization and reciprocal confirmation. Western perspectives, particularly those offered by China studies scholars in the United States, along with the writings by the Western left, have provided nationalist Chinese intellectuals effective justifications for Pax Sinica. The tianxia discourses discussed above, for instance, are filled with copious references to U.S. scholarship on China. In turn, contemporary China studies scholarship in the United States has also continued to exceptionalize Pax Sinica in such disciplines as history, political science, sociology, and anthropology,[77] characterizing China as a "centrifugal empire," where the power radiates outward from the core,[78] or China as a "national empire" and an "empire of nations."[79] Korean historian of China Baik Young-seo, who has criticized this reciprocity between Chinese statist discourse and U.S. China studies scholarship, argues that this reciprocity works as a kind of reinforcement that makes the discourses even more powerful and, thus, by implication, durable and inviolable. Baik breaks down what he calls the contemporary "Chinese discourse of empire" into three varieties of theory of the "civilization-state," the tianxia system, and the tributary system. The "one country, two systems" framework for Hong Kong is, for instance, an example of a new version of the tributary system, as it is something that a nation-state would not have tolerated. However, Baik cautions that, unless China becomes a "good empire" that is beneficial to all of humanity, the negative historical legacy of Chinese discourse of empire as a discourse of domination will always haunt those on the peripheries of China. In a restrained and indirect manner, perhaps because the article was published in China, Baik thus cautions against the pitfalls of the rising Chinese discourse of empire, especially in the East Asia region, and calls for, albeit only in a footnote, the importance of "deconstructing China-centrism."[80] Ultimately, I agree with William Callahan that tianxia presents "a new hegemony where imperial China's hierarchical governance is updated for the twenty-first century"; Zhao and other like-minded nationalist/imperialist intellectuals in China consider it their "yellow man's burden of using China's ethical governance to pacify and civilize the world."[81]

Be that as it may, historians and sociologists of empire who are not China studies scholars have provided broad definitions of empire that offer a useful comparative angle to the political form of contemporary China. To continue to caution against Chinese exceptionalism in Western discourse, I quote just a few definitions of empire drawn from studies *not* about China: empire "is not an epithet but a form of global governance in which a dominant power exercises control over the destiny of others, either through direct territorial rule (colonies) or indirect influence—military, economic, and cultural";[82] empires "are distinguished by having a core area, outlying territories governed directly or indirectly under the aegis of empire, and areas of informal influence, all under the hegemony of a governing elite centered in the core area";[83] and that "empires are expansive, militarized, and multiethnic political organizations that significantly limit the sovereignty of the peoples and polities they conquer." Empires also most often have a "state at their center" and uses a combination of four basic "imperial strategies": premodern land-based empire, modern territorial empire, colonialism, and informal nonterritorial imperialism.[84] Thinking in terms of these broader definitions, China may be considered a premodern land-based empire in the past that has been updated into a modern colonial empire in the present, rewriting the distinction between land-based empires and oceanic empires to show how land-based empires can behave in a similar manner as oceanic empires and may, in fact, surpass oceanic empires in reach and effectiveness. Furthermore, if we consider Chinese economic and political influence in its client states such as Cambodia, Burma, and Laos, as well as in numerous nonclient states around the world, China can also qualify as an informal, nonterritorial empire. All empires claim to be unique, but they are more similar to one another than their denials might indicate. Considering that the tribute system was not unique to China as many claimed since the Roman, Spanish, and Ottoman empires all had tribute systems; that the Chinese discourse of Han racial and civilizational superiority finds its parallels in the West and elsewhere; and that China's multiethnic, supranational polity is similar to other empires in the past and the present, all claims to Chinese exceptionalism must be thoroughly rethought. China and its nationalist intellectuals cannot claim immunity of exceptionalism and neither can the discursive community outside China.

Chinese exceptionalism is as old, if not older, and as potent as European exceptionalism, and in the longue durée of history, may be more enduring and effective in consolidating an empire that is now reaching across the world in a geographical pivot that may surpass all previous empires in human history. The British Empire might have been the largest empire in human history in terms of its geographical scope, but its small imperial core with limited natural resources and population also made its dissolution precipitously fast when the time came. The contemporary PRC, by contrast, has revived a long-held imperial discourse and ideology and acquired the imperial administrative know-how not only from the Manchu Empire, despite its spurious claims to inheritance, but also from the global colonial manual enriched by centuries of European colonialism. The Norweigian scholar Harold Bøckman suggests that China has "the only major imperial geopolitical structure that is still intact today."[85] While Bøckman presumes a problematic notion of "China" as a continuous entity, it is beyond dispute that, having been subjected to Western imperialism during one hundred years of shame and learned from it, and having nurtured imperial ambitions throughout that period and after, the rise of China has in fact been the rise of Chinese empire.

Notes

1. J. M. Blaut, "Geographic Models of Imperialism," *Antipode* 2, no. 1 (August 1970): 65.
2. Blaut, "Geographic Models of Imperialism," 69.
3. Blaut, "Geographic Models of Imperialism," 74. None of this, of course, is news to scholars in postcolonial studies, which for decades critiqued the Eurocentrism underlying all aspects of the operations of Western colonialism and imperialism. However, Blaut's ostensible emphasis on race and a racialized view of imperialism was uniquely prescient for his time, derived from his appreciation of the work of Franz Fanon and C. L. R. James, unlike most other classical Marxist scholars of imperialism, as can be seen in Anthony Brewer's comprehensive summary in *Marxist Theories of Imperialism* (London: Routledge, 1990).
4. A representative example is Odd Arne Westad's *Restless Empire: China and the World Since 1750* (New York: Basic Books, 2012), which is considered a standard book on Chinese empire. While recognizing that China has been an empire for the past two millennia, that Chinese society is a hybrid society, and that "China" as an entity is a changing concept, Westad nevertheless emphasizes, alongside many others, that the Chinese empire is different and needs to be understood via three unique concepts of justice, rules, and centrality, distinct from Western empires. Throughout this long book, not once does the term *Chinese imperialism* appear.
5. One such interruption, perhaps the most famous of them made mostly by Chinese intellectuals, is the discourse on the defects of the Chinese national character in the early twentieth century influenced by Arthur Smith's *Chinese Characteristics* (1890), eugenics, and Yellow Peril discourse, etc. However, these self-disparagements were made for the sake of improving the Han race so that it would ultimately emerge victorious from ruin and over other races.
6. David Palumbo-Liu and Azeezah Kanji have called such a left position a "faux anti-imperialism." See their "The Faux Anti-Imperialism of Denying Anti-Uighur Atrocities," *Aljazeera*, May 14, 2021, https://www.aljazeera.com/opinions/2021/5/14/the-faux-anti-imperialism-of-denying-anti-uighur. Noam Chomsky and Vijay Prashad are two prominent figures who practice this faux anti-imperialism. Left media, such as *Jacobin*, has also predominantly held such views.
7. I discuss this point based on evidence of what had transpired at the Bandung Conference and after in my article, "Race and Relation: The Global Sixties in the South of the South," *Comparative Literature* 68, no. 2 (2016): 141–154.
8. Hence, for Enrique Dussel, decolonial work requires the work of antifetishism. See Enrique Dussel, *Philosophy of Liberation*, trans. Aquilina Martinez and Christine Morkovsky (Eugene, OR: Wipf and Stock, 1985), 95.
9. Giovanni Arrighi, *Adam Smith in Beijing: Lineages of the Twenty-First Century* (London: Verso, 2007), 10.

10. Arrighi, *Adam Smith in Beijing*, chap. 11, 309–350.

11. Arrighi, *Adam Smith in Beijing*, chap. 12, 351–378.

12. Arrighi, *Adam Smith in Beijing*, "Epilogue," 379–389.

13. Aijaz Ahmed, the Indian Marxist scholar who polemically criticized Fredric Jameson's simplistic romanticism toward the Third World in the now famous exchange on Third World literature as national allegory, notes that China is "extremely vulnerable to the United States" both militarily and economically and can never be a rival for the United States. Hence, the sole imperialism of our time is that of the U.S. empire. See Aijaz Ahmed, "Imperialism of Our Time," *Socialist Register* 40 (2004): 51–52.

14. Arif Dirlik, *Complicities: The People's Republic of China in Global Capitalism* (Chicago: Prickly Paradigm, 2017).

15. Jane Burbank and Frederick Cooper, *Empires in World History: Power and the Politics of Difference* (Princeton, NJ: Princeton University Press, 2010), 440–442.

16. Adrian Hadland, "If the Hat Fits: Revisiting Chinese 'Neo-Imperialism' in Africa from a Comparative Historical Perspective," *Asian Politics and Policy* 4, no. 1 (2012): 467–485. The quotation is from 467.

17. Alfred McCoy, *In the Shadow of the American Century* (Chicago: Haymarket Books, 2017).

18. Bat-Ami Bar On provides a summary of the relevant genealogy since Marx and debates about the epistemic privilege of the marginalized in "Marginality and Epistemic Privilege," in *Feminist Epistemologies*, ed. Linda Alcoff and Elizabeth Potter (New York: Routledge, 1993), 83–100.

19. Michele Foucault describes part of the work of genealogy, after Nietzsche, as the excavation of multiple and contradictory pasts. See "Nietzsche, Genealogy, History," in *The Foucault Reader*, ed. Paul Rabinow (New York: Pantheon, 1984), 76–100.

20. Ge Zhaoguang claims that the consciousness of China (Zhongguo) as a national identity first began in the Song dynasty (960–1279). Hence "China" in history has to be understood as a "moving" (yidong) concept. See his *Hewei Zhongguo: jiangyu minzu wenhua yu lishi* (What is China: territory, people, Culture, and history) (Hong Kong: Oxford University Press, 2014), an excellent synthesis of scholarship culled from around the world, especially U.S., Japanese, and European scholarship on China. Hong Kong scholar Kwei-cheung Lo rightly corrects the mistaken attribution that Ge was the originator of the idea that the Song dynasty saw the rise of Chinese national consciousness, when, in fact, it should be attributed to German scholar Rolf Trauzettel. Lo further critiques the notion of China as a national identity as fundamentally Han-centric. See Lo, "Meiyou guojia de minzu: shaoshuzhe de Zhongguo" (People without nation: 'China' of the minority), *Sixiang* (Reflexion) 31 (September 2016): 217–240.

21. Pamela Kyle Crossley, Helen F. Siu, and Donald S. Sutton, eds., "Introduction," in *Empire at the Margins: Culture, Ethnicity, and Frontier in Early Modern China* ed. (Berkeley: University of California Press, 2006), 6.

22. Mark Elliott, *The Manchu Way: The Eight Banners and Ethnic Identity in Late Imperial China* (Stanford, CA: Stanford University Press, 2002).

23. Edward. J. M. Rhoads, *Manchus and Han: Ethnic Relations and Political Power in Late Qing and Early Republican China, 1861–1928* (Seattle: University of Washington Press, 2000), 172.

24. Joanna Waley-Cohen, *The Culture of War in China: Empire and the Military Under the Qing Dynasty* (London: I. B. Tauris, 2006), 8–13

25. Mark Elliott, "Ethnicity in the Qing Eight Banners" in Crossley, Siu, and Sutton, *Empire at the Margins*, 27–57.

26. James L. Millward, *Beyond the Pass: Economy, Ethnicity, and Empire in Qing Central Asia, 1759–1964* (Stanford, CA: Stanford University Press, 1998), 251.

27. Millward, *Beyond the Pass*, 15–18.

28. See Kai-wing Chow, "Imagining Boundaries of Blood: Zhang Binglin and the Invention of the Han Race in Modern China," in *The Construction of Racial Identities in China and Japan*, ed. Frank Dikötter (Honolulu: University of Hawaii Press, 1997), 34–52. Also see Laitinen Kauko, *Chinese Nationalism in the Late Qing Dynasty: Zhang Binglin as an Anti-Manchu Propagandist* (Copenhagen: Nordic Institute of Asian Studies; London: Curzon Press, 1990).

29. Dru Gladney, *Ethnic Identity in China: The Making of a Muslim Minority Nationality* (Belmont, CA: Wadsworth, 1997), 18–19.

30. Due to the confused ways in which ethnicity is distinguished from race, and given how ethnicity often functions like race in China, I use the term *ethnorace* to mark the permeability between the two concepts and to reveal the racial structuration of Chinese society.

31. Drawing from the memoirs published in the early 1960s, Rhoads documents the indiscriminate slaughter in 1911 of Manchus in the garrison city of Xi'an, where half of its total population of twenty thousand Manchus perished. See Rhoads, *Manchus and Han*, 187; 190–193.

32. "Introduction," in in Crossley, Siu, and Sutton, *Empire at the Margins*, 1–24.

33. Colin Mackerras, *China's Minority Cultures: Identities and Integration Since 1912* (New York: Longman, 1995), 40.

34. Nicola Di Cosmo, "Qing Colonial Administration in Inner Asia," *International History Review* 20, no. 2 (1998): 287–309.

35. Joanna Waley-Cohen, *The Culture of War in China: Empire and the Military Under the Qing Dynasty* (London: I. B. Tauris, 2006), 8–13.

36. Di Cosmo specifies the fact that Xinjiang, Tibet, and Mongolia under the Manchus were classified as "outer provinces" (tulergi golo), effectively separate from the China Proper and managed through a politics of difference, similar to the European management of its overseas territories. As to Taiwan and the south, the Manchu Empire aimed to incorporate them into the metropole, in this case similar to the U.S. conquest and colonization of its western territories. The argument that colonialism can only be applied to overseas colonies is, hence, false. See Di Cosmo, "Qing Colonial Administration in Inner Asia."

37. See Pamela Kyle Crossley, *The Manchus* (London: Blackwell, 1997) and Ruth W. Dunnell and James A. Millward, "Introduction," in *New Qing Imperial History*, ed. James Millward, Ruth W. Dunnell, Mark C. Elliott, and Philippe Forêt (London: Routledge Curzon, 2004), 4.

38. See Mark Elliot, "Chuantong Zhongguo shi yige diguo ma?" (Is traditional China a diguo?) *Dushu* 1 (2014): 29–40. Elliot traces the etymology of the Chinese term *diguo* as the translation of the English word *empire* to say that China had not historically used this term to designate itself. In the 1895 Treaty of Shimonoseki, however, the Manchu Empire did call itself the "Great Qing diguo" (Daqing diguo). Furthermore, he cites the late Qing intellectual Yan Fu to show that the English term diguo was by then already used interchangeably with the conventional Chinese term to reference empire as "all-under-heaven" (tianxia).

39. Ge Zhaoguang, *Lishi Zhongguo de nei yu wai: youguan Zhongguo yu zhoubian gainian de zaichengqing* (The inside and outside of historical China: re-clarification of the concepts of "China" and its "peripheries") (Hong Kong: Chinese University of Hong Kong Press, 2017) 121.

40. Ge Zhaoguang, *Here in "China" I Dwell: Reconstructing Historical Discourse of China for Our Time* (20), trans. Jesse Field and Qin Fang (London: Brille, 2017); *He wei Zhongguo: jiangyu, minzu, wenhua yu lishi*; and *Lishi Zhongguo de nei yu wai*.

41. See Julia C. Schneider, *Nation and Ethnicity: Chinese Discourses on History, Historiography, and Nationalism (1900s-1920s)* (London: Brill, 2017), 144. Also see Kauko Laitinen, *Chinese Nationalism in the Late Qing Dynasty: Zhang Binglin as an Anti-Manchu Propagandist* (London: Curzon Press, 1990).

42. Zhang Taiyan, "Explaining 'The Republic of China'" (Zhonghua minguo jie, 1907), trans. Pär Cassel, *Stockholm Journal of East Asian Studies* 8 (1997): 15–40.

43. See the discussion of Zou Rong's work by Jing Tsu in *Failure, Nationalism, and Literature* (Stanford, CA: Stanford University Press, 2005), 41–42.

44. Schneider, *Nation and Ethnicity*, 215–251; 383–384.

45. Quoted in James Leibold, *Reconfiguring Chinese Nationalism: How the Qing Frontier and Its Indigenes Became Chinese* (New York: Palgrave Macmillan, 2007), 43, 57.

46. Julia C. Schneider notes that Liang's article entitled "On the Relationship Between Geography and Civilization" is an excerpted translation of Hegel's "Geographical Basis of History." Schneider, *Nation and Ethnicity*, 111.

47. Liang Qichao, "Lun Zhongguo renzhong zhi jianglai" (The future of the Chinese race), *Qingyibao* 19 (1899): 48–54.

48. Quoted in Schneider, *Nation and Ethnicity*, 115. Liang uses "China Proper" (Zhongguo benbu) to refer to the territory prior to Qing conquest and expansion. China, in this view consists of five parts, China Proper, Xinjiang, Mongolia, Manchuria, and Qinghai-Tibet. See Schneider's summary of Liang's historiography of China in *Nation and Ethnicity*, 106. This term is later inherited by Chinese studies historians in the United States, especially in New Qing history studies.

49. Schneider, *Nation and Ethnicity*, 62.

50. G. W. H. Hegel, *The Philosophy of Right*, trans. T. M. Knox (Oxford: Oxford University Press, 1967), 247–249.

51. Liang Qichao, "Biographies of Eight Great Heroes of Chinese Colonialism," *Xinmin congbao* 3, no. 15 (1905): 84–91. Note how Zheng He, who is, in fact, of Hui ethnicity, is conveniently incorporated into this racial imagination. Hui are assimilated Muslims with a long history of intermarriage with the Han.

52. See Jing Tsu's discussion of these two novels in *Failure, Nationalism, and Literature*, chapter 3, 66–103.

53. See Kean-fung Guan's discussion of late Qing fictions of colonialism, and especially this novel, in his "Hybridity, Adventure, and Reversal—On the Formulation of a Chinese Columbus in He Jiong's "Lion's Blood," *Qinghua zhongwen xuebao* 10 (December 2013): 57–116.

54. Shelly Chan offers an overview of this department's activities in chapter 2 of her book, *Diaspora's Homeland: Modern China in the Age of Global Migration* (Durham, NC: Duke University Press, 2018).

55. Li Changfu, *Zhongguo zhiminshi* (A history of Chinese colonialism, 1937) (Taipei, Taiwan: Shangwu yinshuguan, 1990, rpt.), 50.

56. Yuanfei Wang, in her studies of sixteenth-century texts on Zheng He's voyages, discovered recorded incidents of Chinese cannibalism on these voyages in Southeast Asia, especially one incident where Zheng He ordered Javanese soldiers killed and their flesh consumed. See her "Java in Discord: Unofficial History, Vernacular Fiction, and the Discourse of Imperial Identity in Late Ming China (1574–1620)," forthcoming in *positions: asia critique*.

57. Li, A history of Chinese colonialism, 8–18.

58. Li, A history of Chinese colonialism, 104.

59. Anthony Reid, "Entrepreneurial Minorities, Nationalism, and the State," in *Essential Outsiders: Chinese and Jews in the Modern Tranformation of Southeast Asia and Central Europe*, ed. Daniel Chirot and Anthony Reid (Seattle: University of Washington Press, 1997), 42, 47.

60. Li, A history of Chinese colonialism, chapter 5, 203–353.

61. Shelly Chan, *Diaspora's Homeland: Modern China in the Age of Global Migration* (Durham, NC: Duke University Press, 2018), 51.

62. Chan, *Diaspora's Homeland*, chap. 2, 74.

63. Lucien Pye is credited with the notion of China as a civilization-state, noting that China is "a civilization pretending to be a state." See his "China: Erratic State, Frustrated Society," *Foreign Affairs* 29, no. 4 (Fall 1990): 58. For "empire-state," see Harold Bøckman, "China Deconstructs? The Future of the Chinese Empire-State in a Historical Perspective" in *Reconstructing Twentieth Century China: State Control, Civil Society, and National Identity*, ed. Kjeld E. Brodsgaard and David Strand (Clarendon Press, 1998), 310–345.

64. See Gan Yang, *Wenming guojia daxue* (Civilization, nation, and the university) (Beijing: Joint Publishing, 2012).

65. Among contemporary intellectuals, one of the leading apologists of Chinese empire may be Wang Hui, if only because he has been most ardently admired by Western Marxists as *the* leading intellectual of China and has been most skillful in manipulating a leftism that passes off imperialism as nationalism.

66. John K. Fairbank, "A Preliminary Framework," in *The Chinese World Order: Traditional China's Foreign Relations* (Cambridge: Harvard University Press), 18

67. See Yuri Pines, "Beasts or Humans: Pre-Imperial Origins of the 'Sino-Barbarian' Dichotomy," in *Mongols, Turks, and Others: Eurasian Nomads and the Sedentary World*, eds. R Amitari and Michael Biran (London: Brill, 2004), 59–102.

68. This process began earlier but received more concerted effort in the twentieth century. James Millward notes how the Uyghur Muslims in the Manchu Empire were called *dong-hui* (or East Turkistanis) where the character *hui* was spelled with a dog radical, and later the dog radical was dropped, in a process of transformation from "semicanine barbarians to full members of the imperial polity." See Millward, *Beyond the Pass*, 197.

69. Schneider, *Nation and Ethnicity*, 384–394.

70. For other influential tianxia discourses, see the essays included in Xu Jilin and Liu Qing, eds., *Xin tianxia zhuyi* (New Tianxia-ism) (Shanghai: Shanghai renmin chubanshe, 2015).

71. Zhao Tingyang, *Tianxia tixi* (The Tianxia system) (Nanjing: Jiangsu jiaoyu chubanshe, 2005), 2.

72. Zhao Tingyang, "Rethinking Empire from a Chinese Concept 'All-Under-Heaven' (Tian-xia)," *Social Identities: Journal for the Study of Race, Nation and Culture* 12, no. 1 (2012): 29–41.

73. Han Yuhai, *Tianxia: baona siyi de Zhongguo* (All under heaven: China incorporates four kinds of barbarians) (Beijing: Jiuzhou chubanshe, 2011). I have translated the Chinese title of the book literally because the book cover has a misleadingly innocuous English title printed on it, "Beneath the Skies: An All-Inclusive China."

74. Zhao, *Tianxia tixi*, 34.

75. See the excellent articles included in Thomas S. Mullaney, James Leibold, Stéphane Gros, and Eric Armand Vanden Bussche, eds., *Critical Han Studies: The History, Representation, and Identity of China's Majority* (Berkeley: University of California Press, 2012), especially the introduction drafted by Thomas Mullaney that summarizes the changing views of the Han in terms of civilizational, bioracial, and political-geographic categories, 1–20.

76. Takahiro Nakajima has discussed the persistence of the inherited discourse of Chinese universality in the work of twentieth- and twenty-first-century scholars in China, including Zhao Tingyang. See Takahiro Nakajima, "Chinese Universality in and After Tang Junyi," *Contemporary Philosophy in the Age of Globalization* 4 (2014) 69–91.

77. See Chas W. Freeman Jr., "China's Rise and Transformation: Towards Pax Sinica?" *Washington Journal of Modern China* 10, no. 2(Fall 2012): 1–33, and Yongjin Zhang, "System, Empire and State in Chinese International Relations," *Review of International Studies* 27 (2001): 43–63.

78. Jae Ho Chung, *Centrifugal Empire: Central-Local Relations in China* (New York: Columbia University Press, 2016).

79. For "national empire," see Justin M. Jacobs, *Xinjiang and the Modern Chinese State* (Seattle: University of Washington Press, 2016). For a critical voice on Chinese discourse of tianxia, see William A. Callahan, "Tianxia, Empire, and the World," in *China Orders the World: Normative Soft Power and Foreign Policy*, ed. William A Callahan and Elena Barabantseva (Washington, DC: Woodrow Wilson Center Press, 2011), 91–117.

80. Baik Young-seo, "Zhonghua diguolun zai dongya de yiyi: tansuo pipanxing de Zhongguo yanjiu" (The significance of the discourse of Chinese Empire in East Asia: exploring the possibility of a critical Chinese Studies), *Kaifang Shidai* 253 (January 2014): 79–98.

81. William A. Callahan, "Chinese Visions of World Order: Post-Hegemonic or a New Hegemony?" *International Studies Review* 10 (2008): 749–761. The quotes are from pages 749 and 754.

82. McCoy, *In the Shadow of the American Century*, 40.

83. Patrick Manning, *Navigating World History: Historians Create a Global Past* (New York: Palgrave MacMillan, 2003), 190.

84. George Steinmetz, "The Sociology of Empires, Colonies and Postcolonialism," *Annual Review of Sociology* 40 (2014): 79; 80–81.

85. See Harold Bøckman, "China Deconstructs? The Future of the Chinese Empire-State in a Historical Perspective," in *Reconstructing Twentieth-Century China: State Control, Civil Society, and National Identity*, ed. Kjeld Eric Brødsgaard and David Strand (Oxford: Clarendon Press, 1998), 310–46.

Stonewall Aside

When Queer Theory Meets Sinophone Studies

HOWARD CHIANG

How can the Sinophone concept serve as a heuristic lens for deconstructing the ways in which sexual normativity and contemporary People's Republic of China (PRC) imperialism have been hegemonically produced through one another?[1] This chapter makes a preliminary inquiry into this question around lines of thought lost or overlooked during the canonization of a political turning point in sexuality studies: the Stonewall riots. My thesis is that Sinophone studies ripened in the last two decades as an unruly "queer" (酷兒, *ku'er*) progeny of Chinese studies.[2] The disruptive potential of Sinophone studies is adjacent to the effect of queer approaches on traditional gay and lesbian history and, by implication, Stonewall's capacity to unsettle historical understandings of political change.

Over the last decade, there has been an explosive growth of interest in the intersection of queer theory and Sinophone studies.[3] As this interdisciplinary body of scholarship makes clear, a queer Sinophone intervention activates a multidirectional critique that considers marginalization *itself* as a moving target of analysis. Such geopoliticization of queerness and Chineseness as mutually imbricated, in other words, counters the occlusion of the variant essentialisms—regional, cultural, gender, sexual, or otherwise—that work together to reauthorize disciplinary quandaries. Consider a prototype in the kind of area studies that flourished as an intelligence-gathering force for buttressing U.S. power: The field of postwar China studies has never ceased to generate an "excess of power," whether the signifier "China" has taken on the form of a Cold War enemy, a third world leader, or a neoliberal alibi.[4] As Tani Barlow reminded us nearly three decades ago, "Doubly displaced, colonialism nonetheless made Cold War area studies scholarship possible in the first place."[5]

In a different way, the recent turn to Sinophone studies enables us to undo the erasure of colonialism in "China" studies. The delineation between the so-called Chinese canon (however illusory this notion may be) and Sinophone cultures can be put into a productive dialogue with queer theory to enrich ongoing critiques of queer displacement, mobility, and intersectionality.[6] The queer Sinophone perspective I am advancing further pluralizes our coordinates in understanding the way these hierarchies—of oppression, cultural citizenship, authenticity, and globalization—have been transfigured laterally. This is especially urgent in an increasingly transnational and transcolonial world where the fetishization of a leftist counterhegemonic China is no more tenable than the nostalgic depiction of Stonewall as a crucible of queer liberation. In order to flesh out this multifocal provocation, I outline five reasons why queer theory needs Sinophone studies. Instead of casting the latter as a corrective to the shortcomings of the former, my more immediate goal is to underscore the kaleidoscopic range of illuminations made possible by their generative affinity.

Historicizing Translation

The first reason queer theory needs Sinophone studies is that it offers a rigorous context for historicizing the process of queer translation. A telling example is the history of how the Chinese term *tongzhi* (同志) has been used to translate the Western idea of "gay and lesbian." Tongzhi literally means "comrade" or "common will" in Chinese, and it typically referred to one's ordinary acquaintance in the high socialist period (1949–1976). Over time, however, the term has acquired a more specific, culturally subversive meaning: Chinese queer activists came to promote it as an umbrella category to designate individuals with nonnormative gender and erotic inclinations. Yet, it is worth pointing out that the concept of tongzhi has historically been queered first and foremost in Sinophone locations; its queer appropriation and currency was *then* imported back into mainland China.[7] Based on the existing limited research on queer PRC history, it is not obvious that tongzhi was used by sexual minorities in the Maoist era as either a linguistic marker of identification or an organizing principle for activism.[8] More often than not, people simply used tongzhi to describe each other's comradery, straight or unstraight. In fact, to be historically accurate, the queer notion of tongzhi as we understand it today is the product of a *cultural refraction* via such Sinophone communities as Hong Kong and Taiwan.⁹ Hence, Sinophone communities have served as the principal catalyst in mediating the "glocalization" of LGBTQ identities in East Asia.¹⁰

Many critics have identified the popularization of the term in Sinophone queer cultural activism in the late 1980s and 1990s as a watershed turning point in the history of its lexical dissemination.¹¹ Most famously, the playwright Edward Lam (Lam Yik-Wa 林奕華) used tongzhi to title the first Hong Kong Gay and Lesbian Film Festival in 1989. It is not going too far to argue that tongzhi could only be queered outside its heteronormalized circulation. It was precisely because tongzhi was not a fashionable concept in places like Hong Kong and Taiwan that its Sinophone deployment became a form of cultural subversion. Tongzhi would have never and indeed did not carry a queer-subversive content in Maoist China precisely due to the same reason—from the 1950s to the 1970s, it served to marginalize deviant sexual subjectivity in the mainland. The socialist conception of tongzhi may have stood for class, gender, and other forms of social egalitarianism, but it profoundly alienated sexual minorities (the Maoist period, in fact, condemned the very idea of bourgeois sexuality). So historically speaking, a queer version of tongzhi has survived and circulated not in socialist China but outside it. Elsewhere, I have discussed the conceptual transformation (in particular, transgendering) of tongzhi after the millennium.¹² My point here is that the historical distinction between the PRC, on the one hand, and Sinophone communities such as Hong Kong and Taiwan, on the other, makes possible an understanding of queer/tongzhi China that is linguistically and historically sensitive.¹³

Against Romanticizing China

The second reason queer theory needs Sinophone studies is that it allows us to study queer Asia in a transnational way that does not romanticize China and the non-West. This is a crucial response to another book that has garnered critical attention, *Queer Marxism in Two Chinas* by Petrus Liu. My remark in the previous section suggests that the conceptual stationing of tongzhi in such works has likely flattened the term's social connotation within Chinese history.¹⁴ Here, I wish to put forward another subtle query and ask if its idiosyncratic application in a work like Liu's may have also written off the leftist and radical politics of gay activism outside China, especially in areas where a strong heritage of anticapitalist queer critique exists.

Clearly, the socialist foundation of tongzhi in China presents a partially differentiated genealogy of queer activism in East Asia. That is, it pulls us out of an obsession with European Marxist traditions. One of Liu's main arguments is that "a unique local event has centrally shaped the development of Chinese queer [Marxist] thought: the 1949 division of China into the People's Republic of China (PRC) and the Republic of China on Taiwan (ROC)." This version of queer Marxism, he tells us, "offers a nonliberal alternative to the Euro-American model of queer emancipation grounded in liberal values of privacy, tolerance, individual rights, and diversity."[15] The problem with Liu's assertion is that it blinds us from, rather than bringing us closer to, an understanding of the way global LGBTQ coalition politics has been made possible over time. Liu's version of tongzhi activism—deeply rooted in the views and activities of a highly niche, however radical, and self-referential circle in Taiwan—seems to repudiate the universal, not just liberal, importance of pluralist recognition and redistributive equality.[16]

A Sinophone vantage point recasts the queer rendition of tongzhi as a polyvalent synthesis of global leftist politics and identity politics—rather than something that is produced purely from within Chinese cultural contexts.[17] Historically, the homophile activism of the 1950s and the solidarity of gay and lesbian politics with the student, civil rights, antiwar, feminist, environmental, youth, countercultural, and radical movements of the 1960s and 1970s provide concrete evidence for a leftist genealogy of gay activist history. In academe, the scholarship of John D'Emilio, Lisa Duggan, Kevin Floyd, Diarmaid Kelliher, Peter Drucker, Emily Hobson, Aaron Lecklider, and many others has documented this history with nuance and complexity, and they are all bold proponents of Marxist critique.[18] The power differentials that bring queer resistance and the radical left together—or drive them apart—have always worked in uneven gradations unilaterally on a global scale.

What is decisively missing yet sorely needed is a Marxist analysis of Liu's queer Marxism, as well as an uncovering of the kind of China-centrism it conceals. An instance of Liu's romanticization of China can be seen in his definition of queer theory. By characterizing "queer theory as an incomplete project that is constantly transformed by China," Liu implies not only that the signifier "China" is doing the work of substituting for Marxist analysis but also that China, or Marxism for that matter, is already a complete project or at least one that does not need to be transformed by queer theoretical critique.[19] *Pace* Liu, I argue that what queer theory needs is not China but Sinophone studies.[20]

In this sense, the obsession with a "Chinese materialist queer theory that sets it apart from its Euro-American counterparts" not only begs the question of whose Chineseness is at stake, but it also risks reifying the East-West binary via what I have called self- or re Orientalization.[21] The title of Liu's book suggests that its focus is on both the PRC and the Republic of China

(Taiwan), the homogenized two Chinas. However, Liu's study devotes only ten pages to the work of one PRC-based filmmaker, Cui Zi'en (崔子恩). Despite this skewed representation, Liu speaks of "Chinese" queer theory and Marxism throughout the book without making a distinction between the PRC and Sinophone Taiwan. In Liu's formulation, China is taken as given, self-consistent, internally productive of a bounded queer alternative to Euro-American queer articulations. This unfortunate consequence shares a potential blind spot—and the word *potential* is crucial here—with Kuan-hsing Chen's injunction to use "Asia as method": namely, the essentialization of Asian nativism to turn it into a privileged position for serious intellectual dialogue and thus completely isolates the work that scholars of Asia are doing from the heterogeneity of Western queer studies.[22] This is the very opposite of the disciplinary trap that Rey Chow has identified as ethnic supplementarity. Such marketing of China/Asia "meant that the philosophical and aesthetic investments in Chinese nativism and indigenism were set in motion at a steady pace of deterritorialization, in which the native or indigene, signifying the rooted, local knowledge that is associated with China and Chineseness, took on the exchange value of a marketable, because circulatable, transnational exhibit."[23] Therefore, how can we analyze queer Asia without romanticizing its past and upholding an us-versus-them mentality? Sinophone postcolonial perspectives, as I have been suggesting, provide a way out of that China-versus-the-West binary deadlock. Queer theory needs Sinophone studies in this regard because it reminds us that the challenge to neoliberal capitalism in China is neither exceptional nor exemplary.

Global Indigeneity

The third reason queer theory needs Sinophone studies is that by focusing on *Indigeneity* as a theoretical problem, it allows scholars to draw comparisons and connections across systems of oppression imposed on colonized people all over the world. A regrettable repercussion of the post–Cold War global reordering has been that some Chinese "new left" intellectuals hasten to equate postsocialism with postcolonialism. Sinophone studies breaks from this conceptual ruse by challenging a monolithic postcolonial antipathy toward the West as depicted by predominantly Han Chinese intellectuals.

A queer Sinophone framework builds concerns of gender and sexual injustice into an analysis of how geopolitical others and ethnic minorities have been systematically marginalized by Han centrism. A promising recent development in queer theory synchronizes the power structures behind the definition of *Indigeneity* with those that have come to shape the history of queerness. Scholars working in the field of queer Indigenous studies have delineated the history of epistemic violence and social oppression unduly experienced by North American Native queers.[24] Historically, gender and sexual diversity among native people has been interpreted by white colonists as signs of primitivity. This has bolstered the sedimentation over time of what anthropologist Scott L. Morgensen calls "settler sexuality": "a white national heteronormativity that regulates Indigenous sexuality and gender by supplanting them with sexual modernity of settler subjects."[25] The resistance to white homonationalist citizenship, we might add, is shared by not only oppressed native subjects in the West but also LGBTQ minorities in other areas of the world.[26] Although media scholars such as Jia Tan have advocated for the "transversal queer alliance" between Indigenous studies and area studies, their plea remains a minority.[27]

If the intersection of queerness with Han settler colonialism in Taiwan, the repression of ethnic minorities in the PRC, and the subjugation of migrant workers in Hong Kong, just to name a few, can be broached in conjunction with First Nation studies, queer theory can draw on Sinophone studies to enrich critical discussions of Indigeneity (with its attendant critiques of progress, sovereignty, hierarchy, etc.) on a global and transcultural scale. These are questions that are of significance even for scholars who do not specialize in China. In fact, all of the three examples mentioned above have been studied in depth.[28] And in this way, perhaps the Stonewall revolution can be more appropriately "provincialized"—even criticized—for the way its alleged significance vindicates a template of settler homonationalism that is neither universal nor celebratory for "most of the world."[29] Conversely, we should also be asking why the category of Indigeneity might stumble in certain places (e.g., why does China refuse to recognize Indigenous populations?) and how we can turn such circumspection into a queer analytic of power differentiation within the family resemblance of nation-states (e.g., though home to a vibrant Indigenous and LGBTQ rights movement, Taiwan has been without official nation-state status since 1971). By using Sinophone studies as an analytic lens, we can better diagnose how intersectional minority politics modulates into global (settler) colonial hierarchies and vice versa, depending on the scale, angle, and parameters of our historical thinking.

Queer Sonics

Sinophone studies is also useful for queer theory because it turns our analytic optic toward the queer potential of sound. One of the most powerful tools of queer Sinophone theory that has gone unnoticed, and herein lies my fourth reason, is the way it geopoliticizes the study of queer sonic cultures.[30] The -*phone* suffix in the Sinophone word indicates the speaking of a particular language, but it can also connote broader matters related to the register of sound. To hear queerness requires listening to the surprising ruptures of the norm, and these hearings elicit certain affective responses that could potentially transcend mechanisms of debilitation and social disparagement. Sinophone studies, as a paradigm of historical and cultural critique, contextualizes these lines of inquiry on a concrete geopolitical map. To illustrate what I mean, I would like to return to a crucial juncture in contemporary Chinese history—the 1997 handover of Hong Kong—from which to limn a minor transnational politics of sexuality through a Sinophone sonic lens.[31]

Specifically, I believe that a new queer reading of Wong Kar-wai's epic *Happy Together* (春光乍洩, 1997) is helpful in unmooring the geopolitics of Chineseness from historical queering, not the least because the film is a cultural commentary that is *produced during* as much as it is *about* the postcolonial transition.[32] For instance, the two protagonists' prehandover passports are shown in the film as belonging to the United Kingdom of Great Britain and Northern Ireland. The weight of this colonial document thereby foreshadows the film's strong thematic allegory of borders and their crossings. In fact, as we will see, boundary transgression—sexual, sonic, geopolitical, or otherwise—in the film frequently operates in a south-to-south or minor-to-minor direction. More than two decades after its production, my following reading renders *Happy Together* as both a Sinophone cultural text about its time and a historical product of its time.

Critics have noted that Wong made two evasive, if not misleading, remarks at the time of the film's release. First, despite the film's overt portrayal of a strained relationship between two homosexual men, Wong insisted that *Happy Together* should not be read as a gay film: "In fact I don't like people to see this film as a gay film. It's more like a story about human relationships and somehow the two characters involved are both men."[33] Second, Wong intended to distance the film from Hong Kong's political crisis circa 1997. One reviewer goes so far as to claim that in the film, "Argentina functions as a heterotopic metaphor for Hong Kong."[34] However, Wong subsequently conceded that his decision to film *Happy Together* as far away from Hong Kong as possible turned out to be an ironic failure. This self-defeating move cemented the topic of Hong Kong existentialism as one of the most enduring legacies in the film's critical reception. In his words:

> One of the reasons I chose Argentina was that it is on the other side of the world, and I thought by going there, I would be able to stay away from 1997. But then, as you must understand, once you consciously try to stay

away from something or to forget something, you will never succeed. That something is bound to be hanging in the air, haunting you.[35]

By mapping the disappearance of colonial Hong Kong onto the potential public erasure of homosexuality after the PRC's takeover, *Happy Together* epitomizes the coimbrication of geopolitics and sexuality. This attests to Helen Leung's observation that "in the most innovative films of this period, the postcolonial predicament appears at most as an undercurrent, a not-quite-visible force that nonetheless animates what is amply visible on-screen."[36] Queer sex is often staged in Hong Kong cinema at the juncture of this collision between the visible and the invisible.

Existing readings of *Happy Together* tend to highlight the mainline story revolving around the two protagonists, Lai Yiu-fai and Ho Po-wing, two Hong Kong men who traveled to Argentina with the Iguazu Falls set as their final destination but were ultimately stranded in Buenos Aires when they ran out of money.[37] As Carlos Rojas has shown, a central motif of the plot progression is proclaimed in the opening sequence of the film when Ho suggests to Lai, "Let's start over again."[38] This "seemingly simple and innocent plea . . . [for] *reiteration*," according to Rey Chow, "makes sense only in the [logic of] supplementarity."[39] The perpetual desire to start over embodies the paradoxical nature of the relationship between Lai and Ho: The two men's yearning to start afresh, put the past behind them, and transform their relationship into something more stable is constantly undercut by a recurring complication that drives that yearning in the first place. Throughout the story, Ho's persistent interest in anonymous sex clashes with Lai's strategic maneuvering to contain and domesticate their ostensible monogamy. Ultimately, it is when Lai begins to engage in anonymous sexual relations after Ho leaves him that Lai comes to acknowledge a version of Ho within himself. The recursive impetus to "start over" adumbrates their ultimate fate: Lai eventually returns to Hong Kong (via Taipei), leaving Ho behind to reenact the moments they shared in their old apartment in Buenos Aires. They never visited the Iguazu Falls together.

When I first watched *Happy Together* as a closeted student in high school, my encounter was akin to what Shu-mei Shih later described as her experience in watching Ang Lee's *Crouching Tiger, Hidden Dragon* (臥虎藏龍, 2000): "The linguistic dissonance of the film registers the heterogeneity of Sinitic languages as well as their speakers living in different locales."[40] I say *akin* rather than *identical* because, unlike in *Crouching Tiger, Hidden Dragon*, the characters in *Happy Together* almost never converse in a seemingly unified yet heavily accented Mandarin, or *putonghua* (普通話). Instead, Lai and Ho speak Cantonese to one another (sometimes English to others), and when Lai engages in dialogues with his Taiwanese coworker, Chang, at a Chinese restaurant, he speaks in Cantonese with Chang talking back in Mandarin. The film actually purports Lai's fluency in Mandarin (to be fair, Lai converses in mildly accented Mandarin at times) as well as Chang's ability to understand spoken Cantonese. Nevertheless, we might say that in this way, *Happy Together* is an even more explicitly Sinophone film than *Crouching Tiger, Hidden Dragon*: "The Sinophone frustrates easy suturing, in this case, while foregrounding the value of difficulty, difference, and heterogeneity."[41] The cacophony yet mutual readability of Sinitic language by Lai and Chang presumes a certain familiarity across the popular culture in Taiwan and Hong Kong that has existed since at least the 1950s. Of course, lurking beneath the eclectic verbal bonding between the three male characters in *Happy Together* resides an ever-present threshold of homoerotic intimacy.

I dwell on the significance of the vocal and the sonic to illustrate the new possible angles of reading *Happy Together* based on a Sinophone analytic. To hark back to the minor transnational politics that I discussed earlier, a convincing queer reading of the film emerges from attending to the mutual refraction of *sound* and *minor relationality*. Whereas conventional analyses of the film have focused on the Lai-Ho homosexual relationship, I consider the Lai-Chang homosocial relationship (the film never disambiguates its erotic overtone) as what ultimately disrupts the queer futurity and utopian visions anticipated by the desire to "start over" between Lai and Ho.[42] To begin with, a queer reading is already hinted by my departure from the dominant focus on issues of queer sex, queer stardom, and queer reception centering on the Hong Kong actor Leslie Cheung (張國榮), who played Ho.[43] The heterosexuality of both Tony Leung (梁朝偉), who played Lai, and Chang Cheng (張震), who played Chang, are well-publicized. Thus, the queerness of the Lai-Chang homoromance is accentuated by the actors' minor relationality to the characters in the film: two straight men playing queer and pseudo-queer roles, respectively. What other kinds of queer irruptive reading can *Happy Together* yield from the minor vantage point of the Chang character?

In contrast to the vivid sex scenes in which Lai and Ho are portrayed, the film ultimately concludes with a sentimental portrayal of the Lai-Chang intimacy, with Lai stopping by Taipei and visiting the street stall run by Chang's family. Though Lai and Chang never had sex in the film, this critical sexual absence is perhaps what gives their affective tender ties and, in fact, the overall tenor of the film their queerest edge. The relationship between Lai and Chang is one that constantly subverts even as it contrasts with the major form of relationality that threads the plot development (Lai's gay partnership with Ho). The relevance of queer sound to the Lai-Chang minor relationality is especially evident by way of mutual refraction. Before Chang's departure for Ushuaia, he asks Lai to use his tape recorder to capture Lai's sadness (hinting Chang's sensitivity to Lai's broken relationship with Ho), which he promises to take with him "to the end of the world" and leave it there (see fig. 2.1). Yet, once he reaches Les Eclaireurs Lighthouse, Chang cannot hear anything on the recorder other than "some strange noise, like someone sobbing." Helen Leung has interpreted the inaudibility of Lai's heartbreak as "the sound that we cannot quite hear" that "encapsulates everything that the film is about: loneliness, heartbreak, the futility of love, and the resilience of hope."[44]

I would go further and argue that the *trafficking* of this inaudible sound, which perversely irrupts the Sinitic dialects spoken throughout the film, is as important as its formal quality. The way that the queer Sinophone sound of Lai travels cannot be easily extricated from the minor relational nature of Lai's affect for Chang (and vice versa), a symbol of the minor transnationalism between Hong Kong and Taiwan. It is through Chang that Lai's queer voice arrives at the lighthouse at the end of the world. Moreover, this queer rerouting of non-Cantonese sound unveils the coexistence of multiple Hong Kongs, with Ho, now stranded in Buenos Ares without his prehandover passport (a reminder of the British colonial past), living by another form of queer silence in memory of what could have been—a perpetual "starting over." Though supposedly on his way back to Hong Kong, the final destination for Lai in the film turns out to be Taipei (a symbolic surrogate of homecoming).[45] But when he reaches the street stall run by Chang's family, Lai does not see

Figure 2.1 Chang asks Lai to record Lai's sadness.
Source: *Happy Together* (1997), directed by Wong Kar-wai, produced by Chan Ye-cheng.

Chang there. Instead, Lai sees a photo of Chang at the lighthouse and decides to take it with him, explaining that he does not know when he will see Chang again (figs. 2.2 and 2.3). Reminiscence of the inaudible presence of Lai at the lighthouse scene, Chang claims his silent queer presence in the Taipei night market scene through Lai's Cantonese voiceover. The characters in *Happy Together* carry a certain "sonic" leverage with which to move across borders

Figure 2.2 Lai sees a photograph of Chang at the lighthouse.
Source: *Happy Together* (1997), directed by Wong Kar-wai, produced by Chan Ye-cheng.

Figure 2.3 A photograph of Chang at the lighthouse.
Source: *Happy Together* (1997), directed by Wong Kar-wai, produced by Chan Ye-cheng.

and through which it is possible to trace the transnational mobility of queer Sinophone subjects—in Argentina, Hong Kong, or Taiwan.

Saying No to Straight Sinology

Implicit in my analysis of *Happy Together* lies my fifth reason for merging queer theory with Sinophone studies: to disrupt the spatial and temporal logics that have long defined the homophobic and transphobic contours of area studies, including China studies. By provincializing China, the Sinophone framework enables us to see and think beyond the conventions of China studies. This radical mode of inquiry can be adapted to refuse an epistemological grid of heteronormativity. The rebuttal of *straight*forwardness ensures the continual interrogation of a moving center from the margins of a margin.[46] In terms of the substantive objects of study, a growing number of Sinophone scholars have already ventured into multiple place-based analyses of literary and cinematic examples in a "transpacific" nexus, from Southeast Asia to Hong Kong, Taiwan to North America. These localized examples in literature, film, and popular culture are rarely invoked in Chinese studies, Asian American studies, or other traditional (area studies) disciplines. Sinophone studies, as "the 'study of China' that transcends China" (to borrow the phrase from Mizoguchi Yuzo), empowers those "queer" inquiries excluded from the time-honored Sinology that has formalized alongside the Cold War and its aftermath.[47]

In the spirit of marking out "a space in which unspoken stories and histories may be told,"[48] the queer Sinophone method raises a series of interrelated questions that continue to haunt a "China-centered perspective."[49] These are questions of cultural disparity as much as about geopolitical entanglement.[50] Is the kind of homosexual experience represented in *Happy Together* "Chinese" or "Western" in nature? Homosexuality in whose sense of the term? Is it a foreign import, an expression (and thus internalization) of foreign imperialism, or a long-standing indigenous practice in a new light?[51] In what ways can we give serious attention and due consideration to the administrative reordering of Hong Kong in the late twentieth century? How do we make sense of the special administrative region (SAR) as a newly invented political category? How about the impact of the Tiananmen Square protests on Sinophone communities? Is it possible to speak of an alternative Sinophone modernity that challenges the familiar socialist narrative of twentieth-century Chinese history?[52] Which China is alluded to by the various notions of Chineseness depicted in the films? Is the handover of Hong Kong to the PRC another form of colonial (and imperial) domination? Or does it entail a different ordering of truth regimes and governing practices—what Foucault would call the microsites or "dense transfer point[s]" of power?[53] Evidently, the complexity of the history far exceeds the common terms we use to describe the historical characteristics of postcolonial Hong Kong (or Taiwan, for that matter). To conceive of the PRC in relation to Hong Kong circa 1997 as a regime from the outside or a colonial government only partially accounts for its proto-Chineseness or extra-Chineseness. Precisely due to the lack of a precedent and analogous situations, it is all the more difficult to historicize the social backdrop against which nonnormative desires have been authenticated and circulated through overlapping grids of intelligibility and the "intimate frontiers" of empire.[54]

To Queer China Again

With the rise of China in the twenty-first century, it is all the more pressing to bring the scholarly practice of "queering" to bear on the study of "China." The world is occupied by 1.3 billion native speakers of the Sinitic-language family. That is more than three times the number of people for whom English is the mother tongue. Changing our purview from considering "China" as a national category to envisioning the "Sinophone" as a global concept reflects the fact that the area studies modus operandi of Sinology has long outlived its utility. The danger of criticizing "the West" from a seemingly harmless stance of nativist "China" can easily be neutralized by the self-fashioned postcolonial critic who works from a privileged position to marginalize ethnic, geopolitical, and gender/sexual others.[55] After all, there is no Stonewall in China, but that should not stop us from queering Chinese and Sinophone history. Similar to the way historians have recontextualized Stonewall time and again, queer Sinophone studies dispels the myth of a coherent tongzhi movement past and present. It is perhaps fitting, then, that even though I began with the injunction to treat Stonewall as a lateral event, this chapter concludes with the bid to put China aside or, alternatively put, to queer China again.

The rise of the PRC empire is perhaps one of the most underexplored topics in the critical humanities and social sciences today. Yet, I write about this remiss at a moment when a significant number of historians continue to reference Stonewall as the inception of modern queer politics. My goal has been to consider both the Stonewall hegemony and contemporary Chinese imperialism as interconnected developments in world historiography—an instance of what the Francophone writer Édouard Glissant has called the "poetics of relation."[56] The examples of the Tiananmen incident (1989) and the retrocession of Hong Kong (1997) highlight turning points other than

1969 in the globally intertwined history of dehumanization. In fact, if we bring this narrative to the present, Sinophone communities continue to occasion unforeseen possibilities for queer political action, such as the legalization of same-sex unions in Taiwan and transgender marriage in Hong Kong.[57] Of course, there is no singular consensus on how the direction and contours of these new battles would impact the lives of LGBTQ people in the Asia Pacific.[58] But bringing to focus the geospatial complexities of the Sinitic language populations, at the very least, signals the death of two interconnected positivisms: a linear, evolutionary history of sexual liberation spawned from Stonewall and a neat compartmentalization of the non-West as a differential supplement. In this way, queer theory needs Sinophone studies as a co-produced vector through which to double question its own essentialism defined around any geocultural and temporal unit.

Notes

1. This chapter is a slightly revised excerpt of chapter 2 from Howard Chiang, *Transtopia in the Sinophone Pacific* (New York: Columbia University Press, 2021).

2. The word choice here is intentional: *queer* is translated into Mandarin Chinese by Taiwanese writers in the 1990s as *ku'er*, which literally means a "cool child."

3. This chapter aims to extend the theoretical and empirical horizons explored in Howard Chiang and Ari Heinrich, eds., *Queer Sinophone Cultures* (London: Routledge, 2013); and Howard Chiang and Alvin Wong, eds., *Keywords in Queer Sinophone Studies* (London: Routledge, 2020). See also Fran Martin, "Transnational Queer Sinophone Cultures," in *Routledge Handbook of Sexuality Studies in East Asia*, ed. Mark McLelland and Vera Mackie (London: Routledge, 2014), 35–48; Zoran Lee Pecic, *New Queer Sinophone Cinema: Local Histories, Transnational Connections* (New York: Palgrave Macmillan, 2016); and Ting-Fai Yu, "Queer Sinophone Malaysia: Language, Transnational Activism, and the Role of Taiwan," *Journal of Intercultural Studies* 43 (2022): 303–318.

4. Robert Hall, *Area Studies: With Special Reference to Their Implications for Research in the Social Sciences* (New York: Social Science Research Council, 1947), 82.

5. Tani Barlow, "Colonialism's Career in Postwar China Studies," *positions: east asia cultures critique* 1 (1993): 224–267, on 225.

6. Cindy Patton and Benigno Sánchez-Eppler, eds., *Queer Diasporas* (Durham, NC: Duke University Press, 2000); Arnaldo Cruz-Malavé and Martin Manalansan, eds., *Queer Globalizations: Citizenship and the Afterlife of Colonialism* (New York: New York University Press, 2002); and Eithne Luibhéid and Karma Chávez, eds., *Queer and Trans Migration: Dynamics of Illegalization, Detention, and Deportation* (Urbana: University of Illinois Press, 2020).

7. Martin, "Transnational Queer Sinophone Cultures," 43. On the meaning, history, and politics of the term *tongzhi*, see Wah-shan Chou, *Tongzhi: Politics of Same-Sex Eroticism in Chinese Societies* (New York: Haworth, 2000); and Ta-wei Chi, *Tongzhi wenxueshi: Taiwan de faming* 同志文學史：台灣的發明 (A queer invention in Taiwan: A history of tongzhi

literature) (Taipei: Linking, 2017), 379–392. A parallel example of lexical circulation is the Mandarin vernacular translation of *lesbian* into *lala*.

8. Shana Ye, "A Reparative Return to 'Queer Socialism': Male Same-Sex Desire in the Cultural Revolution," in *Sexuality in China: Histories of Power and Pleasure*, ed. Howard Chiang (Seattle: University of Washington Press, 2018), 142–162; and Wenqing Kang, "Queer Life, Communities, and Activism in Contemporary China," *Cross-Currents: East Asian History and Culture Review* 31 (2019): 226–230.

9. Helen Leung, *Undercurrents: Queer Culture and Postcolonial Hong Kong* (Vancouver: University of British Columbia Press, 2008); Fran Martin, *Situating Sexualities: Queer Representation in Taiwanese Fiction, Film, and Public Culture* (Hong Kong: Hong Kong University Press, 2003); Tze-lan Sang, *The Emerging Lesbian: Female Same-Sex Desire in Modern China* (Chicago: University of Chicago Press, 2003); Howard Chiang and Yin Wang, eds., *Perverse Taiwan* (London: Routledge, 2016).

10. Victor Roudometof, *Glocalization: A Critical Introduction* (London: Routledge, 2016).

11. Song Hwee Lim, "How to be Queer in Taiwan: Translation, Appropriation, and the Construction of a Queer Identity in Taiwan," in *AsiaPacifiQueer: Rethinking Genders and Sexualities*, ed. Fran Martin, Peter Jackson, Mark McLelland, and Audrey Yue (Urbana: University of Illinois, 2004), 235–250.

12. Chiang, *Transtopia in the Sinophone Pacific*, 170–207.

13. On the genealogy of tongzhi in the PRC, see Hongwei Bao, *Queer Comrades: Gay Identity and Tongzhi Activism in Postsocialist China* (Copenhagen: Nordic Institute of Asian Studies Press, 2018).

14. Petrus Liu, *Queer Marxism in Two Chinas* (Durham, NC: Duke University Press, 2015), 41–45.

15. Liu, *Queer Marxism in Two Chinas*, 4, 7.

16. Iris Marion Young, *Justice and the Politics of Difference* (Princeton, NJ: Princeton University Press, 1990); Nancy Fraser, *Justice Interruptus: Critical Reflections on the "Postsocialist" Condition* (London: Routledge, 1997).

17. Alvin Wong, "Queer Sinophone Studies as Anti-Capitalist Critique: Mapping Queer Kinship in the Works of Chen Ran and Wong Bik-wan," in Chiang and Heinrich, *Queer Sinophone Cultures*, 109–129; Howard Chiang and Alvin Wong, "Queering the Transnational Turn: Regionalism and Queer Asias," *Gender, Place & Culture* 23 (2016): 1643–1656; and Alvin Wong, "Queering the Quality of Desire: Perverse Use-Values in Transnational Chinese Cultures," *Culture, Theory and Critique* 58 (2017): 209–225.

18. John D'Emilio, "Capitalism and Gai Identity," in *Powers of Desire: The Politics of Sexuality*, ed. Ann Snitow, Christine Stansell, and Sharon Thompson (New York: Monthly Review Press, 1983), 100–113; Kevin Floyd, *The Reification of Desire: Toward a Queer Marxism* (Minneapolis: University of Minnesota Press, 2009); Peter Drucker, *Warped: Gay Normality and Queer Anti-Capitalism* (Leiden: Brill, 2015); Emily Hobson, *Lavender and Red: Liberalism and Solidarity in the Gay and Lesbian Left* (Oakland: University of California Press, 2016); and Aaron Lecklider, *Love's Next Meeting: The Forgotten History of Homosexuality and the Left in American Culture* (Oakland: University of California Press, 2021).

19. Liu, *Queer Marxism in Two Chinas*, 21.

20. Liu, *Queer Marxism in Two Chinas*, 85–113.

21. Liu, *Queer Marxism in Two Chinas*, 6. On self- or re-Orientalization, see Howard Chiang, *After Eunuchs: Science, Medicine, and the Transformation in Modern China* (New York: Columbia University Press, 2018), 136.

22. Kuan-hsing Chen, *Asia as Method: Toward Deimperialization* (Durham, NC: Duke University Press, 2010).

23. Rey Chow, *Entanglements, or Transmedial Thinking About Capture* (Durham, NC: Duke University Press, 2012), 171.

24. Qwo-Li Driskill, Chris Finley, Brian Joseph Gilley, and Scott Lauria Morgensen, eds., *Queer Indigenous Studies: Critical Interventions in Theory, Politics, and Literature* (Tucson: University of Arizona Press, 2011); Scott Lauria Morgensen, *Spaces Between Us: Queer Settler Colonialism and Indigenous Decolonization* (Minneapolis: University of Minnesota Press, 2011).

25. Scott Lauria Morgensen, "Settler Homonationalism: Theorizing Settler Colonialism within Queer Modernities," *GLQ* 16 (2010): 105–131, on 106.

26. Jasbir Puar, *Terrorist Assemblages: Homonationalism in Queer Times* (Durham, NC: Duke University Press, 2007).

27. Jia Tan, "Beijing Meets Hawai'i: Reflections on *Ku'er*, Indigeneity, and Queer Theory," *GLQ* 23 (2017): 137–150.

28. Wen-Ling Lin, "'Sisters' Making Gender: Between Everyday Work and Social Relations," *Taiwan* 86 (2012): 51–98; Séagh Kehoe and Chelsea E. Hall, "Tibet," in *Global Encyclopedia of Lesbian, Gay, Bisexual, Transgender, and Queer History*, ed. Howard Chiang (Farmington Hills, MI: Charles Scribner's Sons, 2019), 1597–1601; Kyle Shernuk, "A Queerness of Relation: The Plight of the 'Ethnic Minority' in Chan Koon-Chung's *Bare Life*," in Chiang and Wong, *Keywords in Queer Sinophone Studies*, 80–102; and Francisca Yuenki Lai, *Maid to Queer: Asian Labor Migration and Female Same-Sex Desire* (Hong Kong: Hong Kong University Press, 2021).

29. Dipesh Chakrabarty, *Provincializing Europe: Postcolonial Thought and Historical Thought* (Princeton, NJ: Princeton University Press, 2000); Partha Chatterjee, *The Politics of the Governed: Reflections on Popular Politics in Most of the World* (New York: Columbia University Press, 2004).

30. While sound studies represents an emerging field, a sustained scholarly attention to its intersection with queer theory has yet to formalize. For some preliminary investigations, see Drew Daniel, "Queer Sound," *WIRE*, no. 333 (2011): 42–46; and Sarah E. Truman and David Ben Shannon, "Queer Sonic Cultures: An Affective Walking-Composing Project," *Capacious* 1 (2018): 58–77.

31. My approach builds on Audrey Yue, "The Sinophone Cinema of Wong Kar-wai," in *A Companion to Wong Kar-wai*, ed. Martha P. Nochimson (Malden, MA: Wiley-Blackwell, 2016), 232–249; Helen Leung, "New Queer Angles on Wong Kar-wai," in Nochimson, *A Companion to Wong Kar-wai*, 250–271.

32. *Happy Together*, directed by Wong Kar-wai (Hong Kong: Jet Tone, 1997).

33. Quoted in Marc Siegel, "The Intimate Spaces of Wong Kar-wai," in *At Full Speed: Hong Kong Cinema in a Borderless World*, ed. Esther C.M. Yau (Minneapolis: University of Minnesota Press, 2001), 277–294, on 279.

34. Chris Berry, "Happy Alone?" *Journal of Homosexuality* 39 (2000): 187–200, on 193.

35. Jimmy Ngai, "A Dialogue with Wong Kar-wai: Cutting Between Time and Two Cities," in *Wong Kar-wai*, ed. Jean-Marc Lalanne, David Martinez, Ackbar Abbas, and Jimmy Ngai (Paris: Dis Voir, 1997), 83–117, on 112.

36. Helen Leung, "Queerscapes in Contemporary Hong Kong Cinema," *positions: east asia cultures critique* 9 (2001): 423–447, on 424.

37. Rey Chow, "Nostalgia of the New Wave: Structure in Wong Kar-wai's *Happy Together*," *Camera Obscura* 14 (1999): 30–49; Berry, "Happy Alone?"; Leung, "Queerscapes in Contemporary Hong Kong Cinema"; Siegel, "The Intimate Spaces of Wong Kar-wai"; Song Hwee Lim, *Celluloid Comrades: Representations of Male Homosexuality in Contemporary Chinese Cinemas* (Honolulu, University of Hawaii Press, 2006), 99–125; David Eng, *The Feeling of Kinship: Queer Liberalism and the Racialization of Intimacy* (Durham, NC: Duke University Press, 2010), 58–92; Carlos Rojas, "Queer Utopias in Wong Kar-wai's *Happy Together*," in Nochimson, *A Companion to Wong Kar-wai*, 508–521; and Alvin Wong, "Postcoloniality Beyond China-Centrism: Queer Sinophone Transnationalism in Hong Kong Cinema," in Chiang and Wong, *Keywords in Queer Sinophone Studies*, 62–79.

38. Rojas, "Queer Utopias in Wong Kar-wai's *Happy Together*."

39. Chow, "Nostalgia of the New Wave," 34 (emphasis in original).

40. Shu-mei Shih, *Visuality and Identity: Sinophone Articulations Across the Pacific* (Berkeley: University of California Press, 2007), 4.

41. Shih, *Visuality and Identity*, 5.

42. Rojas, "Queer Utopias in Wong Kar-wai's *Happy Together*."

43. Leung, *Undercurrents*, 85–105.

44. Leung, "New Queer Angles on Wong Kar-wai," 269.

45. For insightful analyses of queer kinship and homecoming in the Sinophone contexts, see E. K. Tan, "A Queer Journey Home in *Solos*: Rethinking Kinship in Sinophone Singapore," in Chiang and Heinrich, *Queer Sinophone Cultures*, 130–146; and Wong, "Queer Sinophone Studies as Anti-Capitalist Critique."

46. Shu-mei Shih, "Theory, Asia and the Sinophone," *Postcolonial Studies* 13 (2010): 465–484."

47. Mizoguchi Yuzo, *Ribenren shiyezhong de zhongguoxue* 日本人視野中的中國學 (China as method), trans. Li Suping 李甦平, Gong Ying 龔穎, and Xu Tao 徐滔 (Beijing: Chinese People's University Press, 1996 [1989]), 93.

48. Chen, *Asia as Method*, 120.

49. Paul Cohen, *Discovering History in China: American Historical Writing on the Recent Chinese Past* (New York: Columbia University Press, 1984).

50. Chow, *Entanglements*.

51. On the history of male same-sex relations in China, see Bret Hinsch, *Passions of the Cut Sleeve: The Male Homosexual Tradition in China* (Berkeley: University of California Press, 1990); Wenqing Kang, *Obsession: Male Same-Sex Relations in China, 1900–1950* (Hong Kong: Hong Kong University Press, 2009); and Giovanni Vitiello, *The Libertine's Friend: Homosexuality and Masculinity in Late Imperial China* (Chicago: University of Chicago Press, 2011).

52. Chiang, *After Eunuchs*.

53. Michel Foucault, *The History of Sexuality*, vol. 1: *An Introduction*, trans. Robert Hurley (New York: Vintage, 1990), 103.

54. On "grids of intelligibility," see Hubert Dreyfus and Paul Rabinow, *Michel Foucault: Beyond Structuralism and Hermeneutics* (Chicago: University of Chicago Press, 1982), 120–121. On "intimate frontiers," see Albert Hurtado, *Intimate Frontiers: Sex, Gender, and Culture in Old California* (Albuquerque: University of New Mexico Press, 1999).

55. Kwame Anthony Appiah, "Is the Post- in Postmodernism the Post- in Postcolonial?" *Critical Inquiry* 17 (1991): 336–357.

56. Édouard Glissant, *Poetics of Relation*, trans. Betsy Wing (Ann Arbor: University of Michigan Press, 1997).

57. John Nguyet Erni, "Disrupting the Colonial Transgender/Law Nexus: Reading the Case of W in Hong Kong," *Cultural Studies—Critical Methodologies* 16 (2016): 351–360; Chiang, *Transtopia in the Sinophone Pacific*, 170–207.

58. Joseph Cho and Lucetta Kam, "Same-Sex Marriage in China, Hong Kong and Taiwan: Ideologies, Spaces and Developments," in *Contemporary Issues in International Political Economy*, ed. Fu-Lai Tony Yu and Diana Kwan (Singapore: Palgrave Macmillan, 2019), 289–306.

Written Out

Dance and the Sinophone

EMILY WILCOX

Dance is a field with great potential for Sinophone studies. In particular, as a nonlinguistic medium, dance complicates the established centrality of language in definitions of the Sinophone and suggests new directions for Sinophone studies research. In this essay, I consider the many ways that Sinophone studies and dance studies are already in conversation and assess future prospects for dialogue across dance and the Sinophone.[1]

Existing definitions have often used language as the key identifying parameter for what identifies a cultural work or community as Sinophone. In her introduction to *Sinophone Studies: A Critical Reader*, Shu-mei Shih translates Sinophone literature as "*Huayu yuxi wenxue*, literatures of the Sinitic language family," and she explains that "Sinophone culture . . . is defined not by ethnicity (although ethnicity and language sometimes correspond) but by language."[2] Language also appears centrally in Shih's formulation of Sinophone studies, which states: "Sinophone studies takes as its objects of study the *Sinitic-language* communities and cultures outside China as well as ethnic minority communities and cultures within China *where Mandarin is adopted or imposed*."[3]

Adapting the concept of the Sinophone for film, Audrey Yue and Olivia Khoo's *Sinophone Cinemas* pushes for a deeper investigation of sonic and phonic (as opposed to visual and written) dimensions of Sinophone cinematic expression. Taking a critical approach, its contributors explicitly challenge what Song Hwee Lim called the "lingua-centrism" of Shih's notion of the Sinophone by including silent films and films in non-Sinitic or creole languages such as English and Singlish.[4] Yet, while they expand the scope of the Sinophone, these interventions, in some ways, reinforce the centrality of language as the field's sustained object of attention.

Dance pushes us to further consider what the Sinophone means in the absence of language. Of course, language is essential in many aspects of dance production, consumption, and scholarly work: Choreographers use language to communicate their ideas to dancers, stage and costume designers, composers, and marketers; audiences and critics typically read a performance program and talk or write their reactions verbally; and language is an essential component of most methods of historical documentation and scholarly discourse about dance. Nevertheless, while language is indispensable to the creation, framing, and documentation of dance, it is usually not the primary medium of dance works themselves. By its very definition, dance makes meaning and enacts performative interventions through bodily movements. The sequential unfolding of these movements in time and space—usually with the addition of a music or sound score, lighting, costumes, and stage design—constitutes the creative medium of dance.

Given this, how should one define Sinophone dance? To quote Taiwan-based dance scholar Yatin Lin in her book *Sino-Corporealities*, "[H]ow does this discourse relate to dance studies . . . other than just stating these choreographers' 'Chinese' ethnicity?"[5] Because the Sinophone itself is not a stable concept, but is constantly being debated and revised by scholars with different positions and aims, I argue that there is no single way to conceptualize Sinophone dance. Rather, like other artistic and cultural fields, dance presents a multitude of possible directions for new elaborations and critical reformulations of Sinophone thought and practice. My suggestions in this essay are, thus, not prescriptive but rather seek to stimulate diverse approaches to this rich field.

This essay is divided into three sections, each addressing a different issue for dance and the Sinophone. The first section addresses the basic question: What is Sinophone dance? To this, I provide two possible answers. One, based on the notion of Sinitic-language communities and cultures, considers what dance forms might be the equivalent of Sinitic-language in terms of the styles they use and the communities they address. The other, based on the Sinophone's emphasis on ethnic minorities and places on the margins of or outside China, considers which groups might be seen as Sinophone dance practitioners. It is the intersection of both meanings, I argue, that defines Sinophone dance in its most productive formulation. The second section takes a more metadiscursive approach that is inspired by the historical commitment of Sinophone studies to emphasizing minor practices and overturning entrenched scholarly hierarchies. Looking at both English and Chinese-language dance scholarship, I reflect on how Sinophone dance has both been written into and out of dance research historically. I discuss how specific approaches to Sinophone dance studies may address existing absences. The third section continues this set of concerns by addressing power relationships between dance and language, both in the academic field of Chinese studies and in Chinese and Sinophone dance contexts. I further consider how linguistic barriers pose a challenge for dance practitioners who are able to participate in Sinophone dance but not in the dominant language-based historical and critical discourses surrounding it. Finally, I propose taking bodily discourse, rather than language, as the focus for determining what counts as Sinophone dance.

When bringing the Sinophone into dialogue with dance, it is important to recognize that dance studies as a discipline has developed differently from literary and film studies, where Sinophone studies initially emerged. In English-language dance scholarship, communities traditionally associated with the Sinophone—Taiwan and Hong Kong, Chinese diasporas in Southeast Asia and North America, and Chinese ethnic minorities—have received more attention historically than Han dance communities in mainland China. This means that in English-language dance studies, the "obsession with China" that plagues Chinese literary and film studies and inspired much-needed critique from Sinophone studies is much less prominent, and, in some ways, an opposite trend exists.[6] While a focus on Han communities in China is certainly present in Chinese-language dance scholarship, there is relatively more attention to non-Han dance practitioners within mainland China than to activities in Taiwan, Hong Kong, and the diaspora. Meanwhile, in the field of Chinese studies, dance remains so marginal as a field of study that any attention, even to the most hegemonic of Han mainland choreographers, represents a minor position in the field at large. Thus, just as the medium of dance presents a challenge to language-centered notions of the Sinophone, the distinct histories of scholarly practice around dance likewise push Sinophone studies to continually reassess its assumptions about the hegemonic and the peripheral, margins and centers in the Sinophone world.

What Is Sinophone Dance?

Existing considerations of the Sinophone in relation to dance have tended to focus more on place than form as the factor that makes a dance Sinophone. In *Sino-Corporealities*, the first book-length work to explicitly engage Sinophone studies in relation to dance, Yatin Lin focuses on dance works created in

Taiwan, Hong Kong, and the United States. She frames her investigation by asking, "How do the Sinophone communities they are based in, be it Taipei, Hong Kong, or even New York, nurture, enrich, or shape their choreographies?"[7] For Lin, it is the engagement with Sinophone communities outside or on the margins of China that gives a dance its Sinophone qualities, not the particular style or form in which the dance is created.

While this is one valid way of approaching Sinophone dance studies, I would like to suggest a deeper engagement with dance form, especially as form relates to histories of imperialism and postcoloniality, cultural pluralism, and minoritization. Just as writers in Sinophone spaces write in a multitude of languages, each of which draws upon specific cultural sources and speaks to particular audiences, Sinophone choreographers also create dances in a variety of dance forms that draw upon different cultural experiences and resonate with different audience groups. By not attending to these differences, Sinophone dance studies can run the risk of glossing over imperialist legacies and uncritically reproducing aesthetic hegemonies. Like languages, dance forms carry with them histories of power relations. This necessitates a critical awareness of dance form as one element in the theorization of Sinophone dance studies.

If we take dance in Hong Kong as an example, the political and cultural implications of dance form and its parallels to language become immediately apparent. Prior to the twentieth century, dance in Hong Kong mainly consisted of local community practices brought by migrants from Fujian and Guangzhou. Typical examples included the Fire Dragon 火龍 Dance of Hakka communities and *Chaozhou yingge* 潮州英歌 of Teochew communities. Like the regional topolects of Hakka, Hokkien, and Teochew, these dances are constitutive of local identities as well as transnational Sinophone networks that link Hong Kong, south China, and Sinophone Southeast Asia through family genealogies, clan systems, and native place organizations. During the twentieth century, a number of new dance forms emerged in Hong Kong, each reflecting a different set of cultural and political affiliations and experiences. These included dance styles associated with British and American culture, such as ballet 芭蕾舞, Euro-American modern or contemporary dance 現代舞/當代舞, and ballroom dance 交誼舞/國標舞. Like the adoption of the English language, the local histories of these dance styles are inseparable from British colonization and Cold War American neoimperialism, and their deep-rooted acceptance is part of Hong Kong's postcolonial condition. Twentieth-century Hong Kong also saw the introduction of the newly created Chinese dance or *Zhongguo wu* 中國舞 (also called new dance *xin wudao* 新舞蹈 or national dance *minzu wu* 民族舞), primarily from mainland China but also from Taiwan. Not unlike the linguistic introduction of Mandarin or *putonghua*, these dance forms embody new conceptions of Chinese identity often linked to specific political agendas. These dance styles have been the target of both state censorship and state promotion, depending on the regime. Thus, they show the layering of disparate cultural forces that simultaneously shape dance in Sinophone communities. In the case of Hong Kong, we find dances embodying Chinese migration and settler colonialism, British colonialism, U.S. Cold War imperialism, neoliberal globalization, postcolonial nationalism, and PRC reterritorialization, among others.[8]

Since the 1980s, three professional companies have dominated the Hong Kong concert dance landscape, reflecting what are now the special administrative region's three most predominant and officially recognized concert dance forms. They are the Hong Kong Ballet Company, which performs ballet; the Hong Kong City Contemporary Dance Company, which performs modern or contemporary dance; and the Hong Kong Dance Company, which performs Chinese dance. Although the parallels to language are not exact, an extension of these comparisons between dance forms and languages is telling in contemporary Hong Kong. That is, no major professional ensemble promotes the local forms that might be seen as dance equivalents of regional topolects. Meanwhile, one company promotes what might be seen as the dance equivalent of *putonghua* (Hong Kong Dance Company), and two promote what might be seen as two different dance equivalents of English (Hong Kong Ballet Company and Hong Kong City Contemporary Dance Company). Furthermore, the Hong Kong Ballet Company and Hong Kong City Contemporary Dance Company often collaborate with choreographers and dancers from Europe, Australia, and the United States, while the Hong Kong Dance Company frequently engages artists from China and elsewhere in the Sinophone world.

In its approach to literature and film, Sinophone studies has historically placed significant emphasis on artists and works that employ Sinitic languages. Within literary studies, this is one way Sinophone studies has distinguished itself from English literature and Asian American studies, both of which historically place more emphasis on literature written in English. Moreover, it has been precisely by examining the local distinctions among Sinitic-language literatures from different parts of the Sinophone world—such as *Mahua* literature from Malaysia and its many diverse parallels in Singapore, Hong Kong, Thailand, Tibet, Australia, Taiwan, the United States, and other places—that the potential of the Sinophone as a critical intervention into Chineseness and existing notions of Chinese studies have emerged in their fullest and most potent forms. It has been through careful attention to how such writings differ from work seen more traditionally as Chinese literature (*Zhongguo wenxue*)—whether through the languages being deployed and developed, the experiences being invoked, or the networks being activated—that Sinophone studies scholars have succeeded in effectively challenging once-taken-for-granted models of Chineseness.

The greatest potential for similarly critical approaches in Sinophone dance studies lies, I believe, not in the study of Sinophone artists's engagement with ballet and modern/contemporary dance (although this is, of course, also important and necessary) but rather in the study of what might be called, in keeping with existing Sinophone studies terminologies for literature and film, Sinitic-form dance or Sinophone dance. In the Hong Kong context, this would include the Hong Kong Dance Company and the Chinese dance wing of the Hong Kong Academy of Performing Arts. It would also include dance practices historically linked to Hakka, Teochew, Cantonese, and other place-based topolect communities, many of which are amateur or community-based. Dances performed in connection with Sinitic-language theatrical, entertainment, educational, and ritual activities may also be relevant. Existing English-language scholarship on such topics has already emerged in the contexts of Taiwan, North America, Southeast Asia, and Australia, and they offer promising examples for future work.[9]

Apart from Sinitic-form dance outside mainland China, existing definitions of the Sinophone also invite consideration of dances practiced by non-Han dancers within mainland China, particularly those engaged in networks and discourses of what is known as Chinese dance. Such dance practices may be considered parallel to Sinitic-language literature and film produced by ethnic minority artists in China, which are often addressed in Sinophone studies scholarship. Extensive work on this subject exists in the Chinese-language dance and ethnological literature.[10] In English, there is also an extensive and rapidly growing body of publications on this topic.[11] Like the work on Sinitic-form dance outside China, this area of scholarship contributes in important ways to core concerns of Sinophone studies, such as the critical rethinking of Chineseness as a unified, hegemonic cultural category and the investigation of layered cultural hybridities, minoritizing processes, and negotiations that occur at the interfaces of Han and non-Han communities. Rather than upholding a strict binary between Han and non-Han, much of this scholarship demonstrates the complex interconnections, code-switching, and multiple affiliations that often obtain for ethnic minority artists and their work in China. Because non-Han dance has been incorporated as a central component of state-sponsored hegemonic forms of Chinese dance in many parts of the Sinophone world, how definitions of Chineseness vary across time and place in relation to ethnicity is an important subject of Sinophone dance studies broadly.

The Sinophone in English- and Chinese-Language Dance Studies

Like most academic disciplines, dance studies has its own intellectual trajectories that have developed differently in diverse language communities. I envision Sinophone dance studies as a scholarly intervention that can contribute to dance studies scholarship in both the English- and Chinese-language academic spheres. In both cases, Sinophone dance, as defined above, has been marginalized or written out to a certain extent in existing scholarship, though in distinct ways. Thus, different opportunities exist in each arena for critical Sinophone studies interventions.

English-language dance studies, much like other arts and humanities disciplines, is marked by a history of Euro-American centrism. This means that not only do white and U.S.-and Europe-based dancers and choreographers receive more attention than their nonwhite and non-U.S.- and Europe-based counterparts, but so do the dance forms associated with them. Thus, not only are dancers and choreographers of Chinese descent marginalized in English-language dance scholarship, but those engaged in dance forms associated with Chinese and Sinophone communities are also further marginalized compared to their counterparts who work in dance forms associated with the United States and Europe, such as modern/contemporary dance and ballet. While area studies and ethnic studies have carved out spaces of institutional independence to challenge the Eurocentrism of literary studies in the English-language academy, equivalent spaces in dance studies are extremely limited. This means that dance scholars in the English-speaking academy who work on minoritized dance forms and communities often must make their work legible within conversations centered on the aesthetic and political concerns and histories of white Euro-American dance or risk exclusion, irrelevance, and invisibility.[12] Because of this politics of legibility, all varieties of Chinese and Sinophone dance—whether practiced by Han dancers in mainland China, ethnic minority dancers in mainland China, or Sinitic-language dance communities in other locales—remain on the margins of English-language dance studies.

Because of this predicament, a quite different dynamic exists in the examination of Chineseness in English-language dance studies as compared to literary and film studies. In literature and cinema, Sinophone studies has taken a position of opposition in response to a field that has historically defined Chinese literature and Chinese film to mean the work of writers and directors based in mainland China. In dance, however, the situation is very different. Rather than occupying a central position, dance practices associated with Han dancers and choreographers in mainland China have been more marginalized than dance practices associated with other parts of the Sinophone world. The first research monographs on dance in the Chinese and Sinophone world published in English by dance scholars trained in English-speaking institutions were SanSan Kwan's 2013 *Kinesthetic City: Dance and Movement in Chinese Urban Spaces* and Yatin Lin's 2015 *Sino-Corporealities*. Both books take modern and contemporary dance in Taiwan, Hong Kong, and New York as their primary focus.[13] Routledge's English-language book series, Celebrating Dance in Asia and the Pacific, which has been important in promoting English-language scholarship about dance in Asia, includes books on Singapore, Malaysia, and Taiwan (all of which pay significant attention to Sinophone dance) but not on mainland China. World Dance Alliance, which sponsors the series, also had no mainland China chapter until recently, though it has long-standing chapters in Taiwan, Hong Kong, and Southeast Asia.

Many factors contribute to this situation. Taiwan and Hong Kong both have longer histories of exchange with the Euro-American dance world than mainland China because of British colonialism and the Cold War and, as a result, their dance repertoires have often been more legible to the English-language dance studies community than dance produced in mainland China. There has also been greater scholarly exchange historically between the English-language dance studies community and dance scholars in Taiwan and Hong Kong compared to their counterparts in mainland China. Whereas students from Taiwan have been receiving PhDs in dance studies in English-speaking institutions for decades, the equivalent phenomenon for students from mainland China is much more recent. Even today, many scholars who research dance in mainland China in English-speaking universities are not based in dance departments. Those who are write primarily about modern and contemporary dance, not Chinese dance.

In the Chinese-language dance studies scholarship, a different set of trends exists. Both mainland China and Taiwan have large and very active communities of dance scholars publishing in the Chinese language. In contrast to English-language dance scholarship, Chinese-language dance scholarship places significant emphasis on Sinitic-form dance and on dancers and choreographers active across China and the Sinophone world. Both mainland China and Taiwan-based dance scholars tend to focus on dance activities happening within the political boundaries of their own communities, meaning that Taiwan-based scholars tend to focus more on dancers working in Taiwan, while mainland China-based scholars tend to focus more on dancers working in mainland China. Because China is so much larger and has so many more dance scholars than Taiwan, more Chinese-language dance research is produced on mainland China-related subjects than on other parts of the Sinophone world. As discussed above, there is a great deal of dance studies scholarship produced in mainland China focusing on dance in ethnic minority communities. There have also been book-length Chinese-language publications on dance in Sinophone Southeast Asia published in China, Malaysia, and Singapore.[14] The standard reference book on modern Chinese dance history published in mainland China, Wang Kefen and Long Yinpei's 1999 *Zhongguo jinxiandai dangdai wudao fazhanshi* 中国近现代当代舞蹈发展史 (History of the development of dance in modern and contemporary china) includes long, detailed sections on dance in Hong Kong, Taiwan, and overseas Sinophone communities in Asia, Africa, Australia, Europe, and North America.[15] Recent Chinese-language monographs published in Taiwan also explore Sinophone dance from a transnational perspective.[16]

At times, authors writing in Chinese have questioned the relevance of diasporic Chinese artists' activities abroad to their own work. In a 1947 essay, ironically written during a tour to Sinophone communities in Southeast Asia, Chinese dance pioneer Liang Lun wrote the following about Chinese-Trinidadian dancer Sylvia Si-lan Chen, one of the first internationally-renowned dancers of Chinese descent to create Chinese-themed modern dance: "[Chen] is a very famous dance artist in Russia who frequently performs in Moscow, St. Petersburg, and other places and has received the praise of a great many foreigners. Yet, what does this have to do with Chinese people?"[17] Such explicit dismissals of Sinophone dance outside China are rare in Chinese-language dance scholarship today. Nevertheless, much more research could be done in the Chinese-language scholarship on the place-based dance activities of Sinophone artists working outside mainland China and Taiwan.

The movements of dancers between different Sinophone spaces and the impacts of these movements on the development of Sinophone dance as a simultaneously place-based and transnational phenomenon is another key area that Sinophone approaches can contribute to the Chinese-language dance studies scholarship. Beiyu Zhang's *Chinese Theatre Troupes in Southeast Asia: Touring Diaspora, 1900s–1970s*, offers a useful model in this regard.[18] Such potential directions of inquiry present new challenges to scholars because they necessitate working across multiple languages, dance communities, and political regimes with different investments in the telling of Sinophone stories. Such approaches would unsettle conceptions of the Chinese or Sinophone dance world in which mainland China, and some cases Taiwan, serve as sources of dance knowledge and innovation, spreading unidirectionally outward to people and places further from these imagined centers. Rather, it would draw attention to the many reverse flows, transverse networks, and creative hybridizations that, in fact, sustain a multisited network of multidirectional dance innovation and exchange.[19]

Between Languages and Bodies

As a nonlinguistic medium, dance complicates assumptions about the relationship between language and the Sinophone in Sinophone studies because it allows space for artists to contribute to Sinophone cultural practices without being Sinitic-language speakers themselves. In my book *Revolutionary Bodies: Chinese Dance and the Socialist Legacy*, I argue that several prominent founders of the dance form known today as Chinese dance were members of the diaspora, immigrants, and ethnic minorities with limited command of Sinitic languages. This poses an interesting question: Should work by dancers and choreographers who do not speak or write a Sinitic language or do not identify as ethnically Chinese be considered part of Sinophone dance?

Answering this question necessitates a return to the issue of form, and it requires theorizing bodily discourse as an alternative to language for identifying and analyzing Sinophone dance. As discussed above, language has historically been a privileged category in Sinophone studies. However, this privileging of language is not unique to Sinophone studies. Rather, it is a structuring principle of area and ethnic studies generally, where the language in which a literary or cinematic work is produced often determines the field in which it is researched. By promoting the study of Sinitic-language cultural production created outside Han communities in mainland China, Sinophone studies draws attention to understudied subjects and disrupts the notion of a direct link between language and place that undergirds traditional area studies fields. As Sinophone studies expands beyond literature and cinema, new ways of mapping cultural production as Sinophone will be required to continue this critical endeavor in the absence of language markers. Visual culture, sound, and performance are already receiving greater attention in area studies, and there is a growing recognition of the need to expand scholars' analytical tools to include expressive modalities beyond language and written texts. For dance, this means recognizing bodily expression as a legitimate object of analysis, as well as thinking through ways of defining the Sinophone that shift emphasis from verbal to bodily discourse.

In pursuit of this approach, I find it useful to think of Sinophone bodily discourse in terms of horizons of legibility and communities of recognition rather than absolute distinctions in form, genre, language, nationality, or ethnicity. Just as Sinophone writers introduce words, grammatical structures, and narrative tropes from a variety of different literary traditions in their work, making creolization and hybridity the norm rather than the exception, Sinophone dance practitioners also draw upon a variety of sources and movement lexicons when creating dance performances. Therefore, to identify a dance work or practice as relevant for Sinophone studies analysis, it may be useful to focus on what types of knowledge or aesthetic sensibilities are being activated and which communities of practice and spectatorship are being engaged by particular choices within dance activities.

A common misunderstanding about dance is that because it is nonlinguistic, it somehow constitutes a universal language. In fact, this is not the case. Barriers to participation, legibility, recognition, and appreciation are just as prevalent in dance as they are in other modes of cultural production. Specific ways of holding, moving, adorning, and displaying the body have different associations in different embodied practice communities, and participatory dance activities, in particular, often require a high threshold of bodily expertise for meaningful engagement. Dance, whether experienced as an audience member or embodied as a participant, requires accumulated knowledge to recognize, appreciate, and interpret. This knowledge is necessary to read bodily movements and their interactions with sets, props, costumes, and music; to participate in these movements if the situation calls for it; and to recognize diverse expressive formats and their distinct registers of address, intention, and communication. Thus, just as knowledge of Sinitic languages is necessary to interpret Sinophone literature, knowledge of Sinitic bodily discourse is necessary to interpret Sinophone dance. Similar to language, this knowledge of bodily discourse is often linked to geographic location and national or ethnic identity but is not bound by them. Thus, a dancer who identifies as ethnically Chinese may not practice Sinophone dance and vice versa. What identifies Sinophone dance in this definition is engagement in bodily discourses that activate knowledge and practice systems linked primarily to Sinitic-language cultures and communities. By centering bodily discourse, this approach avoids essentialist understandings that equate ethnic and national identity with dance form. While complicating language, geography, nationality, and ethnic identity as absolute categories of belonging, this approach still promotes attention to understudied dance practices and challenges U.S. and Eurocentrism in English-language dance studies scholarship.

Based on this definition of Sinophone dance in terms of bodily discourse, I emphasize the importance of form in Sinophone dance studies. To return to the example of dance in contemporary Hong Kong, I see the performances of the Hong Kong Ballet Company and Hong Kong City Contemporary Dance Company as potentially less relevant to Sinophone studies analysis because the knowledge required to interpret their bodily discourses is not grounded primarily in Sinitic-language cultures and communities. By contrast, the dance repertoires of the Hong Kong Dance Company and other groups engaged in performances related to Chinese place-based associations, Sinitic-language dialect theater, and other Sinitic-language group activities does often require such knowledge. For this reason, these latter dance activities may be especially relevant for Sinophone studies scholarship aimed at complicating formations of Chineseness in diverse place-based contexts.

The reason I see the diasporic, immigrant, and ethnic minority dance practitioners discussed in *Revolutionary Bodies* as contributors to Sinophone dance is that the dances they performed and created engaged knowledge and practice systems grounded in Sinitic-language communities, regardless of the artists' own linguistic and national identities. In fact, many of the dance styles now recognized as Chinese dance and used to articulate varied local Sinophone experiences across the world are based on dances these individuals developed. In other words, it was with their bodies, more so than their words, that these dancers generated Sinophone expression and knowledge. To gain a full understanding of dance in the Sinophone world, it is essential to look at all forms of dance and to recognize that all forms of dance are capable of exploring and communicating Sinophone experiences and concerns. However, just as Sinophone literary studies attends to Sinitic-language literature created outside or on the margins of China to complicate traditional notions of Chinese literature, Sinophone dance studies can similarly center Sinitic-form dance created outside or on the margins of China as a way to complicate notions of Chinese dance and to understand its varied meanings and reinventions in diverse contexts and communities.

Conclusion

Dance has long played a critical role in the ritual and social life of Sinitic-language communities worldwide. However, these dance practices have rarely garnered the attention of scholars either of dance studies or Chinese studies in the English-language academy. On the one hand, this means that both Chinese and Sinophone dance studies are marginalized fields of study with limited institutional support and scholarly recognition. On the other hand, it also presents an unusual opportunity to productively think through China and the Sinophone together. How does the necessary intervention of Sinophone studies change when modern and contemporary dance companies in Hong Kong, Taiwan, and New York receive more scholarly attention than the most prominent Chinese dance companies in mainland China? How does our understanding of Chinese dance itself change when we learn that its leading architects are diasporic, immigrant, and ethnic minority subjects? By responding to the specificities that dance provides, Sinophone dance studies can build a new field in which the Chinese and the Sinophone are not essentially opposed but rather mutually informing, mutually constituted, and in critical dialogue.

Notes

1. I am grateful to two of my former doctoral students, Elizabeth Chan at the National University of Singapore and Po-Hsien Chu at the University of Maryland, whose work first inspired me to think deeply about dance and performance in Sinophone studies.

2. Shu-mei Shih, introduction to *Sinophone Studies: A Critical Reader*, ed. Shu-mei Shih, Chien-hsin Tsai, and Brian Bernards (New York: Columbia University Press, 2013), 9, 7.

3. Shih, introduction to *Sinophone Studies*, 11 (emphasis added).

4. Audrey Yue and Olivia Khoo, eds., *Sinophone Cinemas* (Basingstoke, UK: Palgrave Macmillan, 2014), 80.

5. Yatin Lin, *Sino-Corporealities: Contemporary Choreographies from Taipei, Hong Kong, and New York* (Taipei: Taipei National University of the Arts, 2015), xiv.

6. Shih, Tsai, and Bernards, *Sinophone Studies*, 17.

7. Lin, *Sino-Corporealities*, xiv.

8. On the history of dance in Hong Kong, see Stephen Kwok and Hong Kong Dance Sector Joint Conference, *Hong Kong Dance History* (Wanchai, Hong Kong: Cosmos Books, 2000); Joanna Lee 李海燕 and Venus Lam 林喜兒, *Shi wu hua: Xianggang wudao koushu lishi (50–70 niandai)* 拾舞話 - 香港舞蹈口述歷史 (五十至七十年代) (*The Unspoken Dance: An Oral History of Hong Kong Dance, 1950s–1970s*) (Hong Kong: City Contemporary Dance Company, 2019).

9. On Taiwan, see, for example, Ya-ping Chen, "Dancing Chinese Nationalism and Anticommunism: The *Minzu Wudao* Movement in 1950s Taiwan," in *Dance, Human Rights, and Social Justice: Dignity in Motion*, ed. Naomi M. Jackson and Toni Samantha Phim (Lanham, MD: Scarecrow Press, 2008), 34–50; Chi-Fang Chao, "Holding Hands to Dance: Movement as Cultural Metaphor in the Dances of Indigenous Peoples in Taiwan," *Journal for the Anthropological Study of Human Movement* 16, nos. 1–2 (2009): https://jashm.press.uillinois.edu/16.1_2/chao.html; Szu-Ching Chang, "Dancing with Nostalgia in Taiwanese Contemporary 'Traditional' Dance" (PhD diss., University of California, Riverside, 2011). On North America, see, for example, William Lau, "The Chinese Dance Experience in Canadian Society: An Investigation of Four Chinese Dance Groups in Toronto" (MFA thesis, York University, Toronto, 1991); Yutian Wong, ed., *Contemporary Directions in Asian American Dance* (Madison: University of Wisconsin Press, 2016); Sau-ling Wong, "Dancing in the Diaspora: Cultural Long-Distance Nationalism and the Staging of Chineseness by San Francisco's Chinese Folk Dance Association," *Journal of Transnational American Studies* 2, no. 1 (2010): https://www.researchgate.net/publication/277829284_Dancing_in_the_Diaspora_Cultural_Long-Distance_Nationalism_and_the_Staging_of_Chineseness_by_San_Francisco%27s_Chinese_Folk_Dance_Association; Hui Wilcox, "Movement in Spaces of Liminality: Chinese Dance and Immigrant Identities," *Ethnic and Racial Studies* 34 (2011): 314–332; Shih-Ming Li Chang and Lynn Frederiksen, *Chinese Dance: In the Vast Land and Beyond* (Middletown, CT: Wesleyan University Press, 2016); Casey Avant, "Claiming Ritual: Female Lion Dancing in Boston's Chinatown" (PhD diss., University of California, Riverside, 2018). On Singapore, see, for example, Soo Pong Chua, "Chinese Dance as Theatre Dance in Singapore: Change and Factors of Change," in *Dance as Cultural Heritage*, vol. 2, ed. Betty True Jones (New York: Congress on Research in Dance, 1985), 131–143; Yu Yun, *A Life in Dance: Lee Shu Fen* (Singapore:

Lee Shu Fen and Dancers Society, 1995); Teresa Lay Hoon Pee, "The Development of Chinese, Indian, and Malay Dance in Singapore to the 1970s" (MA thesis, Queensland University of Technology, 1999); Soo Pong Chua, "Chinese Dance: Cultural Resources and Creative Potentials," in *Evolving Synergies: Celebrating Dance in Singapore*, ed. Stephanie Burridge and Caren Cariño (Routledge, 2014), 17–30; Joey Chua, "The Emergence of Chinese Dance in Postcolonial Singapore, 1960s–1970s," *Dance Chronicle* 40, no. 2 (2017): 131–164; Emily Wilcox, "When Folk Dance Was Radical: Cold War *Yangge*, World Youth Festivals, and Overseas Chinese Leftist Culture in the 1950s and 1960s," *China Perspectives* 120, no. 1 (2020): 33–42. On Malaysia, Thailand, and Australia, see, for example, Sin Wen Lau, "Bodily Offerings of Belonging: Chinese-Australians in Perth," *Asia Pacific Journal of Anthropology* 8, no. 2 (2007): 137–149; Sooi Beng Tan, "The Lion Dances to the Fore: Articulating Chinese Identities in Penang and Medan," in *Authenticity and Cultural Identity, Performing Arts in Southeast Asia*, *Senri Ethnological Reports 65*, ed. Yoshitaka Terada (Osaka: National Museum of Ethnology, 2007), 63–78; Sooi Beng Tan, "Performing Community, Identity, and Change: The Chinese Dragon Leaps to the Beat," in *Sounding the Dance, Moving the Music: Choreomusicological Perspectives on Maritime Southeast Asian Performing Arts*, ed. Mohd Anis Md Nor and Kendra Stepputat (New York: Routledge, 2017); Benjamin Fairfield, "Ethnic and Village Unity: Symbolized or Enacted? Lahu Music-Dance and Ethnic Participation in Ban Musoe, Thailand," *Asian Music* 49, no. 2 (2018): 71–105; and Fung Ying Loo and Fung Chiat Loo, "Dramatizing Malaysia in Contemporary Chinese Lion Dance," *Asian Theater Journal* 33, no. 1 (2016): 130–150.

10. See, for example, Ji Lanwei 纪兰慰 and Qiu Jiurong 邱久荣, *Zhongguo shaoshu minzu wudao shi* 中国少数民族舞蹈史 (History of ethnic minority dance in China) (Beijing: Zhongyang minzu daxue chuban she, 1998); Xu Rui 许锐, *Dangdai Zhongguo minzu minjian wudao chuangzuo de shenmei yu zijue* 当代中国民族民间舞蹈创作的审美与自觉 (The aesthetics and consciousness of contemporary Chinese national folk dance choreography) (Shanghai: Shanghai yinyue chubanshe, 2014).

11. See, for example, Colin Mackerras, "Folksongs and Dances of China's Minority Nationalities: Policy, Tradition, and Professionalization," *Modern China* 10, no. 2 (1984): 187–226; Holly Fairbank, "Chinese Minority Dances: Processors and Preservationists—Part 1," *Journal for the Anthropological Study of Human Movement* 3, no. 4 (1985): 168–189; Holly Fairbank, "Chinese Minority Dances: Processors and Preservationists—Part 2," *Journal for the Anthropological Study of Human Movement* 4, no. 1 (1986): 36–55; Louisa Schein, *Minority Rules: The Miao and the Feminine in China's Cultural Politics* (Durham, NC: Duke University Press, 2000); Carol Pegg, *Mongolian Music, Dance & Oral Narrative: Performing Diverse Identities* (Seattle: University of Washington Press, 2001); Erik Mueggler, "Dancing Fools: Politics of Culture and Place in a Traditional Nationality Festival," *Modern China* 28, no. 1 (2002): 3–38; Yu-Zu Shi et al., "Preservation and Research of Materials of the Traditional Dancing Culture of Yunnan's Minority Groups (Aboriginal)," in *International Dance Conference, Taiwan, August 1–4, 2004: Dance, Identity and Integration: Conference Proceedings*, ed. Janice LaPointe-Crump (Taipei: Congress on Research in Dance, 2004), 215–219; Geoffrey Wall and Philip Feifan Xie, "Authenticating Ethnic Tourism: Li Dancers' Perspectives," *Asia Pacific Journal of Tourism Research* 10, no. 1 (2005): 1–21; Hae-kyung Um, "The Dialectics of Politics and Aesthetics in the Chinese Korean Dance Drama *The Spirit of Changbai Mountain*," *Asian Ethnicity* 6, no.

3 (2005): 203–222; Sara L. M. Davis, "Dance or Else: China's 'Simplifying Project,'" *China Rights Forum* 4 (2006): 38–46; Beida Li, *Dances of the Chinese Minorities* (Beijing: China Intercontinental Press, 2006); Ting-Ting Chang, "Choreographing the Peacock: Gender, Ethnicity, and National Identity in Chinese Ethnic Dance" (PhD diss., University of California, Riverside, 2008); Justin Jacobs, "How Chinese Turkestan Became Chinese: Visualizing Zhang Zhizhong's Tianshan Pictorial and Xinjiang Youth Song and Dance Troupe," *Journal of Asian Studies* 67, no. 2 (2008): 545–591; Anouska Komlosy, "Yunnanese Sounds: Creativity and Alterity in the Dance and Music Scenes of Urban Yunnan," *China: An International Journal* 6, no. 1 (2008): 44–68; Xiaobo Su and Peggy Teo, "Tourism Politics in Lijiang, China: An Analysis of State and Local Interactions in Tourism Development," *Tourism Geographies* 10, no. 2 (2008): 150–168; Holly Fairbank, "Preserving Minority Dance in China: Multiple Meanings and Layers of Intention," *Journal for the Anthropological Study of Human Movement* 16, nos. 1–2 (2009): https://jashm.press.uillinois.edu/16.1_2/fairbank.html; Xianxiang Cui, "Lives of Old Women of Korean Nationality in Beijing: A Case of One Dance Team," *Asian Women* 26, no. 1 (2010): 81–101; Emily Wilcox, "The Dialectics of Virtuosity: Dance in the People's Republic of China, 1949–2009" (PhD diss., University of California, Berkeley, 2011); Jing Li, "The Folkloric, the Spectacular, and the Institutionalized: Touristifying Ethnic Minority Dances on China's Southwest Frontiers," *Journal of Tourism and Cultural Change* 10, no. 1 (2012): 65–83; Qian Liu, et al., "Chinese Tibetan Guozhuang Dance from the Perspective of Sports," *Asian Social Science* 8, no. 7 (2012): 240–246; Emily Wilcox, "Dancers Doing Fieldwork: Socialist Aesthetics and Bodily Experience in the People's Republic of China," *Journal for the Anthropological Study of Human Movement* 17, no. 2 (2012): https://jashm.press.uillinois.edu/17.2/wilcox.html; Jenny Chio, *A Landscape of Travel: The Work of Tourism in Rural Ethnic China* (Seattle: University of Washington Press, 2014); Emily Wilcox, "Beyond Internal Orientalism: Dance and Nationality Discourse in the Early People's Republic of China, 1949–1954," *Journal of Asian Studies* 75, no. 2 (May 2016): 363–386; Amanda Snider, "Meshrep in Our Home . . . Where There is No Meshrep: Contrasting Narratives in the Reinvention of a Uyghur Gathering" (PhD diss., University of Kansas, 2017); Ronald Gilliam, "Performing Community: Memory and Collective Identity on the Uyghur Central Asian Stage" (PhD diss., University of Hawaii, 2018); Emily Wilcox, "Dynamic Inheritance: Representative Works and the Authoring of Tradition in Chinese Dance," *Journal of Folklore Research* 55, no. 1 (2018): 77–112; Emily Wilcox, "The Postcolonial Blind Spot: Chinese Dance in the Era of Third World-Ism, 1949–1965," *positions: asia critique* 26, no. 4 (2018): 781–815; Emily Wilcox, *Revolutionary Bodies: Chinese Dance and the Socialist Legacy* (Oakland: University of California Press, 2018); "Joking After Rebellion: Performing Tibetan-Han Relations in the Chinese Military Dance 'Laundry Song' (1964)," in *Maoist Laughter*, ed. Jason McGrath, Zhuoyi Wang, and Ping Zhu (Hong Kong University Press, 2019), 19–36; Emily Wilcox, "Dance in Wartime China: Liang Lun's Choreographic Migrations of the 1940s," *Journal of Society for Dance Documentation and History* 52 (March 2019): 45–75; Emily Wilcox, "Diasporic Moves: Sinophone Epistemology in the Choreography of Dai Ailian," in *Corporeal Politics: Dancing East Asia*, ed. Katherine Mezur and Emily Wilcox (Ann Arbor: University of Michigan Press, 2020), 115–134; and Ruby MacDougall, "Harnessing Vitality in Kunming: The Intellectual Lineage and Artistic Development in the Yi Compatriots Music and Dance Performance of 1946," *Asian Theatre Journal* 38, no. 2 (2021): 367–394.

12. For discussions of this problem, see, for example, Marta Savigliano, *Tango and the Political Economy of Passion* (Boulder, CO: Westview Press, 1995); Ananya Chatterjea, *Butting Out: Reading Resistive Choreographies Through Works by Jawole Willa Jo Zollar and Chandralekha* (Middletown CT: Wesleyan University Press, 2004); Susan Foster, ed., *Worlding Dance* (Basingstoke, UK: Palgrave Macmillan, 2009); Royona Mitra, *Akram Khan: Dancing New Interculturalism* (New York: Palgrave Macmillan, 2015); Emily Wilcox, "When Place Matters: Provincializing the 'Global,'" in *Rethinking Dance History*, 2nd ed., ed. Larraine Nicholas and Geraldine Morris (London: Routledge, 2018), 160–172.

13. SanSan Kwan, *Kinesthetic City: Dance and Movement in Chinese Urban Spaces* (Oxford: Oxford University Press, 2013); Yatin Lin, *Sino-Corporealities*.

14. See, for example, Ding Bo 丁波, *Fengyu Nanyang xing* 风雨南洋行 (On the road in the South Seas] (Guangzhou: Guangdong renmin chubanshe, 1988); Tang Kwek Leong 鄧國良, *Wuzi xuebu ji* 舞子学步集 (Writings on dance) (Singapore: Soaring Dove Dance Group, 1994); Poh Seng Titt 傅承得, *Gongxiang kongjian: Malaixiya Huaren di yi ge zhuanye wutuan* 共享空间：马来西亚华人第一个专业舞团 (Shared space: Malaysia's first professional Chinese dance ensemble) (Kuala Lampur: Mentor Publishing, 2002); and Yin Qiang 殷强, *Dongmeng wudao yishu* 东盟舞蹈艺术 (Dance art of ASEAN) (Guilin: Guangxi Normal University Press, 2016).

15. Wang Kefen 王克芬 and Long Yinpei 隆荫培, *Zhongguo jinxiandai dangdai wudao fazhanshi* 中国近现代当代舞蹈发展史 (History of the development of dance in modern and contemporary China) (Beijing: Renmin yinyue chubanshe, 1999).

16. See, for example, Chen Ya-ping 陳雅萍, Zhuti de kouwen: xiandai xing. li shi. Taiwan dangdai wudao 主體的叩問 現代性.歷史.臺灣當代舞蹈 (Enquiry into subjectivity: Modernity. History. Taiwan contemporary dance) (Taipei: Taipei National University of the Arts, 2013); Ya-ping Chen, "Putting Minzu Into Perspective: Dance and Its Relation to the Concept of 'Nation,'" *Choreographic Practices* 7, no. 2 (2016): 219–228; and Hsu Wei-Ying 徐瑋瑩, *Luo Ri zhi wu: Taiwan wudao yishu tuohuangzhe de jingyu yu tupo* 落日之舞：台灣舞蹈藝術拓荒者的境遇與突破 1920–1950 (Dance under the setting sun: Conditions and breakthroughs of Taiwan's dance pioneers) (New Taipei City: Linking Publishing, 2018).

17. Liang Lun 梁倫, "Wudao de Zhongguohua wenti" 舞蹈的中國化問題 (The problem of making dance Chinese), *Zhong yi* 中藝 (Malaya 1947), 13 (my translation).

18. Beiyu Zhang, *Chinese Theatre Troupes in Southeast Asia: Touring Diaspora, 1900s–1970s* (London: Routledge, 2021).

19. For a useful methodological model, see Shelly Chan, *Diaspora's Homeland: Modern China in the Age of Global Migration* (Durham, NC: Duke University Press, 2018).

Cantonese Opera and Sino-Soundscape in North America

NANCY YUNHWA RAO

North America has had a vibrant Sinophone soundscape since the nineteenth century, resulting from the migration of Chinese people across the Pacific, the ensuing dispersal of Chinese across the Americas, and the subsequent establishment of Chinese American communities. The soundscape is created through musical practices shaped both by the transnational networks and the locality, deriving from the geographical locations, material conditions, and political context. It is dynamic and always changing. From the period of the mid-nineteenth century to the early twentieth century, the Sinophone soundscape comprised several important forms of musical practices: Cantonese opera performance for ritual practices and theatrical entertainment; procession music for funerals and festivals with *suona*, drums, and gongs; and Taishan *muyu* and other south Chinese narrative songs for storytelling, either in private or in public. They produced a vibrant soundscape for Sinophone communities across North America, leaving indelible imprints on these communities. Traces of this soundscape—drums, playbills, floorplans of Chinese theater, lyrics, costumes—can still be found today in major cities and small towns along California's Mother Lode, such as Oroville and Marysville.

One representative genre during this era was Cantonese opera, the regional genre known to Chinese immigrants who mostly came from the Pearl River Delta of southern China. This chapter will focus on Cantonese opera theaters in North America in the 1920s to consider the historical soundscape of the Sinophone community. To capture the dynamic, complex, and intrinsically social nature of opera performances at these theaters, I will borrow the concept of *musicking*, a term coined by Christopher Small, to bring attention to issues of performativity and reception. The musicking of Cantonese opera, activities that included performing, producing, listening, learning, mimicking, remembering, and sharing, constituted the articulation of soundscape.[1] This essay argues that such a soundscape in the Sinophone communities went beyond what is often narrowly defined as a cultural practice of a single nation-state. In North America, the musicking of the early Sinophone community was, to a large extent, determined by the transpacific movement, policy of immigration, local histories, and the networks of Chinese itinerant performers and social interactions created therein. Through a historical analysis, I will consider how both itinerant musicians and members of the Chinese American communities engage with the articulation of the Sinophone sound world, and I will explore the relationship between singing Cantonese opera and the meaning of being Chinese through the lens of voice. The radio show *The Chinese Hour* in San Francisco in the 1950s sheds light on the inscription of the soundscape on the community, as does the articulation of this soundscape in literary forms in the work of Maxine Hong Kingston. As a whole, this study foregrounds the dynamics of musicking and historicizes the relationship between sonic identities and Sinophone cultural production.

Sino-Soundscape

In a 2016 essay, Tan Sooi Beng and I proposed "Sino-Soundscape" as an organizing title for a special issue of the journal *Ethnomusicology Forum*. The special issue included a set of studies examining performance practices, movement, daily experiences, and musical responses of Chinese immigrants in Australia, British Malaya, Burma, Hong Kong, North America, the Philippines, and Taiwan. In the introduction, we wrote:

> To capture the fluidity and the malleable boundaries of Chineseness, we have borrowed from the term "Sinophone" ... to describe the production of culture by Chinese who live in various spaces outside China. Sinophone culture crosses national borders but is in dialogue with local cultures. In this issue, we propose the concept of Sino-soundscape, adopting also Schafer's notion of "soundscape" (Schafer [1977] 1993), to consider in a more inclusive way the different types of musical and non-musical sounds from the environment that have been amalgamated by Chinese communities in the different locations discussed. Moreover, we build on Steven

Feld's "acoustemology of place" (Feld 2001), where he explores how specific sound-making activities and sonic soundscapes are connected to the culture, social meaning, history and social transformations of a specific place.[2]

This introduction also underscores the importance of treating Chinese migrants and the local society as coeval historical actors. It argues against the cliché that considers music as merely an object transmitted in the network of migration from China to be "transplanted" into the new locality, or the view that as tangential and peripheral sites of cultural production, the immigrant communities mostly "recycled" music of the past.[3] We argue that transnational networks not only sustained the flow of musical practice and culture but also were key players that encouraged border crossings and facilitated bilateral musical relationships and reciprocal musical influences.

In North America, the Sino-soundscape has been shaped by divergent transnational and national social, political, and economic forces; multilingual expressions; cosmopolitan musical encounters; and immigration constraints. These shaping forces came from both sides of the Pacific and involved various types of continuous movements and cultural crossbreeding. The transnational mobility of Cantonese opera performers is of paramount importance to the vitality of the Sino-soundscape. This history of the Sino-soundscape brings a much-needed trans-Pacific perspective to the historiography of American music, dislodging the latter's overt reliance on trans-Atlantic connection, i.e., a history that has long been predicated on America's adherence to European lineage in everything from musical genres to performance practices and cultural institutions. In other words, the notion of Sino-soundscape offers the potential for new and critical ways of understanding American music history. At the same time, the study of Sino-soundscape in North America also casts a new light on the global circulation of Chinese drama, bringing attention to a regional opera genre that has mostly been denied its true significance. In a common myopic view, Cantonese opera is seen merely as a regional genre, marginal and mostly negligible in comparison to the (trans)national prominence of Peking opera. The Sinophone perspective offers an intervention into such a China-centric history of Chinese drama. The notion of Sino-soundscape gains its interpretive power by transcending disciplinary boundaries to form an analytical category that brings together historical, social, national, literary, performative, and musical analysis of the sonic cultural expression. The work of historicizing Sino-soundscape in America is all the more important today given the steady influx of Sinitic-language-speaking immigrants to America "continuing replenishing the coffers of Sinophone cultural productions" and the sweeping success of Chinese

Americans in various performing and creative arts.⁴ Even in stillness, lived experience seems to exert its symbolic relevance. "Their stories," as Michel De Certeau reminds us, "began on the ground level, with footsteps."⁵ In many ways, this essay is an endeavor to hear the "chorus of footsteps" of these musicians and their audiences. By tracing their myriad footsteps and intertwined routes, we can imagine how the sonic culture partook in producing the identity and subjectivity of the Sinophone community, bringing into view previously unidentified layers of inscriptions of Sinophone expression in our time.

Sino-Soundscape in North America

On an unceremonious day in 1917, over a thousand audience members attended a Cantonese opera performance at Gong Sheng Theater, one of Vancouver's three Chinese opera theaters at the time. The business receipt of this day, January 5, records the ticket sales seen in figure 4.1 and table 4.1.

Listed with the sales number was also the opera title of the day and detailed daily expenses for miscellaneous supplies: yards of cotton fabric, bottles of black ink, and packages of five-color powder for stage makeup. Meticulously noted with Suzhou numerals in small prints of ink brush, these tidy characters make visible the musicking of Cantonese opera. The business paper, routine and mundane, connotes the everyday of Chinese theaters. This night, the theater was filled to its full capacity, but otherwise, it was no different

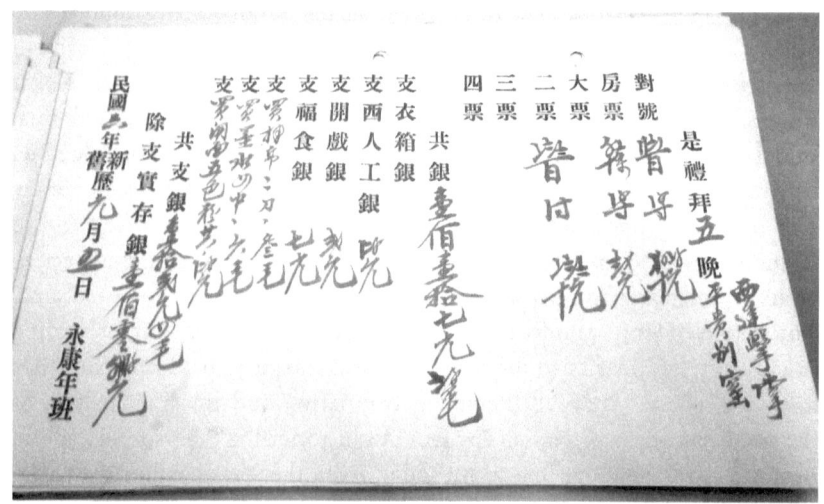

Figure 4.1 Business receipt of the Yong Kang Nian theatrical company, January 5, 1917.

Table 4.1 Business receipt of the Yong Kang Nian theatrical company, January 5, 1917

TYPE	PRICE (CAD)	NUMBER
First tier seat	0.15	271
Box seat	0.15	56
Second tier seat	0.10	687

from other evenings when hundreds of theatergoers gathered to take in an evening of music and drama.

While the value of Chinese theaters cannot be assessed solely by the size of their audiences, the sheer number of nightly audiences is enough to make our inner historian pause: It forces us to grasp the immensity of the opera's influence on the community's collective psyche. The soundscape was driven by the community's desire for pleasure, a desire fulfilled by the reverberant sensation of sound and the immediate experience of the presence of one another. Meanwhile, the sociality, ideology, and moral order connoted by the repertoire were also important. The day's opera was *Pinggui Returning Home*, which, like a few dozen other traditional titles, was a staple of Cantonese opera troupes and ubiquitous in theaters of the nineteenth and early twentieth centuries. In 1875, when Havana's Chinese theater established a new theater at Ciefuego, the company featured the same opera, attracting audiences from neighboring Ranchuelo, Cruces, Lajas, Palmira, etc.[6] This full and expanded rendition of *Pinggui Returning Home* reportedly went on for fifteen days. The opera is based on the classic Tang dynasty story of Xue Pinggui and Wang Baochuan, a pair of lovers who are challenged by societal barriers, poverty, and a call to duty. Through Baochuan's loyalty and perseverance, she is reunited with her husband after eighteen years. A legend that has been told and retold for generations, its rendering into Cantonese opera was more than a musical performance. It is the type of practice that constitutes what Diana Taylor calls "the repertoire," which "enacts embodied memory: performances, gestures, orality, movement, dance, singing—in short, all those acts usually thought of as ephemeral." "Repertoire," Taylor notes, "also allows for individual agency."[7] In myriad ways, the repertoire actively produces, conveys, sustains, and reconstructs cultural memories. Traditional Cantonese opera includes a range of types, from historical legend and military or court dramas to scholar-beauty romance. Performing the repertoire thus both transmitted and reshaped beliefs, values, and cultural symbols.

Sino-soundscape in North America is necessarily complex due to its intrinsic sonic nature and its social inextricability. It straddles between different worlds, and the complexity of its musicking exceeds the common terms we use to describe musical practices. The sonic aspect of the Sinophone world outlasts the written language, such that after the latter's fading into oblivion or even erasure, the sound continues to express what can be recognized as a Sinophone sensibility. A poignant example is in the Chinese theater of the early 1940s in Havana. After the departure of the theater's troupe for the United States, a local opera club founded a new theater troupe by training female descendants to sing. Some of them did not speak Cantonese but memorized the lyrics by phonetic pronunciation. The performing troupe was successful and popular for over a decade.[8] Language affinity is not a requirement in such a soundscape where sonic elements have unique vitality. Chinese Americans need not be what Ian Ang terms "culturalists"—namely, those with "a sense of being the bearers of a cultural heritage handed down from their ancestors"— to identify with this Sino-soundscape.[9] In other words, even while acculturated to the dominant customs of the local society, they could still find the sonic identity and music performance of the Sinophone tradition meaningful and endeavor to reproduce, mimic, reinterpret, reimagine, and reshape the musical practices and expressions in creative ways. These endeavors, through their repetition and persistence, reinscribe the musical practices in the social collective, and the sonic element of the cultural practice becomes embodied and inscribed on the body.

Chinese opera first appeared in California in 1852, during the height of the gold rush. It arrived only a year after the first fully staged European opera, Vincenzo Bellini's *La Sonnambula*, was presented in the city.[10] The two troupes were each making their way across the continent, though in opposite directions. The Chinese opera troupe (Hong Fook Tong) was a Cantonese opera troupe. The occasion of its premiere at San Francisco's American Theater on October 18, 1852, called for the staging of *The Joint Investiture of a Prime Minister of Six Warlords* and *A Birthday Greeting from the Eight Immortals*, an auspicious beginning ritual of Cantonese opera troupes. The 123-member troupe marked the first notable articulation of Sino-soundscape in North America. Many Cantonese opera troupes followed in the nineteenth century, and Chinese theaters quickly thrived in California, fulfilling the need for entertainment in the frontier of the American West. According to public records in 1868, a Chinese theater ranked among the five highest-revenue theaters in San Francisco.[11] By the late 1870s, four Chinese theaters were built, with three running concurrently in San Francisco within several blocks of one another. In the Pacific Northwest, Victoria in British Columbia similarly had three Chinese theaters within two city blocks, according to a fire insurance map of 1885.[12] They constituted the first golden era of the Sino-soundscape in North America.

However, due to anti-Chinese sentiment and a succession of Chinese exclusion laws and restrictions, the entry of Cantonese opera troupes into the United States was halted by the beginning of the twentieth century. Chinatown theaters dwindled or were destroyed during the 1906 earthquake and fire in San Francisco. Professional troupes ceased for more than a dozen years. Only in the early 1920s did the situation change. After successful efforts by savvy legal brokers, the Department of Labor opened the door again for the entry of full-size Cantonese opera troupes. This celebrated outcome involved a complicated cast of players: a trans-Pacific network of merchants, legal brokers, U.S. Immigration officers at the port and in Washington DC, theater agents in Hong Kong, cosmopolitan opera singers, and enthusiastic audiences. All contributed to the formation of this Sinophone performing space. In October 1922, a professional troupe named Renshou Nian arrived to premiere at the Crescent Theater in San Francisco, a former vaudeville/ burlesque theater on Broadway. This was truly significant. Not only was Renshou Nian the first troupe to return in the 1920s, but it was also the first mixed-gender Cantonese opera troupe (*nan-nü ban*) to perform on stage in the United States. (Before the 1910s, actresses were not allowed on stage; Cantonese opera was performed by all-male troupes, as were Chinese theaters in the United States in the nineteenth century.) After the 1922 opening, North America enjoyed a renaissance of Chinese theaters—most prominently, Mandarin Theater and Great China Theater in both San Francisco and Los Angeles, Da Guan Theater and Da Ronghua troupe in Chicago, Le Qianqiu troupe in Boston, and Zhou Min An Theater and Yong Nishang Theater in New York. A busy performing network quickly emerged, facilitating the circulation of Cantonese opera performers, the establishment of theaters in many cities in North America, and linking Sinophone communities through traveling opera performers. Audiences in North America were mesmerized by many of the era's Cantonese opera stars, such as actresses Li Xuefang and Guan Yinglian, and actors Bai Jurong, Xiao Dingxiang, and Ma Shizeng. As leading figures of the profession, they performed newly scripted operas, brought new performing strategies, and invigorated Chinatown theaters. They were raved about by audiences from Guangzhou to Hong Kong and Shanghai, as well as all of the Nanyang region. On U.S. soil, their celebrity status bestowed power on their stage performances, one that imparted considerable subversive potential to the minority status of Chinese immigrants.

At the same time, the stages of Chinatown theaters also inspired various experiments and novel practices, such as characters engaging in multiple mixed-gender cross-dressing in the same plays (at times requiring a chart on the playbill to track who's who in the play), the gender reversal of traditional ritual opera, such as a special gender-reversal performance of *The*

Joint Investiture (thus raising questions about the auspicious function of this ritual opera), new opera of contemporary events (plots involving scenes of interrogation at U.S. immigration stations or the kidnapping of Sun Yat-Sen in London), and stages using montage effects inspired by Hollywood cinema. Working together to produce a different opera nightly, singers, playwrights, and musicians exerted themselves to actualize artistic visions that best expressed their senses of place and their understandings of who they were.

Audiences' relationships with theaters also grew as Cantonese opera was woven into the fabric of social life, anchoring it to features of the community. In one of San Francisco's Chinese-language newspapers, *Young China*, an anonymous author wrote of his new attraction to the theater:

> Allured by the frequent reports of Cantonese opera performers' arrival in the newspapers, I was taken over by a desire to see the opera yesterday and went by car to San Francisco. However, because Bai Jurong is so famous, the tickets for the night were already sold out the previous day, and I nearly left without seeing the opera.... Recently, many famous actors in Guangdong have come to San Francisco, such as Bai Jurong, Zihou Qi, etc.... And if other equally famous performers such as Xue Juexian, Ma Shizeng, Chen Feinong, Xiao Dingxiang... would also come, then fans in Guangdong would certainly be left deprived, while in San Francisco many new fans for Cantonese opera would appear.... What do I listen for? First, I like to listen to the aria sung with clear enunciation and accompanied by expert musicians. Second, I enjoy the visual extravaganza of the elaborate costumes. Whether they are for historical operas or contemporary ones, the costumes are always in gorgeous colors. Sometimes the characters would change costumes simply for the sake of it, while going on a trip or preparing for imprisonment. It's hard to decipher the reasons for such excess sometimes, but they are a feast for the eye, nevertheless. Third, I enjoy watching a large cast. Even though I was often confused by multiple performers who take turns portraying the same character, it is still fascinating to watch.... Finally, the mixed troupe not only makes sense but is also more pleasurable to watch than the all-male troupe.[13]

The theaters' star power attracted a new crop of audiences, and the opera culture gained more popularity. The author's hypothetical musing about more stars quickly became a reality: Xiao Dingxiang would arrive several months later, and Ma Shizeng would arrive in 1930.

Geographically, the performing network had a wide reach in North America. The itinerary of Li Xuefang, for example, extended from San Francisco to New York City, and from Mexicali to Havana. Vancouver, Chicago, Boston,

Portland, and Honolulu also saw many stars' footprints. The Chinatown theaters of North America and the supporting transpacific performing network sustained high-level theatrical productions and were kept very lively. The network created elaborate pathways for concepts and expressive means of Cantonese opera culture—music, ideas, beliefs, stories, songs, martial arts—to become affixed in different locales of the Sinophone community in North America. With a significant transformation of recording technology and the increasing affordability of phonograph records in the late 1920s, a new listening culture quickly developed. It enhanced Cantonese opera's popularity and sent down its roots in even more places. They helped the fans further their appreciation of Cantonese opera and admiration of star singers, introducing the singing voices into homes, workspaces, and streets. If the advertisements for Cantonese opera records are any indication, the scales exploded in 1928, when the phonograph record advertisements began to take up a full page in the newspaper. The record labels included Beka and Odeon (Germany), Victor (United States), New Moon (China), and China Records (issued in Shanghai by a Japanese sponsor). Starting in late 1927, they were joined by a new record label from the Sinophone community—the Oriental Record—a collaboration of San Francisco merchants, the Great China Theater, Hong Kong merchants, and prominent opera performers. The Oriental Record label would go on to produce nearly two hundred titles, according to the extensive advertisement of its catalogs in various Chinese newspapers of the Sinophone community from 1928 to 1930. Its success also reflected the blurring of Chinese theaters and recording studios as a strategy to create a multimodal synergy in the Sino-soundscape.

Sino-Soundscape and Community

The roles that Chinatown theaters and Cantonese opera performances had in the community were complex. The reasons were manifold, including social, historical, demographic, spatial, and multimodal. First, Chinatown theater and Cantonese opera were situated centrally both physically and in the everyday life of Chinese communities, constituting the soundscape for the working and leisure life of the adults and the family. The theaters featured different operas every day, from traditional classics to contemporary stories. They provided news, comic relief, and mixed emotive drama with chivalry and patriotic sentiment. With fluidity in different aspects of opera production—textual, musical, choreographic, and scenographic—the theaters could cater to the community's varying tastes. As the era's racial hostility toward Chinese immigrants in America grew, their activities outside the confines of Chinatown communities were limited, making the presence of Cantonese opera even more welcome. Their embodied experiences at the theaters, memories of these experiences, and sonic sensibilities constituted a way to reconcile with the surrounding world.

Second, the 1920s was a period when the population of second-generation Chinese Americans grew significantly. A quick comparative study of the 1920 and 1930 U.S. census shows the increase in family and second generation in San Francisco's Chinese population: The number of daughters, wives, and sons more than doubled, while its overall male population increased only by 44 percent. The percentage of American-born Chinese grew by 20 percent as a whole. Prompted by the quick growth of second-generation Chinese Americans, San Francisco's Chinatown constructed its first playground. Several Chinese schools were also founded during this decade. With the demographic change, Chinatown theater had a new role as well. As reflected by numerous stories of kids sneaking into the theater by grabbing the coattail of an adult or mothers whispering in children's ears about the plots, going to Cantonese opera was a family activity. At the theater, the family enjoyed performances of melodious tunes, dialogues of humorous exchanges, the wrenching drama of parting and reunions, and the acrobatic movements of battling soldiers. For their part, kids clutched onto stage fronts, ran up and down the aisles, or played hide-and-seek in the stairways. The theaters provided a cross-generation Sinophone expression and fostered a sonic sensibility that informed the shaping of Sinophone identity for the growing number of young people. In the form of collective memory, their musicking offers the possibility of familial belonging, local, and intimate.

Third, the architecture of the purpose-built theaters was designed in the spirit of public arts, reflecting the theater owners' goal to have cultural practice firmly planted in the Sinophone communities. In San Francisco, the Mandarin Theater on Grant Avenue was built in 1924, and the Great China Theater on Washington Street was built in 1925, each with between eight hundred and nine hundred seats. Rather than merely a commercial storefront in the busiest part of Chinatown, both the interiors and exteriors were artfully designed, elevating the buildings to the exalted status of a special public place in the Sinophone community. The facades were designed to simultaneously evoke history and fashion a modern image. These theaters provided significant communal space. As the largest physical space in the community, the theaters were omnipresent in all of the community's public activities—fund-raising initiatives, political rallies against Japanese invasions, public lectures of prominent figures, and patriotic speeches. Often, the theaters assumed a leading role in taking on the civic cause of the public good. They were also the community's most public face, offering featured entertainment for dignitaries, such as diplomats, presidents, or mayors. Cantonese opera served as the most prominent articulation of the Sinophone presence in mainstream society.

Fourth, the circulation of prints (lyrics, anthologies, playbills, and photographs) and sound connected the community's everyday practice in an integral way to Cantonese opera. It grew into a real multimodal cultural production. Glamorous portraits of actresses and spectacular stage photos printed on playbills were suggestive of the musical feasts at the theaters. Working with local burgeoning professional photographers, such as San Francisco's May's Studio, theaters had the portraits of their stars made as artworks (with coloring and sequins) for window displays or other public spaces. Wide circulation of an anthology of lyrics published in San Francisco meant the popularity of the literary text in the Sinophone community in North America. Both the newspapers and playbills regularly provided space for printing laudatory poems written by local fans. The constant presence of discourse about Cantonese opera—troupes, performers, theaters, and repertoire—in daily newspapers, as in news reports, advertisements, and public notices, reveals the deep integration of the theaters and musical practice within the communities. Through visual cues and literary imagination, the visual-textual-auditory interplays were central to the Sino-soundscape. Joint ventures with record companies, such as the Oriental Record, discussed above, also allowed the theaters to facilitate additional modes of musicking of the Sino-soundscape.

The roles of Cantonese opera and theaters and their everyday meaning were continually interpreted by those who attended opera theaters or engaged in various forms of musicking. The sonic sensibility constituted an important sense of place.

Musicking and Inscription of Sino-Soundscape

The constancy of stellar performances was the pillar of the vibrant Chinatown theater culture. In this regard, the transnational mobility of Cantonese opera singers was the key. Most traveled from southern China, their border crossing closely monitored by the U.S. government. They were designated as temporary visitors, as shown by their theater member picture ID cards, which registered the port, steamship name, date of arrival, immigration serial number, and bondsman. However, the significance of these performers in the Sinophone community cannot be measured by either the length of their stay or the legal status of their residency. Stellar opera singers were revered as idols, and the culture of fandom was quickly created by admirers, patrons,

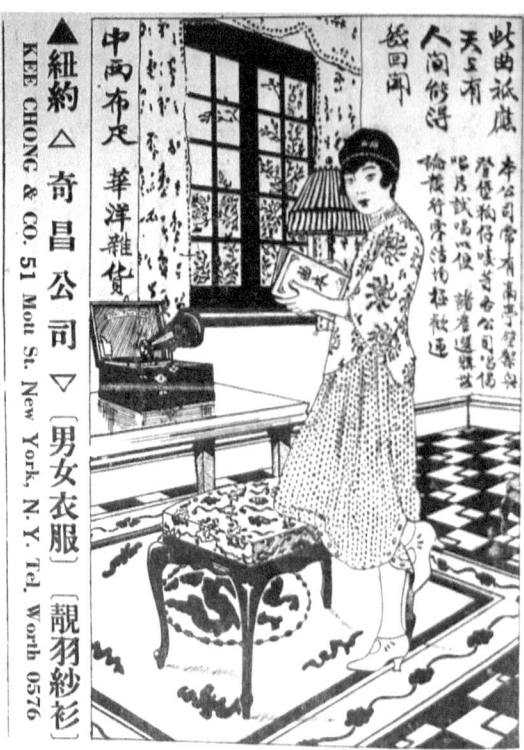

Figure 4.2 The Chinese Nationalist Daily, July 9, 1928.

and various family associations of the community. Their voices—both live performances in the theaters and phonographs heard at the stores, laundries, factories, and homes—permeated throughout the communities. Figure 4.2 reproduces an advertisement from New York's *Chinese Nationalist Daily*, promoting the listening culture as a modern way of life. The stylish female persona is epitomized by the book she holds in her delicate hand whose cover reads "Collection of [Opera] Songs."[14]

Musicologist Nina Eidsheim introduced a useful notion about the study of singing and music, "the voice, listening, sound and music were multisensory phenomena."[15] This notion helps envision the relationship between the singing voice of Cantonese opera of the 1920s and the articulation of Sino-soundscape. The articulation involved multisensory exchanges and social practices. Considering the general size of these Chinese theaters, watching opera performances was inevitably a collective community experience. Unlike the Western convention of reverent listening and mostly quiet spectatorship, the audiences at Chinatown theaters could rejoin or retort, chat or laugh, and move around or snack. One could hum, sing, or tap along to the voices and music from the stage as an act of listening. Going to opera was intrinsically a multisensory and collective experience, which can be characterized as synergetic bodily exchanges that occur both between performers and audiences and among theatergoers. Singing and listening, therefore, are means of relating to other bodies that participate in the complex sonic phenomena of Sino-soundscape. They were also not limited to the confines of theaters.

Inspired by stellar performances at the theaters, some young people sought to emulate their idols' singing voices and learn to perform opera arias and songs. What does it mean for young people to learn to sing Cantonese opera? Learning to sing is to belong and to be intelligible. Musicologist Suzanne Cusick writes, "The act of singing a song is always an act that replicates acceptance of patterns that are intelligible to one's cohort in a culture."[16] From this perspective, we can see that the process of learning to sing and to vocalize in a particular style, such as Cantonese opera, is truly complex, engaging the body in many different ways, which I will explore in the following paragraphs.

Since voices originate from inside the body rather than on the body's surface, they are integral sonic expressions of selfhood. Singing is a performance of the voice. Learning to sing and vocalize in the style of Cantonese opera is to perform the idea of subjectivity. It involves both the subordination of one's voice to the language (or phonetics) of the lyrics to convey meaning in the system of that language and the discipline of one's body to the control of tone, timbre, melodic gesture, and other sonic nuances that connote emotive content. For young adults of the Sinophone community who were likely acculturated in many different vocal and theatrical genres, assuming the task of learning Cantonese opera is a purpose act—one that aims to achieve the embodiment of the particular idea of personhood, a Sinophone articulation. In this act of learning, the person acquires the vocalization both to embody the identity and to be consoled by their intelligibility to others in the Sinophone community. Performing Cantonese opera aria songs can be taken as a means to express the passionate inner self or to "communicate to [their] cohort the depth [they] have allowed cultural norms to penetrate and discipline [their] bodies' interior spaces and interior actions."[17]

To emulate the voice of the idol or sing an opera aria is to perform the subjectivity. The most telling sign of its significance in the Sinophone community is the presence of young students singing Cantonese opera songs at benefit performances or festive occasions. They occurred with some frequency at Chinese schools or gatherings of community associations. More serious students could achieve a professional level of performance. One evening in 1928 in the Great China Theater stands out in this regard. That evening, an Oakland High School student, Guan Yundi, partook in the production of *Mourning of the Chaste Tree Flower*, a signature opera of Bai Jurong, the most famous Cantonese opera singer of the young scholar role type to appear in North America. The theater flyer proudly noted Guan's study with Bai Jurong and his plans to make a recording with the Oriental Record Company.[18]

Learning to sing Cantonese opera aria, therefore, enacted the most immediate and intimate connection to the Sinophone expression for youth who were attracted to not only the music, drama, and emotion but also to discipline their bodies to the Sinophone way of being. Acquiring the singing voice and learning the aria song is to inscribe in one's body the articulation of Sinophone sensibility. The second generation's ability to sing, though to different levels of expertise, shows how deeply the cultural form of the music penetrated their existence and became ingrained in their vocal cords and gestures.

Sino-Soundscape, Social Memory, and Symbolism

The 1920s' vibrant Chinese opera scene formed an important social memory of Sinophone culture in North America. The Sino-soundscape lived on, even after daily performances of Cantonese opera largely ceased. They were continued in different forms of musicking. Generally, from the late 1940s to the 1960s, it remained the musical genre many Chinese communities in North America enjoyed through amateur clubs, popular Cantonese opera films, recordings, and occasional visiting troupes. Yet, the power of the Sino-soundscape in San Francisco persisted, particularly through the radio program *The Chinese Hour*. In the 1950s, this immensely popular daily broadcast mixed news and Cantonese opera programs and aired every weeknight and Saturday afternoon. The rise of radio brought a revolution in the aural environment that prompted a major perceptual and cognitive shift, and the Chinese American community was no exception.

A resident, George Kao, gave a colorful depiction of one day's program. After noting the announcer and Chinese string orchestra that began the program, he wrote:

> For the next full hour, housewives in San Francisco's Chinatown, shopkeepers in Oakland, and laundry and restaurant workers up and down the Peninsula all put away their day's chores and relax with the only all-Chinese news and entertainment radio program broadcast in the United States. It included re-broadcasts (in translation) of President Roosevelt's wartime speeches and the long-popular nightly fare of Cantonese

opera.... Tonight's program, for instance, featured selected arias from the popular production "One Sweet Smile," which tells the bitter-sweet story of a wounded warrior pretending to rebuff his truelove for the sake of her own happiness. Punctuated by tinkling little gongs and staccato beats, the baritone and the soprano sing out a melodious and dramatic duet, while thousands of their unseen audience eat it up word for word by following the lyrics printed in one of the local Chinese papers.[19]

Not unlike the consumerism that accompanied the advancement of radio, *The Chinese Hour* was conceived as an advertising tool for the Golden Star Company to stimulate its sale of radios and furniture through a broadcasting music program. Nevertheless, as a historical actor, the radio program ensured that Cantonese opera was sent over the airwaves throughout the region. It also created an aggregate entity—the audience listening in at the same time—for whom some aspects of live performance and bodily synergy in the theater experience could be simulated. As radio historian Susan Douglass notes, "The fact that we hear not only with our ears but also with our entire bodies—our bones, our innards vibrate, too, to sounds, and certainly to music—means that we are actually feeling similar sensations in our bodies at exactly the same time when we listen as a group."[20] Radio was a prominent medium for enacting the soundscape of Cantonese opera. The radio's airplay became another vibrant mode of musicking, whether hearing passively or actively listening, that fostered collective memory, as we will see in the next example.

Maxine Hong Kingston's grandmother sated her appetite for Cantonese opera through radio. In several interviews, Kingston notes that growing up in Sacramento, her household was filled with Cantonese opera because her grandmother regularly listened to it on the radio. In Kingston's memoir and fiction, Chinese opera and theater constitute a recurring theme, symbolizing an intimate self, ideal, and hope. An episode from her half-memoir, *Woman Warrior*, symbolically connotes the Sino-soundscape. She writes about herself as a Chinese girl in kindergarten who spoke English for the first time at school:

I became silent. A dumbness—a shame—still cracks my voice in two, even when I want to say "hello" casually, or ask an easy question in front of the check-out counter, or ask directions of a bus driver. I stand frozen, or I hold up the line with the complete, grammatical sentence that comes squeaking out at impossible length....

My silence was thickest—total—during the three years that I covered my school paintings with black paint. I painted layers of black over houses and flowers and suns. . . . I was making a stage curtain, and it was the moment before the curtain parted or rose. The teachers called my parents to school, and I saw they had been saving my pictures, curling and cracking, all alike and black. The teachers pointed to the pictures and looked serious, talked seriously too, but my parents did not understand English. . . . My parents took the pictures home. I spread them out (so black and full of possibilities) and pretended the curtains were swinging open, flying up, one after another, sunlight underneath, mighty operas.[21]

The girl's inarticulate self stems from her fear of unintelligibility, namely, the risk of not being legible if she re-enacts the voice and sound of the "ethnicity." She could not discipline her body to sound "natural," like the mainstream American. Her intelligibility is thus symbolized by the visual "thickest" silence, or the black stage curtain. The black stage curtain was, at the same time, ready to fling open to her exuberant imagination, a world of "mighty operas" full of possibilities and filled with sound, light, fantasy, and colorful characters. The mighty opera was a fantastic form of the musicality of her language—the language in which she could be legible. For Kingston, operas stand in for the imaginary connected to the fantasies of opera reconfigured in her artistic identity. Opera's dramatic world symbolizes the young girl's own voice and her cultural identity. The symbol of the black curtain holds a unique significance for Kingston, reappearing in the title of a later book of her writings, *Through the Black Curtain* (1987).[22] This image of opaque black paintwork as a stage curtain concealing colorful opera behind powerfully reflects the influence Cantonese opera exerted on the psyche of the Sinophone community. The influence of the Sino-soundscape might not always be consciously felt, but the symbolism is affixed to the community, and Kingston's allegorical account evokes Cantonese opera as a social memory and aesthetic possibility.

Through her literary practice, Kingston reinvents many aspects of this cultural memory. In her third book, *Tripmaster Monkey: His Fake Book*, Kingston depicts another journey involving a search for identity and freedom of self-representation. Here, Chinese theater constitutes the flux of ethnic identity that the protagonist Wittman wrestles with. He makes a personal crusade to start a new type of theater as an ideal form of self-representation. His search was deeply entwined with Cantonese opera, from its popular stories and characters to its mode of performance. He points to the long history of Chinese theaters in the United States when he underscores the significance of his favorite opera story: "Every matinee or evening for a hundred years, somewhere in America, some acting company was performing *The Oath in the Peach Orchard*." At one point, Wittman thinks, "Whaddayaknow, I've written one of those plays that leave room for actors to do improv, a process as ancient as Chinese opera and as far-out as the theatre of spontaneity."[23] Theater stages symbolized this Chinese American figure's artistic autonomy. While the "fake book" in the novel's subtitle no doubt refers to the term for jazz compilations of tunes, melodies, and chords that musicians improvise from, Kingston considered hers as "a prose book with basic suggestions for social action, for trips." From the perspective of Chinese theater, however, the fake book can also be seen as a contemporary remaking of the synopsis outline called *tigang*, based on which traditional Cantonese opera singers performed. Through the literary genre, music practices of Cantonese opera and jazz meld together, their common aesthetics becoming the ultimate form of the protagonist's expression.

Conclusion

To listen to "the choir of footsteps," this article begins with the study of Cantonese opera in North America as a history of the place and the people who produced, participated in, and were moved by it. Succeeding in circumventing legal constraints, the performing network of Cantonese opera produced and sustained a vibrant Sino-soundscape in North America at a very crucial time—the 1920s. With such prosperity, a sense of creative agency was manifested by Chinese theaters and their performers. Stellar opera singers, though as itinerant musicians and temporary visitors, were an integral part of the Sino-soundscape, whose emplacement ensured the vibrancy of the sound culture, the passing on of repertoire, and their continuation. We also pay close attention to the role of listening and singing, as well as body synergy in theaters and listening in on radio, drawing the Sino-soundscape closer to the messy realm of the body. In the spirit of capturing the soundscape as Sino-sonic sensibility, one created by listening, singing, playing, retelling, emulating, writing, and imagining, we trace its inscription and legibility, both on the body and in metaphors. In so doing, we historicize the backdrop against which Sinophone cultural production in America has been and continues to be circulated and developed.

Notes

1. According to Small, "To music is to take part, in any capacity in a musical performance, whether by performing, by listening, by rehearsing or practicing, by providing material for performance (what is called composition), or by dancing." See Christopher Small, *Musicking: The Meanings of Performance and Listening* (Middletown, CT: Wesleyan University Press, 1998), 9.

2. Sooi Beng Tan and Nancy Yunhwa Rao, "Introduction: Emergent Sino-Soundscapes: Musical Pasts, Transnationalism and Identities," *Ethnomusicology Forum* 26, no. 1 (2016): 1–10.

3. Cecilia J. Pang, "(Re)cycling Culture: Chinese Opera in the United States," *Comparative Drama* 39 nos. 3–4 (2005): 361–396.

4. Shu-mei Shih, "Introduction: What Is Sinophone Studies?" *Sinophone Studies: A Critical Reader*, ed. by Shu-mei Shih, Chien-hsin Tsai, and Brian Bernards (New York: Columbia University Press, 2013), 7.

5. Michel de Certeau, *The Practice of Everyday Life* (Berkeley: University of California Press, 1984), 97.

6. Kathleen López, *Chinese Cubans: A Transnational History* (Chapel Hill: University of North Carolina Press, 2013), 107.

7. Diane Taylor, *The Archive and the Repertoire: Performing Cultural Memory in the Americas* (Durham, NC: Duke University Press, 2003), 20.

8. López, *Chinese Cubans*, 214. A related example is the subject of a documentary film, *Havana Divas*. See *Havana Divas*, directed by S. Luisa Wei (Hong Kong: Blue Queen Cultural Communication, 2018).

9. Ien Ang, "Can One Say No to Chineseness? Pushing the Limits of the Diasporic Paradigm (1998)," in Shih, Tsai, and Bernards, *Sinophone Studies*, 67–68.

10. Much of the following history of Cantonese opera and Chinatown theaters in North America can be found in Nancy Yunhwa Rao, *Chinatown Opera Theater in North America* (Urbana-Champaign: University of Illinois Press, 2017) and *The Oxford Encyclopedia of Asian American Literature and Culture*, ed. Josephine Lee (Oxford: Oxford University Press, 2020), s.v. "Asian Americans in Opera."

11. Receipts of the San Francisco places of amusement, per Internal Revenue returns, extracted from the *Daily Dramatic Chronicle* (San Francisco), January 25 and February, 1868. See table 2.1 in Rao, *Chinatown Opera Theater in North America*, 42.

12. For more information, see Nancy Yunhwa Rao, "Inside Chinese Theater: Cantonese Opera in Canada," *Intersections*, 38 no. 1 (2018): 81–104.

13. Rao, *Chinatown Opera Theater in North America*, 183.

14. For more about such advertisements see Rao, *Chinatown Opera*, 294–296.

15. Nina Sun Eidsheim, *Sensing Sound: Singing & Listening as Vibrational Practice* (Durham, NC: Duke University Press, 2015), 3

16. Suzanne Cusick, "On Musical Performances and Sex," in *Audible Traces: Gender, Identity, and Music*, ed. Elaine Barkin and Lydia Hamessley (Zurich: Carciofoli Verlagshaus, 1999), 25–48.

17. Cusick, "On Musical Performances and Sex," 31.

18. Great China Theater playbill, March 11, 1928, Him Mark Lai Collection, Ethnic Library, University of California, Berkeley. See also Rao, *Chinatown Opera Theater in North America*, 207–209.

19. George Kao, *Cathay by the Bay: Glimpses of San Francisco's Chinatown in the Year 1950* (Hong Kong: Chinese University of Hong Kong Press, 1998), 83–84.

20. Susan J. Douglas, *Listening In: Radio and the American Imagination* (Minneapolis: University of Minnesota Press, 2004), 29–30.

21. Maxine Hong Kingston, *The Woman Warrior* (New York: Vintage, 1975), 65. The following discussion of Kingston's fiction is a modified version of my analysis elsewhere. See the epilogue in Rao, *Chinatown Opera Theater in North America* and "Transnationalism and Everyday Practice: Chinatown Theatres of North America in the 1920s," *Ethnomusicology Forum* 26 no. 1 (2016): 107–130.

22. Maxine Hong Kingston, *Through the Black Curtain* (Berkeley: Friends of the Bancroft Library, 1987).

23. Maxine Hong Kingston, *Tripmaster Monkey: His Fake Book* (New York: Vintage, 1987), 141.

Ann Hui, Hainan, and the Sino-Vietnamese War

A Sinophone Inter-Asian Recasting of Boat People*'s Transpacific Refugee Critique*

BRIAN BERNARDS

Boat People,[1] Ann Hui's politically controversial 1982 docudrama and a widely heralded early work in the Hong Kong auteur's prolific cinematic corpus, opens with a scene of victory: As Viet Cong soldiers march and tanks roll into the streets of Da Nang in central Vietnam, onlooking civilians cheer and wave the yellow-starred red flag of the Socialist Republic of Vietnam from the sidewalks and building windows lining the streets. Da Nang's 1975 liberation is captured by a lone male photojournalist, Japanese protagonist Shiomi Akutagawa (played by Hong Kong actor George Lam), who follows the procession. Akutagawa diverges from the crowded main street to follow a lone boy hobbling on crutches down a narrow side alley, deviating from the collective celebration to the individual suffering and sacrifice caused by the protracted U.S.-Vietnam War within a longer history of imperialism and foreign occupation. The scene fades to black as opening credits run before cutting ahead to 1978 when Akutagawa returns to Vietnam at the government's invitation to observe the new society's progress under unified Communist leadership. A wide-angle shot shows Akutagawa in a picturesque rural hillside environment outside Da Nang, where his party handlers bring him to photograph a model new economic zone (NEZ) highlighting the nation's advances. Outside the NEZ's primary school, smiling schoolchildren perform for Akutagawa, singing "As If Uncle Ho Chi Minh Were Here on the Great Victory Day" (*Như có Bác Hồ trong ngày vui đại thắng*), a patriotic song originally broadcast nationwide on April 30, 1975, Vietnam's Reunification Day.[2]

Writing on the fortieth anniversary of reunification, Vinh Nguyen—a Canadian scholar of global Anglophone diaspora and refugee narratives—revisits Ann Hui's *Boat People* as a standout contribution to the transpacific archive of narratives on the U.S.-Vietnam War and its global aftermath.³ Citing Akutagawa's (and the camera's) deviation from the main street to the side alley and the shift from the jubilant crowd to the hobbling boy, Nguyen describes the opening scene as "a powerful commentary" on "the disjuncture between appearance and reality, the official story against the lived one," symbolic of Hui's emphasis on "the stories rarely seen or heard by the global community, the images not endorsed by governments, the people scarcely understood by asylum host societies."⁴ Highlighting the narrative's anticipatory refugees, Nguyen pushes back against the Cold War political allegory that dominated early critical commentary on *Boat People*: Attributing the film's popular Hong Kong reception to the "1997 factor," this allegory displaced the film's portrayal of the Vietnamese government onto a Communist China emerging from the Cultural Revolution, superimposing the fate of Hong Kong citizens onto the lives of the film's refugees and suggesting that *Boat People* was *really* about prehandover Hong Kong's ambivalence toward impending reunification with the mainland.⁵ Instead, Nguyen emphasizes the "literal" narrative politics of *Boat People*, which foreground (rather than obscure) the "boat people,"⁶ the Hong Kong media's moniker for Vietnamese refugees-in-transit (whose testimonies Hui asked *Boat People*'s screenwriter Tai On-Ping to base his screenplay on). Nguyen's literal reading returns the narrative to Ann Hui's original intention, as described in a 1996 interview: "I was just trying to honestly shoot a Vietnamese story. I never thought I was insinuating anything about mainland China, but when the film came out everyone said it seemed like I was implicating the mainland, to the extent that even I began to feel it, but I really didn't have that intention at the time."⁷ Drawing on recent scholarship rescuing *Boat People* from its overdetermined interpretation as 1997 allegory, Nguyen argues for a repositioning of the film not just within Hong Kong cinematic history but as a rare refugee-centered narrative within a transpacific cinematic archive of the U.S.-Vietnam War largely dominated by Hollywood.⁸

Nguyen's literal reading of the refugee critique in Hui's film critically intervenes in the cinematic politics surrounding the war, given that Hollywood's interest in Vietnamese refugees generally ends with the fall of Saigon, does not extend beyond the actions of (typically white) American soldiers, and denies the U.S. presence of Vietnamese refugees (many of whom arrived via Hong Kong). *Boat People* suggests the backstories of Vietnamese refugees are not just an integral part of the Hong Kong story and its historical self-perception as a site of refuge but also represent fragments of a composite voice diversifying the transpacific cinematic legacy of the U.S.-Vietnam War.⁹

Yet the film's literal narrative politics—its signification as a transpacific refugee critique as opposed to a 1997 handover allegory—should also call attention to another critical context obscured by the film's allegorical reception: the docudrama's Sinophone inter-Asian *production* context that renders its very sense of photojournalistic realism possible. What the above scenes document are not literally the sights and sounds of Da Nang: Needing a shooting location to stand in as Vietnam, Ann Hui, with the cross-border assistance of the government of the People's Republic of China (PRC) and its state film studios, constructed a surrogate Da Nang on China's Hainan Island, situated four hundred kilometers to Da Nang's northeast in the South China Sea. Hui cast both Hong Kong and mainland talent in the roles of Vietnamese. Cantonese dialogue masquerades as Vietnamese, with a notable exception being when the NEZ schoolchildren break into the Vietnamese victory song. Following Hong Kong postproduction conventions at the time, all dialogue is dubbed (regardless of the language in which actors onscreen deliver their lines). The film's extras and minor characters, even the schoolchildren singing in Vietnamese, were performed by mainland Chinese talent.[10] The film's most expensive props, such as the decommissioned army tanks seen in the opening victory celebration, were provided by China's military.[11] That the PRC played such a crucial role in *Boat People*'s material production should call into question an allegorical interpretation in which China is supposedly the big bad Communist other symbolized by Hui's portrayal of an oppressive Vietnamese Communist regime.

Examining the Sinophone inter-Asian surrogacy involved in *Boat People*'s production builds on the literal politics of the film's refugee-centered interrogation of the U.S.-Vietnam War via the film's literal (not simply allegorical) engagement with mainland China. Through the interdisciplinary prisms of Sinophone studies and inter-Asia cultural studies in conversation with transpacific studies and critical refugee studies, the Sino-Vietnamese War of 1979 constitutes a vitally relevant production backdrop obscured by *Boat People*'s critical reception and a narrative backdrop whose implications extend yet complicate its politics of refugee representation. As the first Hong Kong film ever shot in the PRC, thanks to Deng Xiaoping's Open Door policy, *Boat People* was enabled by the geopolitical fallout of the Sino-Vietnamese War. As Hui claims, *Boat People* "opened up a lot of doors" for her,[12] giving her the valuable experience of a Hong Kong-PRC coproduction template that would later define mainstream Hong Kong cinema (and Hui's own filmmaking) in the posthandover era. The PRC's initiation of economic reforms facilitated Hui's Sinophone inter-Asian audiovisual translation, amplification, and photojournalistic dramatization of backstories developed from media reporting on Hong Kong's refugees-in-transit (voices that unsettle Hollywood hegemony in a transpacific cinematic discourse). Many of Hong Kong's so-called boat people at the time were also refugees of the Sino-Vietnamese War: Hui's production implicates this 1979 conflict, one that recalls imperial China's colonial incursions in Annam and foreshadows the PRC's postreform ambitions to reassert military and economic dominance in Southeast Asia, making *Boat People* an important cultural archive of that historical episode today.

Transpacific Refugee and Sinophone Inter-Asian Critique

Critical refugee studies, transpacific studies, inter-Asia cultural studies, and Sinophone studies—all emerging over the last two-plus decades—connote modes of interlocal scholarly inquiry that destabilize nation-state logic and expose its residual Cold War dynamics. Each paradigm supplies lenses through which Ann Hui's *Boat People* can be read, yet it is their discursive intersections that illuminate critical readings between the film's narrative sources and its raw production materials.

Yến Lê Espiritu proposes that critical refugee studies must claim and inhabit spaces outside of or in between nations from which to "articulate the tensions, irresolutions, and contradictions of the promise of citizenship and belonging for those on the social margins," especially by disrupting tropes of "rescue and liberation" that freeze refugee communities in passivity and helplessness.[13] Ann Hui spotlights these contradictions not only with *Boat People* but with the tripartite body of work retroactively classified as her Vietnam Trilogy. In 1978, Hui, with sponsorship from Hong Kong's Immigration Office, directed two episodes of *Under the Lion Rock*, a television program dramatizing the lives of "everyday" Hong Kongers. One of her episodes, "Boy from Vietnam," focuses on recent arrivals with circumscribed rights of residence in the British colony. Airing on Radio Television Hong Kong (RTHK), the episode is a dramatized reenactment of testimonies from quarantined Vietnamese refugees-in-transit, delivered from a Cantonese script by Shu Kei and Wong Chi.[14] Hui further adapted that material for a feature film, *The Story of Woo Viet* (1981), starring budding superstar Chow Yun-fat in the eponymous lead role. Having escaped his home country, Woo Viet is forced to stay in a refugee detention center after his boat reaches Hong Kong before he gains passage to Manila (where most of the film was shot) in search of his lover, where he falls into working as a hired killer.[15] Together composing Hui's Vietnam Trilogy, "Boy from Vietnam," *Woo Viet*, and *Boat People* were each developed from the testimonies of stateless refugees awaiting resettlement in Hong Kong circa 1978–1979.[16] The successful launching of Ann

Hui's career after returning to Hong Kong from film school in London coincided with a decade-plus refugee influx in Hong Kong. To Hui, the refugee crisis was as important to that era's Hong Kong story as Margaret Thatcher's September 1982 visit to Beijing, which initiated talks on Hong Kong's geopolitical fate and which preceded the release of *Boat People* by a month, looming largest as the sociopolitical backdrop informing the film's allegorical interpretation.

The first Vietnamese refugees arrived in Hong Kong aboard "unseaworthy" boats in 1975, followed by another wave in 1978 and peaking with nearly seventy thousand arrivals in 1979. The influxes persisted throughout 1980 and 1981 before Hong Kong implemented a deterrence policy in 1982, by which new arrivals were detained in closed centers run by the Correctional Services Department. As Chan Kwok Bun details, the 1982 "closed camp policy" included "deprivation of personal privacy, stress, hunger strikes, suicides, murders, rapes," and "bouts of interpersonal and group violence among camp residents as well as between camp guards and camp residents." From 1975 through the 1980s, the Hong Kong colonial government finessed a screening policy whose outward purpose was to show its benevolent "humanitarian concern and sympathy" by determining which individuals "were entitled to protection and settlement" but whose "latent (and real) purpose" was to "screen out," to "detain and repatriate, and to solve the refugee problem by discouraging the flow." Screenings were characterized by a denial of adequate legal advice, the absence of counsel during interviews, and a "failure to inform asylum seekers adequately of the reasons for the denial of their claims." Hong Kong public opinion devolved from sympathy to refugee fatigue and antipathy intensified by sensationalized media attention on local Vietnamese gangs.[17] The distressing conditions of the detention centers from where Ann Hui's trilogy derived its narrative sources, coupled with the xenophobia that coursed through Hong Kong as the crisis wore on, should, as Vinh Nguyen proposes, inform critical interpretations of *Boat People*'s refugee backstories more centrally than the 1997 allegory.[18]

Boat People's refugee representation transcends the situation in Hong Kong to critically dialogue with media discourse across the Pacific. In calling for a critical refugee study to not only "take seriously the range of Vietnamese perspectives" on the U.S.-Vietnam War but to unsettle the ideological underpinnings of refugee camp studies that "repeatedly portray refugees as abject" and helpless, Yến Lê Espiritu recognizes the refugee as a paradigm of constricted legibility in mainstream U.S. media that uncritically "remakes the case for US war."[19] Based on Chan Kwok Bun's characterization of Vietnamese detainees as passively awaiting resettlement in their Hong Kong "first asylum" while they "carve out their provisional, minimal existence within the 'cracks' of nation states . . . helplessly watching themselves being classified" by authorities,[20] Lê Espiritu's critique connects the North American refugee paradigm to the Hong Kong one. After all, the United States (55.5 percent) and Canada (18 percent) were the top two countries of resettlement for the more than 100,000 Vietnamese refugees that passed through Hong Kong's detention camps from 1975 to 1988.[21]

In this sense, *Boat People* addresses the transpacific construction of the refugee as paradigm. Viet Thanh Nguyen and Janet Hoskins describe transpacific studies as a space of inquiry that illuminates "the traffic in peoples, cultures, capital, and ideas . . . across the troubled ocean that lends its name to this model" and that underscores the perspectives of those claimed by affectively-charged categories such as refugee, adoptee, war bride, and undocumented migrant.[22] For Lily Wong, the transpacific imagination spans a "charged contact zone," one that "loosens the disciplinary binds" to which certain affective categories or tropes are conventionally affixed and exposes how those tropes are dialogically reconfigured.[23] The transpacific networks implicated by Hui's film unsettle the Vietnamese refugee as an affective media trope. Whereas Hollywood, with its reenactments of the U.S.-Vietnam War in films like Francis Ford Coppola's *Apocalypse Now* (1979), backgrounds the Vietnamese—either to be blown to smithereens or to be rescued (and then forgotten) in American airlifts—and prioritizes the (typically white) U.S. soldier's psyche and subjectivity,[24] Ann Hui foregrounds the transpacific imaginations of her Vietnamese characters, even if *Boat People* mediates such imaginations through Cantonese dialogue and a cast largely composed of Hong Kong and mainland Chinese talent. For example, the character To Minh (played by Andy Lau), a disabled former English-language interpreter forced to engage in dangerous landmine clearance at an NEZ labor camp, divulges to Akutagawa his ambition to flee to New Orleans to open a bar. At a historical moment when Hong Kong, a transnational hub of Sinophone cinema, was witnessing an emergent new wave movement grounded in localism (telling stories affecting "native Hong Kongers"),[25] Ann Hui's narrative formulates what Nguyen and Hoskins call oppositional "translocalism."[26] This refers to how Hui's reconfiguration of the refugee as "local" is informed by multisited inflections (Vietnam backstories) that simultaneously indict both Hollywood and Hong Kong media.

Yet, this oppositional translocalism is multidirectional, not bilateral. Here, the perspectives of Sinophone studies and inter-Asia cultural studies also inform the film's transpacific imagination of the Vietnamese refugee. These interdisciplinary perspectives expose the temporality of the refugee condition, the backdrop of Asian imperialisms, and the limitations of a Cold War interpretative lens that reduces ethnolinguistic and political complexity to binary archetypes of ideology and nationality. Sinophone theory's attentiveness to the temporality of diaspora informs that of the "stateless" refugee, exposing the duration of the condition rather than conferring immutable status as a perpetual foreigner awaiting resettlement or repatriation.[27] Transpacific studies, Sinophone studies, and inter-Asia cultural studies all illuminate Asian imperialisms (and their historical entanglements with European and U.S. imperialisms), such as the roles played by China and Japan as "nations with imperial histories in Asia and the Pacific that predate European and American involvement" and that currently maintain "hegemonic, if not outright imperialist, interests" in the region.[28] Globalization magnifies, rather than obscures, regional and subregional differences in the Asia-Pacific, disrupting an East-West bilateralism treating Asia as a singular entity.[29] Inter-Asia cultural studies, as Kuan-hsing Chen suggests, calls for a "de-cold war" mode of examining relations between and within different Asian societies whose decolonization processes were stunted by expedient Cold War anticommunist/communist alliances compelled by the United States or the USSR.[30]

As the Communist governments of Vietnam and China were, at the time of *Boat People*'s filming, mired in conflict, one cannot simply be superimposed onto the other in a facile gesture of Cold War allegory. Hong Kong's Vietnamese refugees were not ethnolinguistically homogeneous: They included individuals of Chinese descent who spoke various Sinitic languages (including Cantonese) and who were refugees of the Sino-Vietnamese conflict as well as victims of a Cold War equation of ethnicity, nationality, and political identity. The reasons for Vietnamese refugee flight to Hong Kong circa 1979 are linked to U.S. imperialism as well as China's aggression in the Sino-Vietnamese War, a significant Sinophone inter-Asian context that made *Boat People*'s transpacific cinematic imagination materially possible.

The Hong Kong-Hainan-Da Nang Confluences of the Sino-Vietnamese War

Boat People was the first Hong Kong film shot in the PRC, three decades after the nation's establishment, and was facilitated by Deng Xiaoping's Open Door policy reforms starting in 1978. In the early reform years, Hong Kong was the mainland's largest foreign investor and saw itself as playing a vital role in helping China's capitalist transition.[31] With *Boat People*, cinema became another arena of economic coinvestment between Hong Kong and the PRC. The PRC welcomed Ann Hui to Hainan to import Hong Kong's technical expertise and secure opportunities for the film's mainland liaisons, coinvestors, cast, and crew to observe and participate in early state-led capitalist diversification.

Boat People's executive producer was the renowned Shanghai-born, Hong Kong transplant and veteran celebrity of leftist films, Miranda Yang (Xia Meng). Along with Yang's Hong Kong–based Bluebird Film, she used her expansive contacts in the mainland to secure access to PRC shooting locations across the border in Guangdong Province and on Hainan Island, as well as to gain the assistance of PRC state film studios, crew, and talent. *Boat People* was shot on Hainan Island and in the southern Guangdong port city of Zhanjiang from December 1981 to April 1982. Hainan's local government provided the decommissioned People's Liberation Army (PLA) tanks used in the opening scene shot in Haikou. The PLA military in Zhanjiang supplied landmines and other pyrotechnical assistance for explosion scenes, which made the film one of the most expensive productions in Hong Kong cinematic history at the time.[32] Although the mainland's policy toward importing foreign films was still strict in the early reform era, *Boat People*—from a production rather than distribution perspective—was a pioneering forerunner of official coproductions (a classification by which the PRC later granted transnational collaborations domestic status), which, by the 2000s, became a common practice and survival tactic for Hong Kong commercial cinema.

When Ann Hui, Miranda Yang, and their Hong Kong-based talent and crew left for Hainan in late 1981, several roles—such as that of Akutagawa's official Vietnamese government handlers—had yet to be cast. With Yang taking her to the state-run Pearl River Film Studio in Guangzhou to watch film reels of mainland talent, Hui was impressed with the screen presence of veteran actor Qi Mengshi, so she not only cast him in the role of Officer Nguyen but further developed his scenes to make him more of a complex figure.[33] Much like many members of the old cadre in China who studied abroad and retained memories from before the Chinese Civil War (and who were rehabilitated in the early post-Mao era), Officer Nguyen represents the French-educated old guard of the Vietnamese Communist revolution. Though Officer Nguyen was once imprisoned under the South Vietnamese republic propped up by the United States, Nguyen's bourgeois background and Western tastes become suspect in the post-reunification handoff to a younger party guard, represented by Akutagawa's handlers, Comrades Le and Vu (performed by younger mainland actors), who circumscribe the photojournalist's sightseeing itinerary. Officer Nguyen is drawn to Akutagawa for the photojournalist's artistic sensibility and his pursuit of objectivity, while Akutagawa sees in the high-ranking (though imperiled) Officer Nguyen an opportunity to obtain permission to shoot unimpeded and unmonitored in Da Nang. Self-reflexively, this correlates to Ann Hui's cinematic return to mainland China, where, in Hainan, she is subject to the interests of her mainland coinvestors and party handlers.

The close involvement of PRC players in the film's production intimates that if an allegorical interpretation of *Boat People* is merited, perhaps it is not so much Hong Kong's Cold War anxiety toward reunification with the PRC but rather the film's stylistic and thematic resonances with the officially sanctioned scar literature and film trend of early-1980s PRC cultural production. These scar narratives "express bitterness" regarding the worst excesses of the Cultural Revolution, indicting the violence waged by Red Guard clashes on the street and the dislocation and deprivation effected by programs that sent students and members of the old party cadre labeled by Maoist devotees as revisionists and "capitalist roaders," as Deng Xiaoping was, to remote areas for manual labor reform and reeducation (with Hainan Island one such site).[34]

In one scene filmed on Hainan's east coast, Akutagawa and Officer Nguyen stroll along the Da Nang beachside. Conversing in an imagined Vietnamese (Qi Mengshi delivered his lines in Mandarin, which were then dubbed in Cantonese), Officer Nguyen reminisces nostalgically about how, in the French colonial period, this area bustled with economic activity, as hawkers sold food from their boats: "Now they've all fled to Hong Kong or Malaysia. You must have heard about the Vietnamese who left?" Officer Nguyen laments the conditions forcing people to become refugees or be sent to new economic zones (NEZs, kinh tế mới in Vietnamese). As Akutagawa discovers, NEZs are not the emblems of success for collectivized labor reform that his handlers proclaim but are euphemisms for prison labor camps (Officer Nguyen is later "reassigned" to one). Officer Nguyen's sentiments highlight *Boat People*'s scar narrative tone: He even exhibits a physical battle scar on his chest, allowing Akutagawa to photograph it.

Another persecuted scar figure in *Boat People* is To Minh. Labeled by the party as an irredeemable collaborator for his interpretive services to American soldiers, To Minh walks with a permanent limp, an untreated injury recalling the unendorsed image captured by Akutagawa during the liberation celebration. Akutagawa first meets To Minh at the "chicken farm," which euphemizes the execution grounds where party firing squads eliminate Da Nang's "undesirables." Given permission to freely photograph the city, Akutagawa is led here by the adolescent Cam Nuong (played by Hong Kong actor Season Ma in a compelling debut role),[35] a Da Nang resident who captivates his interest when she sticks up her middle finger at his camera. At the chicken farm, Cam Nuong and her brother loot valuables from executed corpses. To Minh attempts to rob Akutagawa for his camera so he can flee the country with earnings from its sale. Grabbing To Minh by his lame leg, Akutagawa slows him down long enough for the police to arrive and detain them both.

Forced together in a cramped, dark holding cell, To Minh conveys his intense fear of returning to the NEZ, signaling to Akutagawa that the photojournalist's handlers have only shown him a model NEZ (where schoolchildren sang a patriotic song for him) exhibited for the government's "foreign friends."

Developed from 1976 to 1980, NEZs were the Hanoi government's population redistribution campaign for central and southern Vietnam modeled on "the Maoist view of cities as obstacles rather than assets in economic development."[36] Its objectives were to ensure food self-sufficiency by creating green belts around urban areas, thus boosting agricultural production on land abandoned during wartime and in uncultivated upland areas. In Vietnam's Central Highlands, NEZs were used to resettle Kinh Vietnamese lowlanders and party loyalists to politically integrate Indigenous upland peoples lumped together under the French "Montagnard" designation, many of who had assisted the U.S. war effort and who the Communists still construed as a security threat.[37] Populations targeted for resettlement included "potentially disruptive elements" such as "civilian personnel in the former South Vietnamese government" and Hoa (Sino-Vietnamese) merchant communities. As Da Nang was one of the fastest-growing urban areas in the final years of the U.S.-Vietnam War, its surrounding countryside was given priority for NEZ resettlement and development.[38] In *Boat People*, Akutagawa tracks To Minh's relocation to a NEZ where "disruptive elements" are forced to clear the terrain of landmines, with many dying or becoming permanently maimed in the process.

Boat People's scar narrative tropes hint at the PRC's own allegorical backdrop, apart from Hong Kong's "1997 factor," which rationalizes authorizing the film's production on its territory. Yet the scale of the atrocities in *Boat People*—like the Vietnamese Coast Guard's mass slaughter of refugees on an escaping boat—and its lack of a forward-looking, cathartic resolution that firmly closes the violent chapter of the past distinguish it from scar narratives sanctioned by the Chinese Communist Party. Given that such spectacles might reinforce the Cold War demonization of the communist other, the PRC's authorization of Ann Hui's Hainan shoot required more than the thawing of UK-China relations or the PRC's ambitions for economic reforms. Retrospectively, such a project seems impossible without three prerequisite historical conditions: the Sino-Vietnamese War of 1979; PRC propaganda that went into that military campaign portraying Vietnam as a renegade Soviet "puppet" on its southern border; and the losses China suffered outweighing any victories it could claim from the conflict. As China simply failed where the United States, France, Japan, and previous Chinese imperial incursions into Annam (during the Han and Tang dynasties) had before it, its leaders supported the use of its territory, raw materials, and talent to dramatize the Vietnamese state's inhumanity in a way that might justify to the outside world (and not to domestic audiences, as the PRC prohibited *Boat People*'s mainland distribution) the deaths of China's soldiers in Vietnam, lest the Chinese Communist Party's legitimacy be questioned by association with another disastrous mass mobilization campaign, like the Great Leap Forward and the Cultural Revolution, whose excesses were now relegated to the past.

To China's leaders, the Sino-Vietnamese War was a "war of self-defense against Vietnam" (*dui Yue ziwei fanji zhan*), while Vietnam's leadership called it a "war against Chinese expansionism" (*chiến tranh chống bành trướng Trung Hoa*). China gave several reasons for its military invasion in early 1979: as retaliation for Vietnam's "liberation" of Cambodia from China's Khmer Rouge allies; to assert territorial claims on the southern border and in the South China Sea (the Spratly Islands); and as a check on Soviet aggression and influence in the region, as Vietnam aligned with the USSR after the Sino-Soviet split in the 1960s.[39] Set in 1978, *Boat People* shows Vietnam's early mobilization in anticipation of the war. On the first day Akutagawa enlists Cam Nuong as his local guide, he meets her on a busy thoroughfare where she collects payments for streetside bicycle parking. When he arrives, Akutagawa notices a long queue outside the Department of Public Security (Sở Công-an) across the street. Cam Nuong tells Akutagawa the government has required all Hoa, including Chinese nationals and diplomats, to register with the authorities, who likely plan to confiscate their property and resettle them in NEZs or "repatriate" them to China. At the time, a combined 67 percent of the Vietnamese Hoa (who made up a significant portion of the 1979 refugee wave to Hong Kong) were either Cantonese or Hainanese,[40] punctuating Ann Hui's use of Cantonese dialogue and the Hainan backdrop to indict Vietnam's anti-Sinitism.

If *Boat People*'s Hong Kong-Hainan-Da Nang confluences mark a pioneering engagement with mainland China that opened doors for Ann Hui's filmmaking career—one prioritizing feminist perspectives in a male-dominated Hong Kong cinematic landscape and understated border-crossing films (such as 2011's *A Simple Life*) contrasting the lavish blockbuster typical of Hong Kong-PRC coproductions—they do so by pivoting on the geopolitical fallout of the Sino-Vietnamese War. These Sinophone inter-Asian confluences do not make Hui complicit with PRC war propaganda but rather acknowledge the leverage such geopolitical fallout gave her to "realistically" translate, dramatize, and stage stories collected from detainees in Hong Kong, thereby complicating dichotomous understandings of the film as a transpacific rebuttal to the absence of Vietnamese voices and stories in Hollywood's rendering of the war experience or as an allegory of Hong Kong's political anxiety about the impending "disappearance" of its local culture following mainland retrocession.

Irresolution

To think of war solely as combat, and its main protagonist as the soldier, who is primarily imagined as male, stunts the understanding of war's identity and works to the advantage of the war machine.... If we no longer accept the identities of our enemies as provided by the authorities, we might find it difficult to accept the identities of the wars those same authorities give us.
–Viet Thanh Nguyen, *Nothing Ever Dies* (2016)

In a transpacific cinematic discourse on the U.S.-Vietnam War, Ann Hui's *Boat People* compels reflection on the subjectivities of the war's "collateral damage" and its legacies in broader demographic and geographic terms than Hollywood's offerings circa 1982, given the latter's fetishization of the combat experiences of American soldiers and its practice of rendering the war's Southeast Asian refugees legible only within anticommunist narratives of rescue that repetitiously justify U.S. military imperialism.[41] With *Boat People*, Hui adapted testimonies of Hong Kong's Vietnamese refugees-in-transit into a cinematic voice of oppositional translocalism, situating them within the historical fabric and identity of Hong Kong and, for many of the refugees, their transpacific destinations of eventual settlement. The film emphasizes not just the stories of those like Cam Nuong, who by the film's end is left in limbo, "defecting on the angry sea" (*touben nuhai*), but also of those loved ones left behind, like Cam Nuong's mother, who commits suicide after party officials publicly expose her affair with a South Korean soldier (who assisted the U.S. and South Vietnamese war effort)—to whom she had turned in economic straits after her husband (Cam Nuong's father) was killed in the war. Foregrounding the noncombatants, Hui treats the stateless subjectivity empathetically without forcing a resolution that must redeem that subjectivity within a nationalist framework.

Yet, a reading that recoups the literal politics of *Boat People*'s refugee-centered narrative should be supplemented by the literal politics of its production context. This is where a Sinophone inter-Asian recasting of its transpacific refugee critique also implicates uneven applications and regimes of power between and within Asian countries, between and within Sinophone sites (Hong Kong and Hainan), and between Asian Communist governments allegorically collapsed into Cold War ideological alignment. Coupled with post-Mao China's economic reforms, the Sino-Vietnamese War authorized

Ann Hui to bring her directorial knowhow from the cosmopolitan Sinophone cinematic hub of Hong Kong to Hainan—an island situated in the geopolitically contested South China Sea—where she cast its tropical backdrop to replicate Da Nang in the genre of documentary realism. The Hong Kong-Hainan-Da Nang confluences of the film's production underscore its indictment of the Vietnamese government's inhumane (and anti-Sinitic) policies, an indictment that serves the PRC's need to outwardly justify its provocation of a border war in Vietnam in 1979. Not only does this border war replay episodes of China's imperial past, such as the Han dynasty general Ma Yuan's suppression and "pacification" of the Trưng sisters' Annam rebellion in the first century CE,[42] but it also perpetuates what Robert Sutter calls a nationalist "Chinese exceptionalism," derived from a self-perception that, having "always followed morally correct foreign policies," China is invariably the aggrieved party to any international conflict.[43] Since the Sino-Vietnamese War of 1979, PRC-Vietnam relations have been fraught with periodic recurrences of the conflict's imperialist underpinnings: In 2014, China sent an oil rig guarded by its navy to islands off Vietnam's coast, where a Chinese state-owned oil company then offered drilling contracts on some areas that Vietnam was already developing. This prompted mass demonstrations with anti-Sinitic overtones in Vietnam that turned violent.[44]

On the fortieth anniversary of the Sino-Vietnamese War, popular PRC cinema has still not reckoned with the conflict in a way that rejects the enemy's identity as construed by China's official history. Popular mainland director Feng Xiaogang's *Youth* (2017), for example, eulogizes the selfless heroism of young Chinese men who joined the war effort: Images of PLA soldiers torching the jungle with flamethrowers while taking on enemy fire make no attempt to show, let alone understand or empathize with, a faceless Vietnamese adversary. To Ann Hui's credit, as a Hong Kong director of several mainland coproductions, she has subtly undermined nationalist discourses that might otherwise saturate the historical content of her films.[45] With *Boat People*, Hui's development of a Japanese character in the leading role of the photojournalist, through whose perspective audiences are introduced to postreunification Vietnam (and yet whose perspective is exceeded by a camera eye that abandons him for healthy portions of the narrative to focus on "a range of subsidiary characters"),[46] is intriguing. Hui initially sought a Japanese actor to play the role.[47] Screenwriter Tai On-Ping attributes Hui's reasoning to several factors: Hui's own part-Japanese background, the necessity for a "third-party" observer role that would have been more difficult for a Chinese national in Vietnam during the Sino-Vietnamese War, and the belief that a Japanese national would more likely have Vietnam "fantasies" that could be "extinguished" by film's end.[48]

These inter-Asian fantasies are embedded in the imperial legacy of the Japanese Pacific War occupation, which, according to Vinh Nguyen, is similarly "complicit in bringing about the contemporary conditions that force escape."[49] Yet, *Boat People* also develops Akutagawa as an anti-imperialist ally: Finding Hui's outline for Akutagawa underdeveloped, Tai On-Ping transformed Akutagawa into an orphan of U.S. Pacific War bombing campaigns in Japan and as a former student who participated in Japan's leftist demonstrations from 1967–1968, thus explaining his initial support for the Vietnamese government's postliberation goals.[50] Given that the Japanese are often caricatured as the fascist aggressor and enemy in both Hong Kong and mainland Chinese war films, Hui's more nuanced depiction—despite the politics of its Sinophone inter-Asian production—subtly resists total cooptation by PRC propaganda seeking to legitimize the Sino-Vietnamese War and the sacrifices thousands of Chinese suffered for it.

Notes

1. *Touben nuhai* (*Boat People*), directed by Ann Hui (Bluebird Film, 1982). *Boat People*'s Sinophone title, meaning "defecting on the angry sea," was conceived by the popular Hong Kong author of martial arts fiction, Jin Yong. Yang Ziyu, *Menghui zhongxia: Xia Meng de dianying he rensheng* (Hong Kong: Hong Kong Open Page, 2017), 236.

2. Pham Tuyen composed the song on April 28, 1975, when he learned the Vietnam People's Air Force had bombed the Tan Son Nhut Air Base in Saigon. Today, the song is played at official government meetings and public school and university assemblies. I thank Qui-Ha Nguyen for this background.

3. Vinh Nguyen, "Ann Hui's *Boat People*: Documenting Vietnamese Refugees in Hong Kong," in *Looking Back on the Vietnam War: Twenty-First-Century Perspectives*, ed. Brenda M. Boyle and Jeehyun Lim (New Brunswick, NJ: Rutgers University Press, 2016), 94. The war's naming conceals the reality that the U.S.-Vietnam War "was not even fought only between the two sides." Viet Thanh Nguyen, *Nothing Ever Dies: Vietnam and the Memory of War* (Cambridge, MA: Harvard University Press, 2016), 8.

4. Nguyen, "Ann Hui's *Boat People*," 103.

5. For a critique of the 1997 allegory, see Mirana M. Szeto, "Ann Hui at the Margin of Mainstream Hong Kong Cinema," in *Hong Kong Screenscapes: From the New Wave to the Digital Frontier*, ed. Esther M. K. Cheung, Gina Marchetti, and Tan See-Kam (Hong Kong: Hong Kong University Press, 2011), 52–55.

6. Nguyen, "Ann Hui's *Boat People*," 95–96.

7. Quoted in Kuang Baowei, *Xu Anhua shuo Xu Anhua* (Shanghai: Fudan University Press, 2017), 41.

8. Nguyen, "Ann Hui's *Boat People*," 95–99. Nguyen sees *Boat People* "as a text that humanizes and makes grievable the 'targets' of American violence . . . that litter the backdrop of American action, both military and filmic" (99).

9. *Boat People* was released in Hong Kong cinemas on October 22, 1982, the same day as the U.S. theatrical release of director Ted Kotcheoff's *First Blood*, the story of Rambo, a former Green Beret of the U.S.-Vietnam War suffering from PTSD following combat duty in Vietnam.

10. Kuang, *Xu Anhua shuo Xu Anhua*, 39.

11. Yang, *Menghui zhongxia*, 237. Hui recalls of the opening scene: "When the army enters the city, it looks like a documentary, but because it was a dramatization, everything was concocted by us" (quoted in Kuang, *Xu Anhua shuo Xu Anhua*, 39).

12. Quoted in Michael Berry, *Speaking in Images: Interviews with Contemporary Chinese Filmmakers* (New York: Columbia University Press, 2005), 430.

13. Yến Lê Espiritu, "Toward a Critical Refugee Study: The Vietnamese Refugee Subject in US Scholarship," *Journal of Vietnamese Studies* 1, nos. 1–2 (2006): 426.

14. Shu Kei, "'Lai ke' qianyin," in *Xu Anhua de Yuenan sanbuqu*, ed. Cheung Chor Yeung (Hong Kong: Qingwen Shuwu, 1983), 196.

15. Ann Hui intentionally developed *Woo Viet* as a "B-movie," a "cheaper version" of a "Hollywood genre film" (Kuang, *Xu Anhua shuo Xu Anhua*, 29–32).

16. *Boat People* screenwriter Tai On-Ping recalls Hui giving him "all the resources" about Hong Kong's Vietnamese refugees that she had gathered in research dating back to "Boy from Vietnam," including "newspaper clippings, casework, and books" (quoted in Shu Kei, "Fangwen Dai Anping," in Kuang, *Xu Anhua de Yuenan sanbuqu*, 3).

17. Chan Kwok Bun, "The Vietnamese Boat People in Hong Kong," in *The Cambridge Survey of World Migration*, ed. Robin Cohen (Cambridge: Cambridge University Press, 1995), 380–383.

18. Nguyen, "Ann Hui's *Boat People*," 100–101.

19. Lê Espiritu, "Toward a Critical Refugee Study," 411–412, 421.

20. Chan, "The Vietnamese Boat People," 384.

21. Chan, "The Vietnamese Boat People," 380–381.

22. Viet Thanh Nguyen and Janet Hoskins, "Transpacific Studies: Critical Perspectives on an Emerging Field," in *Transpacific Studies: Framing an Emerging Field* (Honolulu: University of Hawai'i Press, 2014), 2–3.

23. Rather than the refugee, Wong's focus is the transpacific circulation of the trope of Chineseness as affixed to images, discourses, and narratives of the Chinese sex worker. Lily Wong, *Transpacific Attachments: Sex Work, Media Networks, and Affective Histories of Chineseness* (New York: Columbia University Press, 2018), 7, 14–15.

24. Viet Thanh Nguyen satirizes this in his Pulitzer Prize–winning 2015 novel, *The Sympathizer*. The protagonist, a half-Vietnamese, half-French communist spy living in California, agrees to serve as a cultural informant during the shooting of a film in the Philippines about the U.S.-Vietnam War called *The Hamlet* being made by a famous director simply called The Auteur (a veiled reference to Coppola). The Auteur rejects the protagonist's suggestions to make the nameless "villagers" appear even remotely Vietnamese, saying, "No one gives a shit." Viet Thanh Nguyen, *The Sympathizer* (New York: Grove Atlantic, 2015), 129.

25. Cheuk Pak Tong (Zhuo Botang), *Xianggang xin langchao dianying* (Shanghai: Fudan UP, 2011), 8.

26. Nguyen and Hoskins, "Transpacific Studies," 3.

27. Shu-mei Shih, "Against Diaspora: The Sinophone as Places of Cultural Production," in *Sinophone Studies: A Critical Reader*, ed. Shu-mei Shih, Chien-hsin Tsai, and Brian Bernards (New York: Columbia University Press, 2013), 37.

28. Nguyen and Hoskins, "Transpacific Studies," 4; Shu-mei Shih, "Theory, Asia and the Sinophone," *Postcolonial Studies* 13, no. 4 (2010): 473; Amitav Acharya, "Asia Is Not One," in *Asia Redux: Conceptualising a Region for Our Times*, ed. Prasenjit Duara (Singapore: ISEAS Publishing / New Delhi: Manohar, 2013), 54.

29. Kuan-hsing Chen and Chua Beng Huat, "The Inter-Asia Cultural Studies: Movements Project," in *The Inter-Asia Cultural Studies Reader* (Abingdon, UK: Routledge, 2007), 2.

30. Kuan-hsing Chen, *Asia as Method: Toward Deimperialization* (Durham, NC: Duke University Press, 2010), 120.

31. Robert G. Sutter, *Chinese Foreign Relations: Power and Policy Since the Cold War*, 4th ed. (Lanham, MD: Rowman & Littlefield, 2016), 64–66.

32. Yang, *Menghui zhongxia*, 237–239. At the time, Hainan was still part of Guangdong. It became a separate province and a special economic zone (SEZ) in 1988.

33. Kuang, *Xu Anhua shuo Xu Anhua*, 39.

34. Frank Dikotter, *The Cultural Revolution: A People's History* (London: Bloomsbury, 2017), 197–205. An example of scar literature set in Hainan is Kong Jiesheng's short story, "Zai xiaohe nabian" (On the other side of the stream), in his collection, *Zhuiqiu: Duanpian xiaoshuo ji* (Guangzhou: Guangdong People's Press, 1980). An English translation by Charles W. Hayford appears in *Roses and Thorns: The Second Blooming of the Hundred Flowers in Chinese Fiction, 1979–1980*, ed. Perry Link (Berkeley: University of California Press, 1984), 168–93.

35. Yang, *Menghui zhongxia*, 239.

36. Jacqueline Desbarats, "Population Redistribution in the Socialist Republic of Vietnam," *Population and Development Review* 13, no. 1 (1987): 43–44.

37. Vietnam officially recognizes fifty-three ethnic minority communities. The Kinh, or "ethnic Vietnamese," form the majority. Lan Duong describes how ethnic difference informs the Kinh female gaze through contact with Montagnard populations during resettlement campaigns in post-Doi Moi (renovation) films made by women directors, like Pham Nhuệ Giang's *The Deserted Valley* (2002), which addresses "the implementation of compulsory Kinh education in the highlands and its effects on Kinh characters" who arrive optimistic but end up disillusioned with the goals of the campaign. Lan Duong, "Close Up: The Female Gaze and Ethnic Difference in Two Vietnamese Women's Films," *Journal of Southeast Asian Studies* 46, no. 3 (2015): 457. As an analogous work of PRC scar cinema chronicling encounters between Han and non-Han peoples in the Cultural Revolution's "sent-down" labor reeducation campaign, Zhang Nuanxin's *Sacrificed Youth* (1985) details a young Han woman's labor and reeducation in a Dai village in Yunnan.

38. Desbarats, "Population Redistribution," 46–52.

39. Nicholas Khoo, *Collateral Damage: Sino-Soviet Rivalry and the Termination of the Sino-Vietnamese Alliance* (New York: Columbia University Press, 2011).

40. Tran Khanh, *The Ethnic Chinese and Economic Development in Vietnam* (Singapore: ISEAS, 1993); Chan, "The Vietnamese Boat People," 380.

41. Lê Espiritu, "Toward a Critical Refugee Study," 425.

42. Brian Bernards, *Writing the South Seas: Imagining the Nanyang in Chinese and Southeast Asian Postcolonial Literature* (Seattle: University of Washington Press, 2015), 37.

43. Sutter, *Chinese Foreign Relations*, 47.

44. Sutter, *Chinese Foreign Relations*, 220–221.

45. Gina Marchetti offers an excellent account of how *The Golden Era* (2014), Hui's arthouse coproduction biopic of the modern Chinese author Xiao Hong (1911–1942), accomplishes this. See Gina Marchetti, "The Feminine Touch: Chinese Soft Power Politics and Hong Kong Women Filmmakers," in *Screening China's Soft Power*, ed. Paola Voci and Luo Hui (Abingdon UK: Routledge, 2018), 229–251.

46. Julian Stringer, "*Boat People*: Second Thoughts and Text and Context," in *Chinese Films in Focus: 25 New Takes*, ed. Chris Berry (London: British Film Institute, 2003), 18.

47. Kuang, *Xu Anhua shuo Xu Anhua*, 39.

48. Quoted in Shu, "Fangwen Dai Anping," 4–5. Hui's relationship with her Japanese mother is the subject of her 1990 fictionalized biopic, *Song of the Exile*.

49. Vinh Nguyen, "Ann Hui's *Boat People*," 105.

50. Shu, "Fangwen Dai Anping," 4.

Sinophonic Affects

Kyle Dargan's Anagnorisis *and the Poetics of Infrastructure in Chan Tze Woon's* Yellowing

LILY WONG

This essay brings together Sinophone and affect studies, both critical frameworks that investigate questions of social and identity formation, as inquiries that are emergent, multidirectional, and networked. To be clear, I approach affect as a politics of emotional mobilization—the power to move and be moved by others—that allows for a more flexible framework to study subject and social formation.[1] Affect displays the workings of social meanings; it exhibits the ways conceptions not only operate within identifiable social structures but also move across, push against, and even, at moments, exceed them. It provides the language—of movement, desire, and becoming—that privileges the *potentiality* of meaning over fixed interpretive paths of signs and representation.

Sinophonic inquiry, for instance, allows for an expansive, even if contested, terrain of affective attachments decentered from a singular affective core (e.g., Chineseness). As Shu-mei Shih contends, Sinophone can be a site of "both a longing for and a rejection of various constructions of Chineseness; it can be a site of both nationalism of the long-distance kind, anti-China politics, or even nonrelation with China, whether real or imaginary."[2] That is to say, the Sinophonic framework recognizes differently entangled and often conflicting emotional structures that splinter the centrality of ethno-nationalistic frameworks. Thinking about affect and Sinophone together unsettles more centripetal theorizations of identity (e.g., territory, locality, or nationality) with an emphasis on relationality, dynamism, and temporality.

In this sense, Sinophone can be read as a form of "minor transnationalism": transborder connections across minoritized networks that complicate marketized extraction. Here, I am drawing from Françoise Lionnet and Shu-mei Shih's definition of the term. They argue that minor transnationalism highlights "the complex and multiple forms of cultural expressions of minorities and diasporic peoples and . . . [the] micropractices of transnationality in their multiple, paradoxical, or even irreverent relations with the economic transnationalism of contemporary empires." These minor-to-minor linkages shed light on the jagged forms of transnational connection that recenter the uneven histories and expressions that are often glossed over within the logics of global, marketized connectivity. Comparing it to the melancholic "minor" key in a musical sense, Lionnet and Shih explain that "[minor transnationalism] is perhaps the mode in which the traumas of colonial, imperial, and global hegemonies as well as the affective dimensions of transcolonial solidarities continue to work themselves out and produce new possibilities."[3] It locates more emergent expressions across minoritized networks that, in their entanglements, allow for the navigation and potential redistribution of the historical weights they disproportionately bear.

As such, I approach Sinophone as a form of minor transnationalism that is rallied, maintained, and mediated affectively. I stress the ways Sinophone-as-concept constantly reformulates in relation to the affective pulls between unevenly socialized subjects. How might Sinophone studies activate affective connections that help us envision potential "transcolonial solidarities" across the Asia-Pacific? As an example, this paper reads African American poet Kyle Dargan's 2018 poetry collection *Anagnorisis* in relation to Hong Kong director Chan Tze Woon's (陳梓桓) 2016 documentary *Yellowing* (亂世備忘) to trace emergent forms of Sinophonic affects.

Titled after the moment of self-revelation in Greek tragedy—*Anagnorisis*, Dargan's poetry collection, details the author's reflections on issues of police brutality, Black deaths, and gentrifying displacement in U.S. cities. Sequenced at the middle of the collection is a series of poems—what he names the China Cycle—about his ruminations on Hong Kong, Xinjiang, and his travels in Beijing, Tianjin, and the China-Korea borderlands. Sinophonic affects can be read in Dargan's creative use of Sino-script to convey potential connections with Sinophone communities, particularly in his reflections on Hong Kong's Umbrella Movement (2014). Also depicting the Umbrella Movement, Chan's documentary *Yellowing* connects the personal tales of his fellow protestors during the months-long occupation.

Comparing seemingly distant representations of similar events, I argue that there is political potential in locating Sinophonic affects across aesthetic arrangements—or poetics of infrastructure—that cross divergent mediums (poetry and film) and positionalities. Tracing Sinophonic affects across Dargan's and Chan's work prods us to engage with the reconfiguring relationality and coalitional potential across disciplinarity. Such minor-to-minor linkages challenge and reassemble singular, centripetal, or binary models (e.g., U.S.-China or Afro-Asian) of politico-aesthetic connection often utilized for state-centered use-value or marketized global exchange.

Intimating Across the Pacific

To locate the "transcolonial solidarities" Lionnet and Shih call for, I focus on the uneven convergences of colonial and imperial navigation that appear "linked, but not identical."[4] Lisa Lowe, for instance, argues for the importance of tracking the histories of dispossession across four continents, revealing connections between the emergence of European liberalism, settler colonialism in the Americas, the transatlantic slave trade, and the East Indies and China trades. With this cross-continental scope, she shows how the institutionalization of Euro-American-centered liberal-rights tradition depends on the global divisions of labor, knowledge, and value across differentially situated histories of Indigeneity, slavery, and industry that naturalize social liberties for some and denies access to a majority of others. It is, then, in locating the ongoing unevenness of value and labor, not necessarily the equivalence across difference, that might allow us means to challenge such colonial and postcolonial relations.

Intimacies, to Lowe, are key to unraveling such global asymmetries. She complicates understandings of intimacies as simply sexual or reproductive relations of the "possessive individual" within the liberal private sphere, a defining property of the modern citizen in civil society.[5] Instead, she argues for the tracing of "constellation[s] of asymmetrical and unevenly legible" intimacies in relation to global processes and colonial structures that condition such connections.[6] That is, she compels us to trace networks of intimacies that are often cast as failed, forgotten, illegitimate, irrelevant, deviant, or even too far apart to establish immediate value or correlation. In so doing, she connects what seem to be historically, geographically, and conceptually distant sites to interrogate the "linked, but not identical" practices of dispossession across colonial structures.

In challenging the relation between intimacy and the "possessive individual," Lowe's approach resonates with a genealogy of queer and feminists of color scholars who approach affect and emotions as not simply private states of expression but public practices that constitute intimate relations.[7] Such a relational approach to affect contextualizes conceptions of the "individual" within larger histories of social and material relations. Something as individuated as one's understanding of one's own emotions and desires are, under an affective lens, deprivatized as historically situated notions that are socially tied, not individually owned. Thus, an affective focus on tracing minor-to-minor "intimacies" highlights the malleability and sociality of comparative subject formation.

Scholarship on Afro-Asian relationality, for instance, has long been affectively mediated. By comparatively linking the historical formation of African and Asian diasporas, scholars stress the need to identify the inextricable ties between racial exploitation within imperial nations and transnational imperialistic involvements. When focused on the U.S. context, such relationalities have often been explained through affective binaries of conflict or romanticization as either "perpetual combatants, separated by essential cultural differences, or the quintessential partners for any kind of radical project."[8] The affective charge of this connection is thus often framed in extremes: as "signals that radical politics is all but dead or that the best days between racial minorities are yet to come."[9] Much of this polarizing logic can be understood in relation to histories of "racial triangulation" within the U.S. context in which the uneven oppression of African Americans and Asian Americans have been historically situated (e.g., often being institutionally pit against each other) to uphold and maintain white dominant political and labor structures.[10]

The easy binary of oppositional versus radical partnership, scholars have argued, also risks homogenizing intragroup sameness in order to dramatize intergroup difference for visible consumption and extraction into the global market, or what Jodi Melamed calls "neoliberal multiculturalism."[11] To Melamed, "neoliberal multiculturalism" is a political paradigm that replaces systemic tackling of inequality with institutional management of cultural diversity centered on neoliberal economic policies since the end of the Cold War. In this model, "culture" displaces racial reference, creating essentialized categories of cultural difference that erase histories of racialized exploitation and disguise material patterns of unequal resource distribution.[12] This recoding of racial construction to cultural difference operates on ahistorical logics of leveled playing fields, marketing "culture" as containable forms of difference. Melamed states that this "neoliberal multicultural" paradigm coopts the rhetoric of civil rights to declare economic rights as the most fundamental civil right. It equates individual liberties to individualistic freedoms for consumption and ownership. It portrays neoliberal policies of deregulation and privatization as the key to a postracial world of freedom and opportunity.[13]

Dargan's work on Asia refuses easy extraction into the neoliberal marketplace along commodifiable logics of cultural difference or alliance. In a published roundtable, Dargan joins African American writers—Afaa Michael Weaver, Bro. Yao (Hoke S. Glover), and Aaliyah Bilal—in discussing their writings on China.[14] They discuss how thinking through China offers ways to contemplate not only the United States' continued global exercise of political-economic power but also China's rise as an emerging empire itself.[15] The writers acknowledge the history of Black thinkers who have turned to China for political inspiration, largely during the Cold War.[16] Yet, they emphasize their departure from this genealogy as the material conditions and geopolitics have since shifted.[17]

Dargan, in particular, stresses that his experience in China made him reflect on the contemporary "drive towards capitalist sameness."[18] He elaborates:

> I am not writing with the intent of situating my American minority struggles within the politics of the Chinese people. Though, yes, I do feel a solidarity with many of the people there, but that is mostly economic.... The mutual struggle to govern ourselves and remain human—particularly in the face of late capitalism—is what my writing on China is concerned with.[19]

Here, Dargan rejects the convergence-to-allied-resistance conflation. By not claiming equivalence between his "American minority struggles" and that of the "Chinese people," he articulates a linked but not identical third space: "the mutual struggle to govern ourselves and remain human—particularly in the face of late capitalism." He highlights potential connections that resist simple capital extraction, a literary possibility that is tied to the economic realities of those in China, an intimacy he does not "situate" himself in but "feel[s] a solidarity with."

Framing his writings on China as aspirational critique (not open exchange), Dargan positions his work on China as affective practices that do not claim ownership. In this way, he seems to be tracing the very minor-to-minor "intimacies" that Lowe argues could potentially denaturalize discourses of "possessive individualism," particularly the assumption of one's right to access, know, and marketize culture. Articulating connections that are not easily legible or even "knowable," Dargan's contingent relationality with his own narrations on China defies clear extraction within a neoliberal marketplace. It resists the easy conflation of individual liberties with individualistic freedoms to access consumable difference, a neoliberal multicultural paradigm that Melamed warns us against.

It is in this contingent relation to China that I propose a reading of Dargan's China Cycle through a Sinophonic lens. Sinophone, as defined by Shih, is a network "of cultural production outside China and on the margins of China and Chineseness."[20] It does not refer to an identifiable nation-state, racial, or ethnic positionality as its origin; it connotes a minor transnational relationality linked through the circulation and transmutation of Sinitic-language cultural production. As such, a Sinophonic approach destabilizes the liberal-rights discourse that Lowe is wary of. It unsettles conceptions of subject and social formation away from the possession of citizen-subjecthood, particularly in the ways it is tied to the rights to property and ownership of cultural nationalism.

As a minor transnational methodology that is uniquely equipped to examine China's politico-economic impact from and by its margins, a Sinophonic approach to Dargan's writings on China, I argue, allows for the emergence of the "mutual struggle . . . in the face of late capitalism," which he locates his concerns.[21] Tracing the minor-to-minor "intimacies" in Dargan's China Cycle—what I read as forms of Sinophonic affects—allows for a more expansive, even if contested, terrain of affective attachments that defies easy capital extraction through discourses of cultural difference or multicultural alliance. By examining Sinophonic affects in Dargan's poetry, I highlight the differently entangled emotional structures that enable politico-aesthetic connection; it prompts us to reconfigure the relationalities and potentialities that emerge on and off the page.

Anagnorisis, Sinophonics

Bridging the two halves of *Anagnorisis*, the China Cycle is a series of fourteen poems about Dargan's trip to China in 2014, hosted by the Chinese Writers' Association.[22] Though partially sponsored by the Chinese state, the poems do not sit comfortably with state power, be it the Chinese state or reflections on the United States in comparison to China. An example is the poem "XI. 'Beautiful Country'":

> The hanzi for "hai" (海) I decipher from expressway
> signs above us as we depart the new Port of Binhai.
>
> I ask Dongxia what "Shanghai" then means.
> "No meaning. When it is name, it is just name."
>
> I struggle to swallow her response. I've noticed
> the semantics of Mandarin's myriad characters
>
> harbors the figurative—how "holy" as hanzi
> stacks the character for "other" atop the arboreal
>
> character for "earth," resculpting the metaphor
> in calligraphy (圣). I show Dongxia my strokes

for a character that's caught my eye (京) to ask,
again, for translation. "This means Beijing—

one character." But "bei" I've now memorized
as "north." I follow my finger through my glossary

until it catches on "jing": "capital." North Capital.
Beijing—as much a name as a geographical

distinction. Later, I glean "shang" (上) off street
signs near my lodging. I open the dictionary,

which confesses it means "up," maybe "upper."
Upper Port. Shanghai. North of Hong Kong.

(I plan to tell Dongxia there was a duke
of an old English York. The York that now cradles

Manhattan is the New. I seek similar histories
when I ask what hides behind the hanzi's blades)

Before I fancy myself a sleuth of language
here in the Middle Nation (中国), I must learn

what I mean in Mandarin. After calling myself
"meiguo" (美国) for weeks, I realize that

it can't be simply "America." My book confides
that "mei" means beautiful, that I am "ren"

(人) from the Beautiful Country. I bemoan
the translation, but I was not brought here

to explain all the beauty not found at home.[23]

The speaker articulates a double critique of both U.S. and Chinese state power through a deconstructive engagement with the Mandarin Chinese script.[24] On the one hand, he questions the way he is identified as a "meiguo ren" on Chinese soil. Bemoaning that, to him, "beauty" is not easily ascribed to the way his humanity is, or rather, is *not* seen, as a Black man in America—the supposed "meiguo" ("beautiful country," 美国). On the other hand, he notes that his critique might also not be what he was sponsored to articulate. As his interpreter Dongxia asserts: "When it is name, it is just name," stabilizing the meaning of "Shanghai" on to the supposed fixity, or rules, of the Chinese language.

A Sinophonic approach to Dargan's play on Mandarin Chinese script allows room for "unruly" meanings to emerge. While Sinophone-as-concept unsettles discourses of cultural and historical orthodoxy, a Sinophonic approach to Mandarin Chinese script highlights *the constructed relations* between language and identity formation rather than take for granted naturalized notions of linguistic nativity or political fidelity to the Chinese state.[25] This can be seen in the way Dargan breaks down the meanings associated with graphological character components of 上海 (Shanghai) and 北京 (Beijing), official names of China's financial hub and political capital, respectively. With each query about each character—"hai" (海), "jing" (京), "shang" (上)—the speaker destabilizes the assertion of "When it is name, it is just name." With each question, he detaches the production of meaning from what is often considered its "natural" alignments with "national languages" or the possession of "mother tongues." Language, or in this case, the Mandarin Chinese script, operates as a medium of disputed access rather than a right to identity.[26]

This disorientation between assigned meanings and unauthorized inquiries allows the poem to open up space for minor-to-minor connection and critique. The speaker shows how, in addition to signifying 上海 (Shanghai) a stable designation (noun), the character "shang" (上) also connotes "'up,' maybe 'upper'" a potential directionality (adjective). It is in this deterritorialization of meaning—from proper noun to positional adjective—that he "seeks similar histories," particularly the colonial histories that link the ports of Shanghai, Hong Kong, and New York.

The speaker's desire to "seek" these historical, if not presently apparent or authorized linkages (articulated within parenthesis) allows him to question the stability of meaning inscribed on the page. Compelled to identify as an American in China, or a "'ren'/ (人) from the Beautiful Country," the speaker unsettles this easy association at the end of the poem by complicating the way his identity is presented on the page. He splits the transliteration and the character script for human "ren"/ (人) with a line break, expressing a sense of humanity that extends beyond what is formally legible or allowed.

This reordering of meaning emerges if we approach Dargan's use of Sinoscript as affective infrastructures, not fixated inscription. Here, I draw from Brian Larkin's definition of infrastructures as "built networks that facilitate the flow of goods, people, or ideas and allow for their exchange over space."[27] Infrastructures are mediums through which material (e.g., goods, people) and immaterial (e.g., ideas) values are construed and circulated. They are not simply—in any positivist sense—neutral "things." Infrastructures are organizations of meaning that manifest through material forms and accrue value through spatial arrangements.²⁸

To read Dargan's use of Mandarin Chinese script as affective infrastructures allows us to think of the Sino-script's metaphorical capacities *in relation to* its material arrangements or "to think [infrastructure's] . . . material forms along with their capacities to generate aspiration and expectation."²⁹ Through transliteration and lineation, Dargan unsettles attachments between humanity (人), beauty (美), and the nation-state (国). Asserting that "it can't be simply," the speaker in Dargan's poem unravels not only the national mythologies of America as "meiguo" (beautiful country, 美国) but also China's own fabled positioning as the Middle Nation (中国). It is through the speaker's disorientation—how he bemoans "the beauty not found at home" (be it the United States or the naturalized association between identity, home, and nation more broadly)—that I locate Sinophonic affects in Dargan's poetic infrastructure. Through his spatial orderings on the page, Dargan expresses sentiments that trouble fidelities to national scripts and, by extension, the multiply entangled imperialistic logics they erase and enable.

Sinophonic affects can be further seen in the way Dargan constructs potential connections *with* Sinophone communities (those on the margins of China and Chineseness). An example is the poem "XX. Da Shuo":

> On the other side of the great firewall, the Uyghur Tohti has lost his free life to sentencing with no testimony. Hong Kong nights glimmer with the glow of smartphone faces turned torches in demonstrators' hands. The financial district, its party-tight tycoons, illuminated. The world can see—the world bent to English. Thus I can see. Yet the hanzi here behind the wall cannot align themselves into news of unrest. Unlike America. So much news there that knowing—or caring—is uncouth. Behind this wall, Tianjin's pedestrians pass or smack flush into each other with no knowledge that officials have canceled the National Day fireworks in Hong Kong. Fireworks' news travels widely here. How you hear the human fabric unravel and restitch on this censored side of the wall. A single barrage: a wedding. Two blasts separated by a pause: a funeral. You will not hear the country outgrowing its tailored harmony. (A sound I know from home.) Protesting students have their Instagram eyes gouged out. Unlike with words, there is no subtle way to sanitize the world web's imagebrain. Panoramas of skyscrapers—thirty at a time—rise on this side of the wall. Putin grips Xi standing next to the Next Big Thing on this side of the wall. Rows of dark-suit apparatchiks fold themselves into a mitochondrion on this side of the wall. China Central Television broadcasts the first fifteen channels on this side of the wall, and small women styled with identical bob cuts sit at the anchor desks—words, like quick-setting mortar, pour calmly from their lips.³⁰

The speaker expresses Sinophonic affects as he articulates concerns for the sentencing of Ilham Tohti, a scholar critical of China's policies toward people of his Uighur ethnicity, to life in prison. Connecting what he learns about the Uyghur Tohti's sentencing with the unfolding of Hong Kong's Umbrella Movement, both events marginalized by "the great firewall," the speaker finds himself navigating political and linguistic barriers.

Similar to how Dargan utilizes Sino-script in "Beautiful Country," this poem's title, "Da Shuo"—a pinyin transliteration of Mandarin Chinese with no corresponding Chinese script or English translation— also functions as an affective infrastructure. It creates what some call the "poetics of infrastructures," in which infrastructures are understood as not just technical objects with designated utility but forms of language construction that show how society and social meaning are both already structured and always in (re)formulation.[31] The title "Da Shuo" signifies value not necessarily through the complete transfer of linguistic meaning but rather through the way it takes up space on the page. It affects readers differently according to their own proximity to the language, be it English and/or Mandarin Chinese. Bilingual readers might, for instance, interpret "Da Shuo" to be referring to the characters 大說: a transliteration of the English concept "big talk" (or grandiose statements without substance) that does not directly register in Chinese terminology. Here, Dargan opens spaces between what is visibly portrayed—transliteration on the page—and the uncertain meanings one would need to insinuate (or misread) in order to "hear" ("Da Shuo" as "big talk" without corresponding "Chinese" terminology).

Line by line, the speaker details what is and is not allowed in the dense word block of the central government's "Da Shuo" (big talk). Visually, the poem looks sealed in, flush on both sides of the narrative wall. The wall-like density of the poem's form renders palpable the confinement of the great firewall's data infrastructure. Openings exist, however, when we listen to affective connections that echo beyond the "quick-setting mortar" of words on the page.

This affective focus beckons us to take the "phone" in *Sinophone* seriously.[32] The speaker explains the silencing that accompanies the loudness of state-sanctioned "big talk": to "not hear the country outgrowing its tailored harmony." That "not hearing," or silencing of cacophony, is an experience of sound that the speaker shares. In parentheses, as if in "minor chord," he articulates reverberations through "(A sound I know from home)." Sinophonic affects—the shared "minor chords"—are here activated precisely through the speaker's relinquishing of possessive individualism, particularly in its ties to the rights to property and ownership of cultural nationalism.

Sinophonic affects echo through the poetic infrastructures of the China Cycle, not despite but *due to* Dargan's lack of extractable ownership or easy access into "Chinese culture." Such connections can be read as the very "constellation[s] of asymmetrical and unevenly legible" intimacies that, Lowe argues, form across and possibly against the colonial structures that bind us. It is because of this political potential of minor-to-minor connections that I trace the "linked, but not identical" mobilization of Sinophonic affects across poetic infrastructures in Dargan's China Cycle and Chan Tze Woon's documentary *Yellowing*.[33]

Poetics of Infrastructure in *Yellowing*

Yellowing documents the seventy-nine days of the Umbrella Movement in 2014, the Hong Kong protests that Dargan alludes to in "Da Shuo."[34] Like Dargan's poem, Chan's documentary opens by juxtaposing images of state containment of the protests and China's National Day fireworks. There is an echoing of aesthetic arrangements—poetics of infrastructure—across mediums (poetry and documentary film) and positionalities (Dargan restricted through linguistic and geographical barriers as he writes in Tianjin; Chan with a handheld camera documenting on Hong Kong streets). Although these might seem like distant representations of the same events, links can be intimated if we trace reverberations across their aesthetic infrastructures.

Similar to Dargan's poem, *Yellowing* details "infrastructures" in both the material and metaphorical sense. Dargan alludes to the silencing effect of state-led "Da Shuo" (big talk) through depictions of National Day fireworks within the form of a narrative "firewall" with wall-like density. Such silencing in *Yellowing* is represented through the film's opening montage: scenes of Hong Kong's cityscape that alternate between the firing of tear gas on September 28, 2014, and China's National Day fireworks displayed after signs of protest were mostly cleared away (see fig. 6.1). The sequence concludes with shots of the Mandarin Chinese characters "國榮家盛" (Prosperous nation comes with thriving families) and "慶祝國慶" (Celebrating National Day of the People's Republic of China) lit up on surrounding skyscrapers.

The film's opening seems to end with formal containment—fragmented images of protest concluding in prolonged scenes of national celebration. However, like in Dargan's "Da Shou," we see affective openings created through the film's very aesthetic arrangements.

The sequenced montage produces affective dissonance between scenes of national celebration and that of unrest set against the same material infrastructure: Hong Kong's city streets. Such dissonance is amplified as the sound of National Day fireworks lingers on while the image fades into scenes

Figure 6.1 Opening montage of China's National Day fireworks and the firing of tear gas on Hong Kong streets, ending with National Day slogans projecting off of skyscrapers.

of protestors being teargassed. As the pace of the alternating scenes accelerates, cacophonous noises of fireworks and teargas overlay the images to a point where one is unable to distinguish between the sounds of celebration and protest. Such disorientation prods the viewer to question the cohesion of what is visually chronicled—the montage ending with the tying of family value to the prosperity of the Chinese nation in scenes of towering skyscrapers with "國榮家盛" (Prosperous nation comes with thriving families) lights projecting off of them. Unsettling the sight and sound of nationalist containment, Sinophonic affects echo through aesthetic dissonance despite being seemingly visually foreclosed.

To approach the opening scenes' material (e.g., city streets, skyscrapers) and metaphorical infrastructures (e.g., aesthetic arrangements) with a focus on Sinophonic affects disorients the value of "infrastructure" from state-led developmentalist utility.[35] Larkin notes that while infrastructural projects are often used to represent state power and progress to its citizens, they can also generate divergent emotional investments.[36] He argues that "roads and railways are not just technical objects . . . they encode the dreams of individuals and societies and are the vehicles whereby those fantasies are transmitted and made emotionally real. . . . They form us as subjects not just on a technopolitical level but also through this mobilization of affect."[37] This mobilization of affect can be seen in the way Chan creates affective dissonance through the arrangement of diverging footage set against Hong Kong's cityscape. Echoing how Dargan's poetic form (e.g., deconstructive use of Sino-script, unsettling of sound/script) diffuses the circulation of meaning from state-centered use-value, Chan constructs a poetics of infrastructure which refracts projections of the Chinese state as a centripetal affective core, a decentering I interpret as "Sinophonic affects."

Such a rethinking of "infrastructure"—through Sinophonic affects—is generative, as scholars have detailed how Umbrella Movement protestors recoded the utility of public infrastructures constructed by the state (e.g., highways and streets turned into campsites, organic gardens, and classrooms, etc).[38] Sebastian Veg notes that protesters demonstrated "a claim for public space (the storming of 'civic square,' the public protest space in front of government headquarters that had been closed off) . . . devot[ing] tremendous resources and energy to maintaining spontaneous order (wardens organized security, supply stations provided food and drink, waste disposal and recycling were entirely self-organized)."[39] We see a redistribution of material resources and political aspirations through the occupation and reappropriation of public infrastructure.

In the case of *Yellowing*, this reworking of value is reflected in the director's turn toward the intimate so as to concretize the movement's political impact. Chan starts the film with home videos of his childhood, detailing his relationship to the movement in personal terms. He then goes on to connect his tale with stories of protestors he stands next to while collectively forming a human wall against the police on the night of September 27, 2014 (see fig. 6.2).

In this scene, people literally act as infrastructure. With their hands held high, the protestors form a human wall against the police. While embodying a physical barrier, the protestors try to affectively appeal to the officers in front of them. Choked up in tears, one protestor pleads: "Do you want your children to experience the same fate? Staying out late and waiting to get arrested?" Another protestor follows: "How can you be so indifferent and cold-hearted?... Do police have to be iron-hearted?" The crowd then breaks into song, singing the Cantonese version of "Do You Hear the People Sing" (問誰未發聲). Mirroring the way the protestors line up to physically and emotionally form a human vanguard, Chan links their personal tales to document the effect of collective mobilization.

Chan's approach resonates with what AbdouMaliq Simone terms "people as infrastructure," an extension of the notion of infrastructure to directly include the mobilized engagements and collaborative practices of people.[40] Since the Umbrella Movement unfolded shortly after the start of the Ferguson protests, where the "hands up, don't shoot" gesture was popularized, the common use of the "hands up" gesture by Hong Kong protesters was, at times, interpreted as signs of cross-movement influence.[41] While the intentionality for using such similar protest gestures is debated, an analytical pivot away from

Figure 6.2 Protestors forming human wall against the police with their hands held up.

intentionality to *potentiality* through Simone's concept of "people as infrastructure" might create generative openings.

To read the embodied gestures as infrastructures allows us to view the practice as mediums (not necessarily means with designated utility) through which affect circulates and transfigures. It prods us to analyze the protest gesture's material form in relation to its capacities to generate aspiration and alter expectations. In *Yellowing*, Chan showcases creative mutations of the protest gesture's material arrangements. An example: close-ups of Sino-scripts of *liangxin* (conscience, 良心) and *gongyi* (*justice*, 公義) inscribed on protestors' held-up hands (see fig. 6.3).

In this scene, protestors reutilize public infrastructures by occupying city streets with their hands held up—a gesture that displays the power imbalance between armed police and unarmed citizens—highlighting and challenging the disparate impact of centralized state governance. The protestors embody affective infrastructures, creating sonic and human walls through song, chants, and gestures; in turn, the Mandarin characters of *liangxin* (conscience, 良心) and *gongyi* (justice, 公義) inscribed on their hands transfigure from descriptive pronouncements to questioning provocations.

While a Sinophonic methodology stresses the plasticity of Sinitic languages circulated on the margins of China and Chineseness, Sinophonic affects can be traced across Chan and Dargan's use of Sino-script. Dargan's incorporation of Sino-script in his poetry unsettles attachments among linguistic articulation, cultural possession, and national mythologies of the United States and China. Similarly, Chan displays how Sino-scripts mutate

Figure 6.3 Hands inscribed with the mandarin characters for "conscience" and "justice" while held up in protest.

in utility through the dissenting bodies of protestors who contest conscriptions by the Chinese state on screen. Here, Sinophonic affects reverberate through Dargan and Chan's work, across medial and positional difference. Solidarities and other desires echo despite the lack of visible or extractable connection.

Conclusion: Sinophonic Affects Across Disciplinarity

Tracing Sinophonic affects through Dargan and Chan's aesthetic arrangements—or the poetics of infrastructure—displays the politics of locating minor-to-minor intimacies. In particular, I've argued that minor transnational intimacies between Dargan and Chan's works emerge through the conjunctive pulls of the Sinophonic and affective. An affective approach to the Sinophonic allows us to recognize the differently entangled emotional structures that challenge the dominance of both ethno-nationalism and the operations of racial capitalism.

In this context, Sinophone works less like a stable discipline or identitarian descriptor; it functions as an activating (or affecting) methodology that instigates critical pathways across institutionalized divides. As a relational model, "Sinophonic affects" traced across *Anagnorisis* and *Yellowing* illustrate linkages between anglophone and Sinophonic inquiry, area studies and ethnic studies, as well as literary and media studies. Moreover, analyzing Sinophonic attachments between the two texts with a focus on material and metaphorical infrastructures puts Sinophone studies' strengths in the humanities in dialogue with the social sciences (e.g., studies of infrastructures in anthropology, sociology, geography, landscape architecture, and communications). Such an "undisciplined" approach to Sinophone-as-methodology demonstrates, perhaps, what Chuh calls "critical promiscuity." Chuh argues for the need to "challenge disciplinary divisions and the continuing stultifying consequences of . . . neoliberal multicultural ideologies," which reproduces the subjugation that accompanies institutionalized definitions of the "human," often against minoritized difference.[42]

The urgency to reorder humanistic inquiry away from exploitative structures of racial capitalism, colonialism, and empire is echoed in Dargan's call to locate "the mutual struggle to govern ourselves and remain human—particularly in the face of late capitalism," which he senses potential transpacific solidarity.[43] Identified as an American in China, or a "'ren'/ (人) from the Beautiful Country," Dargan unsettles associations between humanity (人), beauty (美), and the nation-state (国) through his aesthetic arrangements (e.g., use of transliteration, lineation, and Sino script), or what I've read as "affective infrastructures." To approach Dargan's arrangements of poetic form and Sino-script as that of infrastructure allows us to think of language's unstable and destabilizing affective capacities with its material form. In the case of Dargan's China Cycle, we can trace Sinophonic affects through his poetic infrastructure: an activation of shared "minor chords" through which we can hear "the human fabric unravel and restitch" across *contingent relations* to China and Chinesesness.[44]

Sinophonic affects resonate in *Yellowing* as contingent relations between Umbrella Movement protestors and the Chinese state emerge through affective dissonances in filmic form. Similar to Dargan's poems, *Yellowing* details "infrastructures" in both the material (e.g., city streets, skyscrapers, protestors lined up as human walls) and metaphorical sense (e.g., aesthetic arrangements, sonic and affective vanguards). Echoing how Dargan's poetic infrastructure disperses the circulation of meaning away from state-centered utility, Chan constructs a poetics of infrastructure—more specifically, people as infrastructure—which refracts projections of the Chinese state as a centripetal affective core.

Such Sinophonic relationality can be traced across Dargan and Chan's work precisely due to their contingency both to the Chinese state and to each other. Intimacies emerge that are hard to extract through neoliberal multicultural discourses of either incommensurate cultural difference or easily exchangeable multicultural alliance. To read the two works in relation to each other is to trace affective entanglements that do not hinge on the possession of culture or the accessibility of consumable difference.

An affective approach to Sinophone studies allows Sinophonic inquiry to be defined not only by the language and identity of Sinophone subjects, communities, and cultures but also by the relational pulls among unevenly stratified bodies, discourses, and spaces that are put into contact on the margins of China and Chineseness. Sinophonic affects are mobilized both by the identity of its subjects (individuated subjectivity) and their relations in constituting epistemological and political projects (relational agency). For, if solidarities are affective projects, the Sinophonic activates possibilities across the "what-ifs" and the "yet to come."

Notes

1. I am building off of queer/feminists of color and postcolonial theorists who read affect and emotions as intricately tied processes that are not necessarily detached from social constructions (e.g., race, sex, gender formation) but mobilize *in relation* to it. See Lili Hsieh, "Interpellated by Affect: The Move to the Political in Brian Massumi's *Parables for*

the Virtual and Eve Sedgwick's *Touching Feeling*," *Subjectivity* 23 (2008): 219–235; Clare Hemmings, "Invoking Affect: Cultural Theory and the Ontological Turn," *Cultural Studies* 19, no. 5 (2005): 548–567; Sara Ahmed, *The Cultural Politics of Emotion*, 2nd ed. (New York: Routledge, 2015), 204–233; Lily Wong, *Transpacific Attachments: Sex Work, Media Networks, and Affective Histories of Chineseness* (New York: Columbia University Press, 2018), 8–11.

2. Shu-mei Shih, *Visuality and Identity: Sinophone Articulations Across the Pacific* (Berkeley: University of California Press, 2007), 30.

3. Françoise Lionnet and Shu-mei Shih, *Minor Transnationalisms* (Durham, NC: Duke University Press, 2005), 7, 21.

4. Lisa Lowe, *The Intimacies of Four Continents* (Durham, NC: Duke University Press, 2015), 11.

5. Lowe is alluding to political theorist C. B. Macpherson's concept of the "possessive individual." See C. B. Macpherson, *The Political Theory of Possessive Individualism: From Hobbes to Locke* (Oxford: Clarendon, 1962).

6. Lowe, *The Intimacies of Four Continents*, 18.

7. See Ahmed, *The Cultural Politics of Emotion*; Hemmings, "Invoking Affect"; Hsieh, "Interpellated by Affect"; and Wong, *Transpacific Attachments*.

8. Julia H. Lee, *Interracial Encounters: Reciprocal Representations in African and Asian American Literature, 1896–1937* (New York: New York University Press, 2011), 174.

9. Lee, *Interracial Encounters*, 174.

10. See Clare Jean Kim, "The Racial Triangulation of Asian Americans," in *Asian Americans and Politics: Perspectives, Experiences, Prospects*, ed. Gordon H. Chang (Stanford, CA: Stanford University Press, 2001); Helen Heran Jun, *Race for Citizenship: Black Orientalism and Asian Uplift from Pre-Emancipation to Neoliberal America* (New York: New York University Press, 2011); Heike Raphael-Hernandez and Shannon Steen, eds., *AfroAsian Encounters: Culture, History, Politics* (New York: New York University, 2006), 1–6.

11. Jodi Melamed, "The Spirit of Neoliberalism: From Racial Liberalism to Neoliberal Multiculturalism," *Social Text* 89, no. 4 (2006): 1–24.

12. Melamed, "The Spirit of Neoliberalism," 19.

13. Melamed, "The Spirit of Neoliberalism," 1.

14. Kyle Dargan, Aaliyah Bilal, Afaa Michael Weaver, Bro. Yao, and Lily Wong, "African American Writers on China: A Dialogue," *Asian American Literary Review* 7, no. 1 (Spring 2016): 144–165.

15. Dargan et al., "African American Writers on China," 152–159.

16. For more on the history of African American thinkers who have written about or in relation to China, see Robeson Taj Frazier, *The East Is Black: Cold War China in the Black Radical Imagination* (Durham, NC: Duke University Press, 2015); and Fred Ho and Bill V. Mullen, eds., *Afro Asia: Revolutionary Political and Cultural Connections Between African-Americans and Asian-Americans* (Durham, NC: Duke University Press, 2008).

17. Dargan et al., "African American Writers on China," 157–160.

18. Dargan et al., "African American Writers on China," 154.

19. Dargan et al., "African American Writers on China," 158.

20. Shih, *Visuality and Identity*, 4.

21. Dargan et al., "African American Writers on China," 158.

22. Dargan's 2014 visit was his second trip to China, the first being in 2010; both visits were part of the University of Iowa's Life of Discovery program, a joint program between Iowa's International Writing Program and the Chinese Writers' Association that aimed to bring American and Chinese writers together for international exchange.

23. Dargan, *Anagnorisis: Poems* (Chicago: TriQuarterly, 2018), 62–63.

24. I read the speaker of the poems in the China Cycle as versions or extensions of Dargan's voice. For more discussion about the speaker of the collection in relation to Dargan's voice, see Dolapo Demuran, "Conversations with Contributors: Kyle Dargan," *Adroit Journal*, January 24, 2019.

25. For more on the centrality of language, particularly the tensions between sound and script, in understanding the relationship between the concepts of "Sinophone" and "Chinese," see Jing Tsu, *Sound and Script in Chinese Diaspora* (Cambridge, MA: Harvard University Press, 2010).

26. Dargan notes that the lack of tonal accents in his use of pinyin reflects the "flatness" of his experience with the language as he struggled to hear and speak the range of tones in Mandarin Chinese. See Dargan, *Anagnorisis*, 92.

27. Brian Larkin, "The Politics and Poetics of Infrastructure," *Annual Review of Anthropology* 42 (2013): 327–343, quotation on 328.

28. Larkin, "The Politics and Poetics of Infrastructure," 330.

29. Hannah Appel, Nikhil Anand, and Akhil Gupta, "Introduction: The Infrastructure Toolbox," Society for Cultural Anthropology (website), September 24, 2015, https://culanth.org/fieldsights/introduction-the-infrastructure-toolbox.

30. Dargan, *Anagnorisis*, 68.

31. See Larkin, "The Politics and Poetics of Infrastructure," 329–337; and Appel, Anand, and Gupta, "Introduction: The Infrastructure Toolbox."

32. I am alluding to Jing Tsu's call to take the "phone" in *Sinophone* seriously in her piece "Sinophonics and the Nationalization of Chinese," in *Global Chinese Literature*, ed. Jing Tsu and David Der-wei Wang (Leiden: Brill, 2010), 93–114.

33. Lowe, *The Intimacies of Four Continents*, 18, 11.

34. *Yellowing*, directed by Chan Tze Woon (Japan: Uzumasa, 2018).

35. For more on the relation between developments of infrastructures and state power, see Penelope Harvey, "The Topological Quality of Infrastructural Relation: An Ethnographic Approach," *Theory, Culture & Society* 29 (2012): 76–92; Larkin, "The Politics and Poetics of Infrastructure," 332–334.

36. Larkin, "The Politics and Poetics of Infrastructure," 334.

37. Larkin, "The Politics and Poetics of Infrastructure," 333.

38. Francis L. F. Lee and Joseph M. Chan, *Media and Protest Logics in the Digital Era: The Umbrella Movement in Hong Kong* (New York: Oxford University Press, 2018); Sebastian Veg, "Creating a Textual Public Space: Slogans and Texts from Hong Kong's Umbrella Movement," *Journal of Asian Studies* 75, no.3 (August 2016): 673–702.

39. Veg, "Creating a Textual Public Space," 691.

40. AbdouMaliq Simone, "People as Infrastructure: Intersecting Fragments in Johannesburg," *Public Culture* 16, no. 3 (2004): 407–429.

41. Max Fisher, "Hong Kong's Protesters are Using the Same 'Hands Up, Don't Shoot' Gesture Used in Ferguson," *Vox*, September 28, 2014; Carla Murphy, "'Hands Up, Don't Shoot' in Hong Kong Protests?" *Colorlines*, September 29, 2014.

42. Kandice Chuh, *The Difference Aesthetics Makes: On the Humanities "After Man,"* (Durham, NC: Duke University Press, 2019), 129, 4.

43. Dargan, *Anagnorisis*, 158.

44. Dargan, *Anagnorisis*, 68.

THEORIES,
METHODOLOGIES,
CONTROVERSIES

Geocritical Sinophone and Transgressive Community

YINDE ZHANG

Sinophone studies, which has developed over the past fifteen years under the initiative of Professor Shu-mei Shih and other scholars, is defined as a multidimensional critical field. Shih recalled this feature in her essay, *Against Diaspora*, considering the "Sinophone" as a "method" or even an "episteme" that would open up possibilities for a "critical posture" against "statist and imperialist pressure."[1] Her statements update and heighten a corollary notion, that of "sinophone transgression."[2] The critical and transgressive function that characterizes Sinophone studies likely resonates with geocriticism, for which "transgressivity" is also primordial. Inspired by Henri Lefebvre, Gilles Deleuze, and Michel Serres, among others, Bertrand Westphal describes it as a critical approach that enables the transgression of institutions, ideologies, and normativity by contrasting "smooth space" with "striated space," heterogeneity with homogeneity, and nomadism with immobility.[3] In the wake of postcolonial criticism or the Frankfurt School, such an encounter between geocriticism and Sinophone fields is to be expected, as they both advocate the constant crossing of limits, that of closed, frozen, constrained spaces.[4]

Enhancing relations between the two fields is particularly significant in terms of the renewal of Sinophone studies—all the more so, as priority would be given to the perspective of transgressive community. The shared position against centrality, domination, and hegemony seems to be amplified by extending peripheral antagonism to transversal resistance throughout the "inclusive exclusion" principle,[5] leading to a form of transnational, transstatutory, and translocal solidarity. However, such an alliance would distance itself from the topics of globality, which, in the context of the rapid worldwide growth of Chinese literature, appear not to be immune from the risk of an instrumentalized reterritorialization process favorable to Sino-globalization. In this respect, it would be more relevant to invoke the literary nonplace as a form of extraterritoriality that would assert its autonomy facing any established authority while potentially transcending a necessary but insufficient locatedness. Finally, the protest motive, heir to a certain topographical logic, is intended to evolve toward a critical topology, reconfigured ethos, and relational poetics, making it possible to free the diaspora from its ancillary status by taking advantage of its etymological and dynamic sense of dissemination and by mobilizing all living, nomadic, and unassignable forces.

This paper attempts to show the importance of such a transgressive community. It proposes to review a variety of works from Sinophone writers and artists, whether from the diaspora or the mainland, providing a kind of counterfiction that brings them together against ideology, propaganda, and grand narratives. In contrast to the collective dream, positive storytelling,[6] and the Tianxia demagogy, they unfold a disenchanted way of imagination, revealing an undoubtedly anticentralist, antiexpansionist, and antihegemonic tropism. Such an anti-imperial production is disseminated in literary and transmedia creations spanning over two decades since the end of the last millennium. This study will be focused on the cartographic reconfiguration that presents salient features of their works to point out the ways—premonitorily, retrospectively, and self-reflexively—that fictional shaping disputes and undermines the intention to mystify. In the following analysis of an array of contemporary textual and iconographic examples, I argue that Sinophone studies is meant to transgress hierarchic or hegemonic constraints while surpassing its own limitation by building a heterotopia, an open space and a world of possibility.

Deconstructing Centrality

The first observation in this domain is related to resistance against centrality, which is denounced jointly by writers from Taiwan, Hong Kong, and the mainland. Their variable geographical situation does not prevent them from gathering together to challenge the center by protesting against its legitimacy. The subversive operations involve island rehabilitation, bipolar balance, and cartographic distortion.

Insularity appears to be endowed with a militant dimension with Li-Chin Lin, a French-Taiwanese-born cartoonist. She left the island to study art in France at the Ecole Supérieure de l'Image in Angoulême and then enrolled in the Poudrière School for animation in Valencia. After making short animated films, she turned to comics in 2002. Her first graphic novel, *Formosa* (2011),[7] mixes autobiography framed with historical concerns. Inspired by Marjane Satrapi's graphic novel *Persepolis*, Lin's book reveals its difference through geocentric features. The cartographic representation allows the author to display a bildungsroman involved in the historical movement of the island. For a child who had grown up in a multilingual family that included Japanese-speaking grandparents, a Holo- or Hoklo-speaking father, and a Hakka-speaking mother, an education exclusively in Mandarin was experienced as a constraint. Despite the social promotion it promised, the future artist is haunted by the traumatic memory of a violated plural linguistic identity. The book presents the tongue as being jagged, sewn, or gagged. The pages are covered with stomping boots, strapping chains, or injunctive words. The government imposed so-called Chinese culture on local habitants who were brainwashed and enchained, their hands and feet bound. The island territory is assimilated to a crushed tongue, which is bloody, bandaged, and/or muzzled. Such representation deplores without ambiguity the continental centralism under the rule of Generalissimo Chiang Kai-shek. But by googling and manipulating the map, the author intends less to reverse the scale than to get a better focus on a work of memory. *Formosa* crystallizes the scattered events—the February 28 incident, gatherings in Taipei in support of Tiananmen Square students, and many political and ecological scandals, such as electoral fraud or the spoliation of aboriginal lands. The police violence the narrator was subjected to when she participated in a pro-Tibetan demonstration in Geneva, a democratic city par excellence, is transformed into a universal allegory for liberty and a paradigmatic place of resistance against any undemocratic power and a room of restored verb in favor of safeguarding the spaces of freedom.

Liu Suola, a musician and novelist who lives in Beijing and New York, adopts another strategy to deconstruct centrality by creating a bipolar scheme that provokes neutralizing effects. *Nuzhen tang* (The big island of the pig turtles) (2000) constitutes an irreverent uchronia that insularizes China.[8] The story takes place in the year 4000, two millennia after a cataclysm decimating modern civilizations. China proudly remains standing in the middle of the world. A tribe from the West in search of God arrives at the foot of the Great Wall before occupying, by a decree from the emperor of China, an uninhabited island in the Eastern Sea. The community settles on the island while progressively conquering the power on the mainland, perpetuating the bipolar tradition. The so-called unchanging unitary territory is disproved by the story of immigration and recomposition, extending to the rise, in Los Angeles, around the end of the first century of the fourth millennium, of an atavistic "turtle-pig" clan that unearths the archives of the missing island. The island is a counterpower that counteracts a ponderous matrix and the axial monolith. Furthermore, it is animated by chthonic female voices, shaking phallocratic rationalism, official chronicles, and the myth of irradiation.

Rather than a purely geographical element, insularity actually embodies archipelagic thinking and the ethics of relation, according to Edouard Glissant, who contrasts "the island," a figure of fragmentation, with the "continent," that of totality. It is undoubtedly this archipelagic approach that would have inspired Dung Kai-chung in his attempt to compose a puzzle of places and a network of meanings. The Hong Kong writer precedes Lin and Liu in challenging central domination with a truly cartographic reinvention in his unclassifiable *Atlas* (1997).[9] A multitude of "topia" is associated with a malleable map that may influence a territory. For example, the "transtopia" (*zhuanyi di*) designates a light, foldable, and transportable map, which allows the "transferring" of land or making a territory transferable, as evidenced by the well-known Chinese idiom, "When the map was unrolled the dagger was revealed" (*tuqiong bixian*). Such a plan contrasts with the dense, massive, and ponderous earth while permitting its transformation, as exemplified by Antarctica, a territory subject to projection, deformation, enlargement, or narrowing. In this respect, nothing is more eloquent than the ambivalence of *unitopia*, the term implying a double reading in Chinese "unified/unique" (*tongyi di/duli di*):[10] "unified place"—integral, total, collective—couldn't suppress the "unique," i.e., original, unparalleled, personal one. In other words, any map is a recto-verso copy. On one side, it determines what constitutes the integrity of a place by drawing its delimitation, frame, and contour in differentiating itself from what it is not. On the other side, the scale variation may generate, for a place, a double possibility of integration or autonomy: The enlargement makes it possible to perceive the desire to absorb a place, while the reduced version shows the assertion of its individuality. In fact, the plurality of places in Dung Kai-chung's fiction-essay echoes the idea of "transit": a territory is like a meteor, always in motion and in transit, dissolving the weighty matrix. Paradoxically, multiplication leads to a form of "extraterritoriality" (*wailing shuxing*),[11] which contains canceling effects: the "Map of South China" made in 1850 by an anonymous Chinese author shows a big expanse of water instead of the current Hong Kong Island so as to mean, against the British occupation, that "places that do not exist could not be occupied."

Routing Expansionism

The second approach, which is parallel to the anticentralist one, is criticism of territorial expansion. The authors proceed by allegory and rewriting, as cartography rejects territorializing power with contempt, derision, or farce. Beneath irenic appearances and the permanence of debonair myths hides a picture saturated with motives of conquest, colonization, and hegemony. Imaginary cartography brings them to light by demonstrating an inescapable ending of implosion, disruption, and disintegration.

Yan Lianke, well known for his "mytho-realism," formulates sharp criticism against the delusions of grandeur that strike the Chinese collective unconscious today. In *Zhalie Chronicles* (2013), he achieves an allegorical fresco on unbridled developmentalism by imagining a supreme megalopolis born from the hypertrophy of a lost village through thundering prosperity comparable to a cancerous outgrowth. Cartography comes to bring this megalomania to its culmination. Mingyao, the mayor's brother, spends most of his time wandering in the midst of two bronze globes and two gigantic sand tables while hesitating to give a coup de grace to a dying America and a decaying Europe.[12] However, this irrepressible will to conquer cannot escape a blowout before great destiny unfolds. As suggested by the state-village's name, Zhalie, in this eponymous novel, the Sodom that emerges from such uncontrolled and hideous dilatation is fated to be consumed by explosion, dislocation, and evaporation.

The rhetoric of breaking joins that of implosion with authors who opt to revisit some founding myths and legends. Liu Cixin, who stands out in science fiction, seizes the legendary figure of Zheng He (1371–1433) to create a postcolonial fable in "The Western Oceans" (1999).[13] This alternative story, published four years before Gavin Menzies's controversial book, reimagines the discovery of America made by the Muslim eunuch admiral in 1420 and its contemporary fallout. The short story recounts what is happening five centuries later: A Chinese diplomat leaves office in Belfast after the handover of Northern Ireland, a Chinese colony, to England. A new post at the UN is waiting for him in New York, while a commemorative duty delays his departure from Europe. He takes time to meditate, in his son's company, on the heroic "Battle of Paris" in December 1421, which would have seen Zheng He fight out the Allied Army sent by Henry V of England, the duke of Burgundy, and the Holy Roman Empire. From there, the winner would have set sail westward before reaching America, the new Chinese continent, whose lasting wealth contrasts with a miserable Europe. In this adventure story, the colonial past is connected with a contemporary event thanks to a discreet but explicit temporal clue—July 1, 1997. The retrocession in question is then reflected in that of Hong Kong to the People's China in an ironic chiasm that is not without cross-reference to an imperial alternance: By recovering Northern Ireland, England would have perpetuated its imperialist heritage, while by regaining Hong Kong, China would apply a similar method with little concern about the latter's statutory autonomy.

Nevertheless, Liu Cixin refrains from making his alternative narrative a simple protest text. Rather, he seeks to shift the issue that, until now, was focused on the dichotomy between military conquest and commercial mission. His fiction appears, instead, to be more complex. It is built against the model of an adventure novel by showing the impasse at which all imperial pretension inevitably falls. The destination and return are equally invalidated, highlighting the idea of dispossession at the expense of any appropriating will. Here, the reminder of the admiral's eunuch identity acquires an abortive value over the conquering expedition. The physical mutilation, a sign of deficiency in terms of valor, reveals not so much his "vulnerability" as the impossibility of completing the task, linking roads, and mapping routes. Certainly, part of the expeditionary fleet would have crossed the Bering Strait and succeeded in ten years in "closing the world of the great Ming Dynasty's empire where the sun never sets."[14] However, Zheng He would have gone on to the "new continent" definitively as a "foreigner," ruining any glorifying plan for settling or circumnavigation.

The aborted adventure metaphorizes the "rout" of the totalization project, which Han Song tackles, too. As a sci-fi writer, he attacks another symbolic platform by performing a facelift of walls instead of refreshing nautical charts. In "The Great Wall" (2002),[15] a counterfactual fiction, he dismantles its self-protection myth while breaking the chain of expansion it seems to build. The story begins with the discovery of a wall section from beneath the Pentagon destroyed by a terrorist bombing in 2001. A succession of analog detection follows across America and progressively around the world. A belt is formed, like a shield, protecting the planet from any hostility, extending to put an end to wars since these sensational findings seem to accelerate the conclusion of an armistice in Iraq and the dissolution of NATO. The irony is conspicuous because it denotes the author's way of recalling the primordial military function of the construction, to deprecate the cultural vulgate, which tends to assimilate architectural magnificence to irenic beauty. This horizontal widespread network actually recalls Kafka's parable, which reveals a transcendental imperial power aspiring to compete with God for its ambition of totalization.[16] But whatever the overbearingness is, it would never be fulfilled with a connected chain. On the contrary, as once again suggested by Kafka, it would always imply division and fragmentation, making any initiative of totalization impossible.

Disintegrating Hegemony

In addition to these anticentralist and antiexpansionist approaches, the third way one can observe in the literary and artistic imagination consists of sensitive cartography, which contributes to disintegrating the massive symbolic body of an infatuated and reconquering nation. Initiatives have been undertaken to dismantle, purge, and move through attempts of dislocation, self-release, and nomadic movement. The disrupting efforts are perceived as a kind of disincarnating act. That is, at least, what Huang Yong Ping's monumental installation, *Empires*, showed at the Grand Palais in May 2016.[17] A 254-meter-long metal reptile was put alongside a chain of containers facing a giant Napoleonic bicorn hat. The exhibition's name underscores the overlap of historical and renascent empires: The dragon awakened before the great wall of goods in contemplation of the emperor of yesteryear. But gigantism seems like a trompe-l'oeil given the empty containers, fossilized carapace, and especially the spectral hat, which, rather than palpable majesty, appears like ghostly supremacy. The juxtaposition of an inert mass, a disembodied mastodon, and a faceless accessory establishes as much the vanity of power as the fragility of the scarecrow. Such a desymbolizing representation aims to undermine the fantasy of extension and glory, such as shown by a plethora of spontaneous or ordered "patriotic" productions. For example, Cai Guoqiang, a "correct nationalist" (a qualification that he boasts of[18]), created a 1993 pyrotechnic work, *Extend the Great Wall*. It consisted of extending the latter over ten kilometers, beyond the ultimate Jiayu Pass, going as far as the Gobi Desert. This performance is part of a series that is humbly baptized *Project for Extraterrestrials*, conceiving the Great Wall as representative of the whole of humanity or earthlings, licensed to dialogue with aliens.

Han Song shares Huang Yong Ping's skepticism by operating a self-reflexive geo-fiction, which reveals a huge exorcist and liberating virtue. In *Gastronotopia* (2011),[19] he describes a country named Nine Regions, alias Middle Kingdom, to demonstrate that, facing endemic overabundance, its subjects have no choice but to "eat to eat" by means of a stomach prosthesis. These happy, chosen people of the Celestial Empire engage from then on in "humanitarian aid" by attending to the export of their vomit in order to rescue a scrawny England. The new Pantagruelian ogre who spits on the wretched old giant indicates a repulsive revanchism as well as the imperious "abjection,"[20] it is to say rejection out of the body for this imbued Cocagne, as already decried by Mo Yan in *The Republic of Wine*.[21]

In all these cases, it is a question of reinventing a map. Han Han, an unrepentant blogger, tears the old and chauvinistic charts that exclude heterogeneity and diversity.[22] Qiu Zhijie invents new ones. The subtle variations of the world that he tirelessly reconfigures with ink wash are anything but the crystallization of self, the obsession of totality, the fantasy of mastery. The collection *Mapping the World* (2015) seems to be invested with a visual tension between fixation and distancing.[23] The reiterated denominational act on

China could be perceived as ambiguous because of its obsessive and complacent aspects. But it is also the indicator of defetishizing and desubstantializing exertions because of allusions to self-disapproval. The repetition may overlap and saturate while helping submerge and evacuate. The names expose various ideas of utopia: In the northeast of the planet are juxtaposed the Heavenly Kingdom of Peace, the Book of Great Unity, and the Penglai Islands, but they are located in a world that is itself utopian, as evidenced by *Map of Utopia*." Utopianizing the utopia transcends simple dialectic and becomes a deliberately ironic gesture when a pretentious touch of color is added to the onomastic game. A fine melting provokes a semantic shift, which permits the term *world* to be assimilated into a Sinicized universe: "Confucianist Harmonious World" or "Chinese Harmonious World," which is unanimously placed under a "Chinese Sky" and integrated into a globe saturated with "so-called Messiahs."[24] Such egotistic arrogance could not be extricated without the "fabulous" attitude peculiar to the artist-geographer.[25] The ink dilutes narcissistic rigidity while the brush brings out the plasticity of the world. Against the roads, belts, and railway networks prevail the hazards of scale, designations, and positions. There is no victorious markup but eccentric topology that celebrates the "extra-vagance" that implies heterogeneous knowledge, unknown paths, and fantastic encounters.[26]

In substance, the transterritorial Sinophone alliance relies on such writers and artists who actually are "*pantoporos* men," those who are "capable of taking all roads, including prohibited ones"[27] to transform a static and marginalized diaspora into a dynamic and militant nomadism. Far from the ideological utopia, that of all under heaven, China-world, or Sino-globalizing planet, the deterritorialized, fragmented, and "enervated" spaces problematize the grand narrative about the rebirth of the nation, the dream of totality and unitary power, as Chan Koonchung ironically reveals through the portrait of a contemporary "Marco Polo the Small" who is subservient to the atavistic Middle Kingdom.[28] One can't help but wonder if this geocriticism coincides with the reflection of Dung Kai-chung,[29] after Jorge Luis Borges and Umberto Eco, on the map 1/1,[30] insofar as the promoters of all under the heaven are probably reproducing the same mistakes as imperial cartographers owing to the excessiveness of a chimerical representation that is doomed to be ruined. The spaces imagined by our writers and artists are closer to Calvino, for whom insight, through Marco Polo's device, makes the Great Khan understand the vanity of his conquest less because of the impossibility for the suzerain to visit the whole empire than the necessity of conceiving the world as constituted of elsewhere, the multiple and the random.[31] But Calvino also warns us that the invisible is both consubstantial with the unknown and the unpredictable. In this respect, our Sinophone literature is iconoclastic by shaking the collective dream from out of a self-centered Imago Mundi, which is convinced of the principle of the known, the controlled, and the uniform. It especially alerts us to sea serpents (the old chestnut) by reminding us of the virtue of a certain medieval cartography that has lost nothing of its acuteness in the current globalized world with its inscription *Hic sunt dragones*, "Here are dragons":[32] The danger does not come so much from terra incognita as from our unconsciousness or stammering but insufficient consciousness of its power of bewitchment.

Conclusion

Writers and artists, such as those mentioned above, transcend or surpass geographical, ideological, and idiosyncratic restrictions in both critical and (auto)reflexive ways. This general and permanent "transgressivity" confirms the essential aspects related to the Sinophone field while opening some new perspectives. First, it confirms the relevance of the alliance of inside and outside, justified by an efficient common resistance to authority, hierarchy, and hegemony, from as much peripheral as internal opposition. The second reflection is on the criticism of the empire, which must be paradigmatic of that of any system of domination and abuse of power instead of the simple rejection of sinocentrism, as repeatedly highlighted by Shu-mei Shih.[33] In this respect, the geocritical Sinophone would permit the accentuation of transversal approaches since vigilance is necessary over any regime, whether democratic or nondemocratic, for its liberticidal complicity. The third point that would exemplify Sinophone studies seems to lie in its self-surpassing ability, as conservatism, complacency, or compromise are omnipresent, requiring literature to be a battleground against both external power and inner demons. One could recall Han Song's contribution to a flag-waving book,[34] or Qiu Zhijie's link to propagandist discourse.[35] Uncertainties, inconsistencies, and queries precisely transform literary and artistic practices into tension fields or a kind of heterotopia, a space involving the alterity, i.e., critical distance, (auto-)transgressivity, and plurivocality. Their works at least demonstrate the battle against the imposed or spontaneous imperialist temptation. Indeed, what is at stake in a Go game played by the Americans confronted with a Chinese team coming to save America, if not the common fate of sinking into a planetary catastrophe?[36] Is there something similar between the maps in ink by Qiu Zhijie as eccentric and "extra-vagant" "geographer" and the anachronistic "Mongolian Map" of the sixteenth century in the testimony of the Silk Road?[37]

Undoubtedly, there lies the responsibility of Chinese-speaking geocriticism, which, henceforth, must articulate itself with the major issues of the planet, such as ecological crisis or all other challenges facing humankind in the twenty-first century. It is no coincidence that Wu Ming-yi, Chen Qiufan, and Hao Jingfang, each in their own way, thematize the disaster through the common image of waste.[38] They simply seem to join and confirm a general movement where environmental literature will be in the twenty-first century what committed literature was in the twentieth. But it is undermined by an underlying planetary thought that is more ethical and, therefore, more political, as defined by Spivak. For her, the "planet" must be considered rather as a "catachresis," as synonymous with an awareness of otherness, which goes beyond the global—material, tangible, and homogeneous—to reveal a comprehensive but not identical entity.[39] Furthermore, still according to Spivak, to address the "new imperial competitions," the diaspora must meet the challenge of *unheimlich* by "detranscendalizing" cultural origin in order to attempt mysterious and discontinuous experiences, including those of the impossible.[40]

Sinophone literature is shot through with a tension that imposes on such a planetary fiction the work of transfiguration against resurgent ethno-statism, myth of civilization, and fallacious cosmopolitanism. Like Liu Cixin's *Three-Body Problems*,[41] Luo Yijun explores in *Ming dynasty* the imagination of failed civilizations.[42] But the narrative modalities seem to diverge as well as the ethical questionings: The law of the jungle persists, even in a hypothetical mode, in Liu's space opera, while Luo's uchonic fantasy is rather characterized by meanderings and wanderings. On the one hand, an impetuous epic novel, which makes triumph the implacable logic of survival, and, on the other, a weak, amendable, remediable story where the diving into history rhymes with the descent to the bottom of oneself, in some way, a democratic fiction that mixes the representation of fragmented meaning with the questioning of narrative authority. Like Roberto Bolaño,[43] Luo chooses to be exiled from not a country, nor a continent, nor even a local history but an increasingly globalized world—namely, a network that ruins the possible by its measurable ambitions, statistics, and algorithms: He favors the imaginary of possibilities by crossing the territories of evil.

In brief, it is the "topophrenia,"[44] an uneasy awareness of a world in crisis, that the narrative illustrates, referring somewhat to Adorno's negative utopia, insofar as the elsewhere brings a critical look at the triumphalist present. Lucid spatiality makes it possible to thwart the trap of both teleological and alternate times by provoking the literary apocalypse since, as shown in *A Mass for Dream of the Red Chamber* by Chen Chuncheng,[45] the decline of a dynasty, for instance, the Ming, reveals the advent and inalienability of a masterpiece. The King is dead. Long live Literature. Ultimately, Sinophone geocriticism can only reinvent itself if it succeeds in renewing its ability to confront two cartographic models—as they are inscribed in the *Shanhai jing*: static and spatial, on the one hand, and dynamic and sequential, on the other[46]—which are expected to inspire a kind of third space,[47] a transterritorial, creative and free one. The Tribute of Yu (Yugong 禹貢) supposed to justify the imperial order because of its discriminatory circumscription could never erase the "Paces of Yu" (Yubu 禹步), which, instead of cadastralizing, ordering, and hierarchizing, lead to diversify, vivify, and enchant the world.

Notes

1. Shu-mei Shih, *Fan lisan (Against Diaspora: Discourses on Sinophone Studies)* (Taipei: Lianjing, 2017), 50.

2. See Mirana May Szeto, "Intra-Local and Inter-Local Sinophone: Rhizomatic Politics of Hong Kong Writers Saisai and Wong Bik-wan," in *Sinophone Studies. A Critical Reader*, ed. Shu-mei Shih, Chien-hsin Tsai, and Brian Bernards (New York: Columbia University Press, 2013), 198.

3. Bertrand Westphal, *Geocriticism: Real and Fictional Spaces*, trans. Robert T. Tally Jr. (New York: Palgrave Macmillan, 2011), 37–74. See also *Geocritical Explorations. Space, Place, and Mapping in Literary and Cultural Studies*, ed. Robert T. Tally Jr. (New York: Palgrave Macmillan, 2011).

4. Shu-mei Shih proposes "the notion of the artistic arc as a way to connect artworks, spaces, events, and issues—or nodal points of meaning—across a specific trajectory in world history." Shu-mei Shih, "From World History to World Art: Reflections on New Geographics of Feminist Arts," in *Territories and Trajectories: Cultures in Circulation*, ed. Diana Sorensen (Durham, NC: Duke University Press, 2018), 206.

5. Inspired by Eileen Chang's "include me out," in reference to Samuel Goldwyn's famous formula, David Der-wei Wang recommends " including China out." David Der-wei Wang, "Zhongwen xiezuo de yuejie yu huigui: Tan huayu yuxi wenxue" (The transboundary and return of Chinese-language writing: On Sinophone literature), *Shanghai wenxue* (Shanghai literature) 9 (2006): 91–93. See also Zhang Ailing, "Ba wo baokuo zaiwai" (Include me out), in *Wangran ji* (Perplexity), ed. Zhang Ailing (Taipei: Huangguan wenhua chuban gongsi, 2010), 123–124. This posture of committed refusal instead of distant protestation seems to move on a more global vision. See Jing Tsu and David Der-wei Wang, "Introduction: Global Chinese Literature," in *Global Chinese Literature Critical Essays* (Leiden: Brill, 2010), 1–13.

6. See, for example, the recurrent slogan *Jiang hao Zhongguo zhege gushi* (China's story should be correctly told) by exploiting the *zheng nengliang* (positive energy), initiated by Xi Jinping, "Zai wenyi gongzuo zuotanhui shang de jianghua" (speech at the conference on literary and artistic work, Beijing, October 15, 2014), http://www.xinhuanet.com/politics/2015-10/14/c_1116825558.htm.

7. Li-Chin Lin, *Formosa* (Bussy-Saint-Georges: Ca et Là, 2011). A Chinese version was published in Taiwan by Li-Chin Lin's own adaptation. Lin Lijing, *Wo de qingchun. Wo de Formosa* (My youth and my formosa) 2 volumes (Xinbeishi : Wuxian chuban, 2012). For excerpts in English, see Li-Chin Lin, "Tongue-Tied," trans. Edward Gauvin, Words Without Borders

(website), February 25, 2013, https://wordswithoutborders.org/read/article/2013-02/tongue-tied/.

8. Liu Suola, *Nüzhen tang* (The big island of the pig turtles) (Fuzhou: Haixia wenyi chubanshe, 2003).

9. Dung Kai-chung, *Ditu ji* (*Atlas: Archeology of an Imaginary City*) (Taipei : Lianjing, 2011).

10. Dung, *Ditu ji*, 56–57

11. Dung, *Ditu ji*, 34–37

12. Yan Lianke, *The Explosion Chronicles* (*Zhalie zhi*), trans. Carlos Rojas (London: Vintage, 2018), 291–293, 439–440.

13. Liu Cixin, "Xiyang" ("The Western Oceans"), in *Meng zhi hai* (*Sea of Dream*) (Chengdu: Sichuan kexue jishu chubanshe, 2015).

14. Liu, "Xiyang," 41.

15. Han Song, "Changcheng" (The great wall), Nunu shufang https://www.kanunu8.com/book3/6503/129643.html, 2002.

16. Franz Kafka, "The Great Wall of China," trans. Ian Johnston, Johnstonia Texts (website), last updated June 11, 2015, http://johnstoniatexts.x10host.com/kafka/greatwallofchinahtml.html.

17. Huang Yong Ping, *Monumenta 2016/Empires*, Grand Palais, Paris, May 8–June 18, 2016, https://www.grandpalais.fr/fr/evenement/monumenta-2016-huang-yong-ping.

18. Pan Ge, "Cai Guoqiang : Wo meiyou bian, wo reng shi ge zhengque de minzuzhuyi zhe" (Cai Guoqiang: I have not changed, I remain a "correct nationalist"), *New York Times* (Chinese edition), August 12, 2013, https://cn.nytimes.com/culture/20130812/cc12caiguoqiang/.

19. Han Song, "Meishi wutuobang" (Gastronotopia), *Shishang Xiansheng* (Squire) (June 2011): 20–23.

20. Julia Kristeva, *Powers of Horror*, trans. Leon S. Roudiez (New York: Columbia University Press, 1982).

21. Mo Yan, *The Republic of Wine*, trans. Howard Goldblatt (London: Hamish Hamilton, 2000).

22. Han Han, a writer and racing driver, is critical of the chauvinism of his compatriots through his self-deprecation. In the mind of someone like him who walked from the polar village in Mohe in the north until the meridional extremity of Hainan Island, so for one who "did tread all the latitudes of the world "any other country should be given its rightful place only on longitudes." Han Han, "Yaoke fang Tai ji" (Travel notes of a distinguished guest), Sina (blog), December 18, 2012 http://blog.sina.com.cn/s/blog_4701280b0102edcd.html.

23. See his series *Mapping the Word* on his website: http://www.qiuzhijie.com/worksleibie/huihua/2015%20dajihua/e-ditu.htm.

24. See People Claimed to be Messiah Crowding History, Qui Zhijie (website), accessed January 21, 2024, http://www.qiuzhijie.com/worksleibie/huihua/2015%20dajihua/e-ditu.htm.

25. In a work named *Meet Myself in the World*, ink on paper, 2014, Qiu Zhijie populates different sites with fabulous animals partially inspired by *The Classic of Mountains and Seas*, such as Xingtian, teacher, community, mirror, day of being refused, calm, etc., in describing his personal, moral, and emotional states.

26. Clément Rosset, *Le Réel. Traité de l'idiotie* (Paris: Les Editions de Minuit, 2004), 23.

27. Bertrand Westphal, "Entre postmodernisme et post-humanisme: l'espace," *COMPAR(A)ISON* I–II (2014 [2018]): 11.

28. Chan Koonchung (Chen Guanzhong), "Make Boluo" (Marco Polo), *China Digital Times*, February 6, 2018, https://chinadigitaltimes.net/chinese/2018/02/%E9%99%88%E5%86%A0%E4%B8%AD%E6%94%BF%E6%B2%BB%E5%B0%8F%E8%AF%B4%E3%80%8A%E9%A9%AC%E5%8F%AF%E6%B3%A2%E7%BD%97%E3%80%8B%EF%BC%88%E5%85%A8%E6%96%87%EF%BC%89/.

29. Dung Kai-chung, "Dishangdi" (Supertopia), in *Ditu ji*, 44–46.

30. "In that empire, the art of cartography attained such perfection that the map of a single province occupied the entirety of a city, and the map of the empire, the entirety of a province. In time, those unconscionable maps no longer satisfied, and the cartographers guilds struck a map of the empire whose size was that of the empire, and which coincided point for point with it. The following generations, who were not so fond of the study of cartography as their forebears had been, saw that that vast map was useless, and not without some pitilessness was it, that they delivered it up to the inclemencies of sun and winters. In the deserts of the west, there are tattered ruins of that map, inhabited by animals and beggars, in all the land there is no other relic of the disciplines of geography." Jorge Luis Borges, "On Exactitude in Science" in *Collected Fictions*, trans. Andrew Hurley (New York: Viking Penguin, 1998), 325. See also Umberto Eco, "On The Impossibility of Drawing a Map of the Empire on a Scale of 1 to 1" in *How to Travel With a Salmon and Other Essays*, trans. William Weaver (New York: Harcourt Brace, 1994), 95–106; and Lewis Carroll, *Sylvie and Bruno Concluded*, chapter 11, "The Man in the Moon" (London: Macmillan and Co, 1893), 162–174.

31. Italo Calvino, *Invisible Cities*, trans. William Weaver (London: Vintage, 1997).

32. The term is found on the Hunt-Lenox Globe (around 1510) housed by the New York Public Library. It coincides with the eastern coast of Asia.

33. Shih, *Fan lisan*, 223–245.

34. Li Xiguang, Liu Kang, et al., *Yaomohua Zhongguo de beihou* (Behind the demonization of China) (Beijing: Zhongguo shenhui kexue chubanshe, 1996).

35. During one of his recent exhibitions organized by Confucius Institute in Nantes, he tends to advocate Zhao Tingyang's "inclusive utopia" through ambiguous language. See https://asialyst.com/fr/2019/02/14/chine-monde-selon-qiu-zhijie-exposition-nantes-institut-confucius/.

36. Han Song, *Huoxing zhaoyao mei guo* (Red star over America) (Shanghai: Renmin chubanshe, 2012).

37. Qiu Zhijie defines himself as an extravagant "geographer": "I am the detective of paths. That's why every place is my homeland. " "Jiling Theater Portraits, 2010–2016" in *Journeys without Arrivals* (Genève: Mousse Publishing, Centre d'Art Contemporain, 2017), 87. It is a text that accompanies an engraving entitled *Geographer* showing a funny char-compass. The artistic cartography contrasts with the governmental approach: a 30-meter-long roll of silk painting called "Mongolian Map of Mountains and Waters" (Menggu shanshui ditu, Ming Dynasty, sixteenth century) and presenting different sites from the Jiayu Pass to Tianfang (Mecca), was acquired by donation in early 2018 by the Museum of the Forbidden City. In a ceremonial presentation with great pomp to the public, the work was rebaptised "Map of Mountains and Waters Along the Silk Road" (Silu shanshui ditu). Echoing with the

propaganda on the New Silk Road or one belt, one road, it ostentatiously dismisses the crying anachronism on the both historical and denominational level: Abandoned under Ming, the "Silk Road" is a name forged by the German geographer Ferdinand von Richthofen at the end of the nineteenth century.

38. Wu Ming-yi (Wu Mingyi), *Fuyan ren* (The man with the compound eyes), trans. Darryl Sterk (London: Harvill Secker, 2013); Chen Qiufan, *Huangchao* (Waste tide), trans. Ken Liu (New York: Tor Books, 2019); Hao Jingfang, *Beijing zhedie* (Folding Beijing), trans. Ken Liu, in *Invisible Planets: An Anthology of Contemporary Chinese SF in Translation*, ed. Ken Liu (New York: Tor Books, 2016), 219–261.

39. Gayatri Chakravorty Spivak, *Death of a Discipline* (New York: Columbia University Press, 2003), 72.

40. Spivak, *Death of a Discipline*, 86, 102.

41. Liu Cixin, *Santi* (The three-body problem), trans. Ken Liu (New York: Tor Books, 2014); *Hese senlin* (The dark forest), trans. Joel Martinsen (New York: Tor Books, 2015); and *Sishen yongsheng* (Death's end), trans. Ken Liu (New York: Tor Books, 2016).

42. Luo Yijun, *Mingchao* (Ming dynasty) (Taipei: Jing wenxue gufen youxian gongsi, 2019).

43. Roberto Balanō, *2666: A Novel*, trans. NatashaWimmer (New York: Farrar, Straus and Giroux, 2008).

44. Robert Tally, *Topophrenia: Place, Narrative, and the Spatial Imagination* (Bloomington: Indiana University Press, 2019).

45. Chen Chuncheng, *Hongloumeng misa* (A mass for dream of the red chamber), in *Yewan de qianshuiting* (A night submarine) (Shanghai: Sanlian shudian, 2020), 145–194.

46. Vera V. Dorofeeva-Lichtmann, "Conception of Terrestrial Organization in the Shan hai jing Author(s)", *Bulletin de l'École française d'Extrême-Orient* 82 (1995): 57–110

47. Edward William Soja, *Thirdspace: Journeys to Los Angeles and Other Real-and-Imagined Places* (Oxford: Basil Blackwell, 1996).

Sinophone Postloyalism

DAVID DER-WEI WANG

In the wake of Shih's groundbreaking work *Visuality and Identity: Sinophone Articulations Across the Pacific*, there have been waves of attempts to rethink the conditions of Sinophone literature, its spatiotemporal boundaries, its methodological feasibility, and above all, its geopolitical and geopoetic implications. In this essay, I engage with Sinophone Chinese literary studies in three directions. First, I review the strengths and limitations of the extant model proffered by Shih, which is largely predicated on postcolonialism. Second, instead of the postcolonial model, which stresses the politics of spatiality, I introduce postloyalism as a way to tease out the historical bearings of Sinophone discourse, thereby calling forth its inherent politics of temporalities. Third, with fictional examples drawn from Taiwan, Hong Kong, and Malaysia, I highlight the textual and spatial loci where postcolonial and postloyalist inscriptions are intertwined with each other and contend that these loci generate some of the most perplexing Sinophone conditions for further deliberation.

A coinage in the vein of terms such as *Anglophone, Francophone*, and *Hispanophone, Sinophone* was first used in the late twentieth century to refer to the state of "Chinese speaking" or a "Chinese speaking person." Shih brought to the fore the term's colonial undertone, thus igniting its critical power. She contends that, just as is the case of Anglophone, Francophone, or Hispanophone articulations, Sinophone brings to mind the colonizing and colonized conditions in greater China in military, economic, and cultural terms. She criticizes the Han-centered Chinese language policy and the canonical structure of Chinese literature and assigns *Sinophone* to those texts that have been given the "torturous and confusing nomenclature 'literature in Chinese' (*huayu wenxue* 華語文學) as opposed to 'Chinese literature' (*Zhongguo wenxue* 中國文學) written inside China)."[1]

In Shih's endeavor, one can discern a complex range of theoretical attempts, from postcolonial criticism to minority studies, from humanist Marxism to multiculturalism. Of these theories, postcolonialism stands out as her main stake. Shih tackles the common wisdom that colonialism is a modern political and economic maneuvering undertaken only by Western imperialist powers. She calls attention to three types of Chinese colonialism. First, instead of maritime expeditions, the Qing engaged in multiple military and political actions on the borders and adjacent areas of inland China and, as a result, commanded immense territory on the Asian continent. Accordingly, the Qing was an empire thriving on "continental colonialism," and its legacy was inherited by the Republic of China (ROC) and the People's Republic of China (PRC). Second, although the Qing did not develop overseas colonies, the way it ruled minorities *within* the territory of China, making them cower to the hegemonic culture, amounts to "internal colonialism." This phenomenon finds a modern counterpart in contemporary China's rule in areas such as Tibet and Xinjiang. Third, the large influx of Chinese to a target place of immigration may form an emergent force over time, such that it affects local institutional, political, economic, and even demographic structure. Hence, it gives rise to "settler colonialism." Shih's research concludes with the claim that the Sinophone subjectivity is predicated on the disavowal of diaspora. If diaspora studies focuses on issues such as the loss of roots and the yearning for homecoming, Sinophone studies, according to Shih, seeks to pin down the "expiration date" of diaspora.[2]

Shih has made an enormous contribution to Sinophone studies, in particular, her observations of the manifold individual voices, regional soundings, dialectical accents, and local expressions—alternative "mother tongues"— that are in constant negotiation with the standardized, official national language. Meanwhile, her approaches also point to areas where additional critical efforts are desired. Whereas Shih's distinction between (socialist) China and the Sinophone world unwittingly duplicates the polarized agenda of the Cold War era, her support of the politically and ethnically underprivileged embraces a "classic" humanism in both leftist and liberal veins. *Colonialism* has been used as a blanket term to describe variegated forms of conquest, oppression, and hegemony in such a way as to lose its historical specificity and critical rigor. For one thing, in view of the fact that the Qing is an empire established by the Manchus, who by Shih's definition should have been labeled a minority, how do we deal with the paradox that the Han-ethnicity-centered China under the Qing rule is already a colonized polity while exerting its colonial power over other ethnicities? Shih's critique of "settler colonialism" brings into view the predatory side of the narrative of "Chinese diaspora," but it may at the same time downplay the existential circumstance, for good or ill, that underlies overseas Chinese's need for linguistic and ethnic solidarity. Finally, although her concept of "anti-diaspora" projects a desired horizon of multicultural assimilation, the global immigration history, as illustrated by the Hakka and the Jewish people, belies any sanguine belief in the immigrant subjectivity's unilateral "plasticity" in joining a new society.

I would suggest that, despite her interventional efforts, Shih does not go far enough to confront the most polemical dimension of Sinophone studies. In my view, for a Sinophone project to exert its critical potential, one must not engage merely with the domain of conventional overseas Chinese literature plus ethnic literature on the mainland. Rather, one should test its power *within* the nation-state of China. In light of the translingual dynamics on the global scale, one needs to reimagine the cartography of the Chinese center versus the periphery so as to enact a new linguistic and literary arena of contestations. As a matter of fact, to truly subvert the foundation of Chinese national literature, we should no longer consider it apart from the Sinophone literary system. My argument actually derives from Shih's logic. If "Chinese" is not a homogenized entity but a constellation of Sinitic utterances amid the flux of historical changes, a Sinophone scholar can conclude that even the official Han language, however standardized by the state, comprises complex soundings and transformations, therefore, subject to the rhizomic tapestry of Sinoglossia.

Moreover, Shih's discourse treats the Sinophone as a modern phenomenon, resulting from the fragmentation of China when challenged by modern forces. While acknowledging her observations on issues from immigration to diaspora, colonialism, and nationalism, I call for a more serious inquiry into the historical implication of Sinophone discourse, and instead of postcolonialism, I propose the model of postloyalism.[3]

Postloyalism is a coinage derived from a critical reflection on loyalism, or *yimin* 遺民, a unique political and cultural discourse in Chinese history. The term *yimin* originally meant "one who remains loyal to a former dynasty and is ashamed to serve a new dynasty when a change in state power occurs."[4] In Chinese, it is a compound of *yi* 遺—to leave behind or the leftover—and *min* 民—people or subjects. Loyalism is a discourse premised on the politics of anachrony and displacement. When a political subject of ancient times insists on retaining their bereavement for a fallen dynasty or a lost culture against all odds, loyalist sentiment abounds. There underlies a paradox in loyalism, however, as it derives its claim to legitimacy, be it political, cultural, emotional, or ethical, from a reluctant awareness of the loss of that legitimacy. In other words, loyalism gestures toward the belatedness of time and yet gains an unlikely agency in the hope of restoring that which is forever lost. Caught between the desire for the past to be realized in the future and the future to be restored to the past, loyalist plays out a unique politics of time "in fold."

The etymological root of *yi* already contains a sematic ambiguity. *Yi* suggests losing something (*yishi* 遺失) while, at the same time, it means the leaving of something (*canyi* 殘遺); the former points to a total loss, the latter a leftover or a remnant. But *yi* also means giving or bequeathing (*yiliu* 遺留), implying leaving someone a thing or a gift. The three meanings of *yi* speak to the complex historical and affective syndrome that is loyalism: Thrown into the abysmal condition of dynastic cataclysm, a political subject feels entrenched in an irrecoverable loss of their affiliations while cherishing all the more his or her identity as a survivor, a remnant of the loss; more engagingly, they are compelled to preserve the loss as a legacy, a gift, from the past into the future despite the historical fact that suggests otherwise.

When one comes to *post*loyalism, something more complex arises. The prefix *post*, as I am using here, partakes of a postmodernist undertone. Literally, *postloyalism* refers to that which happens, in conceptual, affective, and political terms, *after* loyalism. But insofar as loyalism already implies temporal posteriority and a resultant sense of mourning and nostalgia, the *post* of *postloyalism* doubles the temporal and psychological complexity inherent in loyalism. It could mean either that which is over with or that which is subsequent to loyalism. More intriguingly, in line with the postmodern subversion of the causal sequence of time, *post* loyalism could point to an anticipatory revisioning of the past on behalf of the future, therefore implying a reopening of the pastness of the past. As such, the *post* of *postloyalism* refers to a desire for a timeline that comes prior, rather than posterior, to the extant historical closure: It implies the (renewed) beginning rather than the ending of a desired history.

As a political identity, the loyalist tradition goes back to ancient times. When King Wu (reign 1046–1043 BC) of Zhou (1046–256 BC) conquered the Shang (1760?–1122 BC), he moved all of its peoples to the various states of Song, Wei, and Lu to consolidate Zhou control of the Central Plains. This created the first mass migration of people in China's recorded history. Pining for the former dynasty, the Shang people were unable to control themselves and strove to retain the attire and rituals of the bygone era. Throughout medieval China, loyalist discourse was observed mainly in a descriptive rather than a self-descriptive manner. *Yimin* was invoked in association primarily with the remnants left behind by the fallen dynasty and made only sporadic appearances in records. It was the Song dynasty that witnessed the subtle transformation of loyalist discourse, primarily for two reasons. On the one hand, the rise of neo-Confucianism fostered a totalistic view that links self-cultivation to moral and political integrity vis à vis historical contingencies. On the other hand, the threat of the barbarians from the north gave rise to ethnic and territorial awareness suggestive of an incipient mode of nationhood.

Loyalism since the Song took on a decisively political dimension, reaching its climax at the fall of the Ming. In 1644, when the Manchus stormed the capital, Emperor Chongzhen (1611–1644) hung himself, and the empire changed hands. In an era of dynastic change, the righteous few who refused to surrender to the Qing formed a loyalist solidarity. Only decades later did their cause finally dissolve. The routes taken by these loyalists can be categorized according to a few distinct trends. In some cases, they aspired to recover their former positions of rule (such as Koxinga or Zheng Chenggong 鄭成功 [1624–1664] and Zhang Huangyan 張煌言 [1620–1664]). In other cases, they took a hermitic retreat into the mountains and forests, where they pined for the past (such as Zhang Dai 張岱 [1597–1684]); found refuge from the times in religion and the arts (such as Shi Tao 石濤 [1642–1707] and Zhu Da 朱耷 [aka Bada shanren 八大山人, 1626–1705]); or abandoned themselves to hopelessness or indulged in decadent life (such as Mao Xiang [1611–1693]). Most noticeably, some others, such as Gu Yanwu 顧炎武 (1613–1682) and Huang Zongxi 黃宗羲 (1610–1695), engaged with political and philosophical treatises on the prospects of a civilization's survival, thus opening up a new epistemological dimension of Chinese humanistic studies.[5]

The loyalist consciousness is further complicated when discussed in the light of modernity. By logic, as an ideology closely tied up to dynastic transition and feudal loyalty (and its disavowal), loyalism should have gone extinct after the fall of the Qing, the last Chinese dynasty. When the Republic of China was founded, the seeds of democracy are said to have been planted and the blossoming of equal citizenship projected; to talk about one's unconditional dedication to a royal house was deemed obsolete. Nevertheless, specters of loyalism haunted the republican era, as attested by a lineup of renowned Qing loyalists.

But such a loyalist consciousness need not be aligned merely with conservatism. Insofar as the "modern" is only such because of the term's indication of a violent temporal rupture between past and present, tradition and reform, one can even explore the loyalist dimension embedded in the conceptual makeup of Chinese modernity. Critics have long pointed out that the irony of modernity is both its emphasis on a temporal rupture that creates a distinct "experience of the past" and its exposure of a sense of nostalgia for the irrecoverable past. In one respect, modernity exaggerates the necessity of meanings and values that have no precedent, while in another, it cannot feign the hauntings looming behind radical reforms or ulterior motives. Faced with omens of civilizational rupture, intellectuals of the late Qing expressed shock at the magnitude of "an unprecedented crisis." They were aware that the shock of the "modern" was even more assaulting than the aftermath of another dynastic transition. This indirectly explains the sense of tremendous loss following the founding of the republic.[6]

Politically, loyalism engages itself with the polemics of (dynastic and cultural) legitimacy; it generates the force of its platform from that which has already been overthrown. That is to say, if loyalism is a thought or act predicated on anachronistic desire to turn back the clock so as to return to the primal state of nationhood and selfhood, postloyalism is an exercise that "anachornizes" anachronism. It is aimed to alter or displace a timeline that is already irrecoverably altered or displaced. As such, postloyalism intensifies the precarious nature of loyalism as it seeks to upset—delegitimize—what has already been delegitimized. The result is the opening of Pandora's box, unleashing multiple demons with regard to the politics of recognition and loyalty.

Here, Derrida's notion of "hauntology" finds its complex Eastern parallel.[7] With hauntology, Derrida intended to draw attention to the haunting influence of the "specters of Marx" after the decline of Marxist thought in the West. He criticizes the ontological style of dialectics perpetuated by theorists and philosophers who evade discussion of the shadowy origins of these theories. He writes that "haunting is historical, to be sure, but it is not dated, it is never docilely given a date in the chain of presents, day after day, according to the instituted order of a calendar."[8] In other words, the specter not only comes from the past but also foretells its continuous, lingering presence in the future. Based on Derrida's argument, we can speak of the postloyalist's "refusal to comprehend the mandate." On the one hand, this act ultimately dislodges the loyalist memory from the neat order of time, while on the other hand, it extends and exaggerates the postloyalist ego's a priori attachments to the loyalist consciousness. Time's continuum becomes disjointed, and forms of remembering become unrestricted. The postloyalist's sense of loss and inability to let go of love and resentment are no longer bound by systematic thinking. These feelings rather become endlessly evolving burdens and quagmires—or ghostly seductions.

Now we turn to the Sinosphere and ask how postloyalism can help us better understand the polemics of Sinophone literature. As argued above, despite incessant foreign encroachments, which amount to a colonial threat, since the early nineteenth century, China was not totally colonized except in the cases of Taiwan, Hong Kong, and, partially, Manchukuo. Nor can one describe China as a total colonial power unless one expands the definition of colonialism to cover all hegemonic systems from the empire to the totalitarian regime. One should also look into the fact that, during the colonial periods of Taiwan and Hong Kong, where Japanese and English were mandated as the official language, respectively, Chinese, especially in dialectal forms, appeared to have a firm grip on the society at large. That the Chinese people under colonial rule were still capable of preserving their linguistic and cultural habitus, however hybrid in practice, may have to do with either the colonizer's language policy or merely the duration of the colonial rule. Still, these cases compel one to think beyond the model of (post)colonialism.

One also should pay attention to the case of Sinophone diaspora, particularly in Southeast Asia, where more than thirty million people are of Chinese heritage. Since the late eighteenth century, hundreds and thousands of Chinese have immigrated to Southeast Asia, forming a huge social, economic, and cultural network. As the region went through drastic transformations in political systems, especially from colonialism to nationalism, throughout the twentieth century, the Chinese settlers were forced to cope with various challenges with regard to their ethnic and cultural identities. While the Chinese in countries such as Indonesia and Thailand were assimilated into Indigenous culture as a result of either coercion or gentle naturalization, those in countries such as Malaysia and Singapore were able to preserve their heritages at different degrees of cost.

Shih has used the concept of settler colonialism to describe the Han Chinese immigrants' predatory inclinations in their new space of settlement. For her, "settler colonialism" refers to both overseas Chinese settlers' relocated provincialism and their newly acquired colonial mentality. What we need to stress equally, however, is that these overseas Chinese setters were, in their turn, victims when confronted by ferocious colonial powers (Japanese, Dutch, French, American, English, etc.) and subsequent Indigenous nationalist campaigns. By conventional logic, the Chinese should have succumbed to colonial oppression or nationalist hegemony at the cost of giving up their cultural heritage. Or they should have recognized that they have reached the "destination" of diaspora, for good or ill, and acted out a new identity and linguistic affiliation. The fact, however, is more complicated. Their interaction with the colonial and ingenious cultures has led to varied consequences that cannot be described merely as postcolonial.

This is where the Sinophone becomes an arena between postcolonialism and postloyalism. One sees a range of responses to the use of the Chinese language—and its denial—on the levels of both sound and script, both cognitive recognition and affective negotiation. At the height of the anti-Chinese days in Indonesia, the Chinese language was repressed in the public sphere for fear of affecting national unity. In contemporary Singapore, the Chinese language was acknowledged as one of the mother tongues, only to be ironically learned by Chinese heritage citizens. But the most striking case is in Malaysia, where the Chinese constitute almost one-fourth of the population but occupy an unstable social and political position. The Malaysian government has systematically added pressures to the Chinese language education system since the late 1960s so as to solidify Malay centrism. For the Chinese descendant residents, preserving the Chinese language has become a voluntary cause of sustaining cultural identity and political solidarity.

All these facts remind one that the Sinophone conjuration of "Chineseness" is a matter of hauntology; it involves considerations ranging from sentimental fabulation to political engagement, such that it cannot be streamlined into either resistance or governance. I have, therefore, used postloyalism as a way to engage with these facts. Let me stress again that postloyalism is invoked, in the first place, as a critique of loyalism. But by adding the prefix *post* to *loyalism*, I mean to highlight the temporal anomaly inherent in the concept of loyalism and the doubly anachronistic implication of loyalism in the modern Sinophone context. Psychologically, we may consider postloyalism a deferred effect of the trauma syndrome, even its ghostly double. But in the Sinophone cases to be examined in the following, postloaylism casts something more perplexing—in either conservative or radical vein. Instead of looking merely backward, a Sinophone postloyalist may anticipate a futuristic loss of something they hold valuable now. Or, he or she may preempt such an "anticipatory nostalgia" by projecting—inventing—a memorable object or moment that may have yet to come into existence. Even more paradoxically, where connections with or memories of China have long been suspended or never existed, a Sinophone postloyalist's newborn desire may call for a "prosthetic memory" through the conduit of new media forms.[9] When the future is being mortgaged as if it were the legacy of the past, when the mechanism of memory turns out to be run by a desiring machine, the specter of loyalism reveals its postloyalist thrust.

In the following, I introduce three Sinophone spaces that are rich in both postcolonial and postloyalist traditions: Taiwan, Hong Kong, and (the Sinophone community of) Malaysia. Whereas Taiwan was under Japanese rule from 1895 to1945, Malaysia and Hong Kong were colonized by Britain, respectively, from 1786 to 1957 and from 1842 to1997. While the Chinese people of the three areas each underwent a distinct process of assimilation, they strove to develop their own Sinophone legacies. Decolonization, nevertheless, did not bring these areas a streamlined itinerary of political authenticity or determination.

Taiwan

In light of the dynamics of modern Taiwanese history, one can describe multiple strains of (post)loyalist writing on the island. In the aftermath of 1895, Taiwanese writers exhibited great ambiguity regarding their political allegiances. They directed their loyalist longing toward either the Qing or Ming regimes, either the legacy of the mainland or the local culture of the island. The founding of the republican regime further complicated their loyalist discourse. Taiwanese literature during the colonial period registers the conflict and compromise between colonial discourse and indigenous consciousness; between modern viewpoints achieved via Japanese mediation and revolutionary thoughts brought back from China; and for our concern, between Nipponophone and Sinophone discourses.

In 1949, the Nationalist regime lost the mainland and retreated to Taiwan. By conservative estimates, 1.5 million people made the journey. The majority came to Taiwan as commoners, military personnel of both lower and middle classes, or government employees and teachers. Their mainland backgrounds differed, as did their reasons for coming to Taiwan, but as soon as they arrived on the island, they were lumped into the category of "mainlanders." During times of hardship linking both sides of the straits (both past and present), many found solace in writing. The PRC scholar Li Xiangping describes the narrative and ideological imaginary of Taiwanese writing of this period as a "new loyalist complex."[10]

Li's observation risks oversimplification. It is worth noting that "new loyalist" literature began to undergo qualitative change after the 1970s. As time relegated the mainlanders' migration to Taiwan further into the past, and the numbers of those who made the migration steadily declined, writings about the past became unable to recover the heart-wrenching pain of the early years following their arrival. Yet, the literature changed also because the island's political structure changed, calling a new territorial consciousness into being. The previous "new loyalist" writings no longer bore the stamp of political orthodoxy. Nativist literature's transplantation of attachments from the opposite side of the straits to the Taiwanese side gave rise to a different object of loyalist desire.

For the activists of Taiwan self-determination, the island has always been under colonial rule since the seventeenth century, a condition that could be altered only through declaring independence. Paradoxically, to create a polity free of any Chinese political and cultural influence, they find in (post)loyalism a source of rationale. As the nativists call all preceding ruling forces colonial (whether Chinese, Japanese, Qing, or ROC), they couch their national consciousness in a (Chinese) loyalist discourse they should have disinherited at the outset. Before the idealized Taiwanese Republic can even be founded, they already imagine it as a long-lost utopia. They cast an anticipatory nostalgia for the prehistory of the futuristic nation. As they strive to create a national history predating the founding of their nation, they turn their postloyalism into an uncanny preloyalism.

Meanwhile, a counterexample can be found in the case of Chu Tien-hsin 朱天心 (b. 1958). As an author among the second generation of mainlanders in Taiwan, Chu witnessed the rise of passionate nativism and felt compelled to voice her sense of despondence and estrangement. In *Gudu* 古都 (*The Old Capital*, 1996), the middle-aged female narrator, who seems to be Chu's alter ego, returns from Japan and discovers that if she reexamines Taipei from the perspective of a Japanese tourist, the city where she grew up suddenly seems extremely unfamiliar and even terrifying. Relying on a map from the era of Japanese occupation, she wanders the main streets and narrow alleys of fin-de-siècle Taipei, where sights appear wretched and dilapidated like ruins. She seeks a moment of repose in Taipei but is actually a wandering spirit, migrating along the margins of amnesia and vain hopes in search of the dregs of history.

Lo Yi-chin 駱以軍 (b.1967) is arguably one of the most important writers of contemporary Taiwan. Lo's early writing shows the indirect influence of Chu Tien-hsin. In terms of postloyalist discourse, however, the two are quite different. Chu is forlorn and resentful toward the inevitability of the changing times and the dissolution of values that accompanies it. Lo's works do not put the sequence of time's advance or retreat in such a simple chronological order. He is certainly aware of the ruthlessness of the tricks that time plays, which causes him anxiety, but he does not devote much energy to voicing this anxiety, and he does not assume that he is on the side of justice. Lo's postloyalist complex culminates in *Xixia lüguan* 西夏旅館 (Western Xia Hotel, 2008). The novel parades endless bizarre encounters that occur within the insular space of Western Xia Hotel, from a necrophilic romance to a phantasmal manhunt, from burlesque intrigues to senseless carnivals. Behind the absurdity-turned-quotidian, Lo describes the diasporic experience of a generation of Chinese exiled to Taiwan; the hotel with no exit thus becomes a topos haunted by nostalgia and hysteria. More intriguingly, Lo refers his hotel name to the Western Xia dynasty (1038–1227) of the eleventh century, a dynasty once thriving on a hybrid civilization of Han and non-Han origins. Western Xia was ruined by the Mongols and, as a result, thrown into oblivion, its short-lived cultural splendor becoming an enigma.

At a time when radical Taiwan nativists are seeking a state free from Chinese experience, Lo contemplates not only the position of second-generation mainlanders as adherents—postloyalitsts—to a lost cause but also the fate of Taiwan at large. Once a self-appointed overseas stronghold of Chinese civilization, in the face of the double challenge of self-de-Sinicization on one hand and Chinese political encroachment on the other, will Taiwan become another disappearing Western Xia?

Hong Kong

Despite its colonial status, Hong Kong has served as an unlikely base for Chinese literary production since the 1930s. The colonial government played an intriguing role. It is a well-known fact that during his service as governor of Hong Kong, Cecil Clementi (1875–1947) promoted classical Chinese language literature, which led to the founding of the first Chinese Department at Hong Kong University. Granting his political motivation underneath his pro-Chinese antiquity campaign, Clementi, a sinologist by training, must have harbored his own vocation of Orientalism. Lu Xun, nevertheless, found in the campaign a loyalist overtone, one that was fostered by the colonial ruler: "The foreigners are smarter than us. At this point, not only can we not assimilate them, they are using our culture that is already corrupted to govern us, a corrupted nation."[11]

Thanks to, and in spite of, colonial conditions over the past century, the literary configuration of Hong Kong is closely related to its amorphous status as a *city* short of national identity. As the "deadline" of 1997 loomed over the fin-de-siècle moment, Hong Kong writers were compelled to contemplate their colonial and national identities and reimage the political past and future of their city. Dung Kai-cheung 董啓章 (b. 1967) is one such a case. Since the mid-1990s, Dung has created a series of works about the mysterious V (for Victoria) City. Instead of a nationalist longing, his narrator observes the rise and fall of the metropolis from the perspective of a postapocalyptic future. He recollects its grandeur in the vein of ancient Chinese cities such as Chang'an (Xi'an), Bianliang (Kaifeng) and Hangzhou, pondering the illusory and ephemeral nature of *all* cities in world history. Fiction becomes the final locus where the city can sustain its mesmerizing power.

In particular, in novels such as *Menghualu* 夢華錄 (Dream of splendor) and *Fanshenglu* 繁勝錄 (Account of prosperity), Dung relates in the future perfect sense the splendor and prosperity of V City that will have been ruined by a certain point of time. The titles of the two novels are of special historical significance. "Dream of splendor" brings to mind Meng Yuanlao's 孟元老 (c. 1090–1150) *Dongjing menghualu* 東京夢華錄 (East capital: Dream of splendor), arguably the most famous loyalist account of everyday life in classical Chinese literature. Meng was made a refugee from Kaifeng when the thriving capital of the Northern Song fell to the hands of Jurchen barbarians in 1126. In a quasi-encyclopedic manner, his book catalogs the old capital's commercial life, seasonal products, and festivals, as well as foods, customs, and traditions, all of which had evaporated like a dream. Likewise, "account of prosperity" is derived from *Xihulaoren fanshenglu* 西湖老人繁勝錄 (Account of prosperity by a senior gentleman on the west lake), a book recollecting the bygone urban life of Hangzhou, where the Song royal house built its southern capital after the fall of Kaifeng. By copying the style and structure of the two Song accounts, Dung's novels about life in Hong Kong generate the sensation of a ghostly déjà vu, while the sense of pastness of Hong Kong is projected in the time after 2046, fifty years after her return China.[12]

By the nationalist logic, the people of Hong Kong should have welcomed the restoration of the Chinese regime to the island following 156 years of colonial rule. Dung's fiction reverses such an assumption. On the eve of the handover, according to Dung, Hong Kong was experiencing not so much a wish fulfillment but rather a deeper sense of loss. Instead of the jubilant, postcolonial fervor, Dung entertains a postloyalist nostalgia—most ambiguously—for the lost time of British colonial rule. By "anticipating" Hong Kong to become a ruined city like Kaifeng and Hangzhong, he enacts a historical melancholia, one that speaks to the "eternal return" of a fallen city. Moreover, insofar as both Kaifeng and Hangzhou were Song capitals, Dung's analogy between Hong Kong and the two ancient cities insinuates the political taboo—that Hong Kong might as well enjoy the status of independent sovereignty in its own fantastic moment.

Malaysia

Finally, we come to Sinophone literature in Malaysia. As mentioned above, more than thirty million people of Chinese descent live in the area, demonstrating a variety and vitality of Sinophone cultures that can hardly be homogenized by the conventional paradigm of "overseas Chinese heritage." Particularly in Malaysia, Sinophone language and writing have long served as a token of Chinese ethnic solidarity. However, ever since the 1940s, Malay(si) an Chinese-language authors have had to negotiate between a Chinese identification—fostered by language and the inevitably powerful influence of the Chinese literary tradition—and a sense of belonging to their local environment of Malay(si)a.

Take a look at the case of Li Yung-ping 李永平 (b. 1947). Born and raised in Malaysian Borneo, Li has always harbored a dream of "Mother China," and he went to Taiwan to study in 1967. For him, the island is a miniature projection of the mainland, to which he feels destined to return in the long run. Li's passion is such that he creates a textual phantasmagoria as if only the Chinese script can actualize his loyalist desire. In 1992, he published *Haidong qing* 海東青 (Haidong blues), a work of more than five hundred thousand characters. The novel has no plot to speak of but a detailed account of the nocturnal wandering of a middle-aged scholar and a seven-year-old girl on the streets of Haidong (Taipei) city. Mixing a sensuous expose of the nightlife of the metropolis and an ambiguous narrative of the two characters that bring to mind *Lolita*, the novel impresses more for its fetishistic indulgence in Chinese vocabulary of the most obscure and archaic kind. For Li, this kind of language is the only way to call back the diminishing "essence" of China. Above all, Li frames his novel with an unabashed celebration of the Nationalist regime and its erstwhile leader, Chiang Kai-shek.

The Chinese Malaysian postloyalist tradition takes another turn in the works by Ng Kim-chew. Born in the year that Li Yung-ping embarked on his voyage to Taiwan, Ng grew up witnessing the ever-tightening control of the Malaysian government over the Chinese community. Following Li's steps, Ng went to study in Taiwan in 1986 and ended up settling down on the island. Nevertheless, Ng has engaged in a literary career as if he had never left Malaysia. He remains, to date, a most vehement critic of Chinese Malaysian ethnic culture. On the one hand, he wants to heighten Chinese Malaysians' vigilance regarding their diasporic position vis à vis governmental hegemony; on the other, he lashes out at their longing for transplanting anything Chinese to a new land, likening their effort to a necrophilic ritual. Oscillating between the "wandering Chinese" complex and its disavowal, Ng demonstrates the Sinophone "obsession with China" of the most perplexing kind.

Ng has sought to turn such an "obsession with China" into an interventional move in recent years. One such move can be illustrated by "Yuhai" 魚骸 (Fish bones, 1996), a story about the discovery of the "oracle bones" in relation to Sinophone literary modernity. In 1899, a late-Qing official purchased pieces of medicinal "dragon bones," only to realize that they were animal bones inscribed with the earliest Chinese characters identifiable to date. But the fact that the bones—as well as the history they represent—were not discovered until the turn of the modern century works to synchronize, so to speak, the temporalities of past and present. In Ng's story, a Chinese Malaysian scholar performs a nocturnal ritual of killing tortoises and producing "oracle bones," so as to communicate with the dead and the missing that were lost as a result of colonial rule. Thus, through the medium of the oracle bone inscriptions, his story brings together premodern augural technology and postmodern medial haunting, late-Qing archaeological discovery and fin-de-siècle diasporic nostalgia.[13]

Ng intensifies his Sinophone politics with a series of novels under the title *Nanyang Renmin Gongheguo* 南洋人民共和國 (The people's republic of the South China Sea, 2011–2013). The Republic of the South China Sea is said to be a socialist state that "could have been" founded by Chinese communists on the Malay Peninsula in the 1950s. It is a phantom polity that vanished no sooner than it was conceived by leftist activists. All Ng can do is to describe either the prehistory of the republic, when the leftists underwent all trials to realize their nation-building dream or the posthistory when the leftists were either coopted by the Malaysian government or simply died off as time passed. What was supposed to take place in history—the founding of the People's Republic of the South Sea—remains to be the abysmal lacuna, something that can be captured only by fiction.

Ng's fictional project brings home the aporia of the postloyalist discourse we have discussed so far. It speaks to both the wildest dream and the deepest melancholy of overseas Chinese in regard to their expatriate circumstances. More than sixty years after the establishment of the Federation of Malaya (1957), Ng's characters are seen as wandering ghosts in the "homeland," the Malay Peninsula, which they refuse to call home. They are citizens of the phantom People's Republic of the South Pacific or the aborted Malayan People's Republic—either merely an imagined diasporic mimicry of the People's Republic of China. Nevertheless, at a time when the PRC regime is trying to shed its image as the instigator of leftist insurgencies in Southeast Asia, these characters are destined to be denied by their "spiritual" mother country too. They are postloyalists of the most abject kind.

This essay represents an attempt to broaden the scope and methodology for studying modern Chinese language literature. It does not seek to overwrite the extant imaginary of "China" but rather seeks to tease out its complexity. Is it not a paradox that critics can subscribe to a "politics of marginality" and pontificate about a "clash of empires" and "global contextualization," all the while rigidly marginalizing forms of Chinese/Sinophone modernity and historicity that do not emerge within some preconceived mainstream. If one of the most important lessons one can learn from modern Chinese literature and history is the tortuous nature of Chinese writers' attempts to grapple with a polymorphous reality, then this knowledge can be appreciated in full only through a criticism and literary history equally exempt from formulaic dogma and geopolitical blindness. Through examining two critical models of postcolonialism and postloyalism, I argue that one must genuinely believe that Chinese and Sinophone writers have been, and still are, capable of complex and creative thought, constructing and deconstructing the nation and the world in the literary domain and beyond. Any critical endeavor in the name of Chinese literature must be unafraid to look squarely at this historical reality—a reality of contested Sinophone modernities.

Notes

1. Shu-mei Shih, "The Concept of Sinophone," *PMLA* 126, no. 2 (2011): 709–718.
2. Shih, "The Concept of Sinophone."
3. For a detailed description of postloyalism, see my book in Chinese: David Der-wei Wang, *Houyimin xiezuo: shijian yu jiyi de zhengzhixue* 後遺民寫作：時間與記憶的政治學 (Postloyalist writing: The politics of time and memory) (Taipei: Ryefield Publications, 2007), particularly the first chapter, 23–70.
4. For the definition of a Ming-Qing loyalist, see Lynn Struve, "Ambivalence and Action: Some Frustrated Scholars of the K'ang-hsi Period," in *From Ming to Ch'ing: Conquest, Region, and Continuity in Seventeenth-Century China* (New Haven, CT: Yale University Press, 1979), 327. On the definition of a Song loyalist, see Jennifer W. Jay, *A Change in Dynasties: Loyalism in Thirteenth-Century China* (Bellingham: Western Washington University Press, 1991), 6.
5. Wilt Idema, Wai-yee Li, Ellen Widmer, eds, *Trauma and Transcendence in Early Qing Literature* (Cambridge, MA: Harvard East Asia Monograph Series, 2006). For a study of Ming loyalism from a gender perspective, see Wai-yee Li, *Women and National Trauma in Late Imperial Chinese Literature* (Cambridge, MA: Harvard East Asia Monograph Series, 2014).
6. For instance, the 1927 drowning of Wang Guowei 王國維(1873–1927), one of the most important modern Chinese intellectuals, caused a big controversy as to the cause of his suicide.
7. See Peggy Kamuf, "Violence, Identity, Self-Determination and the Question of Justice: On Specters of Marx," in *Violence, Identity, and Self-Determination*, ed. Hent DeVries and Samuel Weber (Stanford, CA: Stanford University Press, 1997), 271–283, and Nigel Mapp, "Specter and Impurity: History and the Transcendental in Derrida and Adorno," in *Ghosts: Deconstruction, Psychoanalysis, History*, ed. Peter Buse and Andrew Stott (Houndmills: Palgrave Macmillan, 1999), 92–124.
8. Jacques Derrida, *Specters of Marx: The State of the Debt, the Work of Mourning, and the New International*, trans. Peggy Kamuf (New York: Routledge, 1994), 4.
9. Alison Landsberg, *Prosthetic Memory: The Transformation of American Remembrance in the Age of Mass Culture* (New York: Columbia University Press, 2003).
10. Li Xiangping 黎湘萍, *Wenxue Taiwan: Taiwan zhishizhe de wenxue xushi yu lilun xiangxiang*文學台灣：台灣知識者的文學敘事與理論想像(Literary Taiwan: Taiwan intellectuals' literary discourse and theoretical imagination) (Beijing: Renmin wenxue chubanshe, 2003), 292–293.
11. Lu, Xun 魯迅, "Lao diaozi yijing changwan" 老調子已經唱完 (Old tune is over), in *Lu Xun quanji* 魯迅全集 (Complete works of Lu Xun), vol. 7 (Beijing: Renmin wenxue chubanshe, 1981), 324.
12. See my discussion in "Qiannian huaxu zhimeng: Dung Kai-chueng, Meng Yuanlao, Menghuati xushi" 千年華胥之夢：董啓章, 孟元老, 華胥體敘事 (A thousand year old dream of the splendid kingdom of Huaxu: Dung Kai-cheung, Meng Yuanlao and the Huaxu narrative style), in *Kaifeng: Dushi jiyi yu wenhua xiangxiang* 開封：都市記憶與文化想像 (Kaifeng: Urban memory and cultural imaginary), ed. Chen Pingyuan 陳平原, David Wang 王德威, and Guan Aihe 關愛和 (Beijing: Peking University Press, 2013).
13. Kimchew Ng, "Yuhai" 魚骸 (Fish bones) (Taipei, Times publications, 1996), 12–23.

9

Parasite

Conceptualizing a Sinophone Approach and Ethics

E. K. TAN

One way to keep Sinocentric discourse in check is to continue to challenge its power in subsuming and suppressing multivocal Sinophone communities among marginal groups, be it indigenous, ethnic, diasporic, migrant, or queer, into a homologous identitarian presence. As the harbinger of Sinophone studies, Shu-mei Shih frequently reminds us that Sinophone studies needs to turn its attention to the underrepresented local communities around the world. The very notion of "local communities," unfortunately, has been mistaken by some as meaning exclusively the overseas Chinese communities when it comes to Sinophone studies. If we continue to explore deeper into what Shih proposes as the practice of Sinophone studies, it is not hard to deduce that Sinophone studies is relational studies. Shih's engagement with relational studies pays tribute to the late Édouard Glissant and his poetics of relations.[1] This is evident in Shih's essay "Comparison as Relation" in the edited volume *Comparison: Theories, Approaches, Uses*.[2] Another example is Shih's most often quoted line from her 2007 pioneering text for the field, *Visuality and Culture: Sinophone Articulations Across the Pacific*: "[Sinophone studies is] a network of places of cultural production outside China and on the margins of China and Chineseness, where a historical process of heterogenizing and localizing of continental Chinese culture has been taking place for several centuries."[3] If heterogenization and localization are two key concepts pertinent to our investigation of Sinophone expressions, then the focus on the study of a binary oppositional relationship between "China" and the

Sinophone communities is nothing but an intellectual fallacy. Take Sinophone Malaysia as an example. The consideration of a Sinophone expression in Malaysia involves not only a constant negotiation with a displaced, nostalgic overseas Chinese consciousness but also that of the hegemony of an oppressive Malay government toward the Sinophone community and a lingering British colonial presence that continues to haunt the Sinophone subjects. And, in Singapore, contemporary Sinophone communities must negotiate with not only a reconfiguration of racial dynamics among their fellow Malay and Indian citizens but also skilled and migrant workers from south Asia, Southeast Asia, and mainland China. The recent wave of immigration of Chinese nationals to Singapore is an interesting phenomenon to observe. Will this demographic change bring about a re-Sinicization of multicultural Singapore or contribute to the evolution of an existing Sinophone expression in years to come? Furthermore, most Singaporeans, Sinophone or not, by and large still speak with a British colonial tongue. It is this complexity that Sinophone studies strives to examine and address.

Sinophone studies as a network of relations includes the observation of all power actors involved in the shaping of politics, cultural production, and social phenomena of a particular locale. Identifying these power relations is crucial to our valuation and comprehension of the unique experience of distinct Sinophone communities under examination. Hence, as Sinophone scholars, we ask questions such as the following: What does China mean to Taiwan and Hong Kong, and vice-versa, from the perspective of the latter two locales? What does the Malay state mean to Sinophone Malaysians? What does America mean to Sinophone Americans? Furthermore, we dive deeper with queries such as: What does China mean to the Taiwanese indigenous communities, especially within the larger discourse of the cross-straits tension between Taiwan and mainland China? What roles do Chinese settlers play in the racial relations in Malaysia that are beyond the binary tensions between the Sinophone and Malay communities?

We also examine complex political tensions such as the Taiwan Presidential Office Indigenous Historical Justice and Transitional Justice Committee's response to Xi Jinping's claim of the People's Republic of China (PRC) government over Taiwan in his speech on January 2, 2019, commemorating the fortieth anniversary of the Chinese Communist Party's message to Taiwan.[4] In this "Joint Declaration by the Representatives of the Indigenous Peoples of Taiwan Serving on the Indigenous Historical Justice and Transitional Justice Committee," the committee begins with a proclamation of Xi's myopic view of Taiwan. In a simple statement, "Mr. Xi Jinping, you do not know us, so you do not know Taiwan" (習近平先生，你不認識我們，因此你不認識台灣), the committee delegitimizes Xi's entire speech. To further their argument, the committee elaborates on emphasizing the diversity of the Taiwan island made up of multiple racial and ethnic groups vis-à-vis China's hegemonic monocultural state ideology, which promotes national unification regardless of race, ethnicity, and culture, oftentimes through the violent oppression of minorities. To close the statement, the committee vows that Taiwan will not be intimidated by bullying tactics from across the straits.[5] This example points to two issues I want to address in this essay: first, to continue to highlight the critical and generative function of the Sinophone as a theoretical concept that does not simply advocate for a binary relation with China and only China; second, to examine the function of the Sinophone as a parasite to various forms of political and cultural hegemony. The former addresses the common and paradoxical accusation of Sinophone studies as a field that is built upon the tactics of marginalization of China while obsessing over China. The latter encourages scholars to consider how marginal Sinophone communities and groups could benefit from the tactics of occupation to negotiate and demand representation and agency through exploiting dominant bodies.

The fact that there are often multiple power centers among Sinophone communities is, ironically, what makes the field interesting and worth exploring. Instead of seeing China and the various Sinophone communities in oppositional terms of belonging, I propose that Sinophone scholars treat China (or any other power centers) as nodal points of reference in their study of distinct Sinophone expressions. What this does is highlight the power relations that structure and condition what and how a Sinophone community thinks and acts. This will, in fact, redirect Sinophone studies away from the unproductive us-versus-them dynamic of knowledge production to better situate the field within its theoretical propositions.

Before discussing how the concept of parasite functions as a generative approach to rethinking the critical edge of Sinpohone studies, I want to first turn our attention to a quick summary of the criticisms on Sinophone studies that have emerged over the years since Shu-mei Shih published her pioneering monograph in 2007.

As early as 2010, Zhu Chongke, a professor at Sun Yat-sen University in China, published "The Discourse Construction of Sinophone and Some Problems Concerned" to critique the burgeoning field. Zhu stresses the need to establish a "fair and equal dialogue" in the discussion of Sinophone studies from the perspective of scholars located in China in order to clarify "origins and sources." "Fair and equal dialogue" is a curious proposal as it indirectly assumes that literature and scholarship from mainland China and those from Sinophone communities outside China are on equal footing when it comes to processes of production, circulation, reception, recognition, etc. Zhu also chooses to translate the English term "cultural hegemony" (文化霸權) to "cultural leadership" (文化領導權).[6] In Chinese, this underscores an attempt to downplay the top-down power structure and privileged position of a literary center occupied by mainland China over Chinese language literature produced by its overseas communities. In 2013, Huang Weiliang argued that "new literature in Chinese" (漢語新文學) is a much better literary category compared to "Sinophone literature" (華語語系文學) because the former is transnational, inclusive of multiple perspectives, and not restricted by politics. Huang accuses Sinophone scholars based in North America of advocating for a divisive and oppositional ideology that lacks professionalism in academic research.[7] It is not hard to deduce that Huang's argument of Sinophone literature as a divisive category is a reaction to Sinophone studies' critique of the cultural hegemony embedded in the literary center to which Huang and Zhu belong.

Joining the chorus in delegitimatizing the scholarship of Sinophone studies is a prominent professor from Nanking University, Liu Jun. In his essay "The Origin, Development and Criticism of Sinophone Literature," Liu criticizes Shih for her exclusionary rhetoric that he deems as anti-Chinese literary canon and anti-China, and he accuses David Wang's inclusive approach to literary studies of undermining the tradition of Chinese literary history. Liu conveniently dismisses both Shih and Wang's versions of Sinophone studies as lacking in scholarship and grounded in political ideologies.[8] Following a similar line of attack as Liu Jun, Liu Daxian and Huo Yan both accuse Sinophone studies of harboring preconceived biases in its critique of Sinocentrism and the cultural hegemony of China. Liu Daxian openly ridicules the concept of Sinophone literature by claiming that Sinophone literature is "a form of wordplay that is *out of touch with reality*." He further argues that "by adopting new and fancy terms as its rhetoric, [Sinophone studies] reveals its ideological stance hidden behind a theoretical patchwork filled with hundreds of loopholes."[9] Huo Yan accuses Shih of not being self-reflexive in the "rigid" way she imagines "China" in her critique of Sinocentrism. By emphasizing the importance of close reading as a methodology to study primary texts, Huo cautions that "scholars should avoid invoking their personal political beliefs, aesthetic preferences, and personal relations to analyze primary texts out of context." Interestingly, by redirecting us to the literary values and aesthetics of overseas Chinese writings, Huo ends up regurgitating Shih's proposal to focus on local expressions among Sinophone communities, except paying no attention to the contextual implications of the political and cultural hegemony that shapes these Sinophone communities.[10]

Even though scholars in Sinophone studies regard Taiwan as an important site of Sinophone expression and politics, especially among scholars in

Taiwan studies, there is still no shortage of criticism of the field by academics from Taiwan. Two recent examples are Chao Kang, a sociology professor at Tunghai University, and writer and literary critic Ng Kim Chew. Chao Kang's op-ed, "Slave to the West Wind and Peanuts: Critique of Shu-mei Shih's Concept of the Sinophone," appears in *Chaiwan Ben Post*, a biweekly newspaper that focuses on scholarly exchange and news about jobs and educational opportunities across the straits between mainland China and Taiwan; hence, the title of the post—*Chaiwen*.[11] Chao accuses Shih of failing to reflect on American imperialism in her work and contends that before Shih critiques the Chinese empire and calls for the denouncement of Sinocentrism, she should, perhaps, first turn her attention to critique the American empire because of her status as a U.S. academic. Since Chao acknowledges that he has only recently encountered Sinophone studies and has read only one essay by Shih (at least at the time when he writes the piece), he is seemingly unaware that Shih has addressed issues of the American empire elsewhere.[12] More importantly, Chao's last comment reveals a common strategy of criticism and rebuttal—the delegitimatizing of the critic's right to critique by casting Shih as an outsider/other. I am concerned with this type of territorial politics that promotes censorship based on national and regional allegiance. It seems to say because you are a Sinophone scholar in the United States, you should be concerned about Sinophone American literature, not Taiwan literature; by extension, it also implies that you should mind your own business and not partake in any criticism of someone else's home affairs.

This kind of "mind your own business/territory" exclusionary politics Chao hints at is also present in Ng Kim Chew's review of Shih's Chinese monograph *Against Diaspora: Discourses on Sinophone Studies*.[13] Ng accuses Shih of repackaging "Chinese language literature" with a fancy theory and ideology to transform it into a transnational literary and cultural enterprise. Furthermore, he criticizes the way Shih conceptualizes China as an empire that "victimizes" its ethnic minorities and "colonizes" its overseas communities by mobilizing its cultural hegemony in the form of a myth of consanguinity. To Ng, Shih touts a revisionist history that ignores the history of China as a victim to European powers by focusing on its role as a colonizer. On Shih's take on the concept of diaspora, he argues that it is highly problematic to regard Malaysian Chinese as settler colonizers; if anything, they are the victims of the Malay government. I wonder how we come to conclude that one can only be a victim or a victimizer but not both in contested situations. But this is where it gets interesting. At times in this review, Ng takes the position of a native informant to argue against Shih's various renditions of Sinophone theory, especially in instances when Shih uses Sinophone

Malaysia as an example. Sinophone studies is again confronted by a politics of inclusion/exclusion determined by who is "native" enough to speak on behalf of a field and a discipline in Ng's argument. Ng explains with regards to Sinophone Malaysian literature: "Who would know within a decade, our *little industry* (or *street vendor stand*, in Tee Kim Tong's words), would end up becoming part of the Sinophone Transnational Enterprise managed by Shih, the self-proclaimed Executive Director, with many followers in Taiwan and the United States."[14] How do we read the viability of an academic field or theory such as Sinophone studies when research related to the field can only be deemed legitimate based on one's right to represent according to the geopolitical status of the scholar?

What about Sinophone studies warrants this kind of resistance? Why is there a desire to delegitimatize the field and its theoretical propositions, especially among scholars in mainland China and some in Taiwan? Why do some even go to the extent of disputing and rebutting using harsh language such as "ridiculous," "out of touch with reality," and "illogical arguments" to undermine a field that is still negotiating with its own growing pains? How does a relatively new field cause so much reaction and anxiety among scholars from traditional disciplines that have long-established recognition and status in national, regional, or global settings compared to Sinophone studies? What is obvious, perhaps, is that these scholars almost uniformly see in Sinophone studies a position and voice of dissident that they need to suppress to reaffirm the significance of their own fields, be it Chinese literature, Chinese language literature, world literature in Chinese, or Sinophone Malaysian literature in Taiwan (SMLiT).[15] It is hard not to wonder what superior position anti-Sinophone scholars occupy as they speak for the prejudice and injury Sinophone studies has imposed on their fields of study by turning a blind eye to their own privileges and entitlements that have enabled their offensive attack on the burgeoning field. I remember hearing that a Chinese studies scholar asked Shih the following question during the Q&A at an annual conference roundtable on the future of modern Chinese literature and culture in U.S. academia in 2013: Why are we concerned about teaching Sinophone literature when students in U.S. institutions hardly know and care about studying Chinese literature? By "Chinese literature," this scholar is referring to canonical texts, which are largely from mainland China. This is the voice of privilege that ventriloquizes the kind of cultural hegemony and nativist discourse Sinophone scholars question and critique. Scholars like this individual continue to pay lip service to marginal and minority expressions in order to subsume ethnic or Sinophone literature from diverse geographical and cultural backgrounds under the homologous cultural imaginary of a unified China.

The Sinophone as Parasite

If, according to its critics, by existing as a field, Sinophone studies somehow irritates them, then the nuisance we as Sinophone scholars have produced directly or indirectly is, perhaps, accomplishing something. This is where I turn to the concept of the parasite to suggest that we own the nuisance we are continuing to impose on those in power with our presence.

The future of Sinophone studies needs to engage with practices beyond defining distinctive Sinophone localities in order to imagine the Sinophone as a parasite that exists in the form of a continuous nuisance and irritation to the main(stream) body. This will allow us to reconfigure the field and the complex network of power it engages. It is in this sense that the parasitic nature of the Sinophone could enable the burgeoning field to grow in vitality and visibility while forcing power centers to acknowledge its critical energy as a threat. By main or mainstream body, I do not suggest that we fall back to imagining China, by default, as that body in any shape or form. To do that is to reinforce the Sinocentrism that I propose to counter in my earlier work.[16] The body refers to the body of discourse where a Sinophone expression is surrounded and influenced. By claiming the Sinophone as a parasite, I am suggesting that it does not have to be a part of the body in question. However, when it resides in the body, it would allow us to consider questions such as the following: How does the Sinophone continue to negotiate its own growth or departure from this body? And if it departs from this body, what new body of discourse will it latch on for survival?

Borrowing Josephine Ho's metaphor of the parasite in her discussion of the role cultural studies plays in the (re)configuration of disciplinary boundaries in Taiwan's higher education, I propose to treat the critical potential of Sinophone studies as possessing similar parasitic tactics that could destabilize the cultural hegemony from the axes of power over distinct Sinophone communities across the globe. In "Life of a Parasite: One Survival Story in Cultural Studies," Ho explains:

> Though almost always precarious, such existence [of certain critical gatherings of cultural studies within Taiwan's institutions of higher education] penetrates deep into conventional disciplines and may, when the conditions are right, work to reorient the host departments beyond their original disciplinary boundaries. Of course, the precariousness of such "parasitic" existences also keeps the groups on their toes, striving to maintain their professional credibility within prevailing academic conventions while continuing to initiate unconventional intellectual activities as well as social activism.[17]

In a similar fashion, Sinophone studies, as a controversial and nonconformist field, has been negotiating its existence and status quo with traditional disciplines in North American academia for a little more than a decade. Often regarded by these traditional disciplines as too theoretical or too marginal, scholars in Sinophone studies repeatedly struggle to find a way to fit. For example, compared to a scholar of premodern Chinese drama, a Sinophone scholar working on Sinophone Malaysian literature is expected to also exemplify knowledge in areas of Chinese literature at large in addition to their specific area of research to meet the curricular needs of a traditional East Asian studies department. When showcasing their work, Sinophone scholars often find themselves having to make extra effort to justify how their work fits into the large framework of a panel or conference theme. Yet, all of these are the preconditions of the parasitic nature of the Sinophone. First, the expectation of Sinophone scholars as both specialists and generalists highlights the interdisciplinarity of Sinophone studies, a characteristic of the field described in Shih's pioneering work. Sinophone scholars in the United States, Taiwan, Hong Kong, and Singapore are now faculty in an array of departments ranging from Asian studies to comparative literature, English, Asian American studies, history, gender studies, etc. As the field continues to grow and diversify, the potential for critical interventions could help reconfigure disciplinary practices in North America and Sinophone societies in Asia to address issues of power relating to global inequalities and justice more appropriately. In addition to working toward "reorient[ing] the host [or home] departments beyond their original disciplinary boundaries," a network or consortium of Sinophone scholars similar to that of the cultural studies interdisciplinary collective described in Ho's essay could potentially generate international collaboration to "initiate unconventional intellectual activities as well as social activism" that are at times overlooked and undermined by apolitical traditional disciplines.

Ho's concept of the parasite is loosely based on French philosopher and theorist Michel Serres's concept. Serres describes the parasite in three distinct ways: biological, social, and static or interference. For Serres, an example of a biological parasite is the tapeworm, of a social parasite is the sycophant, and an informational parasite is the noise or interference in a system of communication.[18] I borrow Serres's concept of the informational parasite as a theoretical entry point to conceptualize the Sinophone. An important characteristic of the Sinophone is the field's ability to make noise as interference to an established dominant system in order to destabilize and reconfigure it. By how much irritation, annoyance, and even anxiety Sinophone studies has aroused among its critics, the field has somehow adopted the role of the parasite intentionally or not. While Sinophone studies, according to Shih, stresses the importance of localism, the concept of the parasite that I am developing also takes on a spatial dimension: The parasite occupies part of the local/main body and situates itself in relational terms to this body. In other words, the parasite localizes itself vis-à-vis the power relations that define it and that it defines against. Dialogue and exchange can only happen when the parasite is acknowledged, not dismissed. We have already seen what a nuisance the noises made by existing Sinophone scholarship have been to critics in mainland China and Taiwan. Yet, it is important to bear in mind that exchange is not the priority of the parasite; intervention is.

What, then, is the guiding principle of the Sinophone as parasite? The convenient answer, according to its critics, would most likely be the resistance and critique of Sinocentrism. Yet, that is merely a small part of the means, not the end. South Asian scholar Pramod K. Nayar, in his essay "The Transnational Indian Novel in English: Cultural Parasites and Postcolonial Praxis," argues that a postcolonial world largely marred by global migration, neocolonial exploitation, and regional genocide needs a new kind of ethics. Seeing this ethics as the common goal of what he describes as cultural parasites (such as Third-World communities occupying First-World space and Third-World culture, such as Bollywood, invading the First-World cultural arena in the process of reverse globalization), Nayar calls for an awareness among transnational parasites toward "the suffering of the distant Other, respecting the culture of the distant Other, and opposing the exploitation of the strange Other."[19] Sinophone studies can benefit from imagining an ethics of cultural parasite. Under this premise, I propose a Sinophone ethics that can help promote solidarity among Sinophone communities that have experienced a similar history of suffering or injustice to interfere, intervene, resist, and disrupt political and cultural hegemony with "noises" to call for justice and reform.

Having established the role of the Sinophone as parasite and discussed the utility of such conception, I offer examples in politics and activism to illustrate how the Sinophone occupies the parasite as both tactics and metaphor to disrupt political processes and question the legitimacy of these processes.

Parasites and the Sinophone Ethics

On December 2, 2016, barely a month after Donald J. Trump won the presidential election, the president-elect accepted a controversial phone call from Taiwan's President Tsai Ing-wen.[20] As a political and ideological gesture, Tsai's phone call established Taiwan as a democratic and independent country while leaning Taiwan toward the United States and toeing the line of antagonizing

China more than three decades after the United States cut diplomatic ties with Taiwan for mainland China. In less than a week after Trump's fumbling with the United States' One China policy, the concerns and media attention turned to the potential devastation this phone call would have on U.S.–China relations. The tension was especially heightened when Trump publicly stated on December 11: "I don't know why we [the United States] have to be bound by a One China policy unless we make a deal with China having to do with other things, including trade."[21] This revival of a Cold War discourse from the sixties, intentional or not, reaffirms Taiwan's desire to see itself as a Sinophone community outside the purview of China. If there is a positive side to this unprecedented event among the anxieties created, it would be Taiwan's claim to its own status quo on the international stage. Taiwan, no doubt, continues to be a nuisance that China cannot rid itself of other than reclaiming Taiwan as a part of its main body. In the most curious way, my Sinophone reading of this event involving the triangular relationship between Taiwan, the United States, and China places Taiwan in a parasitic relationship with the two power centers in the body of a lingering Cold War narrative. The claim of Taiwan as an independent democratic nation in Tsai's political act of pitting the United States (or perhaps just Trump) against China would have turned out futile if either one of the power centers did not constitute this body of political discourse. Taiwan the parasite destabilizes and weakens the potential amicable relationship between the two leading nations, regardless of how successful Tsai's attempt was. To Taiwan, the United States and China are two nodal points where power lingers and can be redirected. Tsai's phone call functions as a Sinophone parasite that generatively invents, affects, and transforms the relationship between China and the United States.

Launched on September 24, 2014, as a civil disobedience campaign led by Reverend Chu Yiu-ming, Benny Tai, and Dr. Chan Kin-man, the Occupy Central with Love and Peace (OCLP) campaign had been brewing for more than a year. The movement broke out when the advocacy for an electoral system in Hong Kong based on the international standard of universal suffrage and democratic values was stymied by the political influence of the PRC. When the amendments were not made in accordance with democratic procedures to reform the 2017 election process for Hong Kong's fifth chief executive, protests, such as the Black Banner March, the 922 Class Boycott, and the 926 Class Boycott, began to surface starting August 31. As protesters began to gather outside the Central Government Complex beginning on September 27, OCLP campaign organizer Benny Tai announced the beginning of the Occupy Central movement. Within less than a day, the police resorted to using tear gas and pepper sprays on protesters. The persistence of the protesters in the face of police suppression led them to the creative decision to equip themselves with face masks, goggles, and umbrellas to defuse the impact of pepper sprays and tear gas. Hence, the OCLP movement transformed into what is widely known as the Umbrella Movement, which lasted for approximately seventy-nine days. Even though the movement failed to reverse the National People's Congress Standing Committee's (NPCSC) decision to amend the election process, and the three campaign conveners, Chu, Tai, and Chan, eventually surrendered to local authorities on December 3, the extent of this showcase of civil obedience signaled to the PRC government that the Hong Kong people take their democracy and their civil rights seriously from the grassroots level. Hong Kong's status as a special administrative region (SAR) under China's one country, two system governance structure renders the conception of Hong Kong as a parasite possible. In its spatial configuration, we have seen more of a dependent relationship between Hong Kong and the mainland post-1997 handover. It is, however, the OCPL and Umbrella movements in 2014 that have best exemplified Hong Kong as embodying a Sinophone ethics that calls for the resistance to political injustice that jeopardizes democratic values and civil rights of the Hong Kong people. The loud noises made by the protesters of the Umbrella Movement did not simply irritate and annoy the PRC government, but they also put China in the spotlight in global media, raising concerns again among global groups regarding China's unflattering human rights records. Moreover, the Umbrella Movement also emerged as one in the ongoing network of global movements of grassroots solidarity to advocate for democracy, such as the Arab Spring in the Middle East and the Sunflower Movement in Taiwan. One could argue that the Umbrella Movement had not successfully brought change to Hong Kong, especially after the proposition to reform the electoral system was dismissed; yet, aside from the noises and nuisance it has caused the PRC government, the three OCLP organizers had since sworn to invest their time and energy in community work and education—two areas where a Sinophone ethics could be nurtured.

While I began revising this essay for the edited volume, Hong Kong entered another phase of political turmoil. While some deemed the Umbrella Movement short-lived, almost five years after the movement, an amendment to the Hong Kong extradition law introduced by Chief Executive Carrie Lam's government triggered another wave of protests among the Hong Kong people.[22] This time, more than half a million Hong Kongers took to the streets on June 9, 2019, in the first of a series of protests to display their will and resilience as a people. To quote journalist and politician Claudia Mo, "At the end of the Umbrella Movement we said we would be back. And now, we are back."[23] The noise of resistance faded and returned only to become louder and more visible.

While Hong Kong commemorated the Umbrella Movement five years later, on September 28, 2019, by holding a rally in the midst of the recurring protest movement against the extradition bill, protesters embraced the true meaning of commemoration by keeping the spirit of the Umbrella Movement alive.[24] I highlight this continuation of the spirit of civil disobedience among Hong Kongers who believe in their right to protest for the democracy that forms the basis of their society to stress the power of activism from the ground via my analogy of the parasite. The fact that Xi Jinping's government has been interfering and influencing Hong Kong politics, as seen in the case of the OCLP, the Umbrella Movement, and the recent introduction of amendments to the extradition bill, are clear signs of China's disregard of the two-systems rule promised to Hong Kong. Taking Hong Kong as a case study, I direct our focus to Hong Kong and the protesters' resilience instead of the tactics adopted by the PRC government to undermine the region's democracy and the people's right to speech. To do so, I observe some of the major events that followed the initial protest in June 2019.

After multiple protests that included protesters storming into the Legislative Council on the anniversary of the British handover of Hong Kong to China on July 1 and the increasingly violent clashes between the police and the protesters at rally sites,[25] Carrie Lam officially announced the withdrawal of the amendments to the extradition bill on September 4. Although Lam had declared that the bill was dead on July 9, her decision had proven to be too little and too late. The protesters continued to take to the streets to voice their concerns regarding a government that privileged its relationship with China over its duty to the people and to demand that Lam step down from her role as chief executive. In a symbolic way, the protesters embodied the nature of a parasite by transforming the body of resistance to that of the "ordinary citizen" and "girl/boy next door" whose "faceless" persona took on the demands of the collective to advocate for their basic rights as citizens of a democracy.[26] The faceless persona is literally underscored by the fact that protesters wore masks to protect themselves from tear gas and pepper spray used on them by the police. This transformation allowed protesters to occupy the national/regional body with the rhetoric of civil disobedience coming from the people as a nuisance to irritate the body.

One such example is the occupation of the Hong Kong International Airport on August 11, 2019, by prodemocracy protesters.[27] The decision to occupy and disrupt one of the busiest international air travel hubs was triggered by the incident of a woman who was shot in the eye by police during a rally in Tsim Sha Tsui.[28] In addition, Cathay Pacific's decision to comply with China's aviation regulator's demand to suspend one of its pilots, an activist charged with rioting,[29] was also a probable cause. While pacifists might see these disruptions as uncalled-for reactions that would seriously impact Hong Kong's economy by suspending its everyday operations, to the protesters, the occupation allowed them to exploit the status of the interconnected governmental and economic bodies to voice their grievance against a government and corporation (Cathay Pacific) and to parasitically hijack the "international" space of the airport as their stage to draw international attention to their cause.

Next, I turn to Hong Kong's most recent election on November 24, 2019, to argue that the effort of the Hong Kong people in taking to the streets to demonstrate their rights and protest for their beliefs in self-governance and democracy can and have led to positive outcomes. The landslide victory of the prodemocracy parties in this local election cycle is not only proof that the people have spoken but also that they did so with a clear understanding of their individual responsibility and rights as citizens.[30] Of the 452 seats up for grabs in this election, approximately 80 percent of them were won by prodemocracy candidates, successfully turning the pro-Beijing majority of three hundred seats to a minority of merely fifty-eight seats. Prodemocracy parties gained control of a total of seventeen out of eighteen councils in the government.[31] While pessimistic sentiments lingered in the air during the months of protests, with some claiming that most protesters and activists did not have an endgame to their movement, the resilience of those who continued to carry the movement forward had seemingly awakened many ordinary citizens. Hong Kong continues to be a nuisance to the Chinese government, like a parasite that continues to affect the global image of the PRC government.

Conclusion

The Sinophone methodology I invoke here in my reading of politics and activism in the case of Hong Kong and Taiwan is one that embraces a critical approach to seek interventions into political and cultural hegemony in order to uncover issues and problems relating to exploitation and injustice. More importantly, I want to acknowledge the effort of those who creatively test the boundaries and toe the line in the face of injustice or oppression via the tactics and resilience that I describe through the imagery of the parasite. Sinophone studies does not produce these stories or discourse; instead, it is these stories that offer Sinophone studies inspiration to conceptualize a methodology and ethics of critical interventions.

Sinophone as parasite occupies the position of a force that generates energy from its relations to power origins to disturb, interfere, and disrupt political, social, and cultural processes that have been naturalized as dominant and universal. Interference and disturbance can potentially reorder the systems of dominance that have produced these processes. To illustrate how the concept of Sinophone parasite works, I have introduced examples in politics and political activism, such as the response of the Representatives of the Indigenous Peoples of Taiwan to Xi Jinping's speech on the unification of China and Taiwan, the phone call Taiwan's President Tsai Ing-wen made to Donald Trump, and the Hong Kong Umbrella Movement and the anti-extradition bill protests.

Change takes time and is not without multiple setbacks. So, how do we sustain the potential and dynamism of the Sinophone as parasite to continue disrupting dominant political and cultural orders? As a field growing into its second decade, we must keep up with our scholarships while "[out-producing] our critics" and be "more active on the international scene" to advocate for projects that address marginal and under-represented communities and their struggles.[32] Josephine Ho said this so well that I could not but invoke her voice as a call to arms to my fellow Sinophone colleagues: "If nothing else, we need a more concentrated channel for reproduction, and we need to create a more favorable professional environment for those younger scholars and students who may not yet have the staying power to withstand the onslaught of disciplinary pressure or conservative retaliation."[33]

Notes

1. For details, see Édouard Glissant, *Caribbean Discourse*, trans. J. Michael Dash (Charlottesville, VA: Caraf Books, 1989); and *Poetics of Relation*, trans. Betsy Wing (Ann Arbor: University of Michigan Press, 1997).

2. Shu-mei Shih, "Comparison as Relation," in *Comparison: Theories, Approaches, Uses*, ed. Rita Felski and Susan Stanford Friedman (Baltimore, MD: John Hopkins University Press, 2013), 79–98.

3. Shu-mei Shih, *Visuality and Identity: Sinophone Articulations Across the Pacific* (Berkeley: University of California Press, 2007), 4.

4. For the 1979 "Message to Compatriots in Taiwan," see the transcript at http://www.gov.cn/test/2006-02/28/content_213298.htm; for Xi Jinping's 2019 speech in Chinese, see http://www.gov.cn/xinwen/2019-01/02/content_5354223.htm.

5. For the statement in both English and Chinese, Taiwan Presidential Office Indigenous Historical Justice and Transitional Justice Committee, "Indigenous People of Taiwan to President Xi Jinping of China," HackMD@chihao, January 8, 2019, https://g0v.hackmd.io/s/SyKTh6bM4.

6. Zhu Chongke 朱崇科, "The Discourse Construction of Sinophone and Some Problems Concerned," *Xueshu yanjiu* (Academic research), no. 7 (2010): 146–160; quotes are from 147 and 148.

7. Huang Weiliang 黃維樑, "The Proper Name of a Field: 'Sinophone Literature' and 'New Literature in Chinese,'" *Fujian Tribune*, no. 1 (2013): 105–111, at 110.

8. Liu Jun 劉俊, "The Origin, Development and Criticism of Sinophone Literature—Centering on Shu-mei Shih and David Wang," *Wenyi yanjiu* (Literature and art studies), no. 11 (2015): 51–60.

9. Liu Daxian 劉大先, "Sinophone Literature: Theoretical Production and Its Ridiculousness," *Shijie Huawen wenxue luntan* (Forum for Chinese literature of the world), no. 1 (2018): 59–65. (Emphasis mine.), 63

10. Huo Yan 霍艷, "A Different Kind of 'Pride and Prejudice': An Observation and Reflection on Sinophone Studies," *Yangzijiang pinglun* (The Yangtze River criticism), no. 4 (2017): 77–82, 79, 82.

11. Chao Kang 趙剛, "Slave to the West Wind and Peanuts: Critique of Shu-mei Shih's Concept of the Sinophone," *Liangan benbao* (Chaiwan Ben post), no. 162 (2017): http://ben.chinatide.net/?p=13272.

12. See, for example, Shih's position in "Forum 2: Linking Taiwan Studies with the World," *International Journal of Taiwan Studies*, no. 1 (2018): 209–227. Shih specifically discusses her critique of the American empire on page 215.

13. Shu-mei Shih 史書美, *Fan lisan: Huayu yuxi yanjiu* (*Against Diaspora: Discourses on Sinophone Studies*) (Taipei: Linking Publishing), 2017.

14. Ng Kim Chew 黃錦樹, "Such 'Sinophone Studies' Should Quit!—What is Shu-mei Shih's *Against Diaspora* Against?" Sobooks, January 2, 2018, https://sobooks.tw/sinophone-literature-review/.

15. This is a term coined by Tee Kim Tong. Unlike Ng, Tee's attitude toward Sinophone studies is relatively supportive. For details, see Tee Kim Tong, "(Re)mapping Sinophone Literature," in *Global Chinese Literature: Critical Essays*, ed. Jing Tsu and David Der-wei Wang (Boston: Brill, 2010), 77–92.

16. E. K. Tan, *Rethinking Chineseness: Translational Sinophone Identities in the Nanyang Literary World* (New York: Cambria Press, 2013).

17. Josephine Ho, "Life of a Parasite: One Survival Story in Cultural Studies," in *Creativity and Academic Activism: Instituting Cultural Studies*, ed. Meaghan Morris and Mette Hjort (Hong Kong: Hong Kong University Press, 2012), 55.

18. For a quick reading on Michel Serres's concept of the parasite, see Cary Wolfe's introduction, "Bring the Noise: The Parasite and the Multiple Genealogies of Posthumanism" in *The Parasite*, trans. Lawrence Schehr (Minneapolis: University of Minnesota Press, 2013), xi–xxvix.

19. Pramod K. Nayar, "The Transnational Indian Novel in English: Cultural Parasites and Postcolonial Praxis," in *Imagined Identities: Identity Formation in the Age of Globalization*, ed. Gönül Pultar (Syracuse, NY: Syracuse University Press, 2014), 17–32. Nayar uses "transnational parasites" interchangeably with "cultural parasites."

20. "Trump Muddles China Relations with Taiwan Call," *New York Times*, December 3, 2016, A1.

21. Russell Hsian and David An, "What is the U.S. 'One China' Policy?" *National Interest*, December 28, 2016, https://nationalinterest.org/blog/the-buzz/what-the-us-%E2%80%9Cone-china%E2%80%9D-policy-18882.

22. Amendments to the extradition law was first proposed by the Hong Kong Security Bureau in February 2019. The amendments would require the Hong Kong government to surrender anyone (local or foreign) whom the PRC government claimed as a criminal suspect to the mainland for trial. This sets a dangerous precedent, as China has a track record of violating human rights in false accusations and unjust trials held against Hong Kong publishers and bookstore owners. For reports on these cases, see Lai Ying-kit, "Missing, Presumed Detained: Hong Kong Publishers of Books Critical of China Go Missing," *South China Morning Post*, November 12, 2015, https://www.scmp.com/news/hong-kong/law-crime/article/1877932/missing-presumed-detained-hong-kong-publishers-books. Chief Executive Carrie Lam introduced the amendments on April 3, 2019. Carrie Lam held her ground during much back and forth between the prodemocracy and pro-China legislators and an antiextradition bill protest march on the legislative council on April 28 demanding the government withdraw the bill. For timeline on the protests, see Julia Hollingsworth, "Hong Kong Protest Timeline: The Evolution of a Movement," CNN News, August 17, 2019, https://www.cnn.com/2019/08/16/asia/hong-kong-protests-evolution-intl-hnk-trnd/index.html.

23. See James Griffiths, "At the End of the Umbrella Movement We Said We Would be Back!" CNN News, June 12, 2019, https://www.cnn.com/asia/live-news/hong-kong-protests-june-12-intl-hnk/h_ddd6617694298289fcb853c6f3a24cf9.

24. There are several news reports that link the antiextradition bill protest to the Umbrella Movement. For details, see Lily Kuo and Erin Hale, "'Hong Kong Can't Go Back to Normal': Protesters Keep Umbrella Spirit Alive," *The Guardian*, September 28, 2019, https://www.theguardian.com/world/2019/sep/28/hong-kong-cant-go-back-to-normal-protesters-keep-umbrella-spirit-alive; and Adolfo Arranz and Jeffie Lam, "From Occupy 2014 to Protests 2019," *South China Morning Post*, September 28, 2019, https://multimedia.scmp.com/infographics/news/hong-kong/article/3030696/from-occupy-to-hong-kong-protests/index.html.

25. The police began with using tear gas and rubber bullets on protesters. See Jen Kirby, "Police and Protesters Clash as Mass Protests Escalate in Hong Kong," *Vox*, June 12, 2019, https://www.vox.com/2019/6/12/18662677/hong-kong-protests-2019-tear-gas-extradition-bill-legislature-china. As the conflict between the authorities and the protesters escalated, the police resort to brutal means such as beating up nonviolent protesters.

26. See Yuen Yung Sherry Chan, "Hong Kong's Protests Aren't Just About the Extradition Bill Anymore," *The Diplomat*, July 25, 2019, https://thediplomat.com/2019/07/hong-kongs-protests-arent-just-about-the-extradition-bill-anymore/.

27. See Athena Chan, Sum Lok-kei, and Rachel Yeo, "Flights Out of Hong Kong International Airport Cancelled as Anti-Government Protesters Occupy Terminal Building," *South China Morning Post*, August 12, 2019, https://www.scmp.com/news/hong-kong/politics/article/3022411/after-woman-shot-eye-angry-protesters-descend-hong-kong; and Sasha Ingber, "Thousands of Protesters Storm Hong Kong Airport, Shutting Down Flights," NPR, August 12, 2019, https://www.npr.org/2019/08/12/750404354/thousands-of-protesters-storm-hong-kong-airport-shutting-down-flights.

28. See Elizabeth Cheung, "Protesters Call for Mass Hong Kong Airport Demonstration After Woman Shot in Eye During Extradition Bill Unrest in Tsim Sha Tsui," *South China Morning Post*, August 12, 2019, https://www.scmp.com/news/hong-kong/politics/article/3022386/protesters-call-mass-hong-kong-airport-demonstration-after.

29. Danny Lee, "Cathay Pacific Sacks Two Ground Staff over Passenger Information Leak and Says Pilot Charged over Hong Kong Protests Has Been Removed from Flying Duties," *South China Morning Post*, August 10, 2019, https://www.scmp.com/news/hong-kong/transport/article/3022263/cathay-pacific-tells-employees-expect-increased-security.

30. According to a CNN report, Kenneth Chan from Hong Kong Baptist University claimed that the election drew a turnout of more than 70 percent, a historical high record in Hong Kong's election history. See James Griffiths, "Landslide Victory for Hong Kong Pro-Democracy Parties in de Facto Protest Referendum," CNN News, November 25, 2019, https://edition.cnn.com/2019/11/24/asia/hong-kong-district-council-elections-intl/index.html.

31. See Jen Kirby, "Pro-Democracy Candidates Dominate Hong Kong's Local Elections in a Rebuke to China," *Vox*, November 25, 2019, https://www.vox.com/2019/11/25/20981691/hong-kong-district-council-elections-pro-democracy; and Emma Graham-Harrison and Verna Yu, "Hong Kong Voters Deliver Landslide Victory for Pro-Democracy Campaigners," *The Guardian*, November 25, 2019, https://www.theguardian.com/world/2019/nov/24/hong-kong-residents-turn-up-for-local-elections-in-record-numbers.

32. Ho, "Life of a Parasite: One Survival Story in Cultural Studies," 62.

33. Ho, "Life of a Parasite: One Survival Story in Cultural Studies," 65.

Queer Hong Kong as a Sinophone Method

ALVIN K. WONG

Hong Kong often symbolizes the success of Asian modernity in the global cultural imaginary. The late economist Milton Friedman famously proclaimed Hong Kong to be the freest market in the world and said: "If you want to see capitalism in action, go to Hong Kong."[1] Historically, Hong Kong represents what David R. Meyer called "the intermediary of capital," the emporium of trade in the Far East since Britain declared sovereignty over Hong Kong in 1841 under the terms of the Treaty of Nanking at the end of the First Opium War (1839–1842).[2] During the late Qing, when the treaty ports of Amoy, Shanghai, Canton, and Hong Kong were opened up for opium trade, Hong Kong also served as an entrepot for the global coolie trade. For cultural theorist Lisa Lowe, Hong Kong serves as a crucial site for the imperial experiment of free trade and the global coolie trade, both of which are pivotal to the emergence of Western liberal thought and what she terms the "intimacies of four continents."[3]

Despite the rich dynamics of Hong Kong's historical and cultural encounters with global modernity and its Sinophone articulations, the study of Hong Kong in the humanities and social sciences tends to be confined within two intellectual formations, namely postcolonial theory and area studies. Within area studies, it is further ghettoized as a subfield in China studies.[4] Only recently has Hong Kong studies emerged as a legitimate field. Intellectually, the increasing push for academic internationalization means that scholarly studies on China will be prioritized over local studies of Hong Kong. This is, of course, not a situation particular to Hong Kong studies. Shu-mei Shih's theorization of Taiwan's (in)significance within dominant models of globalization, postcolonial studies, and area studies proves highly relevant for Hong Kong. Shih writes, "Taiwan, when any attention is given to it at all, is most often reduced to an object of empirical political analysis, and has been systematically dismissed as a worthwhile object of critical analysis in cultural and other humanistic studies with theoretical import. Taiwan is too small, too marginal, too ambiguous, and thus too insignificant."[5]

It might be helpful to remind ourselves that postcolonial theory, with its poststructuralist posturing of hybridity, colonial mimicry, and in-between-ness, used to provide a legitimate place where most knowledge productions of Hong Kong operate. A dominant view of Hong Kong being sandwiched between two colonizers was a central concern during the heyday of 1990s postcolonial theory. In particular, in the "between colonizers" model by Rey Chow, Hong Kong's postcoloniality marks a situation of being geopolitically and culturally mediated by two colonizers: the British and the incoming People's Republic of China (PRC).[6] The urgency of reclaiming a unique or even "authentic" sense of Hong Kongness is continually threatened by the changing urban space, gentrification, and loss of colonial heritage and landscape due to the tidal wave of "returning to the motherland" discourse.[7] This threat of cultural disappearance due to the consequence of speed in the global city and political uncertainty produces what theorist Ackbar Abbas calls reverse hallucination: "If hallucination means seeing ghosts and apparitions, that is, something that is not there, reverse hallucination means *not* seeing what *is* there."[8] Shu-mei Shih, observing the frenzy for the study of Hong Kong culture around the handover moment, raised the following questions in 2007 that are still urgent now: "What then? What *after* both the fever for Hong Kong cultural studies and the spectacle of the turnover ceremony? What comes *after* nostalgia? How do we theorize the *after*?"[9]

One ambitious effort to theorize Hong Kong culture with a sense of urgency *after* the wave of postcolonial theory on disappearance and colonial in-between-ness comes from Stephen Yiu-wai Chu's book, *Lost in Transition* (the prequel to *Found in Transition*), in which Chu calls for a need "to theorize post-1997 Hong Kong by placing the emphasis not on binary relations but on 'dispersed politics' outside the box of the China-West framework."[10] Building on Stephen Yiu-wai Chu's call that we need to see Hong Kong itself as method,[11] my invocation of "queer Hong Kong as a Sinophone method" does not merely deconstruct Hong Kong and the Sinophone through the de-universalizing impulse of queer theory. Taking my cue from Jose Munoz's phrase that "queerness is not yet here,"[12] and Howard Chiang's concept of transtopia as different "*ways of knowing*,"[13] I theorize queerness as both the geopolitics of desire in Sinophone Hong Kong as well as modes of unknowability, opacity, and indeterminacy that expand the spatial and temporal horizons of queer Sinophone critique.

Though critics have discussed various iterations of "Hong Kong as method," the point of departure remains largely tied to either the 1997 handover on the one hand, or it is heavily shadowed by China-centrism and dominance in the current moment on the other. How might we multiply our existing frames of reference and put Hong Kong into relational comparison with other entities, histories, and desires? Relational comparison is an inherently Sinophone project insofar as it "looks instead at the ways in which texts from different parts of the world are related to each other through their partaking and representation of world historical events."[14] Drawing on Shu-mei Shih's relational model, I understand queerness as the perversity, alternative embodiment, and utopian desire that coexist within neoliberalism, late capitalism, migration, and settler colonialism yet exceed their epistemological grids and disciplinarity through queer Sinophone interventions.[15] In other words, understanding Hong Kong's in-between-ness not simply as a postcolonial predicament, we can now better appreciate Hong Kong's liminal position as structured by multiple power relations; historically by late Qing's geographical marginalization, British opium trade, and the nineteenth-century global discourse of "free trade";[16] a brief but violent episode of Japanese occupation (1941–1945); U.S.-China Cold War political bifurcation and maneuverings; and post-1997 governance by an increasingly authoritarian PRC. Queer Hong Kong, understood in this geo-historical formation of multiple alliances, complicity, and power relations, provides a method to read how social subjects are sexed and gendered within the historical formations of Hong Kong modernity. In turn, queer cultural productions provide alternative methods to read minor histories,[17] bodies, and affects, which serve as queer archival hermeneutics.

Sinophone studies, according to Shu-mei Shih, refers to "a network of places of cultural production outside China and on the margins of China and Chineseness, where a historical process of heterogenizing and localizing of continental Chinese culture has been taking place for several centuries."[18] In a keynote entitled "Empires of the Sinophone," delivered at Harvard University in 2016, Shih places Hong Kong in relational comparison with countries and sites that have always existed between interimperial rivalries and power relationships, such as Burma, Vietnam, and others.[19] Indeed, Hong Kong served as an important colonial entrepot and interimperial middleman during the apex of British imperialism in the nineteenth century.[20] During the Asia-Pacific War, it entered into interimperial rivalry again with the coexistence of the Kuomintang (KMT), Communist, Japanese, and British colonial power bases there. How can we examine this interimperial formation of Hong Kong through Shih's invocation of "empires of the Sinophone"? Furthermore, how might queer theory and Sinophone studies intersect under the interimperial condition?

In order to concretize queer Hong Kong as a Sinophone method, I will turn to three examples that focus on minor acts and gestures, affective history, and queer archive. The first part of my chapter briefly examines Wong Bik-wan's 1999 feminist novel *Lienu Tu* 烈女圖 (Portraits of martyred women), an ambitious narration of Hong Kong women's lives across three generations of women through the force of the minor. In this small section, I will mainly analyze the first and second segments of the novel that narrate feminist survival during WWII and lesbian intimacy among two women workers in the midst of the 1967 Hong Kong riots. Next, I will turn to Jacob Cheung's 1997 film *Intimates* (自梳), which narrates the romance between two women, one a self-combed woman, *zishu nü* (自梳女) and one a courtesan, in mid-twentieth-century Shunde, Guangdong, from a young woman's perspective in contemporary Hong Kong. Self-combing refers to "the lives and life-choices of a group of women called *zishu nü* (自梳女) in the Guangdong Delta region of southern China . . . They were called *zishu nü* or self-combing women because they declared their status as permanently unmarried through a rite which involved combing their hair into a bun similar to that of a married woman."[21] As a cultural text that rewrites the regional practice of self-combing in resisting heterosexual marriage in Guangdong as a missing link for lesbian intimacy during the Asia-Pacific War, the film provides a queer Sinophone approach to Hong Kong modernity through wider spatial and temporal comparisons. Finally, my chapter will conclude with Ma Ka Fai's 2016 novel *Long tou feng wei* 龍頭鳳尾 (Once upon a time in Hong Kong), which presents a story of colonial complicity between a Scottish officer, Morris Davidson, working on the British side and his sexual affair with a local mafia boss called Luk Naam Coi (陸南才). Ma's novel retells Hong Kong's colonial modernity through a queer Sinophone lens that is mediated by the multiple relations of Chinese political forces and British and Japanese empires. At the heart of this interimperial queer desire lies the question of whether Hong Kong literature can serve as a queer archival hermeneutic. My chapter will conclude with some reflections on how queer Hong Kong as a Sinophone method can offer a version of Hong Kong studies more attentive to questions of the minor, affective history, and queer archive.

Wong Bik-wan's Feminist and Lesbian Cartography of Hong Kong

Wong Bik-wan is one of the most prolific writers to have emerged in the late 1980s Hong Kong literary scene. Her writings often combine a startling attention to violence with an understated sensitivity to Hong Kong history and politics. In addition, many of the stories collected in *Wenrou yu baolie* 溫柔與暴烈 (Tenderness and violence), *Qi hou* 其後(Thereafter), and *Mei xing zhe* 媚行者(Beautiful sojourner) are transnational in aspects and constitute what one might describe as the transnationalization of Hong Kong literature. Previous scholarship on Wong have compared her literary style with Zhang Ailing and Lu Xun,[22] or they have illustrated the figurative language of dark violence more generally.[23] The word *lie* (烈), the first word in the Chinese title of *Lienu Tu* 烈女圖 usually connotes a quality of heroism, individual sacrifice for the emperor in Chinese dynastic eras, and those who are deemed fit for enshrinement. In Wong's literary cartography, this normative notion of heroism receives a more humbling and minor treatment. The martyred women did not come from the intellectual class of Hong Kong, nor were they patriotic fighters who fought the Japanese invasion on the eve of the Asia-Pacific War. Rather, Wong resignifies *lie* through its identification with the lower rung of society. On the back cover of the 2004 edition of *Lienu Tu* 烈女圖, the author describes her tough women in the following way: "Born as Chinese women, suffering already becomes the memory of their lives. No matter which era they live in, Chinese women must always be more enduring, hard-working, and forgiving than their men. Those who cannot live already became the dust, and those who endure will survive through each succeeding eras."[24] Beyond the conventional designation of *lie* as piety due to modest and filial modes of conduct, *lie* here points to a politics of surviving through historical and social hardship, compounded by the very fact of being a woman.

Lienu Tu 烈女圖 is a novel full of the trials and tribulations of lower-class women enduring violence and marginalization. Take, for instance, the main protagonists Sung Heung (宋香) and Lam Hing (林卿), who are the first wife and second wife/mistress of Little Moon (阿月仔) in the first segment of the novel. Sung sells cigarettes on the street for a living. Little Moon rarely returns home, and when he makes money, he spends it all on gambling. He even tells others that Sung is his "second wife" when he is married to Lam Hing. After Lam gives birth to a daughter, Little Moon abandons both wives and starts courting a dancing girl at the Red Diamond Café. Lam, losing all hope, decides to drown herself in the ocean. The narrator describes Lam as "your grandmother": "Your grandmother Lam Hing jumps into the sea, kicking a little and swallowing mouthful of salty water. Help! Your grandmother holds onto the mooring and climbs up. She opens her mouth and breathes in deeply. This is not right! I can't be this stupid. Lion doesn't eat me, Japanese soldiers couldn't kill me, I don't want to die."[25] As David Der-wei Wang elaborates on the toughness of the *lienu*, the novel demonstrates "the tenderness in violence: a desire to kill yourself first so that you will live again and a persistence of loving your life even though life is not worth living."[26] Toughness here evokes a sense of resilience at the edge of hopelessness, well knowing that after the loss of hope, one still needs to survive and come up with a means of living.

While *Lienu Tu* 烈女圖 is often read as a nonlinear narrative of Hong Kong women's lives with feminist sensibility, it also constitutes a queer Sinophone method insofar as it maps horizontal alliances among marginalized women, focalizes minor women's histories, and excavates lesbian intimacies as coexisting with the dominant working-class history of Hong Kong's modernization. Wong's queer Sinophone literary aesthetic is akin to what Erin Manning terms the "minor gesture." For Manning, "The minor gesture, allied to Gilles Deleuze and Félix Guattari's concept of the minor, is the gestural force that opens experience to its potential variation. It does this from within experience itself, activating a shift in tone, a difference in quality."[27] For Manning, the minor includes that which is forgotten and cast aside but without which the major and the normative could not have come into being in the first place. Wong Bik-wan's attention to the minor gesture is evident in the novel's textualization of lesbian intimacy during the 1967 Hong Kong riots.

Specifically, as the novel progresses toward the 1960s era of political riots, leftism (mediated by the Cultural Revolution in China), and the rise of working-class women culture, it imagines queer female solidarity. In the second segment of the novel called "My Mother," the narrator centers on two women called Ngan Ji/Yinzhi (銀枝) and Daai Hei/Daixi (帶喜), which literally mean "silver bough" and "bring happiness" or "bring fertility." Working in a textile factory as part of the rising light manufacturing industry that contributed to the modernization of 1950–1970s Hong Kong,[28] these two young female workers commiserate during work time and carry out sisterly romance at night. The narrator describes, "One night, as they walk home after watching a Hollywood film, Daai Hei impersonates the male character in the film and tells Ngan Ji: 'I love you, I will love you my whole life.' Your mother Ngan Ji laughs: 'We will marry men eventually.' Daai Hei wholeheartedly promises: 'even after marriage, I will still love you.' . . . The two of them hold their hands together. If there is no man in this world, how wonderful would it be?"[29] Daai Hei would later crossdress in masculine attire, hold a workers' strike on the street, and drop fake bombs on the road during the 1967 leftist riots. Here, female solidarity is politicized into a "revolution plus queer love" story, while lesbian and female-to-female intimacy is shown alongside a more recognizable form of Hong Kong history that speaks in the name of movement, riots, and class struggle.

Intimates: A Lesbian Erotohistoriography of Hong Kong

I now turn to Jacob Cheung's 1997 film *Intimates* to sketch out another intervention of queer Hong Kong as a Sinophone method, that of a historiography charged with the power of lesbian erotics.[30] The film, while seemingly obsessed with a nostalgic past of lesbian desire in the Guangdong region of Shunde, can be reread anew as a cinematic narrative of lesbian intimacy that crisscrosses different nodes of temporality and the wider transpacific spaces of imagination.

Intimates begins with a panoramic view of the Tsing Ma Bridge in Hong Kong, set to be completed by 1997 when the region is to be returned to China. An independent female architect, Wai, leads a team of engineers and instructs them confidently. One of the other architects is her boyfriend, who soon breaks up with her for someone else. Meanwhile, Wai is given an important task by her father: She is to take an old female servant back to Shunde to seek an old relative. The old female servant is referred to as Auntie Foon and is a self-combed woman. A self-combed woman refers to a regional practice among Shunde and other Canton regions where female industrial participation in the textile and silk industry enabled a large group of women to sustain themselves economically and escape unwanted marriage. While the beginning of the film identifies the old female servant of Wai's family as the self-combed woman, it is only at the end of the film when we discover that the actual self-combed woman, Yee Foon, is the lesbian lover that the servant has been separated from for years due to the Asia-Pacific War. Auntie Foon herself is actually Yu Wan, a courtesan who married the silk factory owner Master Chen as his eighth wife. This was also the factory where all of the self-combed women in the village, including Yee Foon, worked. Wai, the young and independent architect, originally detests Auntie Foon (who is really Yu Wan) and sees her as old-fashioned, nonmodern, and out of touch. Wai eventually becomes sympathetic to the past love shared by Yu Wan and Yee Foon.

How do we understand the intersecting temporalities of contemporary Hong Kong with the past lesbian utopian space of Shunde? What is queer about this lesbian film, and how does it offer a queer Sinophone method? Helen Hok-sze Leung suggests that the film can be read as part of a wave of films about nonnormative sexuality that marks the moment of political anxiety facing 1997 Hong Kong's postcolonial condition. Leung concludes that the narrative structure of nostalgia in the film "remains caught in its attachment to the act of recollection and fails to articulate the significance of this act to the present."[31] In revisiting this classic lesbian film, I am more invested in how this cinematic mode of lesbian erotohistoriography places contemporary Hong Kong and the past Shunde within the material history of female labor, Japanese imperialism, and transpacific mobility.

Queer theorist Elizabeth Freeman defines *erotohistoriography* as "the way queer relations complexly exceed the present, insisting that various queer social practices, especially those involving enjoyable bodily sensations, produce forms of time consciousness—even historical consciousness—that can intervene into the material damage done in the name of development, civilization, and so on."[32] I take Freeman's concept of erotohistoriography further by suggesting that not only do queer forms of time-consciousness perform social practices that counter the material damage of linear historiography, but queer temporality in the film *Intimates* also powerfully invokes lesbian affect in the past as a form of reparative and pedagogical practice for seemingly nonqueer desire in the present. Specifically, in one powerful flashback sequence, Yu Wan, the younger version of Auntie Foon in the past in Shunde, is taken to a business meeting by her husband, Master Chen, the silk factory owner, to meet a powerful Chinese warlord. During the meeting, Yu Wan is asked to rest in a quiet guestroom upstairs only to find out that, in fact, her husband has abandoned her for the night as a "gift" for the warlord whose economic power is enabled by collusion with the Japanese empire. While Yee Foon, the self-combed girl, accompanies her to the meeting, Foon is thrown out of the building by the guard. After two nights of heavy rain and abusive sex, Yu Wan is finally returned to her husband only to find out that Yee Foon had been waiting on the ground outside despite the heavy rain, awaiting her release.

After returning home, Yu Wan finds out that while she was sexually violated by the warlord in return for the business deal, her husband was having sex with a new ninth mistress. Reacting with a feminist statement, Yu Wan lashes out at her husband, Master Chen Yiu Chung: "I was sold to the pander at thirteen; I've tolerated numerous men! Tall, short, old, young.... They don't scare me. I thought I could settle down here under the Chen family's roof, but who knows that this house is a poisonous well!" This flashback sequence is cinematically interwoven with the present when Wai accompanies Yu Wan (mistaken as Auntie Foon) to return to Shunde while Wai herself is told by her cheating boyfriend that he has fallen in love with a new woman. Auntie Foon/Yu Wan assumes the intimate role of caring for the young lady who numbs herself by drinking whiskey, throwing up, and even, at one moment, contemplating suicide.

The temporally interwoven structure of the film lends itself to a queer erotohistoriography in which what seems to be a nostalgic film of lesbian past and ethnographic visuality of the self-combing *zishu nu* turns out to be a pedagogy on the possibility and limit of feminism facing women in both the past Shunde in China and contemporary Hong Kong. Specifically, about two-thirds into the film, narrated in a flashback, Yu Wan leaves the Chen household and briefly sets up a dumpling stall on the street with Yee Foon. As Japanese forces move south after the Nanjing Massacre, various air bombings are heard in the background. Ironically, it is precisely at this moment of impending war that Yu Wan and Yee Foon share a temporary relief from heterosexual domestic violence and betrayal. Yee Foon herself was once pregnant due to premarital sex with her first crush, a man named Ah Shing. Ah Shing was too scared to run away with Yee Foon, and Yee Foon eventually attempted suicide only to be saved at the last moment by Yu Wan. By the time Yee Foon and Yu Wan relocate to a more urban area of Guangzhou, Master Chen tracks down Yu Wan and persuades her to board a steamship with him that would take all wealthy Chinese to the United States to escape the war. Yu Wan accepts the ship ticket but swears to Yee Foon that she will only board the ship if she comes with her. At a critical moment in the narrative, Yu Wan is aboard and finds that Yee Foon is still at the dock, barred by police guards. As the ship starts departing for America, Yu Wan jumps off the deck, much to Master Chen's surprise, and swims across the ocean to reunite with Yee Foon. A loud air bomb is heard, and the film narrative shifts back to the present when Auntie Foon (the older Yu Wan) is retelling her past to Wai.

By recomposing and queering the history of the Second Sino-Japanese War through an aborted transpacific migration to the United States, Jacob Cheung visualizes the intimacy of lesbian utopia precisely at the intersection of war, empire, diaspora, and eventual settlement of the two women across Guangdong and Hong Kong. At once a tale of regional migration, lesbian intimacy, and failed transpacific crossing, the film evokes a vision of what Lisa Yoneyama terms "a decolonial genealogy of the Transpacific." Yoneyama observes "that 'transpacific' as a critical methodology must mean more than the resignification of movements and interfaces across and within the arena that happens to be called the Pacific. Instead, we need to clarify the specific geohistoric conditions under which that space has been constituted as an object of knowledge and nonknowledge."[33] The film's parallel juxtaposition of lesbian intimacy with both WWII and 1990s Hong Kong seeks to redress queer female desire from that which was made unknown to "History" with a capital H.

The cinematic enmeshment of the past Shunde with the present Hong Kong through a tale of war, migration, and displacement thus focalizes what Shelly Chan terms a "diaspora moment," which "erupts and recurs when diaspora time interacts with other temporalities and produces unexpectedly wide reverberations."[34] In Chan's formulation, a diaspora moment disrupts the slow and ongoing movement of migrant lives and histories that, in turn, reconceptualizes what China, nation, and homeland could mean. In my queer inflection, I am drawn to how these diaspora moments of rupture and discontinuity fracture the coherence across bodies, desire, geographies, and Chineseness through queer Sinophone temporality. Overall, the film narrates the flourishing of lesbianism in the regional space of Shunde, the displacement of the two lesbian lovers, Yee Foon and Yu Wan, due to the Asia-Pacific War, and the subsequent possibility of reunion through the help of a Hong Kong girl. In doing so, the film evinces queer Sinophone temporality as a mode of visuality that both cuts across and unites disparate spatial coordinates, sexual orientation, subjectivity, and temporal scales. It offers queer Hong Kong as a Sinophone method that reads the dense layers and intimacy of human desire across time and space.

Queer Hong Kong as a Sinophone Method: Archive Lost and Found

This last portion of my chapter offers a few close readings of Ma Ka Fai's novel *Long tou feng wei* 龍頭鳳尾, which takes queer Hong Kong as a Sinophone method from the affective register to the archival. It insists that the writing of Hong Kong modernity can be a practice of queer archival hermeneutics. Queer Hong Kong as a Sinophone method through Ma's work evinces both a possibility of forming a queer archive and its undoing as well, what Derrida in *Archive Fever* terms the "institutive and conservative" and "revolutionary and traditional" aspects of archive.[35] How does Ma achieve this ambitious goal?

The novel begins with, perhaps, the most quotidian form of queer archive—that of Ma's own family history about his grandfather's secretive homoerotic past. The novel begins with Ma's childhood memory of watching his grandfather chewing on an eight-inch-long curious object while watching the popular TVB show *Enjoy Yourself Tonight* (歡樂今宵). Asking his grandfather what he is chewing on, the old man replies: "It is cow penis. You are still very young, you don't need it yet."[36] Years later, when Ma was studying in Chicago, his sister revealed that their grandfather had a queer past, confirmed through a photograph of him lying lovingly on the chest of a tall, handsome ship captain during the grandfather's years of seafaring. The photograph was discovered by Ma's mother after her father's death. It is noteworthy that Ma's grandfather's queer past is only revealed after his death and through a photograph from his seafaring years. Similar to how Jacob Cheung's film *Intimates* fractures the slow and linear temporality of conventional narratives of migration through queer Sinophone temporality, the queer grandfather's diaspora moment of seafaring tellingly ruptures the assumed heterosexuality of his life and, thus, Ma's family history in Hong Kong. Here, Hong Kong history is interwoven with the expansive layers of queer Sinophone temporality globally.

The reader is soon introduced to a mafia boss named Luk Naam Coi (陸南才), the protagonist of the story. As the narrative unfolds, the narrator traces the childhood of Luk in Mowming city (茂名市), a relatively unknown town in Guangdong. This part of the story details Luk's experience of sexual assault by his older uncle, which he seemed to enjoy (after the fact), and his later arranged marriage to Ah Gyun (阿娟), who constantly demands sex from him but doesn't care about Luk's needs at all. Through twists and turns, Luk leaves for Hong Kong and eventually joins a powerful mafia gang called Hung Mun (洪門) led by Dou Jyut Saang (杜月笙), a historical figure and KMT general with ties to triad societies in Shanghai and Hong Kong. Before joining the triad society and becoming the big boss, Luk works briefly as a rickshaw puller. It is from this experience that he befriends a Scottish police investigator, Morris Davidson, also known as Cheung Dik-san (張迪臣) in Chinese. Davidson works for the British colonial force and will soon become the most important man in Luk's life. Their relationship turns queer when one night, after pulling the rickshaw, Davidson invites Luk home and has sex with him. From then on, all the encounters between Davidson and Luk are both erotic and political in nature—Davidson provides information to Luk so that the mafia gang can watch out for possible police regulation of crimes, while Luk provides information on suspected Chinese collaborators of imperial Japan.

As this dense and layered narrative demonstrates, Ma's novel performs several senses of a queer literary archive. At the level of narrative technique, it eschews the usual voice of the omniscient third-person narrator and instead infuses the author's own family history with Hong Kong colonial history, a narrative device that generates a queer archival fever because the search for the "truth" of his grandfather's sexuality is simply impossible. Was his grandfather "gay"? Why did he marry? Through interweaving the familial with the amorous and little-known fictional history of a queer mafia gang figure, the depiction of queer interracial bond between Luk and Davidson thus imagines queer affect and sexual encounters at the heart of 1930–1940s Hong Kong, a time and place that was caught between multiple imperial formations. Similar to the kind of minor gesture and erotohistoriography of lesbian intimacy evident in Wong's novel and Cheung's film, Ma's novel invents a distinctive mode of narrating a queer Hong Kong past. As Ann Stoler suggests, instead of reading the archive "against the grain" in colonial studies, the complexity of imperialism and the role of sexuality within it also demand that we "explore the grain with care and read along it first."[37]

Reading along the grain shows that Ma's novel both frames Luk and Davidson's queer desire as constitutive of the interimperial situation of 1940s Hong Kong while detailing modes of queer desire that escape normative categorization; hence, the act of literary narration begs the critical question of the "what" and the "how" of a queer Hong Kong archive that verges on ethics of unknowability and opacity. First, Ma's novel places queerness at the heart of the interimperial formation that was Hong Kong. As John M. Carroll points out, Hong Kong, on the eve of the 1941 Japanese invasion, was declared a neutral zone by the British defense policy, which also means that it functioned as an intermediary and strategic zone where the KMT Nationalists and Communists both built their own bases and where pro-Japanese sympathizers built their influence.[38] Hong Kong's situation of being caught among multiple political power and empires (both British and Japanese) thus lends itself to a queer method of reading that is attentive to what Laura Doyle terms interimperiality. Interimperiality refers to "a political and historical set of conditions created by the violent histories of plural interacting empires and by interacting persons moving between and against empires."[39]

Reading along the grain, to heed Stoler's advice, suggests that a queer Sinophone method must be attentive to all the complexity, ellipses, ephemeral acts, and affective tensions within inter-imperiality. In fact, the very title of the novel in Cantonese, "龍頭鳳尾/Lung tau fung mei," connotes the interpenetrability between queerness and interimperial relations. The narrator describes one moment of queer sexual encounter: "Luk can't refuse but obediently lay on his bed, giving his whole back to Davidson and willing to be his excited and crying 'bad boy.' Luk Naam Coi is Syun Hing Society's (孫興社) dragon head, but he is also Davidson's phoenix tail." (170). Specifically, while the term (龍頭) *dragon head* is local Cantonese slang that refers to the status of the gang leader, a title that Luk Naam Coi holds, the "phoenix tail" part hints at the racialized subject position of Luk as the bottom boy. The linguistic naming of him as a "boy" also recalls a certain colonial taxonomy, as black slaves and native men were often described as boys and less of a man within the contexts of slavery and colonialism. If postcolonial theory about Hong Kong hinges on language of in-between-ness, collaborative colonialism, and hybridity, Ma's novel demonstrates that queerness and the erotics of imperialism, in fact, take center stage in the interimperial condition, and that the interimperiality of Luk having multiple allegiances with Davidson, the KMT, and the mafia gang are what constitute him as a particularly useful subject.

If queerness lies at the heart of the interimperiality that is Hong Kong, its place in the archive also escapes normative categorization and traffics in the realm of what Derrida terms "archival violence."[40] The violence of the archive functions to reduce a queer subject like Luk Naam Coi to a status of the non-normative and the perverse, a criminal subject of sexual buggery. In particular, Ma's novel is attentive to this violence of the archive as well as the possibility of rupturing the archive to tell something otherwise. This rupturing of the archive is crucial to my formulation of queer Hong Kong as a Sinophone method, which traffics in modes of unknowability, opacity, and indeterminacy. As the Japanese side is about to surrender in 1945, Luk discovers Morrison's whereabouts in the prisoner-of-war camp and tries to use his influence in the triad society to help Morrison escape. However, once Morrison is able to escape and meet Luk in a secretive place, Morrison brings with him another Chinese boy named Aa Ban (阿斌), whom he met and shared an intimate relationship with in the prison camp. Enraged by this betrayal, Luk decides that he will no longer be Morrison's "bad boy." He promises Morrison to arrange for their escape but informs Japanese military officers that they can catch both Morrison and Aa Ban at the Shek Tong Tsui (石塘咀) harbor. (315). If what cements the smooth functioning of the interimperial logic in the novel is Luk and Morrison's secretive and queer relation, the final evidentiary revelation of Luk as queer in the official archive turns out to be nothing of importance, ironically. It marks him as a perverse Hong Kong subject who simply happens to share a perverse relation with a British officer.

Ma Ka Fai, narrating at the conclusion of the novel in a self-reflexive mode, tells the reader that he found a piece of document at the British National Archives containing the post-WWII legal adjudication of Japanese war crimes. One Japanese officer explains why and how he tortures Morris Davidson to death. He mentions that they torture Davidson to death because he resists the interrogation, and the main reason he resists is because the Japanese officer informs that it was his "Chinese" friend who betrayed him and notified the Japanese of his escape plan. Davidson reasons that Luk can't possibly betray him because "he is mine." When asked by the British interrogator to name who Davidson claims as "his," the Japanese officer writes down the name: "Luk Naam Coi." Ma Ka Fai thus concludes the novel in the following way: "Dear Boss Naam, there is god above our head. No one in the world can live without leaving a trace. Who really cares? Luk Naam Coi, it is because of me Ma Ka Fai that the old neighbors in Wan Chai will forever remember you, maybe not in the way you want to be remembered." (333). By ending the novel with multiple takes on "the archive," Ma seems to suggest that queer figures like Luk, Davidson and others are everywhere in the archive of Hong Kong history but their existence might merely serve as statistics of perversion. Thus, queerness is central to the archive precisely due to its perverse (in)significance.[41]

By turning our attention to three queer Hong Kong texts that illuminate the minor gesture, lesbian erotohistoriography, and queer archive, my chapter provides some clues to what queer Hong Kong as method can offer to Hong Kong studies, Sinophone theory, and queer studies. A queer Hong Kong method is attentive to the minor gesture of queer desire, which takes the form of feminist solidarity, lesbian intimacy, and interimperial sexuality.

It demonstrates how queerness, while often pressed to the fringe of dominant historical narration, also holds critical potential in mapping affective genealogy and clandestine structures of feeling. Queer Hong Kong as a Sinophone method actualizes Shu-mei Shih's claim that "the Sinophone can be considered a way of looking at the world, a theory, perhaps even an epistemology."[42]

Notes

This research is supported by the GRF grant of the Research Grants Council of Hong Kong under the project code: 17613520.

1. Quoted in Stephen W. K. Chiu and Kaxton Y. K. Siu, *Hong Kong Society: High-Definition Stories Beyond the Spectacle of East-Meets-West* (Singapore: Palgrave Macmillan, 2022), 137.
2. David R. Meyer, *Hong Kong as a Global Metropolis* (Cambridge: Cambridge University Press, 2000), 60.
3. Lisa Lowe, *The Intimacies of Four Continents* (Durham, NC: Duke University Press, 2015), 101–133. It is worth pointing out that Lowe devotes one chapter to Hong Kong as the colonial site where both the recruitment and transfer of coolies and the interracial intimacies and differentiation of European and Chinese bodies are simultaneously at work. These forms of colonial and imperial intimacies cover debates of free and unfree labor, vagrancy, and unequal regulations of prostitution and venereal diseases.
4. For a trenchant critique of how both postcolonial theory and area studies are complicit with U.S. empire and fail to critique racism domestically and Asian colonial modernity and imperialism abroad, see Shu-mei Shih, "Racializing Area Studies, Defetishizing China," *positions* 27, no. 1 (2019): 33–65.
5. Shu-mei Shih, "Globalisation and the (In)significance of Taiwan," *Postcolonial Studies* 6, no. 2 (2003): 144.
6. Rey Chow, "Between Colonizers: Hong Kong's Postcolonial Self-Writing in the 1990s," *Diaspora* 2, no. 2 (1992): 151–170.
7. For a study of the demolishing of British colonial buildings and sites like the Star Ferry Pier, Queen's Pier, and other urban landscapes, as well as activism around cultural heritage preservation, see Yun-chung Chen and Mirana M. Szeto, "The Forgotten Road of Progressive Localism: Preservation Movement in Hong Kong," *Inter-Asia Cultural Studies* 16, no. 3 (2015): 436–453.
8. Ackbar Abbas, *Hong Kong: Culture and the Politics of Disappearance* (Minneapolis: University of Minnesota Press, 1997), 6.
9. Shu-mei Shih, *Visuality and Identity: Sinophone Articulations Across the Pacific* (Berkeley: University of California Press, 2007), 141.
10. Yiu-Wai Chu, *Lost in Transition: Hong Kong Culture in the Age of China* (Albany: SUNY Press, 2013), 3.
11. 朱耀偉主編, Chu Yiu-wai, ed. 《香港研究作為方法》 (Hong Kong studies as method) (Hong Kong: Chungwa Publisher, 2016).

12. Jose Esteban Munoz, *Cruising Utopia: The Then and There of Queer Futurity* (New York: NYU Press, 2009), 1.

13. Howard Chiang, *Transtopia in the Sinophone Pacific* (New York: Columbia University Press, 2021), 4.

14. Shu-mei Shih, "Race and Relation: The Global Sixties in the South of the South," *Comparative Literature* 68, no. 2 (2016): 141.

15. For queer Sinophone studies, see Howard Chiang and Ari Larissa Heinrich, eds., *Queer Sinophone Cultures* (London: Routledge, 2014).

16. For an analysis of Hong Kong as a site of colonial intimacy where both discourses of free trade and violent governmentality converge, see Lisa Lowe, *The Intimacies of Four Continents* (Durham, NC: Duke University Press, 2015), 101–133.

17. My invocation of the minor is indebted to the theory of minor transnationalism. See Francoise Lionnet and Shu-mei Shih, eds., *Minor Transnationalism* (Durham, NC: Duke University Press, 2005).

18. Shih, *Visuality and Identity*, 4.

19. Shih, Shu-mei, "Empires of the Sinophone" (lecture, Sinophone Studies: New Direction, Harvard University, Boston, October 14, 2016).

20. Law Wing Sang, *Collaborative Colonial Power: The Making of the Hong Kong Chinese* (Hong Kong: HKU Press, 2009).

21. Ziling Ye, "*Zishu nü* (自梳女): Dutiful Daughters of the Guangdong Delta," *Intersections*, July 17, 2008, http://intersections.anu.edu.au/issue17/ye.htm. See also Janice Stockard, *Daughters of the Canton Delta: Marriage Patterns and Economic Strategies in South China, 1860–1930* (Stanford, CA: Stanford University Press, 1989).

22. Wong Nim Yan (黃念欣), *Wan qi feng ge: Xianggang nu zuo jia san lun* (晚期風格:香港女作家三論) (Hong Kong: Cosmos Books, 2007), 223–242.

23. Joseph Lau, "The 'Little Woman' as Exorcist: Notes on the Fiction of Huang Biyun," *Journal of Modern Literature in Chinese* 2, no. 2 (January 1999): 149–163.

24. Wong Bik-wan, *Lienu Tu* (烈女圖) (Hong Kong: Cosmos Books, 2004).

25. Wong, *Lienu Tu*, 74.

26. David Der-wei Wang (王德威), *Kua shiji fenghua: dangdai xiaoshuo 20 jia* (跨世紀風華：當代小說20家) (Taipei: Rye Field, 2002), 332.

27. Erin Manning, *The Minor Gesture* (Durham, NC: Duke University Press, 2016), 1.

28. Janet W. Salaff, *Working Daughters of Hong Kong: Filial Piety or Power in the Family?* (New York: Columbia University Press, 1995), 20.

29. Wong, *Lienu Tu*, 120.

30. *Zi shu* (*Intimates*), directed by Jacob Cheung (Hong Kong: Orange Sky Golden Harvest, 1997).

31. Helen Hok-sze Leung, "Queerscapes in Contemporary Hong Kong Cinema," *positions* 9, no. 2 (2001): 434.

32. Elizabeth Freeman, *Time Binds: Queer Temporalities, Queer Histories* (Durham, NC: Duke University Press, 2010), 120.

33. Lisa Yoneyama, "Toward a Decolonial Genealogy of the Transpacific," *American Quarterly* 69, no. 3 (2017): 472.

34. Shelly Chan, *Diaspora's Homeland: Modern China in the Age of Global Migration* (Durham, NC: Duke University Press, 2018), 13.

35. Jacques Derrida, *Archive Fever: A Freudian Impression* (Chicago: University of Chicago Press, 1995), 7.

36. Ma, Ka Fai 馬家輝. *Long tou feng wei* 龍頭鳳尾 (Once upon a time in Hong Kong). (Taipei: ThinKingDom Publisher, 2016), 20.

37. Ann Stoler, *Along the Archival Grain: Epistemic Anxieties and Colonial Common Sense* (Princeton, NJ: Princeton University Press, 2009), 50.

38. John M. Carroll, *A Concise History of Hong Kong* (Lanham, MD: Rowman & Littlefield, 2007), 117.

39. Laura Doyle, "Inter-Imperiality: Dialectics in a Postcolonial World History," *Interventions* 16, no. 2 (2014): 160.

40. Jacques Derrida, *Archive Fever*, 7.

41. For a parallel study of the absence and presence of queer sexuality in the colonial archive, see Anjali Arondekar, *For the Record: On Sexuality and the Colonial Archive in India* (Durham, NC: Duke University Press, 2009).

42. Shu-mei Shih, "The Concept of the Sinophone," *PMLA* 126, no. 3 (2011): 717.

Enjoy Your Sinophone!

CHIEN-HENG WU

In a 2018 review published on *Shuo shu* (Speaking of books), the renowned novelist Ng Kim Chew gave readers a piece of his mind regarding the academic recognition accorded to Shu-mei Shih for her theorization of the Sinophone.¹ According to Ng, his engagement with Shih's *Fan lisan* (*Against Diaspora*) was occasioned by the book's inclusion as required reading for his graduate seminar. Experience has taught him that "this kind of book deserves only a skimming-through, for [he] know[s] it that it won't be of any use." But since it is a required reading, Ng was forced to "close-read" *Fan lisan* and, without surprise, found it to be "the most horrible 'academic monograph' in recent years."

This paper is divided into two sections. In the first section, I lay out some of Shih's major assertions and highlight her nuanced formulation of the Sinophone against Ng's reductive reading. My examination focuses on three interrelated topics: the first concerns the idea of Chineseness; the second deals with the definition of *settler colonialism*; finally, I look at the idea of "becoming local" and examine the thin line conjoining and separating the local from the indigenous. In the next section, I will draw out some productive tension in Shih's two theoretical projects, the Sinophone and relational comparison, teasing out the possibility of complementing the Sinophone epistemology with a relational ontology in order to suggest a method of multi-scalar interconnectedness attentive to both the situated *inter*-relationality and its underlying *intra*relationality.

According to Shih, the domain of language is a site of intense cultural and political struggle, and modern China's language policy, far from complying with the standard linguistic classification, imposes a language hierarchy relegating minor languages to the status of regional dialects even when there exists no mutual intelligibility between these languages and the standard Sinitic language of Mandarin. The construction of a unified language makes a series of ideological operations in broader cultural and political spheres possible, all of which contrive to establish a chain of equivalence around the signifier of Chineseness, which, in turn, serves as the basis for the diasporic attachment to an ancestral homeland. This chain of equivalence subordinates the multiplicity of the Sinitic languages and their polyphonic expressions to a standardized version of Hanyu, whose particularity is then disavowed under the overarching banner of Chineseness. Thanks to this process of unification at cultural-linguistic levels, "overseas Chinese" becomes an ideological category, "exploiting racist injuries to their feelings or other forms of alienation [in the land of settlement] that can be easily transfigured into long-distance nationalism for the benefit of China."[2]

For Shih, language, in addition to its linguistic function, also has a politics. The designation of language as dialect by the Chinese state is carried out through deliberate measures of subordination. The critical thrust of the concept of the Sinophone is to "[disrupt] the chain of equivalence established . . . among language, culture, ethnicity and nationality" (710). Therefore, when Shih debunks the myth of the overseas Chinese, the target of her criticism is not diaspora as historical fact but rather diaspora taken *as a set of values* that not only caters to the unifying desire of China's nationalist discourse but also plays into the hands of the racialization discourse of the receiving countries that would most likely interpret the diasporic attachment as a sign of disloyalty or an attempt at disrupting social harmony.[3]

In Ng's reading, Shih's criticism of the overseas Chinese points an accusing finger at those immigrants who are allegedly burdened with "an original sin." To the best of my knowledge, Shih never relies on the discourse of the original sin by labeling those immigrants as the bearers of guilt on account of bloodline descent.[4] Instead, Shih's critique of diaspora aims to expand the scope of possible responses beyond mere nostalgic longing—such that, even with the nostalgic feeling showing up in the land of settlement, this feeling is produced in response to local needs and contingencies—thus, a time-sensitive and place-based formation rather than an a priori attachment to an imaginary homeland.[5] With the concept of the Sinophone, the historical sense of diaspora is fully acknowledged, but values and affects mobilized to reinforce the notion of uniform Chineseness are questioned from the point of view of locality. Simply put, the category of "the overseas Chinese" is criticized for its complicity with ethnocentric reductionism that fosters a vision of the future without prospect, a future predetermined by an imaginary past at the expense of the living present.

In calling for an end to diaspora, the Sinophone also calls for a new politics of time that aims to keep the future open and indeterminate, a future that harbors a spectrum of possibilities, including the thriving and vanishing of the Sinophone culture:

> Sinophone studies take as its premise the plasticity of Sinitic languages to no predetermined destinies, even to the extent that the field of Sinophone studies might reach its demise at the limit. Hence it is important to recognize that Sinophone cultures can be vibrant or vanishing, and neither is a phenomenon to either celebrate or lament.[6]

Contrary to Ng's conspiracy theory, according to which the Sinophone is either part of the United States–led anti-China campaign or the self-serving academic enterprise in the service of global capital, the passage above reveals a rarely acknowledged fact that the person most responsible for the concept's widespread circulation actually holds out the prospect of its disappearance.

Responding to Shih's assertion that many dialects are languages in their own right, Ng acknowledges the tension between dialect and language within a multiethnicity nation but rejects Shih's claim about the homogenizing effect of the language-nationalization campaign that "sought to unify the cacophonous linguistic field in modern China."[7] In Ng's view, this tension is intrinsically linguistic rather than political; its politicization occurs—as when dialect becomes language—only with the colonial introduction and imposition of the modular logic of the nation-state. In the absence of such condition, all that remains is a depoliticized tension between language and dialect. On this view, Shih's translation of the Sinophone as Huayu yuxi wenxue amounts to a monstrous misnomer driven by dubious motivations:

> In substituting Huayu yuxi wenxue for Huawen wenxue, Shih stomps on the established academic convention, ignoring "the given scholarly usage," an act that renders her a capitalist opportunist; there is no solid scholarship, only reckless appropriation, creolization, and a desire to occupy the position of a theoretician.[8]

What follows is a barrage of insults thrown Shih's way as Ng accuses her of acting with business acumen to carve out an academic niche and gain easy access to academic resources (e.g., funding, reputation, etc.). As if the charge of harboring the capitalist mindset is not enough, Ng goes on to declare that the entirety of Shih's theoretical endeavor can be considered an opportunist venture, jumping on the bandwagon of a reinstituted Cold War geopolitics, *all for fear of China's rise on the global stage.*

Let's pause and examine both the stated and unstated assumptions of Ng's argument. It is clear that Ng wishes to keep language (especially the deployment of the term *Sinophone*) as depoliticized as possible. In contrast to Shih's excessive politicization, Ng prides himself on the kind of historical and anthropological fieldwork he has been conducting for Sinophone Malaysian literature. One cannot but respect the contribution he has made to Sinophone Malaysian literature in this regard. Yet, the manner in which Ng presents his case carries a very unsettling implication: Ng wields the authority of a major Sinophone Malaysian writer-scholar to silence Shih's critical engagement in the name of certain methodological and ideological purity. Such bigotry, however, rules out in advance the opportunities opened up by Shih's theorization of the Sinophone. Translating *Sinophone* as "Huayu yuxi wenxue," according to Shih, is an attempt:

> to give a name to those bodies of texts that have been given the torturous and confusing nomenclature "literature in China" (*huayu wenxue*, written outside China) as opposed to "Chinese literature" (*Zhongguo wenxue*, written inside China). The semantic ambiguity of the two terms arises out of the use of "Chinese" in both cases, which is too homogenizing to make any critical work possible.[9]

Such a critical work cannot be achieved without overcoming two blind spots of Chinese diaspora studies: (1) its inability to bypass the idea of Chineseness as the organizing principle and (2) the lack of interaction with other scholarly disciplines.[10] The Siophone's interdisciplinary focus allows it to imbibe elements of criticality from such disciplines as ethnic and postcolonial studies without losing sight of the locality from within which it forms its distinct articulations; moreover, it allows the concept to branch out into different directions in ways that cast a critical glance not only at the debilitating limit of Chineseness but also at those sources where the Sinophone draws its intellectual inspiration. The overcoming of these two obstacles leads not to a negative but rather an affirmative critique that draws on comparable antecedents, structural parallels, and other relevant theoretical insights through cross-disciplinary fertilization, ultimately with the aim of furnishing Chinese diaspora studies with a new lens of awareness.

Another point of contestation raised by Ng regards the question of settler colonialism. In her analysis of China's imperialist formation, Shih brings to the fore the complicity between the Chinese narrative of victimhood, unreflective nationalism, and self-Orientalization, all of which work in concert with the West's production of Chinese uniformity.[11] The importance of this account lies in its identification of *a structure of reversibility* from the position of the victim to that of the oppressor, a perspective that also informs her analysis of settler colonialism.

Take Taiwan, for example. The majority of its current population are the descendants of the Han people who first immigrated to the island around the seventeenth century and later came with Kuomintang (KMT) in the late 1940s. Given the political, economic, and military pressures from China, most of the Han settlers today resist the idea of unification with China and claim a distinct Taiwanese identity. Coupled with the fact that the first-wave Han immigrants had also endured colonial violence under Dutch and Japanese rule—albeit in distinctly different manners and to vastly different degrees from their Indigenous counterparts—the Han population in Taiwan is thus historically endowed with the status of victimhood. This narrative of historical victimization notwithstanding, it should be noted that Taiwan's Han majority today are those who wield enormous clout over others in all spheres of life. So, rather than the standard structure of reversibility (as in the case of China), the situation in Taiwan might be described as the coexistence of the identities of victim and oppressor. Herein lies the limit of a version of the Sinophone that focuses exclusively on the perspective of locality without simultaneously addressing the issue of Indigeneity. In order to put an expiration date on diaspora, the Han have constructed a placed-based identity, but such a construction rarely attends to the prior presence of the Indigenous peoples in Taiwan and fails to acknowledge the contribution of the Indigenous cultures to the formation of Taiwan's local identity. This does not mean that the Indigenous must be subsumed under the local, only that any placed-based definition of a Taiwanese Sinophone identity cannot afford to neglect the perspective of Indigeneity that calls attention to the legacy of settler colonialism.

Here, the Sinophone takes on a rather ambiguous role: In the very gesture of putting an expiration date on diaspora, the Sinophone articulation runs the risk of lapsing into another form of hegemonic exclusion, as the local needs and desires behind the place-based praxis are often realized in total disregard of the values espoused by the island's original inhabitants since those needs and desires have now been dictated by Taiwan's Han majority as the holders of the institutional power in cultural, political, and economic domains. As Shih points out, "The Sinophone [in Taiwan] is the dominant vis-à-vis their indigenous populations."[12] The result is an extremely dismal prospect for Indigenous peoples. "From the indigenous perspective," Shih reminds us, "the history of Taiwan is a history of serial colonialism (Dutch, French, Chinese, Japanese, etc.) that has never ended. *Taiwan has never been postcolonial.*"[13]

If Taiwan has never been postcolonial, it is because settler colonialism is not a specific event but an overall structure that will not end without a radical transformation of the whole system. Here, the thesis of putting an expiration date on diaspora receives an additional twist. Shih supplements the perspective of locality—a corrective to the diasporic discourse—with that of Indigeneity that serves as a critical reminder of two dominant psychodynamics undergirding the mentality of settler colonialism: the amnesia of the past and the disavowal of the present.[14] This formulation offers a vantage point from which the method of the Sinophone critique is on full display. When Shih says that diaspora as value can be criticized from two perspectives—locality and Indigeneity—it is important to understand this claim in terms of trialectics rather than dialectical opposition. That's why Ng's characterization of the Sinophone as evincing the Cold War logic that serves the United States' imperialist interest to delegitimize China's rise to global prominence misses the point because the Sinophone as a critical method brings about "a multiply-mediated and multiply-angulated critique," targeting both the nationalist-qua-imperialist formation of Chineseness and the exclusionary hegemonic culture at the site of settlement.[15]

Shih makes a crucial distinction between the Sinophone as history and the Sinophone as concept—the former, neither inherently progressive nor regressive, referring to the historical fact, whereas the latter suggests a critical epistemology examining the logic of inclusion and exclusion at multiple levels. When the Sinophone is taken as a critical method, its critique cuts both ways, heterogenizing the uniform construction of *both* Chinese and local Sinophone identity. That's why the Sinophone has a trialectical structure, "since mediation is exercised by more agents than one, the so-called perennial other."[16] On this view, the standard dialectical mediation is transformed into a trialectics that complicates the dualistic logic by factoring in the often-neglected perspective of Indigeneity. By emphasizing the multidirectional processes of the Sinophone, Shih manages to bypass the Cold War schema and situates the Sinophone as a critical project problematizing the unifying intent or homogenizing drive of any identity formation.

Having sketched out some of Shih's major points concerning settler colonialism, let us now turn to Ng's counterargument. In Ng's presentation, the relation of power is taken into consideration but only insofar as the Han are on the victimized end of that relationship; otherwise, power relations do not exist. As a result, there is no such thing as settler colonialism.[17] Implicit in such a view is an accusation that Shih has yet again unduly politicized the movement of immigration:

> For Prof. Shih, immigration equals "colonization"; serial waves of immigration equals "serial colonialism"; settlement means "settler colonialism"; given the fact of the nationalist government's presence in Taiwan, it naturally "becomes representative settler colony." According to her definition, the influx of the Vietnamese and Indonesians to Taiwan in recent years are also "settler colonizers."[18]

In Ng's view, the reversibility of victim and oppressor reaches a ridiculous height with Shih's treatment of settler colonialism. Everything is turned topsy-turvy when it gets politicized: Just as a badly victimized China was turned into an aggressive expansionist, the defeated KMT all of a sudden became a settler colonial regime when it fled to Taiwan.

> In Shih's view, Han immigrants are worse than real colonizers because "these colonizers returned to the colonial motherland with the end of colonialism, as with the Japanese in Taiwan or the English in India." Han immigrants, on the other hand, stayed behind without any intention to leave—"settler colonizers stayed and gradually became the majority in population; for example the Han in Taiwan, be they Taiwanese, Hakkas, provincial outsider (*waisheng'ren*), are all settler colonizers from the point of view of the indigenous peoples" and "there is no possibility of decolonization, nor is there any possibility to become postcolonial."

These passages are indicative of Ng's dismissal of the idea of settler colonialism; more importantly, they also confirm Shih's observation of the two prevailing psychodynamics of the settler colonial mentality, as Ng selectively turns a blind eye to the hegemonic dominance of the Han population in Taiwan. To rationalize this will to nonknowledge, Ng even resorts to falsification by grafting the claim—"there is no possibility of decolonization, nor is there any possibility [for the Indigenous peoples in Taiwan] to become postcolonial"—onto an entirely different context:

> In order to fashion immigrants of different ethnic backgrounds into Singaporeans, the Lee Kuan Yew administration thoughtfully adopted English [as the official language] and relegated other languages to the private spheres, an act that offended the most populous Hua. If this is not "against diaspora," what is it then? Claiming that for immigrants "there is no possibility of decolonization, nor is there any possibility to become

postcolonial" reflects a racist point of view on Shih's part. Does she even realize that her "against diaspora" thesis and her "settler colonialism" thesis contradict each other? Or perhaps she does but intends it so?

With this surreptitious substitution of immigrants for the Indigenous peoples, one cannot but suspect that it is rather Ng who is hell-bent on ignoring the critical operation of trialectics that intersects the argument against diaspora with the condition of settler colonialism. Ng's reluctance to acknowledge the indigenous perspective exemplifies the aforementioned twin psychodynamics, as he denies the prior presence of the indigenous population ("the amnesia of the past") and exercises the violence of ableism by likening the minorities to people with disabilities ("the disavowal of the present"):

> Rash and impulsive, [Shih] appropriates whenever she wants, renounces whenever she wants . . . as if she had been endowed with some kind of imperial privilege; just as she is accustomed to occupying the position of the underprivileged minorities, euphemistically known as voicing for their rights, but really more like scrambling for the disabled parking bay.

Just as Ng has difficulty acknowledging the perspective of Indigeneity, he is equally allergic to the idea of locality. For him, Shih's theorization of locality amounts to a simple demand for assimilation—that is, when Shih urges people to put an end to diaspora, she advocates assimilation to the dominant culture in the place of settlement as the be-all-and-end-all solution to all the problems associated with diaspora as value. Following this logic, Sinophone Malaysian writers would have to give up Hanyu as their language of expression because assimilation to the Malay culture is the only way to end diaspora, the only way "to purge settler colonizers of their original sin."

One would be hard-pressed to find such advocacy of assimilation in Shih's work. According to Shih, "Emphasizing that diaspora has an end date is . . . to insist that cultural and political practice is always place-based. *Everyone should be given a chance to become a local.*"[19] "Becoming local" is presented as an ethical choice, and the concept of the Sinophone offers a critical perspective into the condition of possibilities that would render this choice open to all the inhabitants of the community of settlement—an epistemology that acknowledges the ever-changing dynamics in the composition of a Sinophone community, thanks to which, "Sinophone articulations can take as many different positions as possible within the realm of human expression,"[20] including its termination, reinvention, and, of course, everything in between.

It is, therefore, a mistake to interpret the Sinophone as a call for assimilation. Given the process of creolization at the place of settlement, language in a Sinophone community is inevitably multilingual and polyphonic. Ng is thus wrong to assume that Shih urges Malaysian writers to give up Hanyu as their preferred language of expression. When Shih urges that everybody be given a chance to become local, she is not saying that everybody has to be local through assimilation into the dominant culture. An ontological interconnectedness is presupposed and informs the concept of the Sinophone: When a group of inhabitants chooses to become local, the composition of the local changes according to the interactions of all participating agents in this composition; the local, as a result, is an ever-changing configuration, never a fixed entity. The local, then, is not a foundational concept that assimilates those who inhabit the land into its orbit; rather, it is the orbit that constantly rotates and refashions itself around the needs, desires, and contingencies of its inhabitants. The local, in this sense, belongs to what Gilbert Simondon calls the theater of individuation. Bernard Stiegler explains the Simondian concept of individuation as follows:

> If it was [stable], it would be a total ossified crystal, without future or temporality; if it was totally unstable, it would lead to an explosion of the group—atomization, pulverization, entropy, absolute disequilibrium. A group is always between equilibrium and disequilibrium, neither in equilibrium nor in disequilibrium, but rather always at the border of both.[21]

This metastable process in the formation of a *we* (or the local) brings into focus the ontological dimension of the Sinophone that is only tacitly assumed in Shih's account and remains largely subordinated to the primacy of the Sinophone as epistemology. The ontological thus remains an underexplored topic in Shih's theorization of the Sinophone, and it is to this that the next section turns.

Over the years, Shih has tried to refine the concept of the Sinophone by further distinguishing diaspora as history from diaspora as value; the Sinophone as history from the Sinophone as theory. Although these pairs of distinctions help turn our attention away from the vertical genealogy of the sovereign nation-state, they nonetheless do not address the ontological interconnectedness in the composition of a Sinophone locality. This, of course, is not a claim about the absence of an ontology in Shih's conceptualization of the Sinophone, only that the ontological is not prioritized due to certain historical and theoretical exigencies. Nevertheless, a more systematic elaboration of the ontological would help bring the dynamic process of internal composition into sharper relief and contribute to the development of Sinophone studies.

Aside from Shih's conceptualization of the Sinophone as a critical epistemology, relational comparison is another theoretical thread running through several of her publications, starting from "Comparison as Relation" (2013) to a more recent position paper, "Linking Taiwan Studies with the World" (2018). In "Comparison of Relation," Shih turns to Édouard Glissant for a relational ontology to go along with the epistemology of the integrative world history. This odd coupling actually helps illuminate the dynamic composition of a Sinophone identity without falling prey to the vitalist temptation that privileges the ontological becoming as in and of itself constituting the sufficient condition for transformation.

In this article, Shih approaches comparison as relation by bringing two perspectives, one macro and the other micro, to bear on each other. Comparison as relation is first considered from the point of view of the integrative world history as that which "set[s] into motion historical relationalities between entities brought together for comparison, and bring[s] into relation terms that have traditionally been pushed apart from each other."[22] This way of looking at relationality at the world scale attends to both material and nonmaterial differences of each party involved and is strictly historical in nature. Relationality in this historical mode concerns relations *between* given entities in situations fraught with tension and conflicting interests, thus opening up a new avenue where mobility and movement are investigated through an analysis of power relations.[23]

The insight drawn from the integrative world history offers Shih an epistemological model that probes how historical agents enter a relation with each other on a macro scale: "To be sure, not all parts of the network are equally affecting or evenly affected by the global system, but all parts of the network are constitutive of the system itself, and there is no hiding from an interconnectedness that is thoroughly infiltrated by the operation of power."[24] Relationality at this level is probably best described as *inter*relation, establishing horizontal connections whereby Shih is able to trace a plantation arc from the West Indies to the East Indies, then to the American South, and reconstructs "a circuit of interconnected histories of European colonialism" among these sites.[25] Instead of seeing national histories and literatures as discrete and self-contained, this perspective allows Shih to analyze these national histories as elements linked together, though in a highly uneven fashion, on a global scale. This method of thinking relationality lends itself quite well to the conceptualization of the Sinophone as epistemology in that both shift their focus away from the standard genealogy's vertical tracing and cast sidelong glances at comparable instances across different geographical regions. Thus, when Shih says that the Sinophone is "inherently comparative and transnational,"[26] she is referring to a set of horizontal relations across Sinophone communities.

The other major inspiration for Shih's thinking of relationality comes from the Caribbean poet-philosopher Édouard Glissant, who equips Shih with the means to explore the ontological dimension of relationality. According to Glissant, relation is a movement, not the movement of entities that forms an *inter*relation but the movement *immanent* to the ongoing constitution of any given entity. For the sake of convenience, we shall call this mode of relation *intra*relation:

> Like the ecological interdependence of all lands on earth, all people and cultures are interdependent when seen from the viewpoint of Relation. Culture cannot be reduced to prime element, such as prime numbers in mathematics, but are always open and changing through their contacts with other cultures.[27]

The evocation of ecological interdependence suggests a layer of interconnectedness more profound than that derived from the idea of interrelation, which, however dynamic and complex in its determinate unfolding, has already posited the prior existence of the parties involved. Relational ontology, in contrast, draws attention to the fact that higher-level entities come into being only in the wake of a deeper operation of what Karen Barad has termed the agential *intra*-action:

> The neologism "intra-action" *signifies the mutual constitution of entangled agencies*. That is, in contrast to the usual "interaction," which assumes that there are separate individual agencies that precede their interaction, the notion of intra-action recognizes that distinct agencies do not precede, but rather emerge through, their intra-action. It is important to note that the "distinct" agencies are only distinct in a relational, not an absolute, sense, that is, *agencies are only distinct in relation to their mutual entanglement; they don't exist as individual elements*.[28]

Relational ontology inverts the conventional view of causality and instills a recognition that a higher-level entity, from individual to culture, is the result of a metastable formation, "neither in equilibrium nor in disequilibrium," as Stiegler puts it. In a similar fashion, Glissant describes culture as a chaos mode that nonetheless is not chaotic, "neither fusion nor confusion . . . neither the uniform blend . . . nor muddled nothingness."[29] Relation thus conceived "does not precede itself in its action and presupposes no a priori. . . . One does not first enter Relation, as on one might enter a religion."[30]

It is crucial to note that relation in this ontological register is less a claim denying the existence of the prime distinct element than a claim affirming the incessant process of creolization leading up to the emergence of the said distinction. It seems to me that elements of relational ontology are already present in Shih's discussion of the Sinophone, only that it remains a latent assumption. This lack of systematic elaboration of the ontological in Shih's conceptualization of the Sinophone gives the impression that the Sinophone and relational comparison are meant as two separate lines of investigation, a view that has prompted critics as discerning as Kuei-fen Chiu to speak of "a new phase" in Shih's intellectual trajectory:

> True, "relational comparison" is in many ways an extension of "Sinophone as a method" in Shih's theoretical trajectory. Both theoretical articulations seek to construct transnational contexts for the texts under discussion, but underscore at the same time their geographical and temporal specificity. Nevertheless, with "China-centrism" and "Chineseness" [as] the main targets, the Sinophone as a method inevitably falls prey to the "obsession with China" that it seeks to deconstruct.[31]

According to Chiu, in contrast to the concept of the Sinophone bogged down by its obsession with China, relational comparison ushers in a new theoretical direction that helps Taiwan studies forge transnational linkages across a vast array of disciplinary fields without being hamstrung by the default framework of Greater China. While in general agreement with Chiu's appreciative appraisal of relational comparison as "world making,"[32] my reading differs from hers in two important respects. Whereas Chiu considers relational comparison as an advancement from the Sinophone, I see the two more in a mutually informing and mutually reinforcing relationship.[33] Moreover, in Chiu's reading, relationality is seen primarily from the viewpoint of the integrative world history, thereby missing out on the other half of Shih's two-tiered analysis of relationality, that is, relational ontology.

Reading the concept of the Sinophone through the lens of relational ontology affords a more robust theorization of the internal composition of a Sinophone identity as a nongiven and heterogeneously layered formation. It should be emphasized, however, that relational ontology alone is not sufficient, for it risks foreclosing the phenomenological analysis of power. For example, in Glissant's poetics, relation functions like "an intransitive verb," serving as the condition of possibility for the ongoing diversification of the world.[34] It is, in short, "the thing that makes the understanding of every culture limitless."[35] Glissant's claim has a strong ethico-political implication because it matters not whether an individual chooses to enter a relation because it is always already in relation, or rather *it is relation*. It is important to point out that "the thing" in Glissant's account is the power (*puissance*) of the virtual that undercuts the molar power (*pouvoir*) of sovereignty. The question is: How do we move back and forth between *ontological* interconnectedness and *historical* interconnection mediated through asymmetrical relations of power—that is, power as exercised on a macrohistorical scale? Glissant's Deleuze-inspired poetics posits a flat ontology unable to admit the scaling back and forth between different levels of analysis since there is only one plane of immanence with infinite and derivative variations. Consequently, if relation indeed works in the manner of an intransitive verb, there is only relation without relationship *between*. As Peter Hallward argues, relation for Glissant "is a name for self-differentiating reality as such, it is not a 'relationship' between things."[36] This limit of Glissant's relational ontology is also perceived by Shih. Consider the following two passages:

> While Glissant calls Relation an intransitive verb, I would extend it as a transitive verb that acts upon objects, terms, languages, texts, peoples, societies, regions, and so on. This active mode of relation that brings certain entities into relation is an act, a method, and the entities brought together for comparison are then, so to speak, *relationed*.[37]
>
> Glissant notes . . . what the poetics of Relation promises: "The probability: that you come to the bottom of all confluences to mark more strongly your inspirations." *It is surely impossible to reach "the bottom of all confluences," and I doubt there is such a place, however abstract that place may be, but it may be the place where we can work toward, from whichever small or large land mass in the arch-sea.*[38]

In these two passages, Glissant's poetics of relation is modified such that relation is no longer just an intransitive verb but rather one that involves the coming together of two seemingly contradictory postulations: on the one hand, the postulation of a historical agent who acts; on the other, the postulation of the virtual ("the bottom of all confluences") that displaces any such representational agency. An ethics of relation exists at the intersection of these two demands: It insists on historical actuality but works toward its own infinite displacement; it differs from a purely relational ontology in that the virtual is not celebrated in its own right nor posited as some mystical force resisting stasis and uniformity; finally, it appeals to the humanist concept of agency but reworks it in such a radical fashion that it no longer moves toward a teleological end but toward ontological interrelatedness.

In my view, there is a profound reason that before turning to Glissant, Shih constructs her ethics of relation on the ground of the integrative world history, for it is always from the historical ("from whichever small or large land mass in the arch-sea") that one works toward the ontological ("the bottom of all confluences"), not vice versa. Therefore, if the ethical primacy is accorded to relationality, we must take note of its two-tiered translation and understand relationality's interconnectedness not merely as something ontologically affirmed but something to be actualized through a historically determinate doing. Admittedly, the method of relational comparison does draw on this ontological dimension to locate a deeper transformative force. Nonetheless, this ontological force is not posited as a self-generating power but always requires a historical enactment for its actualization. In the end, critique operates on both phenomenological and ontological grounds and has to be strategically calibrated in accordance with the political and ethical priorities of a given field or situation.[39]

Conclusion

The Slovenian philosopher Slavoj Žižek, when he first rose to academic superstardom, was known for his provocative reinterpretation of Lacanian psychoanalysis, particularly the dictum, "Enjoy your symptom." The conventional view treats the symptom as a pathological formation to be dissolved when its hidden meaning is revealed in the analysis. In his reinterpretation, Žižek insists that the idea of symptom not be construed hermeneutically—that is, as a knot of meaning to be interpreted by the analyst and then resolved through analysis. Instead, the symptom is the kernel of one's being that ensures a minimal consistency to one's existence in the world. Hence, psychoanalysis's ethical dictum: Enjoy your symptom.[40]

The concept of the Sinophone can be approached in a similar manner. For example, the Sinophone must not be taken as some pathological formation to be dismissed by a more authentic method (as intended by Ng). And yet, given the possibility of its demise, I would not go so far as to claim a quasi-absolute status ("the kernel of one's being") for the Sinophone. Nonetheless, there is something in the Sinophone that resonates with the idea of minimal consistency. The Sinophone, in the most general sense, is a theory that aims to provide an account of identity formation through a delinking from the paralyzing imagination of an ancestral origin; then through a sustained negotiation between locality and Indigeneity, between the macro analysis of power in one's situated existence and the micro examination of ontological connectedness at the foundation of one's being. Succumbing to neither free-floating becoming nor metaphysical essence, the Sinophone presents a place-based and time-sensitive account of identity formation—at once rejecting the temptation of identarian fixity and enacting a minimal existential consistency; expressing the specificity of a local Sinophone articulation and evincing the generality of the dynamic ontological composition of every living entity. The maintenance of this delicate tension or metastable equilibrium is fundamental to the understanding of the Sinophone as a "world-making" project. With this in mind, enjoy your Sinophone!

Notes

1. Ng Kim Chew, "Zheyang de 'huayu yuxi' lun keyi xiuyi! Shi shu-mei de 'fan lisan' daodi zai fan shenme?" *Shuo shu* (Speaking of books), last modified January 2, 2018, https://sobooks.tw/sinophone-literature-review. All subsequent references to Ng are from the same source. All translations are mine. A backup can be found at https://drive.google.com/file/d/1UDziww8sNnb7N9Fqi1irp8QAEb4OWhFI/view?usp=sharing.

2. Shu-mei Shih, "The Concept of the Sinophone," *PMLA* 126, no. 3 (2011): 710.

3. Shu-mei Shih, "Against Diaspora," in *Sinophone Studies: A Critical Reader*, ed. Brian Bernards, Shu-mei Shih, and Chien-hsing Tsai (New York: Columbia University Press, 2013), 28.

4. She does, however, reference the idea in "Comparison as Relation" to suggest the colonial violence committed by the whites on the blacks and the Indians.

5. Shu-mei Shih, "Introduction: What Is Sinophone Studies?" in Bernards, Shih, and Tsai, *Sinophone Studies: A Critical Reader*, 7.

6. Shih, "Introduction," 11.

7. Shih, "Concept of the Sinophone," 715.

8. On the charge of reengaging Cold War geopolitics, see Shih's rebuttal in "Sinophone Studies Is Irreducible to a Critique of China-Centrism," *Zhongwai wenxue* (Chung Wai literary quarterly) 44, no. 1 (2015): 173–189.

9. Shih, "Introduction," 8.

10. Shih, "Against Diaspora," 30.

11. Shih, "Against Diaspora," 27.

12. Shih, "Concept of the Sinophone," 716.

13. Shih, "Against Diaspora," 31 (emphasis added).

14. Shih, "Introduction," 3–4.

15. Shih, "Against Diaspora," 39.

16. Shih, "Against Diaspora," 33.

17. That is why Ng undersigns himself as "settler colonizer" presumably as an ironic gesture of defiance.

18. It is worth pointing out that Shih does not equate immigration with colonization. For example, in a recent dialogue with Kim Tong Lee, she stresses that Chinese Malaysians should not be considered as settler colonizers in Malaysia because they are neither the demographic majority nor the official wielders of institutional power. The same can be said of the Vietnamese and Indonesians in Taiwan. See Shu-mei Shih and Kim Tong Lee, "Critical Issues in Sinophone Studies," *Concentric: Literary and Cultural Studies* 45, no. 2 (2019): 176.

19. Shih, "Against Diaspora," 37 (emphasis added).

20. Shih, "Concept of the Sinophone," 717.

21. Bernard Stiegler, *Acting Out*, trans. David Barison, Daniel Ross, and Patrick Crogan (Stanford, CA: Stanford University Press, 2009), 79.

22. Shu-mei Shih, "Comparison as Relation," in *Comparison: Theories, Approaches, Uses*, ed. Rita Felski and Susan Stanford Friedman (Baltimore, MD: The John Hopkins University Press, 2013), 79.

23. Shih, "Comparison as Relation," 79.

24. Shih, "Comparison as Relation," 83.

25. Shih, "Comparison as Relation," 86.

26. Shih, "Against Diaspora," 25.

27. Shih, "Comparison as Relation," 84.

28. Karen Barad, *Meeting the Universe Halfway: Quantum Physics and the Entanglement of Matter and Meaning* (Durham, NC: Duke University Press, 2007), 33.

29. Édouard Glissant, *Poetics of Relation*, trans. Betsy Wing (Ann Arbor: University of Michigan Press, 1997), 94.

30. Glissant, *Poetics of Relation*, 172.

31. Kuei-fen Chiu, "Response," *International Journal of Taiwan Studies* 1 (2018): 220.

32. Chiu, "Response," 221.

33. Chiu seems to confuse specificity with necessity. The fact that the Sinophone addresses linguistic communities organized via their specific articulations of Sinitic languages suggests less an obsession with China than an awareness of the community's historical grounding. If "Chineseness" features prominently in Shih's discussion of the Sinophone, even to the degree of appearing inevitable, it is because "Chineseness" constitutes the *specificity* of the Sinophone's historical framing, not because it is posited as the ultimate reference from which the Sinophone comes and to which the Sinophone returns. Given the aforementioned plasticity of Sinitic languages and the corresponding radical politics of time, the Sinophone is best understood as *an effect that has the potential to outgrow its cause*. Therefore, it makes sense not only "through a discursive relationality with 'China-centrism' or the issue of 'Chineseness'" (Chiu, "Response," 220). Rather, it makes sense profusely, in multiple directions and on multiple levels: For example, the sense-generating capacity of the Sinophone can be seen in the dynamics of its local composition; in its relation to other Sinophone communities; or even in its dispersal to different disciplines (sociology, critical race theories, postcolonial theories, Taiwan studies, American studies, etc.). With all of these taken into consideration, the world-opening implications of relational comparison—i.e., "a re-anchoring of Taiwan studies within a variety of disciplinary domains to generate dialogues with international communities at large"—is already the spirit informing Shih's project of the Sinophone. (Chiu, "Response," 220).

Another important observation made by Chiu is that "the move from 'Sinophone' to 'relational comparison' signifies the demise of postcolonial studies and the rise of world studies. The former highlights difference, while the latter emphasizes relationality" (Chiu, "Response," 221). Implicit in such a suggestion is that world studies requires a cosmopolitan framework too complex to be accommodated by concepts such as margins and centers central to both postcolonial and Sinophone studies. While Chiu acknowledges postcolonialism's formative influence at the inception of Taiwan studies, she seems to suggest that the postcolonial perspective is today too narrow for a world-opening endeavor that can only be achieved when we adopt a relational approach. Indeed, we should not ignore the difficulties encountered by postcolonial studies throughout its development. However, the question is: Should this be an either/or choice between difference and relationality? Again, I find such a distinction useful but probably too rigid to cultivate a liberatory ethics. In my view, one of the most underappreciated aspects of Shih's thinking is the Fanonian and Sartrean influence running through her entire oeuvre, from the Sinophone studies to the project of minor transnationalism, and also to the methodology of relational comparison. On her relation to Sartre and Fanon, see "Sinophone Studies Is Irreducible to a Critique of China-Centrism" and the interview conducted by Te-hsing Shan in Shu-mei Shih, *Fan lisan: Huayu yuxi yanjiu lun* (*Against Diaspora: Discourses on Sinophone Studies*) (Taipei: Linkingbooks Publishing, 2017).

34. Glissant, *Poetics of Relation*, 27.

35. Glissant, *Poetics of Relation*, 172.

36. Peter Hallward, *Absolutely Postcolonial: Writing Between the Singular and the Specific* (Manchester: Manchester University Press, 2001), 121.

37. Shu-mei Shih, "Linking Taiwan Studies with the World," *International Journal of Taiwan Studies* 1 (2018): 212.

38. Shih, "Comparison as Relation," 86 (emphasis added).

39. The discourse of posthumanism often presents itself as an advancement from the postcolonial perspective in that the posthuman extends its ethical concern beyond the racial other to include the domain of the nonhuman others (e.g., the environmental and the machinic). This customary understanding of the relationship between posthumanism and postcolonialism, however, has raised concern about its neglect of power differentials among human groups in favor of a formal flat equality of all things. For example, Md. Monirul Islam argues that the attempt to overcome the residual humanism in the postcolonial discourse has given rise to a frenzied displacement of everything human. However, the ontologically liberating discourse of posthumanism, when carried out at the cost of the human other, easily renders itself into a neocolonial practice. Engaging with Shih's defense of humanism, Islam calls to attention the urgent need for situated analysis and strategic prioritization in the face of the leveling ontological parity; failing this, the worst consequences of what appears to be a just theoretical stance is most likely to be borne by the poor and the marginalized human others. See Md. Monirul Islam, "Posthumanism: Through Postcolonial Lens," in *Critical Posthumanism and Planetary Futures*, ed. Debashish Banerji and Makarand R. Paranjape (New Delhi: Springer, 2016), 115–129.

40. Slavoj Žižek, *Sublime Object of Ideology* (London: Verso, 2008), 81.

12

The Lure of Diaspora and Sinophone Malaysian Literature in Taiwan

WAI-SIAM HEE

The Chinese Diaspora, Antilocalization, and Against–Diaspora

The dominant trend in contemporary Malaysian Chinese literary studies is to use diaspora discourse as a way of positioning the field.[1] Ng Kim Chew (hereafter Ng) is one of the main drivers and representatives of this trend. The "Chinese diaspora" theoretical framework informs both academic research on his works and his own research on Malaysian Chinese literature. For example, Jing Tsu uses the concept of Chinese diaspora in her research into Ng and Sinophone Malaysian literature.[2] Although there is nothing inherently wrong with the way the scholar regards Ng, who has become a citizen of the Republic of China (ROC) in Taiwan, as a Chinese diaspora author, I take issue with the increasingly common blanket characterization of local Chinese authors who retain Malaysian citizenship as diaspora Chinese writers due to Ng's influence.

Ng regards Malaysian Chinese literature as a "minor Sinophone literature of diasporic modernity."[3] On multiple occasions, Ng has gone to the Malaysian press to warn Malaysian Chinese authors against overemphasizing localization, lest they pay a heavy price: "In terms of the reality of Malaysia, Malaysian Chinese language literature has no place to talk about the local; that is the privilege of Malay literature of Chinese origin. The local in the context of Malaysia's political reality implies a rejection of the Chinese language."[4] This warning also implies that the sole criterion for the localization of Malaysian Chinese literature is a shift in the Malaysian ethnic-political climate in a direction more favorable to the Chinese ethnicity and language. Actually, the localization of Malaysian Chinese literature flourished in the 1950s and 1960s, when the ethnic political climate was at its most unfavorable. Ng himself went into diaspora in Taiwan in 1986. Taiwan provides rich cultural resources to diaspora Sinophone Malaysians, including scholarships, literary prizes, film sponsorships, publication grants, and writing fees. These constitute a powerful lure, drawing Malaysian Chinese to seek fame and fortune in Taiwan. In contrast, it is harder for Malaysian Chinese to access cultural resources in Malaysia; going into diaspora in Taiwan solves this difficulty.

For many years, Ng has promoted the idea that diasporic Sinophone Malaysian literature, like Taiwanese literature, is a "stateless literature," as in Malaysia, it has been "excluded from the definition of national literature."[5] Shu-mei Shih (hereafter Shih), who has consistently held a position arguing against diaspora, responded by noting that "the necessity of asking whether literature belongs to a country or not springs not from the need to confine literature within a certain region, but from the desire to more accurately understand the complex relationship between locality and transregionality within a literary work."[6] In response, Ng published an online book review mocking Shih's against-diaspora discourse standpoint as being "an extremely foolish argument" that left him "feeling deeply violated." He criticized her book *Against Diaspora* as being "the most frightening 'academic book' I have read in recent years" and questioned whether her application of the theory of "continental colonialism," borrowed from the U.S. discipline of "new Qing history," was, in fact, symptomatic of her conspiring with U.S. neoimperialism. In contrast, he had high praise for Wang Hui's criticism of "new Qing history" in The Rise of Modern Chinese Thought, which he characterized as being a "forcefully and meticulously argued unificationist discourse."[7]

After a literary award ceremony in 2018 at Peking University, Ng restated that he "felt worried about the trend of 'discourses on Sinophone studies' started by Shih in Taiwan and the United States and particularly worried for the Malaysian Chinese who believed they were benefiting from the 'Sinophone.'"[8] Clearly, Ng's escalating critique of Shih demonstrates that he feels that the diaspora discourse he built up has been "violated" by Shih's against-diaspora, localizationalist standpoint.

With China's rise in the twenty-first century, the Chinese government has started to compete with Taiwan in offering scholarships and other inducements to attract Malaysian students to study in China. In recent years, such important international prizes as the Wang Moren-Zhou Anyi World Chinese Literature Prize (organized by Peking University) and the Yu Dafu

Fiction Prize (sponsored by the Zhejiang Writers' Association) have been awarded to Ng. After receiving the prizes, Ng claimed that the Sinophone Malaysian community "has no decent critics" and "unavoidably looks up to the Chinese heartland (中原)."[9] Ng argued that there were two "Chinese heartlands": the larger of the two was mainland China, and the smaller was Taiwan. All of this demonstrates that the diasporic Chinese identity promoted by Ng is approved by and celebrated in the two "Chinese homelands"; more importantly, it shows how the lure of diaspora leads him to publicly mock and deride his fellow Malaysian Chinese. These diaspora discourses flowed back into Malaysia, guiding the perspectives of young local Malaysian Chinese talents.

Shih argues that the term lure implies "both the processes of subjection and sublation."[10] Accordingly, this essay uses the term to describe how diasporic Sinophone Malaysian communities repeat this dual process of subjection and sublation. On the one hand, they are subject to the cosmopolitanism called for by diaspora discourse, while, on the other hand, they comprehensively sublate the talents of local Sinophone Malaysians. This essay argues that diaspora discourse is a powerful lure in the contemporary Malaysian Chinese context: Only by leaving their homeland can Malaysian Chinese prove they are part of an elite. In contrast, those who remain are fools (笨蛋) destined to fail, in Ng's view. Ng often uses insults such as "fools," "idiots" (愚蠢), and being "shameful" (可恥) to describe Malaysian Chinese who disagree with him, questioning whether they "are even capable of understanding anything we've written?"[11]

In Ng's vitriolic discourse, diaspora constitutes a sacred value. He orients himself toward the global diaspora space, constantly constructing a minority discourse of himself as a Malaysian Chinese person. He plays the part of a minor when faced with foreigners and sells Malaysian Chinese trauma using his status as a spokesperson for the diasporic Chinese. However, he plays the role of a strong father figure when faced with insiders, especially Malaysian Chinese. Over many years, he has used crude words and actions to chastise those of his compatriots he believes to be backward or disobedient. This is a sad demonstration of Rey Chow's warning: "For 'third world' intellectuals, the lures of diaspora consist in this masked hegemony."[12]

Now, most Malaysian Chinese reject or avoid discussions of "localization" and regard diaspora as "the new collective identity of Malaysian Chinese."[13] In other words, Malaysian Chinese history, originally regarded as a diaspora experience, has been constructed by diaspora discourse into a "diaspora identity" shared by all Malaysian Chinese. In this view, the diaspora, as criticized by Shih, has become a guiding value of contemporary Malaysian Chinese discourse.[14] Shih holds that diaspora as history is a historical phenomenon:

It is not a question of right or wrong.[15] She criticizes the idea of diaspora as value, which "implies loyalty to and longing for the ancestral 'home,' and bind the diasporic to the so-called homeland."[16] The Chinese author Wang Anyi, when asked how she regarded Malaysian Chinese authors such as Ng, responded that they "have an extremely strong leaning towards China" and "do not identify much with Malaysia." She clearly also believes that being a diasporic Malaysian Chinese author "implies loyalty to and longing for the ancestral home."[17] Her blanket characterization of Malaysian Chinese writers is an example of the way in which the concept of a diasporic Chinese identity promoted by Ng and others has misled Chinese authors in mainland China. This new diaspora discourse of the twenty-first century has crushed the Malaysian Chinese against the one of the past, which called for localization. As a value, diaspora has now been constructed into an important constituent part of contemporary Malaysian Chinese literary ideology.

The renowned Malaysian anthropologist Tan Chee-Beng believes that the phrase "Chinese diaspora," in its broad sense, includes all Chinese outside of China, while in the narrow sense, it refers to recent migrants who maintain close relationships with China and identify with China. However, he states that the term "diasporic Chinese" "does not include early migrants and their descendants, who have already put down roots in another country and become local."[18] In other words, Tan does not consider early migrants from China to Malaysia as "diasporic Chinese." This point resonates with Shih's against-diaspora standpoint.

Cohen cautiously argues that one cannot class all Mexicans, Germans, Cubans, and other nationalities who have put down roots in the United States, or ethnicities which have settled permanently in Europe, as diaspora. Some of the other general features of a diaspora must be shown to be present.[19] He also argues that "not everyone is a diaspora because they say they are. Social structures, historical experiences, prior conceptual understanding, and the opinions of other social actors (among other factors) also influence whether we can legitimately label a particular group a diaspora."[20]

Wang Gung-wu also questions the term diaspora: "Will the word diaspora be used to revive the idea of a single body of Chinese, reminiscent of the old term, the Huaqiao (華僑)? Is this intended by those Chinese who favour its use?"[21] He worries that this concept may "encourage Chinese governments to affirm the idea of a single Chinese diaspora again, along the lines of the earlier concept of huaqiao sojourner for all Chinese overseas."[22] He is also concerned that the term "Chinese diaspora" reminds people of the hoary old cliché of the wealthy Jewish merchant, leading to the equally mistaken impression that the Chinese diaspora is made up of rich traders, controlled behind the scenes by the Chinese government in an effort to build a global business network.

Wang points out that the majority of the Chinese who left China over the last two hundred years were poor. Their harsh circumstances were similar to those of the journeymen today leaving the countryside for urban areas in the hope of a better future. Therefore, Wang is unwilling to link this type of migration with diaspora, which carries implications of wealth.[23]

However, Tee Kim-Tong does regard Malaysian Chinese as "diasporic Chinese." He understands the term "Chinese diaspora" in the broad sense as defined by Tan Chee-Beng above, stating, "When we say 'Malaysian Chinese diaspora,' we are referring to diasporic Chinese, to those whose ancestors left China for Southeast Asia; we do not mean that you are in the process of leaving your country for the diaspora, or that you have not put down local roots."[24] Tee Kim-Tong has stated on multiple occasions that in his view Malaysian Chinese literature is the Sinophone writing of the Chinese diaspora because Malaysian Chinese "cannot leave their diasporic history, culture, and inheritance behind either in name or in substance; this is the history of the Chinese diaspora in Malaysia."[25] Therefore, he believes that "the descendants of the 'Chinese diaspora' are still the 'Chinese diaspora,' even if they are no longer 'diasporic.'"[26]

In his research on early Chinese merchants and their migrations to Southeast Asia and other places across the world, Robin Cohen argues that the Chinese diasporic mode is one that is characterized by trade and business. However, his research on the migration of Chinese to Malaysia stops short around 1963.[27] After Malayan independence in 1957, Chinese people were a minority ethnic group in Malaysia and evidently did not come into the purview of his research on the Chinese diaspora. Cohen adopted the research of William Safran to come up with these nine common features of diaspora:

1. Dispersal from an original homeland, often traumatically, to two or more foreign regions;
2. alternatively or additionally, the expansion from a homeland in search of work, in pursuit of trade or to further colonial ambitions;
3. a collective memory and myth about the homeland, including its location, history, suffering and achievements;
4. an idealization of the real or imagined ancestral home and a collective commitment to its maintenance, restoration, safety and prosperity, even to its creation;
5. the frequent development of a return movement to the homeland that gains collective approbation even if many in the group are satisfied with only a vicarious relationship or intermittent visits to the homeland;
6. a strong ethnic group consciousness sustained over a long time and based on a sense of distinctiveness, a common history, the transmission

of a common cultural and religious heritage and the belief in a common fate;
7. a troubled relationship with host societies, suggesting a lack of acceptance or the possibility that another calamity might be fall the group;
8. a sense of empathy and co-responsibility with co-ethnic members in other countries of settlement even where home has become more vestigial; and
9. the possibility of a distinctive creative, enriching life in host countries with a tolerance for pluralism.[28]

An overview of the diasporic characteristics of texts from various schools of Sinophone Malaysian literary culture in Taiwan reveals that they all possess one or more of these common features. Tee Kim-Tong has demonstrated that Sinophone Malaysian literature in Taiwan is unquestionably a "diaspora literature,"[29] but must all Sinophone Malaysian literature in Malaysia since the beginning of the last century be classed as "diaspora literature"? I believe that diasporic and against-diasporic states coexisted in Malaysian Chinese literary culture across different spaces and times.

Localization, the Cold War, ROC Loyalists, and Malaysian Chinese Writers in Taiwan

Malaysian Chinese literati have been engaged in an against-diaspora discourse distinguishing between "local identity" and "Chinese identity" for nearly a century—from the debates over "art and literature with Nanyang color" in the late 1920s, the promotion of "local Malayan art and literature" in the 1930s, the post-World War II war of words over the "uniqueness of Malayan Chinese art and literature," to the "Malayanization" discourse that gained traction between Malayan independence in 1957 and the founding of Malaysia in 1963. Regarding all of these Malaysian Chinese figures as "diasporic Chinese" risks oversimplifying the formation and development of societal constructs, historical experiences, and local consciousness in Malayan Chinese communities at the time. It cannot be denied that in the 1950s or before, migrants from China and people returning to China from Malaya coexisted in the same Southeast Asian field while also playing with or flowing between two identities: "Malayan Chinese" (馬華) and "overseas Chinese" (華僑). This also signifies that representations and imaginations of Malayan Chinese locality and China in the literature of these two groups were not necessarily diametrically opposed. Rather, they intertwined and shifted: Diaspora and against-diaspora elements coexisted in Sinophone Malaysian literature.

With the onset of the Cold War, Union Press (友聯出版社) intellectuals came to Malaya via Hong Kong to develop their careers. This group combined diaspora and against-diaspora elements. These figures were ROC loyalists who, after the defeat on the mainland, left their homeland, bringing their traumas with them. Chong Fah-hing observes that the Union Press played an important role in the education, media, and publishing fields in an attempt to preserve the Chinese cultural heritage and Confucian traditions overseas. At the same time, they brought the last gasps of the Republican-era literary style to the Malayan literary scene and became the catalyst for Malayan Chinese "Republican" literature.[30] These groups correspond to diaspora features one through four in Cohen's analysis outlined above. However, secretly funded by U.S. cultural aid via the Asia Foundation, Union Press promoted a publishing culture dominated by "Malayanization" in Malaya after the 1950s. They held a series of anti-Communist cultural activities and published a range of highly influential periodicals and textbooks.[31] Using the slogans of localization to long-lasting anti-Communist effect, they became the leaders of the against-diaspora movement. They refused to return to a China under Communist control and, with the support of the Malaysian Chinese Association, gradually monopolized the Chinese publishing market in Malaya. In the process, it swiftly gained a sense of Malayan local and national identity. This clearly contradicts features five and seven in Cohen's list.

Also in the 1950s, many Malayan Chinese teachers, arts workers, and other intellectuals who leaned toward supporting the right-wing ideology of the Kuomintang (KMT) or who had no party affiliation enthusiastically responded to the national ethnic policy of Malayanization as a means to shrug off accusations of racism and Communism leveled at them by the authorities. In this, they were joined by the majority of Chinese merchants and (locally born) Peranakan. These intellectuals, who held modern Western values alongside their support for Malayanization, developed a new vision of Chineseness differing radically from that conceived by the Chinese left wing. In the Cold War, they actively cooperated with the anti-Communist and ethnic policies of those in power and drew a clear line between them and leftist realist Chinese groups who advocated class struggle in Malaya. They supported the Chineseness of the Free China espoused by the KMT in Taiwan and supported by the United States. The main difference between these groups and Malayan left-wing groups lay in their ideological support for or opposition to Communism. These left-wing groups were in the vanguard of against-diaspora Chinese people in promoting localization, from "art and literature with Nanyang color," "local Malayan art and literature," to the "uniqueness of Malayan Chinese art and literature." However, as their anti-imperialist, anticolonial demands for localization were long repressed by the British colonial government, it is perhaps not surprising that they began to lean towards a Communist political ideology. Unfortunately, a large number of leftist figures were detained or deported by the British, either becoming stateless diaspora Chinese people or returning to China. In other words, these Malayan Chinese leftist groups also combined diaspora and against-diaspora characteristics into one. Simply labeling them as patriots or realists does nothing to help us understand the brutal politics of the Cold War.

Once the localization discourse of these leftist groups was hollowed out by Anglo-American imperialism, the same imperialism invited the Union Press intellectuals, via the Malaysian Chinese Association, to come to Malaya in order to fill the vacuum. They cooperated with the British policy of Malayanization and practiced ideas of localization that the British could control. The new generation of Malayan Chinese, who grew up influenced by the Union Press, were the beneficiaries of extremely preferential policies toward overseas Chinese offered by the government in Taiwan, with U.S. aid; they became "a link in the Cold War (anti-Communist) system."[32] Many of them went to Taiwan to study, marking the beginning of diasporic Malaysian Chinese literature in Taiwan. After the 1960s, Malaysian anti-Chinese ethnic politics caused a massive shock to this new generation, who had grown up with the ideologies of Malayanization and Bumiputera privileges.[33] Some remained in Taiwan, gradually exploring new horizons and becoming the core of the postindependence Malaysian Chinese diaspora population in Taiwan.

Based on Ng's broad standards of political identity, the Malaysian Chinese writers in Taiwan can be divided into two groups: The first comprises those who consciously re-sinified themselves by accepting the KMT's anti-Communist Chinese nationalism. Li Yongping (李永平) and Wen Rui'an (溫瑞安) are the foremost figures of this group. The second comprise writers whose political identity remained with Malaysia.[34] Some of these writers returned to Malaysia, such as Pan Yu-tong (潘雨桐).

This broad-brush approach omits the diaspora in Taiwan, the group to which Ng and Tee Kim-Tong both belong, who have chosen a third way, where their political identity flows between their home country and their country of residence, between roots and routes. Ng strongly criticizes Chineseness and Malaysian nationalism and also fiercely opposes the localization of Malaysian Chinese literature. Ng does not completely reject Chineseness. Even if he believes that it is a "burden," he still argues that it "can be an important resource."[35] In the context of the Taiwanese independence movement, Ng has consistently regarded Taiwanese localists who deny Chineseness and support Taiwanese nationalism as opponents.[36] This is also one of the reasons why he has become more and more coopted by the grand unificationist ideas of the mainland Chinese literary world. Unable to rise above the debate between independence and unification in Taiwanese politics, he often transfers his disdain for and criticism of the Taiwanese localists to Sinophone Malaysian localists—despite the manifest differences between the two contexts and their complete lack of comparability.

Ng's diaspora discourse is built on the ethnic identity framework of the traditional diaspora concept. He expands the boundaries of this concept to include the Chinese language in Malaysia, the fortunes of which he regards as equivalent to the fate of the Chinese people in Malaysia. The case of Ng's diaspora discourse corresponds to Safran's characteristics of the traditional diaspora: (1) they, or their ancestors, have been dispersed from a specific original center to two or more peripheral, or foreign, regions; (2) they retain collective memory, vision, or myth about their original homeland—its physical location, history, and achievements; (3) they believe that they are not—and perhaps cannot be—fully accepted by their host society and therefore feel partly alienated and insulated from it; (4) they continue to relate, personally or vicariously, to that homeland in one way or another, and their ethno-communal consciousness and solidarity are importantly defined by the existence of such a relationship.[37]

Ng's expressions of anxiety for his ethnic group are certainly worthy of respect, but by relying solely on racial consciousness to maintain a diasporic relationship with Malaysia, his ethnic identity becomes somewhat homogenous. This is a cause for concern. Floya Anthias believes that the use of ethnicity as the primary analytical framework for diaspora research obscures alliances along class, gender, and transethnic lines.[38] Moreover, the issues in Malaysia around Chinese–Malay relations, such as Bumiputera privileges or national literature, are not ones that concern a single ethnicity. Other dimensions that combine with the multiple identities advocated by modern diaspora discourse, such as class and state affiliation, are eliminated or obscured by Ng's narrative of a homogenous racial identity.

Racism, the Master–Slave Structure, and Chineseness

Shih has observed that Western powers "universalize Chineseness as a racialized boundary marker."[39] This not only rationalized their colonial government but also legitimized the administration of Chinese immigrants as an ethnic minority in contemporary nation-states. As the British colonial government took a long-term divide-and-rule approach to governing Chinese and Malays in Malaya, the majority of the Malay population enjoyed the colonial government's enthusiastic support for Malay-language education alongside special privileges.[40] The Chinese, on the other hand, were administered as an ethnic minority. The authorities discriminated against Chinese language education and Chinese culture, leaving Chinese language education to sink or swim.

In 1948, during the Cold War, the British colonial government announced the Malayan Emergency to put down a proindependence Communist uprising in Malaya. The colonists began joining up with Malay rulers and aristocrats to promote nationality policies, gradually beginning to interfere with the systems and policies of Chinese language education. Chinese language schools that refused to take part in the reforms were accused of being incubators of racism and Communism by the colonists and the Malay aristocracy. Chinese language education, fiercely defended by Chinese language students, as well as the Chineseness they displayed even after putting down roots in Malaya, were both regarded as manifestations of racism in the nationalist perspective of the authorities.

Ng once described Chinese–Malay relations in this way: "You lash out, I am in sorrow. It is a type of master–slave structure in which abuse is dished out and received."[41] The discourse of the traumatic modernity of the diaspora, which Ng proposes, remains limited to his constant repetition of the "master–slave structure" argument. He believes that "Malaysian Chinese, in their history as enslaved citizens, must often face and be subjected to the re-enactment of similar persecutions."[42]

Actually, the theory of the "master–slave structure" lacks a historicizing line of analysis in the Malaysian context; in fact, it has strengthened the Chinese–Malay social contract theory propagated by Malay politicians from the mid-1980s on. As research by Mavis C. Puthucheary shows, Abdullah Ahmad, MP of United Malays National Organisation (UMNO), first imported the term "social contract" in 1986.[43] He used it to explain and rationalize the permanent presence of the Bumiputera privileges in the national constitution while also beginning to defend the privileges using the phrase "Malay dominance." In actual fact, the Bumiputera privileges were part of an "elite bargain" reached between the upper echelons of the UMNO, the Malaysian Chinese Association, and the Malaysian Indian Congress in the Cold War context of Malayan independence; the "bargain" that "was then made was never recorded in any document seen as constituting a legal contract."[44] With the establishment of Malaysia in 1963, this elite bargain was reinterpreted in the constitution without the people of Malaysia having the opportunity to debate it publicly.

Ng's theory of the master–slave structure of Chinese–Malay relations unconsciously restructures this social contract theory. It seems as if Ng has internalized the theory of Malay dominance propagated by these politicians. Ng's fiction and essays are constantly bound by this dichotomous master–slave structure.

In Ng's short story "Tapir" (貘, 1997), a poor Malaysian Chinese mother calls Malays "pigs" because they are so lazy that they don't work hard to earn money but instead ask for assistance from the government, which uses the taxes paid by Chinese to feed the majority ethnic group of Malays.[45] Although this represents the dissatisfaction Malaysian Chinese people feel towards Bumiputera privileges, it also reveals Ng's own racist views as a Han Chinese person: he "animalizes" the other.[46]

In another short story, "My Friend Abdulah" (我的朋友鴨都拉, 2005), Ng stereotypes Abdulah, a Chinese character who has been assimilated into Malay culture, as looking "like a dead *pig* from his head through to his intestines" (emphasis added); an Indian doctor later diagnoses him with having "simultaneously caught three virulent sexual diseases particular to Indians."[47] In addition to demonizing Indian people as carriers of a multitude of sexually transmitted infections, Ng does not even attempt to offer any explanation as to what scientific basis there is for these "sexual diseases particular to Indians." Descriptions of the other in Ng's writings are essentially identical: The other always has serious issues with their appearance and character. These other ethnicities rarely have the opportunity to speak and mainly serve as mouthpieces in Ng's fiction.

In other words, the greatest defect of Ng's fiction is that it is not multivoiced, like truly great writing, and does not have Bakhtin's polyphony: "author's and heroes' discourses interact on equal terms."[48] Ng's short story "Allah's Will" (阿拉的旨意, 2001) also features a Chinese man who has been forcibly assimilated by the Malays. His Malay name is again Abdulah. Before being assimilated, he was sentenced as a traitor for plotting revolt. He was sent to an island by the ruling Malays where he was forced to convert to Islam and bring the land under cultivation. He marries the village chief's daughter and has many children with her. The narrative of the piece is closed and limp: The character of Abdulah is monotonous and completely lacking any evidence of psychological consciousness. Readers have no chance to hear the genuine voice of any of the other characters: The ugly Malay leader supervises Abdulah from on high and repeatedly calls him a "fool" and a "pig."[49] This constitutes the master–slave structure often repeated in Ng's fiction, with its constant simple repetition of a binary good–evil dichotomy and racism.

Another short story, "The Year I Returned to Malaya" (那年我回到馬來亞, 2013), upturns the power hierarchy in the Chinese–Malay master–slave structure in an overly simple manner. In a completely fabricated Malayan history, Ng writes of how Malays became a persecuted community under the rule of the Chinese run Malayan Communist Party. Malays were either forced into exile or fled into the jungle. The story is written in overly plain and direct language, and the narrative logic lacks sufficient awareness of the characters and proper support from details. The first-person narrator is Chinese, which limits the narrator's understanding of the troubles of the Malays. The story also lacks a rounded Malay character—Malays appear only as an amorphous mass. Ng describes a group of Malays trying in vain to revolt against Chinese rule as "jumping around like monkeys." Again, this animalization of the other is a clear demonstration of Ng's racism against Malays; in the story, the Malays also respond in kind, crying out to "kill all of the Chinaman pigs."[50] Both sides fall into hysterical racism. The story is also unfortunate in that it legitimizes Malay fears of Chinese people: As soon as the Chinese take control, the Malays lose their land and homes.

Ng argues that "Malayness is an absolute guiding value. Other ethnicities are not included in the program of the state." He further claims that "except in cases of ideological compromise, Malaysian Chinese literature has the diaspora inborn in it."[51] Here, Ng falls into the trap set by mainstream Malay politicians by naturalizing the diaspora state of Malaysian Chinese people, the most prominent border separating Chinese and Malay people. However, it must be acknowledged that no border contains any natural elements in its existence and birth.[52] Therefore, all current criticisms of Bumiputera privileges, national literature, and the opposition between Malaysian "Chineseness" and "Malayness" must, if they are oriented at the intangible border between "Chineseness" and "Malayness," first acknowledge that the geographical frame of reference for this imagined border originates from Western colonialism.

As Donald Snodgrass has observed, most British colonial officials liked the Malays better than the Chinese or Indians and frequently expressed a romantic admiration for the Malay way of life.[53] The British colonists always took the side of the Malays in issues, including the Bumiputera privileges inscribed in the constitution of the newly independent Malaya, the definition of a Malay, and the reinterpretation of the Bumiputera privileges on the establishment of Malaysia. The borders of the state, ethnic groups, and between Indigenous and non-Indigenous in-habitants in Malaysia today are the product of an elite bargain between the colonists and the Chinese, Malay, and Indian establishments during the Cold War. This bargain has never been publicly debated by the people of Malaysia, no matter what their ethnicity.

Ng's development into a rejection of Malaysian Chinese localization discourse is an extension of this post-Cold War ideology which resets the border between diaspora/local, which contain an elite/commoner dichotomy. Based on the theory of the border, Ng promotes his model of research into Malaysian Chinese diaspora, centered around ethnic identity, without seriously exploring other dimensions of identity, such as class affiliation.

In Ng's discourses on the Malaysian Chinese, limit is a word that appears repeatedly. He has set multiple limits on Chineseness and local consciousness (or, alternatively, localization or locality), but why has he never set any limits on the Malaysian Chinese diaspora discourse that he is constantly mentioning? Not setting a limit in this way implies that Malaysian Chinese diaspora discourse will never go out of date, that the racist Malaysian political environment he decries is permanent, and that the political environment will always continue to develop in a direction unfavorable to Chinese. This type of discourse uses the very real political difficulties faced by Malaysian Chinese over many years as a literary and theoretical bargaining chip. No imaginings of the Malaysian Chinese are allowed to go beyond the wall/border of real politics. This is the border that Ng has drawn decisively around imaginings of Malaysian Chinese literary culture. Whoever goes beyond this wall/border, even slightly, is called an "idiot" or cast as a traitor to their ethnicity.[54] This is what Shih describes as "classic elite exilic sentimentalism, regarding oneself as being on a higher level than the locals."[55] Such ideas are everywhere in Ng's writings. In the border set between self and other in Ng's own consciousness, the binary logic of a sharp divide between enemy and friend can survive and gain legitimacy.

Ng's diaspora discourse appears to call for a borderless, stateless condition, but its borders are the antitheses of diaspora discourse: national identity (whether to his ancestral home China, his early home country of Malaysia, or his adopted home of Taiwan) or class identity (left-wing Chinese language literature or realist literature). As Shih has argued, "Diaspora has an expiration date; one cannot say one is diasporic after three hundred years."[56] In her view, the Sinophone is an against-diaspora cultural and political practice: "When the (im)migrants settle and become localized, many choose to end their state of diaspora by the second or third generation."[57]

The situation of Chinese in Malaysia is rather complex. Although many second- and third-generation Chinese have chosen to end their diasporic state and integrate into local society, many choose to migrate again. From Malayan independence to today, scholars have grouped the remigration of Chinese from Malaysia into three stages. The first stage was in the 1970s, after the government implemented new economic policies designed to assist Malays in the wake of the 513 incident of racial violence. Many Chinese who were dissatisfied with these policies chose to emigrate. Second, during the 1980s, the Malaysian economy went into severe recession. Many Chinese emigrated to developed countries. Third, during the 1990s, the Malaysian economy began to take off. The government gradually began to implement more open policies in the economy and education. Chinese emigration fell noticeably in this period. Overall, between 1957 and 1991, the Malaysian

Chinese population grew by 3.38 million. However, in the same period, net migration amounted to 1.11 million leaving Malaysia; this emigration was greatest in the 1980s, when a number equivalent to half of the growth in the Chinese population left Malaysia.[58]

Ng left Malaysia in 1986 for further education in Taiwan, and his diaspora discourse is valid in the context of the 1980s peak in Malaysian Chinese leaving the country. However, after 1990, and particularly during Asian financial crisis of the late 1990s, the number of Malaysian Chinese emigrating dropped sharply.[59] Malaysia experienced major changes in a whole range of areas after the mid-1990s, including the 1998 Reformasi social and political movement.[60] All these incidents rapidly altered the political map of Malaysia, greatly enhancing Malaysian Chinese people's awareness of political participation and giving them the confidence to put their demands into action. In the 2018 general election, the UMNO-led Barisan Nasional's sixty-one-year tenure in government was brought to an end by the Alliance of Hope. Therefore, should this changed diaspora discourse, elevated in order to decry the permanence of the difficulties of Malaysian Chinese, not also be adjusted and reflected on as the context changes?

Even so, it is undeniable that racial issues are constantly whipped up in the media by some Malaysian politicians. As the contemporary Malaysian scholar of UMNO politics Edmund Terence Gomez has noted, "Racialism has been used as one of the most potent instruments by Malaysian elites to maintain their position and to justify policies implemented."[61] Therefore, Ng's expressions of anxiety for his ethnicity find fertile ground in the local Malaysian Chinese literary and academic worlds.

If the term "diaspora Chinese" is used only to describe "people who are weak minorities in the countries of residence and who may not sustain ties with their ancestral homelands,"[62] then in the context of China's contemporary rise, diaspora will continue to present an ever-stronger lure to marginalized Chinese communities for as long as anti-Chinese sentiment persists across the world.

Notes

1. This work was supported by the Chinese Arts and Culture Research Grant of Singapore Chinese Culture Centre. The sponsored reference number is CACRG-2201. Opinions, findings, conclusions, or recommendations expressed in these materials are those of the author and do not necessarily reflect the views of the Singapore Chinese Cultural Centre.

2. Jing Tsu, *Sound and Script in Chinese Diaspora* (Cambridge, MA: Harvard University Press, 2010), 174–203.

3. Ng Kim Chew, "Minor Sinophone Literature: Diasporic Modernity's Incomplete Journey," trans. Andy Rodekohr, in *Global Chinese Literature: Critical Essays*, ed. Jing Tsu and David Wang (Leiden: Brill, 2010), 15.

4. Ng Kim Chew, *Fenshao* (Burn) (Taipei: Maitian, 2007), 134.

5. Ng Kim Chew, *Huawen xiao wenxue de Malaixiya ge'an* (Sinophone minor literature: A case study on Malaysia) (Taipei: Maitian, 2015), 173.

6. Shu-mei Shih, *Fan lisan: huayu yuxi yanjiu lun* (*Against Diaspora: Discourses on Sinophone Studies*) (Taipei: Linking, 2017), 163.

7. Ng Kim Chew, "Zheyan de 'huayu yuxi' lun keyi xiu yi!—Shi Shumei de fan lisan daodi zai fanshenme?" (Enough of this "Sinophone" theory! What is Shih's "against-diaspora" against?) *Speaking of Books*, November 29, 2018, https://sobooks.tw/sinophone-literature-review.

8. Wang Shuqi, "Daohuozhe Huang Jinshu: ta de fangu you dian ge de huang" (Fire thief Ng: His rebellious bones are a bit too uncomfortable), *Tencent Culture*, accessed November 29, 2018, https://new.qq.com/omn/20180511/20180511A0UKR0.html.

9. Fu Shiye, "Malaixiya zuojia Huang Jinshu: wo zaoyi meiyou guxiang, guxiang zhizai wo de xiezuo li" (Malaysian author Ng: I haven't had a homeland for a long time; my homeland is in my writings), *Jiemian*, accessed November 30, 2018, https://www.jiemian.com/article/2114150.html.

10. Shu-mei Shih, *The Lure of the Modern: Writing Modernism in Semi-Colonial China (1917–1937)* (Berkeley: University of California Press, 2001), xi–xii.

11. Ng Kim Chew, "Aiguozhuyizhe de zhikong" (The allegation from patriots), *Sin Chew Daily*, January 16, 2005, "Xinzhou guangchang" section, 2.

12. Rey Chow, *Writing Diaspora: Tactics of Intervention in Contemporary Cultural Studies* (Bloomington: Indiana University Press, 1993), 118. In the 1990s, Rey Chow called on people to turn "against the lures of diaspora," an earlier warning against diaspora than that of Shih.

13. Cha Pei Yeow, "Mahua lisan wenxue yanjiu: yi Wen Rui'an, Li Yongping, Lin Xingqian ji Huang Jinshu wei yanjiu duixiang" (Research into Malaysian Chinese diaspora literature: On Wen Rui'an, Li Yongping, Lim Chin Chown, and Ng) (master's dissertation, University Tunku Abdul Rahman, 2011), 93.

14. Shu-mei Shih, "The Concept of the Sinophone," *PMLA* 126, no. 3 (2011): 713.

15. Shih, *Fan lisan*, 61.

16. Shih, "The Concept of the Sinophone," 713.

17. Wang Anyi and Zhang Xinying, *Duihualu* (Conversations) (Beijing: Renmin wenxue, 2011), 168.

18. Tan Chee-Beng, "Qianyi, bentuhua yu jiaoliu: cong quanqiu-hua de shijiao kan haiwai huaren" (Migration, localization, and exchange: Overseas Chinese from a globalized perspective), in *Qianyi, bentuhua yu jiaoliu: huaren yimin yu quanqiuhua* (Migration, localization, and exchange: Chinese migrants and globalization), eds. Leo Suryadinata and Neo Peng Fu (Singapore: Huayiguan, 2011), 8.

19. Robin Cohen, *Global Diasporas: An Introduction* (London: Routledge, 2008), 186.

20. Cohen, *Global Diasporas*, 15–16.

21. Wang Gung-wu, "A Single Chinese Diaspora?" in *Diasporic Chinese Ventures: The Life and Work of Wang Gungwu*, ed. Gregor Benton and Liu Hong (London: Routledge Curzon, 2004), 158.

22. Wang, "A Single Chinese Diaspora?" 166.

23. Laurent Malvezin, "The Problems with (Chinese) Diaspora: An Interview with Wang Gungwu," in Benton and Liu, *Diasporic Chinese Ventures*, 49–51.

24. Tee Kim-Tong and Lee Yu-Cheng, "Lisan jingyan: Li You-Cheng yu Zhang Jingzhong duitan" (Diasporic experiences: A conversation between Lee Yu-Cheng and Tee Kim-Tong), in *Lisan* (Diaspora), ed. Lee Yu-Cheng (Taipei: Yunchen, 2013), 174.

25. Tee Kim-Tong, *Malaixiya huayu yuxi wenxue* (On Sinophone Malaysian literature) (Petaling: Youren, 2011), 20–21.

26. Tee Kim-Tong, "Wo yao huijia: houlisan zaitai Mahua wenxue" (I want to go home: Post-diaspora Malaysia Chinese literature in Taiwan, *Sin Chew Daily*, February 8, 2009, "Wenyi chunqiu" section.

27. Cohen, *Global Diasporas*, 84–89.

28. Cohen, *Global Diasporas*, 17.

29. Tee, *Malaixiya huayu yuxi wenxue*, 94–120.

30. Chong Fah-hing, "Zhanhou Mahua minguo wenxue yizhi: wenxueshi zaikancha" (Postwar Malaysian Chinese (Republican) literary sites: A re-investigation of literary history), *Dongnanya xuekan* (Taiwan journal of Southeast Asian Studies) 11, no. 1 (2016): 7.

31. Hee Wai-Siam, "Yazou jijinhui zai xinma de wenhua lenzhan: yi youlian chubanshe he xueshenzoubao weili" (The cultural Cold War of the Asia Foundation in Singapore and Malaysia: The case of the Union Press and the Student Weekly), *Zhongwai wenxue* (Chung Wai literary quarterly), no. 481 (2023): 65–113.

32. Ng, "Huawen xiao wenxue de Malaixiya ge'an," 294.

33. Bumiputera refers to Malays and other Indigenous peoples in Malaysia. Bumiputera privileges are the outcome of a policy that since 1957 has given Bumiputera special immunities and supported the "special position" of ethnic Malays as established in Article 153 of the Federal Constitution of Malaysia in various areas. Malays, as the majority ethnic group, have abused the Bumi putera privileges provided by the constitution as a legal basis on which to legitimize racial discrimination against minority ethnic groups in Malaysia.

34. Ng, "Huawen xiao wenxue de Malaixiya ge'an," 292–293.

35. Ng Kim Chew, *Mahua wenxue yu Zhongguoxing* (Malaysian Chinese literature and Chineseness) (Taipei: Yuanzun wenhua, 1998), 135.

36. Ng, *Fenshao*, 133–136.

37. William Safran, "Diasporas in Modern Societies: Myths of Homeland and Return," *Diaspora: A Journal of Transnational Studies* 1, no. 1 (Spring 1991): 83–84.

38. Floya Anthias, "Evaluating 'Diaspora': Beyond Ethnicity," *Sociology* 32, no. 3 (August 1998): 557.

39. Shu-mei Shih, *Visuality and Identity: Sinophone Articulations Across the Pacific*, (Berkeley: University of California Press, 2007), 24.

40. Lin Yong, "Malaixiya huaren yu Malairen jingji diwei bianhua bijiao yanjiu (1957–2005)" [Comparative study of the change in economic status of ethnic Chinese and Malays in Malaysia [1957–2005]) (Xiamen: Xiamen daxue, 2008), 325.

41. Ng, "Huawen xiao wenxue de Malaixiya ge'an," 240.

42. Ng, "Huawen xiao wenxue de Malaixiya ge'an," 238.

43. Mavis C. Puthucheary, "Malaysia's 'Social Contract': The Invention and Historical Evolution of an Idea," in *Sharing the Nation: Faith, Difference, Power and the State 50 Years after Merdeka*, ed. Norani Othhman, Mavis C. Puthucheary, and Clive S. Kessler (Petaling Jaya: Strategic Information and Research Development Centre, 2008), 12–13.

44. Puthucheary, "Malaysia's 'Social Contract,'" 19.

45. Ng Kim Chew, *Wu an ming* (Dark nights) (Taipei: Jiuge, 1997), 231.

46. Chen, Kuan-Hsing, *Asia as Method: Toward Deimperialization* (Durham, NC: Duke University Press, 2010), 260.

47. Ng Kim Chew, *Tu yu huo* (Earth and fire) (Taipei: Maitian, 2005), 61, 69.

48. Pam Morris, "A Glossary of Key Terms," in *The Bakhtin Reader: Selected Writings of Bakhtin, Medvedev, Voloshinov* (London: Arnold, 1994), 249.

49. Ng Kim Chew, *You dao zhi dao* (From island to island) (Taipei: Maitian, 2001), 87.

50. Ng Kim Chew, *Nanyang renmin gongheguo beiwanglu* (*Memorandums of the South Seas People's Republic*) (Taipei: Lianjing, 2013), 57, 54.

51. Ng, "Huawen xiao wenxue de Malaixiya ge'an," 233–234, 244.

52. John Agnew, "Borders on the Mind: Re-Framing Border Thinking," *Ethics and Global Politics* 1 (2008): 181.

53. Donald R. Snodgrass, *Inequality and Economic Development in Malaysia* (Kuala Lumpur: Oxford University Press, 1980), 34.

54. Ng, "Aiguozhuyizhe de zhikong," 2.

55. Shih, *Fan lisan*, 303.

56. Shih, "The Concept of the Sinophone," 714.

57. Shu-mei Shih, "Against Diaspora: The Sinophone as Places of Cultural Pro duction," in *Global Chinese Literature: Critical Essays*, ed. Jing Tsu and David Wang (Leiden: Brill, 2010), 45.

58. Tang Xiaoli, "Zhanhou Malaixiya huaren zai yimin: shuliang gusuan yu yuanyin fenxi" (Postwar re-migration of Chinese people from Malaysia: estimated volume and analysis of causes) *Huaqiao huaren lishi yanjiu* 3 (September 2012): 37.

59. Tang, "Zhanhou Malaixiya huaren zai yimin," 39.

60. The 1998 Reformasi movement started off as a political campaign calling for the end of corruption and cronyism allegedly associated with the Barisan Nasional Government under the Mahathir Mohamad cabinet.

61. Edmund Terence Gomez, *Politics in Business: UMNO's Corporate Investments* (Kuala Lumpur: Forum Enterprise, 1990), 11.

62. Yow Cheun-hoe, *Guangdong and Chinese Diaspora: The Changing Landscape of Qiaoxiang* (London: Routledge, 2013), 3.

13

Conditions of Theory in Taiwan

Americanism and Settler Colonialism

SHU-MEI SHIH

In the 2014 book, *Latin American Philosophy from Identity to Radical Exteriority*, Alejandro Arturo Vallega claims that the question "Is there Latin American philosophy?" has outlived its rhetorical usefulness because, by all objective measures and practical purposes, there exists a long and rich tradition of Latin American philosophy.[1] Since 2012, I have been involved with and am cofounder of a collective of intellectuals in Taiwan called Knowledge/Taiwan, whose provocation was a parallel statement, "There is no theory in Taiwan."[2] Following Vallega, we may ask if the question—Is there Taiwan theory?—has outlived its rhetorical usefulness. Without getting into the debate about how philosophy relates to theory and vice versa,[3] I do not think this is the case. I believe we are still waiting for the question to outlive its rhetorical usefulness. What I mean by this and how we might go about achieving the end point of waiting for the question to become irrelevant is what energizes this chapter.

This chapter is an invitation to think about theory and theorizing from the perspective of a small, peripheral, minor nation and what it might mean for theory, its nature, production, and circulation, not just as we know it (what exists) or do not know it (what exists but is not recognized or known) but also as we search for the potentialities and limits of our capacity to imagine it (what does not yet exist). My proposal is to think about theory in terms of world history, using a method that I have been calling relational comparison.[4] The basic argument is that it is only through worldliness conceived as interconnectedness—the situatedness of a given location, country, big or small, in a web of relations in the world structured by power—that we can finally come to grips with the question of theory in more egalitarian terms. Considered relationally, the place upon which theory is grounded, be it, say, Paris or Taipei, is always already connected with other places. No theory emerges in a historical vacuum or geographical isolation, and place, understood here as a nodal point of connection, produces and embodies relations on the world scale, however small or marginal it might be. The given place is part of, partakes of, and constitutive of the world, and it is thus not merely a recipient but a coproducer of global processes and, hence, a coproducer of the world as we know it.[5] Comparison, in this sense, is not the juxtaposition of Paris and Taipei but their relationality in the context of world history, which also inevitably implicates multiple interconnected orbits of culture, politics, and economy in their dynamic interaction. The disciplines brought into conjunction here, then, are cultural theory, broadly conceived, in conversation with world history.

So, to begin at the beginning, we may ask the question: What is theory? In its common usage in the humanities and the social sciences, whether in the United States or Taiwan, I presume that by *theory*, we usually mean the concepts, analytical tools, and methods and frameworks that we bring to the analysis of cultural and social texts, where theory is accorded a certain kind of objectivity as well as universality with the capacity to be applied to different texts and contexts. *Theory, by this definition, is objective and universal and is therefore separate from text and context; it exists above and beyond text and context.*

Within this conventional understanding of what theory is, Taiwan, or any other small and marginal nation, may be a text or context but not theory. Since Taiwan is hardly considered universal, Taiwan can never be the site where theory is produced but rather the place to which theory is exported and the object to which theory is applied. Thus, there is no theory in Taiwan. Theory, by implication then, is a Western or metropolitan product, and here, the West refers mainly to Western Europe and the United States. For all practical purposes, it used to be a particular kind of European thought that was translated, deployed, and reinvented in the United States and acquired the status of "theory." In the contemporary context, it appears that Americans have increasingly dominated the production of theory, especially social theory. Consider modernization theory, rational choice theory, theories of neoliberalism, late capitalism, globalization, immigration and diaspora, postcoloniality, transnationalism, and even theories about gender, ethnicity, race, and sexuality, to name just a few. Theory is either American, Americanized French, or, to a lesser extent, Americanized German. It travels through the medium of global English, which is also largely American-inflected. This is the theory that most people seem to read and refer to in the rest of the world, including in Taiwan.

Invoking this conventional narrative of theory and the West-centrism that underlies it is almost a cliché these days. We generally accept the critique that theory, as we know it, is intimately connected to the rise of the West—or, more precisely, the rise of Western colonialism and imperialism around the world—and that empires produce the kind of theory with universal valence and the capacity to travel. Even Edward Said's famous notion of traveling theory, in its emphasis on local adaptation, adheres to the one-way travel narrative of theory in its assumption of theory's origin in the West.[6] In this narrative, the West produces theory, and the Rest receives it, applies it, adapts it, or otherwise consumes it. In today's context of global empire, the situation is, perhaps, even more so. *Hence, the international division of labor in the condition of global empire is not only an economic and political one but also an epistemological one.* Scholars and thinkers situated on the margins of the West, so to speak, have understandably expressed strong condemnation against what they call epistemic racism and even "epistemicide."[7] Within this division, those who are the Humanitas are able to produce theory, while those who are the Anthropos are subhumans who cannot produce theory.[8] According to Portuguese sociologist Bonaventura de Sousa Santos, who has led the charge against epistemicide, the restoration of the world's epistemological diversity is essential in the fight against "cognitive injustice."[9] Similarly, American anthropologists Jean and John Comaroff, in their book *Theory from the South* (2012), have argued for the necessity for Euro-America to evolve toward Africa because it is "the global south that affords privileged insight into the workings of the world at large." It is not at all that the South is "always in deficit, always playing catch-up," but that the South is often the first to feel the effects of world-historical forces," which prefigure "the future of the global north."[10] Here, I am also reminded of Australian sociologist Raewyn Connell's important, earlier book, *Southern Theory* (2007), which draws theory from multiple geographical locations in the Global South: Africa, Latin America, Indigenous Australia, and South and Southwest Asia. Instead of being the West's data mine, the Rest emerges, in her account and at her insistence, as the source of theory.[11]

If we follow the provocations above, the postulation that there is no theory in the Rest (including Taiwan) arises as a consequence of epistemic racism or epistemicide that is deeply embroiled in the global politics of power and knowledge. In this view, it is not that marginal countries like Taiwan do not have theory or cannot produce theory but that it is not discovered, recognized, read, studied, and circulated. If we take this view to its logical implication, *we only need to search, and we will find theory in Taiwan*. It does not help our search that none of the above theorists even remotely mentions Taiwan—Taiwan is the periphery of the periphery when it comes to the question of theory—so the task is entirely left to us, those of us who care about Taiwan. It is the affective investment of the scholars who care that any questions about theory and Taiwan can emerge as questions at all. So then, will we find theory in Taiwan if we look hard? What does looking hard entail? What would we find if we did look very hard?

To answer these questions, I would like to take up the case of so-called critical theory as an example, as it will relate to Taiwan specifically while providing a good (because it is Western, hence, relevant) case study to illustrate how the relational comparison as a method helps us answer the question of theory better. As my collaborator Françoise Lionnet and I have written in the introduction to our book, *Creolization of Theory*, so-called critical theory, considered to have begun in Paris, is, in fact, born of the historical entanglements of the so-called global sixties, broadly conceived to have started in the 1950s and lasting till the 1970s.[12] As we know, Paris May 68 was not an isolated historical event but was closely related to simultaneous movements around the world, such as various decolonial movements across Africa (including the Algerian War) and Asia (consider the Bandung Conference and its inauguration of Third World Alliance and Afro-Asian Solidarity), student demonstrations across Latin America, the civil rights movement and antiwar demonstrations in the United States, Prague Spring and other events in Eastern Europe, and the Cultural Revolution in China that popularized a global Maoism. We should also recall that, biographically, most of the major figures of so-called critical theory were themselves self-conscious participants in this history: Jacques Derrida, Hélène Cixous, and Jacques Ranciere were born in Algeria; Jean-Francois Lyotard taught and Etienne Balibar volunteered in Algeria; Michel Foucault taught in Tunisia; and Henri Lefebvre, of course, was a signee to the 1960 Declaration on the Right of Insubordination in the War in Algeria, the manifesto of 121 drafted by Maurice Blanchot. The signees also included Simon de Beauvoir, Marguerite Duras, Édouard Glissant, Alain Renais, Alain Robbe-Grillet, André Breton, and Jean-Paul Sartre, among others.

How does all of this have anything to do with Taiwan? This is where world history matters and where Taiwan's relationship to critical theory can be illuminated. While the radical narrative presents global revolutions as the prevailing story of the era, the other simultaneous formation that was the constitutive opposite of the radical narrative was, indisputably, the Cold War. The Cold War and its ideological polarizations also saw a wide cross-section of Western intelligentsia turning to Marxism, whether connected to a communist party or not. Of the so-called critical theorists, Louis Althusser was an unapologetic party communist, and Jacque Rancière was a Maoist, while the Tel Quel group's failed love affair with Maoism is also well-known. Of the older generation, Jean-Paul Sartre famously turned to Marxism, along with Simone de Beauvoir, and spent forty-five days as esteemed guests of the People's Republic of China in 1954. Henri Lefebvre was a party member and party theorist while writing the book that would later become a bible of May 68, *The Critique of Everyday Life*, before his repulsion from the party. Of the younger generation from the time, Alain Badiou may still be a theoretical Maoist even today. Furthermore, it is the legacy of the Cold War in Eastern Europe that gave us such theorists as Zygmunt Bauman, not to mention Julia Kristeva and Tzvetan Todorov, both born in Bulgaria. This list is by no means exhaustive, but the picture that I wish to highlight should by now be clear.

For a moment, it is worth reiterating that so-called theory, Western in presumed origin, has been assumed to be a system that reproduces and maintains itself, i.e., a product of autopoiesis, but, as I have tried to show in the brief overview above, is, in fact, born of interrelations and entanglements in world history. The narrative of autopoiesis, then, is a myth built on sanctioned ignorance, or in the words of Raewyn Connell, "grand erasure." Connell argues persuasively, in her aforementioned book *Southern Theory*, that this notion of autonomous theory, in her case social theory, ignores "the whole historical experience of empire and global domination," and by so doing displaces the fact that it is actually born of "the metropole's *action* on the rest of the world" (emphasis mine). By way of proof, she traces the emergence of sociology as a discipline to the last two decades of the nineteenth century, a discipline that actually arose out of "social relations of imperialism" in the sense that original sociology had aimed to understand the difference between the civilization of the West and the primitiveness of the Rest.[13] Similarly, comparative literature as a discipline in the United States also has its imperial, or more precisely, settler colonial, origins in the late nineteenth century,[14] while in Asia, it arose from the condition of Japanese colonialism in Taiwan. It was Shimada Kinji (1901–1993), a professor of English and French at Taipei Imperial University, who taught what would be considered the first comparative literature courses at Taihoku Higher School (the predecessor of National Taiwan Normal University) during the period of Japanese colonialism there (1895–1945). Shimada later founded the first comparative literature department at the University of Tokyo in 1953. Without his experience in the colony, where the superior Japan and the inferior Taiwan collided, comparative literature as a discipline in Japan and across Asia would not have been possible. In this sense, we might say that the origin of comparative literature in Asia is Taiwan and that Taiwan was constitutive of the formation of comparative literature as a worldwide discipline.

As we begin considering the constitutive role played by a marginal nation, in this case, Taiwan, not as a case study but as a site from which broader conversations about theory can be drawn, it is useful to have a basic sense of Taiwan's historical timeline since the end of Japanese colonialism to relate back to the time of emergence of European critical theory. Again, the specificity here is dialectically connected to the general ideas about theory; hence, I solicit the reader's curiosity to learn about Taiwan as an avenue to both specific and general knowledge. At the conclusion of World War II and after "losing" China, so to speak, the Chinese Kuomintang regime exiled itself to Taiwan and enlisted Taiwan at the forefront of the postwar configuration of the Cold War. I suggest that Taiwan's siding with the United States in the anticommunist Cold War constitutes one of its primary world historical roles during this period. Throughout the global sixties, Taiwan was engulfed in Cold War hysteria in the form of the White Terror, when military courts, under martial law, could, without burden of proof, imprison and sentence to death anyone suspected of communist affiliations. The radicalization of Taiwan politics had been gaining momentum since then in the form of the outside party movement (dangwai yundong) against the party-state of the Kuomintang, eventually leading to the lifting of the Martial Law in 1987 and the liberalization of the political sphere. In other words, the radical and the Cold War coexisted in Taiwan, as it did the world over. However the international position of Taiwan during the Cold War was that of a stronghold for American influence, and Taiwan's radical history, whether in the form of outside party politics or Marxist politics, was largely unseen outside Taiwan and, for a long while, was suppressed within Taiwan. From this brief historical outline, I draw three points about theory to consider:

1. The Cold War being the condition of possibility for the radical 1960s, Taiwan, by extension, can be seen as part of the condition of possibility for critical theory.
2. Taiwan's participation in the Cold War may be not so much as an agent but perhaps more as an extension of the United States. This is why only after critical theory was translated into English in the United States did it travel to Taiwan. Very seldom, or almost never, have Taiwan scholars read French and German thought in the original without American mediation. This is part of what I call Taiwan's Americanism, which spells out an itinerary that is followed by many peripheral states when it comes to traveling theory.

3. Critical theory has gradually lost its radicalism through its Americanization, and this also explains why critical theory did not disrupt the social in Taiwan but became largely another academic fashion or trend. Could Taiwan have absorbed it in its radical and political form? It seems that it is the aftermath of critical theory, namely postcolonial theory, that has radicalized the Taiwan intelligentsia, as represented by the work of Chiu Kuei-fen, Liou Liang-ya, and others.[15] Much of the radical impulse among Taiwan's Marxists, however, has seemingly been lost in an outdated, romantic internationalism that discounted the local reality of Taiwan and continues to be anachronistically attached to an increasingly neoliberal China, hence appearing regressive and ultimately conservative in its apologist position on the rise of Chinese empire.[16]

The argument here is that Taiwan's place in world history has, in fact, produced old and new avenues for theory. Below, I will consider two of the historical conditions of theory in Taiwan, Americanism and settler colonialism, not merely as local conditions but as part and parcel to global processes that Taiwan, in turn, helped to produce. To elaborate further Sinophone studies' deconstruction of what I would call Chinese Originalism, the history and idea of Taiwan's primordial connection to China, which had primarily framed Taiwan's knowledge production in terms of Chinese philosophical and epistemological traditions, my purpose here is to examine two other conditions. These two conditions, Americanism and settler colonialism, expose the fallacy of Chinese Originalism as a form of collusion (with U.S. neocolonialism) and a form of disavowal (the fact of Han settler colonialization of Indigenous peoples) by Han settler colonizers in Taiwan. Necessarily, our critique of international division of theory production is simultaneously a critique of West-centrism (the non-West cannot produce theory) and a critique of China-centrism (all theory and knowledge in Taiwan is derived from China).

By Americanism, I refer to the ways in which Taiwan, as a de facto protectorate of the United States, is situated in the international division of knowledge and what theories are possible in such a situation. By settler colonialism, I emphasize the specificity of the settler colonial form, where Han settlers constitute the demographic majority on this archipelago of the Indigenous Austronesian peoples, and how this specificity conditions the production of theory. Both are, to emphasize, world-historical events. The U.S. involvement in Taiwan was an important part of its global Cold War strategy, and Americanism was its cultural consequence. Most importantly, the origin of the international law governing the law of terra nullius—the foundational justification for settler colonialism—has a direct relationship with Taiwan.

Americanism and the Political Economy of Theory

While Americanism has its local consequences in terms of the question of theory in Taiwan, the local nature of this Americanism is always in conversation with its global character, which dates back to the days of the American Revolution when Americanism as such was codified against not only its colonial metropole, England, but also against Europe in general. About one hundred years after the revolution, Theodore Roosevelt published an illuminating essay in April 1894 in *Forum Magazine* entitled "True Americanism," in which Americanism is defined as the "spirit, conviction, and purpose" that an American has. Of the qualities necessary for being American, a major one is letting go of "colonial dependence on, and exaggerated deference to, European opinion," so as not to be a "silly and undesirable citizen." Tautologically, a true American is someone with "an intense and fervid Americanism."[17] Three decades later, during the years between 1929 and 1935, when Italian Marxist Antonio Gramsci was in prison, he wrote a long, though fragmentary, essay entitled "Americanism and Fordism," which was later published in his prison *Quaderni* (*Prison Notebooks*). In this essay, Gramsci argues that Americanism, as exemplified by Fordism, signals a change in the relations of production, which is an "organic extension and an intensification of European civilization."[18] The difference between Americanism and Europeanism is "not one of nature but of degree." Americanism represents a vital force against feudalism, the crushing of parasitic classes who have "no essential function in the world of production," and a new type of liberal state, and ultimately, the rationalization of production and work. European defensive reactions to Americanism are merely the last gasps of the parasitic classes in the "grips of a wave of social panic, dissolution and despair."[19] This Americanism is not all rosy, however, as it regulates the life and leisure (including sexual life) of workers and exploits them in an even more intense fashion, thereby exemplifying the increased "moral coercion exercised by the State and society," leading to "pathological crisis."[20] He reads the tremendous popularity of psychoanalysis at this time as a reflection of the intensified exploitation and moral coercion of workers. Ultimately, those on whom is "imposed the burden of creating with their own suffering the material bases of the new order" must find for themselves an original "system of living," away from this Americanism:[21] Workers must overthrow the system.

Though separated from Roosevelt for almost one hundred years and from Gramsci for half a century, Taiwan's Americanism shares striking similarities with their characterizations. A cursory view of the political economy of Taiwan-U.S. relations is first necessary to understand the reasons why this is the case. We can start the narrative of this relationship with the American support of the Kuomintang during the Sino-Japanese War, the retreat of the Kuomintang to Taiwan (or the recolonization and re-Sinicization of Taiwan by the regime), and the ensuing decades of American aid during the Cold War, both economic and military. The land reform of 1949 to 1953, which distributed land to two million landless farmers, doubled the income of farmers and was a crucial event for the ensuing economic miracle, was spearheaded by the Americans, who, along with a few American-trained Taiwan experts, manned the Joint Commission on Rural Reconstruction.[22] From 1958 to 1965, American aid, in the form of cash grants, poured into Taiwan in the amount of $100 million per year to move Taiwan to free market capitalism, which represented 40 percent of the entire capital formation of Taiwan at the time. Taiwan was, therefore, able to industrialize with great speed, its economy driven by exports to the United States. The strategic interest of the United States in Taiwan during the Cold War is also reflected in the military aid that amounted to a total of $2.4 billion and the patrolling of the Taiwan Strait by the Seventh Fleet. Taiwan formed a crucial part of "an island chain fencing in the Communist camp" until 1979 when the United States established a diplomatic relationship with the People's Republic of China and severed diplomatic ties with Taiwan. Throughout this period, there were only two demonstrations against the United States in Taiwan: one in 1957 when an American army sergeant shot a Taiwanese and was acquitted, and the other in December 1978 to protest the American decision to sever diplomatic relations. The first one signals the legal immunity (or, in the old language, extraterritoriality) of Americans in Taiwan, and the second, the Taiwan people's wish not to be abandoned by the United States. As a matter of fact, Taiwan residents sent no fewer than two hundred thousand letters to President Carter asking the United States not to abandon Taiwan.[23]

As can be gleaned from above, for all practical purposes, Taiwan has been a protectorate of the United States, a protectorate being a sovereign state that is diplomatically or militarily protected against third parties by a stronger state. We do not have to go as far as Chinese premier Zhou Enlai, who repeatedly said during the Cold War that the American presence in Taiwan was an "occupation."[24] Taiwan has enjoyed de-facto, though not de-jure, sovereignty, but to what extent? What does citizenship in Taiwan mean? Has it also been a desire for citizenship in the United States? As exemplified by waves of Taiwanese immigration to the United States, by the number of people who hold dual citizenships, by the petition of Club 51 members to U.S. Congress to turn Taiwan into the fifty-first state of the United States, citizenship in Taiwan has been, for a long time, haunted by the desire for citizenship in America. Oscar-winning film director Ang Lee once remarked that Taiwanese people living in Taiwan are psychological immigrants to the United States.[25] Throughout the Cold War and up to the present, it has been the United States that largely determined the political state of Taiwan. If Taiwan's citizens are not American citizens by nationality, they are, as Roosevelt had said in 1894, by "spirit, conviction, and purpose."[26] Roosevelt's plea that Americans embody true Americanism ironically works quite well for the people in Taiwan, as they might have been more American than Americans in their embrace of Americanism.

Similar to Gramsci's characterization, Americanism in Taiwan points to the changes in the relations of production, namely the economic transformation of Taiwan through land reform and enhanced industrialization, through Fordist rationalization of labor and post-Fordist international division of labor, within which Taiwan plays a specific and productive role. The formative changes in the relations of production were spearheaded by economic aid from the United States. Hence, Americanism was the cause and the effect of Taiwan's industrialization and globalization, and Taiwan may yet be considered the model case where American aid produced the most desirable results, unlike in Africa or the Middle East. In many ways, Taiwan is a *model minority* of the United States in a global formation of multiculturalism, a success story not only for free market capitalism but also democracy.

It is no wonder that Hokkien Taiwanese writer Wang Zhenhe/Wang Chen-ho's representation of Americanism in Taiwan appears as a form of neocolonialism in terms of gendered political economy. In his 1984 novel, *Meigui meigui wo ai ni* (Rose, Rose, I Love You),[27] the title word *meigui* (roses) refers to three things: the prostitutes, who are like roses, in Hualian being trained and readied for the arrival of American GIs during the Vietnam War for R&R; a proximate homonym for *meiguo* (America); and a euphemism for syphilis. Wang would further satirize Americanism using the method of Sinophone transliteration that captures the original word's sound with the target language's sound (homophonic) but in words in the target language that are specifically chosen for sound but different in meaning (homonymic), thus creating Sinophonic multiplicity in sound and word: the name Dorothy is *daolese* (throw away trash), the name T. P. Gu is *tipigu* (kick buttocks), morning becomes *monai* (grope breasts), and "Nation to Nation, People to People" is pronounced as "*neixin dui neixin, pigu dui pigu*" (heart to heart, ass to ass).[28] At stake is also the condition in which American English has become a language of privilege, which is then treated as both the object of love as well as an object of satire. Based on these observations, I propose, tentatively, three new theoretical concepts that can be drawn from Taiwan's experience of Americanism, that is both specific and general:

1. A theory of Sinophone transliteration that is simultaneously homophonic and homonymic: the creative ways in which Han Taiwanese writers

make use of the English language through acts of translating both its sound and meaning on multiply layered registers, as in the examples, to express their anticolonial intent. Across the world, resistance to American hegemony has linguistic registers, and the Taiwan example shows both a specificity that is derived from the unique sound of the two Sinitic languages—Hokkien and Mandarin—and a generality that layered transliteration can smartly register decolonial consciousness.

2. A theory of global multiculturalism where peripheral nations become minorities of global empire. It shows how formal colonialism has given way to the neocolonial and neoliberal form of global multiculturalism in a new international division of knowledge where Taiwan has become a model minority student of American or Americanized theory.[29]

3. A new traveling theory, considered less spatially, more temporally: Distinguished from Edward Said's notion of traveling theory, where local adaptation of Western theory is emphasized, my emphasis here is on the speed of theory's travel. The tendency in Taiwan, as in many other peripheral nations, to import Western theory is a process of condensation and compression, not merely in terms of the ways in which much material is condensed at the moment of importation but also in terms of the speed with which new theories are imported and then discarded, only to be replaced by further new ones. While the detritus of old theories piles up and is littered everywhere, new theories keep coming in. The pronounced characteristic in Taiwan's importation of American literary theories—such as new criticism, reader-response theory, new historicism, psychoanalytic criticism, deconstruction, poststructuralism, postcolonial theory, etc., in successive waves—is less localization, though, of course, localization is important, but more about the temporal process of absorption, application, and abandonment in quick succession. The emphasis on the speed with which Taiwan academia absorbs and moves from one theory to the next constitutes a new notion of traveling theory.

Settler Colonialism and International Law

The similarity between how Americanism applies to the United States and how it applies to Taiwan also arises, in part, from the global formation of settler colonialism that the United States and Taiwan are part of. Just as the United States tried to define itself away from Europe with Americanism, Taiwan has tried to define itself away from China, using strategies and arguments similar in structure. Hence, it is the settler's Taiwan that we have been engaged with in the previous section, the Taiwan constructed as belonging to the Han settlers from China since the seventeenth century. In a different and crucial sense, the condition of possibility for Americanism in Taiwan is further connected to Taiwan's settler colonial condition. The exclusive focus on the Taiwan-U.S. relationship has the danger of absenting the reality of the Indigenous peoples and the substitution of a triangular relationship— the Han settlers, the Indigenous peoples, and the Americans—by a binary one. A settler colony such as Taiwan, where the Han settlers have continuously colonized the Indigenous peoples for several centuries, always evinces a triangular structure: the country of origin where the settlers came from (China), the settlers, and the Indigenous peoples. In the case of Taiwan, because of the Cold War structure, this triangular structure is overlaid with a second triangle: the psychological home country (the United States and its Americanism), the settlers, and the Indigenous peoples. Any understanding of the theory formation in Taiwan must consider the overlapping of these two structures of triangulation. What this implies is that the popular discourse of Taiwan that describes Taiwan being caught between two empires (China and the United States) is a construction that is itself also settler colonial: It makes invisible the reality of settler colonialism, and it displaces the claims of the Indigenous peoples. Recall that one of the classic rationales for settler colonialism is the idea of terra nullius, empty land populated by none; hence, the settler is free to claim the land, though, in reality, the land belongs to the Indigenous peoples. Everywhere, settler colonialism's prime strategy has been to make the Indigenous disappear; in Taiwan, the transformation of the plains Indigenous through assimilation to become Han is one of these methods. Assimilation, as Patrick Wolfe and Lorenzo Veracini have shown, is one of the prime strategies in this regard, so that the settlers become the demographic majority who, due to their sheer size, can never be repatriated.[30] By official count, only 2.3 percent of Taiwan's population is Indigenous Austronesian Taiwanese.[31] However, this percentage does not include the plains Indigenous (pingpu) peoples who have been incorporated into the majority Han Taiwanese, neither does it factor in the pervasive intermarriages between Han Taiwanese and Austronesian peoples over the centuries, leading to a large mixed population that is often only counted as Han.

An example of this "between empires" narrative of Taiwan, though insightful and intriguing, showing how Indigeneity is continuously absented or displaced in the Han Taiwanese imagination, is found in Taiwanese American writer Chang His-kuo's incisive book *Diguo han taike* (Empire and taike), published in Taiwan in 2008. According to Chang, with the rise of China, Taiwan is no longer beholden only to the United States but increasingly more beholden to China. In this context, Taiwan needs to exercise its skills for flexible survival in the manner of a cha-cha dance: The Taiwanese must maintain both distance and emotional intimacy with the empires, as if dancing the cha-cha, in order to create a warm and well-lighted world, to echo the title of Hemingway's famous short story, "A Clean, Well-Lighted Place."[32] Borrowing the metaphor of a comma from Salmon Rushdie, he suggests that Taiwan should embody the grammatical characteristics of a comma in a sentence, connecting the East (China) and the West (United States), always in a process, always incomplete, and never finished. Hence, Taiwan is "neither Chinese nor Western, both Chinese and Western, and sometimes Chinese and sometimes Western."[33] This last statement is conceptually very original: It adds the temporal dimension to a statement that is otherwise about essential qualities. Hence, it very cleverly deconstructs essentialism. Indeed, the book is filled with deconstructions of essentialisms: Taiwan culture is characterized as campy, self-conscious, self-deconstructive, artificial, and imitative; it is *taotaoluoji* (tautological, an example of homophonic translation discussed above) in the sense that it produces questions but answers them without substantive content; it is illogical, and yet, it is also innocent; it inherits the spirit of pirates who use exaggerated gestures but is flexible, creative, and vital. The only time the Indigenous people are mentioned, however, is as an item on a list of inclusive multicultural representation when he discusses the film *Haijiao qihao* (Cape No. 7) as the perfect embodiment of Taike culture. Despite the fact that Taike—a name that the Han Taiwanese sometimes call themselves—means "guests of Taiwan," their entitled sense of ownership of Taiwan and their blatant denial of Indigenous sovereignty is not questioned. The "between empires" narrative is clearly Han settler–centric in its denial of Indigenous dispossession.

Here, I want to emphasize that Taiwan is not a settler colony that is merely similar to other settler colonies, such as the United States, Australia, New Zealand, Canada, and elsewhere, but that *Taiwan was directly connected to the origin of the legal definitions of settler colonialism since the seventeenth century*, which gives further evidence to the significance of Taiwan's place in world history and helps us consider how settler colonialism as a condition of theory for Taiwan must be understood, again, on a world scale. Thus, theory arising out of Taiwan's settler colonial condition is both specific and general at the same time.

Specifically, the connection is to the beginnings of international law regarding settlement and conquest via the Dutch East India Company and the Dutch jurist Hugo Grotius. Hugo Grotius (1583–1645) is the first and foremost theorist who laid the foundation for international law, especially by establishing legal grounds for overseas expansion and settlement, through his immensely influential legal treatises *De Jure Belli ac Pacis libri tres* (*On the Law of War and Peace*; three volumes, 1625), *Mare Liberum* (*The Free Sea*; 1609), and *De Jure Praedae* (On the right of capture, originally *De Indis* [On the Indies], written 1604–1605, published in 1864), coining the term and propagating the law of terra nullius, where the seizure of vacant places is regarded as law of nature, defending the right of conquest and driving out of the natives, the right of punishment of offenders, the right to just war (against savage beasts and then against "men who are like beasts"), and the right to "private war." From Grotius, we have a direct line to the British philosopher John Locke and other theorists of international law. Grotius himself "had relatives among the directors of the Dutch East India Company and Locke was an investor in the Royal Africa Company and in a company trading in the Bahamas."[34] The Dutch East India Company was granted by the states-general of the Netherlands a twenty-one-year monopoly to carry out colonial activities in Asia beginning in 1602, and thus had the right, according to Dutch law, to establish colonies, one of which was Taiwan, or Dutch Formosa (1624–1662). The history of settler colonialism in Taiwan is, therefore, intimately connected to the foundation of international law; it is a world-historical event, and it should be treated thusly.

On the basis of international laws regarding settlement and conquest and drawing from the social contract theory, Carole Pateman has developed the notion of a "settler contract," which is a contract "signed" among settlers themselves and to which both the colonial metropole and the Indigenous peoples are excluded, even though the Indigenous peoples are expected to behave according to the contract designed and executed by the settlers. The Indigenous peoples are not signatories to the contract but are managed and dominated by the contract.[35] The signing of this settler contract among the Han Taiwanese people (whether Hokkien or Hakka) is the determining condition of knowledge production. This determination is the starting point for any consideration of theory in Taiwan or Taiwan in theory.

What this implies is that the utility of a postcolonial theory for Taiwan, after Dutch, Japanese, and second-wave Chinese colonialisms, is largely limited to the Han Taiwanese in Taiwan. Postcolonial theory in Taiwan is a tautology that serves the interest of the Han Taiwanese self, i.e., it is its own prophecy and goal—a self-serving pretense of significant truth. The Indigenous peoples have never been postcolonial. Since settler colonialism is not an event but a structure that can never be thoroughly overturned, as Patrick Wolfe has famously argued,[36] the nature of Han Taiwanese knowledge in Taiwan, though caught among empires (China and the United States), is settler colonial knowledge, and the critique of this knowledge formation will only be the first step toward true decolonization of knowledge in Taiwan.

To extrapolate: A settler colonial theory in Taiwan is akin to that found in other settler colonies around the world but specific to the history of Dutch, Japanese, and Chinese colonization, hence both specific and general. We may, tentatively again, draw the following theoretical points from the settler colonial condition in Taiwan:

1. A theory of tautology (taotao luoji): Settler colonial knowledge in Taiwan is a tautological, self-enhancing truth with no substantive content. It is all form and empty in the center. Hence, it can be easily filled up with imported knowledge from the West. This notion is related to the new notion of the temporality of traveling theory, as discussed above, and it presumes the "emptiness of theory" that Taiwan theorist Liao Chao-yang has propounded.[37] The Han subject is empty; hence, it is forever receptive to Western influence and imposition even while it subjects Indigenous knowledge to repression and oblivion.
2. A theory of imitation: Related to the speediness with which Taiwan academia imports and discards Western theory, the prevailing mode of imitating Western theory again indexes the empty core or the empty center. A new theory of imitation, therefore, needs to be developed not only in the pedagogical sense but also in terms of the neocolonial division of knowledge. An imitation is a copy of an original, and the act of imitation always happens after the time of the original and at an alternative site removed from the origin. An imitation is, therefore, always a copy, happening in an alternate, belated temporality and alternate space. Like a work of translation in the Benjaminian sense, an imitation further extends the life of the original by circulating it, keeping it alive, adjusting it, altering it, and perhaps even perfecting it.
3. Spectralization of the Indigenous: Unlike the predominant ancestralization of the Indigenous in the United States by settlers, whereby the settlers claim to be the inheritors of the land from the Indigenous ancestors who are made to "vanish,"[38] Taiwan's settler colonial imaginary also intends to have the Indigenous vanish, not by claiming to be their descendants and inheritors but by spectralizing their presence. This is part of the settler colonial strategy to make the Indigenous disappear, especially the nonplains Indigenous or mountain Indigenous peoples since the plains Indigenous have been forcefully incorporated into the Han Taiwanese body.[39] In the realm of theory, the lack of settlers' committed engagement with Indigenous knowledge is a clear exemplification of this spectralization, even as the situation is improving.[40]
4. Continentalization of the settler: Concomitant with the spectralization of the Indigenous is the continentalization of the Han settlers. Even

though the earliest waves of Han settlement in Taiwan occurred over three hundred years ago, there persists a strong continental mentality among the Han Taiwanese, as opposed to the seafaring, island, and archipelagic perspective of the Indigenous peoples. This continental mentality, originally expressed as allegiance to China as the Han people's suzerain and their inability to understand what it means to be islanders, is now in crisis as Taiwan's desire for sovereignty becomes more and more pronounced, and as Taiwan confronts and contests the Chinese claim of ownership of Taiwan in the context of the rise of China. Han settlers' continentalism evinces a typical settler colonial affective structure which they are learning to shed in recent decades for strategic reasons in order to achieve settler sovereignty against China's presumed suzerainty.

A Theory of Poverty

In this chapter, I have tried to show that theory arises out of relations in world history by using Taiwan as an example in terms of its two world-historical conditions of Americanism and settler colonialism. Throughout, my aim is to restore the constitutive exteriority—namely, world-historical relations—to that which can be regarded as theory. This is an argument for the importance of rooting theory in the immanent reality, to emphasize theory's embeddedness in the "deep historicism of the social" and the "materialism of the encounter" as Françoise Lionnet and I have argued earlier,[41] but extending the scope to the larger frame of relations in world history. It is an argument for epistemological realism on a world scale. I further argue that to attend to these relations is not merely to understand them as the ground from which to theorize but also to put forth an ethical understanding of what theory is in an unequal international division of knowledge. Inequality, as a form of relation, may be understood as a structuring principle for the production and circulation of theory, and theorizing anywhere must take this structuring principle as a starting point. As our discussions about how colonial expansion was intimately tied to the rise of sociology and comparative literature as disciplines reveal, the kind of theory that is blind to its embeddedness in world history, which is in the most fundamental sense a history of power, cannot in any sense be objective.

Directed at Eurocentric theory, my critique here is, in part, inspired by that of philosopher of science Sandra Harding that any kind of theory that ignores and is not tested by "the majority world"—the world beyond the

West, i.e., the Rest—is fundamentally lacking. Harding argues for "strong objectivity" in science, which she defines as "maximally fair and responsible to the data and to the severest criticism it does and could receive."[42] To achieve this, one must consider both the "cognitive and intellectual norm of objectivity" as well as the "social justice norm of diversity" by seeking out the "underrepresented insights and critical perspectives of economically, socially, and politically vulnerable groups in the West and around the globe."[43] Similarly, Raewyn Connell's method is to "maximize the wealth of materials" and to "multiply, rather than slim down, the theoretical ideas that we have to work with,"[44] and she does this by studying concepts and ideas from, as mentioned earlier, Africa, Latin American, and South and Southwest Asia. For Comaroff and Comaroff, also discussed above, theory has to be based on understanding our world as a "joint becoming" of metropole and colony for it to have any validity at all.[45]

Directed at the peripheral and small nations presumed not to be sites of theory, my proposal is similarly to attend to the world-historical relations but in a different sense. Americanism and settler colonialism are examples of two specific world-historical relations that produce the conditions for theory in Taiwan. As places where world-historical power relations were mostly acutely felt, small island nations like Taiwan are paradoxically endowed with specific epistemic privileges out of conditions of intellectual poverty rather than richness. As Moroccan writer and thinker Adbelkebir Khatibi writes:

> A way of thinking that does not draw its inspiration from its own poverty is always elaborated with the object of dominating and humiliating; thought that is not oriented towards the minority, and marginal, fragmentary, or incomplete is ultimately directed upon ethnocide.[46]

Occupying the position of poverty in the world of knowledge, on the crossroads of theories imported from elsewhere, endowed with the epistemic advantage of the minor, Taiwan and other small nations may thus be the sites of theory-production, the kind of theory which, though forever incomplete, is also always full of potential.

Notes

This chapter is a revised and shortened version of an essay titled "Theory is a Relational World," previously published in *Comparative Literature Studies* 53, no. 4 (2016): 722–746.

1. Alejandro Arturo Vallega, *Latin American Philosphy from Identity to Radical Exteriority* (Bloomington: Indiana University Press, 2014).

2. Shu-mei Shih et al., "Draft Manifesto of the 'Knowledge/Taiwan' Collective" (2012) (in English), in *Zhishi Taiwan: Taiwan Lilun de kenengxing* (Knowledge/Taiwan: The Potentiality of Theory in Taiwan), ed. Shu-mei Shih et al. (Taipei: Ryefield, 2016), 466–468.

3. For a clarifying look at the opposition between philosophy and theory, see John McCumber's important essay, "Philosophy vs. Theory: Reshaping the Debate," August 25, 2009, Mondes Francophones (website), http://mondesfrancophones.com/espaces/philosophies/philosophy-vs-theory-reshaping-the-debate/.

4. See Shu-mei Shih, "Comparison as Relations," in *Comparison: Theories, Approaches, Uses*, ed. Rita Felski and Susan Friedman. (Baltimore, MD: Johns Hopkins University Press, 2013): 79–98. Also see Shu-mei Shih, "World Studies and Relational Comparison," *PMLA* 130, no. 2 (March 2015): 430–438. Even though we work from very different disciplinary locations and were previously unaware of each other's work, geographer Gillian Hart and I have come into dialogue with each other about our respective conceptualizations of the method of relational comparison. Gillian Hart first proposed this notion in "Denaturalizing Dispossession: Critical Ethnography in the Age of Resurgent Imperialism," *Antipode* 38, no. 5 (2006): 976–1004.

5. I am most inspired by Gillian Hart's essay "Denaturalizing Dispossession" as well as her 2016 "Progress in Human Geography" lecture at the annual convention of the American Association of Geography entitled "Relational Comparison Revisited: Marxist Postcolonial Geographies in Practice" (unpublished manuscript) held March 29–April 2 in San Francisco. In addition, I borrow the notion of coproduction from Sheila Jasanoff, "The Idiom of Co-Production," in *States of Knowledge: The Co-Production of Science and Society* (New York: Routledge, 2004), 1–12. Also, see my position paper in the forum, "Linking Taiwan Studies and the World," *International Journal of Taiwan Studies*, inaugural issue, no. 1 (2018): 193–208.

6. Edward Said, "Traveling Theory," in *The World, the Text, and the Critic* (Cambridge, Ma: Harvard University Press, 1983), 226–247.

7. See Bonaventura de Sousa Santos, ed., *Another Knowledge Is Possible: Beyond Northern Epistemologies* (London: Verso, 2008) and Bonaventura de Sousa Santos, ed., *Epistemologies of the South: Justice Against Epistemicide* (Boulder, CO: Paradigm Publishers, 2014).

8. Walter Mignolo has developed this schema drawing inspiration from the work of Sylvia Wynter. See the two works by Walter Mignolo, *Local Histories/Global Designs: Coloniality, Subaltern Knowledges, and Border Thinking*. (Princeton, NJ: Prince University Press, 2000) as well as Walter Mignolo, "I Am Where I Think: Remapping the Order of Knowledge," in *The Creolization of Theory*, ed. Françoise Lionnet and Shu-mei Shih (Durham, NC: Duke University Press, 2011), 159–192. Also see Silvia Wynter, "Unsettling the Coloniality of Being/Power/Truth/Freedom: Towards the Human, After Man, Its Overrepresentation—An Argument," *CR: The New Centennial Review* 3, no. 3 (2003): 257–337.

9. de Sousa Santos, *Epistemologies from the South*.

10. Jean Comaroff and John Comaroff, *Theory from the South: Or, How Euro-America is Evolving Toward Africa* (London: Routledge, 2011), 1, 12.

11. Raewyn Connell, *Southern Theory: The Global Dynamics of Knowledge in Social Science*. (Cambridge: Polity Press, 2007).

12. Shu-mei Shih and Françoise Lionnet, "Introduction: The Creolization of Theory," in *Creolization of Theory*, eds Lionnet and Shih (Durham, NC: Duke University Press, 2011), 1–33.

13. Connell, *Southern Theory*, 44, 33, 45 (emphasis mine), 11.

14. For my critique of the settler colonial origin of comparative literature in the United States, see "Decolonizing U.S. Comparative Literature," *Comparative Literature* 75, no. 3 (September 2023): 237–265.

15. Consider the wide-ranging debate among leading intellectuals in Taiwan in the 1990s on the significance of postcolonial paradigm versus poststructuralism. For a summary of this debate, see Li-chun Hsiao, "Piping de changshi/changshi de piping: lilun, changshi yu gaige" (Theoretical Thinking on the Fault Lines of Theory, Commonsense, and Reform," in Shih et al., *Knowledge/Taiwan*, 177–232.

16. The representative figure who embodies this anachronism is Chen Yingzhen, the Marxist writer who had been the moral conscience from the left during the White Terror era, later defecting to China after China had resoundingly moved to postsocialism with what some would say to be severe neoliberal capitalist tendencies. The particular discourse of internationalism that China continues to promote and Taiwan Marxists like Chen adhere to is largely a hollow propaganda to cover up its settler colonialism in Xinjiang, colonialism in Tibet, and its neocolonial practices in Africa and Southeast Asia.

17. Theodore Roosevelt, "True Americanism" (1894), Great Hearts Institute, accessed August 22, 2014, https://whatsoproudlywehail.org/curriculum/the-meaning-of-america/true-americanism.

18. Antonio Gramsci, "Americanism and Fordism," in Selections from the Prison Notebooks, ed. And trans. Quentin Horare and Geoffrey Nowell Smith (New York: International Publishers, 1971), 318.

19. Gramsci, "Americanism and Fordism," 317.

20. Gramsci, "Americanism and Fordism," 280.

21. Gramsci, "Americanism and Fordism," 317.

22. See Melissa J. Brown, *Is Taiwan Chinese? The Impact of Culture, Power, and Migration on Changing Identities* (Berkeley: University of California Press, 2004), 60–63. Also see Denny Roy, *Taiwan: A Political History* (Ithaca, NY: Cornell University Press 2003), 90–102.

23. Roy, *Taiwan*, 98–151.

24. Roy, *Taiwan*, 121–123.

25. See my discussion of Ang Lee's remarks in relation to his films in Shih, *Visuality and Identity: Sinophone Articulations across the Pacific* (Berkeley: University of California Press, 2007), 40-61.

26. Roosevelt, "True Americanism."

27. Wang Chen-ho, *Meigui meigui wo ai ni* (Rose, Rose, I love you). (Taipei: Hongfan. 1984).

28. The first two homophonic expressions can be found in *Meirentu* (A Portrait of Beauty) and the second two from *Rose, Rose, I Love You*.

29. For earlier discussions of global multiculturalism, see my *Visuality and Identity*, chapter 1 on globalization as minoritization.

30. See Patrick Wolfe, *Settler Colonialism and the Transformation of Anthropology* (London: Cassell, 1999). See also Lorenzo Veracini, *Settler Colonialism: A Theoretical Overview* (London: Palgrave Mcmillan, 2010).

31. See Taiwan government website, accessed September 9, 2016, http://www.taiwan.gov.tw/ct.asp?xItem=126579&ctNode=3698&mp=1.

32. Chang His-kuo, *Empire and Taike* (*diguo han taike*) (Taipei: tianxia zazhi chubanshe, 2008), 7.

33. Chang, *Diguo han taike*, 94.

34. Carole Pateman, "The Settler Contract," in *Contract and Domination*, ed. Carole Pateman and Charles Mills. (Cambridge: Polity Press, 2007), 47–48.

35. Pateman, "The Settler Contract," 35–78.

36. Wolfe, *Settler Colonialism*, 2.

37. Chao-yang Liao, "Theory and Emptiness" (lilun yu xukong), in Shu-mei Shih et al.. *Knowledge/Taiwan*, 141–176.

38. Yael Ben-zvi, "Where Did Red Go? Lewis Henry Morgan's Evolutionary Inheritance and U.S. Racial Imagination," *New Centennial Review* 7, no. 2 (2007): 201–229.

39. Only in recent years, several plains Indigenous (pingpu) tribes who are mostly of mixed heritage have been trying to reclaim their Indigenous status through legal action. The "Declaration of the PingPu Peoples of Taiwan" was made in 2001 at the public hearing for plains Indigenous peoples' identity at the Legislative Assembly, but the efforts have been met with a lot of resistance and legal obstructions. See Jolan Hsieh, *Collective Rights of Indigenous Peoples: Identity-Based Movement of Plain Indigenous in Taiwan* (New York: Routledge, 2013).

40. See, for instance, Shu-mei Shih and Lin-chin T'sai, eds., *Indigenous Knowledge in Taiwan and Beyond* (Singapore: Springer, 2021), which anthologizes some of the most important efforts by indigenous scholars and Western scholars of indigenous knowledge in Taiwan.

41. Shu-mei Shih and Françoise Lionnet, "Introduction: The Creolization of Theory," in Lionnet and Shih, *Creolization of Theory*, 17 and 23.

42. Sandra Harding, *Objectivity and Diversity: Another Logic of Scientic Research* (Chicago: University of Chicago Press, 2015), x.

43. Harding, *Objectivity and Diversity*, 174.

44. Connell, *Southern Theory*, 207.

45. Comaroff and Comaroff, *Theory from the South*, 5.

46. Abdelkebir Khatibi, *Maghreb pluriel* (Paris: Denoël, 1983), 18.

PLACES OF DIFFERENTIATION

Chinese Settler Colonialism

Empire and Life in the Tibetan Borderlands

CAROLE MCGRANAHAN

> The Chinese are like kind parents
> The silver dollars rain down upon us
> —Tibetan saying

One person's frontier is the center of another person's world. Kham is such a place. It is the eastern territory of Tibet, one of the country's three historical regions—Amdo, Kham, and U-Tsang. Kham is both center and frontier and for many people, it is a homeland that precedes and thus transgresses borders and the nations and empires that define them. Kham is a place of diversity and contrast and, like all places, of contradictions. In the current political period, Kham's contradictions are especially relevant, for they illuminate Chinese and Tibetan histories in important, overlooked ways.

In the 1950s, in an imperial move of aggression led by Mao Zedong, the People's Republic of China (PRC) invaded and took over Tibet. In eastern Tibet, the Chinese soldiers were initially kind, offering ordinary Tibetans so many silver coins that these actions were memorialized in the above ditty that older Tibetans still remember today. The government of Tibet, including its leader, the Fourteenth Dalai Lama, protested, but to no avail. Although a sovereign state, Tibet was not a member of the United Nations, and thus, no country substantively came to Tibet's defense. These events unfolded during the Cold War and European decolonization. As countries around the world demanded and gained independence, Tibet ironically lost its independence and became a colony of the communist PRC. In Tibet, including Kham, a key aspect of Chinese communist empire is settler colonialism.

What is settler colonialism? It is imperial territorial acquisition followed by ongoing dispossession and oppression through colonial administration and settlement. Political scientist Glen Coulthard defines settler colonialism as follows: "A settler-colonial relationship is one characterized by a particular form of *domination*; that is, it is a relationship where power—in this case, interrelated discursive and nondiscursive facets of economic, gendered, racial, and state power—has been structured into a relatively secure or sedimented set of hierarchical social relations that continue to facilitate the *dispossession* of Indigenous peoples of their lands and self-determining authority."[1] Settling includes dispossessing others of their land and autonomy. As explained by anthropologist Audra Simpson, it is not just other people settling on native land but also the unsettling of native practices and beliefs.[2] It is to attempt to unmake existing worlds and replace them with imperial ones. In the case of Tibet, it is to replace Tibetan worlds with Chinese ones. In Tibet, Chinese colonial goals include economic and resource extraction, political administration, settlement incentives, the renaming and dividing of lands, cultural assimilation, and (thus far unsuccessful) efforts to eliminate religion in favor of an idealized atheistic socialism.

Imperial formations know no boundaries. They are not limited to certain parts of the world or time periods or types of polities. Thinking of empires as always in formation rather than as steady or coherent states enables needed comparisons across cases in addition to an appreciation of their specificities.[3] Acknowledging that an imperial formation is as likely to be Chinese, communist, and of the twentieth or twenty-first centuries as it is to be English, capitalist, and of the eighteenth or nineteenth centuries is both a historical reality and an analytic argument.[4] It is also a political claim. Claiming the People's Republic of China to be an imperial polity rather than (only) a multiethnic one is to assert an anti-imperial politics and to center a colonized perspective. Given Tibet and China's long tenure as neighboring polities, their shared political history ranges wildly. It has not always been a story of colonialism. Telling the story of Chinese colonialism in Tibet requires assessment of how empire is not only implemented but also how it is lived. Even in the most authoritarian of periods, people rarely respond to or experience colonialism in a singular way. As a structure rather than an event,[5] settler colonialism has shared features but not total coherence across Tibetan areas. Tibetans are colonized by China, but this structural reality has discrete geographic, historic, and political components to it.

Tibet's imperial realities are multiple. In the twentieth century alone, they have quadrupled, including imperial relationships with British India, Qing China, the PRC, and the United States. Going farther back, they include the period when Tibet itself was an empire during the seventh through the ninth centuries, ruling over many of its neighbors, including portions of China, as well as territories further afield.[6] A genealogy of imperial formations related to Tibet over the last millennia thus includes a range of polities, including Tibet itself. The eighth-century arrival of Buddhism in Tibet effectively ended Tibet's imperial structure and activity. Governance, including relations with neighbors, was recalibrated within Buddhist frameworks. Across a vast territory that Tibetans often speak of as historically stretching from Ladakh in the west to Dartsendo in the east, Tibet was a patchwork of social, political, and religious institutions. Such variation was the norm. For example, depending on the village or town in which one lived in Kham, one could be under the administration of a monastic leader, a chiefly family, or a royal family. People living in border areas were sometimes under the influence or even direct rule of neighboring non-Tibetan rulers and vice versa. Local power relations existed alongside other relations of trade, sociality, and religion. The latter was key for Tibet: Buddhist religious ties bound peoples through practices of patronage, pilgrimage, and devotion. Religious institutions and figures were omnipresent in Tibetan economic, social, and political domains. Indeed, the common term for Tibetan systems of governance was *chos srid*, or "religion (and) politics." This combination of religion and politics is a continuing and constant tension for Chinese empire today.

Studying Chinese colonialism in Kham is to ask questions about frontiers, empire, and sovereignty. As Stéphane Gros argues, the eastern Tibetan region of Kham presents a "categorical challenge" to what we think we know about both China and Tibet.[7] Analyzing Chinese colonialism in Kham challenges denials that the PRC is an imperial polity. Instead, it insists on categorizing current Tibetan relationships to China as colonized and asks what changes when we do so. Borderlands, for example, have never been neutral political sites of cultural and economic exchange but are instead areas of political possibility distinct from metropole locations. In this sense, Kham has long been a site for Chinese experiments with imperial policy.[8] For Tibet, centering history and society in Kham means decentering Lhasa, Tibet's capital. Challenging the idea of Lhasa as the national center forces attention to the historical place of regions such as Kham, Amdo, Ngari, or more provocatively, perhaps, areas such as Bhutan (*'Drug yul*) in relation to central Tibet. It also forces a conversation on sovereignty.

Tibetan claims to state sovereignty, and thus to Chinese imperialism in Tibet, can be as productively grounded in Kham as in Lhasa.[9] Kham is a region long associated with a fierce sense of independence, and the people there have continued that tradition in response to the PRC. Since the 1950s, a consistent Tibetan response to Chinese political change has been resistance. As with colonized peoples elsewhere, Tibetan responses to empire exist along a spectrum from consent to refusal, including periods of more active or more passive reactions. Reconfigurations of everyday life under colonialism include consenting to new hegemonic policies and expectations to outright refusal of them.[10] Given structural limits for cultural and political expression in China, consent, resistance, and refusal necessarily coexist. While this may be true for peoples throughout the PRC, the burden of empire places additional forms of oppression on Tibetans as well as Uyghurs and other colonized peoples.[11] For some individuals and communities, consent and refusal might be simultaneous, if contradictory, practices of survival. This is part of the story of the contemporary Tibetan borderlands in Kham.

Settler Colonialism with Chinese Communist Characteristics

Empires take many forms. Settler colonialism is one form, elastic rather than rigid across cultural and historical contexts.[12] It consists of the settling of others' land by the colonizer with the intention of displacing, replacing, or otherwise eliminating the natives of the colonized territory.[13] Classic examples of settler colonialism are Australia, Canada, and the United States. In each instance, there exist drastic policies of both assimilation and destruction, including of native peoples as well as their historical beliefs, practices, and claims to land. Settler colonialism may be one of several strategies or forms an empire takes. While it is often linked to European colonialism and white supremacy, it—like empire in general—is not solely a European or white phenomenon. Settler colonialism is a possible feature of all imperial formations, including that of China.

Is China an empire? If many China studies scholars have been hesitant to call the PRC an empire, Tibetan studies scholars have not hesitated to do so. From political science and international relations,[14] to anthropology, geography, and history,[15] many Tibetan studies scholars portray Tibet's relationship with the PRC as imperial. However, not all scholars do. Some prefer the term *occupied*, a term that calls attention to the problematic and violent nature of Tibet's relationship with the PRC but that falls short of the term *colonized*. This dilemma of naming the socialist state an empire is not limited to China but also exists within Soviet studies. Given the development of colonial and later postcolonial studies from within Marxist frameworks, noncapitalist empires, such as the PRC and USSR, do not fit scholarly imperial models.[16]

While there are similarities in the two cases, the scholarly literatures on these two socialist empires has unfolded differently.

In much of China studies, *empire* is past tense, with important studies focused on the Qing or farther back.[17] Why is this? Avoiding labeling China as imperial draws on a range of possible reasons, including the following: (1) scholarly fears of criticizing the government, and thus potential persecution or loss of research access;[18] (2) Marxist "radical reductionism" or ideological affiliation with or apology for the Chinese communist government;[19] (3) a myopic focus on European empire;[20] and, (4) pervasive "discourse[s] of Chinese victimhood at the hands of Western empires."[21] Within China studies, one important recalibration of the study of empire is through Sinophone studies or the domination of the Chinese language.[22]

Sinophone communities are one way to recognize Chinese empire. Literary scholar Shu-mei Shih identifies three historical processes of imperial consolidation: "the continental colonialism of Manchu and Han Chinese empires that produced internal colonies in today's China; Han settler colonialism in select places such as Taiwan, Singapore and colonial Malaya; and (im)migration out of China that produced minoritized Sinophone communities in different parts of the world such as Australia, Europe, and the Americas."[23] In this formulation, language is central. This holds true in some but not all ways for Tibetan colonial experiences in the PRC. A focus on language misses important historical and theoretical conversations about sovereignty that necessarily ground discussions and experiences of empire in Tibet. In the Tibetan language, the conceptual and imperial other is China (*rGya nag*) and the Chinese (*rGya mi*), not the Chinese language nor the "Han" Chinese. Thus, in addition to a genealogical connection to an imperial formation grounded around language, i.e., the Sinophone, in the case of Tibet, we also need a Tibetan-centered historical and political perspective.

Following World War II, China and the United States both used anti-imperial Cold War rhetoric to reframe empire as something else; for example, to posit imperialism as development or as the liberating spread of either socialism or democracy.[24] In the case of China, the consolidation of the People's Republic of China as socialist empire used and also returned long-standing Chinese tropes of barbarians outside the gates of civilized society as well as new political strategies for and justifications of empire. When the People's Liberation Army invaded Tibet, the initial justification was the need for socialist liberation from feudalism and religion. Later, the Chinese Communist Party added a historical justification to the earlier ideological one: the claim that Tibet was *always* a part of China. Ironically, this historical argument is itself only several decades old. For Xinjiang, in addition to Tibet, anthropologist Kevin Carrico argues that such rhetorical shifts over time maintain the colonial project: "The ideological application of the euphemism of development is particularly pressing in the current western areas of China, where from the Maoist rhetoric of 'liberation' to the post-Maoist rhetoric of 'development' a process of unrelenting Han Chinese colonization has been insistently represented as anything but colonization."[25] Whom does a denial of colonialism serve? Mostly, but not only, those in power.

Under socialism, the Chinese civilizing project has been one of forging national unity and ethnic harmony.[26] In Tibet, one example of this is the ongoing Education Aid for Tibet project, where Chinese citizens travel to Tibetan areas to work as teachers. This labor is seen as moral and part of a civilizing savior complex familiar to colonial situations elsewhere.[27] Moral justifications for the program rest on stereotypical narratives such as "the Han [i.e., Chinese] are superior, central, civilized, and safe and the ethnic minorities [i.e., the Tibetans] are inferior, peripheral, barbaric, and unsafe."[28] In her ethnographic research with teachers in the program, scholar Miaoyan Yang found they understood their participation to be not so much about education for its own sake as education in the service of ethnic unity, national stability, and national integration.[29] Underlying this discourse is the argument that Tibetans are not integrated into the Chinese state and that this is a problem to be fixed. Instead of unity and harmony, Tibetans thus potentially present problems of separatism and splittism to a benevolent imperial state.

Tibet is not an internal colony of China. To call it an "internal colony" would support the fiction that Tibet was historically part of China. An internal colony is a territory inside a state that is administered in a colonial fashion or for which massive economic inequality exists between it and the state center.[30] In the PRC, there are places and peoples whose relation to the state is that of an internal colony.[31] These are mostly non-Han ethnic areas and groups but not necessarily ones that had a sovereign state, as Tibet did. All non-Han peoples are nonetheless grouped into one ethnopolitical category, that of "minority nationalities" or *minzu*, in a way that defines this grouping as natural or inevitable, that is such that "these peoples are officially described as always already a part of China, as if they somehow naturally belonged on this map and did not end up as part of China by being conquered."[32] Anthropologist of China Magnus Fiskesjö argues that this historical revisionism has stark political repercussions: "One formidable effect of this formulation is that it equalizes all the minorities and thereby erases the differences between those who built their own states and empires in the past, such as Tibet, which could easily, like Mongolia, fulfill the criteria for being recognized by the modern world as independent states with their own seat in the United Nations and on the other hand, those minority peoples who never engaged in any such state-building in the past."[33]

Tibet's eighteenth- and nineteenth-century imperial relations were with the Qing (Manchu) empire, which was a non-Han empire of China. Buddhism bound the Qing emperor and Tibetan Dalai Lama together in a "patron-priest" relationship that Tibetans understood as a relation of equals, not one of subordination.[34] Being in an imperial relationship was not the same as being in a colonial one. During the same period, for example, British India also considered Tibet to be in its imperial interest; however, these Great Game politics were not an indicator of loss of sovereignty. In 1913, following the fall of the Qing empire and the efforts of the new Republican government in China to assert claims to Tibet, the Thirteenth Dalai Lama proclaimed Tibet's independence. Tibet never came under the imperial or colonial administration of the Republican government of China. What, then, does current Chinese settler colonialism look like?

Instructions on how to be civilized. Exclusions from certain programs and possibilities. Inclusions in other programs and possibilities. Requirements to perform gratitude, to embrace aspects of socialism, to reject local beliefs and practices, including religious ones—Buddhism in Tibet and Islam in Xinjiang. A visible security presence and invisible but known surveillance methods. State policies based on misunderstandings of native peoples, such as nomadic pastoralists. Alongside these, however, is everyday life. People find ways to live in empire, to live alongside colonizers, to survive and even thrive within limits. Strategies for doing so are multiple.

Within the PRC, Tibetans creatively push back on their state ethnic (*minzu*) categorization at times, and at other times, they operate within proscribed limits.[35] Poetry, literature, art, and song are all important genres for Tibetan cultural and political expression, often with risks of imprisonment and abuse for artists, intellectuals, and even community members.[36] Changes in government policies for nomads, farmers, and urban residents have created new forms of inequality and struggle among Tibetans.[37] Tibetan experiences of nationalist modernity within China are shared across regions. For example, short stories written in Amdo are read by people in Kham. Songs performed by Khampas are beloved by people in Amdo. Poems composed in honor of historical events in Lhasa circulate among Tibetans in all provinces via social media. In the digital era, people have new ways to connect and communicate, including to "undermine political authoritarianism."[38]

Tibetan experiences with Chinese neighbors long precede contemporary empire. Traders, intellectuals, monks, and others regularly traveled to China and other neighboring countries, such as India and Nepal, and resided there sometimes by choice and other times as forced exile. The city of Chengdu in Sichuan, for example, has long had Tibetan residents and is currently being reimagined anew as a Tibetan place within China. While Kham and other

Tibetan regions each have historical and administrative specificities, shared cultural sensibilities and forms have new uses under colonial rule. Understanding Kham thus requires understanding Tibet and vice versa.

Kham: Borderlands, Center, Home

Where is Kham? It is north of Arunachal Pradesh and Burma and Yunnan, south of Amdo, east of Lhasa, and west of Sichuan and China. For Khampa Tibetans in exile, Kham is where they are not. Kham is a dreamt-of homeland, a place kept alive through memory and WeChat. The borders of Kham are not just with China; this is not simply the Sino-Tibetan borderlands. Instead, the borders of Kham and Tibet are also with a range of other peoples. An orientation toward China is only one way to situate Kham, albeit a very potent way, given the current geopolitical situation. However, borders are not only geographic; they are also conceptual and cultural. For example, religious borders in the form of different Buddhist sects stratify much of Tibet and provide impetus to overcome the limits of single sectarian approaches or dominance. Environmental borders of rivers, passes, elevation, and so on challenge and shape human possibility, as do linguistic borders. Kham is an area of religious, environmental, and linguistic diversity, and histories plural that match this diversity. Just as Tibet is not a singular cultural field, neither is Kham. When and how people identify as Khampa is situational and strategic. Nonetheless, in times of loss and change, geopolitical singularities can possess new meanings for people. The current moment is one such time.

A list of possible identities for any individual is always graduated. For an individual in Kham, geopolitical identities are layered and split. One has Tibetan geopolitical identities and now also Chinese administrative ones. Historically, Kham was one of the *chol kha* (regions) of Tibet and was comprised of many *pha yul* (fatherlands) or districts. Each phayul had a central town and many villages and monasteries within its domain. Different Tibetan dialects and even languages are spoken throughout the region, some mutually unintelligible. Under Chinese rule, Tibetan terms were replaced with Chinese administrative units of prefectures, counties, cities, and townships. Nyarong is now Xinlong. Chatreng is Xiangchen. Gyalthang is Shangri-la or Xianggelila. The names shift as the language does; the places reassemble with new boundaries and sensibilities. For some people, the two naming systems coexist; for others, one fades in the face of the other. If your phayul is Nyarong and cholkha is Kham, your county is now Xinlong in the Chinese-established Ganzi Tibetan Autonomous Prefecture in Sichuan Province. Colonizing a place, settling a territory, includes renaming and reshaping its land.

This is not a neutral act. The Tibetan and Chinese languages are not related. They jointly head the Sino-Tibetan language family, but Chinese is the current language of empire. Resistance to this is ongoing.

Insistence on the use of Tibetan languages is one nationalist form of resistance. We see this in numerous projects and forms of activism in the eastern Tibet regions, from the building of schools and the creation of language programs to the Lhakar (White Wednesday) movement's pledge to speak only Tibetan on Wednesdays. Such actions are considered counterrevolutionary by the Chinese government. In May 2018, three years after appearing in a *New York Times* video discussing his work to support the teaching and preservation of the Tibetan language, Tashi Wangchuk was sentenced to five years in prison for "incitement to separatism." His story dissolves important borders: He is from Jyekundo in the historic Tibetan region of Amdo, now known by its Chinese name of Yushu in the province of Qinghai. But his story of linguistic activism and of the state violence that accompanies it could be that of someone in Kham or central Tibet. Becoming visible to the state for advocating for things Tibetan—language, dress, religion, rights—is to take a risk. Even ostensibly safe ways to publicly present and perform Tibetan identities through, for example, "ethnic" song and dance, always include such dangers. Negotiating the risks of state violence is something required under settler colonialism, even for things that, on the surface, seem apolitical.

How can one be unknowable to the state? At Yachen Gar, a religious community of nuns in Kham, women seek ways to be unknowable to, and thus uncontrollable by, the state.[39] This is a project in constant motion, as the nuns build huts in manners and formations designed to deter, confuse, and refuse state mandates to be knowable. Remembering past resistance efforts against the state is also a political project. In exile, as in the PRC, there are prohibitions against narrating the histories of the Kham-centered citizen Chushi Gangdrug army that fought against the PLA for almost two decades.[40] Also discouraged are histories that challenge either Chinese or Tibetan ideas of Kham or even of specific phayul as marginal places rather than centers of their own.[41] The historiography and scholarship produced under such conditions are partial and also political.

Histories written in service to the state or as a form of international relations flatten the complexities of actual people and the often complicated lives they live. For example, the experiences of an individual such as Khampa Tibetan communist Baba Phuntsok Wangyal cannot be reduced to his relationship to socialism or Buddhism or with Mao or the Dalai Lama.[42] Some beliefs are held constant across a lifetime, and others necessarily change over time. Acknowledging the range of subject positions of an individual such as Wangchuk Tempa—monk, bandit, strongman, resistance fighter, Communist

Party member, and Tibetan trying to navigate a Chinese political world—enables a fuller portrait of life in the borderlands, including the sometimes oppositional array of life choices available to individuals.[43] In the twentieth century alone, numerous Khampa Tibetans participated in national political projects from locations both inside and outside of Kham. Some families and individuals gained power through religious rank and accomplishment, others through trade success, and still others through education and literacy (in both Chinese and/or Lhasa Tibetan), which enabled access to and affiliation with new ideological worlds of democracy, nationalism, and/or socialism.

Writing a history of Kham as a borderlands is to posit multiple centers elsewhere. These centers—be they Tibetan, Chinese, Indian, or otherwise—tell different stories of their margins. Some are familiar. The Tibetan state considered its borderlands as places to be both defended and civilized.[44] This language is echoed in Chinese colonial language found in contemporary education and development projects, as well as in both European and Asian Christian missionary discourses in Tibet from the nineteenth century through to the present day.[45] Sources for imperial histories of Kham exist in multiple languages and archives with varying degrees of access throughout the world. Sources for Kham-centered histories exist wherever Khampas are in the world. They are orally narrated, written, and published by Khampa individuals and communities inside Tibet and also in exile. From hagiographies and local histories to diaries and political testimonies and more, available sources are not always accessible inside Tibet.[46] Many documents were destroyed during the 1950s and 1960s. Access to Tibetan archives is controlled by the Chinese government, as is permission for field research. Access to nonarchival sources is limited by fear of imprisonment and abuse for the researcher, the individual speaking and writing, or both. This is a reality of research in a settler colonial region.

Scholarly studies of Kham fall under both Tibetan and Chinese studies. As such, they may have different orientations, research questions, and understandings of Kham in relation to both Tibet and China rather than to only one of the two polities.[47] Over the centuries, Kham's relations with Tibet and China were not commensurate. Kham was not a part of China. It was a part of Tibet. This is a cultural, religious, and historical claim. Prior to the twentieth-century rise of the nation-state around the world, most peoples expressed and recognized identities in locally meaningful ways. People in Kham and throughout Tibet—all regions, not just the Chinese-designated Tibetan Autonomous Region—considered themselves connected to each other through religion and other cultural markers. They were *nang pa* (insiders), meaning practitioners of Tibetan Buddhism. This term exceeded politics, as did another one still in use today: tsampa eaters, people who eat roasted barley flour. As historian Tsering Shakya explains, "If Buddhism provided the atom of Tibetanness, then tsampa provided the sub-particles of Tibetanness. The use of tsampa transcended dialect, sect, gender, and regionalism."[48] Kham is home to tsampa eaters. Yet, as scholar Katia Buffetrille asks about Kham, what happens to the periphery when the center is gone?[49] For if all Tibetans were tsampa eaters, the heart of the Tibetan world in recent times was Lhasa and the Dalai Lama. One answer to her question is that in the periphery, people have created new practices to recenter what has been lost.

Bodies and Borders: A Conclusion

Tibetan brothers and sisters unite. Independence for Tibet. Long life to the Dalai Lama. Dalai Lama return to Tibet. Each of these statements is one made by a Tibetan self-immolator and repeated again and again by others who have self-immolated. As of March 2024, 169 Tibetans have self-immolated. One person self-immolated in China, three in Nepal, and seven people have self-immolated in India; the rest have done so inside Tibet.[50] One hundred and sixty-nine individuals have chosen to end their lives by pouring petrol over their bodies or into their bodies and lighting a match. They have done so consistently as a form of protest against Chinese rule in Tibet. We know this because of the oral and written testimonies they prepared before the act, as well as by the things they have said while they are burning. Of the 158 Tibetans who have self-immolated in Tibet since February 2009, the great majority have done so in "the Sino-Tibetan borderlands." Ninety-six percent of the total self-immolations inside Tibet have been in eastern and northeastern Tibet, in the historic regions of Amdo and Kham, and the current Chinese provinces of Gansu, Qinghai, and Sichuan. Among this group, the majority of the self-immolators are doing so at the borders of Kham and Amdo, near Kirti Monastery in Ngaba, Sichuan. Twenty-five percent of all self-immolations inside Tibet took place in Ngaba. At this Tibetan border, at a monastery where monks come from different areas of Tibet, a new practice of resistance and offering is centered.

Self-immolation is a twentieth-century form of political protest. It does not have a history in Tibet until now.[51] It is now a method—a drastic, bold method—used by Tibetans to speak in a new way to a situation they find untenable. To self-immolate is to kill oneself, but Tibetans widely consider these deaths to be sacrifices rather than suicides. New terminology had to be invented for the act of self-immolation. It is referred to as self-burning in fire (*rang lus me bsregs*), self-offering (*rang lus mchod 'bul*), self-offering in fire (*rang lus me mchod*), or self-giving and burning (*rang lus sbying bsregs*). Acts of self-immolation are framed as religious offerings in the historical sense of fire offerings, of the flame that is always lit on family and monastic altars. They are pleas to the Tibetan community to remain united to defend country and religion, and use the same language to make these pleas that resistance fighters used in the 1950s. And they are protests against the ongoing oppression and violence of Chinese colonialism.

Chinese governmental reactions are predictable. They blame self-immolations on the Dalai Lama and the exile community. They claim that the self-immolators are disturbed individuals. They deny they happened at all. They arrest self-immolators (those who did not die during their attempt) and sometimes also arrest their families. They create policies against self-immolation and launch anti-immolation programs. According to a 2013 report in the *Gansu Daily*, the messages of anti-immolation reeducation campaigns are that "Tibet is an inalienable part of China" and that Tibetan citizens must "uphold the leadership of the Communist Party of China and protect social stability and economic development."[52] At the same time, other forms of protest continue. Detentions continue for all sorts of activism, including linguistic activism, environmental activism, displaying the Tibetan flag or possessing a photo of the Dalai Lama, circulating certain songs or writing them, or offering condolences to the family of a self-immolator. However, amidst the imperial logics of surveillance and detention, life continues in Kham and throughout Tibet, including at its borders. Sometimes, too, when the Chinese government permits, research also takes place.

Academic questions of empire and borderlands are lived by actual peoples. They are not abstractions. Borders and borderlands are thought to be places of possibility, where mixture is possible but where centers and claims to purity are also most strongly defended or illuminated at times. Historically, political practices and possibilities in Kham were not the same as in central Tibet, just as political practices and possibilities in Tibet were not the same as those of China. Today, these Khampa and Tibetan practices and possibilities continue to pose challenges. They challenge specific ideas of nation and empire; they challenge specific structures of power and the people who implement them. In contemporary Tibet, these challenges unfold in a "settler-colonial present," a "deeply unequal scene of articulation" in which people must both live their lives and structure their resistance while also insisting on and acting from another possible understanding of the political.[53] In other words, there is a constant tension between consent and refusal. In Tibet, current Chinese rule is imperial. Self-immolation is one response to imperial rule. It is a refusal to live life in a certain way, a commitment to Tibetan ideas of life plural, and a reminder to all of the impermanence of things, including, eventually, empire.

Notes

1. Glen Coulthard, *Red Skin White Masks: Rejecting the Colonial Politics of Recognition* (Minneapolis: University of Minnesota Press, 2014), 6–7.

2. Audra Simpson, *Mohawk Interruptus: Political Life Across the Borders of Settler States* (Durham, NC: Duke University Press), 2014.

3. Ann Laura Stoler, "On Degrees of Imperial Sovereignty," *Public Culture* 18, no. 1 (2006): 125–146; Ann Laura Stoler and Carole McGranahan, "Introduction: Refiguring Imperial Terrain," in *Imperial Formations*, ed. Ann Laura Stoler, Carole McGranahan, and Peter Perdue (Santa Fe, NM: SAR Press, 2007), 3–42.

4. Carole McGranahan, "Empire Out-of-Bounds: Tibet in the Era of Decolonization," in Stoler, McGranahan, and Perdue, *Imperial Formations*, 173–209.

5. Patrick Wolfe, *Settler Colonialism and the Transformation of Anthropology* (London: Cassell, 1999).

6. Christopher Beckwith, *The Tibetan Empire in Central Asia* (Princeton, NJ: Princeton University Press, 1993).

7. Stéphane Gros, "Frontier (of) Experience: Introduction and Prolegomenon," in *Frontier Tibet: Patterns of Change in the Sino-Tibetan Borderlands* (Amsterdam: Amsterdam University Press, 2019), 41–83.

8. William Coleman IV, " The Uprising at Batang: Khams and Its Significance in Chinese and Tibetan History," in *Khams Pa Histories: Visions of People, Place and Authority*, ed. Lawrence Epstein (Leiden: Brill, 2002), 31–56; Fabienne Jagou, "Liu Manqing: A Sino-Tibetan Adventurer and the Origin of a New Sino-Tibetan Dialogue in the 1930s," *Revue d'Etudes Tibétaines*, no. 17 (2009): 5–20; Hsiao-ting Lin, *Tibet and Nationalist China's Frontier: Intrigues and Ethnopolitics, 1928–1949* (Vancouver: University of British Columbia Press, 2006); Scott Relyea, "Yokes of Gold and Threads of Silk: Sino-Tibetan Competition for Authority in Early Twentieth Century Kham," *Modern Asian Studies* 49, no. 4 (2015): 963–1009; Elliot Sperling, "The Chinese Venture in K'am, 1904–1911, and the Role of Chao Erh-feng," *Tibet Journal* 1, no. 2 (1976): 10–36; Yudru Tsomu, "Taming the Khampas: The Republican Construction of Eastern Tibet," *Modern China* 39, no. 3 (2013): 319–344; Gray Tuttle, *Tibetan Buddhists in the Making of Modern China* (New York: Columbia University Press, 2005); and Xiuyu Wang, *China's Last Imperial Frontier: Late Qing Expansion in Sichuan's Tibetan Borderlands* (Lanham, MD: Lexington Books, 2011).

9. Carole McGranahan, "From Simla to Rongbatsa: The British and the 'Modern' Boundaries of Tibet," *Tibet Journal* 28, no. 4 (2003): 39–60; and "Empire and the Status of Tibet: British, Chinese, and Tibetan Negotiations, 1913–1934," in *The History of Tibet*, Vol. 3, ed. Alex McKay (Richmond, VA: Curzon Press, 2003), 267–295.

10. Simpson, *Mohawk Interruptus*.

11. Darren Byler, "Native Rhythms in the City: Embodied Refusal Among Uyghur Male Migrants in Urumchi," *Central Asian Survey* 37, no. 2 (2018): 191–207; and Ben Hillman and Gray Tuttle, *Ethnic Conflict and Protest in Tibet and Xinjiang: Unrest in China's West* (New York: Columbia University Press, 2016).

12. Lorenzo Veracini, "Settler Colonialism: Career of a Concept," *Journal of Imperial and Commonwealth History* 41, no. 2 (2013): 313–333.

13. Wolfe, *Settler Colonialism*.

14. See, for example, Dibyesh Anand, "Colonization with Chinese Characteristics: Politics of (in)Security in Xinjiang and Tibet," *Central Asian Survey* 38, no. 1 (2019): 129–147; Dawa Norbu, "An Analysis of Sino-Tibetan Relationships, 1245–1911," in *Soundings in Tibetan Civilization*, ed. Barbara Aziz and Matthew Kapstein (Delhi: Manohar, 1985), 176–195.

15. See, for example, Kevin Carrico, "A Colony By Any Other Name: The Cultural Politics of Development in Tibet," *Critical Asian Studies* 50, no. 4 (2018): 639–647; Peter Hansen, "Why Is There No Subaltern Studies for Tibet?" *Tibet Journal* 28, no. 4 (2003): 7–22; Dawa Lokyitsang, "Are Tibetans Indigenous?" *Lhakar Diaries*, December 27, 2017; McGranahan, "Empire Out-of-Bounds"; Emily Yeh, *Taming Tibet: Landscape Transformation and the Gift of Chinese Development* (Ithaca, NY: Cornell University Press, 2013).

16. Sharad Chari and Katherine Verdery, "Thinking Between the Posts: Postcolonialism, Postsocialism, and Ethnography After the Cold War," *Comparative Studies in Society and History* 51, no. 1 (2008): 6–34; Stoler and McGranahan, "Introduction."

17. See, for example, Pamela Crossley, *A Translucent Mirror: History and Identity in Qing Imperial Ideology* (Berkeley: University of California Press, 1999); Laura Hostetler, *Qing Colonial Enterprise: Ethnography and Cartography in Early Modern China* (Chicago: University of Chicago Press, 2005); Peter C. Perdue, *China Marches West: The Qing Conquest of Central Eurasia* (Cambridge, MA: Harvard University Press, 2009).

18. Charlene Makley, "Anthropology and the Anaconda: China Post-2009," *Anthropology News*, April, 2009; James Milward, "Being Blacklisted by China and What Can Be Learned from It," China Beat Blog Archive 2008–2012, August 24, 2011, https://digitalcommons.unl.edu/chinabeatarchive/683/.

19. Emily Yeh, "Tibet and the Problem of Radical Reductionism," *Antipode* 41, no. 5 (2009): 983–1010.

20. Stoler, McGranahan, and Purdue, *Imperial Formations*.

21. Shu-mei Shih, "The Concept of the Sinophone," *PMLA* 126, no. 3 (2011): 709.

22. Shih, "The Concept of the Sinophone"; Shu-mei Shih, "Foreword: The Sinophone as History and the Sinophone as Theory," *Journal of Chinese Cinemas* 6, no. 2 (2012): 5–7; Shu-mei Shih, Chien-hsin Tsai, and Brian Bernards, *Sinophone Studies: A Critical Reader* (New York: Columbia University Press, 2013).

23. Shih "Foreword," 5.

24. McGranahan, "Empire Out-of-Bounds"; Carole McGranahan, "Love and Empire: The CIA, Tibet, and Covert Humanitarianism," in *Ethnographies of US Empire*, ed. Carole McGranahan and John F. Collins (Durham, NC: Duke University Press), 333–349.

25. Carrico, "A Colony By Any Other Name."

26. Stevan Harrell, *Cultural Encounters on China's Ethnic Frontiers* (Seattle: University of Washington Press, 1995).

27. Miaoyan Yang, "Moralities and Contradictories in the Educational Aid for Tibet: Contesting the Multi-Layered Savior Complex," *Journal of Multilingual and Multicultural Development* 41, no. 7 (2019): 620–632.

28. Yang, "Moralities and Contradictories," 5; see also Kevin Carrico, *The Great Han: Race, Nationalism, and Tradition in China Today* (Berkeley: University of California Press, 2017).

29. Yang, "Moralities and Contradictories."

30. Michael Hechter, *Internal Colonialism: The Celtic Fringe in British National Development, 1536–1966* (London: Routledge and Kegan Paul, 1975).

31. Dru Gladney, "Internal Colonialism and the Uyghur Nationality: Chinese Nationalism and Its Subaltern Subjects," *Cahiers d'Etudes sur la Méditerranée Orientale et le monde Turco-Iranien* 25 (1998): 47–63; and Timothy Oakes, "Tourism in Guizhou: The Legacy of Internal Colonialism," in *Tourism in China*, ed. Alan Lew and Lawrence Yu (Boulder, CO: Westview Press, 1995), 203–222.

32. Magnus Fiskesjö, "The Legacy of the Chinese Empires: Beyond 'the West and the Rest,'" *Education About Asia* 22, no. 1 (2017): 7.

33. Fiskesjö, "The Legacy of the Chinese Empires," 7.

34. Fabienne Jagou and Matthew Kapstein, "The Thirteenth Dalai Lama's Visit to Beijing in 1908: In Search of a New Kind of Chaplain-Donor Relationship," in *Buddhism Between Tibet and China*, ed. Matthew Kapstein (Boston: Wisdom Publications, 2009), 349–378; Peter Schwieger, *The Dalai Lama and the Emperor of China: A Political History of the Tibetan Institution of Reincarnation* (New York: Columbia University Press, 2015).

35. David Germano, "Re-Membering the Dismembered Body of Tibet: Contemporary Tibetan Visionary Movements in the People's Republic of China," in *Buddhism in Contemporary Tibet*, ed. Melvyn Goldstein and Matthew Kapstein (Berkeley: University of California Press, 1998), 53–94; Andrew Grant, "'Don't Discriminate Against Minority Nationalities': Practicing Tibetan Ethnicity on Social Media," *Asian Ethnicity* 18, no. 3 (2017): 371–386; Tenzin Jinba, *In the Land of the Eastern Queendom: The Politics of Gender and Ethnicity on the Sino-Tibetan Border* (Seattle: University of Washington Press, 2013); and Charlene Makley, *The Violence of Liberation: Gender and Tibetan Buddhist Revival in Post-Mao China* (Berkeley: University of California Press, 2007).

36. Holly Gayley, "T-Pop and the Lama: Buddhist 'Rites Out of Place" in Tibetan Monastery Produced VCDs," in *Religion and Modernity in the Himalaya*, ed. Megan Sijapati and Jessica Birkenholtz (London: Routledge, 2016), 63–82; Lama Jabb, *Oral and Literary Continuities in Modern Tibetan Literature: The Inescapable Nation* (Lanham, MD: Lexington Books, 2015); Lama Jabb, "The Mingled Melody: Remembering the Tibetan March 10th Uprising," *Revue d'Etudes Tibétaines* 48 (2019): 50–98; and Cameron Warner, "Hope and Sorrow: Uncivil Religion, Tibetan Music Videos, and YouTube," *Ethnos* 78, no. 4 (2013): 543–568.

37. Tsering Bum, "Translocating Ecological Migration Policy: A Conjunctural Analysis of Tibetan Pastoral Resettlement in China," *Critical Asian Studies* 58, no. 4 (2018): 518–536; Huatse Gyal, "'I am Concerned with the Future of My Children': The Project Economy and Shifting Views of Education in a Tibetan Pastoralist Community," *Critical Asian Studies* 51, no. 1 (2019): 12–30; Emilia Sulek, *Trading Caterpillar Fungus in Tibet: When Economic Boom Hits Rural Areas* (Amsterdam: Amsterdam University Press, 2019); and Duojie Zhaxi, "Housing Subsidy Projects in Amdo: Modernity, Governmentality, and Income Inequality in Tibetan Areas of China," *Critical Asian Studies* 51, no. 1 (2019): 31–50.

38. Jabb, "The Mingled Melody," 51.

39. Yasmin Cho, "Yachen as Process: Encampments, Nuns, and Spatial Politics in Post-Mao Kham," in Gros, *Frontier Tibet*, 489–515.

40. Carole McGranahan, *Arrested Histories: Tibet, the CIA, and Memories of a Forgotten War* (Durham, NC: Duke University Press, 2010).

41. Maria Turek, "Return of the Good King: Kingship and Identity Among Yushu Tibetans Since 1951," in Gros, *Frontier Tibet*, 453–488.

42. Melvyn Goldstein, Dawei Sherap, and William Siebenschuh, *A Tibetan Revolutionary: The Political Life and Times of Bapa Phüntso Wangye* (Berkeley: University of California Press, 2004); Heather Stoddard, "Tibet from Buddhism to Communism," *Government and Opposition* 21, no. 1 (1986): 76–95; T. N. Takla, "Notes on Some Early Tibetan Communists," *Tibetan Review* 2, no. 17 (1969): 7–10; Baba Phuntsok Wangyal, *Witness to Tibet's History*, trans. Tenzin Losel, Jane Perkins, Bhuchung D. Sonam, and Tenzin Tsundue (New Delhi: Paljor Publications, 2007).

43. Dáša Pejchar Mortensen, "Harnessing the Power of the Khampa Elites: Political Persuasion and the Consolidation of Communist Party Rule in Gyelthang," in Gros, *Frontier Tibet*, 411–452.

44. Katia Buffetrille, "The Increasing Visibility of the Tibetan 'Borderlands,'" in Gros, *Frontier Tibet*, 85–114.

45. John Bray, "Language, Tradition, and the Tibetan Bible," *Tibet Journal* 16, no. 4 (1991): 28–58; and Brendan Galipeau, "A Tibetan Catholic Christmas in China: Ethnic Identity and Encounters with Ritual and Revitalization," *Asian Ethnology* 77, nos. 1 and 2 (2018): 353–370.

46. See, for example, Lauran Hartley, "The Kingdom of Derge," in *The Tibetan History Reader*, ed. Gray Tuttle and Kurtis Schaeffer (New York: Columbia University Press, 2013), 525–548; Carole McGranahan, "Imperial but Not Colonial: British India, Archival Truths, and the Case of the 'Naughty' Tibetans," *Comparative Studies in Society and History* 59, no. 1 (2017): 68–95; Jamyang Norbu, *Warriors of Tibet: The Story of Aten, and the Khampas' Fight for the Freedom of Their Country* (London: Wisdom Publications, 1986); Tsewang Yishey Pemba, *White Crane, Lend Me Your Wings* (Delhi: Niyogi Books, 2017); and Rinzin Thargyal, *Nomads of Eastern Tibet: Social Organization and Economy of a Pastoral Estate in the Kingdom of Derge* (Leiden: Brill, 2007).

47. Epstein, *Khams Pa Histories*; Gros, *Frontier Tibet*; Wimm Van Spengen and Lama Jabb, *Studies in the History of Eastern Tibet* (Andiast, Switzerland: International Institute for Tibetan and Buddhist Studies, 2009).

48. Tsering Shakya, "Whither the Tsampa Eaters?" *Himal*, September 1, 1993.

49. Buffetrille, "The Increasing Visibility of the Tibetan 'Borderlands.'"

50. "Self-Immolation Fact Sheet," International Campaign for Tibet website, April 6, 2022, https://savetibet.org/tibetan-self-immolations/.

51. Katia Buffetrille and Françoise Robin, "Tibet is Burning. Self-Immolation: Ritual or Political Protest?" special issue of *Revuew d'Etudes Tibétaines* 25 (2012); Tenzin Dorjee, "Foreign Policy and Religion: Tibetan Independence Movement," Oxford Research Encylopedia—Politics, June 26, 2019, https://doi.org/10.1093/acrefore/9780190228637.013.837; Carole McGranahan and Ralph Litzinger, "Self-Immolation in Tibet," special issue of *Cultural Anthropology*, April 8, 2012; Tsering Woeser, *Tibet on Fire: Self-Immolations Against Chinese Rule* (London: Verso, 2016).

52. Tibetan Center for Human Rights and Democracy, "China Uses Religious Propaganda to Counter Tibetan Self-Immolations," *Gansu Daily*, March 20, 2013.

53. Audra Simpson, "Consent's Revenge," *Cultural Anthropology* 31, no. 3 (2016): 326–333.

Beyond Musical, Political, and Linguistic Boundaries

The Influence of the Hong Kong Rock Band Beyond in the PRC in the 1990s and Its Legacy

NATHANEL AMAR

I'll never die
I'll never cry
You'll see
Beyond, "Ngo si fan nou" 我是憤怒

On August 23, 2003, the Hong Kong rock and roll band Beyond played a concert for their twentieth anniversary at Beijing's Workers' Stadium. Only two months after the end of the SARS outbreak in the People's Republic of China (PRC) and Hong Kong, Beyond played one of the first public concerts in Beijing in front of a full house, ten years after the death of their lead singer, Wong Ka-kui 黃家駒. Many PRC newspapers covered the event, citing Beyond as one of the most influential rock bands of the Sinosphere, comparing them to other major rock-and-roll figures of the PRC and Taiwan. *Yunling gesheng* (雲嶺歌聲 China Yunnan music) stated, "Just as Cui Jian 崔健 represents Beijing rock (*yaogun* 搖滾), Lo Ta-yu 羅大佑 created Taiwanese folk music, Beyond brought the dispirited Hong Kong pop music to an era of original innovation.... Someone once said: Hong Kong has no rock and roll, it only has Beyond."[1] An analysis shared by *Xinwen zhoukan* (新聞周刊 China newsweek) said, "Today, Beyond has become one of the three symbols, alongside Cui Jian and Luo Ta-Yu, of Sinophone [Huayu 華

語] pop music."² The *China Daily* (*Zhongguo ribao* 中國日報) stated that, "Beyond, to the Hong Kong music scene, is similar to Cui Jian for China's rock scene or Lo Ta-yu for Taiwan's pop music."³ In 2002, *The World of Music* (*Yinyue tiandi* 音樂天地) had already declared, "Beijing has Cui Jian, so the Chinese don't have to feel ashamed when facing international rock and roll. Taiwan has Lo Ta-yu, so people of the island understand what music is. And in Hong Kong, there is Beyond. . . . This city is worthy of rock and roll because of Beyond."⁴

Besides their prejudices about the state of the Hong Kong music scene, these articles were all trying to integrate Beyond into a larger Sinophone rock and roll community composed of Beijing, Taiwan, and Hong Kong. Despite their linguistic differences, they supposedly all share an authentic rock and roll spirit, as opposed to commercial pop music, coming mainly from Hong Kong and Taiwan. It also shows the despise of these rock and roll critics for Hong Kong pop music sung in Cantonese (Cantopop), a conflict that burst open in 1994 when the Beijing rocker He Yong 何勇 insulted Cantopop and the so-called Four Heavenly Kings during a performance at the Hong Kong Coliseum.⁵ As these articles show, Beyond had an important role in the construction of a Sinophone music world, which is all too often overlooked in the literature. Scholars in Hong Kong mainly focus on the so-called disappearance of Hong Kong Cantopop since 1997, while scholars and music critics analyzing PRC music in general and rock and roll in particular too often minimize the influence of Hong Kong Cantopop or Taiwan Mandopop. As Geremie Barmé puts it, "Mainland critics have generally been blinded by their own linguistic bias, chauvinistic prejudice or lack of resources to appreciate the transformative significance of these formerly peripheral worlds."⁶ Moreover, the concept of Sinophone has rarely been used to understand the circulation of music in the Chinese-speaking world. The example of the influence of the Hong Kong rock band Beyond might help us understand how songs, popular practices, and representations circulate across the border between Hong Kong and the PRC. Through testimonies, scholarly works, archives, and interviews with PRC musicians and citizens who grew up in the 1990s, I want to show how Beyond was understood and appropriated by young people in the PRC— even though they didn't understand Cantonese—and how the language they used to sing these Cantonese songs allowed them to create new identities.

In Search of Sinophone Music

Since it was first coined by Shu-mei Shih in 2007 and further developed in a reader published in 2013,⁷ the concept of the Sinophone has been appropriated and used by scholars covering a range of subjects from literature to cinema to queer culture, but music scholars have so far avoided using the concept. Bringing music back into Sinophone studies may help us understand the global circulation of music but, more importantly, how music consumption can shape various forms of identitiy, sometimes opposed to the ones promoted by local political authorities. Nonetheless, several scholars have offered fruitful analyses on the circulation of music between Hong Kong, the PRC, and Taiwan. Yiu Fai Chow and Jeroen de Kloet's work on global consumption of Hong Kong pop music and Marc L. Moskowitz's analysis of the "counter invasion of the PRC" by Taiwanese Mandopop (pop music sung in Mandarin), have led the foundation of a global study of Sinophone music beyond political and geographical boundaries.[8] Maybe the avoidance of this concept can be linked to a recurring critique addressed to Sinophone studies: the apparent exclusion of China—or, more precisely, the territory governed by the Communist Party of China—and the so-called Han majority who live there. Several authors, such as Alvin Wong, have tried to include China in their understandings of Sinophone studies, not to put the PRC back at the center but, on the contrary, to "decenter the hegemonic aspects of Chineseness."[9] As Shu-mei Shih argues, Sinophone studies allows us to "recogniz[e] a different mode of colonialism for China, of what may be called 'continental colonialism.'"[10] Thus, including China into Sinophone studies allows us to decenter not only China and Chineseness but also to deconstruct the myth of a unified Han majority. Following the footsteps of Dru Gladney,[11] a study of Sinophone music that includes the circulation of music inside and outside of the PRC might help us dislocate China and Hanness and uncover the multiplicity of power relations behind music creation and consumption. This present study of the influence of Beyond in the PRC aims to show how music and language contribute to the creation of new identities and modes of cultural consumption that challenge the dominant Han-centric approach to music in the PRC.

The Invention of Chinese and Hong Kong Rock and Roll

Despite the immense popularity of Beyond in the PRC, the history of Chinese rock did not begin with the Hong Kong band. Chinese rock has a rich and complex history, which started after Mao's death in 1976 and at the beginning of the economic reforms initiated by Deng Xiaoping. In 1979, four students of the Beijing Institute of Foreign Languages formed the first rock band, named Wan Li Ma Wang 萬里馬王, which covered songs by the Beatles and the Bee Gees.[12] The birth of Chinese rock for the general public is, however, said to have taken place on May 1986, when Cui Jian sang the song "Yiwu suoyou" (一無所有 Nothing to my name) for the first time on national television during a charity concert held at the Beijing's Worker Stadium. Cui Jian's song became immensely popular, and three years later, it was the unofficial anthem of the 1989 student democratic movement. Cui Jian himself, like many other Chinese and Taiwanese rockers, performed for the students in May 1989 at Tiananmen. The implication of Chinese rock in the student movement resulted in a crackdown on rock and roll after the June 4 massacre. Cui Jian was forbidden from organizing official concerts in Beijing until 2007—even though he could perform during parties and in provincial cities, as during his 1990 tour for the Asia Games, planned before the Tiananmen crackdown, for instance.[13]

The Hong Kong rock band Beyond was formed in 1983 by lead vocalist Wong Ka-kui and drummer Yip Sai-wing 葉世榮. In 1984, they were joined by Wong Ka-kui's brother, the bassist Wong Ka-keung 黃家強. In 1985, the guitarist Paul Wong 黃貫中 joined the band. Beyond started out as an experimental rock band and produced their first album in 1986, *Goodbye Ideal* (*Zoi gin lei soeng* 再見理想). Their first commercial success came in 1987 with their second album, *Arabian Dancing Girls* (*Aa laai baak tiu mou neoi long* 阿拉伯跳舞女郎). Beyond was not popular among Chinese youth of the 1980s compared to Cui Jian, Lo Ta-yu, or Hou Dejian 侯德健, a Taiwanese folk-rock singer famous for his song "Long de chuanren" (龍的傳人 Descendants of the Dragon) who moved to Beijing in the mid-1980s. Beyond's first concert in Beijing in 1988 was a commercial failure (fig. 15.1) due to Beijingers' lack of interest in rock songs in Cantonese, a stark contrast to their second coming in Beijing at the Worker's Stadium in 2003 in front of a full house. Gene Lau, the lyricist of Beyond, remembers their 1988 tour in Beijing: "In October, Beyond arrived at the Beijing Capital Indoor Stadium for two concerts. At that time in Beijing, nobody knew who Beyond was, which is completely different from today. In the 1980s in China, rock and roll had just appeared, maybe it's the organizer who thought that organizing a rock concert was feasible, that just with the word 'Hong Kong' people would buy tickets. . . . Halfway through the concert, half of the audience had already left."[14] During the Beijing performance, Beyond chose to sing three songs in Mandarin: a new version of their hit song "Grand Earth" (*Daai dei* 大地) translated by Gene Lau, the old Shaanxi folk song turned into a Maoist anthem, "The East is Red" (*Dongfang hong* 東方紅), and Cui Jian's song "Nothing to My Name." Three songs which seem to embody a Sinophone bridge between Hong Kong and the PRC: a rock song in Cantonese translated into Mandarin, a Maoist cultural legacy, and the anthem of the emerging rebellious Beijing rock scene. According to Gene Lau, Cui Jian came to see Beyond before their

Figure 15.1 Poster of the Beyond concerts in Beijing, October 15–16, 1988. Beyond 35th Anniversary.
Source: Hong Kong: Medesign Communication, 2018, 49.

concert, but due to linguistic differences, they couldn't communicate. Cui Jian had to leave before the start of Beyond's concert because he had to perform at the Great Wall that day.[15] A missed opportunity that could have been a pivotal moment for Sinophone rock and roll that epitomized the lack of (linguistic) understanding between Beijing and Hong Kong rockers at that time.

The student protests of 1989 had strong repercussions on Sinophone popular music in the PRC, Hong Kong, and Taiwan. On May 27, 1989, a Concert for Democracy in China was held at the Happy Valley Racecourse in Hong Kong to raise money for the students in Beijing. Famous musicians and artists from Hong Kong and Taiwan participated in the event, including Beyond, who sang "Great Earth" in Cantonese, with a verse in Mandarin (see fig. 15.2).[16] Hou Dejian, who would go back to Tiananmen Square shortly after the concert, came to sing "Descendants of the Dragon"—and changed the lyrics to reflect his experience of the Tiananmen movement[17]—while

Figure 15.2 Beyond singing "Great Earth" at the Concert for Democracy in China in Hong Kong, May 27, 1989.

the Taiwanese pop star Teresa Teng 鄧麗君 sang "Jia zai shan de nabian" (家在山的那邊 My Home Is on the Other Side of the Mountain).[18] After the Tiananmen crackdown, Beyond did a series of concerts in Hong Kong in December 1989 entitled The Real Testament (Zan dik gin zing 真的見證), where they once again covered Cui Jian's song "Nothing to My Name" with a thick Cantonese accent. On stage, Wong Ka-kui dedicated the song to the fallen protesters: "What happened this year, we as Chinese can never forget it. We dedicate this song to all the Chinese blood that was spilled, and the friends who spilled their blood for China."[19] The reference in Wong Ka-kui's speech to a collective pan-Chinese identity—which can also be seen through their choice of Mandarin songs during their 1988 concert in Beijing—is deeply rooted in the zeitgeist of the 1980s, when a reconciliation between Hong Kong and a democratizing China was seen as desirable. A hope shattered in 1989 echoed in Beyond's 1993 song, "Father and Mother" (*Baa baa maa maa* 爸爸媽媽), in which the rock band symbolically dismisses both their father (England) and mother (the PRC), two colonial powers fighting over Hong Kong.

After Deng Xiaoping's southern tour in 1992 and the pursuit of economic reforms, Hong Kong Cantopop and Taiwan Mandopop are said to have invaded the Chinese market because of their apparent nonpolitical aspect—a myth propagated by rock critics and music scholars for whom the authenticity of northern Chinese rock is supposedly superior to southern pop music. This ongoing conflict between Beijing rock and Hong Kong Cantopop, however, conceals popular practices of musical reappropriation, which allowed young people in the PRC, from the 1970s to the 1990s, to discover new musical genres through pirated tapes of Cantopop and Mandopop songs.

"Go With Your Feeling": The Periphery at the Center

In an article published in 1993, Thomas B. Gold relates a joke that circulated in the PRC after the Tiananmen crackdown: "The people go with the Communist Party; the Communist Party goes with the Central Committee; the Central Committee goes with the Politburo; the Politburo goes with the Standing Committee; the Standing Committee goes with Deng Xiaoping; Deng Xiaoping goes with his feelings." "Go with your feeling" (*Genzhe ganjue zou* 跟著感覺走) is a reference to a popular Taiwanese song performed by Julie Sue 蘇芮, revealing "the pervasiveness of popular culture from 'peripheral China' on the mainland core." Since 1978 and the Third Plenum of the 11th Central Committee's decision to reform the economy, smuggled pirated tapes of famous Taiwanese and Hong Kong pop stars invaded the PRC—in the late 1970s, it was said that "Old Deng [Xiaoping] rules by day, little Teng [Lijun] rules by night."[20] This trend did not stop after 1989. Popular singers from Taiwan and Hong Kong toured the PRC in the early 1990s, and pirated cassette tapes from Hong Kong and Taiwan were sold illegally on the streets. The popularity of Taiwan and Hong Kong pop music (also named Gangtai 港台 pop, a contraction of Xiang*gang* and *Tai*wan) in the PRC resides, according to Thomas B. Gold, in its novelty, content, accessibility, foreign character, and escapist aspect. Gangtai pop was, at the same time, foreign and sung in a Sinitic language, modern and accessible, while the lyrics tackled issues such as love and individual feelings, something rarely mentioned during the Maoist era.

With the tight control of Beijing rock and roll by the Communist authorities after 1989, it was difficult for young Chinese people, especially outside of Beijing, to listen to the famous rockers of the 1980s, such as Cui Jian or He Yong. When I was conducting interviews with Chinese punk rockers who grew up in the 1980s and the 1990s, I was expecting them to tell me that Cui Jian was a key reference in their musical education. I was also expecting them to link their experience of foreign music to the apparition of *dakou* 打口—unsold Western CDs and tapes sent by cargo to be recycled but sold on the black market instead.²¹ To my surprise, most of the rockers I interviewed told me that Beyond was the first rock band they listened to in their youth. Cui Jian is barely mentioned, especially by rockers who grew up outside of Beijing. One anecdote about Cui Jian is particularly relevant. It was told by Wu Wei, the singer of the Wuhan punk band SMZB (Shengming zhi bing 生命之餅):

> In the early 1990s, we didn't have any *dakou* in Wuhan; we could only find pirated tapes from Hong Kong and Taiwan. The first rock band I discovered was Beyond, it was very popular. We were all listening to Beyond when we decided to form a band. I've had never heard of Cui Jian at that time. In 1995, I was in Beijing, we were performing in a bar with our band. A friend told me that Cui Jian was attending the show, that he was a very famous rocker, and I should talk to him. I went to Cui Jian and I told him that I was in a band and gave him our demo tape. My friend was surprised that I didn't know Cui Jian, he gave me his tape, and I listened to it at night. The day after, I met Cui Jian again, he told me that he liked my demo. I confessed to him that I never listened to his songs before. Now that I had the chance to listen to his tape, I really liked it. He looked at me, didn't say a word, and left. (Personal interview with Wu Wei, Changsha, December 22, 2012)

Even for underground rockers, Hong Kong Cantopop was an important part of their musical education, far from the stereotypes of Cantopop as being a depoliticized tool used by the Chinese government. Xu Bi, a punk drummer from Changsha, remembers his relation to Hong Kong Cantopop:

> When I was a kid, my parents only listened to Hong Kong Cantopop, that was the only music available before the apparition of *dakou* CDs. I knew I wanted to become a rock star the first time I listened to a *dakou* CD of Nine Inch Nails. But I still cry when I listen to Leslie Cheung's songs, it reminds me of my childhood. (Personal interview with Xu Bi, Wuhan, March 5, 2018)

The rock critic Yang Bo also puts forward Beyond as one of the most influential rock bands of the 1990s, alongside the experimental Cantopop duo Tat Ming Pair 达明一派 and Lo Ta-yu: "At first, we heard some Gangtai rock and roll, like Lo Ta-yu, Beyond, Tat Ming Pair. . . . Afterwards we heard Cui Jian, and through some other methods, we got some foreign rock tapes."²²

These testimonies from rock musicians or critics show the importance of Beyond and Hong Kong music for PRC alternative youth in the 1990s. As

Thomas B. Gold stated, Hong Kong (and Taiwan) were at the center of Chinese popular music from the late 1970s to the mid-1990s. If the periphery of the Sinophone world was in a central position, it was also used and appropriated by China's own cultural periphery, underground musical communities that shared the same musical references to construct their own unique sound in opposition to the hegemony of the *tongsu* music 通俗歌曲—popularized and official music.[23]

Singing Beyond in Cantonese: The Creation of a KTV *Hua*?

By 1997, Beyond was not only a reference for young and rebellious rockers, they were an overall success and were the most popular rock band among Beijing youth, according to one survey.[24] For Z., who grew up in a small town in a Chinese southwest province, Beyond represented the soundtrack of a new era. The last song recorded by Wong Ka-kui before his premature death in 1993, "Boundless Oceans, Vast Skies" (Hoi fut tin hung 海闊天空), on the album *Rock'n'Roll* (*Lok jyu nou* 樂與怒, literally "music and anger," a play on words with the Cantonese pronunciation and the English "rock and roll"), became Beyond's greatest success in the Sinophone world:

> Cui Jian's songs were depressing after 1989. There was no more hope in his lyrics. It didn't embody our spirit at the time. We wanted freedom. And we found it in Beyond's lyrics. "Boundless Oceans, Vast Skies," it's all about individual freedom and love, the hope for a better future. (Personal interview with Z., Beijing, August 9, 2016)

Z.'s statement about Beyond's lyrics is coherent with the findings and obsessions of Chinese scholars who are trying to understand the success in the PRC of a rock band singing in Cantonese. Wu Hai, for instance, argues that "Boundless Oceans, Vast Skies" is popular because it "tries to encourage the youth to constantly strive for a better life."[25] Other scholars analyzed the success of Beyond mainly through a study of the band's lyrics and the musical composition of the songs, but they rarely ask about Beyond's reception by the audience or the meanings individuals give to the songs they listen to. As in Yin Chao's work, these studies try to find the recipe for musical success to improve "the national cultural soft power."[26] However, like Z., many young Chinese were attracted to Beyond because of the expression of individual feelings and freedom in the lyrics, something quite far from the quest for a soft-power recipe highlighted in these studies. Beyond was also foreign— but geographically close—and not approved by the authorities at the time.

Listening to Beyond in the early 1990s or watching Hong Kong television was also a privilege, as Z. recalled:

> I grew up in a small village, but it was a special village. During the Cultural Revolution, the village was treated differently because of its paper industry. Mao's *Little Red Book* was printed here, it was a strategic place, so the workers had many privileges. For example, the local cadres could receive Hong Kong television, and by the end of the 1980s, even the workers could watch Hong Kong TV before everyone else in China. When I was a kid, when one of our parents was out for the evening, we gathered and watched Hong Kong erotic films at night. We were the first to listen to Hong Kong music and to see the music videos. Every time there was a new Beyond song, we watched it, and since we didn't understand Cantonese, we wrote the lyrics on a piece of paper, and went to the city to brag about it, and to show everyone else what the new song was about! (Personal interview with Z., Beijing, August 9, 2016)

Beyond songs, as the erotic movies produced in Hong Kong, were the symbols of modernity and economic reforms. The popularity of Beyond didn't have any provincial borders, everybody knew the lyrics by heart, even if it was in Cantonese, a language unintelligible for the majority:

> If you were from the south and you went to Shandong, for example, there was a lot of misunderstanding and not a lot of common references. The only thing that we had in common was Beyond. If I go to a KTV [karaoke] with a guy from Shandong, I know that I can sing "Boundless Oceans, Vast Skies" with him. Everywhere you go in China, you can find Beyond songs in KTV, and everybody can sing in Cantonese even if they don't speak it! (Personal interview with Z., Beijing, August 9, 2016)

Interviewed by the *China Daily* in 2003, Zhang Nan, a twenty-five-year-old Beyond fan, asserts: "Wong Ka-kui's voice is steady, rhythmical and emotional. Even in Cantonese, which I don't understand, his voice speaks straight to my heart."[27] People were affected by the sound as well as the lyrics, and Wong Ka-kui's voice was as important as the perceived message behind the songs. In the minds of young Chinese of the 1990s, Cantonese became the language of cultural modernity, and people were learning to sing in Cantonese without speaking the language, reproducing the sounds, and deciphering the characters on the music videos. A new language was thus created, a Cantonese sung by non-Cantonese speakers during KTV sessions—a KTV *hua* 話, a minority language that was not Cantonese nor Mandarin, subverting the domination of Mandarin from within, or as Deleuze would say, "a broken language" sung in a large variety of accents mimicking the Cantonese language, "shot with a spray gun of colors."[28] Beyond songs are also the shared KTV *hua* in various Chinese provinces where Mandarin is not the most common language. For instance, Y., from Yunnan, learned to sing Beyond songs during the 1990s: "Beyond was very popular, we could find their CDs on the streets in Kunming. We tried to learn the lyrics by heart, it was difficult, but each time we went to the KTV we would sing Beyond's songs!" (personal interview with Y., Hong Kong, September 24, 2018). It is interesting to note that Beyond is particularly popular outside of Beijing in places where standard Mandarin is not commonly used, such as in Wuhan, Yunnan, or Guangxi. Beyond is also very popular in Xinjiang among Uyghur musicians like the psychedelic rocker Jurat: "I remember in 1994 buying their first album, *Goodbye Ideal*. There was this song, called 'Myth,' I played it all night long while crying, the arrangements were very complicated and beautiful. I didn't know what they were singing, but the music made me feel sad. . . . I found out what kind of music I needed. I sang their songs in bars and clubs, when I went to a KTV I always sang their songs" (personal interview with Jurat, March 24, 2020). As Shu-mei Shih argues, Sinophone studies pays attention to "minority peoples who have acquired or are forced to acquire the standard Sinitic languages of Mandarin, often at the expense of their native language."[29] The example of Beyond and its reappropriation in the PRC through KTV forces us to deconstruct the apparent unicity of Han people by looking at the new language people created inside the four walls of a KTV as it highlights the linguistic and provincial divide of a theoretically unified country. It shouldn't be surprising to observe that Beyond was a KTV hit in the PRC in the 1990s. After all, as Anthony Fung notes, KTVs represent "an adventurous private space devised for expressing suppressed desires and emotions. It allows personal desires to be released without strongly defying social norms." In the safe space provided by KTVs, "sealed off from the social pressures and political forces of control in China," young (and middle-aged) Chinese can express their feelings and political aspirations, which many of them found in the lyrics of Beyond and the Cantonese language.[30]

The general consensus among experts in the field of Cantopop is that after 1997 and the Hong Kong handover to China, Mandopop from the PRC and Taiwan slowly replaced Cantopop in the Sinophone world, provoking an identity crisis among Cantopop stars who began to sing in Mandarin—following the actor and singer Andy Lau 劉德華 who in 1997 released the hit-song "Chinese" (Zhongguo ren 中國人) in Mandarin to celebrate the handover. Beyond, as well as other Cantonese pop and rock bands, is, however, still relevant for Chinese artists and music lovers today. Their influence can still be perceived twenty-five years after the handover, with the creation of a nostalgic discourse idealizing the golden era of Cantopop by a generation whose musical education was shaped by Gangtai pop. But more importantly, references to Beyond in music, discourses, or cultural creations vary from one place to another, from one temporal moment to another. As Shu-mei Shih argues, "The Sinophone spaces are scattered around the world and Sinophone culture is produced in different locations, but in each site the Sinophone is a place-based, local culture, in dialogue with other cultures of that location,"[31] an idea we can also find in Chow and de Kloet's work, who state that "place does matter at the moment of music consumption."[32] The legacy of Beyond changed over time and is not articulated in the same way everywhere.

Beyond After Beyond

Wuhan is known for its climate, hot-and-dry noodles, the vibrant punk-rock community, and the people's favorite sport, running naked through the streets (*luoben* 裸奔) before diving into the Yangzi River. In 2007, the music magazine *So Rock!* (*Wo ai yaogun yue* 我愛搖滾樂) published a photo of a young Wuhan boy jumping naked into the Yangzi, waving a red banner dedicated to Beyond as an homage to the Hong Kong rock band (fig. 15.3).

This obsession with Beyond is, of course, not limited to young people running naked in the streets of Wuhan. The reference to Beyond is still mobilized today for many artists in the PRC who grew up in the 1990s and began their musical education through pirated CDs and tapes of the Hong Kongese rock band. Actor and director Da Peng 大鵬, born in 1982 in Jilin, was notably fascinated with Beyond. The actor, known for his comic TV series *Diors Man* (*Diaosi nanshi* 屌絲男士), participated in 2015 on the variety show *Challenger's Alliance* (*Tiaozhan zhe lianmeng* 挑戰者聯盟). During the last episode, aired in December 2015, Da Peng's challenge was to perform his favorite song in front of the audience. He chose to sing Beyond's famous song "Boundless Oceans, Vast Skies" in Cantonese. Halfway through his performance, Da Peng was unexpectedly joined on stage by Beyond's drummer and singer, Yip Sai-wing, and by the guitarist Paul Wong. Unable to contain his emotion, Da Peng burst into tears and kneeled before the two Hong Kong rockers (fig. 15.4). After this moving performance, Da Peng tells the embarrassed duo that when he first moved to Beijing, he didn't have any money, but he still bought a ticket to their last show Beyond the Story Live 2005 at the Capital Indoor Stadium, singing and crying with all the other fans.[33] In 2017, Da Peng directed his second movie, *City of Rock* (*Fengrenji yuedui* 縫紉機樂隊), set in his hometown of Ji'an, about a failed rock band trying to

Figure 15.3 A Beyond fan from Wuhan jumping naked into the Yangzi River.
Source: *So Rock!* magazine, vol. 66 (2007): 70.

save the city's rock and roll spirit. Throughout the movie, major PRC rockers and bands make a guest appearance, such as the first all-female rock band Cobra (Yanjing she 眼鏡蛇), Xie Tian Xiao, 謝天笑 and Miserable Faith (Tongku de Xinyang 痛苦的信仰). But as the film ends, Da Peng chooses

Figure 15.4 Paul Wong, Da Peng, and Yip Sai-wing on the stage of *Challenger's Alliance*, 2015.

to conclude the movie with an all-cast performance of Beyond's song "No Hesitation" (Bat zoi jau jyu 不再猶豫) in Cantonese, with the guest appearance of Yip Sai-wing and Paul Wong. In a movie centered on the rock spirit of Northern China, Da Peng finds it necessary to pay the most important tribute to the Hong Kong rock band Beyond in Cantonese.

We can find similar discourses among Chinese musicians who promote vintage Hong Kong fashion and sounds in their newest cultural productions. In 2018, the Chengdu indie rock band Mosaic (Masaike 馬賽克) released an album inspired by the 1980s and the 1990s, using iconography close to Beyond's own covers for their last Chinese tour entitled Back to the Future (Huidao weilai 回到未來). The album *Pop Rave* (*Jingge rewu* 勁歌熱舞) displays their musical influences on the cover, each musician holding a vinyl album of their favorite band: Michael Jackson (*Bad*), the Japanese pop band Yellow Magic Orchestra (*Naughty Boys*), and Beyond with their 1993 album *Rock And Roll* (fig. 15.5). Mosaic's album is—like their previous works—sung in Mandarin and English, but surprisingly, the Sichuanese band produced one song in Cantonese, "Cin bui bat zeoi" 千杯不醉, written by Gene Lau, Beyond's lyricist, whom they met thanks to the manager of the "Little Bar," Chengdu's most famous live venue. The band recalls listening to Beyond's songs during their youth, and frequently covering Beyond's

Figure 15.5 Mosaic's last album, *Pop Rave*, Modern Sky, 2018.

294 PLACES OF DIFFERENTIATION

Cantonese songs with their previous group, GT6.³⁴ Cantonese is performed here as a vintage vision of modernity, the Back to the Future of Cantopop.

In a rather odd way, Beyond's influence can also be analyzed through the prism of collective action. There are several cases of collective mobilization by online groups of Beyond fans in the PRC, offended by the misrepresentation of their favorite band on national media. In 2009, World Friends of Laughter (Tianxia xiao you hui 天下笑友會), a comedy act broadcast by Sichuan TV, made fun of Beyond's late singer, Wong Ka-kui. The guest comedian Lollipop (Bangbang tang 棒棒糖) kept referring to Wong Ka-kui 黃家駒 as Wong Ka-gau 黃家狗, transforming the last character of Beyond's late singer into "dog." Beyond fans demanded an apology from Sichuan TV and began to harass the comedian Lollipop on the internet. Sichuan TV quickly published an official apology to Beyond's fans. In 2015, the crosstalk performer Miao Fu 苗阜 made a similar joke during a TV performance, asking when Beyond's singer "Wong Ka-gau" died. After an online campaign against Miao Fu, the performer had to issue an apology on his Weibo account, saying that he didn't want to disrespect Wong Ka-kui, adding that the only song he could sing in Cantonese was Beyond's "Really Love You" (Zan dik ngoi nei 真的愛你). In 2018, he had to apologize again after his 2015 apology mysteriously disappeared from Weibo, saying this time that he used to listen to the song "Boundless Oceans, Vast Skies" every day when he was young.³⁵ Beyond is not only a topic for nostalgic discourses but also an object of online mobilization when fans feel like Wong Ka-kui's image is being attacked publicly.

If Beyond's appropriation by individuals and collectives is place-based and has changed over time, we also have to mention the legacy of Beyond in Hong Kong, which is very different from the PRC for obvious reasons. Beyond's songs have been largely used by the pan-democrats in Hong Kong during protests and vigils. For instance, the song "Glorious Years" (Gwong fai seoi jyut 光輝歲月) was collectively performed by the democrats in 2010 during the Legislative Council by-election when five pan-democrat councilors resigned to trigger a new election. In 2010, students of the Chinese University of Hong Kong (CUHK) again gathered in front of the campus to welcome the Goddess of Democracy—a replica of a statue erected by the students on Tiananmen Square in 1989—transferred from Victoria Park to CUHK. As Gao Yujuan wrote in an essay on the use of Beyond in Hong Kong social movements: "Around midnight, the Goddess of Democracy finally arrived on campus. The students cheered and sang Beyond's '20 Years of War of Resistance' (Kong zin ji sap nin 抗戰二十年), while clapping their hands."³⁶ "Boundless Oceans, Vast Skies" was also often sung during the anti-Hong Kong Express Rail Link movement of January 2010, and Gao Yujuan interviewed participants to understand why they used Beyond's songs during the protests: "These songs are about ideals, freedom, peace and love, and they are truly the songs of the Hong Kong people. They stand for the protection of our land and what we love. There are no other songs more suitable for Hong Kong's social movements, right?"[37] While in the PRC, Beyond stands for hope, modernity, and the longing for a golden era, in Hong Kong, these songs were perceived as symbols "of sincerity and justice, perseverance, resistance to mainstream values and resistance to the establishment."[38] During the 2014 Umbrella Movement, Hong Kong students also sang "Boundless Oceans, Vast Skies," dubbed the unofficial anthem of the Hong Kong protests. But the song, considered a personification of the *zogaau* (leftards), was heavily criticized by more radicals protesters, who "used part of the lyrics from the song to deride collective singing and highlight its ineffectiveness."[39] A debate on the usefulness of Beyond's songs in contemporary social movements in Hong Kong arose among students and protesters. Singing Beyond's songs during protests was seen as an outdated repertoire of action. In 2019, during the anti-ELAB (Anti-Extradition Law Amendment Bill) protests, new songs appeared to replace Beyond's songs, such as the now famous anthem "Glory to Hong Kong" (Jyun wing gwong gwai Hoeng Gong 願榮光歸香港). The musical creativity of the anti-ELAB movement highlights the need for new local songs that can better embody contemporary struggles in Hong Kong. As in the PRC, the uses and references to Beyond's songs in Hong Kong have evolved throughout time. Once a symbol of the democratic movement and hope for a better future, Beyond's songs have been progressively abandoned for more combative anthems.

Conclusion

"Vast sky wide ocean, you and I / Who would change? (Who wouldn't change?) / Many times I've faced the cold shoulder and ridicule / Never have I gave up my heart's hopes and ideals." Beyond's lyrics have been widely commented on, analyzed, and dissected. Several scholars tried to understand the popularity of Beyond in the PRC through a literary analysis of Beyond's songs. If the quality of the lyrics and the musical composition has definitely influenced the popularity of Beyond in the PRC, we also have to look at the historical circumstances of its introduction in the early 1990s. The popularity of the Hong Kong rock band is closely related to the crackdown on Beijing rock and roll after the Tiananmen massacre. It is also related to the growing availability of pirated CDs and tapes from Hong Kong and Taiwan following Deng Xiaoping's Southern Tour in 1992, which led to the pursuit of economic reforms. As Tomas B. Gold noted, the success of Gangtai pop from the 1970s to the 1990s is due to several factors, from its availability and modernity to its escapist aspect.[40] However, if we look at Beyond's popularity through the Sinophone studies paradigm, we can better understand the appeal of Cantonese rock songs as a way to undermine the imposition of the Mandarin language throughout China and can be analyzed as a *minor* appropriation of Cantonese pop culture.

Notes

1. "Beyond Beijing chaoyue ziji" (Beyond beyond themselves in Beijing), *Yunlin gesheng* (China Yunnan Music), September 2003, 6.

2. Li Jianmin, "Beyond ershi nian" (20 years of Beyond), *Xinwen zhoukan* (China newsweek), 16 (2003): 69.

3. "Old band to rock city with new power," *China Daily*, August 21, 2003, https://www.chinadaily.com.cn/en/doc/2003-08/21/content_256807.htm

4. "Beyond Xianggang yinyue de liangxin" (Beyond, the conscience of Hong Kong music), *Yinyue tiandi* (The world of music) (March 2002): 49.

5. Mike Levin, "Chinese Pop Music Lovers Show A Taste For Rock," *Billboard*, January 21, 1995, 45.

6. Geremie Barmé, "Kong-Tai style," in *Encyclopedia of Contemporary Chinese Culture*, ed. Edward L. Davis (London: Routledge, 2005), 431.

7. Shu-mei Shih, *Visuality and Identity. Sinophone Articulations Across the Pacific* (Berkeley: University of California Press, 2007); Shu-mei Shih, Chien-hsin Tsai, and Brian Bernards, eds., *Sinophone Studies. A Critical Reader* (New York: Columbia University Press, 2013).

8. Yiu Fai Chow and Jeroen de Kloet, *Sonic Multiplicities. Hong Kong Pop and the Global Circulation of Sound and Image* (Chicago: Intellect, 2013); Marc L. Moskowitz, *Cries of Joy, Songs of Sorrow. Chinese Pop Music and Its Cultural Connotations* (Honolulu: University of Hawai'i Press, 2010).

9. Alvin K. Wong, "Including China? Postcolonial Hong Kong, Sinophone Studies, and the Gendered Geopolitics of China-Centrism," *Interventions* 20, no. 8 (2018): 1104.

10. Shu-mei Shih, "Introduction: What Is Sinophone Studies?" in Shih, Tsai, and Bernards, *Sinophone Studies. A Critical Reader*, 2.

11. Dru Gladney, *Dislocating China. Muslims, Minorities, and Other Subaltern Subjects* (Chicago: University of Chicago Press, 2004).

12. See Xue Ji, *Yaogun meng xun* (Seeking for the rock dream) (Beijing: Zhongguo dianying chubanshe, 1993).

13. Jonathan Campbell, *Red Rock: The Long, Strange March of Chinese Rock & Roll* (Hong Kong: Earnshaw Books, 2011), 85.

14. Gene Lau, *Beyond zheng zhuan 3.0* (Beyond: The story 3.0) (Beijing, Sanlian shudian, 2018), 42–44.

15. Lau, *Beyond zheng zhuan 3.0*, 45.

16. See the video online: https://www.youtube.com/watch?v=arBjzSDf7Bw, accessed March 6, 2024.

17. Nathanel Amar, "Including Music in the Sinophone, Provincializing Chinese Music," *China Perspectives* 128 (2018): 4–5.

18. See the video online: https://www.youtube.com/watch?v=WONKqNMw6FM

19. Beyond, *1989 zhen de jianzheng yanchanghui* (The 1989 Real Testimony Concert), Kinn's Music, 2015. See the YouTube video, 2:24:10, https://youtu.be/_swCjQxVpps?t=3312 (last access March 6, 2024).

20. Thomas B. Gold, "Go With Your Feelings: Hong Kong and Taiwan Popular Culture in Greater China," *China Quarterly* 136 (1993): 907, 909.

21. See Jeroen de Kloet, "Popular Music and Youth in Urban China: The Dakou Generation," *China Quarterly* 183 (September 2005): 609–626; and Nathanel Amar, "The Lives of Dakou in China: From Waste to Nostalgia," *Études chinoises* 37, no. 2 (2018): 35–60.

22. Yang Bo, "Yaogun jingshen yu women de shidai" (The spirit of rock and our generation), *Aisixiang*, December 11, 2008, http://www.aisixiang.com/data/23172.html, accessed March 6, 2024.

23. Andrew F. Jones, *Like a Knife: Ideology and Genre in Contemporary Chinese Popular Music* (Ithaca, NY: Cornell East Asia Series, 1992).

24. Jeroen de Kloet, "Beyond," in Davis, *Encyclopedia of Contemporary Chinese Culture*, 57.

25. Wu Hai, "Cong Xianggang Beyond yuedui de chenggong tan liuxing yinyue chuangzuo" (A discussion about pop music creation and composition from Hongkong Beyond band's success), *Zunyi shifan xueyuan xuebao* (Journal of Zunyi Normal College) 9, no. 4 (2007): 90.

26. Yin Chao, *A Study of Communication Effects of Beyond from the Perspectives of New Media* (postgraduate thesis, Guilin, Guangxi Normal University, 2013), 6.

27. *China Daily*, "Old Band to Rock City with New Power."

28. Gilles Deleuze and Claire Parnet, *Dialogues II* (New York: Columbia University Press, 2007), 58.

29. Shih, "Introduction: What Is Sinophone Studies?" 3.

30. Anthony Fung, "Consuming Karaoke in China," *Chinese Sociology & Anthropology* 42, no. 2 (2009): 41, 43.

31. Shih, "Introduction. What Is Sinophone Studies?," 8.

32. Chow and de Kloet, *Sonic Multiplicities*, 8.

33. See the video online: https://www.youtube.com/watch?v=mH2cW5i5qL0 (last access March 6, 2024).

34. Personal interview with Mosaic, August 17, 2023.

35. See "Miaofu zaici wei tiaokan Beyond daoqian" (Miaofu apologizes again for teasing Beyond), *KKnews*, October 16, 2018, https://kknews.cc/entertainment/9nry3oj.html (last access March 6, 2024).

36. Gao Yujuan, "Shehui yundong weishenme yao chang Beyond de ge? Beyond suo tixian de yaogun yuan zhenxing ji she qun liliang" (Why does the social movement sing Beyond's songs? Rock authenticity and community power embodied by Beyond), (master of cultural studies thesis, Hong Kong: Lingnan University, 2010).

37. Yujuan, "Shehui yundong weishenme yao chang Beyond de ge?"

38. Yujuan, "Shehui yundong weishenme yao chang Beyond de ge?"

39. Winnie C. Lai, "'Happy Birthday to You': Music as Nonviolent Weapon in the Umbrella Movement," *Hong Kong Studies* 1, no. 1 (March 2018): 70.

40. Thomas B. Gold, "Go With Your Feelings: Hong Kong and Taiwan Popular Culture in Greater China," 909.

Translanguaging as a Transcultural Marker in the Italian Sinophone Play *Tong Men-g*

VALENTINA PEDONE

The focus on language is the very premise of the conceptualization of the Sinophone since Sinophone "foregrounds not the ethnicity or race of the person, but the languages he or she speaks in either vibrant or vanishing communities of those languages."[1] Analytical tools developed in the field of applied linguistics can thus be used within the frame of Sinophone theory to highlight specific power dynamics embedded in language use. The subfield of sociolinguistics, the study of how society affects the use of language, can prove to be especially fruitful for research in Sinophone studies, which, unlike what commonly happens in traditional Chinese studies, focuses on the use of Sinitic languages beyond China. In fact, sociolinguistics takes advantage of concepts such as cultural norms and social attitude to investigate the use of language in the same way that Sinophone studies is interested in how the use of Sinitic languages can stem from specific cultural conflicts among their speakers, such as those against "the hegemonic call of Chineseness" and Chinese "long distance nationalism."[2] In this chapter, I use concepts from sociolinguistics to highlight how Chinese-Italian writer and actor Shi Yang Shi uses language in his Sinophone play *Tong Men-g* (1) to express his fluid cultural identity, (2) to question current hegemonic views on ethnicity in Italy, and (3) to inspire a sense of local belonging in the Chinese-Italian community. This threefold objective, I argue, is pursued in both the content and the form (language). My analysis is rooted in the general perspective of critical Sinophone studies, and I will, therefore, highlight the political dimension of language use in *Tong

Men-g while availing myself of theories recently developed in sociolinguistics on pragmatic aspects of translingual communication and of some analytical tools of traditional sociolinguistics and discourse analysis.

Two key concepts of sociolinguistics can be especially useful in the study of the Sinophone articulations in Italy: speech community and multilingualism. In sociolinguistics, the term *speech community* is used to address a group of people who share common linguistic norms. Although the concept has received occasional negative criticism in its field, especially for being too vague, it is still widely used and is one of the very founding ideas of sociolinguistics, as shown by Hymes's statement that "the natural unit for sociolinguistic taxonomy ... is not the language but the speech community."[3] Today, we tend to perceive speech communities more as flexible contexts whose limits can be designed and adjusted to different research questions rather than as an objective taxonomy to organize groups of speakers globally. Nonetheless, the concept still shows its power, for instance, when used in Sinophone studies to highlight the situatedness and the localized traits of different Sinophone communities. In fact, the Sinophone "registers not only the multiplicity of Sinitic languages but also how they undergo localization and creolization in relation to non-Sinitic languages in a given locality,"[4] which is quite the same scope that could be designed within a sociolinguistics perspective.

As for multilingualism, sociolinguistics offers a wide array of theories, observations, and methodologies aimed at understanding the dynamics that shape contexts such as those commonly touched upon in Sinophone studies: contexts in which a plurality of languages and codes are used for communicative and creative expression. In particular, the most recent developments in the sociolinguistic research in multilingual settings have brought into the field new ideas that are influenced by critical poststructuralism and conceive of language as "a *series of social practices and actions* by speakers who are embedded in a web of social *and* cognitive relations."[5] This perspective's interpretation of language as a "contested space" promises to identify an intriguing common ground on which to further develop Sinophone research. Scholars such as Becker,[6] Garcia and Li,[7] and Creese and Blackledge[8] question the notion of named languages as static, bounded, distinguished entities while "embracing the fluid nature of actual and local language practices."[9] Thus, they adopt the term *languaging*, which, as the practice of language use, "emphasizes the agency of speakers in an ongoing process of interactive meaning-making."[10] In the analysis of *Tong Men-g*, I will show how the author/actor turns to certain language practices (namely translanguaging and code-switching) to purposely address the multilingual Sinophone Italian speech community.

In *Tong Men-g*, writer and actor Shi Yang Shi uses both Italian and Mandarin to perform his life story on stage. The play has been advertised as bilingual, meaning it was intended to address an Italian- and a Mandarin-speaking audience through the repetition of lines in both languages. By considering the sociolinguistic notions of translanguaging, however, we can reveal another dimension of the use of language in the play, which goes well beyond the need to be intelligible to two distinct audiences. Such a dimension can, instead, be related to the evocation of a third space, very much resembling that imagined by Homi Bhabha,[11] one where the author expresses, stages, and celebrates the cultural hybridity of Chinese-Italians and their localization. As will be discussed, in *Tong Men-g*, the interactions between localized language practices (which reflect the personal experience of Shi Yang Shi) and a dynamic third space (that transcends borders between single languages) allow a wide audience to understand most of the content. Sociolinguists such as Auer[12] and Myers-Scotton[13] were among the first in the 1990s to observe how code-switching, the most common term used at the time to address the alternation of two or more distinct languages in the same speech act, can be the default practice in communication among bilinguals. By adopting the translanguaging lens, code-switching is today not only recognized as the norm in certain situations, but it is also viewed as a practice and a strategy that empowers and enables the speaker, or in this case the performer, to address and express their fluid cultural identity. In the case of areas impacted by Chinese migration, such language practices and their creative expressions, which are strongly connected to the localized use of one or more Sinitic languages, are also valuable objects of research in the field of Sinophone studies.

Shi Yang Shi and *Tong Men-g* (Later Titled *Arle-Chino*)

Although Europe has been a relatively recent target of migration when compared to other areas of the globe, today, the continent hosts about 2.5 million Chinese, and Italy is third in the list of European countries for the number of Chinese residents.[14] There are about three hundred thousand Chinese nationals living in Italy today,[15] constituting the country's fourth largest immigrant group. Chinese people have been regularly migrating to Italy for over a century, but only since the 1990s has their number started to surpass that of most other migrant groups.[16] Generally speaking, the Chinese who have been arriving in Italy since the economic reforms of 1980s China have almost exclusively come from southeast Zhejiang province, especially the Wenzhou area, and have not sought to escape poverty like the majority of other migrants. Instead, they have actively pursued financial success through the establishment of small, usually family-run, enterprises. According to this migratory pattern, whose solidity began to falter around 2010, Wenzhounese migrants tended to start up their own enterprises as soon as possible, perceiving any prior subordinate work as a transitional stage before sufficient capital to become self-employed was raised. Consequently, over the years, the newcomers have generally been hired to work in other Wenzhounese-run businesses as employees from the very first moment they landed on Italian soil, virtually avoiding the hurdles of unemployment that are common for other migrant groups when they come to Italy.[17]

Several factors have contributed to demographic changes in the Chinese population in Italy in the past decades. At present, since we are well into the so-called third generation, a certain percentage of Chinese nationals have been born in Italy and have never experienced migration at all.[18] Italy does not automatically award Italian citizenship to children of migrants born on its soil, and the People's Republic of China does not accept dual citizenship. Hence, many Chinese choose to maintain exclusive Chinese citizenship even after residing in Italy for a considerable amount of time or even when born on Italian soil. Because of this double bind, Chinese migrants and their descendants in Italy are currently excluded from many aspects of Italian society (both concrete and symbolic),[19] while they are offered the opportunity to be part of the perennial Chinese diaspora in a dynamic of perpetual belonging to the motherland that deprives them of any "chance to become a local."[20] Rejected, on the one hand, by Italian mainstream cultural discourse, marked as it is by a deeply ingrained Orientalism, and attracted, on the other, by PRC mainstream cultural discourse, which has a strong nationalist and essentialist characterization, a few Chinese Italian writers resorted to the word to express their position in this conflict.

One example of a Chinese Italian who responded with his creativity to this imposed tension is writer/actor Shi Yang Shi (the pen name of Shi Yang). Born near Jinan, in the Shandong province of the People's Republic of China, in 1979, Shi Yang Shi explains in *Tong men-g* how his pen name is formed by the standard Mandarin pronunciation of his name, Shi Yang (IPA ʂɚ jaŋ), and the Italian reading of the alphabetic transcription of his family name (IPA ʃi) that is placed after his name according to Italian convention. After having arrived in Italy with his mother when he was still a child, he grew up in Milan and, as an adult, decided to apply for Italian citizenship, thus giving up his Chinese passport. As an actor, he has starred in dozens of movies, both independent and mainstream, and in many popular TV series.[21] He has acted in a few theatre productions, coauthored the script of *Tong men-g*, and authored the autobiographical novel *Heart of Silk: My Made in China Italian Story* (Cuore di seta: La mia storia italiana made in China).[22] He is also a highly skilled interpreter who often works for the Italian government. Because of his fame, he is frequently a guest on TV and radio talk shows and other entertainment programs, where he offers his views against racism and discrimination, which, as we will see, are dominant themes in his cultural activity.[23]

Tong Men-g is a three-act monologue cowritten by Shi Yang Shi and Cristina Pezzoli and performed entirely and exclusively by Shi Yang Shi. Between 2009 and 2012, the non-Mandarin-speaking theater director, Cristina Pezzoli, led the activities of Compost, a group of artists of various kinds who performed artistic guerrilla actions in the city of Prato.[24] Apart from being the second-largest city in Tuscany after Florence, Prato is also the Italian municipality with the highest percentage of Chinese residents. Most of its Chinese residents work in textile and apparel manufacturing in local Chinese-run sweatshops.[25] From the 1990s to the present day, local right-wing politicians have regularly attempted to gain consensus from the voters during their political campaigns by fueling and encouraging protests against this dense presence of Chinese citizens.[26] Among the most popular activities of Compost, the experimental theatre project called *Sono qui perche: Translator and Traitor of Two Masters* (I am here because) was held in Prato throughout 2011. Its aim was to foster a confrontation between Chinese migrants and the rest of Prato's citizenry through an open and sometimes extremely provoking dialogue by Pezzoli and Shi Yang Shi. These periodic public encounters were attended by over two thousand people in total, more than half of which were Chinese migrants.[27] During these encounters, Shi Yang Shi took on many roles, including, but not exclusively, that of a language interpreter. The project's goal was to collect material for a play to be offered back to the community as a theatrical synthesis of such an experience. *Tong Men-g* is that play, although in the end, it only partially elaborates on the encounters of the *Sono qui perchè* project since it shifts its premise from the collective dimension to an individual one.

Tong men-g debuted in 2011 in Prato and was then performed a dozen more times in different locations throughout Italy and once in Beijing. The title of the monologue is an intricate pun. It is made up of the Latin alphabet with a coda of Chinese characters. The part in Chinese consists of the juxtaposition of two pairs of characters that are almost completely homophones and mean "bronze door" and "same dream." The Latin alphabet part of the title resembles the pinyin alphabetical transliteration of the two pairs of characters, contracted in one invented form; instead of being *tóng mén tóng mèng*, as the correct transliteration of the character version would be, it is *Tong men-g*, a hybrid crafted deviation from accepted transliteration rules. The result is that the title is rather straightforward for Chinese speakers in both forms, while it does not have any meaning for non-Chinese speakers. Non-Chinese speakers have access only to a title they can read but not understand (the alphabetical one) and another they can see but not read (the logographic one), whereas Chinese speakers can gain greater meaning from the two different titles. Differentiated access to language and meaning is, therefore, crucial in the entire work. The difficulty of marketing such an exotic title in the Italian theatre industry might have been the reason behind its change prior to the production's second Italian *tournée* in 2017. The new title was another wordplay: *Arle-Chino: Traduttore e traditore di due padroni* (Arle-Chino: translator and traitor of two masters). Arle-Chino is an invented name that hints at the famous Italian traditional mask Harlequin (Arlecchino), which simultaneously alludes to China and, in the second part, to the famous eighteenth-century comedy by Carlo Goldoni *Arlecchino: Il Servitore di Due Padroni* (*The Servant of Two Masters*). The new title is much more obvious for the Italian-speaking audience not only in terms of readability and pronounceability but also as it hints openly to the content, which can be described as the story of a comedian/translator who is given orders by two different cultural authorities. The cultural and linguistic hybridity that is at the thematic core of the work, however, is perfectly subsumed in the original title and then almost completely lost in the new one.

The play starts with a prelude. The actor walks among the public, holding a tray with a pyramid of gold-foil-wrapped Ferrero Rocher, an Italian chocolate candy that is extremely popular in China. He is dressed in an elegant red suit and pretends to offer the chocolate to people in the public in a very formal fashion. He then puts the tray above his head and tries to balance it while walking toward the stage; a sad melody frames this last movement. He goes backstage and returns holding a gigantic bouncy Ferrero Rocher and starts bouncing it in a choreography closely resembling Chaplin's "dictator and the globe" sequence in *The Great Dictator*. The dance is interrupted by a sudden explosion as if the balloon-like chocolate has burst. The lights go off, and the prelude ends. At the beginning of act 1, we find the actor on a dark stage holding a flashlight. He is dressed as a sort of contemporary harlequin, with a suit made of a patchwork of Chinese and Italian icons (portraits of politicians such as Mao Zedong or Bettino Craxi,[28] national flags, a Vespa scooter, a Tao symbol, and so on). The set design is minimal, except for a thick layer of rice grains covering the stage. He reaches for a pile of rice and finds two small flags in it: Italy's and PRC's. The monologue starts with the actor questioning himself in Italian and Mandarin about his cultural belonging; his Mandarin voice and his Italian voice accuse each other of cultural betrayal:

CH *Wǒ jiào Shí Yáng*
(My name is Shi Yang)
IT *Sono Yang Shi*

(I am Yang Shi)
CH *Bùduì! Wǒ jiào Shí Yáng, wǒ shì Zhōngguórén!*
(Wrong! My name is Shi Yang, I am Chinese!)
IT *No, no, no, io sono Yang Shi e sono italiano!*
(No, no, no, I am Yang Shi and I am Italian!)
CH *Bùduì! Wǒ chūshēng zài Zhōngguó Shāndōng Jǐnán, wǒ de lǎojiā shì Lìjīn, Huáng Hé rù hǎi chù*
(Wrong! I was born in Jinan, in the Chinese province of Shandong, my home is Lijin, where the Yellow River enters the sea)
IT *Ma che dici? Io ho il passaporto italiano, ho scelto la cittadinanza italiana!*
(What are you talking about? I have an Italian passport, I've chosen Italian citizenship!)
CH *Pàntú*
(Traitor)
IT *Traditore*
(Traitor)
CH *Nǐ yǒngyuǎn shì yī gè Zhōngguórén*
(You will always be Chinese!)
IT *Tu essere sempre cinese!*
(You always Chinese! [*Sic!*])
IT *Ma che traditore? Io sono cresciuto in Italia! Mi piace la pizza, gli spaghetti.*
(I am no traitor, I grew up in Italy! I like pizza, spaghetti)
IT *Di soia?*
(Soy spaghetti?)
IT *No, al ragù!*
(No, meat sauce spaghetti!)
CH *Ragù? Bù kěyǐ!* (singing the PRC anthem) *Qǐlai, bù yuàn zuò núlì de rénmín...*
(Meatball sauce? You can't! Arise, you who do not want to be slaves...)
IT (*singing the Italian anthem*) *Fratelli d'Italia, l'Italia s'è desta...*
(Brothers of Italy, Italy has awakened...) (Act 1)²⁹

After going backstage again, the actor comes back as a different character: a funny-looking man dressed in greased blue overalls who carries a bulky bag full of tools and calls himself the "fixer." The fixer is a sort of plumber who, with a clownish broken Italian mixed with a Shandongnese accent, explains to the main character that he must read the book of his ancestors to understand who he really is. This is the only possible way to force the "bronze gate" that prevents him from fully accessing his Chinese heritage and, supposedly, finally feeling at ease with himself. After another costume change into the Harlequin suit, Shi Yang Shi starts pulling up clothes and objects from a chest filled with rice. During the rest of the act, he wears these objects and props to interpret his ancestors. First, he stages the life of his paternal great-grandmother, another character who also includes some Shandongnese expressions in her lines, who was a child-wife and had bound feet. Then, he stages the life of his paternal great-grandfather, who was killed by the Japanese troops during the Second Sino-Japanese War. He moves on to recall the life of his paternal great-great-grandmother, who was a landowner and a businesswoman. After this character, Shi Yang Shi stages some episodes in the life of his maternal grandfather, a doctor who was a victim of persecution during the Cultural Revolution. The last family portrait is his father's, a committed Red Guard in the Cultural Revolution. Each family member performs a monologue in which they narrate their life stories. At the end of act 1, the fixer comes back onstage, demanding to be paid for his job since he supposedly helped Shi Yang Shi "fix his problem," but the actor refuses to pay him because:

IT *Manca un pezzo*
(A piece is missing)
CH *Nǐ huó er méi gàn wán ne !*
(Your job is not done yet) (Act 1).

The second act focuses on the development of Shi Yang Shi's life from his arrival in Italy in 1990, when he was eleven, up to the present day. Here, the author speaks not only about his story but also about the difficulties of the lives of many Chinese migrants in Italy. He remembers his past as a minor working illegally in an Italian restaurant, his precarious lodging conditions, and the scams against his family by Italians. He then moves on to narrate his attempts at being accepted by his peers in school and his subsequent sociocultural and economic emancipation. The narration provides a new perspective on the life of Chinese migrants to Italy: It is filtered through the eyes of a child who experienced it firsthand. While the script and acting are comedic, the evident pain felt by the author throughout past events is extremely compelling and brings the audience to bond with him emotionally. The third act represents Shi Yang Shi's present and focuses on Compost and *Sono qui perchè*. Here, Shi Yang Shi talks about his profession as an interpreter and how it puts him in a difficult position when he has to translate in situations of conflict between Chinese migrants and Italian residents. In this part, he impersonates himself working as an interpreter between imaginary Chinese and Italian interlocutors. He is insulted by both of them for not being able to side with either. The show ends with a shadow play and one last monologue in which the actor compares himself to a vase made according to the traditional Japanese kintsugi art of gold-brazing pottery shards to give them new life. His last words onstage are:

> CH *Zhōngguórén jiào wǒ*
> (Chinese call me)
> IT *I cinesi mi chiamano*
> (Chinese call me)
> CH *Shí Yáng*
> (Shi Yang)
> IT *Gli italiani mi chiamano*
> (Italians call me)
> CH *Yìdàlìrén jiào wǒ Yang Shi.*
> (Italians call me Yang Shi)
> IT *Io mi chiamo*
> (My name is)
> CH *Wǒ jiào Shí*
> (My name is Shi)
> IT *Yang Shi.*
> (Yang Shi) (Act 3).

The actor then collects all the clothes and props used during the show on a shoulder yoke and staggers off the stage. This third act stages the open (violent even) psychological and emotional conflict experienced by the author in his life trajectory, followed by the representation of his newly found way of coping. The audience is drawn by Shi Yang Shi to the final catharsis, and a very moving effect is exerted upon it when the actor finally finishes his long monologue and leaves an empty stage. The dominant theme is thus that of cultural identity negotiation. The following paragraphs discuss how such negotiation is expressed in the play, in terms of both content and form, specifically by means of particular language practices reported in the script.

Translanguaging as an Expressive Resource

As already pointed out, Shi Yang Shi's monologue can be defined as translingual. To further support the idea that in many passages the alternation of the languages in the script works as a transcultural identity marker, we can consider some more detailed similarities between how language is used in the script and how multilingual speakers naturally engage in code-switching. According to Myers Scotton's markedness model,[30] in a given interaction, speakers choose from their linguistic repertoire a single variety that is more appropriate and beneficial to them in the situation. Hence, in multilingual settings, for each interaction, there are unmarked, expected language choices and marked, differential ones: "Speakers do their own 'social work' by using the indexical property of linguistic choices in the negotiation of their own identity and their rights and obligations with others."[31] In other words, when several language varieties are available to speakers in a specific context, the choice of one language variety over another is motivated by the power relations indexed in each variety. Translanguaging, a practice that implies continuous code-switching, can itself be an option in the repertoire of multilingual speakers and function as the unmarked choice in certain environments. The dominant theme of *Tong Men-g* is cultural conflict; hence, the rights and obligations indexed in the two standard languages in the play are unquestionably defined for this context, and the tension between the two languages is clearly and deliberately represented in some of the code-switching occurrences, as in the case of the previously quoted opening lines. However, a third mixed-language variety is also active—the possible unmarked choice in communication among people of Chinese origin in the audience. By observing similarities with code-switching in the phrasing of the script's language alternation, one can maintain that the author had a multilingual audience in mind as well.

Peter Auer argues that, in bilingual conversation, shifting between languages is a conversational act with a communicative function.[32] Multilingual speakers naturally engage in code-switching with expressive, emotional, prosodic, and symbolic intents (as opposed to merely denotative ones). Just as in those contexts wherein code-switching is the unmarked choice, Shi Yang Shi appears to use it in *Tong Men-g* for communicative purposes. For instance, in the play, code-switching often consists of inserting single terms from one language into the other. This is typical of translingual conversation, and it often acts as a transcultural identity marker with the sole purpose of maintaining the translingual flow of speech. The following are some examples from *Tong Men-g*:

> IT *Avevo con me*
> (I had with me)
> CH *Làzhǐ*
> (Wax paper)
> IT *Carta di cera*
> (Wax paper)
> CH *Gāngyìn*
> (Embossing steels)
> IT *Stampi d'acciaio e*
> (Embossing steels and)
> CH *Mòshuǐ*

(Ink)
IT *Inchiostro e potevo stampare giornali dappertutto, anche in mezzo alla campagna più sperduta*
(Ink and I could print newspapers everywhere, even in the middle of the most isolated countryside) (Act 1).
IT *In Cina, per avere il cravattino rosso, bisognava sgomitare per fare i lavori più sporchi come pulire il pavimento, le finestre e anche*
(In China, to wear a red tie, you had to elbow your way to doing the dirtiest jobs, such as cleaning floors, windows and even)
CH *Tányú*
(Spittoon)
IT *La sputacchiera, che era la cosa più schifosa, cosa che mia mamma mi aveva espressamente vietato*
(A spittoon, which was the most disgusting thing, so that my mother forbade me)
CH *Bù kěyǐ*
(Can not)
IT *Di fare perché portava le malattie infettive*
(To do that, because it would bring on infective diseases) (Act 2).

Another typical feature of code-switching in multilingual conversation is the speakers' frequent switching to another language in their repertoire to portray direct speech with a prosodic goal. In fact, the alternation between Italian and Mandarin in *Tong Men-g* occurs quite regularly in correspondence with direct speech. For instance:

IT *Comunque in Italia eravamo caduti in basso: anzi, come diceva mia madre*
(Anyway in Italy we had sunk low: better yet, as my mother used to say)
CH *Cóng tiānshàng diào dào dòng lǐ qùle*
(Fallen from the sky into a hole)
IT *Caduti dal cielo dentro un buco.*
(Fallen from to sky into a hole) (Act 2).
IT *Ho 12 anni ma devo dire che ne ho 16. Se no sono grane*
(I'm 12 years old, but I have to say I'm 16, or it will mean trouble)
CH *Yào shuō nǐ zhǐyǒu 12 suì， yàobù jiù zāole!*
('If you say that you're only 12 it will mean trouble!') (Act 2)

The direct speech can also be only imagined, as in the following example:

IT *In Italia nessuno si alza in piedi; la maestra la chiamavi per nome.*
(In Italy nobody stands up; you called the teacher by her first name)

CH *'Zěnme Yìdàlì tóngxué bù zhànqǐlai gěi lǎoshī dǎ zhāohu ne?'*
('How come Italian students don't stand up to greet the teacher?') (Act 2)

These instances of code-switching have expressive functions, just as in natural multilingual speech when translanguaging is the unmarked, default language choice. In the examples, the message expressed in one language was repeated in the other. In other passages, however, code-switching is used with the same expressive function, but the meanings conveyed by each language are not simply repeated in the other; they are reformulated in a creative manner that reflects the potentials of translanguaging practice:

IT *La mia bisnonna aveva i piedi del loto d'oro*
(My great grandmother had golden lotus feet)
CH *Sāncùnjīnlián, wǒ lǎo lǎolao shì yī wèi xiǎojiǎo nǚrén*
(Three *cun* long golden lotus feet, my old grandmother was a small foot woman)
IT *I piedi del loto d'oro dovevano misurare al massimo dieci centimetri. Come la scarpina di un neonato. I maschi dell'epoca li consideravano irresistibili e sposavano volentieri le proprietarie. 'Si faccia misurare il piede signora':*
(Golden lotus feet had to be at most ten centimeters long. Like a newborn baby's little shoe. Males at the time found it irresistible and were willing to marry their owners. "Please madam, let me measure your foot")
CH *'Zhè dàjiǎo yāzi, shéijia gǎn yào ya!'*
(Such enormous feet, who's gonna want you!)
IT *'Il suo è piede loto di piombo!'.*
('Yours is a lead lotus foot!') (Act 1)
CH *Nàge shídài, rénrén píngděng, Máo zhǔxí shì wǒmen de bǎngyàng, shì tā lǐngdǎo Zhōngguó zhànqǐlai le*
(At that time, all men were equal, President Mao was our model, he led China to rise up)
IT *Di quel periodo, mi manca l'uguaglianza*
(Of that time, I miss equality) (Act 1)
CH *Wǒ liǎng nián méi jiàn de bàba xiàtiān lái kàn women*
(My father, whom I have not seen in two years, comes to see me in the summer)
IT *Dopo due anni che non lo vedevo, viene a trovarci mio padre per le vacanze estive. Lui mi trova più alto di sette centimetri, io lo trovo un po' straniero*
(After two years that I have not seen him, my father comes to see us for the holidays. He finds me seven centimeters taller, I find him a bit of a stranger)
CH *'Zěnme juéde tā yǒudiǎn mòshēngrén de gǎnjué ne? Zhōngguó wèidao zhème nóng!'*

('How come I find him a bit of a stranger? Is the Chinese smell really that strong?') (Act 2)

As a common practice in natural conversations among multilingual speakers, translanguaging enables the expression of a transcultural identity that transcends clear-cut language boundaries. In *Tong men-g*, Shi Yang Shi uses language creatively and engages abundantly in translanguaging with a wide array of expressive functions, as well as with identity-assertion purposes, like when he performs with the accent of his place of origin (Jinan) or when he adopts the typical accent of Prato (e.g., when he acts as an interpreter between Chinese and local authorities in Prato). The result is a play that addresses, expresses, and stages a hybrid cultural identity and does so through a formal linguistic dimension, as the sociolinguistic analysis stresses, and on various other levels (visual, content, structure, and more).

Conclusions

In *Tong Men-g*, Shi Yang Shi stages the life trajectory of a child of Chinese immigrants growing up in Italy by channeling his own life experience. In his narration, he first stresses the cultural conflict that is endured by people with similar backgrounds. He explains how, in coming to terms with such a situation, it was important for him to learn about his Chinese ancestors (act 1). He then moves on to recall the years of his arrival in Italy and the hardships he had to face when adjusting to his new life (act 2). Finally, he stages a specific moment in his adult years when he committed himself to engage in social work as a mediator in disputes between Chinese immigrants and Italy's civil society and institutions. In the end, he formulates a solution to his personal conflict by coming to terms with the fact that where and what he is now is the outcome of the many ruptures he went through, a result that is whole and not fragmented. In a circular movement, the play starts with an image of rupture, the noise of a bursting balloon, and it ends with an image of reconstruction, the patching of a kintsugi vase. The structure seems to propose a juxtaposition between the theme of China (the first act), the theme of Italy (the second act), and the theme of conflict and negotiation between the two (the third act). As it is portrayed in the play, however, China seems rather filtered by Italy's mainstream cultural discourse since act 1 revolves around topics such as foot binding, arranged marriages, and political oppression, which are quite typical in Orientalist discourse on China (as Said summarizes, "the theme of Europe teaching the Orient the meaning of liberty."[33]) Such a reduction of the Chinese experience to a number of stereotypical tropes can be very unfamiliar to the part of the audience of Chinese origin. On the other hand, the Italy evoked onstage is one lived by a young child of Chinese immigrants living at the edge of its society, struggling to be included; an impression of Italy that is particularly familiar to its spectators of Chinese origin but which is mostly unknown by average Italians. The third act, whatever perspective one takes to interpret it, refuses to take sides by rejecting and resisting binary oppositions and advocating for a third space instead.

The theme of cultural identity conflict and negotiation, which is so central in cultural productions by people of Chinese origin in Italy, is treated by Shi Yang Shi in terms of both content and language. In this respect, *Tong men-g* should be considered a translingual play and not a bilingual one since it does not intend to reach out to Italian-speaking and Mandarin-speaking audiences as two different groups. Rather, I contend that Shi Yang Shi engages in a more sophisticated and fluid language use as a means to address a transcultural collective audience. Instances of translanguaging are evident throughout the work. The communication flow is one alone, and it is partially accessible even by those who are monolingual. Monolingual speakers of Italian can follow along, and the effect of hearing unintelligible chunks of speech may actually serve Shi Yang Shi's artistic purposes, as they evoke the sense of estrangement felt by fresh immigrants. On the other hand, monolingual speakers of Mandarin, who rely only on the parts expressed in Mandarin to understand the plot as it unfolds, would be left too much in the dark regarding the narrative content and would find it difficult to follow. Nonetheless, by mixing the languages, Shi Yang Shi reproduces the practice of translanguaging, which is common among people of Chinese origin in Italy, and thus reaches out to the Chinese-Italian part of the audience not on a denotative plane but with the intention of both transcending linguistic and cultural boundaries and expressing belonging (the routes that become roots, as suggested by Shih).[34] The play addresses an audience living in Italy; this is reflected foremost in the choice of Italian as the prevailing language of the script. The Mandarin parts are correspondingly directed to Mandarin speakers living in Italy. It is precisely the use of translanguaging that gives the work its linguistic localization, which would be absent from a monolingual script; the work could be easily rendered completely in Italian, in Mandarin, or in any other language without losing anything at the formal level. It is through the fluid, mixed, hybrid language currently spoken only by people of Chinese origin in Italy that the play manifests its situatedness.

By taking advantage of sociolinguistic concepts and the Sinophone studies theory, we can highlight how the Italian-Sinophone *Tong Men-g* expresses, at the linguistic level, the resistance of people of Chinese origin in Italy to the dual domination of the essentialist views on Chinese and Italian cultures. This struggle is conveyed by the creative use of "fractions of Sinitic languages" to express and address a localized culture, thus questioning the equivalence among language, culture, ethnicity, and nationality.[35] By deliberately imposing a migrant language on the audience, Shi Yang Shi openly claims a space in Italian society for other Chinese descendants; by decoupling such language from the notion of Chineseness through translanguaging, he further claims their right to be perceived as locals.

Notes

1. Shu-mei Shih, "Against Diaspora: The Sinophone as Places of Cultural Production," in *Global Chinese Literature*, ed. Jing Tsu and David Der-wei Wang (Leiden: Brill, 2010), 39.

2. Shu-mei Shih, "The Concept of the Sinophone," *PMLA* 126, no. 3 (Fall 2011): 710.

3. Dell Hathaway Hymes, "Models of the Interaction of Language and Social Life," in *Directions in Sociolinguistics*, ed. John Joseph Gumperz and Dell Hathaway Hymes (New York: Holt, Rinehart and Winston, 1972), 43.

4. Hymes, "Models of the Interaction," 716.

5. Ofelía Garcia and Li Wei, *Translanguaging: Language, Bilingualism and Education* (New York: Palgrave Macmillan, 2014), 9.

6. Alton L. Becker, "Language in Particular: A Lecture," in *Linguistics in Context*, ed. Deborah Tannen (Norwood, NJ: Ablex, 1988), 17–35.

7. Garcia and Li, *Translanguaging*.

8. Angela Creese and Adrian Blackledge, "Translanguaging and Identity in Educational Settings," in *Annual Review of Applied Linguistics* 35, (Winter 2015): 20–35.

9. Garcia and Li, *Translanguaging*, 9.

10. Garcia and Li, *Translanguaging*, 9.

11. Homi K. Bhabha, *The Location of Culture* (London: Routledge, 2004).

12. Peter Auer, *Code-Switching in Conversation: Language, Interaction and Identity* (London: Routledge, 1998).

13. Carol Myers-Scotton, *Codes and Consequences: Choosing Linguistic Varieties* (New York: Oxford University Press, 1998).

14. Kevin Latham and Bin Wu, *Chinese Migration into the EU: New Trends, Dynamics and Implications* (London: Europe China Research and Advice Network, 2013), https://www.chathamhouse.org/sites/default/files/public/Research/Asia/0313ecran_lathamwu.pdf.

15. An exact population of 299,823 as of January 1, 2019, according to Istat (Italian National Institute of Statistics, www.istat.it).

16. Frank Pieke, *Recent Trends in Chinese Migration to Europe: Fujianese Migration in Perspective* (Geneva: IOM, 2002), 17.

17. For a detailed account of the general features of Chinese migration to Italy, refer to Antonella Ceccagno, *City Making and Global Labor Regimes: Chinese Immigrants and Italy's Fast Fashion Industry* (Cham: Palgrave Macmillan, 2017).

18. While there is no comprehensive data on the number of Italian born Chinese citizens, the most recent available figures show that in 2021, 1,877 children were born in Italy from

Chinese parents (Italian Ministry of Labour and Social Policy, RC-Cina-2022, p. 8, www.lavoro.gov.it).

19. For instance, Chinese citizens in Italy cannot vote, receive certain benefits from the government, or open tobacco shops (which are under the government monopoly). They also must apply for a green card regularly just to be legal residents in Italy, even if they were born in the country. This situation is shared by all people born from non-Italian citizens.

20. Shih, "Against Diaspora," 45.

21. See, for example, https://www.imdb.com/name/nm3211285/.

22. Shi Yang Shi, *Cuore di seta: La mia storia italiana made in China* (Heart of silk: My made in China Italian story) (Milano: Mondadori, 2017).

23. Alessio Poeta, "Yang Shi: 'La mia strana storia gay, made in China,'" Gay.it, November 17, 2013, https://www.gay.it/televisione/news/yang-shi-storia-gay-made-in-china-intervista.

24. See, for example, http://incontri-ravvicinati-livorno.blogautore.repubblica.it/intervista-a-cristina-pezzoli-regista-teatrale-e-presidente-di-spazio-compost/.

25. For detailed accounts on Chinese migration to Prato, see Antonella Ceccagno, *City Making and Global Labor Regimes: Chinese Immigrants and Italy's Fast Fashion Industry* (Cham: Palgrave-MacMillan, 2017); Elizabeth L. Krauze, *Tight Knit: Global Families and the Social Life of Fast Fashion* (Chicago: University of Chicago Press, 2018); and Daniele Brigadoi Cologna and Gabi Dei Ottati, "The Chinese in Prato and the Current Outlook on the Chinese-Italian Experience," in *Chinese Migration to Europe. The Case of Prato and Italy*, ed. Loretta Baldassar, Graeme Johanson, Narelle McAuliffe, and Massimo Bressan (London: Palgrave-MacMillan, 2015), 29–48.

26. Fabio Bracci "The 'Chinese Deviant': Building the Perfect Enemy in a Local Arena," in *No Borders: Immigration and the Politics of Fear*, ed. Emma Bell (Chambéry: Éditions del'Université de Savoie, 2012), 97–116; and Zhang Gaoheng, *Migration and the Media: Debating Chinese Migration to Italy, 1992–2012* (Toronto: Toronto University Press, 2019).

27. Riccardo Goretti, "Spazio Compost: la storia della chiusura secondo Cristina Pezzoli," Pratosfera, October 15, 2013, https://www.pratosfera.com/2013/10/15/lettera-aperta-cristina-pezzoli/.

28. Bettino Craxi (1934–2000) was a very influential Italian politician. He was the leader of Italian Socialist Party from 1976 to 1993 and Italy's prime minister from 1983 to 1987. After being prosecuted for bribery and corruption in 1994, he fled to Tunisia where he later died.

29. The script is based on the online video of the performance: Cristina Pezzoli, dir., *Tong men-g*, written and performed by Shi Yang Shi (Teatro Brancaccio, Rome, Italy, September 22, 2014), http://www.e-performance.tv/2014/09/tong-men-g.html. I also own a hard copy of the script, kindly provided by Shi Yang Shi himself for research purposes. All excerpts from the play are from this source.

30. Carol Myers-Scotton, *Social Motivations for Codeswitching: Evidence from Africa* (Oxford: Clarendon Press, 1993).

31. Myers-Scotton, *Social Motivations for Codeswitching*, 100.

32. Peter Auer, "Introduction: Bilingual Conversation Revisited," in Auer, *Code-Switching in Conversation*, 1–24.

33. Edward Said, *Orientalism* (New York: Vintage, 1979), 172.

34. Shih, "Against Diaspora," 46.

35. Shih, "The Concept," 110.

From Multilingualism to Mandarin

Chinese Singaporeans as a Sinophone Community, 1945–1990

JASON LIM

Are Chinese Singaporeans the same as ethnic Han in China? This question was raised during the 2011 general elections in the city-state. It came at a time of an influx of workers, students, and professionals from China. While about three-quarters of the population in Singapore is Chinese, Chinese Singaporeans have a different heritage from the Han in China due to Singapore's modern history. Singapore was a British colony for 140 years until it achieved self-government in 1959. Chinese migrants arrived in large numbers from the southern Chinese provinces of Fujian and Guangdong. Singapore became a settler colony under British colonial rule as the number of Chinese migrants eventually exceeded those of the other ethnic groups.

Before the introduction of Singapore citizenship in 1957, most Chinese in Singapore, whether immigrants or descendants of immigrants born in Singapore, considered China their homeland. However, the Chinese in Singapore did not speak Mandarin. They spoke the languages found in Fujian and Guangdong, with Hokkien (Minnanhua) as the dominant language. In the 1930s, several Chinese community leaders in Singapore promoted the greater use of Mandarin as a medium of instruction in Chinese schools, which became the norm by the 1950s.[1] In addition, there were Chinese Singaporeans classified as Straits-born or Peranakan, descendants from Chinese traders who had arrived in Malaya long before British colonialism and who had married local women. The Peranakans spoke English and Malay; many were English-educated.

Shih Shu-Mei wrote that Sinophone studies is about "the Sinitic-language communities and cultures outside China as well as ethnic minority communities and cultures within China where Mandarin is adopted or imposed."[2] Chinese Singaporeans form a Sinophone community as their roots are in colonial and postcolonial Singapore (not China), with an identity based on different Sinitic languages (with Hokkien as the dominant language and not Mandarin). Singapore Hokkien also absorbed English and Malay words.

During the Cultural Revolution in China from 1966 to 1976, Prime Minister Lee Kuan Yew considered "Chinese cultures of British-ruled Singapore and Hong Kong as legitimate heirs of traditional Chinese culture."[3] It was an attempt by Lee to desinicize China, as it had become a communist state. By the late 1970s, Lee began discouraging the widespread use of all Sinitic languages except Mandarin. This chapter looks at how Chinese Singaporeans have transformed through changing dominant Sinitic languages from the end of World War II in 1945 to the end of the Lee Kuan Yew era in 1990.

The Language(s) of the Singapore Chinese

The language spoken among Chinese in Singapore is an interesting mix of a Sinitic language other than Mandarin, Malay, and English. Therefore, a person classified as Hokkien in the censuses spoke Hokkien with a smattering of English and Malay. For instance, *market* (市場) is not pronounced "chhī-tiūn" but "pa-sat" (from the Malay word *pasar*). Phyllis Chew has compiled a short list of examples of Hokkien words that have absorbed English and Malay.[4] Language was a key identifier for Chinese Singaporeans. It not only revealed the location that an individual had migrated from (or the location of an ancestor), but speaking the language also created a sense of close ties and familiarity. Not surprisingly, when new migrants arrived in Singapore, they started language-based associations, provincial associations, clans, and trade associations centered on a major language.

Research on the Chinese in Singapore has framed the community as part of overseas Chinese or diasporic studies. While the Chinese in Singapore are divided along linguistic lines, these studies link the community with the Qing Empire (and later China) by glossing over language differences. Therefore, Chinese associations are seen to be no different from each other in organization and purpose. Research has also focused on the leadership of these associations and overseas Chinese nationalism before World War II.[5] However, research on the history from 1945 frames the community as a single ethnic group during the nation-building process.[6] Liu Hong considers Chinese associations as similar in outlook and organization because he considers them as one

Chinese people, which is how "Chinese-ness" has been framed in China.[7] The presence of many Sinitic languages is downplayed. For the 1947 census, the British colonial government used the word *tribe* for each community centered around a Sinitic language.[8] This census did not record whether the Chinese in Singapore spoke Mandarin. The five major language groups were Hokkien (39.6 percent), Teochew (21.6 percent), Cantonese (21.6 percent), Hainanese (7.1 percent), and Hakka (5.5 percent).[9] (Chiew 45). Many Chinese community leaders in Singapore also did not speak Mandarin. Despite being called "an overseas Chinese legend," Tan Kah Kee, who was active in the community until he left Singapore in 1950 for China, could not speak Mandarin.[10] He spoke Hokkien.

The importance of Sinitic languages other than Mandarin is a part of life for the Chinese community in colonial Singapore. Different associations using various Sinitic languages organized social and cultural events as part of their Chinese heritage. In such an environment, Mandarin was the language of the educated elite, as they had the opportunity to go to a Chinese school and, if they qualified, Nanyang University, a tertiary institution founded in 1955 that used Mandarin as a medium of instruction. Between the 1947 and 1990 censuses, the five major language groups in Singapore accounted for about 94 percent of the Chinese population, which means that the Chinese Singaporeans "were not representative of the Chinese composition in China."[11] Chen Dung-Sheng notes, "Taiwanese society separated from China" in later years to become a "native society."[12] As nation-building continued with independence, more Chinese people in Singapore considered Singapore home and not China, which is not surprising since the proportion of Singapore-born Chinese increased from about 58 percent in 1947 to 85 percent by 1990.[13]

The diverse business interests that were marked by different dialect groups became a defining characteristic of the Chinese business community in Singapore. With the dominance of the five language groups, it became vital for those involved in business to protect their interests. Cheng Lim-Keak noted that businesses operated according to a "bang" (幫) concept, which he defined as "a Chinese politico-socio-economic grouping based principally on a dialect."[14] As Singapore moved from self-government to statehood, these divisions remained unchanged. For example, Hokkiens dominated nearly all the work available in Singapore, from port workers to rich entrepreneurs, while Teochews were dominant in the pineapple industry, fishing industry, wholesalers and retailers in local produce, and as farmers, goldsmiths, and boatmen. The way these language groups maintained their hold on the trades they had dominated was to organize trade associations that effectively blocked membership to anyone who could not speak the dominant language.[15]

The records of these trade associations reveal very little about conditions in post-1949 China. They reveal the relationship the associations have with the government in colonial and postcolonial Singapore, the relationship these associations have with each other, and the internal dominance of specific language group(s). They are a valuable source for studying Singapore history. After 1945, members of the Singapore Chinese Tea Importers and Exporters Association were concerned with the trade in China and Taiwan, but they saw themselves as Singapore merchants.[16] When trading conditions worsened for Chinese merchants in Singapore, they joined forces for mutual benefit. One example is the "four departments" (四局) comprising four trade associations that held quarterly meetings against British commercial interests.[17] Both instances show the response of Chinese merchants in Singapore to commercial needs. Beyond trades and occupations, many Sinitic languages reflect the heritage of Chinese Singaporeans, for example, through cuisine such as fried Hokkien *mee* (炒福建麵), Teochew *bak chor mee* (潮州肉脞麵), Hainanese chicken rice (海南雞飯), and Hakka *yong yau foo* (客家釀豆腐). Despite references to places and languages in China, these are Singapore dishes.

Dominance of Hokkien

During the colonial period, various language groups had congregated in different parts of Singapore. Although the British had plans for a "Chinese village" in the early years of the colony, it became impossible for all Chinese to congregate in one area due to the overwhelming population. Instead, the Chinese began to live apart from one another in the city. Each area dominated by a language group formed a Chinatown. The Teochews also opened the interior of the island, eventually moving into Punggol and Hougang in northeastern Singapore. As part of nation-building, however, the Lee Kuan Yew government planned to depopulate the city center and move residents to housing estates outside the city. It became possible then for a Hokkien family to have a Hainanese or Teochew neighbor. In the mid-1980s, the Singapore Tourist Promotion Board began plans to redevelop the Cantonese-speaking area for tourism. From many Chinatowns separated by language, Singapore now has one official Chinatown that the government promotes as "Chinese heritage."

With Mandarin taught in Chinese schools, the other Sinitic languages came to be derisively labeled as "dialects," as if these languages were inferior forms of Mandarin, the real or standard language of ethnic Chinese people. Communication between these language groups meant the use of Hokkien as the lingua franca.[18] The Hokkien spoken in Singapore was also unique. Two dictionaries compiled by two China scholars on "Singapore Minnanhua"

(新加坡閩南話) were published in the early 2000s.[19] The dominance of Hokkien can be seen in the organization and activities of the Singapore Chinese Chamber of Commerce (SCCC). The chamber was effectively controlled by the Hokkiens because they dominated trade in colonial Singapore. The executive council was divided equally into "Min" (Fujian) and "Yue" (Guangdong) groups. The former included all members whose ancestors came from Fujian—the Hokkiens, Hokchias, Foochows, and Henghuas. Hokkiens clearly dominated this "Min" group due to their economic dominance in Singapore. The Hokkiens were also numerically superior within the Min group as the Hokchias, Foochows, and Henghuas were very small in numbers—together, they constituted just three percent of the Chinese in Singapore in the 1957 census compared to the Hokkiens at about 41 percent.[20] The Yue group was divided between the Teochews, Cantonese, Hakkas, and Hainanese, with each group of roughly equal economic strength. Since Hokkiens dominated the Min group, and with Hokkien and Teochew sounding almost similar, the Hokkiens dominated the SCCC. Between 1945 and 1993, there were twelve presidents of the SCCC, eight of who were Hokkien, with three Teochews (see table 17.1). SCCC meetings were conducted in Hokkien.[21]

Table 17.1 List of presidents of the SCCC, 1945–1993

NAME	DIALECT GROUP	PERIOD IN OFFICE
Lien Ying Chow 連瀛洲*	Teochew	1941–1942 & 1945–1946
Lee Kong Chian 李光前	Hokkien	1946–1948
Yong Yit Lim 楊溢璘	Hakka	1948–1949
Tan Lark Sye 陳六使	Hokkien	1949–1952
Tan Siak Kew 陳錫九	Teochew	1952–1954
Ko Teck Kin 高德根	Hokkien	1954–1956
Tan Siak Kew 陳錫九	Teochew	1956–1958
Ko Teck Kin 高德根	Hokkien	1958–1964
Soon Peng Yam 孫炳炎	Hokkien	1965–1969
Wee Cho Yow 黃祖耀	Hokkien	1969–1973
Tan Keong Choon 陳共存	Hokkien	1973–1977
Wee Cho Yow 黃祖耀	Hokkien	1977–1979
Lim Kee Meng 林繼民	Teochew	1979–1983
Tan Keong Choon 陳共存	Hokkien	1983–1987
Linn In Hua 林蔭華	Hokkien	1987–1989
Tan Eng Joo 陳永裕	Hokkien	1989–1993

*Lien was elected in 1941, but the Japanese occupation of Singapore from 1942 meant the suspension of his term of office. He returned to Singapore and continued as president of the chamber in 1945.

Minority dialect groups, therefore, faced linguistic challenges within Singapore Chinese society because they spoke a language the majority of the community did not understand. The Henghuas and Hokchias, for instance, arrived in Singapore in the 1880s, and all available trades had been taken up by other groups. During the Japanese occupation, trishaws started to ply the streets of Singapore. The Singapore Hired Trishaw Riders Association was founded in 1950, and it remained an organization dominated by both groups until its closure in 1983. Out of 1,001 members from 1950 to 1976, the association had 429 Henghuas and 347 Hokchias—about 78 percent of the membership.[22] As both groups spoke mutually unintelligible languages, it was compulsory for a Henghua and a Hokchia committee member to be present at the association's office.[23]

"Speak Mandarin"

After Lee Kuan Yew was appointed prime minister in 1959, his government focussed on the greater use of English within a multiracial society to ensure effective communication between people of different ethnic backgrounds. Lee also downplayed his ethnicity by focusing on his nationality. In an interview on an episode of *Meet the Press* on October 22, 1967, a journalist commented that he was "speaking as a Chinese who understands China." Lee replied, "I can't speak as a Chinese because I am a Singaporean . . . with some of the built-in memory programming of the Chinese people."[24] Lee disliked the term "overseas Chinese." Before members of the Chinese Union of Journalists in September 1959, he told them:

> The term "Singapore Chinese" contains an element of chauvinism. In Singapore today there are still many organizations, guilds and schools using the term "Singapore Chinese" or "Overseas Chinese." The organisations registered under such names imply that they will protect the interests of the Chinese, and that other races are barred from joining them. Such terms are detrimental to racial unity.[25]

The government proclaimed four official languages for Singapore: English, Mandarin, Malay, and Tamil. English was the administrative language of government and commerce, while the other three languages were regarded as the mother tongue of the Chinese, Malays, and Indians, respectively. Greater emphasis was placed on English after independence in 1965. In 1966, the Wang Gungwu Report recommended that Nanyang University should have greater use of English and Malay in its curriculum. Wang insisted that the report promoted bilingualism, and it did not call for the end of the use of Mandarin as the medium of instruction.²⁶ In 1981, the Lee government went beyond the recommendations of the report and merged Nanyang University with the University of Singapore to form today's National University of Singapore. However, Chinese Singaporeans already had characteristics that dissociated them from ethnic Han in China. First, while they learned Mandarin if they had attended Chinese schools, they spoke other Sinitic languages outside school. Second, they would be familiar with basic English even if they did not speak it well. Third, they lived in a multiracial and multilingual society that the government wanted to maintain.

In the late 1970s, Lee suddenly decided to promote Mandarin for Chinese Singaporeans when he had been promoting multiracialism and the use of English in the previous decade. He admitted that as a primary school student, "Mandarin was totally alien to me, and unconnected with my life."²⁷ He started learning Mandarin in earnest during the Japanese occupation of Singapore from 1942 to 1945 to read the kanji characters in Japanese and to learn what he suddenly considered to be his language.²⁸ I believe the decision to promote Mandarin was the consequence of his first official visit to China in 1976, where the image of 800 million industrious Chinese left a deep impression on him.²⁹ It is no stretch of the imagination to assume that eight hundred million people could produce results if they spoke a common language. Michael Barr argues that Lee began a Sinicization campaign on February 10, 1978, with a speech to the Historical Society of Nanyang University. One of the themes of this speech was the need for Mandarin to replace all Chinese dialects.³⁰

The Speak Mandarin campaign was launched with great zeal. There were advertisements on radio, television, and newspapers calling on Chinese Singaporeans to stop using dialects and speak what the government considered

LYRICS:	TRANSLATION:
國家要進步，	The country must progress,
語言要溝通，	Language must be communicable,
就從今天起，	From today onwards,
大家說華語。	Let us speak Mandarin.
不分男和女，	Whether male or female,
不分老和少，	Whether old or young,
不再用方言，	Dialect will no longer be used,
大家說華語。	Let us speak Mandarin.
聽一聽，記一記，	Listen and remember,
開口說幾句，	Say a few words,
多情切，多便利，	It is closeness and convenient,
簡單又容易。	It is simple and easy.

to be the language of the Chinese—Mandarin. There was a constant message of "Speak more Mandarin and less dialects" (多講華語，少說方言) through a theme song that was constantly played over radio and television:

Programs using Cantonese from Hong Kong were dubbed into Mandarin. There was even a call for Chinese Singaporeans to "get rid" of their dialect accent when speaking Mandarin.[31] However, the passion, motivation, and drive to promote Mandarin over the other Sinitic languages was not enthusiastically welcomed by all Chinese Singaporeans. Students interviewed by the *Straits Times* a month after the launch of the campaign revealed a chasm over language—for example, while one student said that "it is shameful for a Chinese not to speak Mandarin," another believed "dialects are worth keeping" because "you know where your roots are."[32]

A book published the same month as the launch of the campaign asserts that Mandarin had been the lingua franca of Chinese Singaporeans since the 1930s and that "those who could not converse in it were considered uneducated."[33] The chairman of the Speak Mandarin Campaign of the Singapore Chinese Chamber of Commerce and Industry (SCCCI, the former SCCC) argued that dialects were "ineffective as a medium of communication," so Chinese Singaporeans should speak the "common language," Mandarin.[34] Letters written to the *Straits Times*, probably by English-educated Chinese Singaporeans, wondered aloud about the need to promote Mandarin when English was a common language for all races.

New reasons for the campaign were added over time. The initial reason for the campaign was the concern that, with the increasing use of English, Chinese Singaporeans could become too Westernised and forget their cultural roots. Yet, the government ignored the fact that Hokkien, Teochew, Cantonese, and other Sinitic languages were part of Chinese Singaporeans' cultural roots. Lee Kuan Yew also stressed that the promotion of Mandarin only targeted Chinese Singaporeans and that non-Chinese in Singapore should not see the campaign as an attack on the other three official languages. Indians were spared—Tamil was the official language even though there were Indians (for example, Punjabis, Gujarati, Malayalee, and Ceylonese) who did not speak that language. Lee also appeared not to know that while Malay was the official language, the Malay people included Javanese and Boyanese, who spoke their own language. In a public exchange, a concerned parent told Lee that "although you mentioned that the Malays do not have much problem about this, I think we do have because some of our Malay parents, our grandparents, still talk in their dialect."[35]

Later, government ministers stressed that the learning of Mandarin was a removal of a burden for children. They argued that schoolchildren who spoke dialect at home could not handle the stress of learning English and

Mandarin in schools. Therefore, dialects, deemed to be of low economic and social value, should be eradicated. From 1981 to 1991, Lee's government even insisted that Chinese names be recorded in *hanyu pinyin* rather than dialect.[36] First Deputy Prime Minister Goh Chok Tong—who did not learn Mandarin while at school—said:

> When they [parents] drop dialects in conversation with their children they are recognising that the continued use of dialects will add to the learning burden of their children. So most Chinese parents nowadays speak Mandarin with their children even before they go to kindergarten classes.[37]

Parents were strongly encouraged to communicate with their children using Mandarin. The 1980 census revealed that 71.7 percent of Chinese in Singapore spoke "Chinese dialects" to their parents and siblings, compared to 6.4 percent for Mandarin.[38] Lee Kuan Yew was adamant that "you cannot learn English and Mandarin and speak dialects at home at the same time—it's not possible . . . because it takes up more brain space."[39] Lee stopped giving speeches in Hokkien. Public events used Mandarin instead of dialects. The government also identified places where dialects were continuously used. In 1983, the Ministry of Culture published a booklet called *Names of Food Items Commonly Found in Hawker Centres and Market Places*, where standardized names of vegetables, meat, and cooked food in Mandarin were used to encourage the Singapore Chinese to switch to Mandarin. By 1986, the government became concerned over the preponderant use of Chinese dialects in hawker centers and the Seventh Month auctions. Senior Parliamentary Secretary Ho Kah Leong complained:

> Most of the Chinese who visit these places can speak Mandarin. As a habit or in order to accommodate the hawkers, however, they often speak dialect. Similarly, there are many hawkers who can speak Mandarin, but for the same reason they often continue to speak in dialect. This kind of mutual accommodation between the hawker and his customer in the use of dialect has become a *vicious circle* [sic].[40]

To prevent a "vicious circle," the Lee government produced another booklet, *Names of Items Commonly Found in Hawker Centres, Markets, Restaurants and Zhongyuan Jie Auctions*, that had 697 different items in Mandarin (Chinese characters and *hanyu pinyin*), English, and Malay, in 1986. The impatience of the government to enforce a Mandarin-speaking environment in Singapore was clearly seen when a senior parliamentary secretary said that those who thought it unnecessary to learn Mandarin had an "attitude problem."[41] Some of the Mandarin words spoken in Singapore, however, are different from those used in China, as they are translations of dialect or non-Chinese words. Earlier in this chapter, I mentioned that the Malay word for *market* (*pasar*) had become "pa-sat" in Hokkien; now it has been rendered "bāshā" (巴刹) in Mandarin. The Mandarin term for *cabbage* is "gāolìcài" (高麗菜), which is a written form of the Hokkien "ko-lě-chhài," and not "juǎnxīncài" (捲心菜).

In 1988, Lee Hsien Loong, the minister for trade and industry and Lee Kuan Yew's son, reported that 82 percent of clan associations in Singapore used Mandarin at their meetings (compared to 22 percent before 1979) and that 87 percent of Seventh Month auctions in 1987 used some Mandarin compared to 50 percent in 1986.[42] Lee Hsien Loong did not explain why dialect associations—founded precisely because of the Sinitic language used—should switch to Mandarin. There was little reason for these associations to exist if they were strongly discouraged from using their own language. Not surprisingly, the popularity of the dialect associations declined during the last years of the Lee era, causing Lee to worry about the declining cultural traditions of the Singapore Chinese and resulting in the formation of the Singapore Federation of Chinese Clan Associations (SFCCA) in December 1985. Ironically, since Hokkien was the dominant dialect, it was the chairman of the Hokkien, Huay Kuan (福建會館), who was given the responsibility of setting up the SFCCA.[43] The SFCCA was also seen to be a response by Chinese clan associations to the greater use of English in Singapore, the end of schools using only Mandarin as the medium of instruction, and the "Westernization" of the country through the mass media.[44] The government would use Mandarin to promote Chinese traditions and culture through the SFCCA.

The real tragedy of the Speak Mandarin campaign was the gulf in intergenerational communication. Dialect-speaking grandparents would not be able to converse with their grandchildren. It was the parents sandwiched between who had to act as translators. In his autobiography, Lee Kuan Yew recalls how he and his wife would see parents talking to their children in dialects, and then "they would look embarrassed and switch to Mandarin" when they noticed the Lees. He also believed that "most [grandparents] managed speaking to their grandchildren in dialect and understanding their replies in Mandarin." How he came to this conclusion was not evident in his autobiography.[45]

The rationale for speaking more Mandarin changed again after China embarked on its road of reform and opening up. It became the language to be used to tap an emerging market. With the view that China would soon play a major role in East and Southeast Asia, Lee's government sought to ensure that Chinese Singaporeans should maintain cultural and economic links with China. Minister of Trade and Industry Lee Hsien Loong said:

In recent years, Mandarin has also become more useful as a business language, especially in our dealings with other countries. As China's economy continues to open up and expand, Singaporean businessmen will have more opportunities to do business with China. Those who can speak Mandarin have a chance to trade all over China: those with only dialect will at best have an advantage dealing with one province.[46]

During the tenth anniversary of the campaign in 1989, Lee Kuan Yew said that if not for the campaign, "dialects would continue to dominate as the language of the home and of social discourse between Chinese . . . and the main dialect would have been Hokkien."[47] Lee Kuan Yew considered Chinese dialects, particularly Hokkien, as inferior and debased forms of Mandarin. He believed that "if Hokkien prevails, then the standard of written Chinese will go down." However, as Barr noted, the standard of written Chinese in Hong Kong remained high despite the widespread use of Cantonese.[48] Lee's prejudice against Hokkien is clearly seen when he called it a "vulgar" language with no writing system.[49] Hokkien does have a writing system as evident in Taiwan. Unlike Cantonese, which thrived in Hong Kong, Hokkien was not accepted by the Lee government despite its dominance. Lee told a journalist in 2005, "At the end of the day, it's (all about) the economic value" since "you need to learn enough to do business, to get along with the Chinese in China, because China is going to be economically a big player."[50]

Singapore Chinese Television Programs

In 1982, a drama unit was set up within the Singapore Broadcasting Corporation to produce Mandarin television series. The first television series, *The Flying Fish* (小飛魚), comprising eight episodes, was screened on television in 1983. The second television series, *The Army Series* (新兵小傳), comprising six episodes in 1983, portrayed the adventures (or misadventures) of a new batch of recruits who had been enlisted into the Singapore army for their national service. While there were Mandarin-speaking soldiers in real life, there were also conscripts who spoke Hokkien, earning themselves the nickname "Hok-kiàn-peng" (福建兵). This aspect of conscript life was ignored in the series.

However, it was *The Awakening* (霧鎖南洋) in 1984 that clearly signaled the government's disdain for the use of dialects. The series on the history of the Singapore Chinese community had two parts: The first covered the first half of the twentieth century to the end of the Japanese occupation of Singapore in 1945, and the second covered the period from 1945 to contemporary Singapore. The series was meant to raise awareness of nation-building in Singapore as 1984 marked the twenty-fifth anniversary of full autonomy for Singapore from the British (and twenty-five years of the Lee Kuan Yew government). Despite its attempts to portray the challenges faced by Chinese Singaporeans for nearly a century, the series used only Mandarin. It gave the false impression that every Chinese person who arrived in Singapore from Fujian and Guangdong spoke Mandarin. There were scenes of riots (especially in the second period from 1945 to 1984), but it was only between Mandarin-speaking Chinese students and workers fighting British-led riot police. In one scene, demonstrators facing off the riot police in the 1950s sang "Believe Me, Singapore!" (相信我吧，新加坡!). Not only was the song in Mandarin, but it did also not exist in the 1950s, as the song was composed for *The Army Series* the year before. The message from the series was that the unity of Chinese Singaporeans helped the community overcome all odds (conveniently glossing over the division and rivalry between dialect groups) as Singapore moved from being a colonial port toward nationhood.

Conclusion

The question of what constitutes the identity and heritage of Chinese Singaporeans has been a perennial issue since self-government was attained in 1959. Wang Gungwu believed that "during the first 150 years of Singapore history [from 1819], most of these Chinese considered themselves Chinese, and the question of Chineseness posed no problems for them."[51] However, the Chinese community was not a single ethnic group. It was divided by Sinitic languages that people spoke based on where their forefathers had been born in China. Each "dialect group" contributed to the economy and social fabric of Singapore through the control of various occupations and trades. By 1959, the dominant language of Chinese Singaporeans was Hokkien, largely through the dominance of the island's economy by Hokkien merchants.

In Taiwan, the Kuomintang regime promoted Mandarin at the expense of the Taiwanese language. While this is a case of cultural imperialism through the imposition of a language that originated from outside Taiwan, the promotion of Mandarin in Singapore is largely due to the beliefs of Lee Kuan Yew and the erroneous view that Mandarin has always been the lingua franca of Chinese Singaporeans. Lee never gave Hokkien the same measure of respect he had for Mandarin after his visit to China in 1976. He promoted a Speak Mandarin campaign from 1979, despite never using Mandarin prior to his entry into politics. His government, along with supportive newspaper journalists and Mandarin-speaking teachers and businesspeople, brushed off Hokkien as a crude version of Mandarin. The reality is that for Chinese Singaporeans, Sinitic languages other than Mandarin represent their heritage and identity. The government and Mandarin-speaking elites want Chinese Singaporeans to speak the language of ethnic Han in China. As Ng Kim Chew remarked, "The study of Mandarin is actually the study of a foreign language" in Singapore.[52] Ng correctly noted that the issue is also about the written form of the language—while there is a Mandarin script, the other spoken Sinitic languages have not been written down, "forever banished from the writing system."[53] There has been no written Hokkien because official documents—including records held by the various Chinese associations—are recorded by individuals who had received some education in Mandarin.

The Chinese in Singapore is a Sinophone community. Their roots are in Singapore, and their forefathers did not speak Mandarin unless they had attended Chinese schools. The Lee government from 1959 worked hard to remove the "overseas Chinese" or "Chinese diaspora" tags by encouraging Chinese Singaporeans to think of Singapore as their homeland and not China. Shih wrote that the tag of "diaspora" should expire after about three hundred years, and then "everyone should be given a chance to become a local."[54] While the Chinese in neighboring Malaysia are "perpetually foreign" due to racial discrimination,[55] Lee wanted the "overseas Chinese" label removed quickly as part of building a multiracial nation. Yet, Lee's government worked feverishly to promote the use of Mandarin and push aside the use of other Sinitic languages that were rooted in the migrant experience in Singapore.

Shih once wrote that "the Sinophone is a place-based, everyday practice and experience, and thus it is a historical formation that constantly undergoes transformation that reflects local needs and conditions."[56] Despite the use of Mandarin in official records, the issues discussed within the associations and clans relate mostly to issues within Singapore. These records are a valuable source for a historical study of Singapore, not China. Older records reflected overseas Chinese nationalism simply because there was no Singapore citizenship until 1957. By default, any Chinese person was a citizen of China. By 1990, when Lee left office, his government had completely changed what was normal for Chinese Singaporeans from "Sinophone multilingualism" to Mandarin.[57] However, Sinitic languages other than Mandarin continued to thrive after Lee left office. In 1991, the Workers' Party candidate in the Hougang constituency, Low Thia Khiang, won the seat in the general elections by speaking Teochew at rallies. He defeated the candidate from the ruling People's Action Party who could not speak Teochew. The SCCCI only changed its constitution to ensure Mandarin as its working language on August 10,

1993. For an organization that enthusiastically supported the Speak Mandarin campaign, it took a surprisingly long time to effect this change within the chamber. Major Sinitic languages, such as Hokkien, Teochew, and Cantonese, still thrive because Mandarin is not the foundation of Chinese Singaporean heritage.

Notes

1. Jason Lim, "The Education Concerns and Political Outlook of Lim Keng Lian (1893–1968)," *Journal of Chinese Overseas* 3, no. 2 (2007): 196–197; and Yen Ching-Hwang, *Ethnicities, Personalities and Politics in the Ethnic Chinese Worlds* (Singapore: World Scientific, 2016), 188–190.

2. Shih Shu-Mei, "Introduction: What is Sinophone Studies?" *Sinophone Studies: A Critical Reader*, ed. Shu-Mei Shih, Chien-Hsin Tsai and Brian Bernards (New York: Columbia University Press, 2013), 11.

3. Michael Barr, *Lee Kuan Yew: The Beliefs Behind the Man* (Richmond, Surrey: Curzon Press, 2000), 172.

4. Phyllis Ghim-Lian Chew, *A Sociolinguistic History of Early Identities in Singapore: From Colonialism to Nationalism* (New York: Palgrave Macmillan, 2013), 98–103.

5. Yen Ching-hwang, *Community and Politics: The Chinese in Colonial Singapore and Malaya* (Singapore: Times Academic Press, 1995); Yen Ching-Hwang, *The Ethnic Chinese in East and Southeast Asia: Business, Culture and Politics* (Singapore: Times Academic Press, 2002); C. F. Yong, *Chinese Leadership and Power in Colonial Singapore* (Singapore: Times Academic Press, 1992); and C. F. Yong, *Tan Kah-Kee: The Making of an Overseas Chinese Legend* (Singapore: Oxford University Press, 1987).

6. Cui Guiqiang 崔貴強, *Xinjiapo Huaren—Cong Kaibu Dao Jianguo* (新加坡華人～從開埠到建國) (The Chinese in Singapore: Past and present) (Singapore: Singapore Federation of Chinese Clan Associations and EPB Publishers, 1994).

7. Liu Hong 劉宏, *Zhanhou Xinjiapo Huaren Sheui De Shanbian: Bentu Qinghuai, Quyu Wangluo, Quanqiu Shiye* (戰後新加坡華人社會的嬗變:本土情懷、區域網絡、全球視野) (The transformation of Chinese society in postwar Singapore: Localizing process, regional networking and global perspective) (Xiamen: Xiamen University Press, 2003), 41–79.

8. M. V. Del Tufo, *A Report on the 1947 Census of Population* (London: Crown Agents for the Colonies, 1949), 75.

9. Chiew Seen Kong, "The Chinese in Singapore: From Colonial Times to the Present," in *Southeast Asian Chinese: The Socio-Cultural Dimension*, ed. Leo Suryadinata (Singapore: Times Academic Press, 1995), 45.

10. Yong, *Tan Kah-Kee*, 232.

11. Chiew, "The Chinese in Singapore," 44–45.

12. Chen Dung-Sheng, "Taiwan's Social Changes in the Patterns of Social Solidarity in the 20th Century," in *Taiwan in the Twentieth Century: A Retrospective View*, ed. Richard Louis Edmonds and Steven M Goldstein (Cambridge: Cambridge University Press, 2001), 68.

13. Chiew, "The Chinese in Singapore," 48.

14. Cheng Lim Keak, *Social Change and the Chinese in Singapore: A Socio-Economic Geography with Special Reference to Bang Structure* (Singapore: Singapore University Press, 1985), 23.

15. Ou Rubo (區如柏), *Zuxian De Hangye* (祖先的行業) (Trades of our ancestors) (Singapore: Seng Yew Book Store, 1991); and Thomas Tsu-Wee Tan, *Chinese Dialect Groups: Traits and Trades* (Singapore: Opinion Books, 1990).

16. Jason Lim, *Linking an Asian Transregional Commerce in Tea: Overseas Chinese Merchants in the Fujian-Singapore Trade, 1920–1960* (Leiden: Brill, 2010), 163–187.

17. Singapore Piece Goods Traders Guild, *Xinjiapo Buhang Shangwuju Qingzhu Chengli Bashiwu Zhounian Jinian Tekan* (新加坡布行商務局慶祝成立八十五週年紀念特刊) (85th anniversary souvenir magazine of the Singapore Piece Goods Traders Guild) (Singapore: Singapore Piece Goods Traders Guild, 1993), 101.

18. Chew, *A Sociolinguistic History*, 98; Eddie C. Y. Kuo, "The Speak Mandarin Campaign," in *A General History of the Chinese in Singapore*, ed. Kwa Chong Guan and Kua Bak Lim (Singapore: Singapore Federation of Chinese Clan Associations and World Scientific, 2019), 736.

19. Zhou Changji (周長楫) and Zhou Qinghai (周清海), *Xinjiapo Minnanhua Gaikuang* (新加坡閩南話概況) (Overview of Singapore Hokkien) (Xiamen: Xiamen Daxue Chubanshe, 2000); Zhou Changji (周長楫) and Zhou Qinghai (周清海), *Xinjiapo Minnanhua Cidian* (新加坡閩南話詞典) (Dictionary of Singapore Hokkien) (Beijing: Zhongguo Shehui Kexue Chubanshe, 2002).

20. Cheng Lim Keak, "Pang Trade Specialization in Singapore," in *Review of Southeast Asian Studies (Nanyang Quarterly)*, 8 (1978): 19.

21. Chew, *A Sociolinguistic History*, 98.

22. Jason Lim, *A Slow Ride into the Past: The Chinese Trishaw Industry in Singapore, 1942–1983* (Clayton, Vic.: Monash University Publishing, 2013), 132.

23. Lim, *A Slow Ride into the Past*, 50.

24. Lawrence E. Spivak, "Meet the Press," National Archives of Singapore, October 22, 1967, https://nas.gov.sg/archivesonline/data/pdfdoc/lky19671022.pdf.

25. Lee Kuan Yew "Precis of the Prime Minister's Speech to the Chinese Union of Journalists on Tuesday, 1 September 1959," National Archives of Singapore, September 1, 1959, https://www.nas.gov.sg/archivesonline/data/pdfdoc/lky19590901.pdf.

26. Hong Lysa and Huang Jianli, *The Scripting of A National History: Singapore and Its Pasts* (Singapore: NUS Press, 2008), 133.

27. Lee Kuan Yew, *The Singapore Story: Memoirs of Lee Kuan Yew* (Singapore: Marshall Cavendish Editions and Straits Times Press, 1998), 35.

28. Li Guangyao 李光耀 (Lee Kuan Yew), *Li Guangyao, Wo Yisheng De Tiaozhan: Xinjiapo Shuangyu Zhilu* (李光耀,我一生的挑戰:新加坡雙語之路) (Lee Kuan Yew, my lifelong challenge: Singapore's bilingual journey) (Singapore: Lianhe Zaobao, 2012), 22.

29. Cheong Yip Seng, "Lee: I Carry Back A Great Experience," *New Nation*, May 23, 1976.

30. Barr, *Lee Kuan Yew*, 158.

31. Tan Ban Huat, "How to Get Rid of the Dialect Accent in Your Mandarin," *Straits Times*, November 19, 1979, section 2.

32. Lulin Reutens and Leong Weng Kam, "Dropping Dialects An Easy Decision," *Straits Times*, October 15, 1979.

33. Tan Ban Huat, "Mandarin Becomes the Lingua Franca of the Chinese Here . . .," *Straits Times Bilingual Collection*, vol. 1 (Singapore: Federal Publications, 1979), 44–47.

34. Lee Chin Chuan, "One Common Language for Chinese Vital," *Straits Times*, December 4, 1987.

35. "Fostering Mandarin to 'Converse Across the Dialects,'" *Straits Times*, April 8, 1978.

36. Michael Barr and Zlatko Skrbiš, *Constructing Singapore: Elitism, Ethnicity and the Nation-Building Project* (Copenhagen: NIAS Press, 2008), 98.

37. Goh Chok Tong, "Singapore Government Press Release: Speech by Mr Goh Chok Tong, First Deputy Prime Minister and Minister for Defence, at the launching of the Speak Mandarin campaign at the Singapore Conference Hall on Thursday, 2 October 1986," National Archives of Singapore, October 2, 1986, https://nas.gov.sg/archivesonline/data/pdfdoc/gct19861002s.pdf.

38. Khoo Chian Kim, *Census of Population 1980, Singapore, Release No. 8: Languages Spoken at Home* (Singapore: Department of Statistics, 1981), 4.

39. Chua Chee Lay, ed., *Keeping My Mandarin Alive: Lee Kuan Yew's Language Learning Experience* (Singapore: World Scientific Publishing and Global Publishing, 2005), 30–31.

40. Ho Kah Leong, "Singapore Government Press Release: Speech by Mr Ho Kah Leong, Senior Parliamentary Secretary (Communications and Information), at the launching of the Booklet on 'Names of Items Commonly Found in Hawker Centres, Markets, Restaurants and Zhongyuan Jie Auctions' in Mandarin at the PSA Towers Auditorium on Tuesday, 15 July 1986," National Archives of Singapore, July 15, 1986, https://nas.gov.sg/archivesonline/data/pdfdoc/hkl19860715s.pdf (my emphasis).

41. "Mandarin Drive: Small Group Has Attitude Problem," *Straits Times*, October 26, 1987.

42. Lee Hsien Loong, "Singapore Government Press Release: Speech by the Minister for Trade and Industry, BG Lee Hsien Loong, at the launching ceremony of the Speak Mandarin campaign at the Singapore Conference Hall on 3 October 1988," National Archives of Singapore, October 3, 1988, https://nas.gov.sg/archivesonline/data/pdfdoc/lhl19881003s.pdf.

43. Pang Cheng Lian, "Singapore Federation of Chinese Clan Associations: Revitalising Clan Associations," in *50 Years of the Chinese Community in Singapore*, ed. Pang Cheng Lian (Singapore: World Scientific, 2016), 33.

44. Lin Yuanfu (林源福), "1985-1990 Nian Shiduan Gaishu (1985-1990年時段概述) (Events from 1985 to 1990)," in *Huigu 25: Zongxiang Zonghua Ershiwu Zhounian Wenji* (回顧25: 宗鄉總會二十五周年文輯) (Collection of articles on the twenty-fifth anniversary of the Singapore Federation of Chinese Clan Associations), ed. Li Zhuoran (李焯然) (Singapore: Singapore Federation of Chinese Clan Associations, 2010), 32.

45. Lee Kuan Yew, *From Third World to First—The Singapore Story: 1965–2000* (Singapore: Marshall Cavendish Editions and the Straits Times Press, 2006), 180.

46. Lee, "Singapore Government Press Release."

47. Lee Kuan Yew "Speech by Prime Minister Lee Kuan Yew at the Launching Ceremony of the 'Speak Mandarin Campaign' at the Singapore Conference Hall on Tuesday, 3 October 1989," National Archives of Singapore, October 3, 1989, https://www.nas.gov.sg/archivesonline/data/pdfdoc/lky19891003.pdf.

48. Barr, *Lee Kuan Yew*, 159.

49. Li, *Li Guangyao*, 148.

50. Chua, *Keeping My Mandarin Alive*, 103.

51. Wang Gungwu, "Chineseness: The Dilemmas of Place and Practice," in *Sinophone Studies: A Critical Reader*, ed. Shu-Mei Shih, Chien-Hsin Tsai, and Brian Bernards (New York: Columbia University Press, 2013), 139.

52. Ng Kim Chew, "Sinophone/Chinese: 'The South Where Language Is Lost' and Reinvented," in Shih, Tsai, and Bernards, *Sinophone Studies*, 84.

53. Ng, "Sinophone/Chinese," 88.

54. Shih Shu-Mei, "The Concept of the Sinophone," *PMLA* 126, no. 3 (2011): 714.

55. Shu-Mei Shih, "Against Diaspora: The Sinophone as Places of Cultural Production," in Shih, Tsai, and Bernards, *Sinophone Studies*, 28.

56. Shih, "Against Diaspora," 33.

57. Shih, "Introduction," 7.

Adaptation and Identity Building Among the Ethnic Chinese Communities in Vietnam

A View from Ritual Transformation in Popular Religion

THO NGOC NGUYEN

The ethnic Chinese in Vietnam have a long history of living in the country and have experienced several ups and downs in history. Early on, they understood that integration was the only way to survive and rise in Vietnam. As a culturally defined group, Vietnamese Chinese are now looking for a plausible form of identity as younger generations no longer speak their mother tongues (various Sinitic languages, such as Cantonese, Teochiu, Hokkien, Hakka, Hainan, Ngái, and others).

Shih, Chiang, Chen, and others have established the concept of "Sinophone Studies," with an emphasis on the studies in Chinese communities and their culture outside of the People's Republic of China (PRC) under colonial and postcolonial influences as well as non-Han communities within the PRC and their separate sociocultural development.[1] Scholars such as Rey Chow, Wei-ming Tu, Ha Jin, Ien Ang, Leo Ou-fan Lee, David Wang, Howard Chiang and Alvin K. Wong, etc. have debated on the ontology, structure, sphere, and future of Sinophone studies,[2] while others, such as Gosling, Groppe, Chia and Hoogervorst, and others, directly showcase and discuss the locally born Sinophone sociocultural achievements in Southeast Asia.[3] Research on the ethnic Chinese in Vietnam has long been an academic interest of many scholars (such as Amer, Cooke and Li Chen, Lay, Barrett, Lee, Wheeler, Chan, Nguyen, etc.[4]); however, study from the perspective of Sinophone studies is still a rather new issue and is not enough to paint a complete picture of Vietnamese Chinese culture and its dynamism.

This study synthesizes the viewpoints and research results of the above-mentioned authors on the Vietnamese Chinese, uses field data in the field of cultural studies, and conducts case studies on the symbols and worship of Guandi and Tianhou of the Vietnamese Chinese to demonstrate their views that the Vietnamese Chinese are on their way to shaping their incorporate culture in line with today's Sinophone world. Current research shows that Vietnamese Chinese are actively selecting their own traditional cultural landscapes to build an adaptive ethnic culture—thus vividly demonstrating their wisdom in dealing with the dual goals of social integration and evolution.

Guandi and Tianhou: The Standardized God and Goddess

Standardizing gods has been an important part of East Asian traditions where late imperial rulers strived to tighten and maximize their control over the populations. The study of standardization and orthopraxy in late imperial China has been long discussed and modified by many scholars, such as David K. Jordan, Arthur P. Wolf, James L. Waston, Steven P. Sangren, Liu Zhiwei, Guo Qitao, Richard von Glahn, Donald Sutton, Kenneth Pomeranz, Michael Szonyi, Paul Kartz, David Faure, etc.[5] In their research on the profane power of gods, David K. Jordan and Arthur Wolf affirmed that gods possessed sanctified and worldly powers since the imperial center bestowed them titles, so their images and temples presented iconographic significance with magistrates and bureaucrats.[6]

As demonstrated, the developing and divergent meaning attributed to Guandi and Tianhou was rooted in the very process of late imperial China's standardization policies. As James Watson noted, the "state, aided by a literate elite, sought to bring locals under its influence by co-opting certain popular local deities and guaranteeing that they carried 'all the right messages . . . civilization, order, and loyalty to the state.'"[7] The standardization process, however, was primarily concerned with procedure and ritual acts,[8] much less so with belief and specific meaning. Hence, different social groups could attribute very different meanings to a goddess like Tianhou. The late imperial Chinese states strongly supported standardized cults and rituals based on the view that ritual orthopraxy could be a powerful force for cultural homogenization.[9] While Feuchtwang called this action an "imperial metaphor," Duara dubbed it "superscription."[10] As described by Jordan, gods carry both sacred and profane powers; people worship gods because of their holy efficacy and because they are closely connected to bureaucrats in secular life through the titles bestowed by worldly emperors.[11] Rawski also stressed that in the unification of cultural practices (economic prosperity, educational system, and unified writing system), Chinese culture had become highly integrated.[12]

Many charismatic individuals with "exceptional qualities" in Chinese history evolved into sanctified figures through the process of deification and orthopraxy.[13] Paul Katz similarly emphasized that imperial China gained cultural integration in part thanks to the standardization of culture, such as the promotion of approved deities like Tianhou by state authorities and local elites.[14] Prasenjit Duara used another term to describe such a standardization process, "the superscription," which affirmed that the continuous and discontinuous superscription of Guandi by late imperial emperors accelerated this symbol into a nationwide leading god, thus becoming a special means of state control, which Valerie Hansen called "mechanism of control."[15] Symbolic practices in premodern China, like the cults of Guandi and Tianhou, are undoubtedly the key means of cultural integration, strongly fostered for political purposes by the state and its agents. According to Sutton, state-sanctioned symbols "produced a high degree of cultural unity, transcending social differences in mythic interpretation and variant local ritual practice," which Burkert called "[the] partial reference to something of collective importance."[16] This is undoubtedly the result of orthopraxy, which actively spread the knowledge of national practices and institutions to every village at the grassroots level. Under this policy, local elites and religious specialists "hold rituals to assert the legitimacy of their own interests, even when confronted with state hegemony."[17]

However, the standardization process sometimes turned out to be "pseudo-orthopraxy." Michael Szonyi dubbed it "the illusion of standardizing the gods."[18] Accordingly, under the imperial orthopractic agenda, members of the Five Emperors cult in Fujian adopted the sanctioned cult of Five Manifestations from nearby Jiangxi Province as the "surface" for the unchanged tradition of the local community; however, local elites stood between local officials and local commoners. They flexibly worked for both the will of the state and local interests. Donald Sutton called these pseudo-orthopractic performers "the Janus-faced local elites."[19] Normally, standardization and superscription don't erase older meanings but rather add new elements and interpretative ideas to the symbol, turning them into the so-called interpretive arena of the myth, which comes "to be negotiated and redefined."[20]

In feudal Vietnam, Lê (1428–1527) and Nguyễn (1802–1945) dynasties provided the policy of sanctioning and standardizing the gods as the courts tried to strengthen their authority in each village.[21] However, such processes became degrading and finally ended when the French colonialists imposed their Western mode of control in the late nineteenth century. After 1954,

Vietnam built a socialist nation on the ideological basis of Marxism, and traditional cults and mythical figures were downplayed and decomposed. After the 1986 Đổi Mới policy,[22] the state turned to invest in the so-called national cultural identity, which opened a new pathway for festival traditions, marking the return of mythical gods and spirits.[23]

Though standardized, Chinese culture contained multiple "interpretative areas" where meanings, normative principles, and ways of being were not only imposed by rulers but also contested by commoners who fought to maintain their own lived experience and wisdom of daily life within the shared cultural canon. This was especially so when Chinese cultural symbols were "exported" beyond the boundaries of China. Chinese symbols have, consequently, undergone change and transformation in their journey across East-Asian cultures and civilizations. Ethnic Chinese migrants to Vietnam thus took their traditional culture with them, which served not only as a source of power but also as a medium through which their status was transformed from that of "sojourning aliens" into a "minority group."[24] In the process, the Chinese in Vietnam profoundly changed their way of life and their culture to be accepted within society. At times suffering from domestic repression in the wake of continual dynastic conflicts, they nevertheless integrated into Vietnamese society, producing new cultural forms, some of which we shall explore here.[25]

Guandi (AD 162–220; 關帝, in Vietnamese: Quan Đế), was originally known as Guan Yu (關羽 Quan Vũ) before he received the imperial title Di (帝) by the Ming emperor in 1615 when he was apotheosized as a hero of the period of the Three Kingdoms in China. Chen Shou depicted briefly and vaguely Guan Yu's life in *Sanguozhi* [三國志] sixty years after his death.[26] Prasenjit Duara wrote in his research that "there are references to his vanity, overconfidence, and ignorance on matters of strategy."[27] As a matter of fact, the apotheosized orthopraxy purposively removed these uneasy features of personality.

Guandi was adopted and adapted to many religious settings and millenarian movements, including Confucianism, Buddhism, Daoism, Secret Society (天地會), White Lotus Sect (白蓮教), Taiping Tianguo (太平天國), and others. In Buddhism, Guandi is called Qie Lan pusa (伽藍菩薩 Già Lam Bồ-tát), a protector god of monasteries and temples.[28] Daoism also adopted him as their protector god, especially during the Song (960–1279).[29]

According to Huang Huajie, due to the rise of self-sufficient kin-based communities during the Qing dynasty (1644–1911), Guan Yu faded in local tradition, and he was further superscribed to become a symbol of state loyalty and guardianship. He "inspired an ethic of trust and camaraderie holding together "a society of strangers."[30]

During continuous times of superscription in late imperial China, Guandi became the god of loyalty as well as the god of wealth, the god of literature, the protector god of temples, and the patron god of actors, secret societies, and many others.[31] It is a matter of fact that during the rebellious and warfare times, Guandi was promoted as the symbol of loyalty, righteousness, and comradeship; however, in peaceful times, he was interpreted as the figure who brought luck and practiced exorcism. One may not be surprised when confronting the statue of Guandi in the reception place of a restaurant or a shopping mall in Beijing or Shanghai today. He is popularly known as the god of wealth in modern times.

Tianhou Goddess (in Vietnamese: Thiên Hậu) is a legendary goddess who was originally a shaman woman named Lin Moniang (林默娘). She lived in Fujian during the Song dynasty and used her legendary power to rescue seafarers offshore. After she died at the age of twenty-eight, she was worshipped as a sea goddess by local fishermen and devotees. To strengthen administrative centralization in marginal areas, such as Fujian and Guangdong, the Song emperor started the process of orthopraxy by offering her the title of lady (夫人). The Yuan dynasty then upgraded her title to heavenly concubine (天妃), and the Qing Kangxi emperor sanctioned her as the heavenly empress (Tianhou 天后).[32] Watson added, "by virtue of imperial sponsorship, she eventually became the leading goddess in South China."[33]

The cult of Tianhou followed Chinese merchants and migrants arriving in southern Vietnam in the late seventeenth century.[34] Tianhou is currently worshipped largely by the local Chinese (in Vietnamese: người Hoa) in the Saigon area and the Mekong River Delta. Our fieldwork survey during 2014–2016 shows that there are around 150 Tianhou temples nationwide. The Saigon region has forty-eight temples, while the Mekong River Delta is home to seventy-five temples. Most of the temples are built and operated by the ethnic Teochiu, followed by the Cantonese.[35] The Hokkien, Hainanese, and Hakka each possess three to five temples. Local Vietnamese started adopting the cult during the middle of the twentieth century; consequently, at least eighteen Tianhou temples are found in Saigon and the Mekong River regions. In addition, Tianhou is also coworshipped in around one hundred temples dedicated to Guandi, Xuan Tian Shang Di (玄天上帝), and other gods across the region.[36]

The implication of the Tianhou goddess has greatly changed over the last centuries. She is no longer a sea protector but a land protector, a goddess of blessing, fertility, and wealth in the popular culture of Vietnam (in both the Hoa's and the Viet's traditions). Even though there are dozens of temples built and operated by the Vietnamese, Tianhou is dominantly worshipped by the ethnic Chinese, while Guandi is fairly adored by both ethnic groups. Regarding the difference, I hold the hypothesis that gender, state-sanctioning, and historical embodiment are the main reasons causing the difference.[37]

Both Guandi and Tianhou became part of Vietnamese culture in a process that saw their meanings enhanced, somewhat changed, and with added layers of association and significance—the product of the interpretive schemes brought to their understanding by generations of traditional elites. While these additional meanings did not erase nor negate traditional ones, they did change the place of the gods in the lexicon of social life. Thus, the symbol of Guandi was soon adopted by the Vietnamese elite and government officials to become a critical tool in the creation of national solidarity and, eventually, the spirit of insurrection for a part of the Vietnamese people in the face of Western colonial rule. Tianhou herself, having been standardized by several Chinese emperors prior to the Chinese arrival in Vietnam, was less actively adopted and superscribed by the local Vietnamese. Rather, she was empowered by the ethnic Chinese to become an important identity marker of their unique social and cultural project.

Guandi was, in fact, not able to retain the classical Chinese-style interpretative meanings in his move to Vietnam. Unsure whether to retain or discard attributed meanings to Guandi, the ethnic Chinese in Vietnam eventually accepted him as a symbol of their own integration into Vietnamese society and shared life as a Vietnamese Chinese people (the Hoa of Vietnam). In short, he was de-sinicized and lost his identity-marking character. In contrast, they made Tianhou the symbol of their own identity.

As Clough and Michell conclude, the belief in gods and evils has strengthened in parallel with the rise of modernity.[38] In particular, Keyes, Hardacre, and Kendall argued that East and Southeast Asian countries have deepened into the process of modernization, and "religion has become more, not less, significant."[39] The overseas Chinese brought the profound worldview of gods and evils coexisting to both Vietnam and Southeast Asia. This feature has strongly resonated with the indigenous tradition.

In this paper, we shall explore how Guandi and Tianhou were superscribed by Chinese emperors and how they were transformed into the premodern Vietnamese culture. We will further explore how these transformations reflected the social and psychological aspects of the Hoa people in Vietnam. Finally, we will analyze how the local Vietnamese and ethnic Chinese people made use of these symbols to jointly cross the historical boundaries between Vietnamese and Chinese identities, managing to maintain the dualistic goals of both identity building and national integration.

Ethnic Boundaries As a Historical Legacy in Vietnam

During the mid-twentieth century, the ethnic Chinese experienced an uneasy life that was mainly caused by the historical vulnerability of the Vietnamese people and the serious diplomatic relationship between Vietnam and the PRC. The ethnic Chinese were inactively kept sandwiched between two forces, which generated their cultural vitality and adaptive capacity.

Vietnam was invaded by the Chinese troops many times during its history and was directly ruled during the periods of 111 BCE–938 CE and 1407–1428 CE. This historical vulnerability strongly affected the way Vietnamese behaved toward Chinese people and Chinese-rooted legacies.

Vietnam itself was modeled on the Chinese polity, being culturally influenced by the Chinese and always threatened by it politically. Joseph Buttinger elaborated on this paradoxical relationship: "The more they (Vietnamese) absorbed of the skills, customs, and ideas of the Chinese, the smaller grew the likelihood of their ever becoming part of the Chinese people."[40] According to Holmgren, the first six centuries of Chinese rule in North Vietnam saw more "Vietnamization" of local Chinese than Sinicization of Indigenous Viets.[41] Many Chinese clans "settled into, helped modify, and were finally absorbed into the social, economic and political environment in northern Vietnam."[42] Vietnamese culture took on a deep Chinese coloration, but the ethnic character of the people continued to be Yueh (越), that is, *Viet*, and they inherited and cherished that consciousness of difference in race and desire for separate nationhood (which, in a modified form, has always characterized their more assimilated cousins, the Cantonese.[43]

The Chinese immigrants in Vietnam were generally accepted if they could prove that they wished to permanently settle down in Vietnam. Otherwise, they were subject to strict management regulations for reasons of national defense.

In the Early Le dynasty (980–1009), the Ly dynasty (1009–1225), and the Tran dynasty (1225–1400), the Vietnamese authorities applied a half-hearted policy toward this migrant group. The state was willing to employ talented Chinese migrants who intended to settle down and contribute to the country of Vietnam, but they kept suspicion and applied strict management of foreign traders who came for short-term business activities to prevent the disclosure of national secrets.

According to a Japanese researcher, Fujiwara Riichiro, many Chinese scholars and military talents were recruited as literature mandarins or commanders of the army in Vietnam, where they could introduce the Chinese ideological system and civilization, favoring the Vietnamese state.[44] Vietnamese kings welcomed the Chinese businessmen and ordered local authorities to set up alien shelters in Nha Bi Ward in the Imperial Citadel of Thăng Long and Phố Hiến town.⁴⁵

For the later Le dynasty (1428–1789), after the expulsion of the Ming armies, the wounds in the relationship with China were not yet healed, which heavily affected the policy relating to overseas Chinese immigrants.⁴⁶ In *Ức Trai Thi Tập*, Nguyễn Trãi recorded the fact that King Le forbade overseas Chinese from freely going out and entering the capital. They had to stay in coastal ports such as Vân Đồn, Vạn Ninh, Cần Hải, Hội Thống, Hội Triều, Thông Lĩnh, Phú Lương, Tam Kỳ, and Trúc Hoa.⁴⁷ The Le dynasty imposed strict regulations on the Chinese regardless of whether they intended to settle down and contribute to Vietnam, as they felt that Vietnamese intellectuals were qualified enough to participate in national political activities without overseas Chinese assistance.⁴⁸

Mid-sixteenth-century Vietnam was split into two kingdoms: the Tonkin (Đàng Ngoài) in the north and the Cochinchina (Đàng Trong) in the south. The Cochinchinese started expanding southward as far as the Mekong River Delta in the next two centuries. In Tonkin, Trinh Lords strictly regulated foreigners even if they kept their customs and clothing, banning overseas Vietnamese from living with the Vietnamese.⁴⁹ However, the Nguyen Lords in Cochinchina treated overseas Chinese with kindness and employed them for the purpose of territorial reclamation, economic opening, and international trade development. The Hokkien traders followed the Japanese to set up their living quarters in Hội An in the late seventeenth century, which has been called "the first Minh Hương village" in Cochinchina. In 1669, a Qing Mandarin named Yu Jin reported to emperor Kang Xi (Khang Hy) that "millions of the Chinese evacuated to some refuges (in Cochinchina). Among them, there were many traitors who joined the army to get appointed to some mandarin positions to survive."⁵⁰ Later, after the fall of Zheng Chenggong (鄭成功) in Taiwan Straits, Zheng's viceroys, Mạc Cửu (莫玖), Dương Ngạn Địch (楊彥迪), and Trần Thượng Xuyên (陳上川) asked to reclaim lands in Đồng Nai—Saigon, Mỹ Tho, and Hà Tiên in the Mekong region in 1670s–1980s.⁵¹

In 1698, the Nguyen Lords recognized Minh Hương as "a minority elite,"⁵² inviting famous Chinese monks⁵³ to come to do faith propagation in Cochinchina.⁵⁴

The Tây Sơn dynasty (1789–1802) severely repressed overseas Chinese due to its aversion that overseas Chinese supported Nguyễn Ánh Lord to fight against them. The Tây Sơn attacked Hội An, Đồng Nai, Saigon, and Mỹ Tho during the 1780s, although the state recruited members of Chinese secret societies (天地會) and pirates (such as Tập Đình/習廷 Xi Ting, Lý Tài/李才 Li Cai) to work for them.⁵⁵

The Nguyen dynasty enforced strict citizenship policy and administrative management, but in general, they still favored the overseas Chinese.[56] It is a historical fact that Chinese immigrants owed the Nguyen lords for their resettlement from previous generations; therefore, in the Tây Sơn and Nguyễn Ánh battles, the majority of Chinese people supported Nguyễn Ánh.[57] In 1788, Nguyễn Ánh in Saigon ordered the registration of all the old and new Chinese residents, allowing them to join one of the total five congregations, levied the tax, and forced them to serve the nation as soldiers or civilians.[58] This policy was later abolished.[59] In 1827, Emperor Minh Mang changed the name "Minh Hương" (明香) to "Minh Hương" (明鄉), thus opening and promoting the process of localization among the overseas Chinese.[60] Since then, the Ming Hương people ceased to respect loyalty to the Ming but shifted their focus to ethnicity building, forming a minority elite among the Vietnamese and the overseas Chinese.[61] In 1898, on that basis, King Thành Thái abolished the remnants of Minh Hương village, transforming them completely into Vietnamese identity.[62] In general, the Nguyen dynasty showed a preference for them, but they always had to worry about their contacts with China.[63]

During Western colonialism, the French first put the Chinese community on the periphery, eliminating their intermediary role between Vietnam and China. Thus, unlike other colonies in Southeast Asia, where empires made full use of Chinese communities for business and relationships with the Qing dynasty, the French reduced their influence in Vietnam.[64] French colonists then sharpened the ethnic Chinese dialectic divergence by applying the "divide to rule" policy, which was also continued under Ngô Đình Diệm's reign in the Saigon regime in the 1950s–1960s. Many Chinese communities joined the Vietnamese in anti-French uprising movements but then became apart from the local community because of the colonial policies and manipulation.[65]

Contemporary Vietnam witnessed many ups and downs due to the Indochina wars, deeply affecting the ethnic Chinese community in the country. The Chinese were encouraged to apply for Vietnamese citizenship in northern Vietnam from 1954 to 1975, thanks to the smooth agreement between the Vietnamese state leader and Chinese Prime Minister Zhou Enlai (周恩來) in 1956. In the south, the Saigonese government announced a number of laws to restrain the Chinese's trade capacity and promote application for Vietnamese citizenship.[66] As a matter of fact, the local Chinese in Saigon were always creative and capable of encountering and overcoming the imposing policies; they had enough economic impact to shut down the city's commercial, industrial, and banking systems.[67] The postwar period of 1975–1986 also instilled in the ethnic Chinese a feeling of deep vulnerability, as they were targeted as capitalists, "the fifth column," and impotently caught in the middle of the uneasy Sino-Vietnamese bilateral relations, which led to a large-scale ethnic Chinese exodus by ship and boat from Vietnam during the period.[68] After the 1986 Đổi mới (reform), the ethnic Chinese's economic life was restored. They enjoyed the full rights and obligations of Vietnamese citizens.[69] However, traumatic experience and distrust prevailed, which directly restrained the transracial solidarity in the country.

Nevertheless, postwar ethnic Chinese are striving toward integration and development. Wi-vun Taiffalo Chiung affirmed that this was the mainstream trend of the Chinese community in contemporary Vietnamese society, while Charles Wheeler concluded that "the new identity had a bearing on determining the integration rights and institutional norms of their communities in order to resist the process of erosion into Vietnamese society." The ethnic Chinese truthfully confronted the fading of their political-economic status. Their [the Minh Hương] identity element at least still served as "a useful tool" to form a new status of "a minority elite" in Vietnam.[70] How did it happen? How have the ethnic Chinese built and applied the symbols of Guandi and Tianhou as the mediators and glues to make the transformation?

Acculturation and Adaptability

This study directly relates to the term *acculturation*. Acculturation has long been discussed by social scientists. Redfield, Linton, and Herskovits define it as "phenomena which result when groups of individuals having different cultures come into continuous first-hand contact with subsequent changes in the original culture patterns of either or both groups."[71] In 1954, the Social Science Research Council (SSRC) modified the definition to: "culture change that is initiated by the conjunction of two or more autonomous cultural systems. Its dynamics can be seen as the selective adaptation of value systems, the processes of integration and differentiation, the generation of developmental sequences, and the operation of role determinants and personality factors."[72] The first definition stresses the "continuous first-hand contact," while the second focuses on change and adaptation. Both have had influential impacts on several cultural research works of Western science. After a rather long period, late-twentieth-century scholars suggested the term *biculturalism* to address the community or individuals who are "exposed to two or more cultures" to pursue their interest(s) when encountering cross-ethnic contact.[73] Acculturation may take place in a unilinear or multilinear way—it depends on the dimension and degree of acculturation.[74]

Longstanding processes of acculturation may lead to one of four sequences: *assimilation* (when individuals of the inferior group do not wish to maintain their identity, but instead they seek to be fully integrated into the contributing group); *integration* (individuals of a group try to maintain their original culture while promoting daily intergroup interaction); *separation* (individuals of a group preserve their original culture and avoid interacting with others); and *marginalization* (individuals of a group have little interest in both cultural maintenance and having relationships with others).[75] Regarding the domains of changes, J. W. Berry pointed out that acculturation changes could take place in political, economic, social, cultural, physical, biological, or a combination of all of these kinds of group-level interactions.[76] Nguyen and Benet Martínez and Pfafferott and Brown demonstrated that integration produces the most positive socio-psychological and behavioral outcomes that truly improve life satisfaction if the interests of both the host group and the immigrant group are respected.[77]

In the case of the ethnic Chinese in Vietnam, the contact between the local group, the Vietnamese, and the emigrants, the Chinese, has naturally generalized the process of acculturation. Moreover, the historical legacies and transnational experiences between Vietnam and China have indirectly influenced the process, creating certain boundaries and restraining the acculturative performance.[78] Finally, governmental policies and international relations between Vietnam and China, as well as with the rest of the world, have also strongly affected the transracial interaction and acculturation between the two groups. The consequence of the process turns out to be a special form of integration (in Berry's category), which takes place in almost all of the aspects of life (political, economic, social, cultural, and others).[79]

The premodern overseas Chinese brought the southeastern Chinese cultural tradition to Vietnam and Southeast Asia, which had long been standardized and centralized under imperial Confucian doctrines. There were a number of cultural elites who were instrumental in promoting orthopraxy as a mechanism of control.[80] It is also noticeable that the local elites had to share the local commoners' vision and interest; in return, they could seek to consolidate their positions and reputations among the commoners.

The role of Chinese local elites in organizing and controlling communities on behalf of the emperor and the bureaucratic system has long been analyzed by many scholars. On the one hand, Philip Kuhn affirmed that local elites had enough capacity to create and maintain their influence on the local communities; Joanna Meskill and Keith Schoppa praised the active role of local elites in maximizing the interests of local commoners.[81] On the other hand, Joseph Esherick and Mary Rankin, in their support of Max Weber's theory, stated that local elites used their wisdom to maintain dynamics in local contexts to mediate the gap between the palace and the common people.[82] When the Chinese migrated to Southeast Asia and other regions, the role of the elites became more obviously influential. The elites were normally selected under unified criteria, including seniority in generation and age, social standing, and integrity. Yen Ching-hwang proposed that, in Singapore and Malaya, kinship and dialect ties composed only part of the overseas Chinese social milieu. Instead, class status and class affiliations strongly affected their communal organizing.[83] In her research on Indochinese Chinese during French colonialism, Tracy Barrett also affirmed that prosperous and prominent Chinese merchants and businessmen were dominantly preferred by both the Chinese commoners and the French rulers.[84] It was the local elites who wisely adopted and adjusted the communal interest and evolutionary agenda to meet two goals: in-group solidarity and development and cross-racial social integration.

Overseas Chinese used both classical Confucian virtues and the native place's original tradition as an ideological platform for communal construction. Orthodoxy may not be accurately motivated by Confucian concerns; however, this allowed them to create and foster "the illusion of cultural unity."[85] Among the overseas communities, being a member meant that one had to accept and comply with the already-designed and compromised regulations. Such regulations may change as the acculturative performance takes place. As Gilbert Rozman once stated, cultural identity is not uniform over time or place; it changes when the compromise change.[86]

The Chinese classical standardized tradition has been challenged when it encounters non-Chinese culture in Vietnam. Even though the traditional Vietnamese people were deeply influenced by Chinese Confucian ideology, and feudal dynasties exemplified Chinese models, including spirits-sanctioning policy and orthopraxy, in southern Vietnam, Mahayana Buddhism has been continuously popularized and dominantly prevails in the commoners' spirituality.[87] Buddhist worldview directly affects the way the local Vietnamese view the ethnic Chinese's polytheistic religion and liturgical practices. In addition, the post-war Marxist ideology doesn't really encourage religious faith and religious performance; the so-called standardized tradition of the ethnic Chinese community has become ineffective in the local context. Conversely, some local elites even accuse that Chinese popular religions are too diverse to be systematic and unified.[88] However, the ethnic Chinese people "share [a] deep-rooted Chinese sense of cultural superiority" when getting in contact with the local community.[89] The gap has been accelerated by the fact that the Chinese traders were "accused of manipulating the economy for their own selfish interests while doing nothing for the welfare of the host country."[90]

Some experts proposed that the congruity of the acculturation orientation between host and immigrant groups directly promoted determining adaptation, thus causing a positive transformation.[91] The radical change in viewpoints of both communities truly took place after the 1986 Đổi mới policy, especially when the Cultural Heritage Law was passed in 2001 and modified in 2009. The law gives way to meditating the difference, allowing the Vietnamese to be more tolerant in dealing with the cultural diversity and richness of the Chinese and the Chinese community to give up the long-standing sense of cultural superiority. The following case studies may provide detailed pieces of evidence to support such a hypothesis.

Crossing the Boundaries: Case Studies on the Field

This part of the research presents some typical empirical case studies in southern Vietnam in which Guandi and Tianhou are the two main gods among the ethnic Chinese groups. The liturgical transformation has taken place (or has been emphasized) in recent years thanks to the 1986 Đổi mới policy and the radical change in the worldview of both the Vietnamese and ethnic Chinese communities. Boundaries may not be truly crossed; however, people have learned to live together (with or without ambivalence) by creating and cultivating shared experiences in dealing with gods' sanctity. Though, the case of Guandi is obviously different from Tianhou. The former represents the spirit of patriotism, while the latter calls for ethnic identity solidarity.

Case Study 1: Integral Worship of Guandi

As Stephan Feuchtwang put it, the past "lives with present efficacy," and many parts of the world are living with useful legacies from yesterday.[92] Cairn, as cited in Pham, stated, "Probably for no other people in the world has invasion of their country featured so much in their folklore."[93] Pham Quynh Phuong concluded that during the colonial period in Vietnam, the symbol of Trần Hưng Đạo was understood as the symbol of patriotism rather than as a specific personality,[94] while in southern Vietnam, one can find many symbols of the same category, including the symbol of Guandi.[95]

Guandi has long been adopted and adapted in Vietnamese culture, especially during the anticolonial period. He has been historically empowered as one of the symbols of patriotism in southern Vietnam.[96] In the Cai Lậy District of Tiền Giang Province, local villagers built Guandi Temple and started worshipping Guandi in the early nineteenth century. From 1859 to 1871, the revolutionary movement became vibrant in the region, four local leaders—Trần Công Thận (1825–1871), Nguyễn Thanh Long (1820–1871), Ngô Tấn Đước (?–1871), and Trương Văn Rộng: (?–1871)—organized the revolts in Cai Lậy. The French rulers attempted to smother the revolts by both spy system and armed forces. Having no concrete ideological basis and well-organized party leadership, the four leaders secretly took the popularity of the god of Guandi as the symbol of revolution. They had to shelter in the back hall of Guandi Temple to pursue their goals. Unfortunately, the disguise was leaked, and the French arrested family members of the leaders to lure them. The four leaders finally surrendered and were killed by the French in the temple on December 25, 1871, of the lunar calendar (February 14, 1871). Their bodies were buried behind the temple. Local people deified them as the local guardian gods and organized sacrificial activities for them under the surface of sacrificial activities for the Guandi God on December 25. In 1954, a state-supported temple dedicated to four spirits was annexed to the original Guandi temple, making the whole structure a complex of both heroic worship and popular religion. Currently, both Guandi and four spirits are dedicated during the festival. The cult of the four spirits serves as the deep structure of the complex, while the cult of Guandi acts as the catalyst. Local devotees, including both the Vietnamese and the ethnic Chinese, partake in the anniversary festival for both purposes: paying tribute to the heroes and acquiring god's blessings.

A similar integral compound can be found at Thủ Dầu Một city's Thanh An Temple, where Guandi is worshipped with local Vietnamese historical figures, such as Hùng Vương,[97] Trần Hưng Đạo,[98] Ho Chi Minh, etc. Another compound is at Sóc Trăng city's Võ Đế Thánh Điện, where Guandi is honored together with five local anti-French patriots.[99]

Guandi was localized partially in Vietnamese culture, thus being widely shared between the Vietnamese and the ethnic Chinese. His symbolic meaning transformed from being a martial god among the ruling class into a god of blessing in folk communities. Communal houses, local temples, and Buddhist pagodas worshipped him; new religions (such as Caodaism,[100] Hoahaoism[101]) integrated him; and millennian movements in the late nineteenth century and early twentieth centuries (such as Bửu Sơn Kỳ Hương, Tứ Ân Hiếu Nghĩa, Minh Đức Nho giáo đại đạo and so on[102]) appropriated him. Many Vietnamese families still venerate a statue of Guandi, and many others worship him at home together with Buddhas, other gods, and ancestors.

Unlike imperial China, the process of superscribing Guandi in Vietnam, in many cases, did not start from the ruling class under a standardization agenda. On the contrary, all Vietnamese classes, from the elites to the peasants, triggered, promoted, and controlled the superscription of Guandi. The statue of Guandi was Vietnamized under the context of local anticolonial history in southern Vietnam at the end of the late nineteenth and early twentieth centuries—a time when imperial power and traditional social ideology (Confucianism) faded away under French rule, while the domestic political party did not yet form completely. Thanks to this transformation, Guandi has long become the glue that links people of different backgrounds together.

Case Study 2: The Conflation of Tianhou Rituals and Family Rites in Cà Mau

Unlike Guandi, Tianhou has long been preserved as an icon of Chineseness in southern Vietnam. Over 150 temples of Tianhou have been built in the region, 85 percent of which are owned by ethnic Chinese.[103] Tianhou's main ritual is organized on March 23 of the lunar calendar. This research presents two case studies of Tianhou rituals in two ethnic Chinese dialectic groups, the Teochiu in Cà Mau city and the Hakka in Biên Hòa city. The Teochiu case vividly shows that the local ethnic Chinese elites actively created the illusionary sharing in liturgical practice between the Vietnamese, the ethnic Chinese, and the ethnic Khmer by conflating the new-year Tianhou ceremonies with popular family rites of the Vietnamese people. The Hakka case in Biên Hòa city more dramatically defined, under the strong demand of Chinese in-group solidarity and cross-racial integration, local Hakka elites designated to change the name of the craft-masters temple and the annual festival into the widely-acknowledged Tianhou goddess to achieve the goal of integration and attract more participants while retaining the original worship of the craft gods underneath.

Besides the annual Tianhou birthday celebration held on March 23, the members of Cà Mau Temple organized bigger rituals on the evening of January 3 of the lunar calendar, which they call "Ritual to Welcome Goddess Tianhou's Return to the Temple!"[104] Thousands of devotees, regardless of race (Vietnamese, ethnic Chinese, Khmer, etc.), gender, and age, gather at Tianhou temple from around 10:00 p.m. to 12:00 a.m. to partake in the event.[105]

I found out that the above-mentioned ceremony is just the "goddess returning" ceremony, a part of the twin rituals celebrated before and during the new-year holidays: "Sending Tianhou off to Heaven" and "Welcome Tianhou Back from Heaven." On December 24 of the previous year, devotees perform the farewell ritual to send her to heaven. Noticeably, the day before, December 23, is when Vietnamese people perform the ritual to send the

Kitchen God to heaven. According to folk belief, the Kitchen God is a celestial bureaucrat appointed to dwell in each household. He has to ascend to heaven "to report" all the virtuous and nonvirtuous behaviors and actions of the family members so that the Jade Emperor of Heaven will decide the upcoming status of each family. The Teochiu people actively conflate Tianhou with the Kitchen God to serve the goal of integration. The lunar new year is the time for the family union, both secularly and sacredly. Normally, the Vietnamese welcome the Kitchen God back home together with their own ancestors on the last day of the old year (December 30) in a year-end ritual. Similarly, people observe a ritual to welcome Tianhou back home (the temple) on the evening of the third day of the new year.[106]

Robert J. Foster argued that a "national culture" has not been made by a single voice; instead, it has been "continually imagined, invented, contested and transformed" both by the state and by the agency of individuals.[107] Tianhou is considered a community-binding icon and an ethnic Chinese identity marker by the ethnic Chinese; therefore, there must be another day, especially for her, when the community completes their family rites. Tianhou's returning celebration is thus held after the families set the farewell ritual to send their ancestors back to their world (January 3). Furthermore, Tianhou's native home is in Meizhou (Fujian, China), and she, in turn, is an ancestor of somebody. After fulfilling her celestial missions in heaven, she has to join the family reunion and stay with her family during the holiday. A farewell ritual might be held at her original home in the morning, and it will take time for her to move back to Cà Mau. The evening ceremony is best accepted according to all sources. Obviously, the Teochiu in Cà Mau have developed an articulated ritual that meets the various needs of people of different origins and backgrounds.

Obviously, people use, manipulate, and create culture as part of everyday life within their system of social relations, which requires flexibility in interpreting the idea/faith of the practical performance(s).[108] The ethnic Chinese in Cà Mau city have cultivated new initiatives through the liturgical transformation: The Chinese goddess of Tianhou "acts" like the Kitchen God before the new year and like an ancestor during the new year. The conflation reflects the ethnic Chinese desire to integrate into Vietnamese society as well as to consolidate their internal solidarity. This performance indicates a new attempt to cross boundaries and produce a significant impact on local society.

Represented in the Tianhou's conflation with family rites in Cà Mau are local Chinese tensions between the state and ethnic group, between races, between insiders and outsiders, and between nostalgia and desire of "taking root where landing." Likewise, the resolution for those tensions in the local cult was accommodated by the fact that local Chinese elites willingly promoted and slightly remolded the popular worship of Tianhou. This symbol of celestial power was channeled to convey family values, thereby enabling it to be easily accepted and appreciated. By doing so, the Chinese elite autonomously govern their internal community locally in Cà Mau even when the cross-provincial Teochiu nexus was broken since the late colonial period and the recent erosion of ethnic culture.

Case Study 3: The Liturgical Transformation in a Hakka Craft Village in Biên Hòa

A recent case study shows that the craft-making Hakka Chinese in Bửu Long (Biên Hòa) were previously unable to integrate into mainstream Chinese culture in Vietnam because they worshipped their own craft gods (stone-making, carpentry, and wood-carving) while the others honor Guandi or Tianhou.[109] At the beginning of the twentieth century, they began superimposing the goddess Tianhou on the surface of the original cult of craft masters, thus making a pseudo-orthopractic situation: The surface discourse was the worship of Tianhou, but the structure of the ceremony still maintained under the original platform of the craft gods cult. At the same time, the Hakka people simultaneously adopted both Guandi and Tianhou, but only Tianhou was selected since Tianhou would represent more "Chineseness" values than the locally-adaptive Guandi god.[110]

Normally, Tianhou's birthday festival takes place on the twenty-third of the third lunar month, while the Hakka's Vegetarian Festival lasts from the tenth to the thirteenth of the sixth lunar month in the years of the Tiger, Snake, Monkey, and Pig. Thanks to the popularity of the Tianhou goddess, the superimposed Tianhou cult and Vegetarian Festival can, at least, allow Hakka and non-Hakka Chinese and Vietnamese to live together even with ambiguity and a lack of full understanding.

People can deify a god, so they are able to make a legend and attach it to the god. The annexation of the goddess Tianhou in the original craft masters' worship has been attached with a legend honoring Tianhou. As many informants confirmed, a plague hit the region and took some lives in the early twentieth century. There was no effective medical treatment to stop the epidemic; the craft gods, too, were useless. One mournful morning, as the people gathered at the temple to pray, a local man, Sù Khoòng (曹姜), became abnormal in his gestures and voice, turning his body upside down and walking on two hands straight to the temple main hall. He claimed to be the incarnation of Tianhou for an epidemic-controlling mission.

He asked Hakka devotees to select one hundred types of herbs, categorize them into eight groups, and add other herbal materials to make a medical treatment.[111] The Hakka followed his instructions, and thereupon the plague was controlled. The devotees strongly believed in Tianhou; therefore, they adopted the cult and renamed the temple the Tianhou Ancient Temple. In every three-year cycle, the Hakka organize a vegetarian festival dedicated to her. In fact, as we pointed out after in-depth talks, the legend was gradually composed and added to by the elites in their efforts to institutionalize the gods' transformation.

The Hakka's bottom-up approach to transformation strives not only for the feeling of being integrated but also for evolution. Because ethnic Chinese culture in Vietnam is richly diverse but makes a strong claim to unification, more movements and reforms will take place to eliminate the gaps. However, as there are no logical top-down institutionalized frameworks or criteria to ensure the goals of such movements and reforms, ways of transforming the gods (or popular traditions) vary widely among the subgroups. The Hakka community in Bửu Long compulsorily superimposed the state-sanctioned Tianhou cult on the worship of its craft-master gods for the sake of evolution, which eventually produced a pseudo-standardization.

The transformation of gods and liturgical practices, however, is not always a response to pressure from centralized power. Instead, it should be viewed broadly as the process of empowering the gods of a marginal community to achieve a pragmatic standard status for survival and evolution. The Hakka's liturgical disguise or pseudo-standardization, expressed in the phrase "the caterpillar's spirit under a butterfly's might," has permitted evolution over the past decades and may continue to do so in the future. The haunted vulnerability during the postwar exodus period may partially occupy the civil community; however, the current status and upcoming prospects have enabled them to constitute a prominently optimistic future in a changing Vietnamese society.

Building an Incorporate Ethnic Culture

These above-mentioned case studies all show a prominent tendency in contemporary Vietnam: The long-term outcomes of acculturation are referred to as "adaptation." Numerous writers have generated two kinds of adaptation: psychological adaptations (in mental health and well-being) and sociocultural adaptations (i.e., school adjustment for young people, the work setting, and success in community life).[112] Berry and Sam added the third kind, intercultural adaptation (i.e., the achievement of harmonious intercultural relations).[113] Perhaps the contemporary transformation in the ethnic Chinese community in Vietnam imbues all three types, in which the first two domains refer to the physical changes of social life while the in-depth investigation is necessary to identify the third domain, the intercultural adaptation. The historical superscription of Guandi god in the case of Cai Lậy's heroes worship, the liturgical conflation of Tianhou ritual and family rites in Cà Mau, and the superimposition of Tianhou goddess on the platform of the original crafter gods worship in Biên Hòa all serve as pieces of evidence to support the idea that cultural transformation, as a means for survival and evolution, has been the goal of an endless struggle among the ethnic Chinese in contemporary Vietnam.

Seligman and Weller argued that one cannot absolutely abolish ambiguity but learn to live with it in a different way.[114] Accordingly, people should meditate and take advantage of the interactive relationship between "notation" and "ritual" to attain "shared experience" and handle boundaries. As they put it, ritual teaches us "to live with differences and all their associated ambiguities" and "share lives together." Notation, ritual, and shared experience intermix with one another "to construct alternative historicities and socialities" and promote boundary-crossing even though they can't totally erase the ambivalence and difference.[115] In southern Vietnam, the historical legacy includes both the ethnic Chinese and the Vietnamese struggle to live with ambiguity and difference. In using Seligman and Weller's language, the god of Guandi and goddess of Tianhou can serve as a special form of notation, their worships and liturgical function as the ritual, the local Chinese elites have been creative in adjusting part of their tradition in order to shape the shared experience between two communities. The liturgical transformation may not really reduce or totally abolish the ambivalence between them;[116] However, it actually "shares the potential space of culture created through ritual," as Emile Durkheim once concluded.[117] As a result of transformation, "younger Chinese seem to be more open-minded and more accepting of Vietnamese culture,"[118] while the majority of Vietnamese people are more tolerant and willing to stay hand-in-hand with the local ethnic Chinese community.[119]

Cross-ethnic experience-sharing and ambivalent reduction are not homogeneous in the cases of Guandi and Tianhou. Given the fact that both gods originated from China and have long been parts of ethnic Chinese tradition, the Vietnamese adopted the symbol and the worship of Guandi more than Tianhou; consequently, the interpretations that the Vietnamese had toward the cults are dissimilar. People may have different interests, feelings, and aspirations when they participate in rituals honoring Guandi and Tianhou, thus causing the difference in forms and levels of getting shared experience. In the case of Guandi, two communities share the liturgical experience with less ambiguity and ambivalence—Guandi has truthfully acted as the glue, while Tianhou has performed as the identity marker of the ethnic Chinese in Vietnam even though the Vietnamese people partake in Tianhou rituals with wholehearted enthusiasm.

Notably, all of the above case studies clearly demonstrate that the ethnic dynamism and recent symbolic and religious conversion in Vietnam stemmed from the local Vietnamese Chinese community itself as a result of live movements in the country. Chinese who left Vietnam after the war (approximately 50 percent of Vietnamese boatmen in 1978–1980) are now returning home to visit relatives and invest in Vietnam.[120] Consequently, the new concept of global Chineseness described by Adam McKeown is widespread in the country.[121] A Chinese individual in Vietnam and Southeast Asia (in the Chinese-speaking world) can be different from the past, can have no connection with the PRC, and can actively integrate into the mainstream of local society and get along well with the transformation of globalization. Godley and Coppel, Supang, Wu, Bao, Tan, Chiung, and others revealed various cases of local Chinese in Southeast Asia and the United States involuntarily assimilating into local society and culture while retaining their Chineseness.[122] This process may be slower in Vietnam; however, our field studies strongly support this notion. The ethnic Chinese in Vietnam are thus a part of the research subjects of worldwide Sinophone studies.

Conclusion

Historical vulnerability and cross-ethnic boundaries have taught the ethnic Chinese community in Vietnam to be creative to survive and evolve. Communal elites, under the strong support of their congregational members, had actively drawn a long-term agenda of transformation for the sake of building a transcultural adaptation in the local context, especially when their economic strength was eroding in the postwar period. Public cults and liturgical practices have been transformed dramatically (to compare with domestic cults and other family-based traditions) as the community screens and categorizes components that can function differently: in-group identity rebuilding and out-group boundary-crossing promotion.

Even though both Guandi and Tianhou have been put in the process of liturgical transformation where notation, ritual, and shared experience are widely transmitted, the contextualized Guandi god has actually performed as the glue to build (or rebuild) cross-racial solidarity, while Tianhou goddess has been consolidated as a 'Chineseness' marker or a microcosm of Chinese culture. The anticolonial mentality has faded, while economic aspiration has strongly increased in contemporary Vietnamese society. Consequently, Tianhou has become preferable (to Guandi) among the popular religious followers in the country. Liturgical transformation in popular religions has played an important role in creating multiethnic integration in postsocialist Vietnam. Such a bottom-up integral agenda can ensure a beneficial acculturation procedure even though the state-to-state relationship between Vietnam and China has been unstable in the last two decades. As part of the ongoing Sinophone studies in the world, the Vietnamese Chinese community is developing into a progressive incorporated group in Vietnam and in overseas Chinese communities.[123]

Notes

1. Shu-mei Shih, *Visuality and Identity: Sinophone Articulations Across the Pacific* (Berkeley: University of California Press, 2007); Shu-mei Shih, "The Concept of the Sinophone," *PMLA* 126, no. 3 (2011): 709–718; Howard Chiang, "Sinophone," *Transgender Studies Quarterly* 1, nos. 1–2 (2014): 184–187; Lingchei Letty Chen, "When Does 'Diaspora' End and 'Sinophone' Begin?" *Postcolonial Studies* 18, no. 1 (2015): 52–66.

2. See Shu-mei Shih, Chien-hsin Tsai, and Brian Bernards, *Sinophone Studies: A Critical Reader* (New York: Columbia University Press, 2013); Howard Chiang and Alvin K. Wong, "Introduction: Queer Sinophone Studies: Intellectual Synergies," in *Keywords in Queer Sinophone Studies*, ed. Howard Chiang and Alvin K. Wong (New York: Routledge, Taylor & Francis, 2020).

3. Peter L. A. Gosling, "Changing Chinese Identities in Southeast Asia: An Introductory Review," in *The Chinese in Southeast Asia*, vol. 2: *Identity, Culture and Politics*, ed. Peter L. A. Gosling and Linda Y. C. Lim (Singapore: Maruzen Asia, 1983); Alison M. Groppe, *Sinophone Malaysian Literature: Not Made in China* (Amherst, NY: Cambria Press, 2013); Caroline Chia and Tom Hoogervorst, *Sinophone Southeast Asia: Sinitic Voices Across the Southern Seas* (Leiden: Brill, 2021).

4. Ramses Amer, *The Ethnic Chinese in Vietnam and Sino-Vietnamese Relations* (Kuala Lumpur: Forum, 1991); Ramses Amer, "Vietnam's Policies and the Ethnic Chinese Since 1975," *Journal of Social Issues in Southeast Asia* 11, no.1 (1996): 76–104; Nola Cooke and Li Tana, eds., *Water Frontier: Commerce and the Chinese in the Lower Mekong Region, 1750–1880* (Lanham, MD: Rowman & Littlefield, 2004); Chen Ching Ho, "Mac Thien Tu and Phrayataksin: A Survey on Their Political Stand, Conflict and Background," in *The Chinese Diaspora in the Pacific 1500–1900*, ed. Anthony Reid (Farnham: Ashgate Variorum, 2008), 69–110; Grace Chew Chye Lay, "The Hoa of Phu Quoc in Vietnam: Local Institutions, Education, and Studying Mandarin," *Journal of Chinese Overseas* 6 (2010): 311–332; Tracy Barrett, *The Chinese Diaspora in Southeast Asia—The Overseas Chinese in Indo-China* (London: I. B. Tauris, 2012); Lee Khoon Choy, *Golden Dragon and Purple Phoenix—The Chinese and Their Multi-Ethnic Descendants in Southeast Asia* (Singapore: World Scientific, 2013), 327–368; Charles Wheeler, "Interests, Institutions, and Identity: Strategic Adaptation and the Ethno-Evolution of Minh

Huong (Central Vietnam), 16th–19th Centuries," *Itinerario* 39, no. 1 (2015): 141–166; Yuk Wah Chan, "'Vietnam is My Country Land, China Is My Hometown': Chinese Communities in Transition in the South of Vietnam," *Asian Ethnicity* 19, no. 2 (2018): 163–179; Nguyễn Ngọc Thơ, *Tín ngưỡng Thiên Hậu vùng Tây Nam Bộ* (The cult of Tianhou in the Mekong River Delta) (Hanoi: Chính trị Quốc gia, 2017).

5. David K. Jordan, *Gods, Ghosts and Ancestors: The Folk Religion of a Taiwanese Village* (Berkeley: University of California Press, 1972); Arthur P. Wolf, "Gods, Ghosts and Ancestors," in *Religion and Ritual in Chinese Society* (Stanford, CA: Stanford University Press, 1974), 131–182, 356–357; James L. Watson, "Standardizing the Gods: The Promotion of Tien'hou ("Empress of Heaven") Along the South China Coast, 960–1960," in *Village Life in Hong Kong—Politics, Gender, and Ritual in the New Territories*, ed. James Watson and Rubie S. Watson (Hong Kong: Chinese University Press, 1985), 292–324; Steven Sangren, "Orthodoxy, Heterodoxy, and the Structure of Value in Chinese Ritual," *Modern China* 13, no. 1 (1989): 63–89; Liu Zhiwei, *Zai guojia yu shehui zhi jian-Ming Qing Guangdong lijia fuyi zhidu yanjiu* (Guangzhou: Zhongshan danxue, 1997) (劉志偉.《在國家與神會之間—明清廣東里甲服役制度研究》. 廣州：中山大學, 1997); Guo Qitao, *Exorcism and Money: The Symbolic World of the Five-Fury Spirits in Late Imperial China* (Berkeley: Institute of East Asian Studies, University of California, 2003); Richard von Glahn, *The Sinister Way: The Divine and the Demonic in Chinese Religious Culture* (Berkeley: University of California Press, 2004); Donald S. Sutton, "Introduction to the Special Issue: Ritual, Cultural Standardization, and Orthopraxy in China—Reconsidering James L. Watson's Ideas," *Modern China* 33, no. 1 (2007): 1, 3–21; Kenneth Pomeranz, "Orthopraxy, Orthodoxy, and the Goddess(es) of Taishan," *Modern China* 33, no. 1 (2007): 22–46; Michael Szonyi, "The Illusion of Standardizing the Gods: The Cult of the Five Emperors in Late Imperial China," *Journal of Asian Studies* 56, no. 1 (1997): 113–35; and "Making Claims About Standardization and Orthopraxy in Late Imperial China: Ritual and Cults in the Fuzhou Region in Light of Watson's Theories," *Modern China* 33, no. 1 (2007): 47–71; Paul R. Katz, "Orthopraxy and Heteropraxy Beyond the State—Standardizing Ritual in Chinese Society," *Modern China* 33, no. 1 (2007): 72–90; David Faure, "The Emperor in the Village: Representing the State in South China," in *State and Court Ritual in China*, ed. Joseph P. McDermott (Cambridge: Cambridge University Press, 1999), 267–298.

6. Jordan, *Gods, Ghosts and Ancestors*; Wolf, "Gods, Ghosts and Ancestors"; Adam B. Seligman and Robert P. Weller, *Rethinking Pluralism—Ritual, Experience, and Ambiguity* (Oxford University Press, 2012), 136–137.

7. Watson, "Standardizing the Gods," 323.

8. Robert P. Weller, *Unities and Diversities in Chinese Religion* (London: Macmillan/Seattle: University of Washington Press, 1987).

9. von Glahn, *The Sinister Way*, 251–253.

10. Stephan Feuchtwang, *The Imperial Metaphor: Popular Religion in China* (London: Routledge, 1992), 57–58; Prasenjit Duara, "Superscribing Symbols: The Myth of Guandi, the Chinese God of War," *Journal of Asian Studies* 47, no. 4 (1988): 778–795.

11. Jordan, *Gods, Ghosts and Ancestors*, 1972.

12. Evelyn S. Rawski, "Economic and Social Foundations of the Late Imperial Culture," in *Popular Culture in Late Imperial China*, ed. David Johnson, Andrew J. Nathan, and Evelyn S. Rawski (Berkeley: University of California Press, 1985), 3–33.

13. Janet Hoskins, "The Headhunter as Hero: Local Traditions and their Reinterpretation in National History," *American Ethnologist* 14, no. 4 (1987): 605–622; Pham Quynh Phuong, *Hero and Deity—Tran Hung Dao and the Resurgence of Popular Religion in Vietnam* (Bangkok: Mekong Press, 2009).

14. Katz, "Orthopraxy and Heteropraxy, 72–90.

15. Duara, "Superscribing Symbols," 778–795; Valerie Hansen, *Changing Gods in Medieval China, 1127–1276* (Princeton, NJ: Princeton University Press, 1990).

16. Sutton, "Introduction to the Special Issue," 5; Walter Burkert, *Structure and History in Greek Mythology and Ritual* (Berkeley: University of California Press, 1979), 23.

17. Faure, "The Emperor in the Village," 278.

18. Szonyi, "The Illusion of Standardizing the Gods," 113–135.

19. Sutton, "Introduction to the Special Issue," 9.

20. Duara, "Superscribing Symbols," 780; Pham, *Hero and Deity*, 12.

21. Nguyễn Văn Tố, "Khí giới thờ ở các đền chùa và nghi vệ thời xưa" (Ritual weapons displayed at temples and ancient ceremonies), *Tri Tân* 179 (1945): 7–12; Trần Từ, *Cơ cấu tổ chức của làng Việt cổ truyền ở Bắc bộ* (Organizational structure of traditional viet villages in the north) (Hanoi: Khoa học xã hội, 1984); Pham, *Hero and Deity*, 28.

22. *Đổi mới* means "'reform" in English, or 改革開放 in Chinese.

23. Kirsten W. Endres, "Beautiful Customs, Worthy Tradition: Changing State Discourse on the Role of Vietnamese Culture," *Internationales Asienforum* 33, nos. 3–4 (2002): 303–322.

24. Lee, *Golden Dragon and Purple Phoenix*, 2013; Chan, "'Vietnam Is My Country Land,'" 163–179.

25. Fujiwara Riichiro, "Chính sách đối với dân Trung Hoa di cư của các triều đại Việt Nam" (The policies toward Chinese immigrants of Vietnamese feudal dynasties), *Khảo cổ tập san* 8 (1974): 174.

26. Chen Shou, *Sanguozhi* (History of the three kingdoms), commented by Pei Songzhi (Beijing: Zhonghua Shuju, 1973), 939–942.

27. Duara, "Superscribing Symbols," 780.

28. Inoue Ichii, "Kan'u shibyo no yurai narabi ni hensen" (Origins and development of Guan Yu temples), *Shirin* 26, nos. 1, 2 (1941): 48; Duara, "Superscribing Symbols," 779.

29. Duara, "Superscribing Symbols," 781.

30. Huang Huajie, *Guangongde renge yu shenge* (The human and divine characteristics of Lord Guan) (Taibei: Taiwan Shangwu Yinshuguan, 1968), 100, 122; also cited in Duara, "Superscribing Symbols," 781–787.

31. Duara, "Superscribing Symbols," 781.

32. Liu Tiksang, *The Cult of Tianhou in Hong Kong* (Hong Kong: Joint Publishing, 2000), 26–28.

33. Watson, "Standardizing the Gods," 293–294.

34. Tsai Maw-kuey, *Les Chinois au Sud-Vietnam* (Paris: Bibliothèque Nationale, 1968); Nguyễn, *Tín ngưỡng Thiên Hậu*.

35. In some districts of the Mekong River Delta where the Teochiu are dominant in numbers among the local Chinese, the temple was built and operated mainly by the Teochiu; however, the other Chinese subgroups also join the liturgical activities.

36. Nguyễn, *Tín ngưỡng Thiên Hậu*.

37. Nguyễn Ngọc Thơ, "Biến đổi và tăng quyền trong tín ngưỡng Quan Công ở Nam Bộ" (Transformations and empowerment in the Guandi cult in Southern Vietnam), *Tra Vinh University Journal* 28 (2017): 56–69.

38. Paul Clough and John P. Mitchell, *Power of Good and Evil: Social Transformation and Popular Belief* (Oxford: Berghahn, 2001).

39. Charles Keyes, Helen Hardacre, and Laurel Kendall, "Introduction: Contested Visions of Community in East and Southeast Asia," in *Asian Visions of Authority: Religion and the Modern States of East and Southeast Asia*, ed. Charles Keyes, Laurel Kendall, and Helen Hardacre (Honolulu: University of Hawai'i Press, 1994), 3.

40. J. Buttinger, *Vietnam: A Political History* (New York: Praeger, 1968), 29.

41. 交趾, Chinese term to address ancient Vietnam, referring the Red River Delta Region.

42. Jennifer Holmgren, *Chinese Colonization of Northern Vietnam—Administrative Geography and Political Development in the Tonkin Delta, First to Sixth Centuries A.D.* (Canberra: Australian National University Press, 1980), 172. Cited in Ben Kiernan, *Vietnam—A History from Earliest Times to the Present* (Oxford: Oxford University Press, 2017), 100.

43. C. P. FitzGerald, *The Southern Expansion of the Chinese People* (London: Barrie & Jenkins, 1972), 22.

44. Some typical recruitment details were recorded in *Đại Việt Sử Ký Toàn Thư*, *Quế Hải Ngu hành chí*, and *Văn Hiến Thông khảo*.

45. Riichiro, "Chính sách đối với dân Trung Hoa," 145–148

46. The Ming occupation in Vietnam lasted twenty-one years, from 1407 to 1428. The Ming rulers applied a serious Sinicization policy over the Vietnamese people, including large-scale Vietnamese book burnings (Alexander E. A. Ong, "Contextualizing the Book-Burning Episode During the Ming Invasion and Occupation of Vietnam," in *Southeast Asia in the Fifteenth Century: the China Factor*, ed. Geoff Wade & Sun Laichen [Singapore: Singapore National University Press, 2010], 154–164). After being expulsion, there were 86,640 Chinese soldiers and civilians staying in Northern Vietnam (Riichiro, "Chính sách đối với dân Trung Hoa," 149).

47. All are located in coastal Northeastern Vietnam; see Riichiro, "Chính sách đối với dân Trung Hoa," 150.

48. Chen Ching-Ho, "Mấy điều nhận xét về Minh hương xã và các cổ tích tại Hội An" (Some remarks on Minh Hương village and historical sites in Hoi An), *Việt Nam Khảo cổ tập san* (Vietnam journal of archaeology) 1 (1960): 2; Riichiro, "Chính sách đối với dân Trung Hoa," 151; Sun, *Research on Sino-Vietnam Relation*, 354.

49. Chen, "Mấy điều nhận xét," 4; Riichiro, "Chính sách đối với dân Trung Hoa," 152.

50. Sun, *Research on Sino-Vietnam Relation*, 327.

51. Trịnh Hoài Đức, *Gia Định thành thông chí* (Unified gazetteer of Gia Định Citadel), reprinted 1998 (Hanoi: Education Publishing House, ca. 1818); Christoforo Borri, *Xứ Đàng Trong năm 1621* (Cochinchina in 1621), trans. Hồng Nhuệ, Nguyễn Khắc Xuyên (Ho Chi Minh City: Ho Chi Minh City Publisher, 1998) 92; Nguyễn Chí Trung, *Cư dân Faifo—Hội An trong lịch sử* (Faifo—Hoi An residents in history) (Hanoi: Vietnam National University, 2010), 82; Wheeler, "Interests, Institutions, and Identity," 152.

52. Wheeler, "Interests, Institutions, and Identity," 154.

53. Such as Nguyễn Thiều/元韶, Yuan Shao (1648–1728), Thích Đại Sán/釋大汕, Shi Dashan (1633–1704).

54. Chen, "Mấy điều nhận xét"; Sun, *Research on Sino-Vietnam Relation*, 313, 326; Wheeler, "Interests, Institutions, and Identity," 155–156.

55. Choi Byung Wook, *Southern Vietnam Under the Reign of Minh Mạng (1820–1841): Central Policies and Local Response* (Ithaca, NY: Southeast Asia Program Publications, 2004), 33; Ben Kiernan, *Vietnam—A History*, 258; Huỳnh Ngọc Đáng, *Người Hoa ở Bình Dương* (Chinese people Binh Duong Province) (Hanoi: Chính trị Quốc gia, 2011), 26.

56. Chen, "Mấy điều nhận xét," 5; Riichiro, "Chính sách đối với dân Trung Hoa," 168; Wheeler, "Interests, Institutions, and Identity", 141–166.

57. Sun, *Research on Sino-Vietnam Relation*, 329.

58. Including the Cantonese, Hokkien, Teochiu, Hakka, and Hainan.

59. Dao Trinh Nhat, *Thế lực Khách trú và vấn đề di dân ở Nam Kỳ* (The power of the overseas Chinese and the issue of Vietnamese immigration to Southern Vietnam) (Hanoi: Hội Nhà văn, 1924/2016), 49.

60. Minh Hương (明香) means "worshiping the Ming by the Ming descendants"; Minh Huong (明鄉) refers to the village of those whose ancestors originated from the Ming dynasty from China. See Sun, *Research on Sino-Vietnam Relation*, 363; Dao, *Thế lực Khách trú*, 39.

61. Wheeler, "Interests, Institutions, and Identity," 158.

62. Alain Gerard Marsot, *The Chinese Community in Vietnam Under the French* (San Francisco: EM Text, 1993).

63. Riichiro, "Chính sách đối với dân Trung Hoa," 174.

64. Wheeler, "Interests, Institutions, and Identity," 158.

65. Sun, *Research on Sino-Vietnam Relation*, 333.

66. Accordingly, the local Chinese were prohibited to run eleven professions that had been their prominent Chinese skills (Ramses Amer, *The Ethnic Chinese in Vietnam*, 19–20); Tran Khanh, "Ethnic Chinese in Vietnam and Their Identity," in *Ethnic Chinese as Southeast Asians*, ed. L. Suryadinata (Singapore: Institute of Southeast Asian Studies, 1997), 274.

67. Thomas S. An, "The Overseas Chinese in South Vietnam: A Note," *Vietnam Perspective* 2, no.4 (1967): 13–19.

68. Ramses Amer, *The Ethnic Chinese in Vietnam*, 126–127.

69. Huỳnh, *Người Hoa ở Bình Dương*, 5.

70. Wi-vun Taiffao Chiung, "Identity and Indigenization: Minh Huong People versus Ethnic Chinese in Vietnam," *Taiwan International Studies Quarterly* 9, no. 4 (2013): 87–114; Wheeler, "Interests, Institutions, and Identity," 141–166, 152, 159.

71. R. Redfield, R. Linton, and M. Herskovits, "Memorandum on the Study of Acculturation," *American Anthropologist* 38 (1936): 149.

72. Social Science Research Council, "Acculturation: An Exploratory Formulation," *American Anthropologist* (1953): 974; also cited in Joseph E. Trimble, "Introduction: Social Change and Acculturation," in *Acculturation: Advances in Theory, Measurement, and Applied Research*, ed. Kevin M. Chun, Pamela Balls Organista, and Gerardo Marín (Washington, DC: American Psychological Association, 2003), 6.

73. Timothy P. Johnson, J. B. Jobe, D. O'Rourke, S. Sudman, R. B. Warnecke, N. Chavez, G. Chapa-Resendez, and P. Golden, "Dimensions of Self-Identification Among Multiracial and Multiethnic in Survey Interviews," *Evaluation Review* 21, no. 6 (1997): 671–687; Teresa Lafromboise, Hardin L. K. Coleman, and Jennifer Gerton, "Psychological Impact of

Biculturalism: Evidence and Theory," *Psychological Bulletin* 114, no.3 (1993): 395–412; Maria P. and P. Root, *Love's Revolution: Interracial Marriage* (Philadelphia: Temple University Press, 2001).

74. John W. Berry, "Conceptual Approaches to Acculturation," in *Acculturation: Advances and Theory, Measurement, and Applied Research*, ed. Kevin M. Chun, Pamela Balls Organista, and Gerardo Marín (Washington, DC: American Psychological Association, 2003), 22.

75. John W. Berry, "Marginality, Stress, and Ethnic Identification in an Acculturated Aboriginal Community," *Journal of Cross-Cultural Psychology* 1 (1970): 239–252; E. Sommerlad and J. W. Berry, "The Role of Ethnic Identification in Distinguishing Between Attitudes Towards Assimilation and Integration," *Human Relations* 23 (1970): 23–29.

76. John W. Berry, "Understanding and Managing Multiculturalism," *Journal of Psychology and Developing Societies* 3 (1991): 17–49.

77. A.-M. D. Nguyen and V. Benet-Martínez, "Biculturalism and Adjustment: A Meta-Analysis," *Journal of Cross-Cultural Psychology* 44, no. 1 (2013): 122–159; I. Pfafferott and R. Brown, "Acculturation Preference of Majority and Minority Adolescents in Germany in the Context of Society and Family," *International Journal of Intercultural Relations* 3, no. 6 (2006): 703–717.

78. Chen, "Mấy điều nhận xét," 1–30; Riichiro, "Chính sách đối với dân Trung Hoa," 140–175.

79. Berry, "Marginality, Stress," 239–252.

80. Tu Weiming, Milan Hejtmanek, and Alan Wachman, *The Confucian World Observed: Contemporary Discussion of Confucian Humanism in East Asia* (Honolulu, Hawaii: East-West Center: Distributed by the University of Hawaii Press, 1992), 131.

81. Philip Kuhn, *Rebellion and its Enemies in Late Imperial China: Militarization and Social Structure, 1769–1864* (Cambridge, MA: Harvard University Press, 1980); Joanna Meskill, *A Chinese Pioneer Family: The Lins of Wu-feng, Taiwan, 1729–1895* (Princeton, NJ: Princeton University Press, 1979); Keith Schoppa, *Chinese Elites and Political Change: Zhejiang Province in the Early 20th century* (Cambridge, MA: Harvard University Press, 1982).

82. Joseph Esherick and Mary Rankin, eds., *Chinese Local Elites and Patterns of Dominance* (Berkeley: University of California Press, 1990), cited in Barrett, *The Chinese Diaspora*, 52–6.

83. Yen Ching-hwang, *Community and Politics: The Chinese in Colonial Singapore and Malaya* (Singapore: Times Academic Press, 1995), cited in Barrett, *The Chinese Diaspora*, 54.

84. Barrett, *The Chinese Diaspora*, 33–35.

85. Tu, Hejtmanek, and Wachman, *The Confucian World Observed*, 9–10.

86. G. Rozman, *East Asian National Identities: Common Roots and Chinese Exceptionalism* (Washington, D.C.: Woodrow Wilson Center Press, 2011). Also cited in Tu, Hejtmanek, and Wachman, *The Confucian World Observed*, 41.

87. Alexander Woodside, *Vietnam and the Chinese Model: A Comparative Study of Vietnamese and Chinese Government in the First Half of the Nineteenth Century* (Cambridge, MA: Harvard University Press, 1988).

88. The diversity in popular religions of the ethnic Chinese strongly presents in the splitting of dialects and congregational distribution. The diversity can be found even in one dialectical group. For example, the Teochiu living in the Mekong River Delta don't really unify in popular god worship. The Teochiu communities in Tiền Giang, Long An, Cần Thơ, Hậu

Giang, and An Giang provinces dominantly worship the god Guandi (see Nguyễn Ngọc Thơ, "Biến đổi và tăng quyền ..."); while in Bến Tre, Vĩnh Long, Bạc Liêu, Kiên Giang and Cà Mau they mainly honor Tianhou goddess (see Nguyễn Ngọc Thơ, *Tín ngưỡng Thiên Hậu* ...). In Sóc Trăng they pay the sacrifice to Cảm Thiên Đại Đế God (感天大帝 Gan Tian Da Di) (i.e., Sóc Trăng city, Trần Đề District) and Bắc Đế God (北帝 Bei Di) (i.e., Vinh Chau city). The Cantonese, Hokkien, Hakka, and Hainanese communities have similarly diverse traditions.

89. An, "The Overseas Chinese," 15–16.

90. An, "The Overseas Chinese," 15–16.

91. U. Piontkowski, A. Rohmann, and A. Florack, "Concordance of Acculturation Attitudes and Perceived Threat," *Group Processes and Intergroup Relations* 30 (2002): 751–768; Adam Komisarof and Chan-Hoong Leong, "Acculturation in East and Southeast Asia," *The Cambridge Handbook of Acculturation Psychology*, ed. David L. Sam and John W. Berry (Cambridge: Cambridge University Press, 2016), 248–271.

92. Feuchtwang, *The Imperial Metaphor*, 12.

93. Jim Cairn, *Vietnam: Scorched Earth Reborn* (Camberwell, Victoria: Widescope, 1976), 6, cited in Pham, *Hero and Deity*, 21.

94. Trần Hưng Đạo was the Vietnamese general under the Trần dynasty who defeated the Mongolian invasions in 1258, 1285, and 1288. Vietnamese people of later generations deified him into a god in popular tradition. His life is celebrated each August of the lunar calendar in many places in northern Vietnam (see further Pham, *Hero and Deity*).

95. Pham, *Hero and Deity*, 35.

96. Pham, *Hero and Deity*, 35; Nguyễn, "Biến đổi và tăng quyền," 56–69.

97. Legendary founder(s) of the Vietnamese country.

98. A military general in the Trần dynasty who defeated the Mongolian invasions in 1258, 1285, and 1288. He was deified as a national guardian god by the Vietnamese people of the later generations (see Pham, *Hero and Deity*).

99. Nguyễn, "Biến đổi và tăng quyền", 56–69.

100. Caodaism is a synthetic religion that was founded by Ngô Văn Chiêu (1878–1932) in Tây Ninh, 100 kilometers northwest from Ho Chi Minh City. Caodaism was constructed on the foundation of Buddhism, Confucianism, Taoism, ancestor worship, Catholicism, and other religions. There are around five million followers living in central and southern Vietnam. See Trần Ngọc Thêm, *Tìm về bản sắc văn hóa Việt Nam* (Discovering Vietnamese cultural identity) (Ho Chi Minh City: Tổng hợp, 2001), 559–573; see also Hue-Tam Ho Tai, *Millenarianism and Peasant Politics in Vietnam* (Cambridge, MA: Harvard University Press, 1983), 77–8, 100; and George E. Dutton and Jayne S. Werner, *Sources of Vietnamese Tradition* (New York: Columbia University Press, 2012), 429–430.

101. Also called Hoahao Buddhism, Hoahaoism was founded in 1939 by Huỳnh Phú Sổ (1919–1947) in Hòa Hảo village, Tân Châu District, An Giang Province. Hoahaoism continued Bửu Sơn Kỳ Hương's philosophy; however, it adjusted the structure. Hoahaoism took Mahayana Buddhist philosophy as the foundation and added ancestor worship. See Hue-Tam Ho Tai, *Millenarianism and Peasant Politics*, 17–19, 26–37, 125, 170; also Trần Ngọc Thêm, *Tìm về bản sắc*, 472–475).

102. Bửu Sơn Kỳ Hương is a synthetic religion founded by Đoàn Minh Huyên (1807–1856) in 1849 in Châu Đốc, An Giang Province. Currently, there are around fifteen thousand

followers in the Mekong River Delta (see Hue-Tam Ho Tai, *Millenarianism and Peasant Politics*, 20–27); Tứ Ân Hiếu Nghĩa is a synthetic religion under a branch of Bửu Sơn Kỳ Hương that combines Mahayana Buddhism, Lin-chi tsung (臨濟宗), Tiāntāi-zōng (天台宗), Confucianism, Taoism, ancestor worship, and patriotism. It was founded by Ngô Lợi (1831–1890) in Óc Eo village, Tịnh Biên District, An Giang Province. There are around eighty thousand followers currently living in southern Vietnam (see Hue-Tam Ho Tai, *Millenarianism and Peasant Politics*, 3, 12, 66, 146, 177); Local farmers and rural elites in Trà Vinh Province in southern Vietnam established a folk religious form of Confucianism between 1920 and 1930. Currently, there are hundreds of followers who organize religious activities held at three local temples in the province. This sect also absorbed core principles of Buddhism, Taoism, Caodaism, and local god-worship traditions, yet it is more closely related to Confucianism.

103. Local Vietnamese people built eighteen Tianhou temples where sacrifice and other liturgical practices are regularly held; however, the Vietnamese downgrade her into the same status with other goddesses in the local tradition (Nguyễn Ngọc Thơ, *Tín ngưỡng Thiên Hậu*).

104. This is the Vietnamese transcription: "Lễ Cung thỉnh Thánh mẫu hạ giá hồi cung."

105. Nguyen and Nguyen, "Caterpillar's Spirit Under a Butterfly's Might."

106. Phạm Văn Tú, *Tín ngưỡng thờ Bà Thiên Hậu ở Cà Mau* (The cult of Tianhou in Cà Mau) (Hanoi: Khoa học Xã hội, 2011), 95.

107. Nguyen Ngoc Tho, "The Ritual Incorporation and Cross-Cultural Communication in Camau, Vietnam: A Case Study of the Tianhou Cult," *Culture and Religion* 22, no. 1 (2022): 6–24.

108. Robert J. Foster, "Making National Cultures in the Global Ecumene," *Annual Review of Anthropology* 20 (1991): 235–260; also cited in Pham, *Hero and Deity*, 252.

109. See Weller, *Unities and Diversities*, 172.

110. In Vietnamese, "Hakka Chinese" is *người Hẹ* or *người Hắc Cá*.

111. Nguyen Ngoc Tho and Nguyen Thi Nguyet, "Caterpillar's Spirit Under a Butterfly's Might: Hakka's Liturgical Transformation in Bửu Long, Biên Hòa, Dong Nai," *Journal of Folklore* 1 (2018): 16–28.

112. W. Searle and C. Ward, "The Prediction of Psychological and Socio-Cultural Adjustment During Cross-Cultural Transitions," *International Journal of Inter-Cultural Relations* 14 (1990): 449–464; C. Ward, S. Bochner, and A. Furnham, *The Psychology of Culture Shock* (Hove: Routledge, 2001); C. Ward and A. Kennedy, "Psychological and Socio-Cultural Adjustment During Cross-Cultural Transitions: A Comparison of Secondary Students at Home and Abroad," *International Journal of Psychology* 28 (1993): 129–147.

113. W. J. Berry and D. L. Sam, "Acculturation: Conceptual Background and Theoretical Perspectives," in *Cambridge Handbook of Acculturation Psychology*, 2nd edition (Cambridge: Cambridge University Press), 18.

114. Adam B. Seligman and Robert P. Weller, *Rethinking Pluralism—Ritual, Experience, and Ambiguity* (Oxford: Oxford University Press, 2012), 8–9.

115. Seligman and Weller, *Rethinking Pluralism*, 9.

116. Chee Kiong Tong, *Identity and Ethnic Relations in Southeast Asia: Racializing Chineseness* (New York: Springler, 2010), 188–190.

117. Emile Durkheim, *The Elementary Forms of Religious Life*, 1995 reprint (New York: Free Press, 1912).

118. Tong, *Identity and Ethnic Relations*, 25, 195.

119. Huỳnh, *Người Hoa*, 2011; Nguyễn, "Biến đổi và tăng quyền," 2017.

120. Chan, "'Vietnam Is My Country Land,'" 2018; Minh Thư, "Nạn kiều 1978 Amie Mui Lee: 'Quê hương vẫn là Việt Nam'" (Migrant refugees 1978 Amie Mui Lee: "Vietnam is still the homeland," BBC News, accessed January 16, 2023, https://www.bbc.com/vietnamese/vietnam-47252027.

121. Adam McKeown, "Conceptualizing Chinese Diasporas, 1842–1949," *Journal of Asian Studies* 58, no. 2 (1999): 306–337

122. Michael R. Godley and Charles A. Coppel, "The Indonesian Chinese in Hong Kong: A Preliminary Report on a Minority Community in Transition," *Issues and Studies* 26, no.7 (1990): 94–108; Chantaranich Supang, "From Siamese-Chinese to Chinese-Thai: Political Conditions and Identity Shifts Among the Chinese in Thailand," in *Ethnic Chinese as Southeast Asians*, ed. Leo Suryadmata (Singapore: Institute of Southeast Asian Studies, 1997), 232–259; Lily Wu, "Going Home," in *Cultural Curiosity*, ed. Josephine M. T. Khu (Berkeley: University of California Press, 2001), 201–224; Bao Jiemin, "Chinese-Thai Transmigrants. Reworking Identities and Gender Relations in Thailand and the United States," *Amerasia* 25, no. 2 (1999): 95–115; Tan Chee-Beng, *Chinese Overseas Comparative Cultural Studies* (Hong Kong: Hong Kong University Press, 2004); Chiung, "Identity and Indigenization" 87–114.

For the Chinese in other places, see Chan, "Vietnam Is My Country Land," 163–179; Howard Johnson, "The Chinese in Trinidad in the Late Nineteenth Century," *Ethnic and Racial Studies* 10, no. 1 (1987): 89; and Richard Basham, "Ethnicity and World View in Bangkok," in *Alternate Identities: The Chinese of Contemporary Thailand*, ed. Tong Chee Kiong and Chan Kwok Bun (Singapore: Times Academic Press, 2001), 132.

123. This research is funded by University of Social Sciences and Humanities, Viet Nam National University Ho Chi Minh City under grant number 02/HĐ-NCM-ĐN&QLKH. I also reserve special thanks to (1) Asia Center of Harvard University for offering me the opportunity to work as a visiting scholar at the center during the 2018–2019 academic year, and (2) Professor Adam Seligman (Department of Religion Studies, Boston University) for his kind support of this research.

The Misconstrued Reader

Contemporary Sinophone Literature in Thailand

REBECCA EHRENWIRTH

While there are relatively young Sinophone writers in Myanmar, such as Lan Xiang (b. 1982) and Huang Deming (b. 1986), Sinophone literature in Thailand has "entered a late autumn and early winter" in the twenty-first century, according to Zeng Xin (b. 1938), one of the most prolific Sinophone writers in Thailand.[1] What he means by this metaphor is that the current generation of Sinophone writers in Thailand, including himself, is aged between seventy-five and ninety-five, and since the younger generation does not write (enough) about Thailand anymore, the literature has lost its Thainess, meaning that Sinophone literature in Thailand may die out.

Sinophone literature in Thailand does not just include fewer local characteristics, but the writers have also lost touch with their readers. While Sinophone literature was originally only published locally, by publishing the journal *Taihua wenxue* (Thai-Sinophone literature) online, it now reaches a far wider audience. As I will show in this chapter, the community of Sinophone writers in Thailand still envisions a Chinese reader in China instead of a diverse Sinophone readership across the world. The Sinophone reader of today is multidimensional and diverse in age, gender, occupation, education, and ethnicity; some have read Sinophone literature from other areas, and others are entirely new to it. Since there is a vivid exchange among the community of Sinophone writers in Southeast Asia, their works are read by their peers from Myanmar, the Philippines, Indonesia, and Cambodia. Sinophone writers in Thailand, therefore, know that their audience is not limited to Chinese readers in China; nonetheless, their works often only speak to them.

Zeng Xin's generation of Sinophone writers in Thailand is facing a contradiction: Rejecting the idea that their writings could be seen as a part of Chinese literature, they want to be independent—a Sinophone literature in Thailand—yet they speak to a Chinese reader in China. They not only incorporate their Chineseness but also their Thainess into their writing, giving voice to what Brian Bernards calls a "Sino-Thai biculturalism."[2] They mainly strive to be recognized by readers and critics in China. The aim of this chapter is to argue, therefore, through a reconstruction of the development of Sinophone literature in Thailand and a discussion focusing on the works of two Sinophone authors (Zeng Xin and Sima Gong, b. 1933), that they have a relatively one-dimensional understanding of their expected readers. Their target readership is in China, approximately their age, educated, and (to some extent) interested in Chinese-language literature from Southeast Asia. While their readers are expected to have a profound knowledge of everything "Chinese," especially when it comes to Chinese canonical literature,[3] they do not trust them to know much about Thailand. By creating what I call a "misconstrued reader" in their minds, they limit themselves and their works to a somewhat restricted readership instead of challenging the readers and themselves. Rethinking their ideas about their readership and reflecting upon the readers' capacities and expectations could broaden their work to a larger audience, thus contributing to the survival of Sinophone literature in Thailand.

Of Seeds, Roots, and Fertilizers

Like many of his peers, Zeng Xin himself is second-generation Thai. He was born in 1938 in Bangkok as Setthawong Kriangkai. While his ancestors migrated from Puning in Guangdong Province to Thailand in the nineteenth century, his parents did not speak Cantonese/Teochew, at least not with their children. Zeng Xin started learning Mandarin on his own so he could move to Shantou in 1956 and attend Jimei School for Overseas Chinese students. In 1962, he passed the university entrance exam and continued studying Chinese at Xiamen University. During that time, he discovered his passion for writing; he entered a writing contest for short stories and ended up winning the first prize. In the following years, he experienced the tumultuous period of the Cultural Revolution, during which he was sent to the countryside, and he stopped writing. On returning to Thailand in 1982, he became a merchant. It was only in the 1990s that Zeng Xin took up writing again. Today, he is a board member on many associations, such as the Society of Sinophone Writers in Thailand (Taiguo huawen zuojia xiehui) and the Society of Global Sinophone Writers (Shijie huawen wenxuejia xiehui).

Most of Zeng Xin's peers share a similar life story; they were either sent to school in China at a young age (e.g., Sima Gong[4]) or studied in China and returned to Thailand after the Cultural Revolution, like Zeng Xin. They were born in Thailand and then lived in China for a while, where they experienced the literature. They then returned and put down roots in Thailand. Although their connection to China is still quite strong, having lived most of their lives in Thailand, they do not long for a return to China as previous generations did. They have turned from "fallen leaves returning to the roots" (*yeluo guigen*) to "reach[ing] the ground and grow[ing] roots" (*luodi shenggen*), as Zeng Xin explains.[5] These two phrases became symbolic references to overseas Chinese after the establishment of the People's Republic of China (PRC)—the first hinting at the overseas Chinese (the "fallen leaves") eventually and inevitably returning to China ("the roots"); the second portraying them as "seeds sown in foreign soil," staying wherever they have migrated.[6]

On the one hand, the writers of this generation want to reflect their lives in Thailand for Sinophone readers without exposing them to too much that might be unfamiliar and too Thailand-specific. On the other hand, they do not want to be seen as part of Chinese literature; instead, they want Sinophone literature in Thailand to be recognized as independent and rooted in Thailand. Therefore, they believe they not only need to find the right balance between Chineseness and Thainess so they do not scare the Chinese reader away but also that they should not be too Chinese. This group of second- and third-generation Thai focuses on expressing what the anthropologist Richard J. Coughlin called in the 1960s a "double identity," which enables the Chinese in Thailand to be both Thai and Chinese.[7] They include a local Thai flavor in their Sinophone writing, but they also reconstruct their Sinophone cultural identity by writing literature in or about one of the Chinese minority languages or topolects, which is, in many cases, Teochew (Chaozhou hua). They choose to write in a language that is often not their mother tongue Thai, and they utilize what John Guillory has called "cultural capital,"[8] for instance, by including intertextual references to canonical Chinese texts.

Returning to their roots and spending a significant time in China was as if they had been "fertilized in China." The experience in China provided them with the necessary—what I will call—"nutrients" for their literary creativity, such as Teochew, Chinese history, and the Chinese classics, as well as the art of writing, which make up their Chineseness. If these writers had not been exposed to an education in China, they probably would not have started to write (again) in Thailand. However, it also made them feel dependent on China not only as their enricher but also as their audience. They do not necessarily connect their Chineseness with the PRC as a whole but instead a certain area in the mainland where the authors' ancestors are from; I therefore refer to this as "local Chineseness." This can be seen when they, for instance, use Cantonese expressions, such as *chongliang* for "taking a bath,"[9] or when they talk about Chaozhou (a city in Guangdong Province) or the Chaoshan region.[10] Their Chineseness neither embraces the idea of one Chinese culture or language—that of the Han-majority—as opposed to different local cultures and languages within the mainland, nor does it automatically include patriotism and blind obedience to modern China. However, it certainly shows a strong attachment to China without scrutinizing or explicitly criticizing it. Therefore, there is sometimes a political preference for the PRC visible in their work, even though the authors themselves may deny this.

Their misconstrued reader neither wants to hear criticism about China nor do they want to see "the Chinese" negatively portrayed. Therefore, the writers censor themselves. Although some of the Chinese characters are painted as conservative and narrow-minded at the start of the stories, they are always depicted as dynamic characters capable of change, at least to some extent. For instance, when the wife of the nameless protagonist in Zeng Xin's short story "Lan yanjing" (Blue Eyes) hears that her son, who has gone to study at Harvard, wants to bring home his girlfriend (Li Ma), she is very afraid that she might not be Chinese.[11] It would be unacceptable for her son to marry a foreigner. Although Li Ma turns out to be a foreigner with blue eyes, the mother accepts her in the end, but only because she can speak Mandarin. The protagonist in Sima Gong's short story "Jiantizi" (Simplified Chinese) is also portrayed as a conservative Chinese reader in Thailand who does not want to accept the shift from traditional to simplified Chinese characters.[12] However, after seeing how his Thai grandson (Tilacai) learns simplified Chinese characters, he begins to realize that they may be easier to remember and changes his mind about simplified Chinese.

Both stories highlight the importance of language but a very particular language: the one written and spoken by the majority of Chinese in China—Mandarin, in simplified characters. While Sima Gong's story begins by discussing the difficulties of shifting from traditional to simplified Chinese in particular, within the Sinophone community in Thailand, it fails to acknowledge that traditional characters still play an important role today, even in Thailand. (It is worth mentioning here that parts of the thaisinoliterature website are still in traditional characters.)

A Trip to Thailand

Following the history of Chinese migration to Thailand and the integration in and—at times—exclusion of immigrants from Thai society, we can see a shift from an initial nationalistic feeling of belonging to their country of origin (China) to a predominantly cultural attachment. Sinophone and Thai literature also mirror the slow assimilation and integration of the Chinese into Thai society.

> Small road is crowded by *Jek* [Chinese] and Thai,[13]
> Unavoidably mingling, clashing with one another.
> *Jek* mix with Thai beyond recognition,
> Who is who?
> One can't help but wonder.
> Modern times deviantly mess up the place.
> *Jin* [Chinese] cut off their pigtails and become Thai undetectably.[14]
> What an unconventional abnormality,
> People surprisingly reverse their ethnicity.[15]

These lines from the poem "Niras Sampheng" (A trip to Sampheng market) by the famous Thai author Nai Busya, written in 1920, show how Chinese immigrants slowly became Thai. The poem not only portrays the busy Chinatown in Bangkok in the early twentieth century but also speaks to an uncanny assimilation of the Chinese into Thai society. The lyrical I talks of an inversion of the Chinese ethnicity (line 9) and describes this as abnormal (line 8) since it will lead to chaos and problems within society, as predicted at the start of the poem (line 2). This is, of course, the perspective of a Thai writer at the start of the twentieth century when Thai nationalism was propagated by the government. Therefore, this impressively reflects a superficial assimilation of what is perceived as "the other" (in this case, the Chinese immigrant) and the anxieties that come with this in an atmosphere of heightened nationalism on both sides.

While "in Southeast Asian historiography, the Kingdom of Thailand is commonly portrayed as a 'success story' for its integration of Chinese immigrants and settlers into the national culture," as Bernards has summarized,[16] the development of Sinophone literature in Thailand has undergone various highs and lows. Before the turn of the twentieth century, Chinese immigrants were welcomed in Thailand, but the political atmosphere in Thailand radically changed when Vajiravudh came to power, becoming King Rama VI in 1910: "He made the Chinese immigrants, whom his father [Chulalongkorn] had deliberately imported, the target of nationalism, rather than complain about the influence of Britain, which controlled 90 per cent of Siam's trade."[17] Fighting Chinese nationalism with Thai nationalism became the political focus at the time. Vajiravudh called the Chinese "Jews of the East," commenting that while the Jews had no homeland, the Chinese were worse since "they come to work here [in Thailand] but send money back home to their country."[18] Chinese-language literature had just emerged in Thailand and was widely published. I call this literature "Chinese-language literature" because it was very Chinese, meaning that it did not include any local characteristics and was originally aimed at China, as Sima Gong (one of the most prominent Sinophone writers in Thailand and the long-term president of the Society of Sinophone Writers in Thailand) states.[19] It was even seen as a part of Chinese literature: "Chinese-language literature in Thailand at that time was regarded as [Chinese] literature by Overseas Chinese in Thailand."[20] Not only were the first serialized novels published in Chinese newspapers in Bangkok, such as *Hanjing ribao* (Hanjing daily; established in 1903) and *Meinan ribao* (Maenam daily), which were financed by donations from overseas Chinese, but the newspapers also belonged to different political factions and were used to voice their respective propaganda to support Chinese nationalism, according to Zhang Guopei.[21] This did not include local characteristics since most of the writers were loyal overseas Chinese.

The expected readership at the time was other immigrants from China, and many of the newspapers also had literary supplements (*wenyi fukan*) that published literature written by these immigrants. These newspapers, with their literary supplements, laid the ground for the subsequent development from Chinese-language literature, which was not very different from literature written in China, to a more independent Sinophone literature with increasingly local characteristics. This gradual development reached its first peak at the end of the 1920s and the start of the 1930s when the first wave of intellectuals from south China arrived in Thailand. Influenced by the New Culture movement and the subsequent May Fourth movement in China, different genres such as "new poems" (*xin shi*), short stories (*duanpian xiaoshuo*), and miscellaneous essays (*zawen*) emerged, and Sinophone literature in Thailand blossomed. The genre of "new poems" written in free verse, as propagated by Hu Shi, gained popularity among Sinophone writers. Lin Dieyi (1907–2004), a first-generation Thai and one of the first-generation writers, remains one of the most well-respected Sinophone authors. Inspired by literary trends from China, he wrote several "new poems," such as *Pengyou ni bu hui wangji ba* (Don't forget, my friend!, 1928). He also established the Panghuang xueshe (Wandering Society), and the first poetry collections were published in Thailand in that period, such as Lin Dieyi's *Po meng ji* (Collection of broken dreams, 1933).

Since the writers could not publish their work anywhere other than Thailand, their intended readership was the Sinophone community in Thailand. Most of the works still reflected what Zeng Xin calls the "body in Thailand, heart in China" feeling of the 1920s and 1930s.[22] What he means by this is that most of this generation's writers still wanted to return to the roots, i.e., China, and they still did not feel at home in Thailand, even though they were born in Thailand. Lin Dieyi's poems exactly mirror this generation's homesickness and longing to return to China. Although the writers of this period are still very much orientated toward China, this can be seen as the start of Sinophone literature in Thailand since the writers of this period not only wrote about China but also about their experiences as aliens living in a foreign land. Like the lyrical I in Nai Busya's poem, the writers reflect in the literature how they experience their assimilation into Thailand.

With the restrictions imposed on the Chinese community, the closing of Chinese schools and newspapers under the military rule of General Phibun (prime minister from 1938–1944 and 1948–1957), the emergent Sinophone literature had to go underground, and, at the same time, it became more Sinocentric. Very little was published, with poetry vanishing almost entirely. Yet, at this time, the first novels (*xiaoshuo*) and essays (*sanwen*) were being written. Since China was struggling under the Japanese invasion in the Second Sino-Japanese War, most of the literary works of that time were very patriotic. Sinophone writers were influenced by the anti-Japanese literature of the mainland, and in their work, they expressed their support for the Chinese against the Japanese. One example of such literature is Tian Jiang's poem *Wo zuzhou, wo tanxi!* (I curse, I sigh!). With its rapid rhythm, the poem reads as if the words are being fired from a machine gun. In the 1940s, Sinophone literature in Thailand was also influenced by realism, which can be seen most clearly in the novels, for instance, in Chen Kaixiu's (penname: Tie Ma) *Meigui ting* (Hall of roses), in which corruption among the overseas Chinese is caricatured.

The establishment of the PRC in 1949 led to a second wave of Chinese immigrants in Thailand, who were termed "new Chinese" (*xin Tang*).[23] Among them were a few aspiring young writers who fused with the group of older writers, leading to a flourishing period for literature. Mainly, novels, essays, and longer short stories were produced, all of which were more oriented toward life in Thailand than reminiscing about China. For instance, Chen Ding's (1932–1974) novel *San pin guniang*, (Three married off girls, 1954) is about Chinese families in Bangkok's Chinatown, reflecting on the lives and customs of the Chinese community in Thailand. The collaboratively written novel *Fengyu Yaohuali* (Stormy Yaowarat Road) discusses the life of a young couple who went to Thailand to find work.[24] The story reflects the highs and lows of the Chinese working class in Bangkok during the 1950s and 1960s, and it became an influential work for later generations not only because of its collective nature and its success in Thailand (it was even translated into Thai) but also because it was one of the first works published outside Thailand.[25]

The community of Sinophone writers in Thailand was beginning to realize that there was an even bigger audience they could reach outside Thailand. While these "new Chinese" writers had not yet fully put down roots in Thailand, they still felt very connected and rooted in areas with largely Chinese populations, such as Chinatown. As such, the returning-to-the-roots ideology of the previous peak gradually began shifting to a reach-the-ground-and-take-roots orientation. The diasporic consciousness of the previous generation had slowly vanished, and the works of this generation of writers had acquired strong local characteristics. While many Chinese-born authors became fluent in Thai, those born in Thailand for whom Thai was their mother tongue also acquired Chinese as their second language. In addition to the works written locally in the Sinitic script, Chinese literature (from China) was also increasingly translated into Thai by bilingual authors. More writers who were born in Thailand or had obtained Thai citizenship joined the community of Sinophone writers in the 1960s, although the Society of Sinophone Writers had not been formally established yet.

This peak was followed by a long period of low production, which lasted until the early 1980s. Zeng Xin describes this period as follows: "Sinophone literature in Thailand survived silently under water."[26] Many writers and editors were under surveillance by the Thai government in those years due to anti-Chinese sentiment, and the writers assumed political orientation as well as their links to Communist China. Most of the works were, therefore, published in Hong Kong, Taiwan, or Singapore. Like Sima Gong, many writers and intellectuals turned to business and gave up writing altogether.

When the Thai government began lifting its restrictions on Chinese schools and Chinese language learning in the late 1980s, a third wave of Chinese immigrants came to Thailand; among them were a couple of enthusiastic writers. What followed was another peak, which lasted until the start of the twenty-first century. Many of the writers who had turned to business also started writing again. In 1986, the Society of Sinophone Writers in Thailand was established with Fang Siruo as its first president. At the same time, many students who had studied in China or Taiwan returned to Thailand. This marked the start not only of the longest and most fruitful period for Sinophone literature in Thailand but also of a new target readership. While previous generations mainly wrote for other Sinophone immigrants in Thailand, this generation made it their aim to write for readers in China. Not only had they all gathered substantial China experience by living there at some point in their lives, but they also felt like they needed to (re-)connect with China and reactivate their local Chineseness. For the sake of brevity, in the next section, I will focus on the analysis of the works of two writers in particular, illustrating what I mean by "local Chineseness."

Paradigms of Sinophone Writers in Thailand: Zeng Xin and Sima Gong

From the way Zeng Xin's stories are written, including the annotations, explanations, and twists in the plots, we can clearly see that he envisions his main readership to be in China. Although Sima Gong does not use the same techniques as Zeng Xin, his topics also clearly show that his target readership is based in China. The topics may range from differences in languages (Teochew and Thai) to more historical and political themes, such as the Nanjing Massacre or the Olympic Games of 2008. Both authors do not touch on politically sensitive topics because they want to be read and critiqued in China and not sanctioned or banned. Due to the balance between reconstructing China and showing local Thai characteristics, their works can be seen as paradigms of contemporary Sinophone literature.

For them, as for many of these writers of their generation, "feeling Chinese" is not equivalent to "being Chinese," but to being from the Chaoshan region, speaking Teochew, and keeping Chaoshan customs alive since most of the authors of this generation are descendants of immigrants from this region. "Regarding quantity and quality, he [Sima Gong] is the number one among Sinophone writers in Thailand," states Zhang Guopei.[27] Sima Gong has a very high reputation among Sinophone writers in Thailand since he is considered original and progressive. As president of the Society of Sinophone Writers in Thailand, he was, for instance, responsible for the introduction and spread of flash fiction as a genre among his peers. One year after the Society of Sinophone Writers in Thailand was established in 1986, Sima Gong became a member. Just three years later, he became its president, and he retained this role for the next twenty years.

Yet, Sima Gong's works are not just unique because he is a somewhat avant-garde writer but also because, in many of his works, he humorously brings Thai and Teochew together. For instance, the short story "Ta zaiye bushi yi ge xiaohua le" (He is no longer a joke) is about a Chinese person (Sha Tonghai) who has just moved to Bangkok. The narrator introduces the protagonist by calling him "*xin Tang xiong*," which refers to the "new Chinese" immigrants who came to Thailand in the 1950s. The name Yuesha (literally, "south Chinese sand"), which the protagonist's surname "Sha" comes from, is a common term for the Chinese in Thailand, as Sima Gong explained to me in an email. The story is thereby set in 1950s Bangkok, but the protagonist's name emphasizes his Chinese origins.

In the following three passages, the narrator describes how Sha Tonghai finds his way in Bangkok by referring to some street names, such as Sampeng Lane and Yaowarat Road in Chinatown. After strolling around for a while, Sha Tonghai reflects on the Thai language: "It [Thai] is Teochew with a little bit of 'salt' or accentuated a bit."[28] While Teochew is indeed similar to Thai pronunciation, it is wrong to assume that a speaker of Teochew can automatically speak and understand Thai. It is, in the end, the protagonist's presumption that he can easily communicate with the locals that leads him to be put in jail because he cannot prove his identity to the police after he gets into a fight with a taxi driver whose Thai he does not understand. The story takes a sudden turn at this point because, in prison, he becomes acquainted with a known criminal whose daughter he later marries, making him rich. Sha Tonghai is, therefore, a dynamic character who develops from a somewhat arrogant "new Chinese" into a criminal and billionaire. It is worth highlighting that the protagonist's arrogance toward differences in languages sends him to jail.

Like Zeng Xin, Sima Gong includes Thai street or place names, such as Yaowarat Road, but only after the narrator mentions to the reader that the setting is Thailand/Bangkok. This suggests they do not believe the reader would otherwise understand their description; in this, they underestimate the reader. In another example, we find that Sima Gong includes the Thai word for "hello" (*Sawatdekap* or *shayueli* in Chinese characters) several times in the version published in Bangkok in 1991 but not in the version published in a short story collection in China in 2008.[29] With this self-censorship, he takes away the exoticizing effect for the reader by making it less Thai and to accommodate the Chinese reader. The authors have built an antiquated image of their intended reader and, therefore, only cater to these readers' needs. While they show their ability to adapt when it comes to new literary forms, such as flash fiction, they are shy of revisiting their ideas about their readers. Their misconstrued reader still exists, but, like them, they are getting older.

When Zeng Xin, on the other hand, provides the reader with annotations explaining Thai words, expressions, or circumstances, he also draws attention to the fact that the Sinophone world is multilingual, as Shu-mei Shih has stated.[30] This is also emphasized in Zeng Xin's short story "Li Sao." The story's protagonist is Li Sao, an elderly woman who sells fruit on the streets of Bangkok. Since she went to school in Bangkok but spoke Teochew at home, she does not know there are different Chinese languages and topolects. At the start of the story, the narrator describes how important it is for Li Sao to keep "Chinese" alive by asking her children to only talk to her in Chinese, i.e., Teochew. One day, however, a customer starts talking to her in a language she cannot understand. Another customer explains to her that the woman is talking in Chinese—Mandarin. The narrator explains: "When Li Sao heard Mandarin for the first time, she thought it is a foreign language. She always thought *Tangren* [Chinese] are [all the] Chinese and *Tanghua* [here: Teochew] is Chinese."³¹ The story contains several messages: First, it is important to keep Teochew culture alive by teaching it to children. Second, Mandarin and many other Sinitic languages and topolects are all part of the Sinophone. What "Chinese" language is depends on the speaker.

Yet, the story takes a sudden turn when Li Sao decides she must learn Mandarin now and that her children and grandchildren should learn it, too. In this story, Zeng Xin carefully interweaves fiction with reality by providing the reader with information about the development of Chinese-language education in Thailand. The narrator explains the setting with statements such as, "In 1994, Chinese schools sprang up like mushrooms all over Thailand."³² This unexpected turn and the explanations of the narrator, however, also draw attention to the expected readership: Mandarin-speaking Chinese. Why else would the protagonist, who so candidly believed in Teochew at the start of the story, suddenly want to learn Mandarin? And why end the story with her demanding that her offspring give up Teochew in favor of Mandarin? The story was written in 2001, just after the so-called Chinese-heat reached Thailand. This is also the narrator's explanation for why Li Sao suddenly wants to learn Mandarin. The story wants to reflect reality on the one hand, but it also caters to the needs of China on the other because it confirms that this campaign, initiated by China to promote Mandarin in Thailand, was somewhat successful. By including this turn in the story, Zeng Xin adapts the story for the misconstrued reader.

Sima Gong's flash fiction "Boshi" (Ph.D.), on the other hand, is a rare example of the reader being challenged. The I-narrator in this story is Dr. Liu Yinsi, who is sent from Hong Kong to Bangkok by his boss. On the plane, he speculates about why his boss chose him for the business trip: "Maybe because I speak Teochew. Or because I have a Ph.D. in Economics."³³ After he arrives in Bangkok, his business partner invites him to a dinner where he can network. To his surprise, nine out of the twenty guests also have doctoral degrees. After a couple of days, the protagonist meets up with his business partner again and asks him in Teochew, "which science" (*na ke*) and "which institute" (*na xi*) he got his Ph.D. from. In response to his question, the man turns red and furiously storms off, leaving the astonished Liu Yinsi behind. Liu Yinsi asks his secretary why the man was so furious, telling her what he had asked. His secretary begins to laugh, saying: "Mr. Liu, you asked him ... in Thai these words mean ... I can't tell you! You will understand later." What

Dr. Liu Yinsi did not know (and what the readers will also only understand if they understand Teochew and Thai) was that the two words *ke* and *kuai*, as pronounced in Teochew, and *xi* and *hi*, sound similar to vulgar words for male and female genitals in Thai, effectively "cock" and "cunt." Again, Sima Gong shows that Teochew may be similar to Thai, but this does not mean speakers of Teochew can communicate with Thai speakers. As a speaker of both languages and a former businessman himself, Sima Gong uses his knowledge of both languages to draw attention to presumptuous Chinese who believe that all Chinese is the same and who do not consider that language used incorrectly can be offensive.

The reader is challenged because Sima Gong does not offer any explanation for the two words that lead to the misunderstanding between the protagonist and his business partner. Like the protagonist, the reader is left in the dark about the meanings of the words in Thai when pronounced in Teochew. With this example, which was published in Bangkok, Sima Gong shows that he trusts in the readers' ability to find out the meaning themselves. While for the misconstrued reader, he would have added an explanation, he refrains from doing so here, thereby reflecting an acknowledgment and appreciation for their local readership.

The "New" Reader Is Diverse

Readership began to expand and diversify in the 1980s when many Sinophone works were published not only in Thailand but also in China, Taiwan, and Hong Kong.[34] Not only did the readership broaden but more was being published. In the first two years of the twenty-first century, according to Zeng Xin, a total of eighty-eight books, including novels, flash fiction, poetry, and essays, were published, which equated to almost 15 percent of the six hundred works of Sinophone Thai literature that had been published since 1920.[35] Many Sinophone writing communities also moved to the internet and published their works online.

With this change in accessibility, there also came a new readership: Younger readers from different areas could now read, like, and discuss Sinophone literature from almost every part of the world. However, while the readership changed, the intended readership of the Sinophone authors in Thailand did not. Even with a new generation of Sinophone writers, the reader still seems to be a misconstrued one, although now slightly younger. Works by young authors such as Xiao Yun (also Wen Xiaoyun), who was born in 1968 in Jiexi (Guangdong Province) and moved to Bangkok in 1989, show a drastic shift in theme and lack of local flavor. Since writers like her have yet to acclimate to their new environments, they have not yet taken root in Thailand. This can be seen, for instance, in her poem "Shijian qu nali" (Where did the time go?), in which she recalls her childhood friends in China. In an afterword to the poem, she writes, "When I went back home, I saw my two childhood friends."[36] By calling China her home, she emphasizes her feeling of belonging to China rather than Thailand, and with this, she caters to the Chinese reader in China who wants to hear more about her loyalty to China.

To describe this group of writers in Zeng Xin's words, they are still "floating like [a] water lotus" (*shuilian piaofu*).[37] Their works include very emotional and personal feelings toward life in general, society, and their new living conditions. They reflect on their situation as immigrants and process their own experiences. For instance, in the novella *Ran bu jin de huoyan* (Inexhaustible flame) by Mo Fan (also Chen Shaodong or Lan Yan), a couple moves to Thailand to start a new life along with their teacher and his son. While they overcome the first difficulties they are confronted by on their arrival in Thailand, such as the language barrier, they soon face problems with their ID cards. Life in Thailand is described as complicated and stressful, as they are frequently harassed by the police. In the end, the first-person narrator asks himself: "How can this be the life of the new immigrants? Can these be the dreams of the new immigrants? Fate is teasing people, times are deceiving people, reality is destroying people."[38] These and other works—such as Chen Yu's poem "Yu du" (Rain passing through)—by this generation of writers reflect the depression and loneliness that some of the new immigrants felt when they first moved to Thailand. They also illustrate the authors' understandings of being an immigrant in a foreign country and emphasize that they have not yet settled in Thailand.

However, we can take a closer look at later works, such as Mo Fan's flash fiction "Xia beizi" (In the next life), in which a parent takes their child to see the Buddhist temple Wat Arun in Bangkok. On the way there, the parent asks the child what they want to be in their next life.[39] After the child answers that they want to be "the father's child," the parent suggests that it would be better to become a panda instead of a human being. Not only is the panda a symbol of China, but the parent even talks about the two Chinese pandas in the Bangkok Zoo who live luxurious lives. This example shows that the new generation of Sinophone writers in Thailand has adapted in response to the criticisms of the older authors, such as Zeng Xin and Sima Gong, in order to be seen as part of Sinophone literature in Thailand. They include local characteristics in, for instance, the setting of their stories, and they also include China. However, as these stories show, they fail to reevaluate their readership and continue accommodating the misconstrued reader.

This new generation of writers has also not yet found a balance between exploring their own feelings in reminiscing about China and experiencing

Thailand. Their experiences as migrants and their perception of Chineseness are very different from those of the older generations, as often their Chineseness is not "local" anymore, and it is not attached to a certain place in China, such as Chaoshan. This wave of Sinophone literature reflects the difficulties and, at times, also the unwillingness to assimilate and integrate into Thai society. Therefore, their integration of Thai local flavor is occasionally rather superficial, e.g., when they only include Thailand as the setting. Fan Jun, who was born in 1972 in Shandong and came to Thailand sometime after 2004, writes in a comment on his poem "Ta xiang" (Foreign land): "I have been living in Thailand for a long time and gotten used to everything here. Therefore I often have the illusion that 'this foreign land is my homeland.'"[40] This comment testifies to the argument that this group of writers has not yet integrated into Thailand and still regards China as their motherland. It does not imply, however, that they will one day view Thailand as their home. On the contrary, it rather emphasizes that they might just get used to their life in Thailand. This also shows that their literature is geared toward China. Therefore, for them, the intended readership is still "the Chinese" in China instead of Sinophone readers around the world.

Notes

1. Zeng Xin, *Gei Taihua wenxue bamai* (Feel the pulse of Sinophone literature in Thailand) (Xiamen: Xiamen daxue chubanshe, 2005), 9. All the page numbers mentioned here refer to a personal digital copy that Zeng Xin gave me in 2012.

2. Brian Bernards, *Writing the South Seas: Imagining the Nanyang in Chinese and Southeast Asian Postcolonial Literature* (Seattle: University of Washington Press, 2015), 167.

3. For a discussion of the use of intertextuality in their works, see Rebecca Ehrenwirth, "Playing with the Canon: The Uncanny Pleasure of Intertextuality in the Works of Sinophone Thai Writers Sima Gong and Zeng Xin," *Modern Chinese Literature and Culture*, 32, no. 2 (Fall 2020): 136–178.

4. Born in 1933 as Kriangchao Durongsang in Bangkok, Sima Gong was sent to school in Shantou, living with relatives, when he was only six years old. His ancestors were from Guangdong and the men of his family had been merchants for many generations. When he was twenty, he returned to Thailand, but it was only in 1966 that he began writing. To earn money and continue the family business, he took a ten-year break from writing in the mid-1970s.

5. Zeng, *Gei Taihua wenxue bamai*, 12.

6. L. Ling-chi Wang, "Roots and Changing Identity of the Chinese in the United States," *Daedalus* 120, no. 2 (Spring 1991): 183.

7. Richard Coughlin, *Double Identity: The Chinese in Modern Thailand* (Hong Kong: Hong Kong University Press, 1960).

8. John Guillory, *Cultural Capital: The Problem of Literary Canon Formation* (Chicago: University of Chicago Press, 1993).

9. Zeng Xin, "Yi tong shui" (A bucket of water), in *Lan yanjing* (Blue eyes) (Bangkok: Shidai luntan chubanshe, 2002), 62.

10. The term Chaoshan refers to the cities of Chaozhou, Jieyang, and Shantou in Guangdong Province. This is the origin of the Minnan Chaoshan topolect or Teochew.

11. Zeng Xin, "Lan yanjing" (Blue eyes), in *Lan yanjing*, 13.

12. Sima Gong, "Jiantizi" (Simplified Chinese), in *Sima Gong weixing xiaoshuo zixuanji* (Selected short stories by Sima Gong) (Shanghai: Shanghai wenyi chubanshe, 2008), 145.

13. First- or second-generation Chinese immigrants in Thailand were called *Jek*. First, this was a neutral designation, but later it became derogatory. See Thak Chaloemtiarana, "Are We Them? Textual and Literary Representations of the Chinese in Twentieth-Century Thailand," *Chinese Southern Diaspora Studies* 7 (2014): 167.

[14]. Chinese immigrants wearing a queue or cue were called *Jin* in Thai. However, according to Tejapira, there were different names, such as Jin phrai and Jin khun nang. See Kasian Tejapira, "Imagined Uncommunity: The Lookjin Middle Class and Thai Official Nationalism," in *Essential Outsiders: Chinese and Jews in the Modern Transformation of Southeast Asia and Central Europe*, ed. Daniel Chirot and Anthony Reid (Seattle: University of Washington Press, 2001), 58–59.

15. Translated from Thai by Kasian Tejapira (1992), cited from Supang Chantavanich, "From Siamese-Chinese to Chinese-Thai: Political Conditions and Identity Shifts Among the Chinese in Thailand," in *Ethnic Chinese as Southeast Asians*, ed. Leo Suryadinata (Singapore: Institute of Southeast Asian Studies, 1997), 256.

16. Bernards, *Writing the South Seas*, 164.

17. Leo Suryadinata, *The Making of Southeast Asian Nations: State, Ethnicity, Indigenism and Citizenship* (Singapore: World Scientific, 2015), 138.

18. Chris Baker and Pasuk Phongpaichit, *A History of Thailand*, 3rd ed. (Cambridge: Cambridge University Press, 2014), 129.

19. Sima Gong, *Taihua wenxue mantan* (An informal discussion of Sinophone literature in Thailand) (Bangkok: Bayin chubanshe, 1994), 11.

20. Sima, *Taihua wenxue mantan*, 11.

21. Zhang Guopei, *20shiji Taiguo huawen wenxue shi* (A history of Sinophone literature in Thailand in the 20th century) (Shantou: Shantou daxue, 2007), 20.

22. Zeng, *Gei Taihua wenxue bamai*, 25.

23. Zeng, *Gei Taihua wenxue bamai*, 13.

24. A total of nine authors contributed to this collaboration by writing one chapter each. Among them were Fang Siruo (also Nai Fang or Phonglachet Kitaworanat, 1931–1999), and Ni Zhangyou (also Ni Longsheng or Yi She, 1927–2012). The group included not only first-generation immigrants but also younger writers who were born in Thailand.

25. The serialized novel was published in 1963 and 1964 in the Chinese-language newspaper *Huafeng zhoubao* (Sinophone news weekly). It was also published in Hong Kong in the 1970s, as well as in China. For a detailed analysis of the novel, see Bernards, *Writing the South Seas*, 176–181.

26. Zeng, *Gei Taihua wenxue bamai*, 13.

27. Zhang, *20shiji Taiguo huawen wenxue shi*, 127.

28. Sima, "Ta zaiye bushi yi ge xiaohua le" (He is no longer a joke), in *Yanyuan* (Performer) (Bangkok: Bayin chubaneshe, 1991), 74–77; Sima, "Jia zai fujin" (Neighborhood), in *Yanyuan*, 18–20.

29. Sima, "Jia zai fujin", in *Sima Gong weixing xiaoshuo zixuanji* (Selected short stories by Sima Gong) (Shanghai: Shanghai wenyi chubanshe, 2008), 61.

30. Shu-mei Shih, "Against Diaspora: The Sinophone as Places of Cultural Production," in *Sinophone Studies: A Critical Reader*, ed. Shu-mei Shih, Chien-Hsin Tsai, and Brian Bernards (New York: Columbia University Press, 2013), 32.

31. Zeng Xin, "Li Sao" (Li Sao), in *Lan yanjing*, 94.

32. Zeng, "Li Sao," 94.

33. Sima, "Boshi" (Ph.D.), in *Guqi* (Courageous spirit) (Bangkok: Taihua wenxue chubanshe, 2008), 47–48.

34. Zeng, *Gei Taihua wenxue bamai*, 13.

35. Zeng, *Gei Taihua wenxue bamai*, 13.

36. Wen Xiaoyun, "Shijian qu nali" (Where did the time go?) in *Xin shiji Dongnanya huawen xiaoshi jingxuan* (A selection of Sinophone short poetry in Southeast Asia in the new century), ed. Zhu Wenbin and Zeng Xin (Hangzhou: Zhejiang Gongshang University Press, 2018), 124.

37. Zeng, *Gei Taihua wenxue bamai*, 25.

38. I only have a personal copy of this story provided by the author.

39. Mo Fan, "Xia beizi" (In the next life), in Zhu and Zeng, *Xin shiji Dongnanya huawen shan xiaoshuo jingxuan*, 209–210.

40. Fan Jun, "Ta xiang" (Foreign land), in Zhu and Zeng, *Xin shiji Dongnanya huawen xiaoshi jingxuan*, 135.

Contributors

NATHANEL AMAR is the director of the Taipei antenna of the French Centre for Research on Contemporary China (CEFC) at Academia Sinica. His research focuses on the circulation of Sinophone popular music and music censorship. He is the author of *Scream for Life: L'invention d'une contre-culture punk en Chine populaire* (Scream for life: The invention of a punk counter-culture in contemporary China; 2022), and the editor of two special issues of *China Perspectives* on Sinophone musical worlds (2019 and 2020).

BRIAN BERNARDS is associate professor of East Asian languages and cultures and comparative literature at the University of Southern California. He is author of *Writing the South Seas: Imagining the Nanyang in Chinese and Southeast Asian Postcolonial Literature* (2015) and coeditor of *Sinophone Studies: A Critical Reader* (2013). His articles have appeared in journals, such as *Inter-Asia Cultural Studies*, *Prism: Theory and Modern Chinese Literature*, *positions: asia critique*, and *Asian Cinema*.

HOWARD CHIANG is the Lai Ho and Wu Cho-liu Endowed Chair in Taiwan Studies, professor of East Asian languages and cultural studies, and director of the Center for Taiwan Studies at the University of California, Santa Barbara. He holds a PhD in history from Princeton University. His recent publications include *After Eunuchs: Science, Medicine, and the Transformation of Sex in Modern China* (2018), *The Making of the Human Sciences in China: Historical and Conceptual Foundations* (ed., 2019), *The Global Encyclopedia of LGBTQ History* (ed., 2019), *Keywords in Queer Sinophone Studies* (ed. with Alvin K. Wong, 2020), *Transtopia in the Sinophone Pacific* (2021), and *Sinoglossia* (ed. with Andrea Bachner and Yu-lin Lee, 2023). From 2019 to 2022, he served as the founding chair of the Society of Sinophone Studies. With James Welker, he coedits the Global Queer Asias book series published by the University of Michigan Press.

REBECCA EHRENWIRTH is assistant professor of translation (Chinese-German) at the University of Applied Sciences/SDI Munich. She is the author of "Playing with the Canon: The Uncanny Pleasure of Intertextuality in Sinophone Literature from Thailand" (2020), "Journey to a Foreign Land: Imagining Migration in Sinophone Literature from Thailand" (2023), and the coeditor of the book *Contemporary German-Chinese Cultures in Dialogue* (2023). She is a founding member and the current secretary-treasurer of the Society of Sinophone Studies.

WAI-SIAM HEE is associate professor in the School of Humanities at Nanyang Technological University, Singapore. He has authored four scholarly monographs and coedited five volumes. His recent published monograph is *Remapping the Sinophone: The Cultural Production of Chinese-Language Cinema in Singapore and Malaya Before and During the Cold War* (2019). He has also published essays in *Cultural Critique*, *Interventions: International Journal of Postcolonial Studies*, *Inter-Asia Cultural Studies*, and *Modern Chinese Literature and Culture*, and *Journal of Chinese Cinemas*.

JASON LIM, PHD, FRHISTS, is senior lecturer in Asian history at the University of Wollongong in Australia. He graduated with a PhD in history and Asian studies at the University of Western Australia in 2007. He is the author of two books: *Linking an Asian Transregional Commerce in Tea: Overseas Chinese Merchants in the Fujian-Singapore Trade, 1920–1960* (2010) and *A Slow Ride into the Past: The Chinese Trishaw Industry in Singapore, 1942–1983* (2013). His research interests are Southeast Asia during the Cold War and the history of the Chinese communities in Malaysia and Singapore after World War II.

CAROLE MCGRANAHAN is professor of anthropology at the University of Colorado. She holds a PhD in anthropology and history from the University of Michigan (2001). Dr. McGranahan is a scholar of contemporary Tibet and the USA. She is author of *Arrested Histories: Tibet, the CIA, and Memories of a Forgotten War* (2010), coeditor of *Imperial Formations* (with Ann Stoler and Peter Perdue, 2007) and *Ethnographies of U.S. Empire* (with John Collins, 2018).

NGOC THO NGUYEN is associate professor in cultural studies at Vietnam National University—Ho Chi Minh City, majoring in Chinese Studies and Vietnamese folklore and social ritual studies. He concentrates on rituals, customs, and daily life of the Vietnamese and ethnic Chinese peoples under the East Asian perspective. He obtained his PhD degree at Vietnam National University—Ho Chi Minh City, and was a visiting scholar to Sun Yat-sen University in 2008, the Harvard Yenching Institute during the 2017–2018 academic year, Harvard University's Asia Centre in 2018–2019, Boston University in 2019–2020, and Brandeis University in 2020–2021. He is currently a senior faculty member of the University of Social Sciences and Humanities, Vietnam National University—Ho Chi Minh City. Nguyen Ngoc Tho is the author of seven books, a dozen book chapters, and more than forty journal articles published in Vietnam and overseas (the United States, Europe, PRC, Taiwan, Cambodia, etc.). He is also a member of the Standing Committee of the National Foundation for Science and Technology Development (NAFOSTED) of Vietnam (Council of Culture, Arts, and Mass Media).

VALENTINA PEDONE is an associate professor of Chinese studies at the University of Florence, Italy. Her academic interests encompass sociolinguistic phenomena within Sinophone migrant communities in Italy, focusing on translanguaging and heritage language maintenance. Her research also delves into the cultural productions stemming from Chinese migration to Italy and Europe, with a focus on Italian Orientalism, Sinophobia, and cultural discourse within Sinophone diasporas. She is the author of *A Journey to the West: Observations on the Chinese Migration to Italy* (2013), which explores various cultural aspects of China-Italy mobility since the 1980s. Her second book project, currently in progress, involves the study of literary works by individuals of Chinese descent living in Italy, with the aim of creating a new literary archive that showcases contemporary Sino-Italian expression while considering the works' position within the broader Italian literary landscape.

SHU-MEI SHIH is the Irving and Jean Stone Chair of Humanities, with a joint appointment in the departments of Comparative Literature, Asian Languages and Cultures, and Asian American Studies at the University of California, Los Angeles. She was the past president of the American Comparative Literature Association (2021–2022) and holds an honorary chair professorship at National Taiwan Normal University. Among other works, her 2007 book, *Visuality and Identity: Sinophone Articulations Across the Pacific* has been attributed as having inaugurated the field of Sinophone studies, and *Sinophone Studies: A Critical Reader* is the first reader in the field that she coedited in 2013. She works at the intersection of area studies, ethnic studies, and comparative literature, and has published on subjects ranging from transnationalism, critical theory, critical race studies, and Indigenous knowledge to Taiwan studies and Sinophone studies. Her recent books include *Against Diaspora: Discourse on Sinophone Studies* (反離散：華語語系研究論, 2017) and *Theorizing Across Borders* (跨界理論, 2023).

E. K. TAN is associate professor of comparative literature and cultural studies in the departments of English and Asian & Asian American Studies at Stony Brook University. He specializes in the intersections of Anglophone and Sinophone literature, cinema, and culture from Southeast Asia, postcolonial studies, diaspora studies, queer Asian studies, world literature, and cinema. He is the author of *Rethinking Chineseness: Translational Sinophone Identities in the Nanyang Literary World* (2013). He is currently working on two separate projects tentatively titled *Queer Homecoming: Translocal Remapping of Sinophone Kinship* and *Mandarinization and Its Impact on Sinophone Cultural Production.*

DAVID DER-WEI WANG is Edward C. Henderson Professor in Chinese literature and comparative literature at Harvard University. Wang specializes in modern and contemporary Chinese/Sinophone literature and comparative literary theory. His recent English publications include *The Lyrical in Epic Time: Modern Chinese Intellectuals and Artists Through the 1949 Crisis* (2014), *Harvard New Literary History of Modern China* (ed., 2017), and *Why Fiction Matters in Contemporary China* (2020).

EMILY WILCOX is associate professor of Chinese studies at William & Mary. She is the author of *Revolutionary Bodies: Chinese Dance and the Socialist Legacy* (2018, winner of the 2019 DSA de la Torre Bueno Prize), which was published in Chinese translation by Fudan University Press in 2023. Wilcox is coeditor of three collections: *Corporeal Politics: Dancing East Asia* (2020); *Inter-Asia in Motion: Dance as Method* (2023), and *Teaching Film from the People's Republic of China* (2024). She is cocreator of the University of Michigan Chinese Dance Collection and cocurator of the exhibit *Chinese Dance: National Movements in a Revolutionary Age, 1945–1965*. Wilcox has published over thirty academic articles and book chapters on dance and Asian studies in both English and Chinese and frequently teaches and lectures internationally on these subjects.

ALVIN K. WONG is assistant professor in the Department of Comparative Literature and the director of the Center for the Study of Globalization and Cultures at the University of Hong Kong. His research spans across the fields of Hong Kong literature and cinema, Chinese literary and cultural studies, Sinophone studies, queer theory, transnational feminism, and the environmental humanities. Wong's book *Unruly Comparison: Queerness, Hong Kong, and the Sinophone* is forthcoming from Duke University Press. He has published in journals such as *Journal of Lesbian Studies; Gender, Place & Culture; Culture, Theory, and Critique; Concentric; Cultural Dynamics; Continuum; JCMS; Journal of Chinese Cinemas;* and *Interventions* and in edited volumes such as *Transgender China, Queer Sinophone Cultures, Filming the Everyday, Fredric Jameson and Film Theory, Sinophone Utopias,* and *Queer TV China*. He also coedited the volume *Keywords in Queer Sinophone Studies* (2020). He currently serves as vice-chair of the Society of Sinophone Studies (SSS). With Daniel Elam, Wong is the coeditor of the HKU Press book series, Entanglements: Rethinking Comparison in the Long Contemporary.

LILY WONG is an associate professor in the departments of Literature and Critical Race Gender & Culture Studies at American University. She also serves as an associate director of AU's Antiracist Research and Policy Center. Her research focuses on the politics of affective labor, racial capitalism, minor-transnational coalitional movements, as well as media formations of transpacific Chinese, Sinophone, and Asian American communities. She is one of the founding board members of the Society of Sinophone Studies, serves on the advisory board of *Verge: Studies in Global Asias*, and supports AAPI Women Lead's Intergenerational Participatory Action Research as an advisor. She is the author of the book *Transpacific Attachments: Sex Work, Media Networks, and Affective Histories of Chineseness* (2018) and is coeditor (with Eric Tang) of "Dimensions of Violence, Resistance, and Becoming: Asian Americans and the 'Opening' of the COVID-era" special issue in *Journal of Asian American Studies* (2022), and coeditor (with Christopher B. Patterson and Chien-ting Lin) of the anthology *Transpacific, Undisciplined* (2024).

CHIEN-HENG WU is associate professor of foreign languages and literature at National Tsing Hua University. With a keen intellectual focus on the intersections of multiple disciplines, his research interests are expansive and interdisciplinary, including political philosophy, cybernetics, postcolonial theory, and Taiwan studies.

YINDE ZHANG is professor of Chinese studies at the University of Sorbonne Nouvelle-Paris 3 and research director of the Comparative Literature Studies Center for Comparative Literature (CERC). His main research interest is the Chinese-Western literary relationship in the twentieth and twenty-first centuries and the Chinese contemporary literature, with a focus on comparative approach and political imagination. His publications include *Le monde romanesque chinois au XXe siècle. Mondernités et identités* (The Chinese fiction world in the twentieth century, 2003), *Littérature comparée et perspectives chinoises* (Comparative literature and Chinese perspectives, 2008), *Mo Yan. Le lieu de la fiction* (Mo Yan: The place of fiction, 2014), and *Utopia and Utopianism in the Contemporary Chinese Context: Texts, Ideas, Spaces* (ed. with David Der-wei Wang and Angela Ki Che Leung, 2020).

Index

Abbas, Ackbar, 194
acculturation, 94, 101; and adaptation, 349–350; and group-level interactions, 342; and positive transformation, 344; Vietnamese Chinese, 341–344
Adam Smith in Beijing (Arrighi), 27
adaptations/adaptability: and acculturation, 341–344, 349–350; defined, 349; intercultural, 349–350; psychological, 349; sociocultural, 349; transcultural, 351; Vietnamese Chinese, 341–344
Afaa Michael, Weaver, 128–129
affect studies, 7, 125
against–diaspora, 226–231
Against Diaspora: Discourse on Sinophone Studies (Shih), 11, 147, 180, 227
Ahmad, Abdullah, 235
Ahmed, Aijaz, 50n13
"Allah's Will" (Ng), 236
Althusser, Louis, 247
Americanism, 12, 243–259; and American Revolution, 250; defined, 250; and Europeanism, 250; Gramsci on, 250, 252; Wang Zhenhe on, 252

"Americanism and Fordism" (Gramsci), 250
American Revolution, 250
Anagnorisis (Dargan), 7, 126, 130–135
ancestor worship, 358n100, 358–359n102
Ang, Ian, 94
Ang Lee, 62, 251
Anglo-American imperialism, 233
Anglophone, 17, 109, 140, 161
Anthias, Floya, 234
anticipatory nostalgia, 168, 170
anti-Extradition Amendment Bill protest, 9–10
antilocalization, 226–231
Apocalypse Now, 113
Arabian Dancing Girls, 284
"archival violence," 204
Archive Fever (Derrida), 202
Arlecchino: Il Servitore di Due Padroni (*The Servant of Two Masters*) (Goldoni), 304
Army Series, The, 325–326
Arrighi, Giovanni, 27–29, 33
Asia Foundation, 232
Asian imperialism, 6, 113–114, 206n4
Asia-Pacific War, 195, 196–197

assimilation, 12, 342; civilizational, 44–45; cultural, 13, 216–217, 266; multicultural, 163; of races, 36; and settler colonialism, 254, 268; superficial, 365; violent, 46
atheistic socialism, 266
Auer, Peter, 301, 308
Auzhou lixianji, 39
Awakening, The, 325

Baba Phuntsok Wangyal, 273
Badiou, Alain, 247
Bai Jurong, 95, 102
Balibar, Etienne, 246
Barad, Karen, 219
Barlow, Tani, 56
Barmé, Geremie, 282
Barr, Michael, 321, 325
Barrett, Tracy, 343
Bauman, Zygmunt, 247
Beatles, 283
Bee Gees, 283
Beijing Institute of Foreign Languages, 283
Beiyu Zhang, 81
"Believe Me, Singapore!," 326
Bellini, Vincenzo, 94
Bernards, Brian, 362
Berry, J. W., 342
Bettino Craxi, 304, 314n28
Beyond (Hong Kong rock and roll band), 281–296; after Beyond, 292–296; creation of a KTV *Hua*, 289–292; singing in Cantonese, 289–292
Bhabha, Homi, 301
biculturalism, 341, 362
Biên Hoa: Hakka Craft Village in, 348–349; liturgical transformation in, 348–349
Bilal, Aaliyah, 129
biological parasite, 183
Birthday Greeting from the Eight Immortals, A, 94
Blanchot, Maurice, 246
Blaut, J. M., 23–24, 49n3
Boat People (Hui), 6–7, 108–121; critical refugee studies, 111–114; Hong Kong-Hainan-Da Nang confluences, 114–119; literal narrative politics, 110, 119; scar narrative, 116–117; transpacific imagination, 113; Vinh Nguyen on, 109
Bøckman, Harold, 48–49
bodies and borders, 275–276
Bodies: Chinese Dance and the Socialist Legacy (Wilcox), 82
Bolaño, Roberto, 156
Bonaventura de Sousa Santos, 245
boundaries: linguistic, 281–296; musical, 281–296; political, 281–296
"Boundless Oceans, Vast Skies," 289, 292, 295, 296
Breton, André, 246
British: colonialism, 10, 77, 80, 315; imperialism, 195
Bro. Yao, 129
Buddhism: and Caodaism, 358n100; Guandi in, 335; and Hoahaoism/Hoahao, 345, 358n101; Mahayana, 343, 358n101, 358–359n102; Tibetan, 267, 271, 272, 273, 274–275; worldview, 343
Buffetrille, Katia, 275
Burbank, Jane, 29
Burkert, Walter, 334
Buttinger, Joseph, 338

Cai Guoqiang, 153
Callahan, William, 47
Cà Mau, family rites in, 346–348
Cantonese, 328; creation of a KTV *Hua*, 289–292; singing Beyond in, 289–292
Cantonese opera, 3, 5–6, 89–105; advertisements for, 97; culture, 97; in North America, 89–105; and radio, 103; Renshou Nian, 95; role in community, 97–99; San Francisco, 94–96; singing and vocalizing in style of, 101; troupes entry halted in U.S., 95. *See also* Chinese opera
Cantonese pop culture, 296
Cantonese rock songs, 14, 296
Caodaism, 345, 358n100
capitalism: free market, 251–252; global, 28–29; late, 129–130, 140, 195, 244; neoliberal, 28, 59; racial, 140; Western, 26
Carrico, Kevin, 269
Carroll, John M., 204

Carter, Jimmy, 251
cartography, 151, 159n30
Catholicism, 358n100
Celebrating Dance in Asia and the Pacific, 80
centrality: deconstructing, 148–150; geocritical Sinophone, 148–150
Chaiwan Ben Post, 180
Challenger's Alliance, 292, 293
Chan, Shelly, 201
Chang His-kuo, 254
Chan Kin-man, 185
Chan Koonchung, 8, 154
Chan Kwok Bun, 112
Chan Tze Woon, 7, 126
Chao Kang, 180
Chaoshan, 17, 364, 369, 374, 375n10
Chaozhou yingge of Teochew communities, 76
Chen Chuncheng, 156
Chen Ding, 367
Chen Dung-Sheng, 317
Cheng Lim-Keak, 317
Cheung, Jacob, 10, 196, 199, 201, 202
Cheung, Leslie, 63
Chia, Caroline, 332
Chiang, Howard, 194, 332
China. *See* People's Republic of China (PRC)
China Daily, 290
Chinatown culture, 6
Chinatown theaters, 97–99; culture, 99
Chinese Characteristics (Smith), 49n5
Chinese colonialism, 35, 38, 162, 276; historiography on, 41; periods of, 40–41
Chinese Communist Party. *See* Communist Party of China
Chinese Confucian ideology, 343
Chinese cultural symbols, 335
Chinese dance/dancers, 5, 76–78, 80–82, 84. *See also* dance
Chinese diaspora, 163, 226–231
Chinese empire, 23–49; Dirlik on, 29; discursive injunction against, 25; Han race, 24–25, 27; Manchu Empire, 28, 30–35; Pax Sinica, 35–49
Chinese exceptionalism, 26, 47–48, 120
Chinese hegemony, 10
Chinese Hour, The, 90, 102–103

Chinese immigrants, 16, 82, 89, 90, 95, 97, 234, 311–312, 375n14; and Cantonese opera, 89; Han, 167; minority status of, 95; racial hostility, in America, 97–98; in Thailand, 365, 367–369, 375n13; in Vietnam, 338–340
Chinese imperialism, 6, 23–25, 49n4, 55, 67, 267
Chinese-language dance studies, 79–81
Chinese Malaysian culture, 12, 173
Chinese Malaysian migration, 11–12
Chinese migrants, 15, 91, 231, 302–303, 306, 315, 335–336, 338, 374
Chinese nationalism, 26, 316, 327, 366
Chineseness, 1, 4–5, 7, 9, 11, 16, 59, 168, 209–210, 234–239; geopoliticization of, 55; and Sinophone, 77–78; theory of tianxia, 45
Chinese opera, 6, 103, 105; in California, 94; Cantonese opera troupe, 94; popularity of, 6; and Sinophone culture, 102. *See also* Cantonese opera
Chinese Originalism, 249
Chinese rock and roll, 283–287
Chinese settler colonialism, 265–276
Chinese Singaporeans: and Hokkien, 318–320; language(s) of, 316–318; Peranakan, 315; as Sinophone community, 315–328; and Speak Mandarin campaign, 320–325; Straits-born, 315; television programs, 325–326
Chinese Theatre Troupes in Southeast Asia: Touring Diaspora, 1900s–1970s (Beiyu Zhang), 81
Chinese Union of Journalists, 320
Chinese University of Hong Kong (CUHK), 295
Chiu, Kuei-fen, 220, 224–225n33
Chong Fah-hing, 232
Chow, Rey, 59, 62
Chu Tien-hsin, 170
Chu Yiu-ming, 185
civilizational assimilation, 44–45
civilization-state, 43, 47
Cixous, Hélène, 246
"Clean, Well-Lighted Place, A" (Hemingway), 255

Clementi, Cecil, 171
code-switching, 78, 300–301, 307–310
cognitive injustice, 245
Cohen, Robin, 230, 232
Cold War, 25, 27, 76, 55–56, 109, 111, 113, 129, 162, 232, 235, 237, 246–249; anticommunist/communist alliances, 114, 117, 119; and British colonialism, 80, geopolitics, 212; imperialism, 77; and Taiwan, 231–234, 251, 254
colonialism, 162; British, 10, 77, 80, 315; continental, 162; Dutch in Taiwan, 13; internal, 162; in Pax Sinica, 35–49; settler, 60, 162–163, 167, 243–259. *See also* Chinese colonialism
Columbus, Christopher, 39
Comaroff, Jean, 245
Comaroff, John, 245
Communism, 232, 235
communist(s): Asia, 7, 119; Chinese, 14, 109–110, 114, 117, 174, 232–233, 266, 268–272, 287, 316, 368; and Cold War, 114, 117, 119; Kuomintang, 195, 204; Malaysia, 235–236; Vietnam, 6–7, 108, 110, 114–115
Communist Party of China, 34, 117, 269, 276, 283; mass mobilization campaign, 118. *See also* Cultural Revolution; People's Republic of China (PRC)
community/ies: Cantonese opera's role in, 97–99; and Sino-soundscape, 97–99; transgressive, 147–157
"Comparison as Relation" (Shih), 176, 218
Complicities: The People's Republic of China in Global Capitalism (Dirlik), 29
Compost (group of artists), 303, 306
conditions of theory in Taiwan, 243–259
Confucian doctrines, 342
Confucianism, 335, 346, 358n100, 358–359n102
Confucian virtues, 343
Connell, Raewyn, 245, 247, 259
continental colonialism, 162, 227
continentalization of the settler, 257–258
Cooper, Frederick, 29
Coppola, Francis Ford, 113

Coulthard, Glen, 265
Court of Colonial Affairs, 33
Creolization of Theory, 246
critical promiscuity, 140
critical theory, 8, 246, 248–249
Critique of Everyday Life, The (Lefebvre), 247
Crouching Tiger, Hidden Dragon (Ang Lee), 62–63
Cui Jian, 284–285, 286, 287
Cui Zi'en, 59
cultural assimilation, 13, 216–217, 266
cultural hegemony, 9, 15, 178–182, 184, 188
cultural imperialism, 326
culturalists, 94
cultural leadership, 179
cultural parasite, 184
Cultural Revolution, 109, 116, 118, 123n37, 198, 246, 290, 306, 316, 362–363
culture: American, 76; Cantonese opera, 97; Cantonese pop, 296; Chinatown, 6; Chinatown theater, 99; Chinese, 15, 35, 135, 149, 176, 178, 181, 195, 235, 312, 334–335, 338–340, 348–349, 364, 365, 367–368; and Chinese hegemony, 10; Chinese Malaysian, 12; Chinese Malaysian ethnic, 173; East-Asian, 335; ethnic, 349–351; exclusionary hegemonic, 214; Han, 29, 46; hegemonic, 162; Hong Kong, 194; Indigenous, 167, 213; Italian, 312; karaoke, 14; Malay, 216, 236; Malaysian Chinese literary, 231, 238; marketing, 128–129; opera, 96; popular, 14, 63, 66, 336; queer, 283; queer sonic, 61; Sinitic-language, 1, 13, 17, 73–74, 83, 316; Sinophone, 8, 11, 16–17, 56, 90, 102, 172, 211, 292, 368; sonic, 92; Taike, 255; Taiwan, 255; Teochew, 371; Third-World, 184; Vietnamese, 16, 337–338, 344–345; Vietnamese Chinese, 332; visual, 82; working-class women, 198
Cusick, Suzanne, 101

da Gama, Vasco, 39
Dalai Lama, 265, 273, 275

dance, 93; cha-cha, 255; ethnic, 273; history, 3; and language, 74, 83; and Sinitic-language communities, 84; and Sinophone, 73–84; and Sinophone studies, 73–74. *See also* Sinophone dance
Daoism, 335; and Caodaism, 358n100; and Tứ Ân Hiếu Nghĩa, 358–359n102
Da Peng, 292–293
Dargan, Kyle, 7, 126, 128–135
Davidson, Morris, 196
de Beauvoir, Simon, 246–247
Debray, Régis, 45
De Certeau, Michel, 92
Declaration on the Right of Insubordination in the War in Algeria, 246
de-Cold War, 7, 114
De Jure Belli ac Pacis libri tres (Grotius), 256
De Jure Praedae (Grotius), 256
de Kloet, Jeroen, 283, 292
Deleuze, Gilles, 147, 198, 291
D'Emilio, John, 58
Deming, Huang, 361
Deng Xiaoping, 110, 114, 116, 283, 286, 287, 296
Derrida, Jacques, 166, 202, 204, 246
Der-wei Wang, David, 197
"Descendants of the Dragon," 284–285
Dian Shijie, 39
diaspora: Chinese, 163, 226–231; Taiwan, 226–239
"diaspora moment," 201
Diguo han taike (Chang His-kuo), 254
Diors Man, 292
Dirlik, Arif, 28–29
disciplinarity, 140–141
Dongjing menghualu (Meng Yuanlao), 171
Douglass, Susan, 103
Doyle, Laura, 204
Drucker, Peter, 58
Duara, Prasenjit, 333, 334
Du ciel à la terre: la chine et l'occident (Debray and Zhao), 45
Duggan, Lisa, 58
Dung Kai-cheung, 8, 150, 171–172
Duras, Marguerite, 246
Dussel, Enrique, 27
Dutch East India Company, 255, 256

East-Asian culture, 335
"East is Red, The," 284
Education Aid for Tibet project, 14, 270
Eidsheim, Nina, 100
Empire (Hardt and Negri), 45–46
Empire and life in the Tibetan borderlands, 265–276
Empires (Huang Yong Ping), 153
empire-state, 43
English-language dance studies, 79–81
Enjoy Yourself Tonight, 202
epistemic racism, 245
erotohistoriography: defined, 200; lesbian, 199–200, 205; queer, 200
Esherick, Joseph, 342
Espiritu, Yến Lê, 111–113
ethics: of opacity, 204; of relation, 150, 221; Sinophone, 184–188; of unknowability, 204
ethnic boundaries, 338–341
ethnic culture, 349–351
Ethnomusicology Forum, 90
Euro-Americans: centrism, 5, 79; liberal-rights tradition, 127; model of queer emancipation, 58; modern/contemporary dance, 76–77; queer articulations, 59
Eurocentrism, 3, 26, 79
Europeanism, 250
European opera, 94
European "scramble for Africa," 29
exclusionary hegemonic culture, 214
expansionism, 150–152
"Explaining 'The Republic of China,'" 36
expressive resource, translanguaging as, 307–311
Extend the Great Wall (Cai Guoqiang), 153

Fairbank, John K., 43
family rites in Cà Mau, 346–348
Fang Siruo, 368, 375n24
Fan Jun, 374; "Ta xiang," 374
Fan lisan (*Against Diaspora*), 209
Fanshenglu (Dung Kai-cheung), 171
"Father and Mother," 286
Faure, David, 333
Feng Xiaogang, 120

Fengyu Yaohuali, 367
fetishism, 24, 27
Feuchtwang, Stephan, 333, 344
Fire Dragon Dance of Hakka communities, 76
First Opium War (1839–1842), 193
Fiskesjö, Magnus, 270
Floyd, Kevin, 58
Flying Fish, The, 325
Foochows, 319
Fordism, 250. *See also* Americanism
Formosa (Lin), 149
Forum Magazine, 250
Foster, Robert J., 347
Foucault, Michel, 67, 246
Four Heavenly Kings, 282
Francophone, 17, 161
Freeman, Elizabeth, 200
free market capitalism, 251–252
Friedman, Milton, 193
Fung, Anthony, 291
"Future of the Chinese Race, The" (Liang), 37

Gansu Daily, 276
Ganzi Tibetan Autonomous Prefecture in Sichuan Province, 272–273
Gao Yujuan, 295
Gastronotopia (Han Song), 153
Gene Lau, 284, 294
geocritical Sinophone, 8, 147–157; deconstructing centrality, 148–150; hegemony, 152–155; territorial expansion, 150–152. *See also* Sinophone; Sinophone studies
Ge Zhaoguang, 34–35, 50n20
Gladney, Dru, 283
Glissant, Édouard, 67, 150, 218–221, 246
global capitalism, 28–29
global Maoism, 246
global multiculturalism, 252–253
Global South, 28, 30, 245
"Glorious Years," 295
"Glory to Hong Kong," 296
god(s), 149, 152; defying, 348; Kitchen God, 347; standardized, 333–337. *See also* Guandi
goddess(es): annexation of, 348; standardized, 333–337. *See also* Tianhou

Goh Chok Tong, 323
Gold, Thomas B., 287, 289, 296
Goldoni, Carlo, 304
Gomez, Edmund Terence, 239
Gong Sheng Theater, Vancouver, 92
Goodbye Ideal, 284, 291
Gosling, Peter L. A., 332
Gramsci, Antonio, 250, 252
"Grand Earth," 284–285
Great China Theater, 95, 97–98, 102
Great Dictator, The, 304
Greater China, 161, 220
Great Game politics, 271
Great Leap Forward, 118
"Great Wall, The," 152
Groppe, Alison M., 332
Gros, Stéphane, 267
Grotius, Hugo, 255–256
GT6, 294
Guandi: in Buddhism, 335; standardized god and goddess, 333–337; worship of, 333, 336–337, 344–346, 350
Guan Yinglian, 95
Guan Yundi, 102
Guattari, Félix, 198
Guo Qitao, 333
Gu Yanwu, 165

Hadland, Adrian, 29
Haidong qing (Li Yung-ping), 173
Haijiao qihao, 255
Hainanese, 319
Ha Jin, 332
Hakkas, 319
hallucination, reverse, 194
Hallward, Peter, 221
Han centrism, 34, 44, 59
Han Chinese immigrants, 167
Han culture, 29, 46
Han dance/dancers, 75, 79. *See also* dance
Han ethnoracialism, 33
Han immigrants, 213, 215
Han race/Chinese, 14, 27, 29, 36–37; innate capacity as colonizers, 38; racism, 44; superiority to white people, 37–38
Hansen, Valerie, 334

Han Song, 8, 153
Han Taiwanese, 256; and Austronesian peoples, 254; imagination, 254; Indigenous (pingpu) peoples, 254; knowledge, 256; writers, 252–253
Han Yuhai, 45
Happy Together (Wong Kar-wai), 4, 61–66
Harding, Sandra, 258–259
Hardt, Michael, 45–46
hauntology, 166, 168
Heart of Silk: My Made in China Italian Story (Shi), 302
hegemonic culture, 162
hegemony: Chinese, 10; cultural, 9, 15, 178–182, 184, 188; geocritical Sinophone, 152–155
Hemingway, Ernest, 255
Henghuas, 319–320
Herskovits, M., 341
He Yong, 282, 287
Hispanophone, 17, 161
historical consciousness, 200
historical opera, 96
Ho, Josephine, 182–183
Hoahaoism/Hoahao, 345, 358n101
Hobson, Emily, 58
Ho Kah Leong, 323
Hokchias, 319–320
Hokkien language, 253, 315, 328, 332, 336; Chinese Singaporeans, 322, 326; dominance of, 318–320; and SCCC meetings, 319; in Singapore, 318–320
homosexuality, 62, 66
Hong Kong: concert dance, 77; culture, 194; dance/dance forms in, 76; democracy protest, 7; and Euro-American dance world, 80; existentialism, 61–62; lesbian erotohistoriography of, 199–202, 205; modernity, 195, 202; postloyalism, 171–172; queer sex in, 62; rock and roll, 283–287; social movements in, 9; special administrative region, 186; Umbrella Movement, 7, 9–11; Vietnamese refugees, 111–114; Wong Bik-wan's feminist/lesbian cartography of, 196–198
Hong Kong Academy of Performing Arts, 78
Hong Kong Ballet Company, 77, 83
Hong Kong Cantopop, 282, 286–287, 288
Hong Kong City Contemporary Dance Company, 77, 83
Hong Kong Coliseum, 282
Hong Kong Dance Company, 78
Hoogervorst, Tom, 332
Ho Po-wing, 62
Hoskins, Janet, 113
Hou Dejian, 285
Huafeng zhoubao, 375n25
Huang Huajie, 335
Huangjin shijie, 39
Huang Weiliang, 179
Huang Yong Ping, 153
Huang Zongxi, 165
Hui, Ann, 6–7, 108–121
Huo Yan, 179
Hymes, Dell Hathaway, 300

identity: and ethnic Chinese Communities in Vietnam, 332–352; Taiwanese, 213
Ien Ang, 332
Imago Mundi, 155
immigrants: Chinese, 16, 82, 89, 90, 95, 97, 234, 311–312; Han, 213, 215; Han Chinese, 167; Sinitic-language-speaking, 91
imperialism: Anglo-American, 233; Asian, 6, 113–114, 206n4; British, 195; Chinese, 6, 23–25, 49n4, 55, 67, 267; cultural, 326; informal nonterritorial, 48; Japanese, 200; "neo-imperialism," 30; U.S., 77, 114, 119, 180; Western, 23–27, 32, 46, 49, 49n3, 245
"inclusive exclusion" principle, 147
incorporate ethnic culture, 349–351
Indigeneity: global, 59–60; and queerness, 59–60
Indigenous: culture, 167, 213; rights movement, 9; spectralization of, 257
informal non-territorial imperialism, 48
informational parasite, 183
infrastructure, 135–140
insularity, 148–150
integration, 150, 270, 342; cross-racial, 343, 346; cultural, 334; multiethnic, 352; social, 333, 343

intercultural adaptations, 349–350
interimperiality, 10, 204
internal colonialism, 162
international law, and settler colonialism, 253–258
intimacies, 127; minor-to-minor, 128–129; and possessive individual, 127
Intimates, 10, 196, 199–200, 202
Islam, Monirul, 225n39
Italy, 15; Chinese nationals living in, 301–302, 306, 311–312; culture, 312; ethnicity in, 299; Sinophone articulations in, 300; Sinophone studies, 3; *Tong men-g*, 303, 312

Jameson, Fredric, 50n13
Japanese: colonialism, 247–248; imperialism, 200; occupation, 170, 195, 320–321, 325
Joint Commission on Rural Reconstruction, 251
Joint Investiture of a Prime Minister of Six Warlords, The, 94
Jordan, David K., 333

Kao, George, 102
karaoke culture, 14
Katz, Paul, 333–334
Kelliher, Diarmaid, 58
Kham, 265–267; borderlands, 272–275; center, 272–275; Chinese colonialism in, 267; geopolitical identities, 272; home, 272–275; imperial histories of, 274; scholarly studies of, 274–275; and state sovereignty, 267–268
Khampa Tibetans, 272, 274
Khatibi, Adbelkebir, 259
Khoo, Olivia, 73
Kinesthetic City: Dance and Movement in Chinese Urban Spaces (SanSan Kwan), 80
King Rama VI, 365
Kingston, Maxine Hong, 90, 103–104
King Wu of Zhou, 164
Kitchen God, 347
Knowledge/Taiwan, 243
Kristeva, Julia, 247
KTV *Hua*, 289–292
Kuan-hsing Chen, 59

Kuhn, Philip, 342
Kuomintang (KMT), 195, 203–204, 213, 215, 232; anti-Communist Chinese nationalism, 233

Lacanian psychoanalysis, 222
Lai Yiu-fai, 62
Lam, Carrie, 186, 187
Lam, Edward, 57
language(s): and dance, 74, 83; of Singapore Chinese, 316–318; and Sinophone studies, 82–84; Tibetan, 273. *See also* Hokkien language; Mandarin language; Sinitic-language
Lan Xiang, 361
La Sonnambula (Bellini), 94
late capitalism, 129–130, 140, 195, 244
Latin American philosophy, 243
Latin American Philosophy from Identity to Radical Exteriority (Vallega), 243
Lau, Andy, 291
law: Cultural Heritage law, 344; Hong Kong extradition law, 186, 191n22; international, 253–258; Martial Law, 248
Lecklider, Aaron, 58
Lê dynasty, 334, 338–339
Lee-chin Lin, 8
Lee Hsien Loong, 324
Lee Kuan Yew, 15, 316, 318, 322
Lefebvre, Henri, 147, 246, 247
leftism, 53n65, 198
Leo Ou-fan Lee, 332
lesbian erotohistoriography, 199–200, 205
Leung, Helen, 62
Leung, Tony, 63
LGBTQ: coalition politics, 58; minorities, 60; rights movement, 60
Liang Lun, 81
Liang Qichao, 35; on Chinese colonialism, 38; on global voyages of Zheng He, 39; on superiority of Han Chinese race, 37–38
Liao Chao-yang, 257
Li Changfu, 35, 40; on Chinese immigration as colonization, 42; historiography on Chinese colonialism, 41
Li-Chin Lin, 148–149

Lienu Tu, 196–198
Lin, Yatin, 74, 75–76
Lin-chi tsung, 358–359n102
Lin Dieyi, 367
lingua-centrism, 73–74
linguistic boundaries, 281–296
"Linking Taiwan Studies with the World" (Shih), 218
Lin Moniang, 336
Linton, R., 341
Lionnet, Françoise, 126, 127, 246, 258
"Li Sao" (Zeng Xin), 370–371
liturgical transformation in Hakka Craft Village, 348–349
Liu, Petrus, 57–59
Liu Cixin, 8, 151–152, 156
Liu Daxian, 179
Liu Hong, 316
Liu Jun, 179
Liu Shipei, 36–37
Liu Zhiwei, 333
Li Xiangping, 169
Li Xuefang, 95, 96–97
Li Yung-ping, 172–173
local communities, 176, 342
localization, and Taiwan, 231–234
Locke, John, 256
"Long de chuanren," 284
Long tou feng wei, 196, 202
Long Yinpei, 81
Lost in Transition (Yiu-wai Chu), 194
Lowe, Lisa, 127, 129–130, 193
Low Thia Khiang, 327
loyalism, 163–164; and politics, 166; and Song dynasty, 165. *See also* postloyalism
loyalist consciousness, 165–166
Luk Naam Coi, 196, 203–205
Luo Yijun, 156
Lu Xun, 171, 197
Ly dynasty, 338
Lyotard, Jean-Francois, 246

MacKinder, Halford J., 30
Magellan, Ferdinand, 39
Mahayana Buddhism, 343, 358n101, 358–359n102

Mahua literature, 77
Mainlandization, 10
Ma Kai Fai, 10, 196, 202
Malayan Chinese leftist groups, 233
Malaysia: communist, 235–236; independence, 230–231, 235, 238; Malay culture, 216, 236; postloyalism, 172–174; Sinophone, 177
Malaysian Chinese Association, 232, 233, 235
Malaysian Chinese literary culture, 231, 238
Malaysian Chinese literary studies, 226
Malaysian Chinese literature, 226
Malaysian Chinese writers in Taiwan, 231–234
Manchu Empire, 28, 30–35; Court of Colonial Affairs, 33; Han people, 32; as military empire, 33
Mandarin Chinese script, 131–133
Mandarin language, 210, 253, 290–291, 315–328; and educated elite, 317; as legitimate Chinese language, 15; in popular music, 14; and Singapore Chinese, 316–318; Speak Mandarin campaign, 320–328; taught in Chinese schools, 318–319; television series, 325–326
Mandarin Theater, 95, 98
Manning, Erin, 198
Maoism, 246, 247
Mao Zedong, 265, 273, 283, 304
Mapping the World (Qiu Zhijie), 153
Mare Liberum (Grotius), 256
marginalization, 55, 178, 195, 197, 342
Marxism, 59, 246–247, 335
Ma Shizeng, 95, 96
Mass for Dream of the Red Chamber, A (Chen Chuncheng), 156
"master–slave structure," 234–239
McCoy, Alfred, 30
McKeown, Adam, 351
"mechanism of control," 334
Meigui meigui wo ai ni, 252
Meigui ting (Tie Ma), 367
Mei xing zhe, 197
Melamed, Jodi, 128
Menghualu (Dung Kai-cheung), 171
Meng Yuanlao, 171–172
Meskill, Joanna, 342

Meyer, David R., 193
"mighty operas," 104
migrant(s), 301–302, 338; Chinese, 15, 91, 231, 302–303, 306, 315, 335–336, 338, 374; experience in Singapore, 327; subjugation of workers in Hong Kong, 60; workers from south Asia, 177
Ming China, 40
Minh Hương, 339
"minor gesture," 198
Mo, Claudia, 186
Mo Fan, 373
Mongol Empire, 40–41
Morgensen, Scott L., 60
Mosaic (Chengdu indie rock band), 294
Moskowitz, Marc L., 283
multicultural assimilation, 163
multiculturalism, 46, 162; global, 252–253; neoliberal, 128
multilingualism, 300, 315–328
multi-systemic state, 43
Munoz, Jose, 194
musical boundaries, 281–296
musicking, 94; of Cantonese opera, 90, 92; defined, 90; and inscription of Sino-soundscape, 99–102
Myers-Scotton, 301
"My Friend Abdulah" (Ng), 236
mytho-realism, 151

Nai Busya, 365, 367
Names of Food Items Commonly Found in Hawker Centres and Market Places, 323
Names of Items Commonly Found in Hawker Centres, Markets, Restaurants and Zhongyuan Jie Auctions, 323
Nanyang Renmin Gongheguo (Ng Kim-chew), 174
Nationalist Daily, 100
National People's Congress Standing Committee's (NPCSC), 186
Nayar, Pramod K., 184
Negri, Antonio, 45–46
neo-Confucianism, 165
neo-imperialism, 30
neoliberal capitalism, 28, 59

neoliberal multiculturalism, 128
"new Chinese" immigrants, 367–368
New York Times, 273
Ng Kim Chew, 11–12, 173–174, 180–181, 209, 226, 327
Ngô Tấn Đước, 345
Nguyễn dynasty, 334
Nguyễn Thanh Long, 345
"Niras Sampheng" (Nai Busya), 365
Ni Zhangyou, 375n24
non-Han dance, 75, 78
North America: Cantonese opera in, 89–105; Sino-soundscape in, 89–105
North American Native queers, 60

Occupy Central with Love and Peace (OCLP) campaign, 185–186
Once Upon a Time in Hong Kong (Ma Kai Fai), 10
One Belt, One Road Initiative, 30, 159–160n37
One China policy, 185
Open Door policy, 110, 114
opera: Cantonese, 3, 5–6, 89–105; Chinese, 6, 94, 102–103, 105; culture, 96; European, 94; historical, 96; "mighty operas," 104; Peking, 6, 91
Opium Wars, 24
Orientalism, 302
Oriental Record Company, 97, 102
"Origin, Development and Criticism of Sinophone Literature, The" (Liu Jun), 179

parasite: biological, 183; cultural, 184; informational, 183; Sinophone as, 182–184; and Sinophone ethics, 184–188; social, 183; transnational, 184
Pateman, Carole, 256
patriotism, 358–359n102
Paul Wong, 284
Pax Sinica: colonialism in, 35–49; race in, 35–49
Peking opera, 6, 91
people as infrastructure, 139
People's Liberation Army (PLA), 13, 115, 269

People's Republic of China (PRC), 3–4; and African relations, 29–30; Arrighi on, 27–28; Chinese opera, 6, 94, 102–103, 105; communist, 14, 109–110, 114, 117, 174, 232–233, 266, 268–272, 287, 316, 368; culture, 15, 35, 135, 149, 176, 178, 181, 195, 235, 312, 334–335, 338–340, 348–349, 364, 365, 367–368; One Belt, One Road Initiative, 30, 159–160n37; One China policy, 185; as ontological alternative to capitalist world, 28; Open Door policy, 110, 114; parasitic relationship with Taiwan, 185; and postloyalism, 9; socialism in, 27, 29; Third Worldism, 3, 28; Uyghur genocide, 25; and Vietnam relations, 120; Western imperialism, 23; Western Right racialized vilification of, 4

Persepolis (Satrapi), 149
Pezzoli, Cristina, 303
Phyllis Chew, 316
Pinggui Returning Home, 93
place-based differentiation, 13–17
poetics of relation, 67
political boundaries, 281–296
Pomeranz, Kenneth, 333
Pop Rave, 294
popular culture, 14, 63, 66, 336
Portraits of Martyred Women (Wong Bik-wan), 10
possessive individual, 129; and intimacies, 127
posthumanism, 225n39
postloyalism, 8–9; and China, 9; defined, 163, 164; Hong Kong, 171–172; Malaysia, 172–174; Sinophone, 8, 166–168
Prague Spring, 246
Project for Extraterrestrials, 153
prosthetic memory, 168
"pseudo-orthopraxy," 334
psychological adaptations, 349
Puthucheary, Mavis C., 235

Qi hou, 197
Qi Mengshi, 115
Qiu Zhijie, 8, 153, 155, 159n37
Quaderni (*Prison Notebooks*), 250

queer: culture, 283; erotohistoriography, 200; Marxism, 58; sonic culture, 61; sonics, 60–66; translation, 56–57
queer Hong Kong: archive lost and found, 202–206; as Sinophone method, 193–206. *See also* Hong Kong
Queer Marxism in Two Chinas (Liu), 57
queerness: geopoliticization of, 55; and Han settler colonialism, 60; and Indigeneity, 59–60
queer theory: Chinese, 59; Liu's characterization of, 58; and Sinophone studies, 4, 55–67

race: assimilation of, 36; in Pax Sinica, 35–49. *See also* Han race/Chinese
racial capitalism, 140
racism, 234–239; epistemic, 245; Han race/Chinese, 44
radio, and Cantonese opera, 103
Radio Television Hong Kong (RTHK), 111
Ran bu jin de huoyan (Mo Fan), 373
Rancière, Jacque, 246–247
Rangshu (Liu Shipei), 37
Rankin, Mary, 342
Rawski, Evelyn S., 333
"Really Love You," 295
Redfield, R., 341
refugee(s): Southeast Asian, 119; studies, 110; transpacific, 111–114; Vietnamese, 6–7, 109, 111–114, 119
relational ontology, 209, 219–220
Renais, Alain, 246
Renshou Nian, 95
Republic of the Central Hua, 36. *See also* People's Republic of China (PRC)
Restless Empire: China and the World Since 1750 (Westad), 49n4
reverse hallucination, 194
Rey Chow, 194, 228, 332
Riichiro, Fujiwara, 338
Robbe-Grillet, Alain, 246
Rock And Roll, 294
ROC Loyalists, 231–234
Rojas, Carlos, 62
Roosevelt, Theodore, 250, 252

Royal Africa Company, 256
Rozman, Gilbert, 343
Rushdie, Salman, 255

Said, Edward, 245, 253
San Francisco: Cantonese opera, 94–96; Mandarin Theater on Grant Avenue, 98
Sangren, Steven P., 333
San pin guniang (Chen Ding), 367
SanSan Kwan, 80
Sartre, Jean-Paul, 246–247
Satrapi, Marjane, 149
Schoppa, Keith, 342
Scotton, Myers, 307
Second Sino-Japanese War, 201, 306, 367
Secret Society, 335
self-combing, 196, 200
self-immolation, 275–276
Seligman, Adam B., 350
separation, 342
Serres, Michel, 147, 183
settler colonialism, 60, 162–163, 167, 209, 243–259; and assimilation, 254, 268; Chinese, 265–276; with Chinese Communist characteristics, 268–272; defined, 266; and international law, 253–258
settler sexuality, 60
Shakya, Tsering, 275
Shih, Shu-mei, 3, 8, 12, 18n1, 62, 125, 126–127, 147, 155, 157n4, 178, 194, 206, 209; on diaspora, 227; on Han-centered Chinese language policy, 161–162; on imperial consolidation, 269; relational model, 195; on settler colonialism, 163, 167; on Sinophone literature, 73, 125, 176, 209, 282–283, 291, 370; theorization of Taiwan, 194
"Shijian qu nali" (Xia Yun), 373
Shimada Kinji, 247
Shi Yang Shi, 15, 299, 301–307
Shizi hou, 39
Shizi xie (He Jiong), 39
Shu Kei, 111
Shuo shu (Speaking of books), 209
Si-lan Chen, Sylvia, 81

Sima Gong, 362, 364, 366, 368, 369–372; background, 374n4; literary narrativity, 17; target readership, 369
Simondon, Gilbert, 217
Simone, AbdouMaliq, 138–139
Simpson, Audra, 266
Singapore, 3, 15; as British colony, 315–316; Chinese population in, 15; contemporary Sinophone communities in, 177; Han settler colonies of, 10; Hokkien in, 318–320; independence of, 15; Japanese occupation of, 321; merchants, 318; official languages for, 320–321; Singapore Broadcasting Corporation, 325; Singapore Hired Trishaw Riders Association, 320; Singapore Tourist Promotion Board, 318; Speak Mandarin campaign, 15
Singapore Broadcasting Corporation, 325
Singapore Chinese: language(s) of, 316–318; and Mandarin language, 316–318; television programs, 325–326
Singapore Chinese Chamber of Commerce and Industry (SCCCI), 319, 322, 327
Singapore Chinese Tea Importers and Exporters Association, 318
Singapore Federation of Chinese Clan Associations (SFCCA), 15, 324
Singapore Hired Trishaw Riders Association, 320
Sinicization thesis, 31–32
Sinitic-form dance, 78, 80
Sinitic-language culture, 1, 13, 17, 73–74, 83, 316
Sinitic-languages, 301, 317; communities, 1, 17, 73–74, 79, 83–84; cultures, 1, 13, 17, 73–74, 83; and dance, 84; literatures, 77–78, 84
Sinitic-language-speaking immigrants, 91
Sinocentrism, 155, 179–180, 182, 184
Sino-Corporealities (Lin), 74, 75
Sino-Japanese War, 250
Sinophone, 161–162; community, Chinese Singaporeans as, 315–328; defined, 126, 129; and disciplinarity, 140–141; epistemology, 8, 11, 209; geocritical,

147–157; as parasite, 182–184; postloyalism, 8, 166–168; Shu-mei Shih on, 125
Sinophone Cinemas (Yue and Khoo), 73
Sinophone culture, 8, 11, 16–17, 56, 73, 90, 102, 172, 211, 292, 368; and Chinese canon, 56; diversity of, 17; and national borders, 90; in North America, 102; thriving and vanishing of, 211; variety and vitality of, 172
Sinophone dance, 5, 15, 74–75; critical approaches in, 78; English- and Chinese-language dance studies, 79–81; overview, 75–78; and Sinitic bodily discourse, 83
Sinophone ethics, and parasite, 184–188
Sinophone literature, 361–374; of seeds, roots, and fertilizers, 362–364; in Thailand, 361–374
Sinophone Malaysian communities, 228
Sinophone Malaysian literature, 181, 212, 226–239
Sinophone Malaysians, 227; community, 228; diaspora, 227; localists, 234; writers, 216
Sinophone method: queer Hong Kong as, 193–206
Sinophone multilingualism, 327
Sinophone music, 282–283
Sinophone postloyalism, 8, 161–174
Sinophone resistance, 7
Sinophone studies, 18n1, 147–148, 177; conceptualization of power, 2–3; criticisms on, 178–180; and cultural parasite, 184; defined, 1; historical and historiographical time of, 17; interdisciplinarity, 7–8; and language, 82–84; musical performance, 5; and queer theory, 4, 55–67
Sinophone writers in Thailand, 369–372
Sinophonic affects, 140–141
Sinophonic inquiry, 125, 140–141
Sino-soundscape, 5–6; and community, 97–99; history of, 91; inscription of, 99–102; in North America, 89–105; and social memory, 102–105; and symbolism, 102–105
"Sino-Thai biculturalism," 362

Sino-Vietnamese War, 6, 110–111, 117–118; Hong Kong-Hainan-Da Nang confluences of, 114–119
Small, Christopher, 90
Smith, Arthur, 49n5
Snodgrass, Donald, 237
socialism, 29, 274; atheistic, 266; and Baba Phuntsok Wangyal, 273; in China, 27, 29; and Chinese civilizing project, 270; high, 16
social memory, and Sino-soundscape, 102–105
social parasite, 183
Social Science Research Council (SSRC), 341
Society of Global Sinophone Writers, 363
Society of Sinophone Writers in Thailand, 16–17, 363, 366, 368, 369
sociocultural adaptations, 349
sociolinguistics, 299–300
Song Hwee Lim, 73–74
sonic culture, 92
Sono qui Arle-Chino: Translator and Traitor of Two Masters, 303
So Rock!, 292
Southeast Asia, 16–17, 28, 35, 38, 40–42, 66, 80–81, 119, 167, 174, 230–231, 332, 337, 342–343, 351
Southern Theory (Connell), 245, 247
Speak Mandarin campaign, 15, 320–328
spectralization of the Indigenous, 257
speech community, 300
standardized god/goddess, 333–337
Stanley, Henry Morton, 39
Stiegler, Bernard, 217
Stonewall riots, 55, 67
Story of Woo Viet, The, 111
Straits Times, 322
Sui dynasty, 31
Sun Yat-sen, 32, 37, 96
Suola, Liu, 149
superficial assimilation, 365
Sutton, Donald, 333, 334
symbolism, and Sino-soundscape, 102–105
Szonyi, Michael, 333, 334

Tai, Benny, 185
Taihua wenxue, 361

Taike culture, 255
Taiping Tianguo, 335
Taiwan, 12–13; Americanism, 12, 243–259; and Cold War, 231–234, 251, 254; conditions of theory in, 243–259; culture, 255; diaspora, 226–239; Dutch colonialism in, 13; and Euro-American dance world, 80; Han settler colonies of, 10; and localization, 231–234; Malaysian Chinese writers in, 231–234; Martial Law in 1987, 248; parasitic relationship with China, 185; parasitic relationship with United States, 185; postloyalism, 169–171; queerness and Han settler colonialism, 60; ROC Loyalists, 231–234; Sinophone Malaysian literature in, 226–239; social movements in, 9
Taiwanese identity, 213
Taiwan Mandopop, 282–283, 286–287
Tan, Jia, 60
Tan Chee-Beng, 229, 230
Tan Kah Kee, 317
Tan Sooi Beng, 89
Taoism. *See* Daoism
"Tapir" (Ng), 236
Tashi Wangchuk, 273
"Ta xiang" (Foreign land) (Fan Jun), 374, 374
Taylor, Diana, 93
Tây Sơn dynasty, 339
Tee Kim-Tong, 230, 231
Teochew, 15–17, 317–319, 322, 327–328, 362–363, 369–372
Teresa Teng, 286
territorial expansion, 150–152
Thailand, 16–17; Chinese immigrants in, 365, 367–369, 375n13; diversified readership, 372–374; and Sima Gong, 373; Sinophone literature in, 361–374; Sinophone writers in, 369–374; Zeng Xin and Sima Gong, 369–373
Thai nationalism, 365–366
theater of individuation, 217
Theory from the South (Comaroff and Comaroff), 243
theory of imitation, 257

theory of poverty, 258–259
theory of tautology, 257
Third-World, 50n13; communities, 184; countries, 26; culture, 184; literature, 50n13; solidarity, 4; Third World Alliance, 246
Third-World culture, 184
Thirteenth Dalai Lama, 271
Three-Body Problems (Liu Cixin), 156
Through the Black Curtain (Kingston), 104
Tiananmen Square incident/crackdown, 4, 14, 67–68, 285, 287
Tianhou, 351; rituals, 346–348; standardized god and goddess, 333–337
Tian Jiang, 367
Tiāntāi-zōng, 358–359n102
tianxia, 43–45, 148
Tianxia: baona siyi de Zhongguo (Han Yuhai), 45
Tianxia tixi (Zhao Tingyang), 46
Tibet, 13–14; Chinese imperialism in, 267–268; eighteenth- and nineteenth-century imperial relations, 271; Empire and life in, 265–276; Han settler colonies of, 10; imperial realities, 267; as "internal colony," 270; languages, 273; state sovereignty, 267–268
Tibetan Autonomous Region, 274
Tibetan borderlands, 265–276
Tibetan Buddhism, 274
Tibetan Dalai Lama, 271
Tie Ma, 367
time consciousness, 200
"Today's Tibet, Tomorrow's Hong Kong," 14
Todorov, Tzvetan, 247
Tohti, Ilham, 134
Tong Men-g (*Arle-Chino*), 15, 301–307; and Shi Yang Shi, 301–307; translanguaging as transcultural marker in, 299–313
tongzhi, 4, 56–57; activism, 58; queer rendition of, 58
Trần Công Thận, 345
Tran dynasty, 338, 358n94, 358n98
transcolonial solidarities, 126–127
transcultural adaptation, 351
transgressive community, 147–157

translanguaging: as expressive resource, 307–311; as transcultural marker in *Tong Men-g*, 299–313
"Transnational Indian Novel in English: Cultural Parasites and Postcolonial Praxis, The" (Nayar), 184
transnational parasites, 184
transpacific refugees, 111–114
transtopia, 150, 194
transversal queer alliance, 60
traveling theory, 253
Treaty of Nanking, 193
Tripmaster Monkey: His Fake Book (Kingston), 104
"True Americanism" (Roosevelt), 250
Trump, Donald J., 184
Trương Văn Rộng, 345
Tsai Ing-wen, 184
Tứ Ân Hiếu Nghĩa, 358–359n102

Ức Trai Thi Tập, Nguyễn Tr.i, 339
Umbrella Movement, Hong Kong, 7, 9–11, 126, 186–187, 296; "Today's Tibet, Tomorrow's Hong Kong," 14; *Yellowing*, 135–140
Under the Lion Rock, 111
Union Press, 232
United Malays National Organisation (UMNO), 235, 239
United Nations, 44, 265, 270
United States: Chinese exclusion laws and restrictions, 95; Chinese theaters in, 94; culture, 76; imperialism, 77, 114, 119, 180; left-leaning China studies, 25–26; parasitic relationship with Taiwan, 185; Vietnam War, 108–110, 112–113, 117, 119, 252
U.S.-China Cold War, 195
U.S.-Vietnam War. *See* Vietnam War
Uyghur genocide, 25

Vallega, Alejandro Arturo, 243
Veracini, Lorenzo, 254
Vietnam, 41–42; aligning with USSR, 118; anti-Sinitic overtones, 120; Chinese immigrants in, 338–340; communist, 6–7, 108, 110, 114–115; culture, 16, 337–338, 344–345; ethnic boundaries as historical legacy in, 338–341; ethnic Chinese Communities in, 332–352; Hakka Craft Village in Biên H.a, 348–349; integral worship of Guandi, 344–346; and PRC relations, 120; Sinophone religious communities in, 16; Tianhou rituals and family rites in Cà Mau, 346–348
Vietnamese Chinese: acculturation and adaptability, 341–344; case studies on the field, 344–349; crossing the boundaries, 344–349; culture, 332; ethnic boundaries as historical legacy, 338–341; Guandi and Tianhou, 333–337; incorporate ethnic culture, 349–351; standardized god/goddess, 333–337
Vietnamese refugees, 6–7, 109, 111–114, 119
Vietnam War, 108–110, 112–113, 117, 119, 252
Viet Thanh Nguyen, 113
Vinh Nguyen, 109, 112, 121
violent assimilation, 46
visual culture, 82
Visuality and Identity: Sinophone Articulations Across the Pacific (Shih), 161
von Glahn, Richard, 333

Wang, David, 179, 332
Wang Anyi, 229
Wang Gung-wu, 229–230, 326
Wang Hui, 53n65, 227
Wang Kefen, 81
Wang Zhenhe/Wang Chen-ho, 252
Wan Li Ma Wang, 283
Waston, James L., 333
Weber, Max, 342
Weiming Tu, 332
Weller, Robert P., 350
Wenrou yu baolie, 197
Wen Xiongfei, 42
Westad, Odd Arne, 49n4
Western: capitalism, 26; colonialism, 237, 340; imperialism, 23–27, 32, 46, 49, 49n3, 245

Western Left, 47; Giovanni Arrighi on, 27; ideological purism, 4; intellectuals, 25; moralism, 4; romanticism toward China, 28
Western Right, and racialized vilification of China, 4
Wheeler, Charles, 341
White Lotus Sect, 335
White Terror, 248
Wolf, Arthur P., 333
Wolfe, Patrick, 254, 256
Woman Warrior (Kingston), 103
Wong, Alvin K., 283, 332
Wong Bik-wan, 10, 196; feminist cartography of Hong Kong, 196–198; lesbian cartography of Hong Kong, 196–198
Wong Chi, 111
Wong Ka-keung, 284
Wong Ka-kui, 281, 284, 286, 289, 295
Wong Kar-wai, 4, 61
working-class women culture, 198
World Dance Alliance, 80
World Friends of Laughter, 295
World of Music, The, 282
world system, 44
World War II, 196, 201, 248, 269, 316
worship: ancestor, 358n100, 358–359n102; of Guandi, 333, 336–337, 344–346, 350; of Tianhou, 333, 336–337, 348–350
Wo zuzhou, wo tanxi! (Tian Jiang), 367
Wu Hai, 289

Xiao Dingxiang, 95, 96
Xiao Yun, 372–373; "Shijian qu nali," 373
Xi Jinping, 177–178, 187
Xin Jiyuan, 39
Xinwen zhoukan, 281
Xixia lüguan, 170
Xu Bi, 288

Yachen Gar, 273
Yang, Miranda, 115

Yan Lianke, 8, 151
"Year I Returned to Malaya, The" (Ng), 236
Yellowing (Chan Tze Woon), 7, 126; poetics of infrastructure, 135–140
Yen Ching-hwang, 343
yimin. See postloyalism
Yin Chao, 289
Yip Sai-wing, 284
Yiu Fai Chow, 283
Yiu-wai Chu, Stephen, 194
"Yiwu suoyou," 284
Yoneyama, Lisa, 201
Yong Kang Nian theatrical company, 93
Young China, 96
Youth, 120
Yuanfei Wang, 53n56
Yue, Audrey, 73
Yunling gesheng, 281

Zeng Xin, 361–363, 367, 368, 369–372, 373
Zhalie Chronicles (Yan Lianke), 151
Zhang Ailing, 197
Zhang Guopei, 366, 369
Zhang Huangyan, 165
Zhang Nan, 290
Zhang Taiyan, 32, 35–36
Zhao Tingyang, 35, 44–45
"Zheng chouman lun" (Zhang), 35
Zheng He, 40–41, 53n56
Zhongguo jinxiandai dangdai wudao fazhanshi (Wang Kefen and Long Yinpei), 81
Zhongguo minzu zhi (Liu Shipei), 37
Zhongguo wu, 76
"Zhongguo zhimin bada weiren zhuan," 38
Zhongguo zhimin shi (Li Changfu), 40
Zhou Enlai, 251, 340
Zhu Chongke, 178–179
Zhu Da, 165
Žižek, Slavoj, 222
Zou Rong, 36

GPSR Authorized Representative: Easy Access System Europe, Mustamäe tee
50, 10621 Tallinn, Estonia, gpsr.requests@easproject.com

www.ingramcontent.com/pod-product-compliance
Lightning Source LLC
Chambersburg PA
CBHW022025290426
44109CB00014B/750